# INTERNATIONAL MACROECONOMICS

To the memory of Rudi Dornbusch

# INTERNATIONAL MACROECONOMICS

## Peter J. Montiel
*Williams College*

WILEY-BLACKWELL

A John Wiley & Sons, Ltd., Publication

This edition first published 2009
© 2009 Peter J. Montiel

Blackwell Publishing was acquired by John Wiley & Sons in February 2007. Blackwell's publishing program has been merged with Wiley's global Scientific, Technical, and Medical business to form Wiley-Blackwell.

*Registered Office*
John Wiley & Sons Ltd, The Atrium, Southern Gate, Chichester, West Sussex, PO19 8SQ, United Kingdom

*Editorial Offices*
350 Main Street, Malden, MA 02148-5020, USA
9600 Garsington Road, Oxford, OX4 2DQ, UK
The Atrium, Southern Gate, Chichester, West Sussex, PO19 8SQ, UK

For details of our global editorial offices, for customer services, and for information about how to apply for permission to reuse the copyright material in this book please see our website at www.wiley.com/wiley-blackwell.

The right of Peter J. Montiel to be identified as the author of this work has been asserted in accordance with the Copyright, Designs and Patents Act 1988.

*Library of Congress Cataloging-in-Publication Data*
has been applied for

ISBN 9781405183864 (hbk)

A catalogue record for this book is available from the British Library.

Set in 10.5/12pt Times Roman by SPi Publisher Services, Pondicherry, India
Printed in Singapore

 M WEP229764 290923

# Contents

## Part 2    Fixed Exchange Rates                                         113

# Preface

........................................................................................................................................

As I write this in early 2009, evidence of how intensely integrated the world economy has become is all around us. The financial crisis through which we are currently living has touched almost every corner of the world, and the international dimension of the required policy response is widely acknowledged. While the current crisis has emphasized the internationalization of macroeconomics in a dramatic way, the international aspects of macroeconomics have been growing rapidly in importance throughout the world over the past two decades. As the world becomes more integrated economically, this process is likely to accelerate. It is easy to predict that issues related to the international aspects of macroeconomics will become increasingly visible and urgent to students in years to come.

In this context, an understanding of the macroeconomics of open economies is likely to become an integral part of the education of students of economics, public policy, business, and international relations, among other disciplines. What makes this study at once fascinating and challenging is that so much of what determines how open economies behave macroeconomically depends on the specific circumstances of each country: its size, degree of macroeconomic openness in both goods and financial markets, the exchange rate and monetary policies that it pursues, the types of economic disturbances that it tends to experience, and so on. In the face of this diversity, the challenge that instructors face in teaching this subject is to provide their students with a versatile analytical framework that they can use to think clearly about the wide range of open-economy macroeconomic issues that they will invariably encounter in the future, whether as citizens, in their professional lives, or as policymakers.

## Special Features of this Book

This book is intended to help facilitate that task. I became motivated to write it as the result of many years of teaching this subject at a diverse set of academic institutions as well as of seeing it applied first-hand during a long stint in the Research Department of the International Monetary Fund. My objective has been to present, in as clear a language as possible, a comprehensive, but *unified* analytical approach to the subject, organized along lines motivated by current policy issues and buttressed by a large number of real-world applications and illustrations.

The book is based on the premise that the models that we use to study international macroeconomics share a common analytical core, and that what may often appear to be disparate models are actually special cases drawn from that common core and customized to fit the circumstances that specific countries find themselves in at particular times. I believe that it is important for students to understand both the common analytical core as well as how to do the customization. This approach has the pedagogic virtue that students only need to learn one general framework as well as the algorithms for knowing how to adapt it to specific cases – exactly the process that researchers and policymakers go through in thinking about these issues.

The underlying analytical core on which the models in this book are based consists of a generalized and modernized version of the original Mundell-Fleming model. This version retains the Mundell-Fleming assumptions of complete specialization in production, short-run price stickiness, and behavioral functions based on simple decision rules. It departs from the original, however, in paying careful attention to the specification of stocks and flows as well as to the role of expectations, and its behavioral functions are specified in a manner that provides a natural segue to the optimizing models that are currently used by researchers in this field, a segue that is provided in the final chapter of the book. This analytical framework has two virtues that recommend it for an upper-level undergraduate textbook. First, it has long been – and continues to be – the workhorse for policy analysis and discussion of monetary and exchange rate issues in international macroeconomics. Consequently, it provides students with analytical tools that they will encounter beyond the classroom, especially in the financial press. Second, when stocks and flows are treated correctly, the framework is a natural extension of the standard IS-LM model used in intermediate macroeconomics that will be familiar to most undergraduate students.

In addition to its unified analytical treatment of the subject, the book introduces several innovations to teaching important topics in international macroeconomics. For example:

1 It provides a textbook treatment of imperfect capital mobility under fixed exchange rates from a portfolio-balance perspective that makes appropriate distinctions between stocks and flows.
2 It models expected future exchange rates as the outcome of a rational expectations-formation process, and shows how these expectations are influenced by the expected duration of shocks, as well as by the nature of goods-market adjustment.
3 It provides a new textbook version of a large-country model, again extracted from the general framework, that can be used to think about issues of international policy coordination among industrial countries.
4 It bases the analysis of optimal exchange rate regimes squarely within the analytical framework that students used earlier in the book to analyze fixed and floating rates separately, using a single diagram to illustrate how the economy responds to different types of shocks under alternative exchange rate regimes.

Finally, this book shares with other textbooks on the subject a concern with showing students how the models it develops can be used to understand the world by applying them to a wide range of real-world examples. However, while the anticipated audience of the book mandates a disproportionate representation of the macroeconomic experience of the

United States in these applications, I have tried to broaden these examples to encompass the experience of a large number of other countries. In addition to such direct applications of the models, almost all chapters also contain a unique textbook feature: optional empirical studies at the end of the chapter. These are intended to illustrate the methods that researchers in international macroeconomics have used to learn about specific aspects of the real world that are covered in that chapter.

## Organization

The book is divided into five parts, with a structure designed to follow a sequence that I have found to be pedagogically very useful.

Part 1 makes the transition from the largely closed-economy approach of intermediate macroeconomics to the context of macroeconomic openness. This provides an opportunity to address many fundamental open-economy issues early in the book (e.g. the effects of various open-economy variables on economic welfare, the distinction between accounting and economic relationships in open-economy macroeconomics, and the generality of various open-economy parity conditions). All of these are explicitly motivated as building blocks for the construction of a general framework that can be used to think about all of these issues. The virtue of that approach is that hopefully it will serve to place all of these topics in context for the students.

Part 2 of the book, on fixed exchange rates, allows students to gradually build up their familiarity with the analytical framework that will be used for the rest of the book by starting out with the simplest applications of that framework. But the fixed exchange rate topics are not covered just because of their pedagogical role in developing students' understanding of the basic model. This part of the book addresses issues (e.g., ''hard'' and ''soft'' pegs, currency boards, and the macroeconomics of capital account restrictions) that, while they may currently be of policy relevance primarily outside of the United States, will be recognized by knowledgeable students as being of topical interest in many places around the world. The issues treated in these chapters have also been of historical importance for the United States, and they continue to be taken seriously in proposed reforms of the inter-national monetary system.

The heart of the book is Part 3, where floating exchange rates are considered in detail. In these chapters, specific adaptations of the floating rate version of the general model are shown to be required, depending on the expected duration of the shocks that affect the domestic economy, on the monetary policy regime that is in place, on the economy's supply-side response, and on its size. Having explored the macroeconomics of fixed and floating exchange rates, the last chapter in Part 3 considers the question of optimal exchange rate regimes – i.e., how the exchange rate regime should be chosen. Because the macro-economic interactions in these models are more intricate than those in the models of Part 2, this material is introduced only after students have acquired some familiarity with the basic analytical framework.

Part 4 takes up several topics of current interest that have in common a single theme: the optimal design of international monetary arrangements. This part includes chapters on reform of the international financial architecture, G-8 policy coordination, and monetary unification. Important by-products are the extension of the analytical model to the more complicated large-country case and a description of the emergence of the euro in the chapter on monetary unification.

The book concludes in Part 5 with an extension of the analytical framework to encompass intertemporal optimizing behavior on the part of the private sector, the paradigm that currently dominates research in this field. The chapter explains how optimizing models are related to the models based on behavioral decision rules that are used in the rest of the book.

## Alternative Teaching Strategies

The material just described comprises 19 chapters, and this may often be too much to cover in a quarter or a short semester. Because the various models studied in the book are all individual special cases of the framework developed in Chapter 4, there are various ways to compile the chapters into shorter courses. For example, Chapters 1–11 plus 17 and 18 could be covered in a short semester, and would include models appropriate for emerging-market economies that intervene heavily in foreign exchange markets, industrial countries such as Japan, the UK, and Canada that maintain floating rates, the United States (a large economy whose actions affect the rest of the world), and countries such as those in Western Europe that participate in a monetary union. Alternatively, by skipping Chapters 5–9 but including Chapters 10–14, 17, and 19, the book can be adapted to a quarter-long US-oriented course that focuses on floating exchange rates only.

## Level

This book is intended for students that have completed an intermediate-level course in macroeconomics – i.e., for an audience that will typically consist of junior and senior undergraduates as well as Master's level students in Economics and related disciplines. Although the relevant goods- and financial-market equilibrium conditions are derived from the ground up, the book presumes familiarity with the standard closed-economy IS-LM and derivative models that are featured prominently in most intermediate-level textbooks in macroeconomics. While it makes no use of calculus, the analysis is more advanced and detailed than that in the standard International Economics texts. Though most of the analysis is graphical, models are always presented in equation form and solution algorithms are described in mathematical terms. This means that, even though no more advanced mathematical tools are required than those typically needed to master most intermediate-level textbooks in macroeconomics, and even though I have tried to develop the material as clearly and transparently as possible, the book is likely to speak more clearly to students with some mathematical sophistication in their backgrounds.

## Supplements and the '08–'09 Meltdown

Three types of web-based materials for instructors are available as supplements to the book. First, all of the book's analytical figures are available in the form of Powerpoint slides for use in lectures. Second, answers are provided to all of the end-of-chapter exercises. Finally, there are also suggestions for using the analytical tools provided in the text for teaching students about the 2008–2009 international financial meltdown. While these events occurred too recently to treat them in the manuscript, there are several places where the models developed in the book can be very usefully employed to shed light on the macro-economic implications of the crisis, both for the United States as well as for countries in a variety of other macroeconomic situations that have been affected by the crisis in different ways. These applications are linked to the chapters in the book where they can most usefully be introduced.

## Acknowledgements

No project of this magnitude could possibly be brought to fruition without the combined efforts of a large number of people, and this book is certainly no exception. I owe a special debt of gratitude to my students, who have not only helped me learn about this subject over many years, but many of whom have also offered constructive comments on earlier drafts of this manuscript. My wife Susan, my daughter Ruth, and my son Alex have been supportive and patient through a long gestation process. I owe a special debt of gratitude to Rudi Dornbusch, to whose memory this book is dedicated, for inspiring my initial appreciation for small macroeconomic models as well as for his sustained encouragement and support. My editor George Lobell made suggestions for the inclusion of material that greatly improved the book. Last, but not least, I am greatly indebted to several reviewers, including:

Rodolphe Desbordes, University of Strathclyde
Bernardo Guimaraes, London School of Economics
Kenneth Kasa, Simon Fraser University
Fabio Milani, University of California, Irvine
Marc-Andreas Muendler, University of California, San Diego
David Shepherd, Westminster Business School
Watanabe Shinichi, International University of Japan
Grigor M. Sukiassyan, California State University, Fullerton

for their careful reading of the manuscript and large number of perceptive comments.

Peter Montiel, Williams College
Peter.J. Montiel@williams.edu

# Part 1
# Foundations

# 1

# An Overview of the Book

........................................................................................................................................

*Globalization – the extension of the division of labor and specialization beyond national borders – is patently a key to understanding much of our recent economic history. (Alan Greenspan)*

The international economic system has undergone a profound transformation over the past several decades. At the beginning of the 21st century many of the most important economies around the world – and many smaller economies as well – are trading goods and services, financial assets, and even the services of factors of production such as labor and capital much more intensively with each other than they had been doing over most of the 20th century. This ongoing process, colloquially known as **globalization**, has meant that markets for many commodities and for a wide range of financial assets are becoming increasingly international in scope, rather than being restricted to the confines of a single country. It is hard to believe that such a process would not fundamentally change the economies that have been engaged in it, and indeed the quote above from Alan Greenspan, the former Chairman of the Board of Governors of the US Federal Reserve System, suggests that it may not be possible to understand macroeconomic developments even in as large an economy as that of the United States without taking into account this continually intensifying process of international economic integration.

This book is about how international economic integration affects domestic macroeconomic performance. It is therefore motivated by one fundamental question: How does the intensification of trade across international boundaries in both goods and services as well as in financial assets affect the way the economy works? As we will see, the answer to this question is the same as that to many other interesting questions in economics: it depends. Factors such as the size of the economy, the degree to which it is integrated with the world economy in different markets, the policies that it adopts toward the value of its currency in terms of the currencies of other countries, and how it conducts its monetary and fiscal policies all influence how the process of globalization affects macroeconomic performance. The objective of this book is to provide you with a set of analytical tools that will help you think in an orderly way about how all of these factors interact to affect an open economy's macroeconomic performance, and thus prepare you to better understand how the process of globalization will continue to affect the way not only that your own economy works, but also the diverse economies of the many countries that you will eventually have reason to care about in our increasingly integrated global environment.

In this first chapter we will go over some fundamental concepts to help establish a framework for the rest of the book. We will also consider some of the topics that we will be investigating together. Finally, we will take a brief tour of the book's contents to give you an overview of its structure and a sense of how the topics to be examined in it fit together.

## 1.1    What Is International Macroeconomics?

### Short-run Macroeconomics

Macroeconomics is the study of an economy's aggregate performance. Macroeconomists typically concern themselves with two sets of issues, which fall into the general categories of **long-run macroeconomics** (or *growth theory*) and **short-run macroeconomics**. In long-run macroeconomics we study the evolution of an economy's productive capacity over time, while in short-run macroeconomics the focus is instead on the factors that determine how fully the economy *uses* its productive capacity at any moment in time, as well as on the behavior of other macroeconomic variables that are affected by the rate of capacity utilization, such as changes in the rate of inflation.

The reason that macroeconomists worry about these things is not just to learn how the world works, but also to understand how to design policies that will enhance the economy's ability to do what it is supposed to do: provide the goods and services that satisfy our society's material needs. To attain that goal, we want to make sure that our economy achieves an optimal rate of growth of productive capacity over time while fully utilizing the productive capacity that it possesses at each moment in time.

In short-run macroeconomics, which is the subject of this book, our main concern is with **stabilization**, which means keeping the economy's actual level of production as close as possible to its productive capacity. The trick involved in doing so is that the economy is continually subjected to a variety of unpredictable changes, either in the economic environment or in the behavior of economic agents, that tend to drive the actual level of production, measured by real gross domestic product (GDP), away from the level of productive capacity, as measured by potential, or full-employment real GDP.[1] Macroeconomists refer to such unpredictable changes as **shocks** to the economy. These shocks tend to generate booms and busts in the level of economic activity, which may destabilize the average price level or create prolonged periods of underutilization of productive capacity. Since shocks are unavoidable, the policy issue that is the focus of short-run macroeconomics is how the economy can be stabilized in the face of such shocks, either by adopting institutional arrangements that make it less vulnerable to shocks or by taking countervailing

---

[1]    Full employment GDP is sometimes also referred to as the *natural* level of real GDP.

policy measures in response to shocks when they arrive, usually in the form of fiscal and/or monetary policies.

This all sounds pretty straightforward, but in practice this problem can get fairly complicated. The effects of shocks on the economy may be quite complex, depending not just on their magnitudes, but also on their origin (that is, the specific macroeconomic market in which their effect is initially felt), their expected duration, and the extent to which they were anticipated or not before they happened. Moreover, different macroeconomic institutional arrangements may be more effective in countering the effects of some shocks than others, and some arrangements may ameliorate the effects of some shocks while magnifying those of others.[2] Finally, far from serving just to stabilize the economy in the face of shocks, policies may themselves be the sources of shocks in many cases, and even when they are conducted with an eye to the achievement of macroeconomic stabilization, their effectiveness in doing so may depend on various characteristics of the economy, including its institutional environment.

The bottom line, then, is that life in short-run macroeconomics is complicated. The point of studying short-run macroeconomics is to sort out these complications by mastering an analytical framework (a "model") that allows us to identify what is important and to clear away irrelevant detail, so that we can think about all of these issues in an orderly and systematic way.

## Closed versus Open Economies

Unfortunately, the frameworks that most students learn for this purpose in intermediate macroeconomics tend to be deficient in one important respect. Intermediate-level macroeconomics textbooks are usually dominated by **closed-economy macroeconomic models**. This is an analytical framework in which residents of the domestic economy are assumed to trade goods and services, financial assets, and factor services only with each other. As suggested above, that assumption has been rendered increasingly irrelevant by the forces of globalization that have gathered strength in recent years. The phenomenon of globalization requires that macroeconomic issues be analyzed in a setting that takes into account the fact that domestic and foreign residents trade often and sometimes very extensively with each other. The study of macroeconomic issues in an open-economy setting in which such links are taken into account is sometimes referred to as **international monetary economics**, **open-economy macroeconomics**, or **international macroeconomics**. These terms are used interchangeably throughout this book.

What kind of trade does the term macroeconomic openness take into account? Closed-economy macroeconomics typically considers trade in four types of commodities: goods and services, money, interest-bearing financial assets (bonds), and labor. A short-run macroeconomic equilibrium is one in which the markets for all of these commodities are simultaneously in equilibrium, and the purpose of a short-run macroeconomic model is to

---

[2]    For example, a central bank policy of keeping the money supply constant in the face of shocks to the demand for domestic output would tend to make real GDP more stable than a policy of keeping the interest rate constant. But keeping the money supply constant would actually make real GDP *less* stable than keeping the interest rate constant if the shocks affecting the economy primarily involve changes in the demand for money.

explain how this **general equilibrium** determines the values of real GDP, the interest rate, the price level, and the level of employment, among other variables of interest. In the real world, all of these commodities are actively traded across national boundaries, in the sense that people who live in one country consume goods and services produced in other countries, hold money and other types of financial assets issued in other countries, and sometimes work in other countries or hire foreign workers. All of these transactions create economic links across countries that, as we will see in this book, may substantially change the ways that economies behave. Thus, a theory that adequately describes the behavior of any real economy that is "open" in any of these ways must take transactions of these types into account. This book will consider how doing so changes our understanding of short-run macroeconomics.

## The Issues of Concern

In this context, the questions that we are going to be interested in are in part the standard ones asked in closed-economy macroeconomics. In closed-economy macroeconomics the key endogenous variables are the level of real economic activity (real GDP) and the price level.[3] We care about these things because we believe that they are related to the country's level of economic well-being. We want to explain their behavior, in the sense that we seek to understand how they are affected by changes in exogenous variables (the macroeconomic shocks that we discussed previously), as well as by policy variables that can be controlled by governments.

When we open the economy up to external commerce, the analysis of how these key endogenous variables are determined has to be modified. In particular, the following questions arise:

1   How are the effects of domestic exogenous shocks on the macroeconomic variables that we care about affected by macroeconomic openness?

For example, we know that the US economy is subject to occasional fluctuations in real GDP that are often triggered by changes in domestic variables, such as the expectations of consumers or firms. These are usually referred to as **business cycles**. How is the behavior of US business cycles likely to be affected in the future by the increased openness of the US economy? To take a specific example, if the residents of a country become more optimistic about their future economic prospects and consequently decide to spend more, how do the effects of those spending decisions on the level of domestic economic activity depend on how much the economy trades with the rest of the world? How do they depend on whether domestic residents can borrow from the rest of the world to finance their additional spending, or on the policies that the domestic central bank has adopted toward the value of the domestic currency?

---

[3]   It may be worth briefly recalling the distinction between **exogenous** and **endogenous** variables in economics. The relationship between them is that of cause and effect. Exogenous variables play the role of independent causes in economic theories: they affect other variables, but are not themselves affected by those variables. Thus, their behavior is not explained by the theory. Endogenous variables, by contrast, are those whose behavior is explained by a theory.

2    Are there new exogenous shocks that may influence these variables in the open-economy environment?

For example, it is sometimes said that when the United States sneezes, Latin America catches pneumonia. A tightening of monetary policy in the United States in the early 1980s was indeed associated with the outbreak of a debt crisis that resulted in a "lost decade" of economic growth in Latin America during the 1980s. Why did this happen? Are such effects the unavoidable consequence of macroeconomic openness, or did their emergence depend on the policies that were being pursued by the affected countries? As additional examples, should firms in Argentina care if the US dollar becomes more expensive in terms of European euros or Japanese yen? Should residents of Thailand be happy, sad, or indifferent if the Japanese central bank decides to lower interest rates to stimulate the Japanese economy? Should the European Central Bank change interest rates in Europe when interest rates fall in the United States? Under what conditions should other Asian countries care if the Chinese central bank chooses to buy large amounts of US Treasury bills? In short, how do macroeconomic events in other countries affect open economies, and how is the transmission of these effects affected by the policies followed in the home economy?

3    How is the effectiveness of policies affected by macroeconomic openness?

Much of intermediate macroeconomics is taken up by the study of fiscal and monetary policies. How do the impacts of these policies depend on how open the country is to trade in financial assets with the rest of the world? How do they depend on the institutional arrangements that govern the central bank's behavior in the foreign exchange market? Are they affected by the size of the domestic economy relative to that of its trading partners? As examples, can Bulgaria use monetary policy to stimulate its economy if world demand for its exports contracts? Does expansionary fiscal policy in Switzerland lose its ability to affect the economy because any additional demand created by the fiscal expansion is simply channeled to the purchase of foreign goods?

4    Are there new policy options in an open macroeconomic environment?

Domestic monetary policy involves the buying or selling of domestic government securities by the central bank (open market operations). But in an open economy, the central bank can also buy or sell *foreign* securities. Do these transactions have the same effect on the economy as open market operations? Why have the central banks of many countries been buying large amounts of US Treasury bills in recent years? Similarly, countries may have a choice about how open they are to trade with the rest of the world through the regulations and taxes that they implement on such trades. What are the macroeconomic effects of such measures?

The questions just posed suggest that we may have to rethink our interpretation of the way the economy works from a macroeconomic perspective when we take openness into account. As economies around the world have become increasingly open, macroeconomists have had to confront this possibility when thinking about a broad range of macroeconomic issues. As an illustration, Empirical Study 1.1 at the end of this chapter describes one such case: the impact of openness on the behavior of the inflation rate.

In addition to potentially altering the ways that familiar macro variables like the inflation rate may behave, macroeconomic openness also complicates matters by generating new endogenous variables that will typically be of concern to policymakers – in particular, the foreign exchange value of the domestic currency and a variety of balance of payments concepts. As in the closed-economy case, we will want to know:

1   How do these variables affect the country's economic well-being?

For example, when a new currency, the euro, was introduced by ten members of the European Union in 1999, that currency initially lost a substantial amount of value against the US dollar, and subsequently reversed that performance and actually gained value against the US dollar, right up until the time of writing (early 2008). How did such fluctuations in the value of the euro affect the economic well-being of residents of the European Union? As a second example, the United States currently spends much more on goods and services produced by the rest of the world than the rest of the world spends on goods and services produced in the United States (to the tune of nearly 6 percent of US GDP in 2007, a very high figure by historical standards). How does a deficit of this size in this category of international transactions affect the well-being of US residents?

2   What determines the behavior of these variables?

Just why did the euro decrease and then increase in value the way it did? As we will see, such swings in the value of individual currencies have not been unusual, and sometimes they are much more dramatic. For example, in 1997 the value of the currency of Thailand (the *baht*) fell by more than 30 percent in less than a month, and such dramatic **currency crises** (sudden changes in currency values) have not been unusual. Why do they happen?

3   How can policymakers affect their behavior if they desire to do so?

If all of these international variables indeed matter for the well-being of the residents of a country, is there anything that policymakers can do to influence them? How do the conventional fiscal and monetary policy tools affect them? Are there other, new policy tools that can be brought to bear on these international variables? If policymakers can indeed influence these variables, what effects – if any – do their actions have on the more familiar domestic macroeconomic variables?

As all these issues make clear, both because it alters the way that familiar macroeconomic endogenous variables behave, and because it produces new issues of concern to policy-makers, macroeconomic openness requires us to modify the toolkit used in the study of closed economies.

## International Macroeconomics and International Finance

At this point, you may be wondering how international macroeconomics differs from something else you may have heard about: international finance. International finance is essentially the analysis of the process of arbitrage among financial assets issued in different political jurisdictions, and usually denominated in different currencies. By contrast, as we have seen, international macroeconomics is the analysis of macroeconomic issues in the context of an economy that is open to various types of trade with the rest of the world. What is the relationship between them?

A financial asset issued by a resident of country A, say, gives the person who buys it – say a resident of country B – a legal claim on the income of the person who issues it.

The size of that claim (i.e., the contractual rate of return on the asset) and the likelihood that it will be satisfied when it is due (the riskiness of the asset) both depend on the macroeconomic conditions in country A. Thus, macroeconomic conditions affect asset prices. You cannot know how much you should pay for an asset issued by a resident of country A unless you understand the conditions that determine the return that the asset is likely to yield.

At the same time, however, the terms on which an individual in country A can borrow abroad will affect the terms on which borrowing and lending take place at home, in country A, because dealing with residents of other countries represents an alternative source of funds for domestic borrowers and lenders. In turn, this affects whether domestic households choose to consume more or domestic firms choose to buy more physical capital, which will in turn affect their country's macroeconomic performance. Thus, international asset prices affect domestic macroeconomic conditions.

The bottom line is that the prices at which assets trade are both affected by and themselves affect domestic macroeconomic conditions. In other words, asset markets interact with the other markets that make up a general macroeconomic equilibrium. What this means is that *international finance is a part of international macroeconomics*. It follows that, since the underlying macroeconomic performance of the economy is what ultimately determines the prices of financial assets that are traded internationally, even if your primary interest is international finance, you have no choice but to care about international macroeconomics. In short, the tools that we will develop in this book will help deepen your understanding of international finance.

## 1.2    The International Macroeconomics Toolkit

These tools will consist of a set of open-economy macroeconomic models that will be applicable in different circumstances. Thus, we will spend a lot of our time building analytical macroeconomic models. Why should we do so? *The reason is that the answers to the questions posed previously tend to depend not only on a variety of characteristics of the domestic economy, but also on the specific ways that that economy is linked to the rest of the world.* For example, in closed-economy macroeconomics, an important characteristic of the domestic economy in determining how it responds to shocks and policy changes is the extent of wage-price flexibility, which determines the slope of the economy's aggregate supply curve. While this may be a purely domestic phenomenon, it is just as important in affecting macroeconomic behavior in the context of an open economy. But in addition, the economy's behavior is also affected by several new considerations of an international nature, including:

1    The rules that govern the behavior of the domestic central bank, not only in the domestic securities market (the **monetary policy regime**), but also in the foreign exchange market (the **exchange rate regime**).
2    The degree of integration of the domestic economy with world markets for goods and services.
3    The degree of integration of the domestic economy with world financial markets (typically referred to as the degree of **capital mobility**).

It turns out that all of these characteristics have significant effects on how open economies "work" from a macroeconomic perspective. What is particularly important for our purposes, however, is that these characteristics have tended to differ not only across countries, but also for the same country at different points in time. For example, some countries (such as United Arab Emirates as of early 2008) keep the value of their currencies rigidly tied to that of the US dollar, while others (such as New Zealand) allow the values of their currencies to be fully determined by the market (in the case of New Zealand, since 1985). In some large developing countries, such as Brazil and India, international trade represents a relatively small fraction of GDP, while in others, such as Singapore and Malaysia, the volume of trade is actually larger than the economy's GDP. Some developing countries (referred to as **emerging-market economies**, or (**emerging economies** for short) are highly integrated with world financial markets, while others have remained relatively isolated financially from the rest of the world. These differences mean that, in analyzing the macroeconomic behavior of open economies, we need to consider several cases, depending on which of these characteristics holds. That is what creates the need to analyze several different models.

## 1.3    The Contents of this Book

However, it would be tedious and not very illuminating to take a purely taxonomic approach, considering alternative combinations of characteristics one at a time and seeing how the economy works under each particular combination. Instead, we will proceed by developing a general framework from which specific models can be derived as special cases, and the specific special cases that we will study will be ones that reflect the characteristics of important groups of countries around the world.

### Structure

In keeping with this approach, the book will be divided into six main parts:

Part 1.    Foundations
In the first part of the book, we will introduce and interpret many of the international macroeconomic concepts that will be used throughout the book. Specifically, we will examine the balance of payments accounts and their links to the national income accounts, we will explore arbitrage conditions that have been applied to trade in goods and services as well as in financial assets, and we will develop the general analytical framework described above.

Part 2.    Fixed exchange rates
To develop our modeling tools gradually, we will begin the analytical portion of the book with what is arguably the simplest model to understand: one in which a country is highly integrated financially with the rest of the world, its central bank is committed to maintaining a fixed value of its currency in terms of some foreign currency, and in which there are institutional mechanisms in place to limit the central bank's discretion in buying and selling domestic securities. The last two of these conditions are the components of what is sometimes referred to as a **"hard" exchange rate peg**. While there are several

contemporary versions of hard exchange rate pegs, the most important historical application of this type of exchange rate regime was during the time of the classical gold standard (1880–1914), and we will begin our study of international macroeconomic models in Chapters 5 and 6 by analyzing how the gold standard worked.

The gold standard was eventually succeeded after World War II by a world monetary system designed at an international conference held in Bretton Woods, New Hampshire in 1944. This system, known as the Bretton Woods system, remained in place from 1946 to 1973. In Chapters 6 and 7 we will examine macroeconomics under the Bretton Woods system. Like the gold standard, this system featured fixed exchange rates. However, unlike the gold standard, the fixed exchange rates that prevailed under the Bretton Woods system are best described as **"soft" exchange rate pegs**. A soft peg is an exchange rate regime in which the central bank maintains a fixed, officially announced exchange rate, but retains substantial discretion over the value of the official exchange rate as well as over monetary policy. Another major difference from the conditions that prevailed under the gold standard was that during the Bretton Woods period links among national capital markets were very imperfect. Thus the analytical focus of Chapters 6 and 7 is on the macroeconomic behavior of an economy that is characterized by imperfect integration with world financial markets and operates a soft fixed exchange rate. As you will see, this is a subject that is not just of historical interest, because these characteristics describe rather well the conditions that prevail among most developing countries today.

However, as previously mentioned, the process of globalization has resulted in increasing integration among national financial markets, making capital much more mobile internationally for both industrial as well as for many middle-income developing countries. Consequently, in Chapter 8 we conclude our examination of fixed exchange rates by turning to the analysis of fixed exchange rates under high capital mobility. As we will see there, many international macroeconomists have come to question the sustainability of soft exchange rate pegs as countries become increasingly integrated financially with the rest of the world, because many countries that have gone through this process have been led to abandon such pegs in recent years, often under crisis circumstances. These economists have argued that if such countries want to retain a fixed exchange rate, they will have to adopt a modern version of a hard exchange rate peg. Chapter 8 will thus conclude our examination of macroeconomics under fixed exchange rates by describing the modern versions of hard pegs and exploring the considerations that may influence the choice between soft and hard pegs in a financially integrated world.

Part 3.   Floating exchange rates

Most readers of this book, however, will probably be living under a different set of macroeconomic circumstances, one that tends to prevail among the major industrial countries and the largest emerging-market economies. Such economies are characterized by very high capital mobility, no central bank commitment to defend any particular value of the exchange rate by intervening in foreign exchange markets (floating exchange rates), and a substantial degree of discretion on the part of the central bank in its conduct of monetary policy. The analysis of macroeconomic behavior under such circumstances will receive the most attention in this book. It is the subject of Part 3.

As we will see, an important complicating factor that arises when exchange rates are perceived as free to move in the future is that the expected *future* value of the exchange rate will affect today's macroeconomic outcomes. Since long-lasting shocks to the economy will tend to affect the exchange rate that prevails in the future, the effects of shocks will thus depend on how long they are expected to last. Accordingly, in this part of the book we will separately analyze the cases of transitory, intermediate, and permanent shocks to the economy, and will also consider how macroeconomic responses to permanent shocks are affected when the economy's asset markets adjust much more quickly than the markets for goods and services, as is indeed likely to be the case in the real world. Chapter 10 will examine the effects of transitory shocks in a floating-rate model, while Chapter 11 will consider longer-lived shocks. Chapter 12 examines the implications of asymmetries in the speed of adjustment in the markets for goods and services and those for financial assets.

Those chapters will be based on a sticky-price "Keynesian" framework of the type that is usually employed for the analysis of short-run stabilization issues in macroeconomics. In this framework, the aggregate price level is perceived as adjusting slowly, so to a first approximation it is constant in the short run – that is, it does not immediately adjust in response to shocks. Over a long enough time horizon, however, the aggregate price level becomes an endogenous variable. Thus, to round out our analysis of macroeconomics under floating exchange rates, Chapter 13 will examine how the economy responds to shocks over a horizon that is long enough for all price-level adjustments to be completed. However, not all international macroeconomists subscribe to this Keynesian perspective on the speed of price level adjustment. Consequently, this part of the book concludes with a separate examination in Chapter 14 of how floating exchange rates work under a more "classical" perspective that allows for full short-run wage and price flexibility.

Having separately considered how open economies behave under fixed and floating exchange rates, it is natural to ask which exchange rate regime countries *should* adopt. In Chapter 15 we will consider what criteria can be used in evaluating exchange rate regimes. We will then apply these criteria together with the analyses of the first two parts of the book to consider what factors should influence the type of exchange rate regime that it may be optimal for a specific country to adopt.

Part 4.   International monetary cooperation

For most of the book, we will conduct our analysis from the perspective of a single country. That is, we will analyze how an *individual* economy behaves under a variety of circumstances. The nation-state is, after all, the context in which macroeconomic policy decisions are typically made. But sometimes countries may choose to enter into international agreements that have the effect of constraining the policy decisions that they can make. In Chapters 16–18, we will explore why they may find it desirable to do so.

We will consider a variety of arrangements for international monetary coordination that place differing degrees of constraint on domestic policy decisions in the participating countries. Chapter 16 considers the least constraining type of coordination, consisting of the establishment of certain "rules of the game" to govern both international capital flows as well as the behavior of international financial institutions. Proposals affecting these issues feature prominently in contemporary debates over how to redesign the international financial system to create a new international "financial architecture."

In Chapter 17, we will consider the types of cooperation that may be called for when macroeconomic developments in a single country have important effects on partner countries. The analysis of this situation, which currently prevails among the G-3 "countries" (the United States, the European countries constituting the Eurozone, and Japan) will require modifying earlier models to handle the case of a country that is sufficiently large so that its actions are capable of influencing the international environment in which it operates. The policy spillovers generated in these circumstances create a case for international cooperation beyond the mere agreeing on "rules of the game": countries will want to induce other countries to take into account – at least in a loose way – these spillover effects when they formulate their domestic macroeconomic policies.

Finally, the most ambitious form of cooperation, in the sense that it seeks to impose the strongest international constraints on domestic macroeconomic policies, involves the coordination of exchange rate policies, particularly in the extreme form of **monetary unification**, the adoption of a common currency. We will explore this type of coordination in Chapter 18, with a specific focus on the evolution of a single European currency, the euro.

Part 5. The new international macroeconomics

Finally, in the book's last chapter, we will explore the implications of incorporating into our basic analytical framework more sophisticated assumptions about the way that macroeconomic agents behave, based on explicit microeconomic foundations. This alternative description of the way economic agents behave highlights the role of intertemporal issues – decisions about the allocation of spending and production across different points in time – in international macroeconomics. It has formed the basis of a "new international macroeconomics" that has guided academic research in the field during recent years.

## Techniques

Because most of our work will consist of building and analyzing models, it is worth saying a word or two about the analytical techniques that will be used throughout the book. As is invariably the case in modern macroeconomics (and particularly in most intermediate macroeconomics textbooks), the models that we will study will be developed and summarized in equation form. But, again as in intermediate macroeconomics, we will generally analyze these models using graphical tools, which you will likely find very familiar. The exception will be in Chapter 14, in which we analyze flexible-price versions of floating exchange rate models. In that context, the analysis will rely on simple algebra applied to log-linear versions of the models.[4] You may want to brush up on the basic properties of natural logarithms before reading those chapters especially, though natural logs will also be used (sparingly) in various other places in the book. While calculus is not used explicitly, those of you who are familiar with it will occasionally recognize reasoning that is derived from basic concepts of calculus.

---

**Empirical Study 1.1   Globalization and Inflation**

As we will discover in this book, there are many ways that increased openness can affect macroeconomic performance, but the links are sometimes subtle, and they depend both on the type of openness that a country experiences, as well as on the

*(Continued)*

---

[4]   A log-linear model is one whose equations are linear functions of the logarithms of the variables in the model.

**Empirical Study 1.1**    *(Continued)*

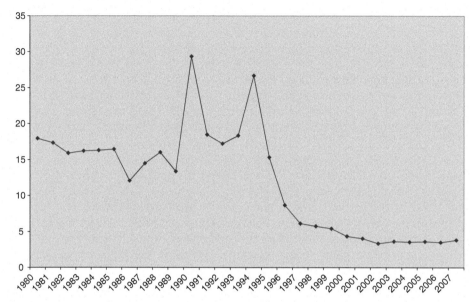

**Figure 1.1**    World inflation rate, 1980–2007 (in percent)
*Source*: International Monetary Fund, *International Financial Statistics*.

macroeconomic policies that it pursues. Understanding how such factors interact in affecting a country's macroeconomic performance is a key objective of this book.

As an illustration, consider an issue that has been debated by economists in recent years: the effect of globalization on inflation. Of particular interest is the role that globalization may have played in bringing about the "great disinflation" – the dramatic decrease in inflation rates that many countries experienced in the period since the early 1990s. Figure 1.1 displays the average annual world inflation rate over the period 1980–2007, based on consumer price indexes. As shown in the chart, the average rate of inflation in the world remained relatively high until the mid-1990s. After that time, it has fallen rather dramatically. Why might this have happened?

There are many possible explanations. Some economists emphasize the role of institutional changes in the ways that monetary and fiscal policies are conducted in many countries around the world. Improved productivity performance may also have contributed. But several observers have pointed to a potential effect of globalization.

There are several ways that globalization may affect a country's "normal" rate of inflation. For example, consider the effects of increased "real" openness, in the form of increased integration of markets for goods and services. Such integration increases the intensity of competition faced by domestic producers. This much is clear. But how does this increased competition affect the sensitivity of domestic prices to domestic demand? One argument is that when domestic demand is high, foreign competition prevents domestic producers from raising prices as much as they otherwise would, because consumers would simply buy foreign goods; similarly, when domestic demand is low, domestic producers would not need to lower prices as much as they otherwise would, because they can sell some of their output abroad. This argument implies that domestic inflation would be less responsive to domestic demand in open economies, and it has been cited to explain why US inflation may have stayed low during recent periods of rapid growth, such as the late 1990s.

One problem with this story, though, is that it assumes that the behavior of the prices of foreign goods (measured in domestic currency) does not change when domestic inflation does. If the prices of foreign goods moved in tandem with that of domestic goods whenever domestic demand changed, the story would not hold. But is there any reason why we should expect that to happen? One such reason is that the domestic currency may lose value relative to foreign currencies when domestic inflation rises, making foreign goods become more expensive when their prices are measured in domestic currency. Similarly, the domestic currency may gain value relative to foreign currencies when domestic inflation falls, making foreign goods less expensive in domestic currency terms. Is this what normally happens? To answer this question, and therefore to understand how globalization may affect the behavior of inflation, we need to understand what determines the relative values of world currencies, one of the central issues that we will consider in this book.

Increased financial openness may have had a role to play as well. Money growth is often the result of excessively expansionary fiscal policies, since governments that need to finance large fiscal deficits generally pressure central banks to print money with which to purchase government debt. Under increased financial openness, governments that run large fiscal deficits are likely to face high interest rates on their debt, because the higher risks faced by their creditors would cause them to shift their lending overseas unless they are compensated by the government for bearing the increased risk by being paid higher interest rates. The higher interest rates that the government has to pay would tend to discourage excessively expansionary fiscal policies, thus reducing pressures on central banks to expand the money supply.

There is substantial empirical evidence on the relationship between openness and inflation. The key reference is Romer (1993), who found that more open economies (measured in terms of commercial openness) have tended to experience lower inflation. More recently, Wynne and Kersting (2007) have documented the effects of commercial openness on the behavior of inflation in the United States. Specifically, they have shown that changes in the rate of inflation in the United States are positively correlated with high levels of economic activity in the country's main trading partners. This implies that, in a globalized context, changes in the US inflation rate are affected not just by domestic economic conditions, but also by economic conditions in US trading partners.

## 1.4  Summary

As the phenomenon of globalization has intensified during recent years, it has become increasingly important for the analysis of macroeconomic issues to be conducted in an open-economy context. Openness affects the ways that variables of concern to policymakers respond to exogenous changes in the economic environment, influences the effectiveness of familiar macroeconomic policies, and introduces new objectives of policy as well as new policy instruments. The objective of this book is to develop an analytical framework to help us understand exactly how openness affects macroeconomic performance.

We begin that task in the next part of the book by defining some open-economy macroeconomic concepts, exploring the foreign exchange market in more detail, and developing the general analytical framework that will provide the foundation on which the analysis of the rest of the book will be built.

## Further Reading and References

### On the openness of the US economy

Cooper, Richard N. (1986) "The United States as an Open Economy," in *How Open is the U.S. Economy?*, Proceedings of the Tenth Annual Economic Policy Conference of the Federal Reserve Bank of St. Louis (December), pp. 3–24.

### On globalization and inflation

Fieleke, Norman S. (1997), "Popular Myths about the World Economy," Federal Reserve Bank of Boston, *New England Economic Review* (July/August), pp. 17–26.

Rogoff, Kenneth (2003), "Globalization and Global Disinflation," Federal Reserve Bank of Kansas City *Economic Review* (Fourth quarter), pp. 45–78.

Romer, David (1993), "Openness and Inflation: Theory and Evidence," *Quarterly Journal of Economics*, Vol. 108 (November), pp. 869–903.

Tootell, Geoffrey M.B. (1998), "Globalization and U.S. Inflation," Federal Reserve Bank of Boston *New England Economic Review* (July/August), pp. 21–33.

Wynne, Mark A. and Erasmus K. Kersting (2007), "Openness and Inflation," Federal Reserve Bank of Dallas *Staff Papers*, No. 2 (April).

### On the "internationalization" of US capital

Quinlan, Joseph and Marc Chandler (2001), "The U.S. Trade deficit: A Dangerous Obsession," *Foreign Affairs* (May/June), pp. 87–98.

# 2

# Open-economy Macroeconomic Accounting

...........................................................................................................................

In order to analyze the macroeconomics of open economies, you will need to become familiar with a wide variety of concepts used by international macroeconomists. The next two chapters are intended to help you do so. This chapter defines some of these concepts and explores the **identities** (definitional relationships) that link them to each other. By classifying international transactions into different types and showing how they are linked to each other, these identities provide a foundation for clarifying and disciplining our thinking about international macroeconomic issues. In Chapter 3 we will begin to explore the economic motivations that underlie each of these types of transactions. Together, therefore, these two chapters provide fundamental building blocks for the general analytical framework that we will construct in Chapter 4.

Our point of departure in this chapter is a country's **balance of payments (BOP) accounts**. Recall from the last chapter that macroeconomic openness involves trade between domestic and foreign residents in goods and services as well as in financial assets. The balance of payments accounts are the record of all such trades. In this chapter we will explore the balance of payments accounts and examine how they are linked with the national income and product accounts. While the basic purpose of doing this is to acquaint you with some fundamental concepts in international macroeconomics, it turns out that we can actually extract some very useful and very powerful economics from the basic relationships that we will be examining in this chapter. It is hard to resist the urge to take advantage of this opportunity, so we will indeed pause to explore some of these economic applications as we go along.

## 2.1   The Balance of Payments Accounts

The term ''balance of payments (BOP) accounts'' refers to the system of accounts kept by each country that tracks payments to and receipts from nonresidents by residents of the country. The entries in the balance of payments accounts, like those in the national income and product accounts, represent economic **flows** (which are quantities measured in units of currency or goods *per unit of time*), rather than **stocks** (which are quantities measured at fixed points in time). In this section we will go over the basic rules that govern how these flows are recorded in the balance of payments accounts and will identify the different types of transactions that are tracked in these accounts.

### Rules of Balance of Payments Accounting

Since the balance of payments accounts keep track of economic transactions between residents of the domestic economy and those of other economies, we need to first define who is considered a resident and who is not. Residents are economic agents (such as households, firms, or governments) who *normally* reside in a country, even if they are temporarily abroad, such as tourists, diplomats, military personnel, migrant workers, or students. In the balance of payments accounts of the United States, for example, the term ''resident'' *does not* include branches or subsidiaries of US companies that happen to be located in foreign countries (subsidiaries are legally incorporated there, branches are not). These are assumed to be residents of the foreign country, because they normally conduct their business (and therefore ''reside'') there, regardless of their legal status. Under this definition of residence, **international transactions** are transactions between residents and nonresidents.

The balance of payments accounts that track these transactions obey the basic rule of double-entry bookkeeping: because every transaction involves an exchange of equal values, every international transaction gives rise to two entries in the BOP accounts, one recording the value of what is received by the domestic resident, as well as one recording the value of what the domestic resident gives up. One exception to the ''exchange of equal values'' principle might immediately occur to you: gifts exchanged between residents and nonresidents. But even in this case, to maintain the double-entry principle, it is assumed that the transaction actually involves an exchange – what is exchanged for the item given away is conventionally assumed to consist of ''goodwill'' that is equal in monetary value to the gift. Under this convention, there are no exceptions to the rule that every transaction involves an exchange of equal values.

The basic rule for recording international transactions is that any transaction resulting in the receipt of something of value *from* foreigners (thus creating an obligation to foreigners, or an ''account payable'' to foreigners by domestic residents) is classified as a **debit**, and is entered with a negative sign, while any transaction resulting in a transfer of something of value *to* foreigners (creating an ''account receivable'' from foreigners by domestic residents) is classified as a **credit**, and is entered with a positive sign. Notice that, because every transaction in the balance of payments accounts thus generates a debit as well as a credit that exactly offsets it in value, *the sum of all transactions recorded in the BOP accounts must be equal to zero.*

**Table 2.1**    US international transactions, 2007

|  | *$ bn* |
|---|---|
| Exports of goods | 1149 |
| Imports of goods | −1965 |
| Exports of services | 479 |
| Imports of services | −372 |
| Income receipts | 782 |
| Income payments | −708 |
| Unilateral current transfers, net | −104 |
| US Government grants | −33 |
| US Government pensions and other transfers | −7 |
| Private remittances and other transfers | −65 |
| Unilateral capital transfers, net | −2 |
| US-owned assets abroad, net (increase/financial outflow (−)) | −1206 |
| US official reserve assets, net | −1 |
| US Government assets, other than official reserve assets, net | −23 |
| US private assets, net | −1183 |
| Foreign-owned assets in the United States, net (increase/financial inflow ( + )) | 1864 |
| Foreign official assets in the United States, net | 413 |
| Other foreign assets in the United States, net | 1451 |
| Statistical discrepancy (sum of above items with sign reversed) | 84 |

*Source*: US Department of Commerce.

## Types of Transactions

Table 2.1 summarizes the external transactions of the United States for the year 2007. You can see that transactions in the accounts are classified into several (six) types:

**a    Exports and imports of goods**. Sales of goods to foreigners, referred to as *exports* of goods, transfer something of value to foreigners, so they give rise to credit entries, while purchases of goods from foreigners (*imports* of goods) involve the receipt of value by domestic residents, so they are recorded as debits. Note that what is recorded here is the actual transfer of the good, whether from domestic to foreign residents (exports) or vice versa (imports). The payment for the good is typically entered somewhere else in the accounts. In 2007, the United States exported $1149 billion worth of goods to the rest of the world, but imported much more, $1965 billion.

**b    Exports and imports of services**. Services that are traded between domestic and foreign residents include tourism, transportation (both passenger and freight), royalties and licenses, and insurance and financial services. The same accounting principle applies as for goods in classifying entries as debits or credits. You can see from Table 2.1 that, in contrast with goods, the United States was a net *exporter* of services to the rest of the world.

**c    Receipts and payments of investment income** (interest and profits). Investment income is the compensation that the owner of capital receives for the use by someone else of the services of that capital. These are recorded as ''income receipts'' and ''income payments'' in Table 2.1. An *entitlement* to the receipt of investment income, in the form of profits or interest, is entered as a credit, because it arises as the result of the transfer to foreigners of the services of capital that is owned by domestic residents, while the *obligation* to make a payment for investment income is entered as a debit (because domestic residents are using capital services that are produced by foreign-owned capital). Again, it is important to remember that what is entered here is the value of the services provided (which gives rise to the entitlement to receive payment or the obligation to make payment), not the form in which those services are paid for.[1]

**d    Unilateral transfers.** As mentioned above, a gift from a domestic resident to a foreign resident is considered an import of something of value (goodwill), so transfers (gifts) given to foreigners are entered as debits, while transfers received are credits. Thus, this item records the transfer of goodwill, not of the commodity that generates that goodwill. In Table 2.1, unilateral transfers are reported on a net basis (credits minus debits). As you can see, in 2007 the United States provided more transfers than it received in that year. Thus, according to the BOP accounts, at any rate, the country was a net importer of goodwill from the rest of the world![2]

**e    Purchases and sales of physical or financial assets.** Sales of physical assets or financial claims by domestic residents to foreign residents, *whether those financial claims are themselves on domestic or on foreign residents*, involve giving up something of value and are therefore entered as credits. Correspondingly, purchases of physical assets or financial claims by domestic residents from foreign residents are debits. In the BOP accounts, domestic and foreign residents are classified into central banks, governments, and private agents. Financial assets held by central banks are called "official assets." These are treated in the same way as the corresponding asset transactions by other agents (private and government), but are simply tracked separately, for reasons to be explained later in this chapter. Thus, the acquisition of financial claims by the domestic central bank on residents of the rest of the world is entered as a debit, while the sale of such claims by the domestic central bank is entered as a credit. Similarly, the acquisition of a claim on a domestic resident by a foreign central bank is a credit in the domestic balance of payments, while the sale of such a claim is a debit.

**f    Statistical discrepancy.** Since every transaction recorded in the balance of payments accounts gives rise to equal and offsetting credit and debit entries, the sum of all of the transactions recorded in the accounts should in principle be zero, as we noted previously. However, because the data in the accounts are collected from different sources, measurement errors (including unrecorded transactions) and timing problems prevent this from literally being true in the recorded data. The "statistical discrepancy" (also called "errors and omissions") line in Table 2.1 captures the net effects of these errors, so that the sum of all entries will indeed add to zero when this line is included.

It is worth pausing for a moment to define some terms that are frequently used in discussing the financial transactions in the BOP accounts. Sales of financial claims (assets) to foreign residents by domestic residents are called **capital inflows**, and as mentioned

---

[1]    The United States received more payments for the services of capital in 2007 than it paid to the rest of the world. This is something of a puzzle, because the United States has actually borrowed more from the rest of the world than it has loaned to the rest of the world, as we will see later in this chapter. We will consider then how this can be reconciled with the data in Table 2.1.

[2]    For an extended discussion of the role of unilateral transfers in the balance of payments of the United States and other countries, see Fieleke (1996).

above, these are entered with a positive sign, since something of value (the claim) has been exported. Similarly, purchases of financial assets by domestic residents from foreign residents are called **capital outflows** and are entered with a negative sign, since something of value has been imported. A special term is often used for capital inflows that take the form of the sale by a domestic resident of a financial claim on a foreign resident to either the same or another foreign resident. This type of transaction is referred to as **capital repatriation**, since it entails returning resources to the domestic economy that were at some point in the past made available to the foreign economy.

As discussed in Chapter 1, globalization has involved increased trade not just in goods and services, but also in financial assets. An important dimension of such trade is the scale of capital inflows to developing countries. These capital inflows represent additional resources that these countries can use to invest in increasing their productive capacities or to consume more than they could do, based just on their own resources. But fluctuations in such capital inflows have been large, and have at times been associated with episodes of severe macroeconomic instability in such countries, as we will see at various times in this book. Figure 2.1 shows both the increasing scale of these inflows in recent years, as well as their volatility. Note in particular the drop-off in capital inflows during the early 1980s and late 1990s. We will come back to these episodes at various places in this book.

International financial transactions come in a variety of forms. A fundamental distinction is between financial claims that take the form of equity and those that take the form of debt. **Debt claims** contractually stipulate specific payments that debtors have to make to their creditors, and they do not convey ownership rights that entitle the creditor to an equal say over the affairs of a firm as its shareholders. Debt claims can take the form of **bonds**, which

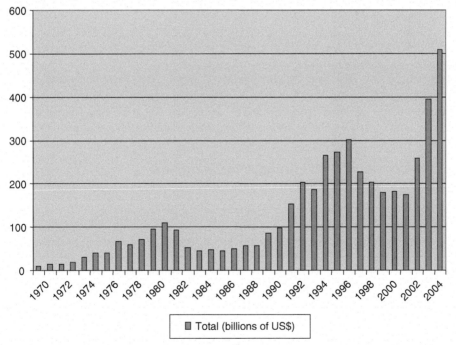

**Figure 2.1**  Developing countries: total capital inflows
*Source*: World Bank, *World Development Indicators*.

are marketable securities, or **loans**, which are typically not marketable and are usually provided by banks. **Equity claims**, by contrast, are ownership shares. They entitle the buyer of the claim to a voice in appointing the firm's board of directors (which in turn appoints the firm's management) and of a share to the firm's profits after the servicing of debt. Since debt holders get paid from a firm's revenues before equity holders do, the latter are often described as having a "residual claim" on the firm's income.

In the balance of payments accounts, data sources such as the International Monetary Fund (IMF) and World Bank typically classify financial transactions into three types:

1   When purchases of equity by foreigners transfer direct control over an enterprise to the buyers of that equity, this type of capital flow is referred to as **foreign direct investment (FDI)** into the country where the enterprise is located. Sales of equity to foreign residents by enterprises already controlled by foreign residents are also FDI. What "control" means is a fuzzy concept. Conventionally, purchases of equity associated with ownership of at least 10 percent of the market capitalization (value) of a firm are treated as FDI.
2   The purchase or sale of marketable financial assets across countries is called a **portfolio flow**. Purchases and sales of equity that do not entail control of domestic firms by foreigners or of foreign firms by domestic residents are referred to as **portfolio equity flows**, while international purchases and sales of bonds are called **portfolio bond flows**. The sale of equity (stocks) and bonds by domestic to foreign residents constitutes a **portfolio capital inflow**, while the purchase of such assets by domestic from foreign residents represents a **portfolio capital outflow**.
3   The final type of financial transaction is **lending**. As indicated above, this consists of nonmarketable loans, typically extended by banks, but also by other lenders such as governments and international financial institutions.

In addition to this three-way classification, financial transactions are also occasionally classified by the maturity of the financial instrument that is traded.[3] When financial claims (bonds or loans) have an original maturity of less than a year, they are considered short term, and trading in such claims is referred to as **short-term capital flows**. When claims have original maturities of more than a year, or when they have no specified maturity (for example, FDI or portfolio equity claims), they are dubbed **long-term capital flows**.

## 2.2   Sub-accounts in the Balance of Payments

The balance of payments accounts are organized into several sub-accounts, which include selected categories of transactions. Notice that, unlike the overall balance, the balance in these sub-accounts need not be zero; since they only contain a subset of all transactions, the balancing transaction may lie outside the included subset. For example, suppose that a US resident imports a foreign good and pays for it by writing a check to the foreign exporter. The import of the good gives rise to a debit in the US balance of payments, but the transfer of the ownership of a claim on the US importer's bank from a domestic to a foreign resident gives rise to an exactly offsetting credit. However, if these two sides of the transaction are

---

[3]   A financial instrument is just a promise to make payments in the future. The maturity of the instrument is the length of time during which those payments are to be made.

recorded in different sub-accounts, then there is no reason for the entries in the sub-accounts to sum to zero, even though in total all the entries in the balance of payments will do so.

As we shall see, it is these sub-accounts of the overall balance of payments accounts that actually have important economic implications. As you will see below, an important distinction among the sub-accounts is between those that contain only *current* transactions (transactions in currently produced goods and services, factor income, and transfers) and those that contain only *financial* transactions (transactions in existing physical assets or financial claims).

## Definitions

Table 2.2 lists the various sub-accounts of the balance of payments for the United States in 2007. They consist of the following:

**a    The balance on merchandise trade.** This is the narrowest of the sub-accounts that contain only current transactions. It consists of exports of goods minus imports of goods. This account recorded a **deficit** (an excess of debits over credits) of $816 billion in the United States in 2007. However, economists don't usually draw strong distinctions between trade in goods and in services, which makes this very narrow sub-account of limited practical relevance.

**b    The balance on goods and services.** This is a more inclusive concept that consists of the balance on merchandise trade plus *net* service exports (exports of services minus imports

**Table 2.2**    Sub-accounts of the US balance of payments, 2007

|  | $ bn |
| --- | --- |
| Current account (*CA*) | −739 |
| Balance on goods, services, and investment income | −635 |
| Balance on goods and services (*N*) | −709 |
| Balance on merchandise trade | −816 |
| Exports of goods | 1149 |
| Imports of goods | −1965 |
| Balance on services | 107 |
| Exports of services | 479 |
| Imports of services | −372 |
| Net investment income (*NINV*) | 74 |
| Income receipts | 782 |
| Income payments | −708 |
| Unilateral transfers, net (*NUT*) | −104 |
| Capital and financial account | 656 |
| Capital account | −2 |
| Nonreserve financial account (*NFA*) | 245 |
| Official reserves settlements balance (*ORS*) | 413 |
| US official reserve assets, net | 0 |
| Foreign official assets in the United States, net | 413 |
| Statistical discrepancy | 83 |

of services). As we will see, this is a more meaningful concept. In fact, since we will actually use it in building our open-economy macroeconomic models, this is a good time to begin to introduce some notation. Since it is the difference between exports and imports of goods and services, we will often refer to the balance on goods and services in this book as **net exports**. Let $X$ denote the dollar value of exports of goods and services, and $IM$ the corresponding dollar value of imports. Then the dollar value of the balance on goods and services, which we will call $N$ (for net exports), is given by:

$$N = X - IM$$

In 2007 exports of goods and services from the United States amounted to \$1628 billion, while imports of goods and services were \$2337 billion, so the balance of goods and services recorded a deficit of \$709 billion. This is not unusual. While the United States has not always run deficits in the balance on goods and services, it has tended to do so for many years. This sub-account receives substantial attention in the press, where positive values of or increases in $N$ are considered to be good economic news, while negative values or decreases are treated as cause for concern.[4]

   c   **The balance on goods, services, and investment income.** Adding net investment income (the difference between income receipts and income payments in Table 2.2, which we can denote $NINV$) to $N$ yields the balance on good, services, and investment income.
   d   **The current account.** This is the most inclusive – and most important – of the BOP sub-accounts relating to current transactions (hence the name). It consists of the balance on goods, services, and investment income plus net unrequited transfers ($NUT$). Using the symbol $CA$ to denote its US dollar value, the current account is defined as:

$$CA = N + NINV + NUT$$

As you can see from Table 2.2, in 2007 the United States recorded a current account deficit of \$739 billion, dominated by a large deficit in the balance on goods and services. We will explore the economic significance of the current account later in this chapter.
   There are also a variety of sub-accounts on the asset (capital) side of the BOP ledger. This side of the BOP accounts is referred to as the **capital and financial account**, consisting of the **capital account** and the **financial account**.
   The capital account is a relatively minor item. It records unrequited transfers of existing assets (rather than of currently produced goods and services) as well as transactions involving the purchase or sale of nonproduced, nonfinancial assets such as patents, franchises, or leases that are not accounted for elsewhere in the BOP accounts. To keep things as simple as possible, we will omit separate consideration of the capital account in the rest of this book by just assuming (realistically) that it is approximately zero.
   The financial account is much larger and more important. It records transactions in the different types of financial claims mentioned above (that is, FDI, portfolio flows, and

---

[4]   As we will soon see, there is some justification for all of this attention. Not only does this particular BOP concept play an important macroeconomic role, but because a large part of the information on these transactions is drawn from customs data, it is available and published relatively frequently (on a monthly basis) compared to some of the other data in the BOP accounts, which are compiled quarterly.

lending). These transactions can be undertaken by the private sector, by governments, and by central banks. As shown in Table 2.2, the BOP accounts track these individually. For analytical purposes, it is useful to consider separately those transactions involving the private sector and governments, on the one hand, and those involving central banks, on the other. Financial claims on nonresidents held by central banks are called **official foreign exchange reserves**, or just "reserves" for short.[5] Accordingly, the purchase or sale of financial assets by the private sector or governments is entered in the **nonreserve financial account**, while those involving central banks are entered in the **official reserves settlements accounts**. This gives us our last two subaccounts.

e   **The nonreserve financial account balance** *(NFA)*. As we saw previously, sales of physical assets and financial claims by domestic (non-central bank) residents to foreign (non-central bank) residents are called capital inflows *(KI)*, while purchases of physical assets or financial claims by domestic (non-central bank) residents from foreign (non-central bank) residents are called capital outflows *(KO)*. The former are entered as credits, and the latter as debits, in the balance of payments accounts. The difference between the two is the **nonreserve financial account balance** *(NFA)*:[6]

$$NFA = KI - KO$$

Table 2.2 shows that the United States ran a nonreserve financial account surplus of $245 billion in 2007. This means that nonofficial US residents in the aggregate borrowed this much more than they loaned to the rest of the world. This is in part how the country managed to pay for the excess of the goods and services that it bought from the rest of the world over the goods and services that it sold to the rest of the world, plus its net payment of investment income and unilateral transfers to the rest of the world.

f   **Official reserve settlements balance** *(ORS)*. Purchases and sales of foreign financial assets by central banks are called **official foreign exchange intervention**. The *net* change in official reserve assets (net increase in financial claims on domestic residents held by foreign central banks minus the net increase in claims on foreign residents held by the domestic central bank) is called the **official reserve settlement balance**. We will refer to this subaccount as *ORS*.

It is important to note that the United States is in a somewhat unusual position regarding *ORS*, because of the role of the US dollar as the dominant international "vehicle"

---

[5]   These consist of gold, foreign interest-bearing assets, special drawing rights (SDRs), and other claims on the International Monetary Fund (IMF), all of which can be exchanged for foreign currency. The IMF is described in Chapter 6, and SDRs in Chapter 7.

[6]   There is a semantic issue that is important to mention at this point. The terminology used in this chapter for the capital and financial account and its subaccounts is relatively new. It is the product of a revision to the IMF's official *Balance of Payments Manual* adopted in 1999. Before then, the term "capital account" was applied to what was called above the "nonreserve financial account," and most of the items currently included in the capital account were included under transfers in the current account. The reason this is important is because many economists continue to refer to the nonreserve financial account as the "capital account" of the balance of payments, and you will often encounter this usage in both the press as well as in the policy and professional literature.

currency.[7] Generally, central banks hold foreign exchange reserves in order to have the option to engage in **foreign exchange market intervention** (to buy or sell their own currencies in the foreign exchange market). Such reserves are usually maintained in the form of vehicle currencies, such as the US dollar.[8] That means that the central banks of other countries typically hold financial claims on US residents (usually these take the form of Treasury bills issued by the US government).[9] Thus, in calculating the country's *net* international reserve position, the international reserves held by the United States have to be netted out against the claims on US residents held by foreign central banks. Indeed, as you can see from Table 2.2, in 2007 the official reserves settlements balance for the United States was driven entirely by the accumulation of claims on the US by foreign central banks. But because a very small number of currencies serve as vehicle currencies, this situation is the exception rather than the rule. Generally, international reserves of other central banks consist only of the net foreign assets held by those central banks themselves.

## Interpreting the Sub-accounts

Since the current account, the nonreserve financial account, and the official reserve settlement balance together exhaust all of the transactions that comprise the balance of payments, in the absence of statistical discrepancies these three sub-accounts should sum to zero.[10] That is:

$$CA + NFA + ORS = 0$$

This is referred to as the **balance of payments identity**. However, remember that the components of this sum do not *individually* have to be equal to zero. Should we care what values these sub-accounts take? The answer is yes, and our next task is to explain why.

*Why the current account matters*    From the identity above, a current account surplus must be offset by a deficit on the sum of the nonreserve financial account and *ORS*, and a current account deficit must be offset by a surplus on the sum of the nonfinancial capital account and *ORS*:

$$CA = -(NFA + ORS)$$

---

[7]    Traders in the foreign exchange market tend to quote prices in terms of a small number of currencies, and to use those currencies as common means of exchange – that is, as the international "moneys" for which other currencies are bought and sold. The currencies that play this role are called "vehicle" currencies. According to the Bank for International Settlements (2005), in 2004 fully 89 percent of all foreign exchange transactions around the world involved US dollars.

[8]    While most international reserves are held in the form of US dollars, some countries also hold reserves in the form of euros, Japanese yen, or British pounds. According to the IMF, in 2005 about 66 percent of the world's total reserves were held in US dollars, 25 percent in euros, 4 percent in yen, and 3 percent in pounds. The countries that issue these currencies are in a similar position to that of the United States.

[9]    In recent years, several countries that have accumulated large amounts of reserves have created special institutions to invest these reserves in a wider array of assets, hoping for higher returns than are available on government securities. These institutions are called **sovereign wealth funds**.

[10]    Recall that we are assuming that the capital account balance is zero.

Thus, if CA is positive, NFA + ORS must be negative and equal in magnitude. In other words, *a current account surplus represents an exactly equal accumulation of net financial claims by domestic residents on the rest of the world*. This explains why the current account surplus is often referred to as the economy's **net foreign investment**. It is one way that the domestic economy can accumulate wealth. On the other hand, if the current account balance is negative, there is an equal accumulation of net financial claims by the rest of the world on the domestic economy. Thus, *a current account deficit corresponds to an exactly equal accumulation of net financial liabilities to the rest of the world*, and is referred to as **net foreign borrowing**.

The net financial claims that all the residents of a country in the aggregate have on the rest of the world (that is, their claims on the rest of the world minus the rest of the world's claims on them) are referred to as the country's **international investment position**, which we will call *IIP*. Because these net financial claims generate income for domestic residents (in the form of interest, dividends, capital gains, and so on), the country's international investment position is a component of its national wealth in exactly the same sense that its stock of productive physical capital is. What we have shown is that, just as the country's stock of physical capital is the sum of its past net investment, its net international investment position is the sum of its past current account surpluses and deficits. As a component of a country's wealth at a moment of time, the international investment position is a *stock*, rather than a flow.

Table 2.3 shows the international investment position, as a fraction of the country's GDP, for a group of industrial and developing countries in 2004. The investment position was estimated by accumulating each country's current account surpluses and deficits. Notice that it varies substantially among countries. Most industrial countries are net creditors to the

**Table 2.3**    Net international creditor positions of selected countries, 2004 (ratio to GDP)

| *Industrial countries* | *IIP/GDP* | *Developing countries* | *IIP/GDP* |
|---|---|---|---|
| Australia | −0.64 | Argentina | −0.48 |
| Austria | −0.17 | Brazil | −0.49 |
| Belgium | 0.31 | Chile | −0.37 |
| Canada | −0.13 | China | 0.08 |
| Finland | −0.12 | Colombia | −0.35 |
| France | 0.05 | India | −0.11 |
| Germany | 0.08 | Indonesia | −0.52 |
| Italy | −0.18 | Korea | −0.04 |
| Japan | 0.38 | Kuwait | 2.43 |
| Netherlands | −0.06 | Mexico | −0.43 |
| New Zealand | −0.92 | Peru | −0.53 |
| Norway | 0.65 | Philippines | −0.59 |
| Sweden | −0.10 | Saudi Arabia | 0.64 |
| Switzerland | 1.30 | Singapore | 1.75 |
| United Kingdom | −0.13 | South Africa | −0.05 |
| United States | −0.23 | Syria | −0.54 |
| | | Thailand | −0.29 |
| | | Venezuela | 0.17 |
| | | Zimbabwe | −0.61 |

*Source*: Lane and Milesi-Ferretti (2006).

rest of the world, though there are some exceptions. The United States, as the world's largest debtor, is an important one.[11] But sparsely populated industrial countries with substantial natural resources such as Australia, Canada, New Zealand, and several Scandinavian countries are also net international debtors. We will discuss later on in the chapter why this might be so (see Box 2.5). Similarly, developing countries tend to be net international borrowers, but there are also exceptions to this pattern – in particular, several sparsely populated oil-producing countries in the Middle East. We will look at one such example, Kuwait, in Box 2.2.

We have just seen that the current account matters because it determines the *change in the economy's international investment position*. Does that mean that current account deficits – which increase the country's net debt to the rest of the world – are always bad? We will see in the following section that this depends on what is financed with the borrowing that is associated with current account deficits.

*Why the "balance of payments" matters*    Economists often use the term "overall" balance of payments (or just balance of payments for short) to refer to a particular sub-account: the sum of the current and nonreserve financial accounts. Thus:

$$BOP = CA + NFA$$

From the balance of payments identity, we can see that:

$$BOP = -ORS$$

Thus the overall balance of payments is just the negative of the official reserves settlement balance.

Why should we care about this particular sub-account? As already mentioned, central banks often decide to intervene in foreign exchange markets by buying or selling their own currencies in exchange for foreign currencies, typically US dollars (we will see why they do this in the next chapter). While they can always sell their own currencies in exchange for foreign currencies, however (since they can print it in amounts that are unlimited in principle), they can only buy their own currency if they have the foreign exchange with which to do so. Since they can not print foreign exchange (only foreign central banks can do that) they often maintain a stock of foreign exchange reserves for this purpose, as we saw previously. These reserves take the form of financial assets that can quickly be turned into foreign currency, such as gold, liquid financial assets issued by foreign governments, the country's reserve position at the IMF, and its stock of special drawing rights (SDRs). We will discuss the role of gold in Chapter 5 and of reserve positions at the IMF as well as of SDRs in Chapters 7 and 8.

---

[11]    Remember that we previously noted that the United States had a surplus on net investment income in 2007. How can this be, if the rest of the world owns more financial claims on the United States than the United States does on the rest of the world? One part of the answer is that the international investment position of the United States calculated by summing US current account deficits/surpluses over time probably understates the true value of *IIP* for the United States, because many of these assets are relatively old, and have probably increased substantially in market value over time. Another part is that a larger share of US claims on the rest of the world than of the rest of the world's claims on the United States are in the form of high-yielding assets like FDI rather than lower-yielding ones like Treasury bills.

This means that the stock of foreign exchange reserves that a central bank holds determines its ability to buy its currency in the foreign exchange market. The importance of the overall balance of payments, which we denoted *BOP* above, emerges from this fact. Assuming that foreign central banks do not hold claims on the domestic economy, the relationship above indicates that *BOP* surpluses/deficits correspond to increases/decreases in the central bank's liquid foreign assets. A *BOP* surplus means that *ORS* must be negative, so the domestic central bank must be acquiring net claims on the rest of the world and thus accumulating net foreign exchange reserves. Conversely, a *BOP* deficit means that *ORS* is positive, so the central bank must be selling claims to the rest of the world and thus losing reserves. *BOP* deficits are thus worrisome because they signify decreases in the central bank's stock of foreign exchange reserves, which would imply a reduced ability by the central bank to buy its own currency with foreign currency.

## 2.3   Basic BOP Facts for the United States

We saw in the previous chapter that macroeconomic openness is likely to alter the way an economy works, and we have learned in this chapter that the current account of the balance of payments accounts is important because it serves as an indicator of the change in a country's net international creditor position. How open is the US economy, and how has its current account balance been behaving over time?

A good indicator of the degree of an economy's openness in the market for goods and services is the ratio of the sum of its exports and imports of goods and services to its GDP. The larger that exports are as a share of GDP, the larger the share of domestic production that is purchased by foreigners, and the larger that imports are as a share of GDP, the larger the share of domestic spending that is devoted to buying foreign goods and services. As Figure 2.2 shows, this ratio has more than doubled in the United States over the past four decades, from less than 10 percent of GDP in the early 1960s, to nearly 30 percent of GDP by the year 2007. By this measure, the US economy is clearly becoming significantly more open over time.

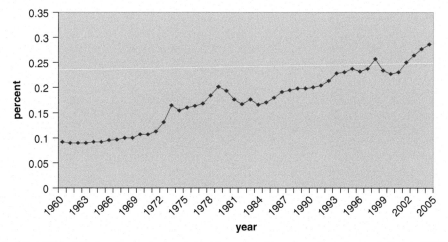

**Figure 2.2**   United States: Sum of exports and imports of goods and services relative to GDP

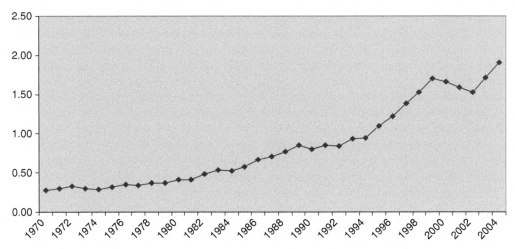

**Figure 2.3**    United States: Sum of external assets and liabilities relative to GDP

With regard to financial openness, a widely used indicator is the ratio of the sum of a country's external assets and liabilities to GDP. Figure 2.3 shows this ratio for the United States. The picture for financial openness is even more dramatic than that for commercial openness. In this case, the data start only in 1970, and end in 2004. But over this 35-year period, the ratio of the United States' external assets and liabilities to GDP increased from just over 25 percent to nearly 200 percent, suggesting much more extensive cross-border trade in financial assets over time.

Turning to the current account performance of the United States, as Figure 2.4 indicates, that performance has been erratic over recent decades. Relative to the size of its economy (as measured by GDP), the United States had a declining current account surplus during the 1960s, had periods of surpluses as well as deficits during the 1970s, and began to record massive deficits during the first half of the 1980s. Overall, current account deficits tended to

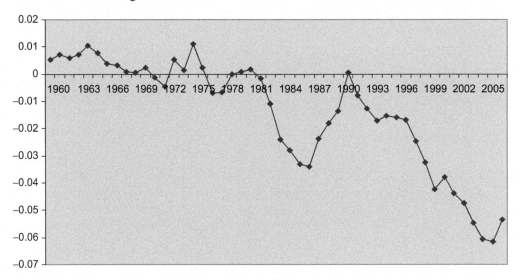

**Figure 2.4**    US current account balance relative to GDP

be small and temporary until about 1982 or so, but the situation has changed since then. While current account balance was temporarily restored in the early 1990s, in recent years the deficit has again widened significantly and persistently, amounting to a high over this 40-year period of over 6 percent of GDP by 2006. The upshot is that the United States has been a large net international borrower for more than two decades. Consequently, the US international financial position has evolved from a net creditor position of about 14 percent of GDP in 1980 to a net debtor position, which, according to Table 2.3, amounted to about 23 percent of GDP by 2004.

In short, the United States is becoming increasingly open and is also becoming an increasingly larger net international debtor. Are these two developments linked in some way? Is the increased openness of the United States somehow causing it to become an ever-larger net international debtor? The answer is probably not. There are many countries in Table 2.2 – for example, Germany and Switzerland – that are much more open than the United States but are net international *creditors*. We will explore the factors driving the large current account deficits that the United States has accumulated since the early 1980s in Chapters 10, 17, and 19.

## 2.4    The NIPA in an Open Economy: Aggregate Identities

The relationships among the various components of GDP are described in a system of accounts called the **National Income and Product Accounts (NIPA)**. In this section, we will examine the relationship between the BOP accounts and the more familiar closed-economy NIPA accounts.

### Closed-economy Macroeconomic Identities

In a closed economy, we can write the basic NIPA identity as:

$$GDP = C + I + G$$

where *GDP* is the dollar (nominal) value of GDP, and all other variables (aggregate private consumption, $C$, private investment, $I$, and government spending, $G$) are also measured in current dollars. This identity holds because any output that is not sold to willing buyers in the marketplace is automatically considered to be ''sold'' to firms in the form of unintended inventory investment, so private investment is actually *defined* as $I = GDP - C - G$. Defining gross domestic saving as:[12]

$$S = GDP - C - G$$

The basic NIPA identity also implies the familiar closed-economy identity:

$$S = I$$

---

[12]    This definition assumes that all of government spending $G$ is devoted to consumption. If this is not the case (as it usually is not), we can simply redefine $I$ to include the investment component of government spending, and refer to $I$ as domestic (rather than private) investment.

This identity states that wealth accumulation (saving) in a closed economy must take the form of the accumulation of real productive assets (investment).

Now let's see what happens to these relationships in the context of an open economy.

## Open-economy Macroeconomic Identities

As we have seen, in an open economy, domestic residents can trade both goods and services as well as financial assets with the rest of the world. This introduces several changes to the two identities above.

First, in an open economy we need to distinguish between *total spending by domestic residents* and *total spending on domestic goods by both domestic and foreign residents*. Total spending by domestic residents is called **absorption** (*A*), and is given by:

$$A = C + I + G$$

Why is this no longer the same as total spending on domestic goods? First, what domestic residents spend is not necessarily spent on domestic goods. What they actually spend on domestic goods is their total spending, $C + I + G$, minus what they spend on foreign goods (imports of goods and services, *IM*). Second, foreign residents also buy domestic goods (in the form of exports of goods and services, *X*). Thus, total spending on domestic goods is given by:

$$GDP = [(C + I + G) - IM] + X$$

where the first term on the right-hand side of the identity corresponds to total spending on domestic goods and services by domestic residents, and the second to spending on domestic goods and services by foreign residents.

This can equivalently be written as:

$$GDP = (C + I + G) + (X - IM)$$
$$= A + N$$

Recall that *N* denotes net exports (the balance on goods and services). Thus, we have our first link between the BOP and NIPA accounts. *GDP* must be equal to *domestic absorption* plus *net exports*. The latter is the second of the two BOP sub-accounts we discussed previously, and this identity shows why the balance on goods and services is an important macroeconomic concept: it is one of the key components of aggregate demand. Other links will refer to progressively broader sub-accounts, as we shall see subsequently.[13]

Next, we need to draw a distinction between gross *domestic* product (*GDP*) and gross *national* product (*GNP*). Recall that gross domestic product is defined as the total value of all final goods and services produced in the domestic economy during a given period, valued at market prices. What is the difference between this concept and that of *GNP*? The answer

---

[13]   What about links involving the narrowest sub-account, the balance on merchandise trade? Since the NIPA does not draw a distinction between the production of goods and that of services, there is no link between the trade balance and the NIPA accounts corresponding to the one described above for the balance on goods and services.

is that *GNP* is *GDP* plus net investment income, to correct for the fact that some of the domestic *GDP* is produced by foreign capital (that is, by capital owned by foreign residents) and some foreign *GDP* is produced by domestic capital:

$$GNP = GDP + NINV$$

Using the basic NIPA identity from above and adding net investment income to both sides we have:

$$GNP = (C + I + G) + (N + NINV)$$

Notice that this links the next broader balance of payments sub-account (the balance on goods, services, and investment income) to the national income and product accounts.

Finally, adding net unilateral transfers:

$$GNP + NUT = (C + I + G) + (N + NINV + NUT)$$
$$= (C + I + G) + CA$$

While the quantity $GNP + NUT$ corresponds to *gross national income.*[14]

If we assume that $NUT = 0$ (as we will do from now on), we can write:

$$GNP = (C + I + G) + CA$$

Notice that we can also write:

$$CA = GNP - A$$

Thus the current account is the difference between a country's income and the goods and services that it absorbs. This particular identity has played an important role in the development of international macroeconomics (see Box 2.1).

## The Disposition of National Saving in an Open Economy

Recall that in the closed-economy NIPA, domestic saving was defined as $S = GDP - C - G$. In an open economy, our definition of saving must be modified to:

$$S = GNP - C - G$$

---

[14]   Actually, we can draw a second distinction between *GNP* and national income (*NI*). In the national income and product accounts, national income is defined as GNP minus depreciation (DEP) plus unilateral transfers received from abroad (e.g., pensions, reparation payments, and foreign aid):

$$NI = GNP - DEP + NUT$$

This tells us the amount of income that domestic residents actually have available for consumption and net investment.

## Box 2.1    The Absorption Approach to the Balance of Payments

The relationship between GDP, domestic absorption, and the balance on goods and services (net exports) played an important role in the development of open-economy macroeconomics. In the early 1960s, an economist at the International Monetary Fund named Sydney Alexander formulated what became known as the *absorption approach* to the balance of payments (actually, it should have been called the absorption approach to the balance on goods and services, but that wouldn't have been a very elegant name).

Prior to Alexander's contribution, most economists had tended to analyze adjustment in the balance on goods and services from a *partial equilibrium* perspective – that is, by looking at the markets for exports and imports in isolation and disregarding the consequences of developments in these markets for the rest of the economy. Based on the identity linking GDP, domestic absorption, and the balance on goods and services, Alexander noted that net exports could only improve (that is, record a larger surplus or smaller deficit) if domestic absorption declined relative to GDP. This emphasized the point that adjustments in a country's external trade had an important general-equilibrium (macroeconomic) dimension and could not be analyzed in isolation from the rest of the economy. The absorption approach shows that since either GDP or absorption (or both) must change when net exports change, a credible explanation of what determines changes in net exports must be able to also account for the unavoidable associated changes in GDP and/or domestic absorption.

As you will see, we will use the absorption approach quite frequently in the chapters that follow. Often we will want to know how shocks to the domestic economy affect the equilibrium value of net exports. There will be times when a simple partial-equilibrium examination of the determinants of exports and imports will give an ambiguous answer. But a consideration of the general-equilibrium perspective using the absorption approach will in many cases help us pin down what will happen to the equilibrium value of net exports. This early insight into the general-equilibrium implications of macroeconomic openness thus remains quite useful today.

which is called gross *national* (instead of *domestic*) saving. This definition allows us to derive a very important identity relating national saving, investment, and the current account:

$$S = I + CA$$

As it turns out, this identity yields a number of important economic insights. First, written in this form, the identity shows that while a closed economy can only accumulate wealth by building real (nonfinancial) capital, an open economy can do so by building real capital at home or by acquiring financial claims on the rest of the world. Domestic investment and current account surpluses (often appropriately called foreign investment) are two different ways in which a country can use current output to increase future income. Notice that wealth accumulation equals saving, no matter what form wealth accumulation takes.

This raises an obvious question: how *should* an economy accumulate wealth, from a social welfare-maximizing perspective? The answer is that the size of the national "pie" is maximized if wealth is accumulated in the form that yields the highest social return, whether it is real investment in the domestic economy or the accumulation of financial claims on the rest of the world. This simple observation can provide some useful economic insights. Boxes 2.2 and 2.3 provide two instances, relating to the disposition of oil revenues in

## Box 2.2    The Disposition of Oil Revenue in Kuwait

Over the past three decades, Kuwait has pumped out a substantial amount of oil from its reserves and sold it on the world market, presumably on the view that the oil is more valuable if sold in the present than if kept in the ground and sold in the future. It is easy to see that, other things being equal, from an NIPA perspective the act of pumping oil from the ground for sale in the world market would tend to increase not only the country's exports, *EX*, but also the value of its production and income, *GNP*. Now let's consider what the country could have done with that oil revenue, and how its decisions regarding the disposition of its oil revenues would have affected its national income accounts.

In principle, the revenues from oil exports could have been consumed or saved. If saved, they could have been invested in increasing the domestic capital stock or in acquiring claims on the rest of the world. To see how the country's national income and product accounts are affected by different decisions about the disposition of the revenues, assume for simplicity that any changes in absorption by Kuwaitis would have been devoted to the purchase of foreign goods. Now consider the following three possibilities.

If the oil revenues had been fully devoted to consumption, consumption and imports would have risen by the same amount as the increase in exports. In that case, the increase in oil revenues would have induced no change in national saving, investment, or the current account of the balance of payments. GNP and consumption would have risen by the same amount; exports and imports would also have increased by that amount. On the other hand, saving, investment, and the current account would have remained unchanged.

If the increase in revenues had been fully devoted to investment, investment and imports would have increased by the same amount as exports. In this case, national saving would also have risen by that amount, but the current account would have remained unchanged.

Finally, suppose that consumption and investment remained unchanged. Then both GNP and national saving would have increased by the amount of the increase in exports, as would the country's current account surplus.

What *should* a country do in such circumstances? We'll investigate this question in Chapter 19. As to what actually happened, while part of the revenue was indeed consumed, much of it was not, so the Kuwaiti national saving rate has tended to be very high. And while domestic investment has also been high, so has the country's current account surplus, reflecting a diversification of the national wealth portfolio into real capital in Kuwait as well as to the acquisition of financial claims on the rest of the world. Thus, as shown in Table 2.2, Kuwait has become a substantial net creditor to the rest of the world.

## Box 2.3    Capital Flight from Latin America in the Early 1980s

During the decades of the late 1970s and early 1980s, many countries in Latin America experienced massive **capital flight**, meaning that domestic residents opted to take their savings abroad (often to Miami), rather than invest them at home. How does this affect the countries' national income accounts, and what are the implications of capital flight for economic welfare?

Notice first that the emergence of such a phenomenon would tend to leave saving unchanged (since capital flight does not concern changes in consumption, but rather in the allocation of saving). Since domestic residents were choosing to acquire claims on the rest of the world rather than to invest in domestic physical capital, however, domestic investment would have decreased and the current account increased by equal amounts.

Was this a bad thing for the countries involved? It does not necessarily have to have been so. For example, it would not have been a bad thing if it simply reflected a relatively low social return on domestic capital compared to the higher returns available to domestic savers abroad. So why, then, were so many people worried about this phenomenon at the time? There could have been a variety of reasons, some of which are not immediately relevant for us in the present context. But one possible reason is worth mentioning. It may have been that, while *social* rates of return were actually higher at home than abroad, capital flight happened anyway. In that case, capital flight would have made the countries from which capital "flew" poorer than if the money had been invested at home. How could such a situation arise? It could have been due to the perception by those engaged in capital flight that *private* rates of return to savers were not as high in the domestic economy as the private (and social) rates of return available abroad. This can happen as the result of policies pursued toward the financial system and/or the risk of expropriation by financially strapped governments. If domestic banks are not permitted to pay savers interest rates that reflect the high returns available on domestic capital investment, or if capitalists have reason to fear that these returns may be appropriated by the government, they may well prefer to take their money to Miami. In the presence of such distortions, domestic wealth would have indeed been misallocated through capital flight.

Kuwait and the phenomenon of capital flight in Latin America during the late 1970s and early 1980s.

## The Financing of Domestic Investment in an Open Economy

The identity derived above can be written two other ways, and both of them offer additional economic insights.

First, it can be written as:

$$I = S - CA$$

This tells us that, *while a closed economy must finance investment by saving, an open economy can do so either by saving or by reducing its net foreign wealth* (borrowing abroad). This is an important form of the identity. It explains, for example, why many developing countries are attracted by macroeconomic openness: by giving them access to external funds, it provides them with the means to sustain a higher level of investment and economic growth than they could achieve on the basis solely of their own national saving. This observation fundamentally alters the role of national saving in long-run growth. Rather than saving being required to make a given level of investment possible, what saving by domestic residents actually does is to alter the way that domestic investment is financed, that is, it alters the composition of investment financing between domestic and foreign sources. This change in perspective is not always easy for economists to adopt, as Box 2.4 illustrates.

### The Composition of the Current Account

Finally, we can write the same identity as:

$$-CA = I - S$$

This says that the current account deficit ($-CA$) is the difference between investment and saving. For example, we saw previously that a current account deficit represents the use of foreign saving, that is, net borrowing from abroad that increases a country's net international indebtedness. Does this mean that a current account deficit is bad?

In part the answer depends on whether it reflects increased investment or reduced saving. If it reflects an increase in investment *with yields exceeding the cost of external borrowing*, then it can be a good thing, in the sense that it can increase the country's future consumption opportunities, because the returns that domestic residents receive on the funds they have borrowed exceeds the amount that they have to pay for those funds, leaving more resources available for future consumption. If it reflects low saving resulting from higher current consumption, however (as in Mexico in the early 1990s; see Box 2.4), then repaying the accumulated debt will require a downward correction in future consumption, since there is no increase in future income in this case with which to repay the debt. This is desirable only if an extra unit of current consumption is worth more to the economy than the future consumption that it would have to give up to repay the debt. This is likely to be the case, for example, when the economy's income is unusually low, such as in the event of a natural disaster that temporarily impairs a country's productive capacity.

This form of the identity is used frequently by international macroeconomists to discipline our thinking about the likely causes and sustainability of current account deficits in both industrial and developing countries. Three cases are described in Boxes 2.5 to 2.7.

## 2.5    Sectoral Identities

So far, we have been analyzing open-economy macroeconomic identities from the perspective of the country as a whole. Next, we will divide the country into private and public

**Box 2.4   Saving and Growth in Post-reform Mexico, 1994**

In the early 1990s, the international financial institutions (the International Monetary Fund and World Bank) considered Mexico to be a model country. After a period of poor macroeconomic performance during the 1980s, Mexico had reformed many of its policies in a manner consistent with advice widely proffered by those institutions. Yet by 1994 many observers of the Mexican economy had become worried about the low growth registered by the Mexican economy despite its widespread policy reforms. Low growth was blamed in part on the relatively low rates of investment that Mexico had achieved after implementing these reforms. The question was why investment remained low despite what was widely perceived as a substantial improvement in the policy environment. In answering this question, many observers focused on the low rates of national saving that were also observed in Mexico at the same time.

But does it make sense to blame low saving for the unsatisfactory investment performance of the Mexican economy? As we have seen, in an open economy investment need not be constrained by the level of national saving. Mexico was indeed a very open economy during this time and had received very substantial capital inflows during the early part of the decade of the 1990s. The identity $I = S - CA$ suggests that, since Mexico is a highly open economy, if more investment was desired, it could have been financed by additional external borrowing. Thus, low saving by domestic residents was not necessarily a constraint on investment in Mexico. Instead, while low investment was indeed a problem for growth, it likely existed for independent reasons affecting the demand for investment, not the supply of financing for investment in Mexico. Observers should have been worried about a reduced *demand* for investment, not a reduced availability of funds for investment.

The low saving rate turns out to have been a problem, but for other reasons. The low saving rate resulted in a large current account deficit in the balance of payments, despite Mexico's low investment rate. This current account deficit resulted in a buildup of external debt that contributed to a severe financial crisis by the end of 1994. Observers were right to have worried about Mexico's low saving rate, not because of its effect on investment, but rather because of its implications for the country's current account deficit.

sectors. In particular, let $NT$ denote the net taxes paid by the private sector to the government, and suppose that we define:

$$S^P = GNP - NT - C$$

and

$$S^G = NT - G$$

## Box 2.5   The Balance-of-payments Stages Hypothesis and the US Current Account Deficit in the Late 1990s

A familiar perspective that is often applied to developing countries argues that at low levels of income per capita, the return to capital is high because labor is plentiful relative to capital (a diminishing marginal returns story), but precisely because incomes are very low, the national saving rate may also be low. Countries in those circumstances may be expected to import capital from the rest of the world, so they should be expected to have a high current account deficit. As countries accumulate capital and their income per capita rises, their domestic investment opportunities should diminish (again due to diminishing returns), and their saving rates should rise, reducing their current account deficits. This suggests that "mature" economies with very high levels of income per capita would tend to have high saving rates and, because they would also have few remaining domestic investment opportunities, would tend to exhibit current account surpluses (for example, this was the situation of the United Kingdom in the second half of the 19th century).

This may help explain why in Table 2.3 industrial countries tend to be net international creditors more often than developing countries do. However, we also saw in Table 2.3 that resource-rich and relatively underpopulated industrial countries were an exception to this rule. The **balance-of-payments stages hypothesis** suggests that in such a context the marginal product of capital may remain high (i.e., while these economies may be rich, they are not necessarily "mature" economies), so that it makes sense for them to continue to borrow from the rest of the world to finance domestic investment.

We have seen that the United States ran a large current account deficit in the late 1990s and into the first decade of the 21st century. That means that one of the richest countries in the world was borrowing massively from the rest of the world. Does it make sense for that to happen? The answer has two parts. First, it certainly may be a good thing from the perspective of the United States, since the American saving rate is so low that without external borrowing the United States would be hard put to finance reasonable levels of domestic investment. But second, it could conceivably be a good thing from the perspective of the world as a whole, despite the balance-of-payments stages hypothesis. It would be so, in particular, if technological developments during the second half of the 1990s made investment in the United States more productive than in lower-income countries. Indeed, a burst in productivity in the United States because of technological developments would be consistent with both lower saving rates as well as higher investment rates, for reasons that we will explore in Chapter 19. The role of productivity improvements in driving the US current account deficit during the last half of the decade of the 1990s is discussed in the papers by Pakko (1999), Holman (2001), and Mann (2002) listed under "Further Reading" at the end of the chapter.

The former is *private* saving (saving by households and private firms, identified by the superscript P), while the latter is *government* saving, or the surplus in the government's budget (that is, the fiscal surplus, given the superscript G). We can easily verify that the sum of the two is total national saving.

**Box 2.6    The Developing Country Debt Crisis of the 1980s**

During the late 1970s, many developing countries, especially in Latin America, accumulated a large amount of external debt. Part of this accumulation was in the form of *gross* rather than *net* external liabilities, since it essentially financed capital flight, as discussed in Box 2.3. As such, it would not have been associated with current account deficits.

But many of these countries did increase their net external indebtedness during this time, through current account deficits. What was this debt used for? The answer is that it largely reflected an increase in investment, possibly driven by optimistic views of the future outlook for commodity prices, which was in turn driven by expected future natural-resource scarcity (remember that developing countries tend to be *sellers* of products based on natural resources). Disappointing commodity prices, together with domestic mismanagement, made much of the accumulated capital unprofitable, implying that, in order to generate the current account surpluses required to service the debt when it came due, the indebted countries would have had to generate additional saving by reducing consumption, rather than counting on higher future incomes. Their inability/unwillingness to do so resulted in the subsequent debt crisis, in the form of a failure on the part of these countries to service their debts on the contractually agreed terms and their being cut off from having recourse to new borrowing. For an accessible real-time description of the developing country debt crisis see Fieleke (1982).

Adding these two identities together yields:

$$S^P + S^G = GNP - C - G$$
$$= I + CA$$

This permits us to write:

$$S^P = I + CA + (G - NT)$$

Thus *private saving must be used to finance domestic investment, foreign investment, or the government deficit.*

We can also write this last identity as:

$$CA = (S^P - I) + (NT - G)$$

Notice that this remains just another identity. That means that it must hold no matter what the economic relationships might be among its constituent parts. In turn, this implies that this relationship cannot tell us anything about those economic relationships. For example, despite a common misconception, this identity cannot tell us that a $1 reduction in the government's fiscal surplus (increase in the fiscal deficit) will tend to increase the deficit in the current account of the balance of payments deficit by $1. For this to happen, everything else in the equation would have to remain equal. Whether everything else – in the form of $S^P$ and $I$ – would indeed remain unchanged in the face of an increase in the deficit would

## Box 2.7   Current Account Deficits in Mexico and Thailand

In December 1994, Mexico was hit by a financial crisis in the form of an unwillingness on the part of its external creditors to continue to lend to Mexico. At the time, many observers blamed the country's large current account deficit for the emergence of the crisis. Yet Thailand had a similarly large current account deficit at the time (relative to the size of its economy) and did not experience a similar crisis. Why not?

One argument made at the time was that the difference between the two countries was that the Mexican current account deficits were driven by a **consumption boom** (i.e., a sharp reduction in the saving rate). The story was that, because a consumption-driven deficit would not automatically generate the future income required to service the debt that the country was incurring, a reduction in future consumption would be called for when the time came to reverse the current account deficit so as to repay these loans, and Mexico might have been no more willing/able to do so then than it had been in the debt crisis of the 1980s. However, Thailand's deficit reflected an investment rather than consumption boom, and thus the debt incurred could be serviced in the future out of higher incomes produced with the additional capital, rather than through reduced consumption, making it more likely that the debt would indeed be paid.

Nonetheless, Thailand had its own severe crisis just a few years later, triggering the Asian crisis of 1997, which spread through several countries in the region with dramatic effects on currency values and levels of real output. Though the causes of this crisis remain under debate among international macroeconomists, one interpretation of why Thailand suffered Mexico's fate despite its higher investment rates is that, for a variety of reasons, the newly created capital was being misallocated. As a result, it yielded very low returns, and in that sense was the equivalent of consumption.

depend on the structure of the economy. In Chapter 11 we will see an example in which this (misnamed) "fiscal approach to the balance of payments" would indeed be correct, but as we shall also see later, this result is not general. Box 2.8 describes an application of the "fiscal approach to the balance of payments" to an interpretation of US current account deficits during the early 1980s.

## 2.6   Summary

In this chapter, we have examined how the transactions associated with macroeconomic openness – trade in goods and services as well as in financial claims – between residents and nonresidents are tracked in a country's balance of payments (BOP) accounts. We also saw that two sub-accounts of the balance of payments accounts are of particular economic importance: the current account, because it determines the change in a country's net international creditor position (its net financial claims on the rest of the world), and the official reserve settlements balance (also known as the overall balance of payments), because it determines the change in the central bank's stock of foreign exchange reserves, which is the key determinant of the central bank's ability to intervene in the foreign exchange market to buy its own currency.

## Box 2.8    The US Current Account Deficit in the Early 1980s

The argument in this section criticized the "fiscal approach to the balance of payments" based on the identity $CA = (S^P - I) + (NT - G)$. Nonetheless, just such a framework has been used to discuss the emergence of a current account deficit in the United States during the early 1980s (shown in Figure 2.3). This current account deficit had as its counterpart a reduction in the private saving rate and increase in the budget deficit, with little change in investment (see Hakkio 1995, for a decomposition). Because the swing in the fiscal deficit was larger than that in the private saving rate, some observers came to refer to the fiscal and current account deficits as the "twin deficits," and blamed the latter on the former.

Is this wrong? Not necessarily. The criticism in the text does not claim that increases in fiscal deficits cannot cause increases in current account deficits, but only that they cannot be *assumed* to do so on a one-for-one basis on grounds of the identity above. To establish the direction of causation and the magnitude of the effect, it is necessary to make an *economic* argument that fiscal deficits are exogenous, and determine the extent to which private surpluses (excesses of private saving over investment) may offset their effects on the current account. To do so we need an economic model.

Indeed, the experience of the United States can also be used to illustrate the point that the relationship between fiscal and current account deficits is more complicated than a naive interpretation of the identity would suggest. Recall that in Box 2.5 we offered a possible interpretation of the reemergence of a large US current account deficit during the late 1990s as the product of the technology boom and its associated productivity gains. The technology boom was accompanied by a private investment boom and a low private saving rate (due to wealth effects associated with the boom), resulting in a substantial current account deficit. As shown in Figure 2.5, this deficit emerged despite the simultaneous emergence of a fiscal surplus in the late 1990s. In fact, the fiscal surplus that emerged during these years may itself have partly been caused by the technology boom, through higher tax receipts associated with the capital gains emerging from the technology-driven stock market boom. You can read more about the US experience in the early 1980s in Friedman (1985), Chrystal and Wood (1988) and Fieleke (1990).

We have also reviewed the relationship between *current* transactions in the balance of payments accounts and the national income and product accounts. This led to the following observations:

- Openness in the market for goods and services requires us to modify the standard identity that accounts for the disposition of a country's production to take into account purchases of domestic production by foreigners (exports of goods and services) and purchases of foreign output by domestic residents (imports of goods and services). As we will see in Chapter 4, this means that the balance on goods and services is a key component of aggregate demand for domestic output.
- In an open economy, national saving can be expressed as the sum of domestic investment and the current account of the balance of payments. As we saw, this relationship

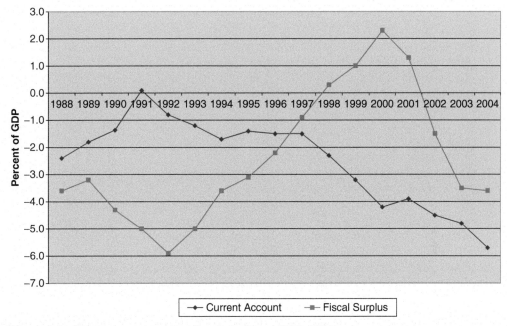

**Figure 2.5** US current account and fiscal surpluses, 1988–2004

can be expressed in three different ways, and these alternative expressions can be used to shed valuable insights on a variety of open-economy macroeconomic phenomena even before we introduce any formal behavioral content into our analytical framework.

The balance of payments and open-economy national income and product accounts provide an organizing framework for our analysis of open-economy macroeconomics. The next step is to begin to build a theory that explains the behavior of the variables that we have introduced in this chapter. The first task, which we will undertake in the next chapter, is to examine the motivations that induce economic agents to undertake each of the transactions we have identified in this chapter, and to explore how these transactions interact to influence the behavior of the foreign exchange market.

## Questions

For questions 1–9, explain how each of the transactions described would be entered in the balance of payments accounts of the United States:

1  A loan of $10 million is made by a US bank to the government of Honduras. The loan is funded by creating a $10 million deposit in the US bank.
2  The Honduran government uses the proceeds of the loan to buy vaccines from a US firm.
3  A Danish firm pays $100,000 in interest to an American who holds bonds issued by that firm in a prior year. The $100,000 is deposited in a Danish bank.
4  A US tourist travels to Mexico, buys $2500 worth of Mexican pesos with a check written on an American bank, and spends the full amount during the trip.
5  An American charity gives $100,000 worth of food to a non-governmental organization (NGO) in Darfur.

6   A foreign student pays tuition of $25,000 to a domestic university. The payment is made from a bank account that the student's parents have in a bank in their own country.

7   An overseas subsidiary of a domestic firm remits $1 million in profits to its parent company by writing a check drawn on its account on a domestic bank.

8   The domestic central bank acquires a deposit in a foreign commercial bank worth the equivalent of $10 million by paying for it with a check drawn on a domestic commercial bank.

9   A US resident imports $1 million of wine from the Republic of Georgia, paying with a check drawn on a US bank. The Georgian exporter uses the funds to purchase Georgian currency from the Georgian central bank.

10  If only one sub-account of the balance of payments account could be published, which do you think it should be, and why?

11  The United States maintains a floating exchange rate, but many countries peg their exchange rates against the US dollar. Assuming that the Fed never intervenes in the foreign exchange market, would you expect the official reserve settlements balance (ORS) of the US balance of payments to always be zero? Explain why or why not. Would your answer be different if the country in question were Uganda (which also maintains a floating exchange rate) rather than the United States? Why or why not?

12  As you will learn in Chapter 7, during the period when the Bretton Woods exchange rate regime was in place, loans made to countries by the International Monetary Fund were supposed to finance "temporary deficits" in the balance of payments without changing their exchange rates. Since the balance of payments accounts definitionally sum to zero, this must have referred to some sub-account of the balance of payments accounts. Which one did it refer to, and why was that particular sub-account, instead of some other, of concern to the IMF?

13  The United States is currently (as of 2008) running a current account deficit of over 5 percent of GDP. Should this be a source of concern to American policymakers? Explain why they should or should not be worried about it. Whatever your answer to this question, can you conceive of empirical circumstances under which you would have given a different answer? What would those circumstances be, and why?

14  An important open-economy macroeconomic identity relates the current account surplus to the difference between domestic saving and investment. Some observers have interpreted this as implying that every $1 reduction in the fiscal deficit would reduce the current account deficit by $1. Based on what you have learned so far, would you agree or disagree? Explain.

15  What does the "absorption approach" imply about the macroeconomic changes that would have to accompany a reduction in the current account deficit in the United States?

## Further Reading and References

### On BOP accounting

Fieleke, Norman S. (1996), "Unilateral International Transfers: Unrequited and Generally Unheeded," Federal Reserve Bank of Boston, *New England Economic Review* (November/December), pp. 27–37.

## On the history of international borrowing and lending

Fieleke, Norman (1982), "International Lending in Historical Perspective," *New England Economic Review* (November/December), pp. 5–12.


## On interpreting the US current account deficit

*a. The experience of the 1980s*

Chrystal, K. Alec and Geoffrey E. Wood (1988), "Are Trade Deficits a Problem?" Federal Reserve Bank of St. Louis *Review* (January/February), pp. 3–11.

Fieleke, Norman S. (1990), "The United States in Debt," Federal Reserve Bank of Boston, *New England Economic Review* (September/October), pp. 34–55.

Friedman, Benjamin M. (1985), "Implications of the U.S. Net Capital Inflow," Chapter 4 in R. Hafer, ed., *How Open Is the U.S. Economy?* Federal Reserve Bank of St. Louis, Proceedings of the Tenth Annual Economic Policy Conference, pp. 137–61.


*b. The experience of the 1990s*

Hakkio, Craig S. (1995), "The US Current Account: The Other Deficit," Federal Reserve Bank of Kansas City *Economic Review* (Third Quarter), pp. 11–24.

Holman, Jill (2001), "Is the US Current Account Deficit Sustainable?" Federal Reserve Bank of Kansas City *Economic Review* (First Quarter), pp. 5–24.

Mann, Catherine L. (2002), "Perspectives on the U.S. Current Account Deficit and Sustainability," *Journal of Economic Perspectives* Vol. 16, No. 3 (Summer), pp. 131–52.

Pakko, Michael R. (1999), "The US Trade Deficit and the New Economy" Federal Reserve Bank of St. Louis *Review* (September/October), pp. 11–20.


## On the current account and the international investment position

Bank for International Settlements (2005), *Triennial Central Bank Survey* (Basle: Bank for International Settlements).

Lane, Philip, and Gian Maria Milesi-Ferretti (1999), "The External Wealth of Nations: Measures of Foreign Assets and Liabilities for Industrial and Developing Countries," International Monetary Fund, Working Paper WP/99/115 (August).

Lane, Philip R. and Gian Maria Milesi-Ferretti (2006), "The External Wealth of Nations Mark II: Revised and Extended Estimates of Foreign Assets and Liabilities, 1970–2004", IMF Working Paper, 06/69.


## On the international investment position of the United States

Nguyen, Elena L. (2007), "The International Investment Position of the United States at end-2006," *Survey of Current Business*, Bureau of Economic Analysis, U.S. Department of Commerce, pp. 10–19.

# 3

# Macroeconomic Influences on the Foreign Exchange Market

........................................................................................................................

In the last chapter we explored the types of transactions that take place between domestic and foreign residents in open economies, as summarized in the balance of payments accounts. In transactions of this sort the sellers typically expect to be paid in their own currencies, just as they do in purely domestic transactions. Since domestic residents don't normally hold foreign currencies and foreign residents don't normally hold domestic currency, this means that buyers in each country have to acquire the currency of the other country in order to make payments. They can buy foreign currencies, usually referred to as **foreign exchange**, in the **foreign exchange market** – the market in which currencies are traded for each other. The foreign exchange market is an additional market that interacts with the markets for labor, good and services and financial assets in open-economy macroeconomics.

In the foreign exchange market, the supply and demand for foreign exchange arise from the three types of transactions we examined in Chapter 2: current account transactions, nonreserve financial account transactions, and official reserve transactions. In this chapter we will explore some of the key determinants of the demand for and supply of foreign exchange arising from these different types of transactions. In particular, leaving a fuller description for later chapters, we will focus specifically on the factors that influence the choices that domestic and foreign residents make between buying domestic or foreign goods and services, thus motivating current account transactions, as well as between acquiring domestic or foreign financial assets, which motivate nonreserve financial account and official reserve transactions.[1] As we will see, in the case of goods, the key factor is the *relative price* of the two types of goods. However, in the case of assets the factors involved depend on whether the economic agent whose behavior we are considering is a private agent or a central bank. Private agents are primarily concerned with the *relative returns* and other properties of the two types of assets. On the other hand, the conditions under which central banks participate as buyers and sellers in the foreign exchange market are determined by macroeconomic *policy* considerations. In the process of exploring the relative price, relative return, and policy considerations that motivate the three types of transactions that constitute the foreign exchange market, we will introduce several key concepts in international macroeconomics that will be used throughout the rest of this book.

## 3.1 Exchange Rate Concepts

Just as with any other market, the foreign exchange market determines an equilibrium price and quantity traded. The equilibrium price defines the terms on which units of the foreign and domestic currencies can be exchanged for each other. This price is called the **exchange rate**. It can be expressed as the *domestic-currency price of foreign currency* (units of domestic currency per unit of foreign currency), or as the *foreign-currency price of domestic currency* (units of foreign currency per unit of domestic currency). As you can see, these are the reciprocal of each other. Because it tends to be the version favored by most international macroeconomists, in this book we will define the exchange rate as the price of foreign currency measured in units of domestic currency. From the perspective of the United States, for example, we will measure the exchange rate in units of dollars per euro, dollars per yen, and so on.

Several exchange rate concepts are used in international macroeconomics. The exchange rate between the domestic currency and any single other foreign currency is called the **bilateral exchange rate** between those two currencies. Clearly, from the perspective of any single currency, there are as many bilateral exchange rates as there are other currencies in the world. However, sometimes we may be interested in what is happening to the value of a currency not against any single other currency, but against the currencies of all other countries together, or against the currencies of some specific group of countries. Since different bilateral exchange rates may be moving in opposite directions, no single bilateral exchange rate can convey this information. Instead, economists use **multilateral** (most often called **"effective"**) exchange rate indices, which are essentially weighted averages of indices of bilateral exchange rates of the currency we are interested in against various other currencies. Box 3.1 describes how effective exchange rate indexes are constructed.

Because reciprocal definitions of the exchange rate are widely used, it is generally not a good idea to describe movements in exchange rates as "increases" or "decreases," since these words have different implications for the value of the currency depending on which definition is being used. Thus, a special terminology is used to describe exchange rate

---

[1]    For brevity, from now on I will use the term "goods" instead of "goods and services." You should therefore understand the term "goods" to refer to all of the commodities – whether they are goods or services – that economies produce.

## Box 3.1    Construction of Effective Exchange Rate Indexes

Effective exchange rate indices are constructed in three steps. First, the relevant bilateral exchange rates for a particular country are converted into indexes, using a common base year. Next, a set of weights is chosen to be applied to each of the bilateral indexes. Finally, the bilateral indexes are averaged together using these weights. This seems straightforward. However, in following this procedure, several choices have to be made:

### 1.   Geometric or Arithmetic Weighting

The first choice is whether to use **arithmetic** or **geometric** weighting. Arithmetic weighting involves defining the index as the weighted *sum* of the ratios of the value of the exchange rate in each year to its value in the base year. Geometric weighting, on the other hand, constructs the index by raising each bilateral index to a power equal to the weight assigned to it, and *multiplying* together the resulting values for all of the bilateral indexes used.

Geometric weighting is broadly agreed to be the appropriate approach. To see why, suppose that two sets of currencies are judged to be equally important for the home country, so they are assigned equal weight in the effective exchange rate basket. If the home country's currency doubles in value against the first set, while the second set doubles in value against the home currency, then we would want the index to show the average value of the home currency remaining unchanged. This would happen with the geometric index, but not with the arithmetic one. The geometric index has the desirable property that a 1 percent depreciation of the domestic currency against the currency of any other country causes a percentage change in the index that is equal to the weight assigned to that country.

### 2.   Choice of Weights

The next choice has to do with the weights to be used. The first question in this regard concerns what types of international transactions should be used to assess the relative importance of specific bilateral exchange rates for the home country. The answer depends on the purpose for which the index is to be used. Because effective exchange rate indexes are most often used to assess a country's competitiveness in trade in goods and services – i.e., the relative price of its products compared to the products of the rest of the world – most effective exchange rate indexes use total trade in goods and services as weights, ignoring trade in financial assets. But some indexes include only merchandise trade (not services) and others (e.g., the index compiled by JP Morgan). include only trade in manufactures. The choice depends on just how broad a measure of competitiveness we are interested in.

Given that trade weights are to be used, a second issue is whether the weights should reflect only bilateral trade flows with the home country (i.e., the share of each country in the home country's total trade) or total multilateral trade flows (the share of each country in total world trade). While the former might seem to be the obvious choice for a measure of competitiveness, the latter may better capture the effects of competition among countries in third markets. For example, if country A does not trade much with country B directly, but country B exports products that are directly competitive with those exported by country A, then a depreciation of country B's currency relative to that of country A may have a significant effect on country A's overall competitiveness by making country A's products less competitive in third markets. This effect would not be picked up by an index based on bilateral trade weights.

### 3. Number of Currencies

In principle, because effective exchange rate indexes are usually used to measure competitiveness, they should account for changes in the bilateral exchange rate against the currencies of *all* the countries with which the home country conducts trade. In practice, however, data limitations often create a tradeoff between broad country coverage and the length of the time series that can be used to construct the index.

### 4. Base Year for Weights

Finally, a decision has to be made about the reference period to be used to construct the trade weights. The problem is that the shares of trade with specific trading partners are likely to change from one period to the next. This creates a choice among the use of fixed weights, weights that are updated periodically, or weights that are updated every period.

The problem with using fixed weights is that they can become outdated if trade patterns shift dramatically. The problem with updating every period, on the other hand, is that the source of changes in multilateral exchange rates can become obfuscated between changes in weights and changes in exchange rates. Occasional updating represents a commonly used compromise.

As can be seen from this description, the choices to be made in constructing effective exchange rate indexes are not always unambiguous. Consequently, different choices have been made by different practitioners, and a variety of effective exchange rate indexes are likely to be in wide use at any one time for any particular country. The readings listed at the end of this chapter compare several broadly used effective exchange rate indexes for the US dollar. Somewhat frustratingly, it turns out that different indexes sometimes provide different interpretations of the behavior of the US dollar, and indexes that may appear to be superior on theoretical grounds (e.g., more comprehensive ones) do not always outperform the others empirically. The best advice in choosing an effective exchange rate index is to think carefully about the use to which the index is to be put.

movements. A reduction in the value of the domestic currency (an increase in the value of the foreign currency) is referred to as a **depreciation** of the domestic currency. Notice that a depreciation is associated with an *increase* in the exchange rate as we have defined it, because when the domestic currency loses value, more units of the domestic currency have to be given up for each unit of the foreign currency. An increase in the value of the domestic currency is referred to as an **appreciation** of the domestic currency. This is associated with a *decrease* in the value of the exchange rate as we have defined it.

To illustrate how these terms are used, consider the recent behavior of the US dollar. Figure 3.1 shows the bilateral exchange rate of the dollar against the Japanese yen and

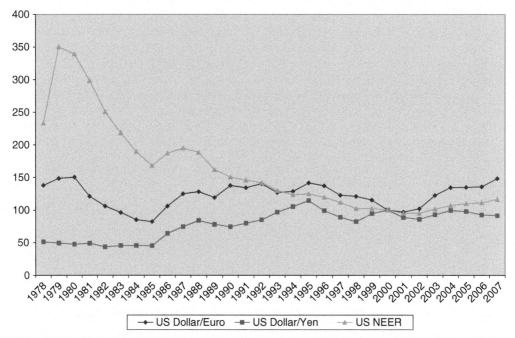

**Figure 3.1** Bilateral and effective exchange rates for the US dollar, 1978–2007

European euro in the years 1978 to 2007, expressed as indices. Notice that after appreciating slightly against the yen from 1978 until 1985, the dollar depreciated very strongly against the yen for about a decade, from 1986 to 1995. A sharp appreciation followed for three years, and over the last nine years in the chart the dollar fluctuated within a fairly narrow range against the yen. The pattern was somewhat different against the euro. In particular, the dollar appreciated much more sharply from 1980 to 1985, depreciated from 1985 to 1995, and then appreciated again until 2000. Since that time it has been depreciating rather sharply, in contrast to its relative stability against the yen. This illustrates the point that bilateral exchange rates do not necessarily move in tandem with each other.

Figure 3.1 also shows the evolution of the effective exchange rate for the US dollar, that is, the value of the dollar in terms of a broader basket of foreign currencies (NEER). The three episodes mentioned above are easily discernible, but the pattern differs somewhat from the two bilateral rates. First, compared to the two bilateral rates, the dollar's appreciation in effective terms from 1981 to about 1985 is much stronger. This is then followed by depreciation in 1986–7, but instead of continued depreciation until 1995, the effective value of the dollar appreciated gradually from 1987 to 2001. After that period the nominal effective rate follows the two bilateral rates in a gradual but continued depreciation until the end of the sample. The implication is that there were broad swings in the value of the dollar from 1987 until about 1995 that did not simply reflect bilateral movements against the euro and yen.

## 3.2  Supply and Demand for Foreign Exchange

Why has the exchange rate of the dollar varied in this way? The determination of exchange rates is one of the central questions that concern international macroeconomists. Since the exchange rate is the relative price that adjusts to achieve equilibrium in the foreign exchange market, it must be determined by the same mechanism that determines equilibrium prices in other markets: equality of supply and demand. To explain exchange rate movements we would therefore need to explain what determines the supply and demand for foreign exchange – that is, the foreign demand for domestic goods, services, and assets, and the domestic demand for foreign goods, services, and assets. The factors that do so will determine the shapes and positions of the supply and demand curves for foreign exchange and thus the exchange rate.

Exploring the factors that determine the positions of these curves is a topic that will concern us for most of the rest of this book. We will approach this task in two steps. Recall from Chapter 2 that balance of payments transactions can be classified into three sub-accounts: current account transactions (*CA*), nonreserve financial capital account transactions (*NFA*), and central bank transactions (*ORS*). Accordingly, transactions in the foreign exchange market take the form of buying and selling of goods, buying and selling of financial assets other than by central banks, and transactions involving official reserves. Our first step will be to ask in each of these cases what motivates domestic and foreign residents to trade with each other – and therefore to enter the foreign exchange market – rather than with residents of their own countries. Thus to derive the supply and demand for foreign exchange, we first need to address three questions, corresponding to each of the sub-accounts just mentioned:

1   What determines the relative attractiveness of domestic versus foreign goods (for current account transactions)?
2   What determines the relative attractiveness of domestic and foreign assets (for capital account transactions)?
3   What rules govern central bank transactions in the foreign exchange market (for the official reserves settlement balance)?[2]

These questions will occupy us for the rest of this chapter. We will investigate them one at a time in each of the following sections.

But answering these questions is not enough to explain the determination of the exchange rate. Knowing how domestic residents decide how to allocate their spending on goods between domestic and foreign goods, for example, will not tell us the total demand for imports (and thus for the foreign exchange with which to buy them) unless we also know how much domestic residents intend to spend on *all* goods (domestic and foreign). Similarly, knowing how domestic residents decide to allocate their bond holdings between domestic and foreign bonds does not tell us their total demand for foreign bonds (and thus for the foreign exchange with which to acquire them) unless we also know how they plan to allocate their financial portfolios between money and bonds. These are standard questions in macroeconomics, and to answer them we will need to build a full macroeconomic model. That is the second step in our exploration of exchange rate determination, and will be the task of the next chapter.

---

[2]   It is worth noting at this point that the reason that transactions by central banks are treated differently in the balance of payments accounts from other capital account transactions is precisely that central bank actions in the foreign exchange market are governed by different considerations than those that influence private agents or the nonfinancial agencies of the public sector.

## 3.3    Relative Prices of Domestic and Foreign Goods: The Real Exchange Rate

The relative attractiveness of domestic goods compared to foreign goods depends primarily on their relative price. We can think of this relative price as the number of domestic goods that must be given up to acquire one foreign good. This relative price is called the **real exchange rate**. To distinguish it from the relative price of two *currencies*, we will refer to the latter as the **nominal exchange rate**.

### The Real Exchange Rate and the Nominal Exchange Rate

What is the relationship between the real exchange rate between goods and the nominal exchange rate between currencies? Suppose that domestic goods (think of this as a representative basket of goods produced in the home country) sell for the domestic-currency price $P$, foreign goods (again, a representative basket) sell for the foreign-currency price $P^*$, and the bilateral exchange rate between the domestic and foreign currency (units of domestic currency per unit of the foreign currency) is denoted $S$. Then we can derive the real exchange rate ($Q$), the relative price of the foreign good in terms of the domestic good, simply as the money price of the foreign good divided by the money price of the domestic good, with *both money prices expressed in the same currency*. To express the price of the foreign good in domestic currency we simply have to multiply its foreign currency price $P^*$ by the price of foreign currency in terms of domestic currency, that is, by the exchange rate $S$. That means that the real exchange rate can be written as:

$$Q = SP^*/P \tag{3.1}$$

For example, suppose that a representative basket of Japanese goods costs ¥100,000, and a representative basket of American goods costs $50, while the nominal exchange rate is ¥100 yen per dollar (that is, $0.01 per yen). Then the dollar price of the Japanese basket is $1000 (0.01 dollars per yen $\times$ ¥100,000) and the real exchange rate would be 20 ($1000/$50) American baskets per Japanese basket.[3]

Because natural logarithms have a number of desirable properties, it will be convenient at various places throughout this book to work with variables in the form of natural logarithms (logs).[4] Using lowercase letters to denote the log of a variable (that is, $x = \log X$) we can express the real exchange rate in terms of logarithms by taking logs of both sides of equation 3.1. This yields:

$$q = s + p^* - p \tag{3.1'}$$

---

[3]   Measuring the real exchange rate empirically is not as straightforward as measuring the nominal exchange rate. The latter can be observed directly, while the former requires choosing a specific price index to measure the price level in the home country and its trading partner. Which index is appropriate depends on which domestic-foreign relative price we want to measure – e.g., that of manufactures, that of internationally traded goods and services more generally, or that of all goods and services produced in the domestic and foreign economies.

[4]   The key property of logs that will prove useful to us is that the change in the log of a variable can be interpreted as the percentage change in that variable. Appendix 3.1 provides a brief review of the properties of logs.

Just as in the case of the nominal exchange rate, this real exchange rate can be expressed in bilateral and multilateral (or effective) terms. The **multilateral real exchange rate** (or the **real effective exchange rate** – the two terms are synonymous and are both in common use) is constructed from bilateral real exchange rates just as the effective nominal exchange rate is constructed from bilateral nominal exchange rates. It is simply the geometrically weighted average of the relevant set of bilateral real exchange rates.

Notice that a country's nominal and real exchange rates do not have to move in the same direction. As can be seen from the definition of the real exchange rate in levels (equation 3.1) or in logs (equation 3.1′), changes in the bilateral real exchange rate depend on two different factors: changes in the nominal exchange rate and changes in a country's price level relative to that of its trading partner. In terms of equation 3.1, for example, an increase in $Q$ (a real exchange rate depreciation) can be brought about either by an increase in $S$ (a nominal depreciation) or by an increase in $P^*/P$ (a *reduction* in a country's price level relative to that of its trading partner). But it is possible, say, for $Q$ to fall (to appreciate) while $S$ is rising (depreciating) if $P^*/P$ falls by more than enough to offset the increase in $S$. For example, in many developing countries that experienced high inflation during the decades of the 1980s and 1990s, it was not at all uncommon for their bilateral real exchange rates against the US dollar to appreciate significantly at the same time that their nominal exchange rates were depreciating, simply because their domestic inflation rates were so much higher than the inflation rate in the United States.

The behavior of the real effective exchange rate of the United States over the period 1980–2007 is shown in Figure 3.2. The real effective value of the US dollar has been through several phases over that period. The dollar began the period appreciating strongly in real effective terms from 1980 to 1985. This was subsequently reversed and followed by a sharp depreciation from 1986 to about 1988. From 1988 to about 1995, the dollar's value was relatively stable in real effective terms. However, a new cycle began around that time, with a period of real effective dollar appreciation from 1995 to about 2000, followed by fairly continuous depreciation since then. We will have occasion to return to this pattern, in order to try to explain it, at several times in this book.

The role of the inflation differentials mentioned above show up in the relative behavior of the US nominal and real effective exchange rates in Figure 3.2. As you can see from the

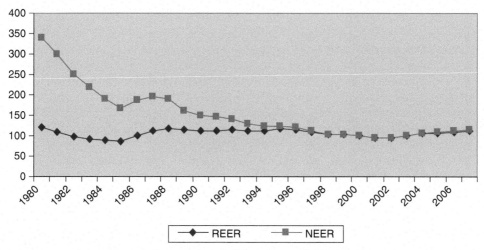

**Figure 3.2**  US nominal and real effective exchange rates, 1980–2007
*Source*: IMF, International Financial Statistics.

chart, the US nominal effective exchange rate (NEER) was much more depreciated than the real effective exchange rate at the beginning of the period, but the gap between the two narrowed progressively over time, effectively disappearing by the mid-1990s. This reflects the much higher inflation rates of several major US trading partners than that of the United States during the beginning of the period, and the gradual convergence of inflation rates by the mid-1990s. During the early part of the period the currencies of the high-inflation trading partners were depreciating sharply against the US dollar, causing a strong appreciation of the US nominal effective exchange rate.

But as the inflation rates of these countries and that of the United States converged, relative price levels in the United States and its trading partners tended to stabilize, and movements in the US real effective exchange rate therefore became dominated by changes in its *nominal* effective exchange rate.

## Purchasing Power Parity

An important question that will concern us in subsequent chapters is the extent to which domestic markets for goods and services are integrated with foreign markets. Markets are integrated when the prices of domestically produced goods are linked to the prices of foreign-produced goods through **arbitrage**, the process of buying cheap and selling dear. This process tends to equalize prices in different markets by lowering them where they are high and raising them where they are low, an outcome referred to as the **law of one price (LOOP)**. As we will see subsequently, the degree of goods-market integration between two economies – that is, the scope for commodity arbitrage between them – will have an important impact on the behavior of the real exchange rate that captures the relative price of the goods produced in the two economies.

The extent to which arbitrage can operate between domestic and foreign goods depends on two factors:

1   Do the domestic and foreign (rest-of-the-world) economies produce identical goods? In other words, do consumers at home and abroad consider the domestic and foreign goods to be **perfect substitutes** for each other? If they are perfect substitutes, we would expect the pressures of arbitrage to drive their money prices into equality with each other (when expressed in the same currency), and thus for the law of one price to hold. If the goods are not identical – that is, if they are **imperfect substitutes** – then there is no reason for their money prices to be equalized by arbitrage, and their relative price (the real exchange rate) should be determined by the usual market supply and demand consider-ations. For example, a bushel of soybeans of a defined type grown in the United States is a perfect substitute for a bushel grown in Brazil, but American and Brazilian cars will not tend to be perfect substitutes for each other.
2   To the extent that the domestic and foreign economies produce goods that are identical to each other, are there any barriers to the process of arbitrage between them that would prevent their prices from being equalized? Such barriers could be natural in origin or they could be created by policies. Natural barriers include imperfect information or transportation costs, for example, while policy barriers could take many forms, such as ''voluntary'' export restraints, import quotas, or other quantitative restriction on cross-border trade in goods and services.

The answers to these questions have an important bearing on the behavior of the real exchange rate. As a useful frame of reference to explore their implications, we can organize the discussion around the concept of *purchasing power parity (PPP)*, a venerable theory about the determination of the real exchange rate. There are two versions of this theory: absolute PPP and relative PPP.

*Absolute PPP*    The first, strongest version, known as **absolute PPP**, states that the domestic and foreign bundles of goods should sell for the same price when expressed in a common currency – that is, the real exchange rate should *on average* be equal to one:

$$Q = SP^*/P = 1 \tag{3.2}$$

This should seem like a very surprising proposition, since it makes a strong quantitative prediction about the behavior of the real exchange rate. Why should anyone expect it to be true?

To see why one might expect this relationship to hold, note that in the real world $P$ and $P^*$ would correspond to aggregate price indices, such as the consumer price index (CPI), which measures the domestic-currency price of a basket of goods and services purchased by consumers. The theory is motivated by an arbitrage argument applied to these consumption baskets. It claims that the purchasing power of $1 (the number of units of a ''representative'' consumption basket that $1 can buy) should be the same whether the $1 is spent at home or abroad. Since $1/P$ is the purchasing power of $1 over the price of the domestic consumption bundle, and since $1 is worth $1/S$ units of the foreign currency, each of which can buy $1/P^*$ consumption bundles abroad, if the purchasing power of $1 is equalized at home and abroad, this means:

$$1/P = (1/S)(1/P^*), \text{ which implies } SP^*/P = Q = 1$$

But why should the purchasing power of $1 be equalized in this way (that is, be at parity)? The argument is that if it were not, each consumer would presumably spend the $1 where it can buy more units of the consumption bundle. For example, if $1/P$ is less than $1/SP^*$, then $1 could buy more goods abroad than at home. Thus, people would spend their money abroad instead of at home. In turn, this would raise foreign prices and lower domestic prices (or depreciate the domestic currency as people try to acquire the foreign exchange with which to buy the foreign goods) until the parity is restored.

This theory has some important implications. First, if $Q = 1$, then it follows that $S = P/P^*$. Thus, if the domestic and foreign price levels are somehow determined independently, then PPP becomes a theory about what determines the equilibrium value of the nominal exchange rate. Second, if this theory about the behavior of the real exchange rate holds continuously, any model we build to explain the determination of net exports could not rely on changes in the real exchange rate to affect whether domestic and foreign residents choose to buy domestic and foreign goods, because the real exchange rate would be constant. But is the theory indeed right?

A glance at Figure 3.2, a depiction of the US multilateral real exchange rate, might make one skeptical. The theory suggests that the real exchange rate should fluctuate randomly around a constant value, yet the multilateral real exchange rate shown here seems to exhibit much more systematic long swings, as described above. ''Eyeball'' tests such as this are not always the most reliable, however, and more rigorous tests are clearly desirable. Empirical

Study 3.1 at the end of this chapter describes how such tests can be performed. Unfortunately, their results are not very favorable to the absolute PPP hypothesis over time periods similar to those in Figure 3.2.

This means that something must be wrong with the arbitrage argument. But what could that be? Actually, several things. Even assuming that the law of one price holds (that is, that arbitrage equalizes the prices of identical individual consumption goods when these prices are expressed in a common currency), the theory faces the problem that the representative domestic and foreign consumption bundles that go into the respective CPIs are typically different. They give different weights to the same goods, reflecting differences in consumer preferences. Because many Hindus are vegetarian, for example, the representative consumption bundle in India contains much less meat than it does in Pakistan, a predominantly Muslim country. Thus, *even if the arbitrage argument holds true and LOOP holds for each individual good in the basket, the different weights used in constructing the domestic and foreign baskets would mean that the baskets refer to different composite goods.* Because there is no arbitrage reason to expect the prices of different composite goods to be equalized, different amounts of the "representative" basket in each country could be purchased with $1.

There are two ways to respond to this challenge. First, if one indeed wants to use the theory to explain the nominal exchange rate, one could use as the counterparts of $P$ and $P^*$ not the prices of the typical consumption bundles in each country, but those of the *same* basket of goods priced in each country's currency. The nominal exchange rate consistent with PPP, say $S_{PPP}$, would then be the exchange rate that would be required to equalize the common-currency price of the uniform basket of goods in the two countries. Suppose that the domestic-currency price of this uniform basket is $P_S$, and its foreign-currency price is $P_S^*$. Then the PPP exchange rate is defined as:

$$S_{PPP} = P_S/P_S^*$$

An approach to the theory of PPP along these lines that is interesting (and entertaining) to explore has been implemented by the *Economist* magazine in the form of its "Big Mac" index, as described in Box 3.2.

## Box 3.2    The "Big Mac" Index

The *Economist* magazine uses a version of PPP based on a uniform consumption bundle, in the form of the "Big Mac" sandwich sold by McDonald's, to evaluate whether currencies around the world are **overvalued** or **undervalued** when measured against the dollar. A currency is said to be "overvalued" if its current value is appreciated relative to its equilibrium rate, meaning that the currency will have to depreciate (lose value) in the future in order to move to its equilibrium rate. It is "undervalued" if it is depreciated relative to its equilibrium rate, so it will have to appreciate (gain value) to move to its equilibrium rate. Under the modified version of the PPP hypothesis that applies it to a *uniform* bundle of goods, the equilibrium rate is that which equalizes the price of the uniform bundle at home and abroad (i.e., the exchange rate that ensures that $1 buys the same number of bundles everywhere).

The *Economist* (in a somewhat tongue-in-cheek manner) considers the Big Mac as one such uniform bundle, since the sandwich is pretty much the same everywhere that it is sold. Moreover, since globalization has made Big Macs available in many places around the world, comparing the US dollar prices of Big Macs in different countries should allow us to draw some inferences about whether the currencies of those countries are at their equilibrium values. (More recently a Starbucks latte has been used for the same purpose.)

Table 3.1 summarizes a recent application of the Big Mac index in the *Economist*. The first and second columns of the table give the prices of Big Macs in each country in local currency and in US dollars, converted from local currency using the currently prevailing market exchange rate. The third column gives the hypothetical exchange rate that would be required in order for the dollar price of a Big Mac in the country in question to be the same as it is in the United States. This is the PPP exchange rate – i.e., the exchange rate that equalizes the dollar price of Big Macs at home and abroad. Column 4 provides the actual market exchange rate, and the last column calculates the percentage excess of the PPP exchange rate over the market exchange rate, expressed as a proportion of the market rate. This serves a measure of **overvaluation** if positive (the PPP rate is *more* depreciated than the market exchange rate, so the market rate has to *depreciate* in order to achieve PPP) and of **undervaluation** if negative (the PPP rate is *less* depreciated than the market rate, so the market rate has to *appreciate* in order to achieve PPP).

Consider, for example, the case of the Argentine peso. In February 2007, a Big Mac cost $3.22 on average in the United States. According to Table 3.1, a Big Mac sold for 8.25 pesos in Buenos Aires at the same time (column 1). For these prices to be equal in dollars, the peso/dollar exchange rate would have to be 2.56 (column 3 – the local price of a Big Mac divided by the price of the Big Mac in the US, or 8.25/3.22). This is the implied PPP equilibrium exchange rate. The *actual* peso-dollar exchange rate in February 2007 was 3.11 (column 4). Since the actual exchange rate for the peso was more depreciated than the estimated equilibrium one, the peso is judged to be undervalued by 18 percent [(2.56 – 3.11)/3.11] (column 5). This suggests that the peso should be expected to appreciate to return to its equilibrium value.

How reliable should we expect the Big Mac standard to be as a guide to the equilibrium values of currencies? There are at least two potential problems. First, while Big Macs are relatively uniform in composition, they are not perfectly so (for example, Big Macs in India do not contain beef). Even to the extent that the components are similar, their *quality* may not be uniform. Second, even allowing for uniformity in composition and quality, the dollar prices of the components of the sandwich may not be easily arbitraged across national boundaries, since the price of a Big Mac covers not just the cost of the ingredients that go into making the sandwich, but also includes other costs, such as wages, rent, and utility payments. These are costs of factors of production that may not even be easily arbitraged within national boundaries. This explains why, since the prices of such factors vary significantly across the United States, the *Economist* calculates the average price of a Big Mac from prices in several US cities.

**Table 3.1** The Hamburger standard

| Countries | Big Mac prices | | Implied PPP* of the dollar | Actual dollar exchange rate January 31, 2007 | Under (−)/over (+) valuation against the dollar, % |
| --- | --- | --- | --- | --- | --- |
| | In local currency | In dollars | | | |
| United States† | $3.22 | 3.22 | | | |
| Argentina | Peso 8.25 | 2.65 | 2.56 | 3.11 | −18 |
| Australia | A$3.45 | 2.67 | 1.07 | 1.29 | −17 |
| Brazil | Real 6.40 | 3.01 | 1.99 | 2.13 | −6 |
| Britain‡ | £1.99 | 3.90 | 1.62 | 1.96 | +21 |
| Canada | C$3.63 | 3.08 | 1.13 | 1.18 | −4 |
| Chile | Peso 1,670 | 3.07 | 519 | 544 | −5 |
| China | Yuan 11.00 | 1.41 | 3.42 | 7.77 | −56 |
| Colombia | Peso 6,900 | 3.06 | 2,143 | 2,254 | −5 |
| Costa Rica | Colones 1,130 | 2.18 | 351 | 519 | −32 |
| Czech Rep | Koruna 52.10 | 3.06 | 16.2 | 21.6 | −25 |
| Denmark | DKr27.75 | 2.18 | 8.62 | 5.74 | +50 |
| Egypt | Pound 9.09 | 2.41 | 2.82 | 5.70 | −50 |
| Estonia | Kroon 30 | 2.49 | 9.32 | 12.0 | −23 |
| Euro area§ | ??2.94 | 3.82 | 1.10 | 1.30 | +19 |
| Hong Kong | HK$12.00 | 1.54 | 3.73 | 7.81 | −52 |
| Hungary | Forint 590 | 3.00 | 183 | 197 | −7 |
| Iceland | Kronur 509 | 7.44 | 158 | 68.4 | +131 |
| Indonesia | Rupiah 15,900 | 1.75 | 4.938 | 9,100 | −46 |
| Japan | ¥280 | 2.31 | 87.0 | 121 | −28 |
| Latvia | Lats 1.35 | 2.52 | 0.42 | 0.54 | −22 |
| Lithuania | Litas 6.50 | 2.45 | 2.02 | 2.65 | −24 |
| Malaysia | Ringgit 5.50 | 1.57 | 1.71 | 3.50 | −51 |
| Mexico | Peso 29.0 | 2.66 | 9.01 | 10.9 | −17 |
| New Zealand | NZ$4.60 | 3.16 | 1.43 | 1.45 | −2 |
| Norway | Kroner 41.5 | 6.63 | 12.9 | 6.26 | +106 |
| Pakistan | Rupee 140 | 2.31 | 43.5 | 60.7 | −28 |
| Paraguay | Guarani 10,000 | 1.90 | 3,106 | 5,250 | −41 |

| | | | | | |
|---|---|---|---|---|---|
| Peru | New Sol 9.50 | 2.97 | 2.95 | 3.20 | −8 |
| Philippines | Peso 85.00 | 1.74 | 26.4 | 48.9 | −46 |
| Poland | Zloty 6.90 | 2.29 | 2.14 | 3.01 | −29 |
| Russia | Rouble 49.00 | 1.85 | 15.2 | 26.5 | −43 |
| Saudi Arabia | Riyal 9.00 | 2.40 | 2.80 | 3.75 | −25 |
| Singapore | S$3.60 | 2.34 | 1.12 | 1.54 | −27 |
| Slovakia | Crown 57.98 | 2.13 | 18.0 | 27.2 | −34 |
| South Africa | Rand 15.50 | 2.14 | 4.81 | 7.25 | −34 |
| South Korea | Won 2,900 | 3.08 | 901 | 942 | −4 |
| Sri Lanka | Rupee 1.90 | 1.75 | 59.0 | 109 | −46 |
| Sweden | SKr32.00 | 4.59 | 9.94 | 6.97 | +43 |
| Switzerland | SFr6.30 | 5.05 | 1.96 | 1.25 | +57 |
| Taiwan | NT$75.00 | 2.28 | 23.3 | 32.9 | −29 |
| Thailand | Baht 62.00 | 1.78 | 19.3 | 34.7 | −45 |
| Turkey | Lire 4.55 | 3.22 | 1.41 | 1.41 | – |
| UAE | Dirhams 10.00 | 2.72 | 3.11 | 3.67 | −15 |
| Ukraine | Hryvnia 9.00 | 1.71 | 2.80 | 5.27 | −47 |
| Uruguay | Peso 55.00 | 2.17 | 17.1 | 25.3 | −33 |
| Venezuela | Bolivar 6,800 | 1.58 | 2,112 | 4,307 | −51 |

* Purchasing power parity; local price divided by price in United States.
† Average of New York, Atlanta, Chicago, and San Francisco.
‡ Dollars per pound.
§ Dollars per euro.
*Source: The Economist.*

*Relative PPP*    Alternatively, suppose that instead of redefining the basket, we use the standard consumer price index (CPI) for our measures of $P$ and $P^*$. A less stringent (weaker) version of PPP, called **relative PPP**, acknowledges that because they refer to different bundles of goods, the absolute prices of these consumption baskets may not be equalized, but notes that as long as the individual components of the basket obey the arbitrage argument and the composition of the bundle does not change, the ratio between the quantity of the domestic bundle that can be purchased with $1 and the quantity of the foreign bundle that can be purchased with the same amount of money should be constant:

$$Q = SP^*/P = K$$

where $K$ is the ratio between the quantity of the domestic bundle and the quantity of the foreign bundle that can be purchased with $1.[5]

Unfortunately for the relative PPP theory, this would be true only under a rather stringent assumption: that the *relative* prices of goods included in the commodity bundles used to compute the price indices $P$ and $P^*$ do not change. If they do, then even if all similar goods are arbitraged to sell for the same price in the same currency, the relative prices of the two bundles of goods will change – that is, $K$ will not be a constant.

For example, suppose that the foreign country's basket of goods contains more expensive goods on average than the domestic basket. Then $K$ would tend to be greater than unity (it would take more than one domestic basket to buy a foreign basket). What would happen if the world relative price of expensive goods increased? Then the relative price of the foreign basket in terms of the domestic basket would rise, because it contains more such goods, and $K$ would increase. The bottom line is that $K$ will change whenever world relative prices of goods change, even if similar goods always sell for the same common-currency price everywhere in the world.

In the models that we will build in this book, the real exchange rate will change endogenously precisely because shocks to the economy give rise to changing relative prices of goods – that is, we will assume that the prices of individual goods are indeed perfectly arbitraged (they sell for the same common-currency price everywhere), but that the representative baskets of goods produced at home and abroad are fundamentally different.

It is worth noting, however, that in the real world the arbitrage argument need not hold even for individual goods – that is, the same good need not sell for the same common-currency price everywhere.[6] Why not? There are several reasons, including the existence of transportation costs, commercial policies that impose barriers to trade, and price discrimination. Some goods, especially those with transportation costs so high that they become **nontraded** (consumed only in the economy where they are produced), can sell at very different prices (measured in the same currency) in different countries, because it is too expensive for consumers to acquire these goods in countries where their price is lower. In addition, commercial policies that impose barriers to trade in the form of tariffs and quotas may prevent arbitrage. Finally, when firms have monopoly power in the markets for the products they sell, they may practice price discrimination among national markets to maximize monopoly profits. For all these reasons, even the same consumption bundle can sell for different prices (expressed in the same currency) in different countries. As Box 3.2 suggested, this may be the case for Big Macs.

---

[5]   Notice that absolute PPP implies relative PPP, but not vice versa.
[6]   Indeed, the LOOP itself has not held up well across countries in empirical tests.

The implication is that standardizing the basket to which the price indices refer does not salvage the use of PPP as an indicator of the equilibrium value of two currencies. However, it is worth noting that there are other uses for an exchange rate parity calculated in this way. Box 3.3 explains why an artificial exchange rate parity of this type is actually the appropriate conversion factor to use in converting the incomes of different countries into a common currency for the purpose of making international comparisons of living standards, and Box 3.4 provides a specific application: to the assessment of the impact of Indonesia's 1997–8 currency crisis on living standards in that country.

## Box 3.3 International Comparisons of Living Standards

The PPP concept should not be dismissed as useless simply because PPP does not work very well as a theory of real exchange rate movements. In fact – somewhat paradoxically – something called the **PPP exchange rate** has proven to be a useful concept precisely *because* PPP is not a very good theory of real exchange rate determination.

The term PPP exchange rate refers to a particular exchange rate computed by the University of Pennsylvania's Center for International Comparisons. It is the exchange rate that would be required to equalize the price in US dollars of a representative "world" consumption bundle, consisting of approximately 150 different goods, in different countries. The usefulness of this concept arises from the fact that, *when PPP fails, the PPP exchange rate is the right exchange rate to use in making international comparisons of living standards*.

To see why, notice that in comparing living standards across countries what we actually want to know is how many units of some *uniform* consumption basket people in different countries can afford to consume, given their income per person. Suppose the domestic economy's income per person, measured in domestic currency terms, is $Y$, and the corresponding value for the foreign country, in foreign currency, is $Y^*$. Then, using the notation in the text for the prices of uniform consumption baskets, the "typical" domestic resident can consume $Y/P_S$ standard consumption bundles, while the typical foreign resident can consume $Y^*/P_S^*$ bundles. The relative standard of living is thus:

$$\frac{Y^*/P_S^*}{Y/P_S} = (P_S/P_S^*)Y^*/Y = S_{PPP}Y^*/Y$$

where $S_{PPP} = P_S / P_S^*$ is the PPP exchange rate, the exchange rate that would equalize the cost of the standard consumption bundle in the two countries, when expressed in the same currency. This means that to compare living standards between the foreign and domestic economies, the foreign income should be converted at the exchange rate $S_{PPP}$ rather than at the prevailing market exchange rate $S$. If, for example, the representative consumption basket costs twice as much in US dollars as in Indian rupees ($P_S / P_S^* = 2$), to convert Indian rupee incomes into dollars for the purpose of

*(Continued)*

**Box 3.3**   *(Continued)*

comparing living standards in the two countries, we would want to use an exchange rate of two dollars per rupee ($S_{PPP} = 2$) to reflect the fact that each rupee of income in India can be used to buy twice as much of the standard consumption basket in India as a dollar could buy in the United States. Notice that:

1   This measure is completely independent of market exchange rates. It is computed only from the ratio of the prices in different currencies of the same consumption basket.
2   The market exchange rate $S$ and $S_{PPP}$ will be different only if $S$ and $P_S/P_S^*$ are not the same – that is, as long as $SP_S^*$ is different from $P_S$, which in turn means that the same consumption bundle has different domestic-currency prices in the home and foreign countries. Another way of saying this is that comparing incomes using $S_{PPP}$ will provide a different answer from using market exchange rates – thus making $S_{PPP}$ a useful concept – precisely when PPP *does not* hold.

Table 3.2 provides comparisons of calculations of the US dollar gross national income (GNI) per capita for a sample of countries using market-based and PPP-based exchange rates in 2006. Notice that the figures can be quite different, especially for the lowest-income countries. For example, GNI per capita for countries such as China and India is more than twice as high when computed using $S_{PPP}$ than when using market exchange rates. The reason is that in poor countries the prices of representative consumption bundles, measured in a common currency, tend to be much lower than in rich countries.

This pattern is confirmed for a much larger group of countries in Figure 3.3, which plots the ratio of PPP-based GNI per capita to market-based GNI per capita against market-based GNI per capita. You can see that the relationship between these two variables is highly nonlinear, with the ratio rising dramatically as incomes per person fall to very low levels. Thus, using market-based measures of income per person tends to severely understate the incomes of the lowest-income countries, where low wages make the prices of goods that are not easily traded across international boundaries much lower than in rich countries. These results provide a dramatic confirmation of the fact that, contrary to the arbitrage argument for PPP, the same goods do not sell for the same common-currency price everywhere around the world.

The bottom line is that, for a variety of reasons, the real exchange rate is not in fact continuously pinned down by PPP. Deviations from the value of the real exchange rate that would be consistent with relative PPP (that is, from $Q = K$) can be large and persistent. We can indeed build models in which the relative prices of domestic and foreign goods can diverge, either because the compositions of the domestic and foreign goods are different (as in the models in the rest of this book) or because natural or artificial barriers to trade make arbitrage across national boundaries difficult. In models with such features, changes in relative prices can cause people to change the composition of their spending.

**Table 3.2**    Dollar values of gross national income (GNI) per capita with market-based and PPP-based exchange rates in selected countries, 2006

| Country | GNI per capita (market-based) | GNI per capita (PPP-based) |
|---|---|---|
| Argentina | 5332 | 11672 |
| Bangladesh | 423 | 1230 |
| Brazil | 5483 | 8702 |
| China | 2025 | 4664 |
| Egypt, Arab Rep. | 1446 | 4941 |
| France | 36984 | 32240 |
| Germany | 35561 | 32684 |
| Haiti | 459 | 1066 |
| India | 817 | 2466 |
| Indonesia | 1655 | 3305 |
| Italy | 31370 | 28974 |
| Japan | 35153 | 32843 |
| Korea, Rep. | 18370 | 22988 |
| Malaysia | 55195 | 12156 |
| Mexico | 7926 | 11186 |
| Nigeria | 696 | 1407 |
| Pakistan | 813 | 2408 |
| Philippines | 1434 | 3434 |
| Poland | 8533 | 14251 |
| Russian Federation | 6726 | 12736 |
| Spain | 27321 | 28199 |
| Thailand | 3186 | 7443 |
| Turkey | 5513 | 8410 |
| United Kingdom | 39919 | 33645 |
| United States | 44074 | 44074 |

*Source*: World Bank, World Development Indicators.

## 3.4    Relative Returns on Domestic and Foreign Assets: Interest Parity Conditions

We looked at relative prices of goods because these are an important factor in determining whether people buy domestic or foreign goods, which in turn is an important input into the determination of the current account of the balance of payments. Similarly, we will now look at expected relative rates of return on domestic and foreign financial assets, because these determine whether people choose to buy domestic or foreign assets. This in turn is an important input into the determination of the nonreserve financial account of the balance of payments.

### Uncovered Interest Parity (UIP)

What determines these relative returns? Consider the return to a domestic resident from investing $1 in a domestic asset versus investing it in a foreign asset. Buying the domestic

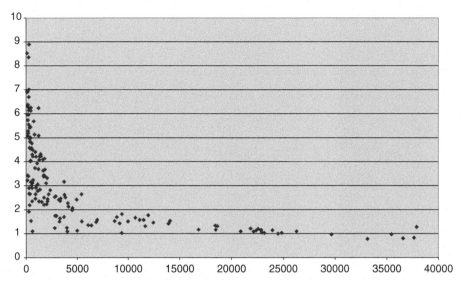

**Figure 3.3**    Ratio of PPP-based and market exchange rate-based measures of GNI per capita as a function of income levels

asset will produce $1 + R$ dollars in a year, where $R$ is the domestic **nominal interest rate** (the interest rate measured in terms of money). To buy a foreign asset, the domestic resident first has to buy foreign exchange. For $1, she can obtain $(1/S)$ units of the foreign currency, where $S$ is the exchange rate. This can then be used to purchase whatever amount of the foreign asset this will buy. This investment will yield $(1/S)(1 + R^{*})$ units of foreign currency in a year, where $R^{*}$ is the foreign nominal interest rate. To compare this to the return obtainable by buying the domestic asset, this amount has to be converted back into domestic currency, at the price expected to prevail in a year, when the foreign currency proceeds of the investment are sold. Because this is unknown today, we can call this price $S^{e}_{+1}$, where the superscript "e" refers to an expectation that is formed today (which is when the decision is being made about where to allocate the funds), and the subscript $+1$ refers to the number of periods in the future to which the expectation applies. The *expected* US dollar return on the foreign asset is thus $(1 + R^{*}) S^{e}_{+1}/S$.

What relationship – if any – should we expect to hold in equilibrium between the returns on domestic and foreign assets? In parallel with PPP theory, there is an arbitrage argument suggesting that these returns should be equalized, so that on average we should observe:

$$1 + R = (1 + R^{*})S^{e}_{+1}/S \tag{3.3}$$

or:

$$R = (1 + R^{*})S^{e}_{+1}/S - 1 \tag{3.3$'$}$$

This condition is called **uncovered interest parity (UIP)**, and we shall call the interest rate $R' = (1 + R^{*}) S^{e}_{+1}/S - 1$ the **uncovered interest parity interest rate (UIP interest rate)**. We will see where the "uncovered" part of this term comes from later in this section (see n. 6).

Notice that, by dividing both sides of equation (3.3) by $(1 + R^{*})$ and replacing $S^{e}_{+1}/S$ by the equivalent expression $[1 + (S^{e}_{+1} - S)/S]$, we can rewrite the UIP condition as:

## Box 3.4   By How Much Did the 1997–8 Currency Crisis Lower Living Standards in Indonesia?

As mentioned in Chapter 1, many countries have in recent years undergone sudden and dramatic depreciations in the foreign-exchange value of their currencies, in episodes known as **currency crises**. Though this has not always been the case, such crises have often been accompanied by severe contractions in real GDP, with serious impact on the living standards of the population. But how serious have those impacts been? Journalists often report the incomes of residents of the crisis countries by converting the domestic-currency values of those incomes to, say, US dollars, at market exchange rates. But as we have seen, this can be very misleading, because when the domestic currency depreciates drastically against the dollar, the dollar value of incomes in the affected country will fall drastically as well, but so will the dollar cost of the bundle of goods and services consumed by the residents of the affected country. A better measure of the effect of the crisis on living standards is obtained by converting domestic-currency incomes into dollars using PPP-adjusted exchange rates.

   The 1997–8 currency crisis in Indonesia provides a dramatic example. The Indonesian currency, the *rupiah*, depreciated from 2,450 *rupiah* per dollar at the end of June 1997 to 10,375 by the end of January 1998. The currency crisis was associated with a severe contraction in economic activity in Indonesia in 1998 that created tremendous economic hardship in the country. But how large was the contraction in Indonesia's living standards? Figure 3.4 provides two answers. Converting income per capita to dollars at the official exchange rate yields the bottom curve in this chart. By this measure, Indonesia's per-capita income was extremely low throughout the period 1970–97, but had been increasing since 1987. However, as the result of the crisis the country would appear to have lost the equivalent of 10 years of growth in a single year, with income per capita undergoing a decrease of more than 50 percent in 1998. The top curve, which converts income to dollars using PPP-adjusted exchange rates, gives a different picture: by this measure Indonesia had grown continuously since 1975, and by 1996 had reached a level of income per capita almost three times higher than would have appeared using market exchange rates, consistent with what we saw in Table 3.2. But notice that the impact of the crisis on living standards, while still severe, is dramatically reduced by this measure. The contraction in living standards is approximately 16 percent in 1998 by this measure – still an economic calamity, but the equivalent of three years of growth, rather than the full decade implied by conversion at market rates.

$$(1 + R)/(1 + R^*) = \left[1 + \left(S_{+1}^e - S\right)/S\right]$$

Taking logs of both sides of this equation, the UIP condition can be approximated as:

$$R - R^* = \left(S_{+1}^e - S\right)/S \tag{3.4}$$

This equation reveals that UIP essentially requires that interest rate differentials be equal to expected future (percentage) exchange rate changes.

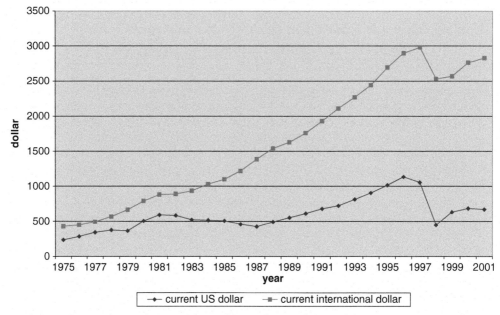

**Figure 3.4**    Indonesia: gross national income per capita, 1975–2001

Why might we expect uncovered interest parity to hold? As with PPP, the explanation involves arbitrage. The basic observation is that if these are essentially the same asset, they should yield the same return. Otherwise people would move their funds into the asset that yields the higher return, and that process would itself tend to equalize the returns. For example, suppose $(1 + R^*) S^e_{+1}/S > (1 + R)$. Then funds would leave the domestic economy and flow abroad. Given $S^e_{+1}$, sales of domestic assets would depress their price and raise their interest rates, causing the right-hand side of the inequality to increase. At the same time, purchases of the foreign currency to buy foreign assets would increase $S$, while purchases of foreign assets would raise their price and lower their rates of return $R^*$. Both effects would decrease the left-hand side of the inequality. This process would continue until equality is achieved between the two rates of return.

But as with PPP, the question is: are they indeed the same asset? The general answer is that they may not be. Even when they are otherwise identical (that is, they have the same maturities and promise the same future payments), domestic and foreign assets are likely to differ by risk characteristics. In particular, they are usually denominated in different currencies. Moreover, they are issued in different political jurisdictions and by different debtors. These characteristics suggest that the two assets may differ due to at least three different kinds of risk:

- **Exchange rate risk:** This is the risk attached to the possibility that the future exchange rate will turn out to be different from the value $S^e_{+1}$ expected when the transaction was initially undertaken.[7]

[7]  Individuals can eliminate exchange rate risk by agreeing today to sell the foreign-currency returns on the foreign assets they purchase for a domestic-currency future price that is agreed upon today. The markets on which such future currency transactions are carried out are called forward markets, and the agreed price is the forward

- **Political (or country) risk:** This is the differential risk that the authority in the foreign country may enact policies (such as capital controls or confiscation) that would impair the value of the foreign asset.
- **Commercial (or credit) risk:** This is the risk that, without any change in policies, the foreign agent that issued the asset may not honor it fully.

But even if these risk differences exist, people may not care about them (that is, they may be **risk neutral**). Thus, for the assets to be truly different in a way that would affect their relative returns, they have to differ in risk *and* people have to care about risk (that is, they may be **risk averse** or **risk loving**).

In the case of PPP, objections to the theory were based not only on differences between the representative consumption bundles at home and abroad, but also on transportation costs and trade barriers that prevented arbitrage. Their counterparts in the case of assets are transaction costs. Buying a foreign asset and redeeming the proceeds involves three separate transactions (buying the foreign exchange, buying the asset, and selling the foreign exchange when the asset matures). Even when there are no official restrictions on buying and selling bonds across international boundaries (**capital controls**), each of these transactions will involve brokerage fees, so in principle transaction costs could eliminate some arbitrage profits that could otherwise be available when there is a gap between the domestic and foreign returns. Thus, even if individuals expect to receive, say, a rate of return that is 1 percent higher by investing in foreign than in domestic assets, and they don't care about risk, if the brokerage costs involved in executing the three transactions required to do so exceed 1 percent, then it will not prove worthwhile for them to invest abroad. The implication is that it would not be profitable to arbitrage away return **differentials** (gaps) that are smaller than transaction costs. But in reality, these transaction costs are very small, and the scope for return differentials arising from this source is not great in the absence of official prohibitions (capital controls), unlike in the case of goods and services. When capital controls are present, though, these can represent serious obstacles to the arbitrage transactions required to establish UIP.

## Imperfect Substitutability

What is the alternative to UIP? If domestic and foreign interest-bearing assets are imperfect substitutes (they have different risk characteristics and people actually care about risk), then we can expect that peoples' choice between holding one type of asset or the other should depend on a comparison of their rates of return. In particular, the choice of whether to hold the riskier asset would depend on whether the return on that asset exceeds that on the safer asset by a large enough margin so as to compensate the holder for the higher risk involved in holding that asset. The excess return on the riskier asset is called the **risk premium**. Thus whether arbitrage takes place should depend on whether the risk premium is sufficiently large. In general, we would expect that the greater the share of the risky asset in private portfolios, the greater the risk premium that portfolio managers would demand on that asset in order to willingly hold such a large share of that asset in their portfolios.

---

price, or forward exchange rate. The interest parity condition that holds when the forward exchange rate replaces the expected future exchange rate in equation (3.3) is called the covered interest parity (CIP) condition, because the transaction is "covered" for exchange rate risk. By contrast, therefore, the transactions underlying (3.3) are "uncovered."

We can express this as follows. Let $B_P$ and $F_P^*$ respectively represent the stock of domestic and foreign bonds held by the domestic private sector. Since foreign bonds are denominated in the foreign currency, $F_P^*$ represents their foreign-currency value, and their domestic-currency value is therefore given by $SF_P^*$. Then we would expect the ratio of domestic to foreign bonds in private portfolios to be given by:

$$B_P/SF_P^* = B[\underset{+}{R}, (1 + \bar{R}^*)S_{+1}^e/S - 1]$$

where $B[\ ]$ denotes the function that describes the ratio of domestic to foreign bonds that domestic residents wish to hold in their financial portfolios, and the signs under the arguments of the function $B[\ ]$ indicate the direction in which an increase in that variable affects the function. Thus, in equilibrium, the ratio of domestic to foreign bonds is an *increasing* function of the rate of return on domestic bonds $(R)$, and a *decreasing* function of the expected rate of return on foreign bonds $((1 + R^*) S_{+1}^e/S - 1)$. This becomes the parity condition in the case of imperfect substitutability, replacing UIP.

## Modeling Financial Links

In building our various models, we will need to make alternative assumptions about how closely the domestic economy is integrated with world financial markets. How to measure such integration is somewhat problematic, however. For macro modeling purposes what we are interested in is whether the relative rates of returns on domestic and foreign assets are affected by the relative supplies of the two types of assets. But this can happen in two ways. One way in which it can happen is if the assets are quite similar, but there are barriers to arbitrage between domestic and foreign financial markets that essentially create segmented markets. An alternative way in which it can happen is if the two types of assets have perceived risk characteristics that depend on the political jurisdictions in which they are issued, making domestic and foreign assets different from each other, and thus preventing arbitrage from equalizing their rates of return.

While these two sources of persistent return differentials are conceptually distinct, they have the common implication that relative asset returns will depend on relative asset supplies. To capture this property, we will adopt the degree of *effective* arbitrage that prevails between domestic and foreign interest-bearing assets as our summary measure of the extent to which the domestic economy is financially integrated with the rest of the world. We will consider three possibilities: no arbitrage at all (financial autarky), imperfect arbitrage, and perfect arbitrage.

*No Arbitrage between Domestic and Foreign Assets*    If restrictions on financial transactions between domestic and foreign residents completely rule out the possibility of arbitrage between domestic and foreign financial assets, the domestic economy becomes financially closed. In this case, the demand for domestic bonds $(B_P)$ can be written in closed-economy intermediate-macroeconomics fashion:

$$B_P = W_P - PL$$

where $W_P$ is domestic private sector's financial wealth (consisting of domestic bonds and money, but no foreign bonds), $P$ is the domestic price level, and $L$ is the real demand for money, making *PL* the nominal demand for money. In effect, the domestic private sector's demand for domestic bonds becomes a residual demand. The private sector decides how much money it wants to hold, and then devotes the rest of its financial portfolio to holding domestic bonds.

*Imperfect arbitrage* When arbitrage is imperfect, the rate of return on domestic assets is influenced by that prevailing on foreign assets, but the two are not linked rigidly together. We should expect that the larger the arbitrage flows, the more closely the returns on domestic assets should move with that on foreign assets.

Consequently, we will model imperfect arbitrage as arising from imperfect substitutability between domestic and foreign assets. This is the case that we considered in the last subsection. We saw that when domestic and foreign interest-bearing assets are imperfect substitutes, the demand for domestic bonds relative to foreign bonds depended on their relative rates of return, so we can write the demand for domestic bonds as:

$$B_P = B\left[R, (1 + R^*)S_{+1}^e/S - 1\right]SF_P$$

In the next chapter we will see how different degrees of financial integration can be represented with an equation of this type.

*Perfect substitutability* Finally, when domestic and foreign bonds are perfect substitutes there can be no well-defined demand for domestic bonds, since they are indistinguishable from foreign bonds. Instead, to determine the equilibrium rate of return on domestic bonds we use the arbitrage condition derived from UIP:

$$R = (1 + R^*)S_{+1}^e/S - 1$$

As shown in Empirical Study 4.2, UIP tends to hold only imperfectly among industrial countries for short-maturity assets. However, in the analysis of floating exchange rates in Part 3 of the book, we will make the assumption that UIP holds under current international conditions. The reason is that though deviations from UIP are the rule rather than the exception over short time horizons (see Empirical Study 4.2), for the longer-term interest rates that primarily influence spending decisions such deviations do not appear to be sufficiently large in practice, at least among industrial countries, as to warrant the additional complication that they would introduce into our floating exchange rate models.

Which countries fall into our various categories of financial integration? There is no easy answer to this question since, as mentioned above, tests of financial integration can be difficult to interpret. Table 3.3, taken from Obstfeld (2004), provides an approximate classification. The countries in this table are classified as (financially) advanced (highly integrated with world capital markets), emerging (imperfectly integrated with world capital markets) and insular (essentially unable to access world capital markets). As you can see, the first group tends to consist of the high-income industrial countries, the second is dominated by middle-income developing countries, and the last consists of the lowest-income countries of the world. An important point to take away from this table, however, is that while for many countries the process of globalization has undoubtedly greatly increased the effective degree of integration with world financial markets, the vast majority of countries still remains only imperfectly integrated – at best – with world financial markets.

**Table 3.3**   Classification of countries by degree of integration with world financial markets

| Advanced | Emerging | Insular | |
| --- | --- | --- | --- |
| Antigua | Argentina | Algeria | Lesotho |
| Australia | Bolivia | Angola | Madagascar |
| Austria | Brazil | Bangladesh | Malawi |
| Barbados | Chile | Belize | Mali |
| Belgium | China | Benin | Mauritania |
| Canada | Colombia | Botswana | Mauritius |
| Cyprus | Ecuador | Burkina Faso | Mozambique |
| Denmark | Egypt | Burundi | Namibia |
| Finland | Guatemala | Cameroon | Nepal |
| France | Hungary | Cape Verde | Nicaragua |
| Germany | India | Central African Rep. | Niger |
| Greece | Indonesia | Chad | Nigeria |
| Hong Kong | Israel | Comoros | Papua New Guinea |
| Iceland | Jordan | Congo, Dem. Rep. | Paraguay |
| Ireland | Korea | Congo, Rep. | Romania |
| Italy | Malaysia | Costa Rica | Rwanda |
| Japan | Mexico | Cote d'Ivoire | Sao Tome and Principe |
| Luxembourg | Morocco | Dominica | Senegal |
| Netherlands | Pakistan | Dominican Rep. | Sierra Leone |
| New Zealand | Panama | El Salvador | Sri Lanka |
| Norway | Peru | Equatorial Guinea | St.Kitts and Nevis |
| Portugal | Philippines | Ethiopia | St. Lucia |
| Puerto Rico | Poland | Fiji | St. Vincent & Grenadines |
| Singapore | Seychelles | Gabon | Syria |
| Spain | South Africa | Gambia | Tanzania |
| Sweden | Taiwan | Ghana | Togo |
| Switzerland | Thailand | Grenada | Trinidad and Tobago |
| United Kingdom | Turkey | Guinea-Bissau | Tunisia |
| United States | Uruguay | Guyana | Uganda |
| | Venezuela | Haiti | Zambia |
| | | Honduras | Zimbabwe |
| | | Iran | |
| | | Jamaica | |
| | | Kenya | |

*Source*: Obstfeld (2004).

## 3.5   Central Bank Intervention in the Foreign Exchange Market: Exchange Rate Regimes

In a closed economy the central bank can affect macroeconomic performance through its purchases and sales of domestic securities, or **open market operations**, which represent the central bank's instrument for conducting monetary policy. As we have seen, in an open economy the central bank can also buy or sell foreign exchange. Thus it can intervene in both the domestic bond market as well as in the foreign exchange market. The buying or selling of foreign exchange is referred to as the central bank's **exchange rate policy**. The relationship between exchange rate policy and monetary policy (that is, the central bank's interventions in the two markets in which it can act) will be one of our major concerns throughout this book. We will begin to discuss this issue in Chapter 4, but for now we need to clarify some terms pertaining to exchange rate policy and its implications for the central bank's behavior in the foreign exchange market.

## Central Bank Behavior

So far, we have looked at the relative prices and rates of return that influence the behavior of private agents in the foreign exchange market in the form of current and capital account transactions respectively. We now want to examine the factors that influence the behavior of central banks in the foreign exchange market, that is, the purchases and sales of foreign exchange by central banks that are the transactions appearing in the "official reserves settlements" (*ORS*) portion of the BOP accounts. It turns out, as we will see in the rest of the book, that the macroeconomics of open economies depends critically on the behavior of central banks in the foreign exchange market.

Recall that transactions by the central bank are treated differently from those of other agents in the balance of payments accounts because central bank behavior is assumed to be motivated by different factors than those that motivate other participants in the foreign exchange markets. Specifically, central bank transactions reflect *policy* decisions, while the transactions of other participants are assumed to reflect their *private* interests.

Factors governing the behavior of central banks in the foreign exchange market can be classified into two types:

1   General rules of behavior governing central bank intervention in the foreign exchange market. These are referred to as the **foreign exchange regime**. The foreign exchange regime determines the conditions under which the central bank intervenes in the foreign exchange market. In general, these rules constituting the foreign exchange regime determine the amount of discretion central banks have in their foreign exchange operations.
2   The second set of factors concerns how the central bank uses the discretion allotted to it by the foreign exchange regime. This is referred to as **exchange rate management**.

Just as we have discussed only one of the factors affecting each of the current and capital accounts so far (the real exchange rate and the uncovered interest parity condition), putting off the rest until we begin to build our analytical framework, we will discuss just the first set of factors governing central bank behavior – the foreign exchange regime – for now, leaving aside the issue of exchange rate management until we build models in which this issue arises.

*Exchange Rate Regimes*   The historical pattern regarding foreign exchange regimes is that most of the world's major trading economies have tended to adopt similar types of foreign exchange regimes at the same time. The term **international monetary system** is used to denote the prevailing dominant exchange rate regime together with the international institutions and informal codes of conduct that exist to support its operation. Since the last quarter of the 19th century, prevailing exchange rate arrangements among the major trading countries have consisted of a commodity (gold) standard, the Bretton Woods system, and floating exchange rates. We will discuss the gold standard and the Bretton Woods system in Chapters 5 and 7 respectively, and will consider how the international monetary system functions under floating exchange rates in Chapters 16 and 17.

*Fixed Exchange Rate Regimes*    The gold standard and the Bretton Woods systems are examples of what are commonly known as **fixed exchange rate regimes**, although a better name might be **officially determined exchange rate regimes**. Under such regimes, the central bank is committed to buying and selling an unlimited amount of reserves (gold or foreign exchange, respectively) at an officially determined price in terms of its own currency. That price may indeed be fixed in the sense of being unchanging, but it need not be. It is, however, always "fixed" in the sense of being determined by the central bank or other official authority.

One distinction between commodity standards such as the gold standard and more conventional fixed exchange rate regimes such as the Bretton Woods system is that under the former, the central bank is committed to intervening in the private market for some commodity, such as gold bullion, rather than directly in the foreign exchange market. Nonetheless the effects of both regimes on the exchange rate and the determination of *ORS* turn out to be exactly the same. Under a commodity standard, as long as two central banks are committed to fixing the price of the same commodity, private agents in one country can always acquire the currency of the other country by buying the commodity in their own country, shipping it to the other country, and selling it to the central bank in that country in exchange for foreign currency. This has two implications:

1   The price of the foreign currency in the foreign exchange market cannot exceed the cost of acquiring the currency in this manner, and similarly for the price of the domestic currency in terms of the foreign one, so the exchange rate between the two currencies essentially becomes circumscribed within very narrow bounds by the commodity prices established by the two central banks.
2   As a result of this kind of arbitrage, excess flow supplies or demands in the overall balance of payments (*CA + NFA*), which give rise to incipient changes in nominal exchange rates, result instead in commodity flows between central banks (*ORS*). However, these flows occur not at the discretion of central banks, but that of other economic agents (individuals, firms, or governments) who are engaged in international transactions. That is so because it is the net effect of the actions of these agents that determines whether an excess supply or excess demand for foreign exchange emerges that causes the commodity whose price is being fixed by the central banks to be shipped for arbitrage purposes. It follows that under these circumstances, central banks have no discretion over *ORS*. Their actions are restricted to maintaining the official commodity price that they have announced by engaging in the commodity transactions requested of them by other agents at that price. *ORS* simply records the net effect of such transactions on the central bank's reserve stocks of the commodity the price of which it is setting. Since the net effect of those transactions is given by the sum of the current and capital accounts of the balance of payments, we have:

$$-ORS = CA + NFA$$

Because the central bank has no discretion over *ORS* under a commodity standard, *ORS* is not a **policy variable** (a variable whose behavior is determined by policymakers) under such a regime.

A conventional fixed exchange rate regime, such as that established under Bretton Woods, operates in very much the same way, except that the ''commodity'' is foreign exchange. The implications are that the equilibrium exchange rate that prevails in the foreign exchange market will be circumscribed by the central bank's buying and selling rates for foreign exchange, and *ORS* will not be a policy variable.

*Floating Exchange Rate Regimes*    A **floating exchange rate regime**, by contrast, is one in which the central bank makes no commitment to establish the price either of a commodity or foreign exchange. There are two broad types of floating exchange rate regimes. In the case of a **clean float**, the central bank is committed not to intervene in the foreign exchange market at all. In that case, the exchange rate is purely market-determined, though the central bank can influence it indirectly through monetary policy, as we shall see in Part 3 of the book. With regard to *ORS*, since the central bank neither buys nor sells foreign exchange, *ORS* must be zero. Thus we have:

$$ORS = 0 = CA + NFA^8$$

Finally, under a **dirty float**, the central bank neither commits itself to fixing the price of anything nor to refraining from intervention in the foreign exchange market. Thus the central bank can influence the exchange rate both directly as well as indirectly. With regard to *ORS*, it simply reflects the central bank's discretionary policy decisions. Thus we have:

$$CA + NFA + ORS = 0$$

where, since *ORS* is a policy variable, it takes on the value determined by the central bank.

*Varieties of Fixes and Floats*    In the real world, fixed and floating exchange rate regimes can be further subdivided into various types. For example, an extreme case of a fixed exchange rate regime occurs when one country simply adopts the currency of another country or participates in a multilateral monetary union. In these cases, referred to as **dollarization** (whether or not the currency adopted happens to be the US dollar) and **monetary unification** respectively, the exchange rate between the domestic and foreign currencies is unity by definition. Ecuador and El Salvador, for example, recently abandoned their national currencies in favor of the US dollar, and several countries in Western Europe adopted a new currency, the euro, in place of their national currencies.

A less extreme form of a fixed exchange rate regime is one in which a central bank announces a fixed exchange rate parity, which is supported by institutional arrangements (such as constitutional provisions establishing an official exchange rate or requirements for legislative supermajorities to change the established exchange rate) that not only make it

---

[8]    Notice the implication that under a clean float, the current account must be the negative of the nonreserve financial account. We will make use of this result frequently when analyzing floating exchange rates.

very difficult for the exchange rate parity ever to be changed, but also subsume monetary policy to the defense of the exchange rate regime. Such arrangements are the defining characteristics of a **currency board**. From 1991 to 2001, for example, Argentina operated a currency board under which the value of an Argentine peso was set equal to one US dollar, and this parity could not be changed by the central bank. It required an act of the legislature to change the exchange rate.

A still less extreme version, a **soft peg**, consists of a central bank announcement about the value of the exchange rate that it will defend in the foreign exchange market, but with the central bank retaining discretion to change this parity in the future and to conduct its domestic monetary policy as it sees fit.

There are also exchange rate regimes that are essentially hybrid combinations of fixed and floating rate regimes. Under **exchange rate bands**, for example, the exchange rate floats within a band of values circumscribed by officially announced upper and lower bounds determined with reference to an official exchange rate parity. The limits of the band are usually expressed as a percentage of that parity. If the exchange rate reaches one of the bounds, the central bank intervenes in the foreign exchange market to make sure that it does not pass through it. From 1993 to the time of the creation of the euro in 1999, for example, the Western European countries that subsequently adopted the euro operated with exchange rate bands that allowed their exchange rates to fluctuate by 15 percent above or below a central parity before their central banks were obligated to intervene in the foreign exchange market. There can be various types of bands, depending on whether the central parity is literally fixed or is continually adjusted (the latter is referred to as a **crawling band**), on the band width, on the rules that govern foreign exchange market intervention by the central bank inside the band, and so on.

Figure 3.5 shows a frequency distribution of official exchange rate regimes across countries at the end of 2007. These are defined as the regimes that countries report to the International Monetary Fund that they have adopted. As the chart demonstrates, there is no uniformity in exchange rate regimes across countries. While formal bands (identified as "pegged exchange rate with horizontal bands" and "crawling bands" in the chart) are

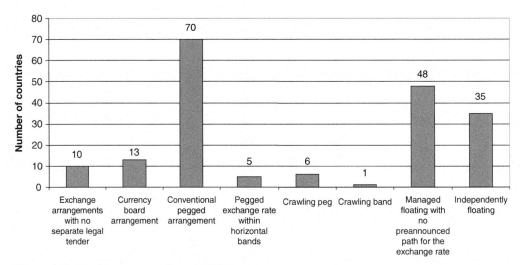

**Figure 3.5**  Exchange rate regimes in 2007

relatively rare, roughly the same number of countries describe themselves as pursuing some kind of floating exchange rate arrangement ("independently floating" and "managed floating with no preannounced path for the exchange rate," totaling 83 countries) as operating under an officially determined or fixed exchange rate ("exchange rate arrangements with no separate legal tender," "currency boards," and "conventional (soft) pegs," amounting to 93 countries).

---

## Empirical Study 3.1   Testing PPP

One way to test absolute PPP more rigorously is as follows. Begin by expressing the hypothesis in logs by taking logs of both sides of equation (3.2):

$$q = s + p^* - p = 0$$

or:

$$s = p - p^*. \tag{3.2'}$$

Now consider a general empirical specification for the nominal exchange rate such as:

$$s = \beta_0 + \beta_1 p + \beta_2 p^* + \epsilon \tag{3.2''}$$

where the $\beta$s are unknown parameters to be estimated empirically and $\epsilon$ is a **random variable** (a variable whose value is determined by chance). If absolute PPP is right, then equation (3.2') suggests that in the real world we should observe that $\beta_0 = 0$, $\beta_1 = 1$, $\beta_2 = -1$, and $\epsilon$ should fluctuate around a mean value of zero (that is, $\epsilon$ should be **mean-reverting**). If these conditions are true, then the log of the real exchange rate ($s - p + p^*$) would tend to fluctuate randomly around an **equilibrium** value (the value to which the market will eventually drive it) of zero, as implied by equation (3.2').

Using **econometrics** (statistical methods for estimating economic parameters and testing hypotheses about them), these hypotheses can be tested for consistency with real-world data. Unfortunately, it turns out that the theory does not hold up very well in the face of such tests. Econometric estimates of equation (3.2') for individual countries over the post-World War II period (referred to as *short-span time series tests*), tend to find that if the parameter values $\beta_0 = 0$, $\beta_1 = 1$, $\beta_2 = -1$ are imposed in equation (3.2''), the random term $\epsilon$ does not tend to be mean-reverting. On the other hand, when those parameters are left unconstrained, then whenever $\epsilon$ tends to be mean-reverting, the estimated values of those parameters are far from the theoretical values of $\beta_0 = 0$, $\beta_1 = 1$, $\beta_2 = -1$ (see Montiel 1999).

*Long-span* tests – spanning periods approaching a century or more – appear to be more favorable to the PPP hypothesis, in the sense that the empirical predictions described above are not as frequently rejected by the data. Thus the implication seems to be that the real exchange rate appears to be centered on a stable value over very long periods, but exhibits systematic swings over shorter periods lasting several years or even decades. To read more about testing PPP, see Rogoff (1996).

## Empirical Study 3.2    Testing Uncovered Interest Parity (UIP)

There is a large literature in international macroeconomics that attempts to test empirically whether the uncovered interest parity (UIP) condition has been empirically valid in a wide variety of countries and over different periods of time. It turns out that this is not easy to do.

To see how tests of UIP can be conducted, notice first that, by dividing both sides of equation (3.3) by $(1 + R^*)$ and replacing $S^e_{+1}/S$ by the equivalent expression $[1 + (S^e_{+1} - S)/S]$, we can rewrite the UIP condition as:

$$(1 + R)/(1 + R^*) = \left[1 + \left(S^e_{+1} - S\right)/S\right]$$

Taking logs of both sides of this equation, the condition can be approximated as:

$$\begin{aligned} R - R^* &= \left(S^e_{+1} - S\right)/S \\ &= \left(s^e_{+1} - s\right) \end{aligned} \tag{3.4}$$

where $s^e_{+1} = \log(S^e_{+1})$ and $s = \log(S)$. Thus the UIP condition implies that the expected future (percentage) change in the exchange rate over some specific time horizon should be equal to the differential between the domestic and foreign rates of return on bonds with maturity corresponding to that horizon.

The difficulty in testing whether this is true is that expected exchange rate changes are not directly observable. Because of this, tests of UIP thus invariably involve a secondary hypothesis about what determines this expectation. That makes the evidence on this issue hard to interpret, since rejection of both hypotheses together need not imply rejection of UIP itself.

A common approach to empirical testing is to assume that expectations of future exchange rates are **rational**, meaning that such expectations are formed using all available information. If this is true, then while such expectations may turn out to be incorrect, they should not be *systematically* incorrect, since people forming expectations would notice any systematic errors and take them into account in forming their expectations in the future, thereby eliminating such errors. This is equivalent to saying that the expectation of the future exchange rate formed in the current period should be an *unbiased* predictor of the actual exchange rate that is eventually observed in the future:

$$s_{t+1} = s^e_{t+1} + u_{t+1}$$

where $u_{t+1}$ is a mean-zero, serially uncorrelated random variable. Under this assumption, the UIP condition becomes:

$$s_{t+1} - s_t = R_t - R^*_t + u_{t+1}$$

That is, the interest rate differential should be an unbiased predictor of future exchange rate changes. This hypothesis can be tested by estimating the regression:

$$s_{t+1} - s_t = a + b\left(R_t - R^*_t\right) + u_{t+1}$$

If UIP is correct, we should find that $a = 0$, $b = 2$, and $u_{t+1}$ is serially uncorrelated.

Empirical estimates of this equation have yielded several results. First, interest rate differentials do not explain very much of the future variation in exchange rates. In other words, most of the variation in exchange rates is unanticipated, or the result of "news." Second, when this equation is estimated over short horizons (i.e., when it is applied to short-term interest rates and correspondingly short-run exchange rate movements), researchers frequently find that interest rate differentials *underpredict* future exchange rate changes, or that the exchange rate even moves in a direction *opposite* to what the theory would predict.[9] In other words, countries with high interest rates tend to have *appreciating*, rather than depreciating currencies. Third, when the interest rate differentials being considered pertain to assets with maturity longer than one year, such differentials do a much better job of predicting future exchange rate changes, consistent with UIP.[10] Thus, tests of UIP tend to be more supportive of the hypothesis over longer than over shorter horizons.

The failure of UIP over short horizons is one of the unresolved puzzles of international macroeconomics. There are several possible interpretations. A key question is whether such tests fail because UIP fails to hold, because the assumption made in such tests about the link between actual and expected exchange rate changes (rational expectations) is wrong, or for some other reason that is consistent with UIP and rational expectations. Such reasons could include, for example, an expected exchange rate change that eventually occurs, but not within the sample period (a situation referred to as the **peso problem**), the possibility that monetary policy causes the interest rate differential to be a function of expected future exchange rate changes (which would create a **simultaneity bias** in estimation), or the effects of rational learning.[11] The resolution of these questions remains a topic for research.

## 3.6   Summary

When the domestic economy is open, domestic residents can trade goods and services as well as financial claims with foreign residents, so that they have to decide whether to buy domestic or foreign goods and services and whether to hold domestic or foreign financial assets. The decisions that they make in this regard have important effects on the domestic market for goods and services as well as on domestic financial markets.

At the same time, the choices that domestic and foreign residents make concerning the purchase of domestic or foreign goods influence the current account of the balance of payments, while the choices that they make whether to hold domestic or foreign financial assets influence the nonreserve financial account and the official reserves settlement balance. Since these three types of transactions determine the supply and demand for foreign exchange, these choices will determine the equilibrium outcome in the foreign exchange market.

In this chapter we have examined an important subset of factors that influence these choices. The real exchange rate, defined as the number of domestic goods that must be given

---

[9]   The evidence is surveyed by Engel (1996).
[10]   See Chinn and Meredith (2005).
[11]   Isard (2006) discusses these possibilities.

up to acquire one foreign good, is the key variable that influences the composition of spending between domestic and foreign goods and services, while differentials between domestic and foreign rates of return play the corresponding role in influencing the decision by private agents whether to hold domestic or foreign financial assets. The behavior of central banks in the foreign exchange market, on the other hand, is a policy decision that depends in the first instance on the foreign exchange regime that the country has adopted.

We shall see in the rest of this book that the exchange rate regime adopted by a country has a significant effect on how that country's economy is affected by macroeconomic shocks and how standard macroeconomic policies such as fiscal and monetary policies affect the economy. This should not be too surprising if you recall from intermediate macroeconomics that the type of monetary policy followed by the central bank (such as fixing the money supply or fixing the interest rate) made a huge difference as well. Consequently, given the diversity of exchange rate regimes that are actually in use around the world, to do justice to the macroeconomics of open economies we will have to analyze macroeconomic performance under a variety of exchange rate arrangements. In Parts 2 and 3 of the book, we will explore the difference that the central bank's behavior in the foreign exchange market makes by separately analyzing open-economy macroeconomics under fixed and floating exchange rates. But before doing so, we need to set out the basic economic framework that we will be using to conduct the analysis. Chapter 4 turns to that task by describing how the fundamental concepts introduced in this chapter – the real exchange rate, the interest parity condition, and the exchange rate regime – fit into the general macroeconomic framework that we will be using to analyze international macro-economic issues in the rest of the book.

## Questions

1   "International capital mobility tends to equalize interest rates in different countries." Do you agree or disagree? Why?
2   Two important "parity" conditions are often used in open-economy macroeconomics: purchasing-power parity and uncovered interest parity. Explain what each of these is and under what conditions you might expect them to be empirically valid in the real world.
3   What is the "purchasing power parity exchange rate", how is it used, and what makes it suited for that purpose?
4   How seriously should we take the *Economist* magazine's Big Mac standard as a guide to the equilibrium values of currencies? Explain what aspects of the Big Mac standard make it a potentially useful indicator of equilibrium currency values, and why we nevertheless would not necessarily expect the Big Mac standard to provide an accurate guide to the equilibrium values of nominal exchange rates.
5   Shortly after the Asian currency crisis in the summer of 1997, the price of the US dollar in terms of the Indonesian *rupiah* increased fourfold. Using market exchange rates to make the conversion into US dollars, this meant that GDP per person in Indonesia, measured in US dollars, fell to a quarter of its pre-crisis value. Does this mean that the crisis caused living standards in Indonesia to contract by 75 percent? Explain why or why not.
6   Consider the foreign exchange market for a particular currency, say the Botswanan *pula*. Show how the equilibrium value of the *pula* in this market would be affected by a commitment by the central bank of Botswana to buy or sell the *pula* in unlimited amount

at a specific central bank-determined exchange rate. Under what conditions can the central bank make such a commitment?

7　What do we mean by the phrase "the foreign exchange value of the dollar"? Explain why economists prefer to use multilateral exchange rates rather than bilateral ones to measure this concept.

8　When a small country maintains a fixed exchange rate against the currency of a larger country, which in turn maintains a floating exchange rate against the currencies of the rest of the world, is the small country's exchange rate fixed of floating? Explain your answer.

9　Economists have often found that purchasing power parity gives a closer approximation to reality during periods of very high inflation than during "normal" times. Can you provide an explanation for why this might be so?

## Further Reading and References

### On the structure of foreign exchange markets

Chrystal, K. Alec (1984), "A Guide to Foreign Exchange Markets," Federal Reserve Bank of St. Louis *Review* (March), pp. 5–18.

### On multilateral (effective) exchange rates

Acree, Bryan (1999), "Revising the Atlanta Fed Dollar Index," Federal Reserve Bank of Atlanta *Economic Review* (Third Quarter), pp. 40–51.

Batten, Dallas S. and Belongia, Michael T. (1987), "Do the New Exchange Rate Indexes Offer Better Answers to Old Questions?" Federal Reserve Bank of St. Louis *Review* (May), pp. 5–17.

Coughlin, Cletus C. and Pollard, Patricia S. (1996), "A Question of Measurement: Is the Dollar Rising or Falling?" Federal Reserve Bank of St. Louis *Review* (July/August), pp. 3–18.

Cox, Michael W. (1986), "A New Alternative Trade-Weighted Dollar Exchange Rate Index," Federal Reserve Bank of Dallas *Economic Review* (September), pp. 20–8.

Ott, Mack (1987), "The Dollar's Effective Exchange Rate: Assessing the Impact of Alternative Weighting Schemes," Federal Reserve Bank of St. Louis *Review* (February), pp. 5–14.

Rosensweig, Jeffrey A. (1987), "Constructing and Using Exchange Rate Indexes," Federal Reserve Bank of Atlanta *Economic Review* 72 (Summer), pp. 4–16.

### On the Big Mac index

Pakko, Michael R., and Pollard, Patricia (1996), "For Here or To Go? Purchasing Power Parity and the Big Mac," Federal Reserve Bank of St. Louis *Review* (January/February), pp. 3–22.

Pakko, Michael R., and Pollard, Patricia (2003), "Burgernomics: A Big Mac Guide to Purchasing Power Parity" Federal Reserve Bank of St. Louis *Review* (November/December), pp. 9–27.

### On testing PPP

Montiel, Peter J. (1999), "Estimating Equilibrium Exchange Rates: An Overview," in L. Hinkle and P. Montiel, eds., *Exchange Rate Misalignment: Concepts and Measurement for Developing Countries* (Oxford: Oxford University Press).

Rogoff, Kenneth (1996), "The Purchasing Power Parity Puzzle," *Journal of Economic Literature* Vol. XXXIV (June), pp. 647–68.

**On financial flows**

Aurelio, Marcella Meirelles (2006), "Going Global: The Changing Pattern of U.S. Investment Abroad," Federal Reserve Bank of Kansas City *Economic Review*, Third Quarter, pp. 5–32.

**On financial arbitrage**

Chinn, Menzie D. and Meredith, Guy (2005), "Testing Uncovered Interest Parity at Short and Long Horizons during the Post-Bretton Woods Era," NBER Working Paper 11077 (January).
Engel, Charles (1996), "The Forward Discount Anomaly and the Risk Premium: A Survey of Recent Evidence," *Journal of Empirical Finance* 3, pp. 123–92.
Isard, Peter (2006), "Uncovered Interest Parity," IMF Working Paper WP/06/96 (April).
Obstfeld, Maurice (2004), "Globalization, Macroeconomic Performance, and the Exchange Rate of Emerging Economies," NBER Working Paper 10849 (October).

**On central bank intervention**

Bonser-Neal, Catherine (1996), "Does Central Bank Intervention Stabilize Foreign Exchange Rates?" Federal Reserve Bank of Kansas City *Economic Review* (First Quarter), pp. 43–57.
Humpage, Owen (1994), "Institutional Aspects of US Intervention," Federal Reserve Bank of Cleveland *Economic Review* Quarter 1, pp. 1–19.
Neely, Christopher J. (2000), "Are Changes in Foreign Exchange Reserves Well Correlated with Official Intervention?" Federal Reserve Bank of St. Louis *Review* (September/October), pp. 17–31.
Neely, Christopher J. (2001), "The Practice of Central Bank Intervention: Looking under the Hood," Federal Reserve Bank of St. Louis *Review* (May/June), pp. 1–10.

**On the size of foreign exchange markets**

Bank for International Settlements (2005), *Triennial Central Bank Survey* (Basle: Bank for International Settlements).

## Appendix 3.1   Properties of Logarithms

Suppose that some number $a$ can be expressed as some other number $b$ raised to a power given by yet a third number $c$, so that $a = b^c$. The number $b$ is referred to as the *base*. Using any positive number greater than one as the base, we can express any positive number $a$ in this way by a suitable choice of the power $c$. The power $c$ to which $b$ has to be raised in order to equal $a$ is referred to as the *logarithm* of $a$ using $b$ as the base, or as the *base-b logarithm* of $a$, which is written as:

$$\log_b a = c$$

where the shorthand "log" stands for logarithm and the subscript identifies the number that functions as the base.

Logarithms have several desirable properties that can be derived from the properties of the powers of numbers. Suppose that for some other number $x$ we have that $\log_b x = y$. Then:

1   Since $ax = b^c b^y = b^{c+y}$, it follows that $\log_b (ax) = \log_b (b^{c+y}) = c + y = \log_b a + \log_b x$.
2   Since $a/x = b^c / b^y = b^{c-y}$, it follows that $\log_b (a/x) = \log_b (b^{c-y}) = c - y = \log_b a - \log_b x$.

3 Since $a^n = (b^c)^n = b^{cn}$, it follows that $\log_b a^n = \log_b (b^{cn}) = cn = n \log_b a$.

While logarithms can be expressed using any positive number greater than one as a base, a particularly useful base is the mathematical constant $e$, approximately equal to 2.718.[12] Logarithms expressed with base $e$ are called **natural logarithms**.

Remember that we use lowercase letters to denote the logs of the corresponding ''level'' variables (e.g., $x = \log (X)$ ) and that an attractive feature of working in logs is that changes in logs can be interpreted as percentages. That means that when $y$ and $x$ are the logs of $Y$ and $X$, respectively, a relationship such as $y = x^a$ indicates that a 1 percent change in $X$ is associated with an $a$ percent change in $Y$. When the parameter $a$ is unity, a 1 percent change in $X$ is associated with a 1 percent change in $Y$, so changes in $Y$ are *proportional* to changes in $X$.

[12] Just like the mathematical constant $\pi$ (also an irrational number) is defined as the ratio of the circumference of a circle to its diameter, e is defined as the unique real number such that the function $e^x$ has the same value as the slope of a line tangent to the function at $x$, for any real number $x$.

# 4

# The Macroeconomic Framework

...................................................................................................................

In the last chapter we looked at some of the most important determinants of the three components of the balance of payments accounts: the current account ($CA$), the nonreserve financial account ($NFA$), and the official reserves settlements balance ($ORS$). We saw that the supply and demand for foreign exchange that interact in the foreign exchange market originate in the various types of transactions that are recorded in these sub-accounts, and that each of the sub-accounts in turn is affected by a different set of factors, such as the relative price of domestic and foreign goods, the relative rates of return on domestic and foreign financial assets, and the rules that govern central bank intervention in the foreign exchange market.

You would be justified in supposing that the logical next step in our analysis would be to put these three sources of supply and demand for foreign exchange together to ask how the foreign exchange market – the market in which currencies are traded for each other – works as a whole, taking all three types of transactions into account. The purpose of such an analysis would be to explain how the price of foreign exchange (the nominal exchange rate $S$) is determined, as well as what determines the aggregate quantity of foreign exchange bought and sold in the market.

Unfortunately, matters are not quite so straightforward. The problem with proceeding in that way is that the behavior of the foreign exchange market cannot be understood in isolation from what is going on in the rest of the economy. In other words, to understand the determination of equilibrium in the foreign exchange market, we have to investigate how that market interacts with the whole economy. Because the exchange rate and domestic macroeconomic variables such as the level of output, the price level, and interest rates are **jointly endogenous** variables (variables whose values are determined at the same time by other variables), we have to explain their determination simultaneously.[1]

In this chapter we will develop a general analytical framework that will help us to do just that. Because there are important differences in the ways that individual countries interact with the international economy – differences such as the size of the country, how well integrated it is with the rest of the world both commercially and financially, how it conducts its exchange rate and monetary policies, and so on – international macroeconomists have to use different macroeconomic models to analyze different country circumstances. While these models appear superficially very different from each other, they tend to share a common analytical core. Indeed, as you will see in the rest of this book, most of them are essentially special cases drawn from a common analytical framework. One of the most important objectives of this book is to help you master that analytical core, so you can understand how the various models that international macroeconomists use fit together. The purpose of this chapter is to familiarize you with that core. In the rest of the book you will learn how to adapt the general analytical framework that you will study in this chapter to fit the circumstances of specific countries.

The framework that we will be adopting is one that is in wide use among international macroeconomists. Just as in closed-economy macroeconomics, it describes how financial markets, goods markets, and factor markets interact to determine the behavior of the macroeconomic variables that we are interested in, including the exchange rate and other open-economy macro variables. We will begin by describing some basic characteristics of the framework, examining how equilibrium is attained first in the economy's financial markets and then in its goods and factor markets. Each of these markets will be in equilibrium only when certain endogenous variables take on specific values (not surprisingly, called their **equilibrium** values). Thus, what we will be investigating is what the values of the endogenous variables have to be in order for all macroeconomic markets to be in equilibrium at the same time. This process will be familiar to you, since it is essentially what you did in studying how simultaneous equilibrium in financial, goods, and labor markets determined the values of real GDP, the interest rate, and the price level in intermediate closed-economy macroeconomics.

As is always true in macroeconomic models, we will find that if we want to explain many things (that is, we want to have many endogenous variables in our model) we have to know a lot about the economy – in other words, we have to be able to describe a large number of conditions that the equilibrium values of the endogenous variables have to satisfy. Thus our next step will be to consider reasonable sets of additional conditions that can be imposed on our framework to help us pin down a unique set of equilibrium values for the large number of endogenous variables that we will try to explain in this book. We will see that different sets of these ancillary assumptions will apply in different circumstances, and it is by imposing different sets of ancillary assumptions that we will be able to produce special

---

[1]  Remember that endogenous variables are those whose behavior is explained by a theory, while exogenous variables are the factors that serve as ultimate causes in the theory. They affect the endogenous variables, but are not in turn affected by them.

cases of our general framework – specific **macroeconomic models** – that are tailor-made for the study of different country circumstances.

This may all seem pretty abstract at present, but because it is standard macroeconomic methodology, you are likely to find it all quite familiar as we go along. You should know, though, that this chapter is an important one that merits a particularly careful read, because much of what you will learn in the rest of the book builds directly on what we will do here.

## 4.1    Production Structure and Economic Agents

The first step in constructing our analytical framework is to describe the economy's production structure and the strength of trading links between the domestic and foreign goods markets. We will assume that the bundle of goods and services produced by the domestic economy is different from (is an imperfect substitute for) the goods and services produced by the rest of the world, but that the price of the domestic bundle, when expressed in a common currency, is the same at home and abroad. The same is true for the foreign bundle. In other words, there are no barriers to arbitrage – natural or policy-induced – between the domestic economy and the rest of the world. In the language of Chapter 3, purchasing power parity (PPP) will fail to hold in our framework not because the same goods sell for different common-currency prices in different countries, but because the domestic economy and the rest of the world produce different things.[2] This is not the only way to describe "real" (goods-market) links between the domestic and foreign economies, but it is the simplest framework that enables us to analyze many of the interesting problems that arise in international macroeconomics.[3]

How should we think about goods-market integration in this context? A particularly simple and intuitive way to do so is to consider that the goods markets of two economies are closely integrated when arbitrage ties the prices of the *aggregate* bundles they produce closely to each other (when measured in a common currency). This is particularly appealing because the two aggregate price levels will be tied closely together when the range of individual goods in the two economies that satisfies the law of one price is large, meaning that many of the goods produced in the two economies are essentially traded in a single market. Thus when the goods markets of two economies are highly integrated, small changes in the relative price of the bundles of goods that they produce (i.e., in the real exchange rate) will cause large reallocations of demand for the two goods by the residents

---

[2]    For example, Singapore and Botswana produce very different bundles of goods, with services and manufactured goods representing a much larger share of Singapore's output, while diamonds and agricultural goods represent a much larger share of the output of Botswana. As a consequence, even if all goods sold for the same common-currency price in both countries, the relative price of Singapore's output in terms of Botswana's output could change. In that case, the real exchange rate between the two countries would change and PPP would fail (see Chapter 3).

[3]    This particular set of assumptions about the production structure of the domestic economy and the rest of the world is the defining characteristic of the Mundell–Fleming model, an analytical framework developed by two economists, Robert Mundell and J. Marcus Fleming, at the International Monetary Fund's Research Department during the early 1960s. Because the model proved to be the workhorse analytical framework for international macroeconomics for several decades, Robert Mundell was awarded the Nobel Prize for its development in 1999.

of both countries. Empirical Study 4.1 at the end of the chapter examines the issue of goods market integration in more detail.

Next we need to consider whose behavior we will be describing in our framework. Small open economy macroeconomic models typically consider four distinct sets of agents:

1   The domestic (nonfinancial) household sector, which produces output and receives the income from production, pays taxes, buys domestic and foreign goods for consumption and investment purposes, and manages a financial portfolio.
2   The domestic government, which buys domestic goods and services, levies taxes, and issues debt.
3   The domestic central bank, which buys foreign exchange and domestic bonds by printing money.
4   The rest of the world, which trades goods and financial assets with the domestic economy.

Our next task is to examine how these agents interact with each other in markets for financial assets as well as in markets for goods and services. We will begin by considering how equilibrium is attained in asset markets (Section 4.2) and will then turn to describing equilibrium in goods markets (Section 4.3).

## 4.2   Equilibrium in the Market for Financial Assets

To keep the financial side of our framework as simple as possible, there will be no financial intermediaries such as banks. We will begin by considering the menu of financial assets that the agents in our economy can hold, then we will consider how they decide how much of each asset to hold, and will finally examine the conditions that must be satisfied in order for the demand for each asset to be equal to its supply.

### Financial Balance Sheets

The domestic household sector's **net financial wealth** is the difference between the value of the financial assets that it owns and that of its financial liabilities. Since we will assume that it has no financial liabilities, its net worth will consist of the total value of the financial assets that it owns. These consist of domestic money (currency, denoted $M$), domestic bonds ($B$), and foreign bonds ($F^*$).[4] Foreign bonds are assumed to be denominated in the foreign currency, so the domestic-currency value of these bonds is given by $SF_P^*$. This makes the domestic household sector's total financial wealth, denoted $W_P$, equal to:

$$W_P = M + B_P + SF_P^*$$

The subscript P attached to $B$ and $F$ indicates that these are the amounts of domestic and foreign bonds, respectively, that are held by the domestic household (private)

---

[4]   An asterisk will be used to denote a variable that is denominated in foreign exchange.

sector; no subscript is attached to $M$, since only the domestic household sector holds domestic currency.

The government, in contrast to the household sector, owns no financial assets, but does have financial liabilities in the form of the cumulative value of the debt that it has issued over time to finance its past fiscal deficits. Because this debt represents a liability of the government, the financial wealth of the government, which we will call $W_G$, consists of the *negative* of the public debt:

$$W_G = -B$$

where $B$ is the cumulative stock of bonds issued by the domestic government. The bonds issued by the government are assumed to be nominal (nonindexed) bonds that pay variable interest rates and have a face value of \$1; thus $B$ denotes both the number of domestic bonds as well as their value outstanding. You can think of the government bonds in our model as being similar to very short-term (say three-month) Treasury bills.

With respect to the central bank, we will assume that it has no net financial wealth, because it never saves or dissaves.[5] This means that, while the central bank has both assets and liabilities, the value of its assets is always equal to that of its liabilities. The central bank's net financial wealth, $W_C$, thus takes the form:

$$W_C = 0 = SF_C^* + B_C - M \tag{4.1}$$

where $F_C^*$ is the central bank's holdings of foreign assets (official foreign exchange reserves) and $B_C$ is its holdings of domestic bonds, both of which it acquires by issuing domestic currency $M$.

Notice that if we add together the net financial wealth of all domestic residents, including the private sector, the government, and the central bank, we have:

$$
\begin{aligned}
W_P + W_G + W_C &= \left(M + B_P + SF_P^*\right) - B + \left(SF_C^* + B_C - M\right) \\
&= S\left(F_C^* + F_P^*\right) + \left(B_P + B_C - B\right)
\end{aligned}
$$

which can be written as:[6]

$$W_P + W_G + W_C = S\left(F_C^* + F_P^*\right) - B_F$$

where $B_F$ is the amount of domestically issued bonds held by foreigners. That is, the net financial wealth of all the residents of a country added together – and thus the country's total net financial wealth – is equal to the total financial claims of domestic residents on the rest of the world (given by $S\left(F_C^* + F_P^*\right)$) minus the rest of the world's financial claims on domestic residents ($B_F$). In Chapter 2, we referred to this as the country's international investment position, and denoted it as *IIP*.

---

[5]   This will be the case, for example, if any returns earned by the central bank on the financial assets that it holds are automatically transferred to the country's treasury.

[6]   This equality follows from the fact that the total supply of domestic bonds outstanding must be held by the domestic central bank, the domestic private sector, or the rest of the world, so $B_C + B_P + B_F = B$.

## Portfolio Allocations

We can now turn to **portfolio allocations**. This term refers to the decisions that each agent has to make concerning how to allocate his or her wealth among the available financial assets and/or liabilities. Notice that the government has no such choice to make, since it issues only one type of financial liability. On the other hand, since it holds two different kinds of assets and one type of liability, the central bank does have choices to make. But since the central bank is a public agency, these are not portfolio choices, made for the purpose of maximizing the value of its portfolio, but rather *policy* choices. The central bank has to decide the total *size* of its financial portfolio (which will be given by the amount of its monetary liabilities $M$ that it chooses to issue), as well as the *composition* of that portfolio between foreign and domestic bonds. As discussed in Chapter 3, the choice of $F_C^*$, the central bank's holdings of foreign exchange arising from central bank intervention in the foreign exchange market, represents **exchange rate policy**, while the choice of $M$, the total amount of the central bank's monetary liabilities outstanding, represents **monetary policy**.

The household sector, however, does face choices about how to allocate its financial wealth so as to maximize the value of its portfolio. The resulting choices can be described in the form of **asset demand functions** (equations that describe how the household sector decides how much of each asset to hold) for each of the three assets that the household sector can hold.

Consider first the demand for money. We will assume that money is held as a medium of exchange (that is, for transactions purposes) only, and not as a store of value. Under this assumption, the demand for money by the domestic household sector, which we will call $M^d$, is given by the intermediate macroeconomics expression

$$M^d = PL(\underset{-}{R}, \underset{+}{Y}, \ldots)$$

This equation states that the nominal demand for money $M^d$ increases *in proportion* to the domestic price level $P$ (because a higher average price level increases the average value of the transactions that have to be undertaken by the private sector in the same proportion). Consequently, changes in the domestic price level do not affect the *real* demand for money, which is given by $M^d/P = L$. The latter is a decreasing function of the opportunity cost of holding money, given by the interest rate on domestic bonds ($R$) and an increasing function of real GDP ($Y$), which determines the volume of transactions for which the household sector needs to hold money. The ellipsis dots represent other (unspecified) factors that may affect the demand for money. We will refer to changes in any other such factors as exogenous demand for money "shocks."[7]

The demand for money is illustrated graphically in Figure 4.1. Since it is a decreasing function of the domestic interest rate, it can be drawn as a curve, labeled $PL$, with a negative slope in $R$-$M$ space. This curve is flatter the more responsive the demand for money is to changes in the domestic interest rate, and steeper the less responsive it is. The position of the curve is determined by variables other than $R$ that may affect the demand for money.

---

[7] Shifts in the demand for money are not uncommon. They can arise, for example, as the result of institutional and technological innovations that allow individuals to shift between money and non-money assets at lower cost (e.g., online banking) or that allow them to make the same volume of transactions while holding less cash or smaller checking accounts (e.g., credit cards and ATM cards linked to savings accounts).

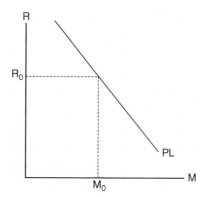

**Figure 4.1**    The demand for money

For example, because changes in the domestic price level change the nominal demand for money in the same proportion, changes in $P$ would shift the curve *horizontally* in the same proportion as the change in $P$ (an $x\%$ increase in $P$ would shift the curve rightward by $x\%$, while an $x\%$ decrease in $P$ would shift it leftward by $x\%$). Similarly, increases (decreases) in real GDP ($Y$) would shift the curve to the right (left) by an amount that depends on the magnitude of the change in $Y$ as well as on how sensitive the demand for money is to changes in $Y$. The position of the curve is also affected by money demand shocks. Positive shocks, representing increases in money demand, shift the curve to the right, while negative ones shift it to the left.

Once the household sector has decided how much money to hold, it next has to decide how to allocate the rest of its nonmonetary wealth (given by $W_P - PL = B_P + SF_P^*$) between domestic and foreign bonds. In Chapter 3, we saw that this decision depends on how closely substitutable these two types of bonds are for each other (which is our measure of the strength of financial links between the domestic economy and the rest of the world). In the most general case, in which domestic and foreign bonds are imperfect substitutes, we assumed that the ratio of domestic to foreign bonds in private portfolios would depend on the rates of return on the two types of bonds, expressed in the same currency, that is:

$$B_P = B[\underset{+}{R}, \ (1 + \underset{-}{R^*})S_{+1}^e/S - 1, \ \ldots]SF_P^*$$

The ellipsis dots represent unobservable factors that may affect preferences between domestic and foreign bonds, such as changing perceptions of the respect for bondholders' property rights in the political jurisdictions in which the bonds are issued.

It will be more convenient, however, to express the demands for $B_P$ and $F_P^*$ not in terms of each other, as in the equation above, but as functions of the factors that ultimately determine how much of each asset the private sector wants to hold – that is, the relative rates of return and the amount of private nonmonetary wealth $W_P - PL$ to be allocated between the two assets.

To transform the equation above into this form and derive the separate demands for domestic and foreign bonds, first divide both sides by the function $B[\ ]$ to solve the equation for the demand for foreign bonds $SF_P^*$. This yields $SF_P^* = (1/B[\ ])B_P$. Substituting this into the definition of nonmonetary wealth $W_P - PL = B_P + SF_P^*$, we have:

$$W_P - PL = B_P + (1/B[\ ])B_P = \{(1 + B[\ ])/B[\ ]\}B_P$$

Dividing both sides of this equation by $(1 + B[\ ])/B[\ ]$ produces:

$$B_P = \frac{B[\ ]}{1 + B[\ ]}(W_P - PL)$$

Notice that since the function $B[\ ]$ depends only on rates of return, this equation expresses the demand for domestic bonds as a function of the rates of return on the two types of bonds as well as the total amount of nonmonetary wealth that the domestic household sector has available to be allocated between domestic and foreign bonds, which is what we want. To simplify the notation, we can write the demand for domestic bonds as follows:

$$B_P = H[\underset{+}{R}, (1 + \underset{-}{R^*})S^e_{+1}/S - 1](W_P - PL(R, Y))$$

where $H[\ ] = B[\ ]/(1 + B[\ ])$.[8] It is easy to see that it must be possible to express the domestic private sector's demand for foreign bonds in a similar way. We will write it as:

$$SF^*_P = F[\underset{-}{R}, (1 + R^*)S^e_{+1}/S - 1](W_P - PL(R, Y))$$

where $F[\ ] = 1/(1 + B[\ ])$.[9]

To summarize our description of private asset demands, the household sector first decides how much of its wealth to hold as money (the first equation above), and then allocates the remainder (its nonmonetary wealth, $W_P - PL$) between domestic and foreign bonds depending on the rates of return $R$ and $(1 + R^*) S^e_{+1}/S - 1$. Notice that the allocation of nonmonetary wealth between domestic and foreign assets respects the principles that we discussed in Chapter 3 – when domestic and foreign assets are different and people care about the difference, the relative attractiveness of domestic and foreign assets depends on their relative rates of return, or on interest rate differentials.[10]

The demand for domestic bonds by the rest of the world is determined in the same way as are domestic asset demands. It is thus given by:

$$B_F/S = H^*[R, (1 + R^*)S^e_{+1}/S - 1](W^*_F - P^*L^*(R^*, Y^*))$$

or:

$$B_F = H^*[\underset{+}{R}, (1 + \underset{-}{R^*})S^e_{+1}/S - 1]S(W^*_F - P^*L^*(\underset{-}{R^*}, \underset{+}{Y^*}))$$

---

[8]  The properties of the function $H[\ ]$ follow from those of $B[\ ]$ and the fact that $H[\ ] = B[\ ]/1 + B[\ ]$. In particular, you can easily verify that $H$ will be increasing in the domestic interest rate and decreasing in the rate of return on the foreign asset, as indicated above.

[9]  Since the portion of each person's nonmonetary wealth not devoted to domestic bonds must be devoted to foreign bonds, it must be the case that $F = 1 - H$. From the definitions of the functions $H$ and $F$ you can readily verify that this is so.

[10]  Notice that the function $B[\ ]$ from the previous chapter can be recovered from the two asset demand functions above by taking the ratio of the demand for $B_P$ to that for $SF^*_P$.

where $B_F$ is foreigners' demand for domestic bonds, $H^*[\ ]$ is the function describing the share of domestic bonds in foreigners' nonmonetary wealth, $W_F^*$ is foreigners' financial wealth, $L^*[\ ]$ is the foreign demand for money function, and $Y^*$ is foreign real GDP.

## Asset Market Equilibrium

In asset-market equilibrium, the supply of each asset must be equal to the demand for that asset. In the case of domestic money, since it is only held by domestic residents, this means that $M = M^d$, which we can write as:

$$M = PL(R, Y) \tag{4.2}$$

The domestic bond market, in turn, will be in equilibrium when the stock of bonds that the government has issued is willingly held by the central bank, domestic residents, and foreign residents – in other words, when:

$$B = B_C + B_P + B_F$$

Using the asset demand functions that we derived before, we can write this as:

$$
\begin{aligned}
B - B_C = & H\big[R, (1 + R^*)S_{+1}^e/S - 1\big](W_P - PL(R, Y)) \\
& + H^*\big[R, (1 + R^*)S_{+1}^e/S - 1\big]S\big(W_F^* - P^*L^*(R^*, Y^*)\big)
\end{aligned}
\tag{4.3a}
$$

Finally, with respect to foreign bonds, we will assume that the supply of foreign bonds to the domestic economy by the rest of the world is perfectly elastic at the foreign interest rate $R^*$, that is, domestic residents can acquire as many of these bonds as they like at the exogenously determined foreign interest rate, essentially because the domestic economy is small in the market for such bonds. In that case, there is no independent supply of foreign bonds: the supply of foreign bonds is determined by the domestic private sector's demand for such bonds. The stock of foreign bonds held by the domestic household sector is given by:

$$SF_P^* = F\big[R, (1 + R^*)S_{+1}^e/S - 1\big](W_P - PL(R, Y))$$

Rather than an equilibrium condition, this equation simply describes one component of the total world demand for foreign bonds.[11]

It is useful to consider equation (4.3a) a little more carefully. It can be plotted as shown in Figure 4.2. The left-hand side of the equation is the supply of bonds to the domestic and foreign private sectors, and the right-hand side is the demand for bonds, which is labeled $B_P + B_F$ in the figure. The former is a vertical straight line, because according to our assumptions, neither the total amount of domestic bonds outstanding at any moment of time nor the amount that the central bank chooses to hold depends on the domestic interest rate. The latter is upward sloping, suggesting that the demand for domestic bonds increases when the return on domestic bonds rises. This arises from two separate effects:

---

[11]    This equation remains unnumbered because it is not an independent equilibrium condition.

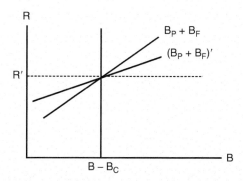

**Figure 4.2** Domestic bond market equilibrium under imperfect substitutability

1 As $R$ rises, domestic residents reduce their demand for money. Thus $PL$ falls and the nonmonetary wealth that they have available to allocate to the holding of domestic and foreign bonds increases. Since a fraction $H$ of this increase in the nonmonetary component of wealth is devoted to holding domestic bonds, the demand for domestic bonds rises.
2 As $R$ rises, both domestic and foreign residents switch away from foreign into domestic bonds.

In equilibrium, the intersection of demand and supply determines the domestic interest rate, which is arbitrarily drawn in the figure as equal to the foreign uncovered interest parity (UIP) interest rate, $R' = (1 + R^*) S_{+1}^e / S - 1$.

Notice what happens in Figure 4.2 as domestic and foreign bonds become closer substitutes with each other – i.e., when the domestic economy becomes more integrated financially with the rest of the world. When the two types of bonds are very similar, the effect of a given change in $R$ on the demand for domestic bonds becomes stronger, because people are more willing to replace foreign bonds with domestic bonds. This makes the demand curve for domestic bonds flatter, causing it to rotate clockwise to a position such as $(B_P + B_F)'$. You can see what must happen in the limit, when the two types of bonds become perfect substitutes: the demand curve for domestic bonds must become perfectly flat, and the domestic interest rate must be equal to the UIP interest rate. In this case, equation (4.3a) would be replaced by:

$$R = R' = (1 + R^*) S_{+1}^e / S - 1 \qquad (4.3b)$$

Thus, asset market equilibrium yields three equations for our model: the central bank balance sheet (4.1), the money-market equilibrium condition (4.2), and the bond-market equilibrium condition, given by (4.3a) in the imperfect-substitute case and by (4.3b) in the perfect-substitute case.

## 4.3 Equilibrium in the Market for Domestic Goods

Having described equilibrium in financial markets, we can now turn to the market for domestically produced goods and services (recall that we are referring to these as just goods). We will describe separately the determination of aggregate demand for and supply of domestic goods, and will complete our framework by incorporating into it definitions of the real exchange rate as well as of the real interest rate.

From the open-economy national income and product accounts (NIPA) identity that we discussed in Chapter 2, we have:

$$Y = GDP = C + I + G + X - IM$$

There are two points worth noting about this identity. The first concerns the units in which it is measured. In Chapter 2 the variables in this equation were measured in domestic currency (dollars) per unit of time. But suppose that we want to measure the identity above in units of the domestic good, instead of domestic currency. How would we do this? To convert units from dollars into units of goods, we have to divide each variable by the domestic-currency price of the domestic good. This permits us to write the equation in *real* terms – that is, in units of the domestic good per period of time.

If we do this, the variable *IM* denotes spending on imports measured in units of the domestic good. But it is often more convenient to measure such spending in units of the good being bought, that is, foreign goods. To do so, we can express total spending on imports measured in units of the domestic good as:

$$IM = QZ^*$$

where $Z^*$ denotes spending on imports in units of the foreign good and $Q$ denotes the real exchange rate (relative price of the foreign good in terms of the domestic good), as in Chapter 3. In other words, total spending on imports in units of the domestic good is the total amount of foreign goods bought times the relative price of foreign goods in terms of the domestic good (the real exchange rate). Using this expression, our identity becomes:

$$Y = C + I + G + X - QZ^*$$

The second issue that we have to take up is what it means for this to be an *identity* in the first place. As indicated in Chapter 2, what makes this equation an identity is that in effect it defines aggregate domestic investment, *I*, as:

$$I = Y - C - G - X + QZ^*$$

That is, whatever is not bought becomes investment. This is because total investment includes the accumulation of inventories by firms. Thus, unsold goods become investment in the form of unintended inventory accumulation (or depletion, when sales actually *exceed* production).

To make the identity into an equation that describes the aggregate demand for domestic goods, which we will denote *AD*, we need to restrict the definition of *I* to include *desired* investment only, which we denote *I'*:

$$AD = C + I' + G + X - QZ^*$$

Setting aggregate demand equal to real GDP, we have:

$$Y = AD$$
$$= C + I' + G + X - QZ^*$$

In this form, what was simply an identity becomes the **domestic goods market equilibrium condition**. That is, the market for domestically produced goods will be in equilibrium when the supply of domestic goods, given by $Y$, is equal to the total desired demand for domestic goods by all agents in the model, given by $AD$. The demand for domestic goods by domestic agents is given by $C + I' + G - QZ^*$, while that by foreign agents is simply $X$.

## Determinants of Absorption

In the next step, we need to describe what determines the demand for domestic goods by the various agents in the economy. To begin with, we will use standard intermediate-macro-economics behavior to explain what determines the amount of the domestic good that domestic residents wish to buy. Beginning with domestic households and firms, we will describe real private domestic absorption, $A$, as:

$$A = C + I' = A(\underset{+}{Y - T}, \underset{-}{r}, \dots)$$

where $T$ represents the real tax revenues collected by the government, and $r$ is the **real interest rate**, defined as the rate of return, measured in terms of goods, obtainable by saving one good today. Thus, private absorption is assumed to increase when household disposable income increases and to fall when the domestic real interest rate rises. We will assume, again in standard intermediate-macroeconomics fashion, that the marginal propensity to absorb (the change in absorption associated with a one-unit change in income) is less than one.[12] The ellipsis dots represent other determinants of absorption, which we will refer to as exogenous shocks to domestic spending. We will explore the microeconomic underpinnings of this relationship in Chapter 19, and will see there that changing expectations of future income may be an important source of such shocks. For now, however, we will subsume such expectation effects on current spending into the unspecified ''shocks'' that may affect current private absorption.

Figure 4.3 plots absorption as a function of income. As we have assumed that absorption increases with disposable income, the curve has a positive slope. The slope of the absorption function reflects the marginal propensity to absorb. Since we have assumed that this is less than one, the absorption function has a slope that is flatter than a 45-degree line through the origin. The vertical height of the function depends on the level of taxation, the real interest rate, and on shocks to absorption. Increases in taxes and in the real interest rate shift the absorption function down (since these shocks would reduce the level of absorption at any income level), while tax cuts and reductions in the real interest rate shift it up.

---

[12] At subsequent points in the text – for example, when we want to distinguish between consumption and investment spending and when we want to focus on intertemporal issues in Chapter 19 – we will need to modify our description of what determines private spending.

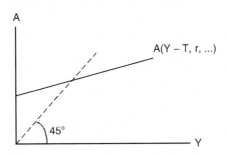

**Figure 4.3**    Absorption and income

Similarly, positive absorption shocks displace the curve upward, while negative ones displace it downward.

## The Composition of Absorption

Now that we have explained the factors that determine how much domestic private residents want to spend in total – that is, the *level* of domestic absorption – we have to ask how they allocate their spending between domestic and foreign goods – that is, what determines the *composition* of absorption. We have already seen in Chapter 3 that this should depend on the relative price of foreign goods in terms of domestic goods, that is, on the real exchange rate, $Q$. The simplest way to capture this dependence is to assume that the fraction $\varphi$ of its total spending that the private sector devotes to domestic goods is a function of the real exchange rate. Thus, we can write the share of spending devoted to domestic goods as:

$$\varphi = \varphi(\underset{+}{Q}, \dots),$$

where $0 < \varphi < 1$. The positive sign under the function $\varphi(\ )$ indicates that the share of private spending devoted to domestic goods is larger the cheaper domestic goods are relative to foreign goods, that is, the more depreciated the real exchange rate. Once again, the ellipsis dots serve to remind us that other factors may come into play that we are not including in our model. We will refer to these as exogenous shocks to the composition of absorption.

It is worth pausing to consider the likely effects of increasing international integration in goods markets on the fraction $\varphi$. In general we would expect that:

1    The more open the economy, the larger the share of domestic spending that would tend to be devoted to imports (that is, the *smaller* $\varphi$ should be).
2    As discussed in Section 4.1, the more open the economy, the higher the degree of substitutability between domestic and foreign goods, so increased openness should increase the sensitivity of $\varphi$ to changes in $Q$.

We will come back to these observations in the next chapter.

Since the domestic private sector's total spending is given by $A(Y - T, r)$ and a share $\varphi(Q)$ of this spending is devoted to domestic goods, its demand for domestic goods must be given by $\varphi(Q)\,A(Y{-}T,\,r)$, and its demand for foreign goods (imports) *measured in units of the domestic good* $(QZ^*)$ must therefore be:

$$QZ^* = (1 - \varphi(Q))A(Y - T, r)$$

## Exports

What about exports? To keep things simple, we will assume that exports depend positively on the real exchange rate (that is, foreigners demand more of the home country's goods when those goods are cheaper) and that they also depend on a variety of other exogenous factors. These factors, which we will lump together into a catch-all variable denoted by the Greek symbol $\theta$, include things like foreign incomes, tastes, and foreign government policies that affect how much foreigners want to import. Since all of these things are exogenous to our model and affect the domestic economy only through their effect on its exports, we do not gain much from distinguishing among them. Thus we will write exports as:

$$X = X(\underset{+}{Q^*}, \underset{+}{\theta})$$

where it is assumed, as a convention, that an increase in $\theta$ increases exports. Again, we would expect that the more open the economy the larger the share of exports should be in GDP (this would correspond to larger values of $\theta$), and the more sensitive $X$ should be to changes in the values of both $Q$ and $\theta$.

## Aggregate Demand

We are now in a position to see what determines the aggregate demand for domestic goods. Recall that we previously expressed aggregate demand as:

$$AD = C + I' + G + X - QZ^*$$

Using the definition of private absorption, this becomes:

$$AD = A + G + X - QZ^*$$

But since $QZ^* = (1 - \varphi)\,A$, we can simplify this to $Y = \varphi A + G + X$. Finally, writing this out with all of its determinants, our expression for aggregate demand for domestic goods is:

$$AD = \underset{+}{\varphi(Q)}A(\underset{+}{Y - T}, \underset{-}{r}) + G + \underset{++}{X(Q, \theta)}$$

which can be summarized as:

$$AD = AD(\underset{+}{Y - T}, \underset{-}{r}, \underset{+}{G}, \underset{+}{Q}, \underset{+}{\theta})$$

Notice that:

1   Since an increase in domestic income increases domestic absorption, it would tend to increase aggregate demand for domestic goods. But for every unit of increase in income the increase in aggregate demand would be less than one unit, both because the marginal propensity to absorb is less than one and because only a fraction $\varphi$ of any increase in absorption is devoted to spending on domestic goods.
2   An increase in government spending and a reduction in taxes would both tend to increase aggregate demand. These represent two types of **expansionary fiscal policy**.
3   Similarly, a reduction in the domestic real interest rate is also expansionary. This is the traditional channel of transmission for monetary policy in closed-economy macroeconomics.

In open economies we have three new influences on aggregate demand, however:

1   The level of aggregate demand depends on the real exchange rate. A depreciation in the real exchange rate (an increase in $Q$) will increase aggregate demand for domestic goods through a mechanism that is referred to as **expenditure switching**. By making domestic goods cheaper relative to foreign goods, an increase in $Q$ induces both domestic and foreign residents to switch from buying foreign to buying domestic goods, given their total levels of spending. Thus, real exchange rate depreciation is also expansionary in our model.
2   Exogenous shocks to a country's exports, captured by the variable $\theta$, will affect aggregate demand in the same way as exogenous changes in government spending do. The more open the economy's goods market is to trade with the rest of the world, the more frequent and larger such shocks are likely to be. For example, Mexico's increased trade integration with the United States after the passage of NAFTA (the North American Free Trade Agreement) in 1993 has made the Mexican economy much more sensitive to US business cycles in recent years than it used to be.
3   Exogenous changes in domestic residents' preferences between domestic and foreign goods (shocks to the function $\varphi(\ )$) will also affect aggregate demand. Such shocks would include, for example, not just simple changes in tastes, but also government policies, such as quotas on imports, intended to change the composition of spending by domestic residents.

The behavior of aggregate demand is depicted in Figure 4.4. Because an increase in income increases absorption, the aggregate demand curve AD has a positive slope. However, since the increase in aggregate demand is less than the increase in income for the reasons we saw above, this slope is less than one. Because an increase in $G$ or $\theta$ would tend to increase spending at any given level of income, each of these changes would shift the AD curve upward. Similarly, an increase in taxes or in the domestic real interest rate would decrease spending at any given level of income, thus causing the curve to shift downward. Finally a depreciation in the real exchange rate $Q$ would leave the level of domestic spending unchanged, but would switch both domestic and foreign spending toward domestic goods, thus increasing the aggregate demand for such goods and causing the AD curve to shift upward.

   Finally, to derive the conditions under which the domestic goods market is in equilibrium, we simply set aggregate demand equal to aggregate supply:

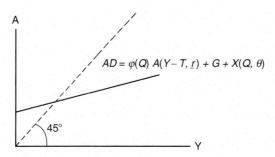

**Figure 4.4**   Aggregate demand

$$Y = \varphi(Q)A(Y - T, r) + G + X(Q, \theta) \tag{4.4}$$
$$\quad\; + \qquad\quad +\quad - \qquad\qquad\; +\;\; +$$

We will refer to this equation as the **goods market equilibrium condition**.

## Net Exports

Before leaving the goods market, it is useful to pause and consider the determination of the balance on goods and services, or net exports ($N$). Measured in units of the domestic good, the balance on goods and services is:

$$N = X - QZ^*$$

Now that we have explained the determinants of both exports and imports, we can write this as:

$$N(Q, Y - T, r, \theta) = X(Q, \theta) - (1 - \varphi(Q))A(Y - T, r)$$
$$\quad + \quad - \quad +\; + $$

Note in particular that a real exchange rate depreciation will ''improve'' the balance on goods and services (that is, cause it to become more positive), both by increasing exports as well as by reducing imports. This effect of the real exchange rate on net exports is referred to as **expenditure switching**. Empirical Study 4.2 and 4.3 at the end of this chapter describe two particularly interesting applications of our explanation of the determination of net exports, concerning respectively the effects of the real appreciation in the US dollar during the first half of the 1980s on the fate of the US manufacturing sector and explanations of the deterioration of net exports in the United States during the early 1980s and late 1990s.

For future reference, notice that using this definition of net exports, the goods market equilibrium condition (4.4) can be written as:

$$\begin{aligned} Y &= \varphi A + G + X \\ &= \varphi A + G + N + (1 - \varphi)A \\ &= A + G + N \end{aligned} \tag{4.4$'$}$$

We can now proceed with the construction of the rest of our model by including in it our definition of the real exchange rate, introducing a definition of the real interest rate, and describing the behavior of aggregate supply.

### The Real Exchange Rate and Real Interest Rate

To keep track of the definitions of the real exchange rate and real interest rate, we can formally incorporate these definitions into our framework. In Chapter 3 we defined the real exchange rate as:

$$Q = SP^*/P \tag{4.5}$$

However, we have not yet given a formal definition of the real interest rate.

Informally, we defined it as the rate of return in the future, measured in terms of goods, obtainable by saving the equivalent of one good today. To see how the real interest rate is linked to the other variables in our model, consider that saving one good today is equivalent to saving $P$ dollars, since $P$ is the price of the good in dollars. Investing this amount in a domestic bond yields $P(1 + R)$ future dollars, which can be used to buy goods in the future. How many goods can be purchased in the future with $P(1 + R)$ dollars? The answer depends on the future price of goods. The number of goods that can be purchased with $P(1 + R)$ dollars is just $P(1 + R)$ divided by the future price of goods. Since that price is unknown at the present time, we can denote the *expected* future price of goods $P^e_{+1}$, where the subscript indicates that the price pertains to one period in the future, and the superscript that $P^e_{+1}$ is an *expected* price. Thus, the amount of future goods that one can expect to obtain by saving one good today is just $P(1 + R)/ P^e_{+1}$. Subtracting the amount of the original good foregone (which is just one) from this quantity gives the *extra* amount of future goods that can be obtained by saving one good today, which is what an interest rate means. Thus the real interest rate r is given by:

$$r = P(1+R)\left(1/P^e_{+1}\right) - 1 \tag{4.6}$$

The definition of the real interest rate is sometimes referred to as the **Fisher equation**, after the Yale economist Irving Fisher, who first gave it prominence.

### Aggregate Supply

In developing our framework, we have not yet said anything about what determines aggregate supply in our economy. Notice, in particular, that the equality between aggregate demand and supply in the goods market equilibrium condition captured in equation (4.4) must hold no matter how aggregate supply is determined. The next step in building our framework is to consider the determination of aggregate supply.

A useful point of departure is the observation that an economy's capacity to produce goods and services depends on its endowment of productive factors such as capital and labor, as well as on the productivity of its technology. These factors of production tend to be accumulated slowly over time. As noted in Chapter 1, the level of real output that the economy produces when these factors of production are fully employed is variously referred to as its "full employment," "potential," or "natural" level of output.

Shifts in aggregate demand may affect whether the economy fully utilizes this productive capacity. Such shifts represent a change in the value of the domestic price level that is required to sustain a given level of real demand for domestic output. To sustain real output at its full-employment level in the face of a shift in aggregate demand therefore requires an adjustment in the domestic price level. Most macroeconomists believe, however, that for a variety of microeconomic reasons, the aggregate price level tends to be "sticky" in the short run – that is, it adjusts slowly over time in response to aggregate demand shocks. Consequently, when aggregate demand for domestic goods is subjected to a shock, the average price of domestic goods does not immediately change. Instead, what changes immediately is the level of production. Since labor tends to be the only variable factor of production in the short run, these changes in the level of production are accompanied by changes in the level of employment. During the time it takes for the price level to adjust, therefore, both production and employment may deviate from their full-employment levels. Over time, however, the price level adjusts, so that more and more of the effect of the change in aggregate demand shows up in the form of a change in the price level, and less in the form of a change in the levels of production and employment. Eventually, after a long enough time period has passed, the full response of the economy to the change in aggregate demand takes the form of a change in the average price level, and the level of production returns to its "natural", or full-employment, level.

The focus of this book is on short-run macroeconomics, and we will therefore take the economy's level of productive capacity as given. To capture the price level dynamics just described in the simplest possible way, it is useful to consider just two extreme cases in our model: the **short run**, defined as a period that is so short that the price level does not have time to adjust at all when aggregate demand shifts, so that all adjustment takes the form of a change in production, and the **medium run**, a period that is long enough for all price level adjustments to be complete and for production to have returned to its natural level, but short enough that the capacity level of output remains unchanged.

The short-run stickiness of the price level can be captured in our framework by adding to it the new equation:

$$P = \bar{P} \tag{4.7a}$$

Assuming, for simplicity, that the short run extends into the next period as well, we also have:

$$P^e_{+1} = \bar{P} \tag{4.8a}$$

Since in the medium run the price level adjusts so as to bring the economy back to its natural level of output, in the medium run equation (4.7a) is replaced by:

$$Y = \bar{Y} \tag{4.7b}$$

And since all price adjustments are completed in the medium run, we also have:

$$P^e_{+1} = P \tag{4.8b}$$

This completes the description of our analytical framework. Almost all of the analytical work that we will do in the rest of the book will be based on this framework. While it may seem complicated, remember that we will be working only with special cases of this general framework. These special cases will be much simpler, but, as you will see, they will nevertheless yield a large number of powerful analytical insights. In fact, the very flexibility of this framework is one of its attractive features, and has made it the workhorse tool for policy analysis in open-economy macroeconomics. It is worth noting, however, that this framework does have some limitations, and there is a set of issues – essentially involving the optimal allocation of spending over time – that will require us to extend it by modifying the simple assumptions that we have made in this chapter about the behavior of private absorption. We will extend the framework to explore these issues in Chapter 19.

## 4.4    Equations and Unknowns: Imposing Additional Structure

Our general framework is summarized in Boxes 4.1 and 4.2. Box 4.1 lists and defines the variables that we introduced in the last section. As you can see from the box, there are 20 such variables ($B$, $W_P$, $S$, $F_C^*$, $B_C$, $M$, $R$, $Y$, $P$, $R^*$, $S_{+1}^e$, $P^*$, $\theta$, $W_F^*$, $Y^*$, $r$, $G$, $T$, $P_{+1}^e$ and $Q$). But as shown in Box 4.2, there are only 8 equations to restrict the values that these variables can take on. In general, to solve an analytical model we need as many independent equations as we have variables to solve for (unknowns). Intuitively, this is because each equation pins down a unique value of a single variable, conditional on the values of all the others. Thus, we need exactly as many equations as we have variables whose values we want to pin down.

---

### Box 4.1    Definition of Model Variables

| | |
|---|---|
| $B$ | Stock of domestic government bonds outstanding (domestic bonds). |
| $W_P$ | Total financial wealth of the domestic private sector. |
| $S$ | The nominal exchange rate (units of domestic currency per unit of the foreign currency). |
| $F_C^*$ | Stock of foreign bonds held by the domestic central bank (foreign exchange reserves), measured in units of the foreign currency. |
| $B_C$ | Stock of domestic government bonds held by the domestic central bank. |
| $M$ | Stock of currency issued by the domestic central bank (money supply). |
| $R$ | Interest rate on domestic bonds. |
| $Y$ | Domestic real GDP. |
| $P$ | Domestic price level. |
| $R^*$ | Interest rate on foreign bonds. |
| $S_{+1}^e$ | Expected future exchange rate. |
| $P^*$ | Foreign price level. |
| $\theta$ | "Shift" variable in the demand for domestic exports. |
| $W_F^*$ | Foreign financial wealth (measured in foreign currency). |
| $Y^*$ | Foreign real GDP (measured in units of the foreign good). |
| $R$ | Real interest rate. |
| $G$ | Domestic government demand for domestic goods. |
| $T$ | Domestic tax revenue. |
| $P_{+1}^e$ | Expected future value of domestic price level. |
| $Q$ | Real exchange rate (units of domestic good per unit of the foreign good). |

## Box 4.2    Equations

**Central bank balance sheet**

$$SF_C^* + B_C = M \tag{4.1}$$

**Money market equilibrium**

$$M = PL(R, Y) \tag{4.2}$$

**Domestic bond market equilibrium**

$$\begin{aligned}
B - B_C = &H\big[R,\, (1+R^*)S_{+1}^e/S - 1\big](W_P - PL(R, Y)) \\
&+ H^*\big[R,(1+R^*)S_{+1}^e/S - 1\big]S\big(W_F^* - P^*L^*(R^*, Y^*)\big)
\end{aligned} \tag{4.3a}$$

or:

$$R = R' = (1+R^*)S_{+1}^e/S - 1 \tag{4.3b}$$

**Domestic goods market equilibrium**

$$Y = \varphi(Q)A(Y - T, r) + G + X(Q, \theta) \tag{4.4}$$

**Definition of the real exchange rate**

$$Q = SP^*/P \tag{4.5}$$

**Definition of the real interest rate**

$$r = P(1 + R)\big(1/P_{+1}^e\big) - 1 \tag{4.6}$$

**Short-run aggregate supply**

$$P = \bar{P} \tag{4.7a}$$
$$P_{+1}^e = \bar{P} \tag{4.8a}$$

**Long-run aggregate supply**

$$Y = \bar{Y} \tag{4.7b}$$
$$P_{+1}^e = P \tag{4.8b}$$

This means that the framework that we have described so far is not a coherent model of any economy. To extract a specific model economy from this framework we need to impose more structure on it – that is, we need additional restrictions on the values that the variables can take, so we can actually succeed in pinning them down. The special cases that we will consider in the rest of the book are in each case obtained by imposing alternative sets of restrictions, adapted to the characteristics of specific economies.

Before moving on to these special cases, however, we need to discuss three particular sets of restrictions that will play special roles in our analysis. The first two of these – that the country under analysis is "small" in an economic sense, and that some variables are set exogenously by the government – are worth emphasizing now because we will be imposing them consistently throughout most of the book (except for Chapter 17, where we will examine the "large" country case). The third set of restrictions – those that we will use to identify the foreign exchange regime – is also worth discussing now because it will provide the organizing principle for much of the rest of the book.

## The Small-Country Assumption

For most of this text, we will assume that the country that we are analyzing is a "small" one. This word is in quotation marks because it refers to smallness not in terms of the country's geographic size or population, but rather in the economic sense that the country's economy is so small relative to the world economy that it can have no perceptible effect on the world economic environment. This means that, from the perspective of the domestic economy, the variables $\theta$, $P^*$, $Y^*$, and $R^*$, which capture different aspects of the international economic environment facing the country, can be taken as exogenous. This is not a good assumption for the United States or the European Union, each of which accounts for about a fifth of the world economy and can thus perceptibly affect economic variables in the rest of the world, but it is reasonable for just about every other country in the world. As mentioned above, we will come back to the large-country case in Chapter 17. For now, we note that the effect of making the small-country assumption is to take away 4 unknowns, leaving us with 16 variables to determine with our 8 equations.

## Predetermined Variables

Our focus in this book is on short-run macroeconomic stabilization issues. Consequently, the specific models that we will be using will all be short-run macroeconomic models. This means that we will be taking as given over the time frame of the analysis any variables that represent stocks of assets or liabilities that are accumulated as the result of past saving or dissaving decisions. Because such variables are inherited from the past, their current values do not have to be explained by the short-run models that we will be using.[13] Such variables are referred to as **predetermined**.

As we shall see, this applies to $W_P$ (domestic private wealth), $W_F^*$ (foreign private wealth) and $B$ (government debt). With respect to domestic private wealth, the domestic private

---

[13]    As mentioned before, a country's capital stock is an example of a predetermined variable. It changes slowly over time as the result of net investment (new capital constructed minus old capital lost to wear and tear), but because this change is gradual, in short-run macroeconomics we typically take the capital stock as given, or predetermined.

sector accumulates financial wealth over time by saving (a flow), and its current financial wealth $W_P$ (a stock) represents the accumulated value of all its past saving. But because each period's saving represents only a small part of the private sector's total accumulated wealth, the *current* period's saving has a negligible effect on total private financial wealth. Consequently, $W_P$ can effectively be taken as fixed at any given moment of time (in the absence of exchange rate changes). A similar argument establishes that foreign private wealth, $W_F^*$, must be a predetermined variable too. Similarly, since it represents the cumulative value of all past government fiscal deficits and surpluses, and thus can be changed only slowly as the government runs new deficits and surpluses, domestic government debt $B$ is also a predetermined variable. Thus we can take $W_P$, $W_F^*$, and $B$ as given – that is, as the equivalent of exogenous variables for the purpose of solving the model. That leaves us with 13 endogenous variables and 8 equations.

## Identification of Policy Variables

Notice that we have not yet said anything about policy variables: those variables that are controlled directly by the government. As in intermediate macroeconomics, we will assume that $G$ and $T$ are policy variables, thus making them exogenous as well. These variables will be our measures of fiscal policy. These assumptions about $G$ and $T$ leave us with 11 endogenous variables and 8 equations.

What about monetary policy? This will be an important question throughout this book. In principle, the central bank can control $B_C$ (through open market operations), but it may not be able to choose the value of $B_C$ exogenously if it has committed itself to altering $B_C$ as necessary to achieve some other goal. This is a familiar observation from closed-economy macroeconomics, of course, where $B_C$ is not an exogenous policy variable if the central bank conducts monetary policy by targeting the value of a short-term interest rate.

If $B_C$ can be chosen exogenously and the central bank chooses to do so, we will treat it as a policy variable. That will leave us with 10 endogenous variables to solve for with our 8 equations. If it cannot be chosen exogenously or the central bank chooses not to do so, then we will have to add an equation to the model that describes how $B_C$ is determined. In that case, we will still have 11 endogenous variables, but will then have 9 equations to work with. In either case, we will be two equations short.

## Foreign Exchange Regime

The final set of restrictions will depend on the foreign exchange regime, so we will have to discuss these as we come across them in subsequent chapters. Just to prepare you, though, the forms those restrictions will take depend on whether the central bank maintains a fixed exchange rate or a floating exchange rate.

*Fixed Exchange Rate*    As we saw in Chapter 3, under fixed exchange rates, the market exchange rate is equal to the rate announced by the central bank. Thus, under fixed exchange rates, we need to add the equations:

$$S = \bar{S} \tag{4.9}$$

$$S_{+1}^e = \bar{S} \tag{4.10}$$

Notice that under this regime, the stock of foreign exchange reserves, $F_C^*$, remains an endogenous variable. This leaves us with 10 equations and 10 unknowns, a model that we can actually solve.

*Floating Exchange Rate*    In the case of floating exchange rates, $S$ and $S_{+1}^e$ remain endogenous variables, and the stock of foreign exchange reserves, $F_C^*$, becomes exogenous. This leaves us with 8 equations and 9 unknowns. You will see how we deal with this problem when we turn to the analysis of floating exchange rates. In brief, we will distinguish between *transitory* and *permanent* shocks to the economy. The former will affect $S$, but will leave $S_{+1}^e$ unchanged. When shocks are transitory, then, $S_{+1}^e$ will essentially become a constant, leaving us with 8 equations and 8 unknowns. When shocks are permanent, on the other hand, any effects on $S$ will tend to persist into the indefinite future, so we can impose:

$$S = S_{+1}^e$$

The addition of this equation will leave us with 9 equations and 9 unknowns.

We are now ready to apply our framework.

---

## Empirical Study 4.1    Measuring Goods Market Integration

Measuring the degree of integration between the goods markets in different countries is not an easy task. We already saw, when discussing purchasing-power parity (PPP) in the last chapter, that the representative production bundles of different countries may fail to sell for the same common-currency price because the composition of the bundles may be different, and because even when they are not different, the law of one price (LOOP) may fail to hold between identical goods in different countries, as the result of natural or policy-induced barriers to goods-market arbitrage. The former include imperfect information, transportation costs, and monopoly power, while the latter include a variety of trade barriers imposed by governments. As mentioned in the text, we will be assuming that PPP fails to hold because of imperfect substitutability, rather than because of trade barriers preventing effective goods-market arbitrage. But how can we assess how important natural and policy-induced barriers to trade may be in the real world?

One way to do so is examining the extent to which changes in a country's nominal exchange rates are passed through to the domestic-currency prices of its imports. If trade barriers are unimportant, two identical goods should sell for the same common-currency price in the home and foreign country, so if a change in the exchange rate leaves the price of an imported good unchanged, an $x$ percent depreciation in the home country's exchange rate should cause its import prices to rise by $x$ percent, and an $x$ percent appreciation should cause them to fall by $x$ percent.

A particularly revealing time to conduct such a test would be when exchange rate movements are large. The strong appreciation of the US dollar in the early 1980s provides a good example. Fieleke (1985) conducted such an exercise, computing "import price relatives" that essentially compared the change from 1980 to 1984 in the dollar price of US imports of manufactured goods from Canada, Germany and Japan to the foreign-currency producer price index for manufactures in those countries. A strict application of the law of one price would suggest that the former should have been smaller than the latter by the amount of US dollar appreciation against each of the relevant currencies. Fieleke found that the relative prices of most imported items from all three countries did decline significantly over the period as predicted, resulting in a sharp decline in the dollar prices in the average prices of imported manufactured goods from those countries relative to the US domestic producer price index for manufactures, even though there was a substantial amount of variation in the extent to which dollar appreciation was passed through to the prices of individual manufactured imports. The upshot is that the arbitrage mechanism described in the text was a useful first approximation for imports of manufactures into the United States during this period.

More formal tests of the effects of exchange rate changes on import prices have been conducted using econometric estimations of the factors determining "real" import prices (i.e., domestic-currency import prices deflated by a domestic price index). Such specifications typically allow real import prices to depend on the "real" prices of competing goods and on real domestic expenditure on imports and competing goods together, and they allow for the real import price to adjust gradually over time. An example is Olivei (2002). Olivei estimates an equation of the form:

$$p_t^{\text{imp}} = b_0 + b_1(w_t^* + s_t) + b_2 p_t^C + b_3 c_t + u_t$$

where $p_t^{\text{imp}}$ is the logarithm of an import price index, $w_t^*$ is the log of an index of foreign producers' costs measured in foreign currency, $s_t$ is the log of the nominal exchange rate, $p_t^C$ is the log of an index of the prices of goods that compete with imports in consumer demand in the domestic economy, $c_t$ is the log of aggregate consumer expenditure on imports and competing goods, and $u_t$ is a random term. The key parameter here is $b_1$, which measures the extent to which exchange rate changes are passed on to the domestic-currency prices of imports. Consistent with the case study described above, Olivei found, as have several other such studies, that exchange rate pass-through is significant but, at least in the case of manufactured imports into the United States, is not complete, as would be suggested by the law of one price. The exercise of monopoly power is a leading interpretation: when the importing country's currency appreciates, for example, the foreign producer's costs measured in units of the importing country's currency fall, but the foreign producer may respond partly by lowering prices in the importing country and partly by increasing markups.

Pass-through is much more complete in the case of commodities such as oil, metals, and agricultural products, which are more homogeneous than manufactures and generally trade in more competitive markets.

## Empirical Study 4.2    Real Exchange Rates and Deindustrialization in the United States

In the framework that we are developing in this chapter, changes in the real exchange rate are assumed to be associated with **expenditure-switching** – a change in the composition of demand between domestic and foreign goods – both in the domestic economy as well as in the country's trading partners. Thus, a real exchange rate appreciation would be expected to be associated with a decline in demand for domestic goods and increase in demand for foreign goods. This link between the real exchange rate and the composition of demand gave rise to the view in the United States during the mid-1980s that the strong appreciation of the dollar during the first half of the decade (see Figure 3.2) had been responsible for a loss in price competitiveness in US manufacturing, and a consequent contraction of the US manufacturing that would culminate in the "deindustrialization" of the United States.

Manufacturing activity indeed tends to be more exposed to foreign competition than activities such as services, for which trade barriers such as transportation costs are much more important (It would be very expensive to import an Indian barber to provide a haircut in Omaha!), but some observers have nonetheless questioned whether the strong dollar appreciation during the first half of the 1980s indeed contributed to poor manufacturing performance in the United States, pointing out among other things that during this period US manufacturing output increased more rapidly than that of the country's trading partners(Tatom 1988).

However, this outcome is affected by the more rapid growth of the American economy than that of US trading partners during that time. Since markets for manufactured goods are not perfectly integrated, this would result in more rapid increase in demand for US manufactured output, even if US manufactures were becoming less competitive. The fact that the US manufacturing trade balance (exports minus imports) as a ratio of total shipments from manufacturing indeed deteriorated significantly from 1979 to 1985 is indeed suggestive of a strong role for faster growth of absorption in the United States. Krugman and Hatsopoulos (1987) construct a market share index for US manufacturing from 1970 to 1985 based on the ratio of US sales in each market to what those sales would have been had the US share of each market been the same as it was in 1980, thereby correcting for the effects of differential growth rates in various markets. They find that, after having been relatively stable from 1970 to 1980, the index declined by about 8 percent from 1980 to 1985. Their conclusion was that US dollar appreciation was indeed associated with declining US competitiveness in manufacturing, as the expenditure-switching perspective would predict.

Other economists have provided microeconomic evidence of the effects of dollar appreciation on US manufacturing performance during this period. For example, Little (1989) found that, within the US manufacturing sector, labor tended to shift out of mature industries and into high-tech activities in which the US has a comparative advantage during the first half of the 1980s, as well as out of the production-related jobs that are most susceptible to import competition and into service-oriented manufacturing activities that were less vulnerable to foreign competition. Overall, then, the evidence is consistent with the view that the strong dollar appreciation during the early

1980s indeed induced expenditure switching from domestic to foreign manufactured goods in the United States.

## Empirical Study 4.3 Explaining the US Trade Deficit

Our net export equation specifies a set of factors that are likely to be important in determining the performance of a country's net exports. These factors include the nominal exchange rate $S$, relative prices at home and abroad $P^*/P$, domestic household disposable income $Y - T$, and the catch-all variable $\theta$ that represents a variety of potential influences on foreign demand for the exports of the domestic economy. These influences are likely to include, for example, factors that affect foreign absorption, such as real incomes in a country's trading partners.

To what extent can factors such as these explain the sharp deterioration of net exports in the United States in the early 1980s and late 1990s? This question has been addressed in a large number of studies. The early-1980s episode was examined, for example, by Bergstrand (1987). He estimated separate regressions for US exports to and imports from Canada, Japan, Germany, the United Kingdom, and France from the second quarter of 1960 to the fourth quarter of 1982, using US and foreign GDP, the US and foreign price levels, and the exchange rate between the dollar and the foreign currency to explain these trade flows. He found that the estimated coefficients on each of these variables was consistent with the theoretical assumptions we have made in this chapter, and more importantly, that the estimated equation was able to explain a very high proportion of fluctuations in US exports and imports to each of these countries over the sample period. Bergstrand then used these estimated equations to explain the behavior of US exports and imports from 1982 to 1985, conditional on the actual behavior of US and foreign GDP, the US and foreign price levels, and the exchange rate between the dollar and each of the foreign currencies during that period. Again, he found that such variables were able to explain the post-1982 behavior of US trade flows quite well. He concluded that the deterioration of US net exports after 1982 could be fully explained by the real appreciation of the US dollar and faster growth in the United States than in the country's trading partners during that time.

The deterioration of US net exports in the late 1990s was studied by Papaioannou and Yi (2001). Motivated by the analytical approach captured in our net export equation, they noted that, since the US economy grew much faster than those of Japan and Western Europe during 1996–9, a substantial part of the deterioration in US net exports could have arisen from cyclical factors. This is an important issue, because to the extent that cyclical factors were important, some part of the deterioration of US net exports would tend to be temporary, and would tend to be reverted once the US and its trading partners returned to more normal levels of capacity utilization. Their specific interest, therefore, was in determining how much of the fall in US net exports during that period could be attributed to cyclical factors. Using estimates of potential output in the US and its main trading partners, as well as of the income elasticity of demand for imports in the various countries, they estimated that cyclical factors could

*(Continued)*

---

**Empirical Study 4.3**    *(Continued)*

account for about 57 percent of the decline in US net exports in 1996–7, but by 1999 such factors could explain only about 14 percent of the decline. The remainder must have been due to factors such as high levels of absorption relative to income in the United States, as well as to the real appreciation of the US dollar during the period.

---

## 4.5   Summary

In this chapter we have put together the analytical framework that we will be using to study international macroeconomics in this book. As is standard in macroeconomic models, it consists of a set of equilibrium conditions for different markets in the economy, focusing specifically on financial markets and goods markets, as in the standard closed-economy models. The main modifications to that framework involve explaining the macroeconomic roles of trade with the rest of the world in goods and services as well as in financial assets. This requires introducing a bond market equilibrium equation (or an uncovered interest parity relationship) as a feature of financial market equilibrium, as well as distinguishing in the goods market between domestic absorption and aggregate demand for domestic goods.

An important message to take away from the analytical framework introduced in this chapter is that the behavior of an open economy in response to macroeconomic shocks will depend very much on the structure of the economy and the policy regime pursued by the central bank. The key structural features that will prove to be important are the economy's degree of "real" (goods-market) and financial integration with the rest of the world, as well as the shape of its aggregate supply curve (i.e., the degree of domestic wage-price flexibility). The key aspects of the policy regime are whether the central bank maintains a fixed or floating exchange rate regime, and how it conducts monetary policy. In subsequent chapters we will consider specific variations on these themes that are important in different types of open economies.

### Questions

1   Explain why the determination of the equilibrium exchange rate in the foreign exchange market is a macroeconomic phenomenon.
2   Consider an economy that is producing at full employment, so equation (4.7b) holds, that is perfectly integrated financially with the rest of the world, so (4.3b) holds, and that maintains a fixed exchange rate, so both (4.9) and (4.10) hold. What endogenous variables are left in this framework? What equation(s) pin down the values of this (these) endogenous variables(s)?
3   Under the conditions specified in problem (2), can the central bank treat $B_C$ as an exogenous policy variable? Explain why or why not.
4   Suppose that the economy that we are interested in modeling is *not* a small open economy, so that the macro variables that describe the external economic environment have to be treated as endogenous. What additional types of conditions do you think we

would have to add to our framework in order to be able to explain the behavior of these variables?

5   Suppose that the economy in problem (1) experiences an increase in government spending. How would you expect the response of the real exchange rate to this shock to depend on how integrated the domestic goods market is with the rest of the world?

## Further Reading and References

### On exchange rates and import prices

Fieleke, Norman S. (1985), "Dollar Appreciation and U.S. Import Prices," Federal Reserve Bank of Boston *New England Economic Review* (November/December), pp. 49–54.

Goldberg, Pineloppi K. and Michael M. Knetter (1997), "Goods Prices and Exchange Rates: What Have We Learned?" *Journal of Economic Literature* 35 (September), pp. 1243–72.

Olivei, Giovanni P. (2002), "Exchange Rates and the Prices of Manufacturing Products Imported into the United States," Federal Reserve Bank of Boston, *New England Economic Review* (First Quarter), pp. 3–18.

### On the real exchange rate and deindustrialization in the United States

Krugman, P.K. and G.N. Hatsopoulus (1987), "The Problem of US Manufacturing," *New England Economic Review* (January), pp. 18–29.

Little, Jane Sneddon (1989), "Exchange Rates and Structural Change in US Manufacturing Employment," *New England Economic Review* (March), pp. 56–70.

Tatom, John A. (1988), "The Link Between the Value of the Dollar, U.S. Trade and Manufacturing Output: Some Recent Evidence," Federal Reserve Bank of St. Louis *Review*, pp. 24–37.

### On the real exchange rate and net exports in the United States

Bergstrand, Jeffrey H. (1987), "The U.S. Trade Deficit: A Perspective from Selected Bilateral Trade Models," Federal Reserve Bank of Boston, *New England Economic Review* (May/June), pp. 19–31.

Papaioannou, Stefaan and Kei-Mu Yi (2001), "The Effects of a Booming Economy on the U.S. Trade Deficit," Federal Reserve Bank of New York, *Current Issues in Economics and Finance* (February), pp. 1–6.

## Appendix 4.1   The Marshall–Lerner Condition

The specification of the demand for imports that we have adopted in this chapter is somewhat different from that which is most commonly found in textbooks on international macroeconomics. We have defined total spending on imports, measured in units of domestic goods, as:

$$QZ^* = (1 - \varphi(Q))A$$
$$+$$

The more common specification, and the one that appeared in the original Mundell–Fleming model, is:

$$QZ^* = QZ(Q, Y)$$
$$\underset{-}{\phantom{Q}} \quad \underset{+}{\phantom{Y}}$$

That is, the demand for imports, measured in units of the *foreign* good $(Z^*)$, is taken to depend negatively on the real exchange rate $Q$ and positively on domestic income $Y$. Why the difference, and how does it matter?

The traditional specification has the undesirable property that, holding the real exchange rate and real income constant, any changes in spending by the domestic private sector (caused, say, by changes in taxation or in real interest rates), would leave imports unchanged, implying that such changes in spending would have to affect only domestic goods. This is unappealing because there is no reason to believe that changes in taxes or real interest rates should affect tastes for domestic as opposed to foreign goods, so such changes should affect spending on both types of goods. An implication of our specification is that changes in taxation and in real interest rates will have direct effects on net exports in our model that do not appear in the traditional specification.

Another implication is that the conditions for real exchange rate depreciation to increase net exports are simpler in our model than under the traditional specification. Notice that under the traditional specification a depreciation of the real exchange rate (an increase in $Q$) could actually *increase* spending on imports measured in units of the domestic goods. The reason is that, while fewer foreign goods would be bought when $Q$ rises, each foreign good purchased costs more in units of the domestic good. Because for every 1 percent increase in $Q$ the cost of each imported good *increases* by 1 percent, while the quantity of foreign goods imported *decreases* by a percentage equal to the elasticity of demand for imports, the percentage change in total spending on imports will increase by one minus the elasticity of demand for imports ($\eta_Z$). The total change in import spending, measured in units of the domestic good, will therefore be equal to $(1 - \eta_Z)QZ^*$. Since the percentage change in exports is given by the elasticity of demand for exports $\eta_X$, the total change in exports is $\eta_X X$. Thus the change in net exports $\Delta N$ must be given by:

$$\Delta N = \eta_X X - (1 - \eta_Z)QZ^*$$

If trade is initially balanced, so that $X = QZ^*$, then this expression becomes:

$$\Delta N = X(\eta_X + \eta_Z - 1)$$

and the condition for a real exchange rate depreciation to increase net exports is $\eta_X + \eta_Z - 1 > 0$. This expression is called the **Marshall–Lerner condition**, after the British economist Alfred Marshall and Swedish economist Abba Lerner who developed it.

Why don't we need to impose the Marshall–Lerner condition in our model? The answer is that by assuming that the share of spending on imports is a decreasing function of the real exchange rate, we have implicitly assumed that the elasticity of demand for imports is greater than unity. This means that the Marshall–Lerner condition is automatically satisfied.

## Appendix 4.2    The Framework in Log-Linear Form

For future reference, it will be useful to express the perfect-capital mobility version of our framework (i.e., the version that uses equation 4.3b) in log-linear form. We will be using models based on this form in Chapters 13 and 14. To do so, notice that the goods market equilibrium condition (4.4) can be written as:

$$Y = \varphi(Q)A(Y - T, r) + G + X(Q, \theta)$$
$$\phantom{Y =} {}^{+} \phantom{\varphi(Q)A(} {}^{+} \phantom{Y - T,} {}^{-} \phantom{) + G +} {}^{+} \phantom{X(Q,} {}^{+}$$
$$= D(r, Q, G, T, \theta)$$
$$\phantom{= D(} {}^{-} \phantom{r,} {}^{+} \phantom{Q,} {}^{+} \phantom{G,} {}^{-} \phantom{T,} {}^{+}$$

We can write this in log-linear form as:

$$y = b_0 - b_1 r + b_2 q + b_3 g - b_4 t + b_5 \theta \tag{A4.4}$$

We have already seen that the definition of the real exchange rate is written in logs as:

$$q = s + p^* - p \tag{A4.5}$$

Writing (4.6) as:

$$1 + r = P(1 + R)\left(1/P^e_{+1}\right)$$

and taking logs of both sides, we can write the definition of the real interest rate as:

$$r = R - \left(p^e_{+1} - p\right) \tag{A4.6}$$

We previously derived the log form of uncovered interest parity:

$$R = R^* + \left(s^e_{+1} - s\right) \tag{A4.3b}$$

In log-linear form the money market equilibrium condition becomes:

$$m - p = c_0 - c_1 R + c_2 y \tag{A4.2}$$

Finally, the two aggregate supply relationships can be written as:

$$p = \bar{p} \tag{A4.7a}$$
$$y = \bar{y} \tag{A4.7b}$$

# Part 2
# Fixed Exchange Rates

# 5

# The Classical Gold Standard

...................................................................................................................

Now that we have established the analytical foundations that we will be relying on in this book, we can turn to the main task at hand: analyzing macroeconomic behavior in open economies. As suggested in Chapter 1, the effects of openness on macroeconomic behavior are not the same under all circumstances. Instead, the way that economies behave at a macro level when they are open to trade in goods and financial assets with the rest of the world depends critically on several factors, the most important of which are the degree of integration that the country has achieved with world goods and financial markets and the type of exchange rate regime adopted by the central bank. Specific combinations of these factors have been historically most important and remain most relevant today. In this part of the book we will begin to investigate how openness affects macroeconomic outcomes by focusing specifically on a fixed exchange rate regime and considering the alternative cases of perfect and imperfect integration with world financial markets. Fixed exchange rates have indeed been adopted by countries with varying degrees of integration with world financial markets historically, and that continues to be true – especially among developing countries – at the present time.

As we saw in Chapter 3, many countries in the world currently maintain some form of fixed exchange rate regime. However, not all fixed exchange rates are the same. International macroeconomists classify fixed exchange rates into two types: hard and soft pegs. They can be distinguished from each other by two characteristics: (1) the conditions under which the exchange rate can be changed and (2) the amount of discretion that the central bank retains over its conduct of monetary policy. A hard exchange rate peg is a fixed exchange rate regime with institutional features that make it very difficult for the central bank to alter the value of the exchange rate and that compel money supply growth to reflect changes in the central bank's stock of foreign exchange reserves. Under a soft exchange rate peg, by contrast, the central bank retains substantial discretion to alter the exchange rate as it sees fit and can conduct an independent monetary policy, under which there need be no link between changes in the central bank's foreign exchange reserves and changes in the domestic money supply.

There are many examples of hard exchange rate pegs. They differ from each other with respect to the specific mechanisms that are used to make it difficult to change the exchange rate and to link money supply growth to the change in the central bank's reserves. The best-known example of a hard peg was the classical gold standard that prevailed among the world's major trading countries during approximately 1880 to 1914. For several reasons, it is useful to begin our study of macroeconomics in open economies by analyzing how the gold standard worked.

First, since the period of the classical gold standard was the first one during which all of the world's major trading nations abided by a common set of rules in international monetary affairs, and since many observers have concluded that during this time the international economy worked reasonably well, the gold standard continues to be an important point of reference in contemporary discussions of international monetary arrangements. To make sense of these discussions, therefore, you need to understand how the gold standard worked.

Second, as you will see in Chapter 9, there are modern versions of hard pegs that are designed to mimic certain characteristics of the classical gold standard for individual economies. Many economists have advocated the adoption of such exchange rate regimes for a variety of emerging-market economies, and they have indeed been implemented in several important countries – for example in Argentina and Hong Kong. Thus, the economics of hard pegs is an important contemporary topic in international macroeconomics.

Finally, because hard pegs can be analyzed with the simplest version of the analytical framework that we developed in Chapter 4, the study of how hard pegs work provides a useful introduction to the type of macroeconomic analysis that we will be conducting throughout the rest of this book.

We begin the chapter with some historical background that will help us understand how the gold standard evolved. We then turn to exploring central bank behavior under the gold standard. In the next chapter we will turn to "hard peg" macroeconomics.

## 5.1  Evolution of the International Gold Standard

In this section, we will review how the gold standard arose. Tracing the evolution of the gold standard provides a useful insight into what made this exchange rate regime a "hard" peg – specifically, why the official price of gold (which, as we will see, determined the official exchange rate under the gold standard) was not regarded by central banks as a policy variable to be adjusted at their discretion.

### Precious Metals as Money

In ancient times, countries and city-states generally operated on what economists refer to as a **specie commodity standard**, consisting of the use of precious metals as money. In the West, the use of precious metals as money can be dated back to the 24th century BCE in Mesopotamia. The innovation of money in the form of a generally acceptable medium of exchange yielded important social benefits over simple barter, because it avoided wastage of resources in the form of the transaction costs incurred in seeking out a "double coincidence of wants" in trade. But why use precious metals in particular – instead of something else – as money?

In fact, many different types of commodities have functioned as money across human history. These include cloth, grain, silk, cows, cowrie shells, wampum (beads on string), tobacco, cigarettes, and more exotic items such as massive stones and even human skulls! But precious metals have been used most commonly. Precious metals are attractive as money because they have intrinsic value, that is, their value makes it likely that others will accept them in exchange, which makes people more likely to accept them as means of payment. By contrast, commodities with little or no intrinsic value would not be accepted in exchange unless people felt that others would *also* accept them in exchange. This requires either the emergence of a social convention or the discretionary action – the *fiat* – of some governing authority.[1] However, the former would be difficult to coordinate and the latter difficult to enforce, especially for long-distance trade between individuals in different political jurisdictions.

However, commodities other than precious metals have intrinsic value as well. Why should precious metals be preferred as a means of exchange over other commodities? The answer is that such metals have certain important advantages over other commodities for this purpose. Some of the advantages of precious metals are that:

- Precious metals are *portable* (they have a high value-to-weight ratio). The scarcity of precious metals such as gold and silver ensures that this is so and makes such metals relatively less costly to transport than other commodities. This is important, since money has to be transported in the process of exchange.
- They are *divisible into standardized units*, which permits their use in a wide range of small and large transactions.
- They are *storable* (durable), which reduces the cost of holding money between transactions.
- They are reasonably *homogeneous*, which permits their value to be easily identified.

Among precious metals, gold has particular advantages in the form of a high value per unit of weight, which makes it cheaper to transport and store a given value of money. However, the high value of gold also means that it is of limited usefulness for low-value transactions, which has historically implied that lower-valued metals, such as silver and copper, have tended to be used as money simultaneously with gold.

## Coinage

In Mesopotamia and Egypt, precious metals (primarily silver) were used in trade in the form of **bullion**, bars or ingots of precious metals usually cast in standardized sizes. This meant that it was necessary to weigh and grade the metal during transactions. The need to do so added to the cost of making transactions using precious metals as money. Obvious gains in efficiency were thus available through **coinage**, the recasting of precious metals into quantities of standardized weight and fineness. Official coinage was first introduced in the West in Lydia (located in Asia Minor) during the 7th century BCE to get around the costs

---

[1]   The term "fiat money" is often used to denote a form of money based on a commodity with little intrinsic value.

associated with the homogeneity issue.[2] Coins were stamped by the sovereign according to metal weight and fineness.[3] This represented a gain in efficiency because the metal only needed to be weighed and tested once, instead of in every transaction. Thus, governments essentially provided information about the quantity and quality of the metal that traders previously had needed to collect for themselves as a public good.[4]

Yet why should anyone believe what the government had stamped on the coin? To ensure its credibility, the government had to stand ready to supply the equivalent amount of bullion in exchange (that is, coins had to be redeemable in, or **convertible** to, bullion). This is what originally caused units of account to have names corresponding to weights (pounds, pesos, and so on), and resulted in the emergence of **commodity standards** for national currencies.

## Paper Money

Officially issued paper money made its appearance in China during the reign of Hien Tsung (806–821 CE). For about a thousand years prior to that time, Chinese money had taken the form of round copper coins with a square hole in the middle.[5] Privately issued paper money also seems to have been widely used for the first time in China. It appears to have emerged initially during the Song dynasty (960–1279) in the form of privately issued liabilities (that is, as certificates that entitled the bearer to receive payment in coin) that enabled merchants engaged in long-distance trade to avoid the cost of transporting coins. In the 12th century, under the Mongol Yuan dynasty (1206–1367 CE), metallic coins were prohibited from circulating and paper money was used exclusively as the means of payment, a phenomenon that was perceived as a marvel by the visiting European traveler Marco Polo.

In the West, banking first emerged as a specialized profession in Italy in the last part of the 13th century, but paper money began to circulate widely only in the 16th century, through the activities of merchants and goldsmiths, whose acceptance of coins for safe-keeping evolved into their undertaking financial activities. The standard story suggests that a durability problem (in the form of theft) caused people to store coins with goldsmiths. Because they worked with precious metals and needed to maintain inventories of such metals, goldsmiths could take advantage of scale economies in providing secure storage.[6] They issued receipts for the metal that they safeguarded, which also began to circulate as money, since they were backed up by the precious metal on demand and were thus "as good as gold." But goldsmiths quickly discovered that as long as their promises to redeem their receipts in gold were credible, they did not actually have to keep 100 percent reserves against their receipts, since the receipts themselves could circulate as money without people

---

[2]   Rulers may have been motivated by the advantage that these reduced costs gave to local traders, which would have implied increased revenues for the king.

[3]   The original Lydian coins were not made of gold, but of a metal called *electrum*, which was an alloy of gold and silver; see Bernstein (2000). Gold and silver coinage was also introduced by the Lydians. The Lydian king Croesus, who reigned between 560 and 547 BC, began to mint gold and silver coins in the 6th century BC. Croesus' wealth was legendary. Even today, someone who is very wealthy is sometimes said to be "as rich as Croesus."

[4]   The use of coinage appears to have arisen approximately contemporaneously in China, in the form of bronze spade and knife money issued by the Zhou kings in the late 7th or early 6th century BCE (see Williams 1997).

[5]   Bernstein (2000) attributes the innovation of officially issued paper money to the emergence of a shortage of copper.

[6]   In other words, these individuals required secure means of storage for precious metals for their own commercial purposes, so it was relatively inexpensive for them to provide those facilities to others.

first having to redeem them in gold. The goldsmiths could thus make money by lending out their "free" reserves, and they thus evolved into banks: financial institutions whose liabilities functioned as money.

The result of this evolution was the widespread use of paper money, a form of money with no intrinsic value, but which was valuable because of someone's promise to exchange it at a fixed price for something of known value. This was an important social innovation, because it reduced the resource costs to the economy of producing money. Since the intrinsic value of the paper in paper money was much less than its face value, fewer resources were required to produce a given stock of money the larger the share of that stock consisting of paper money. The resources saved in this way were free to be used in other socially productive ways.

A further evolution occurred when the government itself began to issue paper money, either directly or through a central bank.[7] The attraction of banking for the government was the same as that for the goldsmiths – the ability to gain command over real resources by issuing pieces of paper. The constraint that operated on the government's ability to do this was also the same as that to which the goldsmiths were subjected: convertibility into a precious metal. The government did not necessarily monopolize the issue of notes, but it could secure an important competitive advantage for its own notes by declaring them to be **legal tender**, that is, payable in discharge of legal obligations. Note that while this would oblige people to accept the government's paper money as payment, it did not force them to *hold* this money. For people to be willing to do that, they would have to be confident that the government's money would retain its value. For this to happen, in turn, the central bank in this system had to stand ready to redeem its own notes in precious metals at the officially announced price in any amount required by the private sector. You can see why maintaining the metal value of the government's paper money became such an important concern for the monetary authorities.

## The US Dollar

The story of the US dollar began with the Coinage Act of 1792, which established the US Mint, adopted the dollar as the US monetary unit, and gave it a fixed value in terms of *both* silver and gold, creating a **bimetallic standard**. The dollar was set equal to 24.75 grains of fine gold and 371.25 grains of fine silver, so a troy ounce (480 grains) of gold was worth $19.394 (480/24.75), and a troy ounce of silver was worth $1.293 (480/371.25). Thus the price ratio between silver and gold was 15:1 (ounces of silver per ounce of gold).

Why did the United States adopt a bimetallic standard? As mentioned above, one reason is that it was not practical to mint gold coins of small enough denomination to be useful for everyday transactions. Since a silver coin of the same weight would be worth only one-fifteenth as much as a gold coin, the minting of silver coins met the demand for small-denomination coinage.

However, bimetallic standards are inherently unstable. The international price of gold increased at the end of the 18th century, and other countries that adopted a bimetallic standard after the Napoleonic Wars (1803–15) consequently did so with a higher silver/gold ratio (15.5:1) than prevailed in the United States. The result was to make gold more valuable in foreign mints than in the United States.

---

[7] The first paper money in what would become the United States was issued by the colony of Massachusetts in 1690.

The predictable result of this situation was for gold to flow out of the United States and silver to flow in. To make a payment abroad in foreign exchange, for example, US residents found it cheaper to acquire the foreign exchange by shipping gold rather than silver overseas (since gold was cheaper in the United States, a smaller dollar value of gold than of silver was required to obtain a given quantity of foreign exchange). Foreign residents, in turn, preferred to ship silver to the United States, because by doing so it cost them less in foreign currency to make a given payment in dollars. The result was that gold flowed out of the United States while silver flowed in, causing the latter to replace the former in circulation. Thus, the United States ended up on a *de facto* monometallic (silver) standard. The US Congress tried to rectify things in 1834, raising the mint ratio to 16:1 by raising the price of gold to $20.67 per ounce. But because the ratio abroad remained unchanged, the situation was simply reversed: now gold became relatively expensive in the United States, and gold flowed in while silver flowed out.

This experience is not unusual for dual-standard systems, as we will see throughout this book. Such systems always have the problem that when market forces cause the relative price of the two standards to change, the relatively more expensive one (the one with a higher price in the marketplace than at the mint) will be driven out of circulation, since it is more valuable in other uses than as money. This is an application of **Gresham's law** (usually stated as ''bad money drives out good'').

The United States continued to operate a metallic standard until 1861, when convertibility of dollars into gold was suspended during the Civil War, and the government issued paper money (called ''greenbacks''), which carried no obligation for redemption in precious metals. Why was convertibility suspended? Actually, the experience in the United States was not unique in this regard. The United Kingdom had also suspended convertibility during the Napoleonic Wars and the major trading nations suspended it again during World War I (see Box 5.1). The reason is that to maintain the credibility of the promise to redeem notes in gold, central banks, like the goldsmiths, had to maintain a certain ratio of gold reserves to the amount of notes outstanding. We will show more formally in the next section that keeping such a fixed ratio meant that the central bank lost its discretion in monetary policy, that is, its discretion over when it could issue paper money to buy government bonds. The central bank could only print notes when people brought it gold, and had to redeem notes in gold when people did not want to hold them. The upshot was that the central bank could not print notes freely to buy the government's bonds – and thus help to finance the government's fiscal deficits – when the government needed to pay for the war effort. To restore this discretion and make it possible for the central bank to print money when the government needed it, instead of when the balance of payments dictated it, convertibility was suspended. In 1879, convertibility to gold was restored in the United States at the pre-Civil War parity, but not to silver. This event ushered in the classical gold standard as an international monetary system.

## 5.2    Central Bank Behavior under the Gold Standard

The **gold standard era** was a period of time during which most of the world's major trading countries maintained a gold standard domestically and conducted exchange rate and monetary policies roughly according to certain practices that we will explore shortly. It prevailed internationally from about 1880 to the outbreak of World War I in 1914. As noted in Box 5.1, Britain adopted the gold standard after the Resumption Act of 1819 (as

## Box 5.1    Monetary Standards in British Monetary History

### The Great Recoinage

The issue of restoring the value of the monetary standard has been a recurrent one in British monetary history. While the silver content of the basic unit of account – the shilling – was determined by the mint price of silver during the 17th century, during the course of that century the metallic content of shilling coins was continually debased by clipping, a common practice in which small amounts of silver were scraped away from the edge of the coin and melted down into bullion, thus reducing the acceptability of the coins in trade. The major obstacle to a recoinage (replacing the old worn coins with new coins of full metal weight) was determining whether the old coins would be exchanged for new ones at face value or at the mint value of the metal they contained. The former would have entailed retaining the mint price of silver, but would have required the government to purchase the additional silver required to increase the silver content of the coinage so as to make the metallic value of the coins equal to their face value. The latter would have involved raising the mint price of silver, in order to permit the government to issue new shilling coins with a lower silver content. This question was hotly debated in Britain at the end of the 17th century and was ultimately decided in the Great Recoinage of 1695 in favor of the first option – retaining the mint parity – on the grounds, strongly advocated by the philosopher John Locke, that the government was bound by its prior commitments regarding the silver content of the shilling.

### The Bullion controversy

A similar dilemma arose at the conclusion of the Napoleonic wars. Fears of a French invasion had caused a run on gold from the Bank of England that forced the suspension of convertibility of Bank of England notes into gold in 1797, leaving the country on a paper standard during the Napoleonic Wars. Monetary financing of the war effort caused the price level in Britain to double between 1797 and the surrender of Napoleon in 1815. A return to the gold standard was advocated by the Bullion Committee to restore price stability, but the question was at what level to set the mint price of gold, in view of the increase in the price level that had taken place since convertibility was suspended. As in the recoinage controversy, the issue was hotly debated, and again convertibility was ultimately restored on the basis of the old parity, but not until 1821, by which time postwar deflation had returned the average price level to its 1797 value.

### Britain's return to gold in 1925

As noted in the text, convertibility into gold was suspended worldwide (except in the United States) with the outbreak of World War I. The United States, which was a

*(Continued)*

**Box 5.1**  *(Continued)*

nonbelligerent during the first part of the war, stayed fixed against gold, but since other countries did not, the gold standard effectively remained suspended during the war. The European countries sustained much higher inflation than the United States over the course of the war (the cost of living increased 1.7 times in the United States, 2.2 times in the United Kingdom, 2.7 times in France, and 4 times in Germany). The question for the postwar international financial system, then, was at what parity to restore the gold standard. In the meantime, exchange rates floated internationally during the years 1919 to 1925.

The higher United States price level with a fixed dollar price of gold put downward pressure on dollar prices. In the United Kingdom, the issue of whether to restore the prewar parity became heatedly debated once again. In 1918, the Cunliffe Committee advocated restoration of the prewar parity. This position was strongly attacked by economist John Maynard Keynes for its potential contractionary effects, but eventually the United Kingdom reestablished the 1913 parity in 1925 under Churchill. Despite postwar deflation, by 1925 the price level in the United Kingdom was still double its prewar level, while that in the United States was only 40 percent higher. The result was that sterling was overvalued relative to the US dollar. As predicted by Keynes, the high relative prices of British goods resulted in a severe recession in Britain due to the country's loss of competitiveness.

mentioned previously, convertibility to gold had been suspended during the Napoleonic Wars), setting the price of gold at 4.25 pounds sterling per ounce. Germany adopted the gold standard in 1871, and the United States followed in 1879, setting the price of gold at $20.67 per ounce. By 1880, Australia, Belgium, Canada, Denmark, Finland, France, Holland, Italy, New Zealand, Norway, Sweden, South Africa, and Switzerland had all adopted the gold standard. Russia and Japan did so in 1897, and Argentina, Austria-Hungary, and India did so at the turn of the century.

Since our interest is in using the gold standard to learn how hard pegs work, our next task is to examine how the central bank's behavior can be expected to have affected macroeconomic performance under the gold standard. In this section, we look at the rules governing the central bank's behavior and explore their implications for the foreign exchange market as well as for the conduct of domestic monetary policy.

### The "Rules of the Game"

You should think of the gold standard as essentially a set of rules governing the behavior of central banks – that is, determining their conduct of exchange rate and monetary policies. These have come to be known as the gold standard "rules of the game." The "rules of the game" consisted of the following:

1   The government announced a price at which it stood ready to exchange its currency for gold (since this was referred to as *convertibility*, and the currencies involved were called *convertible* currencies).

2    Imports and exports of gold by private citizens were unrestricted.
3    The central bank ''backed'' its domestic currency by holding a stock of reserves in gold
     and convertible currencies that was proportional to the amount of currency it had issued.
     Specifically, if we let $P_G$ be the price of gold in units of domestic currency determined
     by the domestic central bank under rule 1, and let $Au$ (the chemical symbol for gold) be
     the amount of gold (and convertible currencies) held by the central bank, and if a
     fraction $\sigma$ of each unit of currency issued by the central bank is backed by gold and
     convertible currencies, this rule means that:

$$P_G Au = \sigma M$$

where M is the stock of currency issued by the central bank.[8]

## Effects on the Foreign Exchange Market

The adoption of gold standard rules had two effects on the foreign exchange market: (1) it
affected the equilibrium price of foreign exchange, and (2) it affected the central bank's
discretion with respect to the official reserves settlements balance (*ORS*).

*Effects on the Exchange Rate*    With regard to the exchange rate, notice that under the gold
standard the central bank did not fix the exchange rate (the price of foreign currency in terms
of domestic currency) but instead fixed the price of gold. As long as other countries did the
same, and as long as the free shipment of gold was permitted (that is, as long as the first two
''rules of the game'' were observed), this had the effect of establishing fixed exchange rates
among the participating countries.

To see why, note that under the first two rules of the game, an American resident who
wanted to buy British pounds could do so by shipping gold to England. To buy one pound,
the US resident would have to ship an amount of gold equal to 1/(price of an ounce of gold in
pounds) to the Bank of England. Since each ounce of gold costs an amount equal to the price
of gold in dollars at the US Treasury, the cost of acquiring one pound by shipping gold is:

*Price of gold in dollars* $\times$ (1/*Price of gold in pounds*)

Since this expresses the price of pounds in terms of dollars, it is essentially an exchange rate
available through the central banks of the two countries. It is called the **mint parity**. Notice
that the mint parity amounts to a fixed exchange rate between the two currencies as long as
the price of gold is unchanged in the two countries. The reason is that, in the absence of
shipping costs, arbitrage in the foreign exchange market would ensure that the equilibrium
price of foreign exchange must be equal to the mint parity.[9]

To see why, suppose that the market exchange rate deviates from the mint parity and
assume no shipping costs for gold.[10] If the exchange rate $S$ were greater than the mint parity,

[8]    For the United States, $\sigma$ was about 0.12 during the gold standard period (see Bordo 1981).
[9]    The price of gold in US dollars was $20.67 per ounce, while the price of gold in pounds sterling was set at
4.25 per ounce; thus the ''mint parity'' exchange rate between the dollar and the pound was $4.87 per pound.
[10]    The so-called **gold points** around the mint parity – the margin of deviation from the parity beyond which it
became profitable to ship gold – were determined by shipping costs.

then US citizens would find it cheaper to acquire pounds by buying gold from the US Treasury, shipping it to the United Kingdom, and selling it to the Bank of England for pounds, than by buying them in the foreign exchange market. Indeed, under these circumstances even individuals who did not need to make payments to nonresidents could make profits selling dollars to buy gold from the Treasury, shipping it to the United Kingdom for pounds from Bank of England, and selling the pounds in the foreign exchange market. In effect, people would buy pounds at the mint parity and sell them at the market price. This arbitrage process would cause the pound to depreciate in the foreign exchange market until the mint parity was restored. We conclude that under gold standard rules the exchange rate between the domestic and foreign currencies would be determined as:

$$S = P_G/P_G^*$$

where $P_G^*$ is the price of gold in the foreign currency.

It is worth noting that, since the market price of foreign exchange is determined by the mint parity, a country could effectively devalue its currency by raising the domestic-currency price of gold. However, the exchange rate would remain fixed as long as the price of gold was fixed. We will examine the macroeconomic implications of changes in the price of gold in Chapter 6.

*Effects on the Official Reserves Settlements Balance*    The "rules of the game" also ensured that the official reserves settlements balance (*ORS*) would be determined by $CA + NFA$, meaning the central banks had no discretion over *ORS*. When $CA + NFA$ is a negative number, there is an excess demand for foreign exchange (debits exceed credits in the current and nonreserve financial account balances together). This would drive up the price of foreign currency in the foreign exchange market, triggering the arbitrage process described previously. But as shown in that discussion, this process results in an outflow of gold from the domestic central bank, that is, a positive and exactly offsetting value of *ORS*. The upshot is that the central bank has no discretion over the determination of *ORS*. *ORS* is determined entirely by what happens to $CA + NFA$, which determines whether an incipient excess demand or excess supply emerges in the foreign exchange market. The gold standard, therefore, was a regime under which the "rules of the game" allowed central banks no discretion over *ORS*.

## Effects on Domestic Monetary Policy

If the third rule of the game required only that the central bank maintain a stock of reserves of gold and convertible currencies sufficient to sustain its commitment to defend a specific price of gold, it would not be a separate "rule" at all, since the need to keep such a stock is implied by the first rule. Unless the central bank has access to stocks of gold that it can sell when needed, it cannot credibly fix the price of gold in terms of domestic currency.

However, the need to have access to gold with which to redeem its currency in the market does not require the central bank to "back" its currency by gold in any fixed proportion. It is true that the amount of gold to which the central bank has to have access should be expected to depend on the amount of currency that it has issued, since the value of the outstanding currency represents the sum total of the potential claims on the central bank's stock of gold.

But the amount of gold "backing" for each unit of currency outstanding required to make the currency "as good as gold" is certainly not one-for-one, since the public is unlikely to ever want to exchange all of its currency into gold. Indeed, the amount of gold required is not even likely to be unique (unchanging). It depends on the likelihood that the public will actually want to convert currency into gold, which in turn depends on how committed the public perceives the central bank to be to its announced gold price. The more committed the central bank is perceived to be, the smaller the amount of gold to which it will need to have access.

Instead of making sure that the central bank had enough reserves to back a given stock of money, the third "rule" actually supported the gold standard in a more indirect way: by regulating the conduct of monetary policy. Indeed, you can readily see that if the third rule of the game had been followed exactly under the gold standard, central banks would have had absolutely no discretion over monetary policy. Since the money stock would have been tied to their gold reserves, they would have been able to expand the money supply only when people brought them gold and to contract it only when people pulled gold out of the central bank.

To see how the third rule would tend to affect monetary policy, let's examine what it implies about the central bank's discretion over the amount of government bonds ($B_C$) that it holds. When reserves are held in the form of gold and convertible currencies, the central bank's balance sheet takes the form:

$$P_G Au + B_C = M \tag{5.1}$$

Recall that our specification of the third rule requires:

$$P_G Au = \sigma M \tag{5.1a}$$

Solving this expression for $M$, substituting in (5.1), and then solving for $B_C$, the third rule can therefore be shown to imply:

$$B_C = (1/\sigma - 1)P_G Au \tag{5.1b}$$

Since $\sigma$ is a positive fraction, $(1/\sigma - 1)$ is a positive number. Thus, $B_C$ must be *proportional* to $P_G Au$. This means that:

1   If the central bank has no discretion over its holdings of gold and convertible currencies, $Au$, it also cannot have discretion over its holdings of domestic bonds, $B_C$.
2   Since $(1/\sigma - 1)$ is positive, domestic monetary policy must act to *reinforce* the effects of movements in foreign exchange reserves on the domestic money supply (since $B_C$ and $Au$ have to move in the same direction).

This characteristic of the gold standard – that in addition to removing discretion over the exchange rate it also removes discretion over domestic monetary policy – is what makes it an example of a hard peg. To incorporate this feature into our formal framework, we can summarize money-supply determination under the gold standard as:

$$M = P_G Au/\sigma$$

That is, the money supply is proportional to the central bank's stock of gold and convertible currencies.

Most economists agree that this third "rule" was not literally adhered to very closely during the gold standard era. As we will see in the next chapter, however, the role of the third rule is to sustain the credibility of the gold parity. Departures from this rule, therefore, would not have materially affected the macroeconomic implications of the gold standard as long as such deviations were not large enough and persistent enough to imperil a central bank's ability to defend its gold parity – i.e. to abide by the first rule. But why would countries have done so? Empirical Study 5.1 explores one possible reason. We will consider others in Chapter 6.

The hard-peg property of the gold standard still makes it attractive to some people as an international monetary system. Moreover, as we will see in Chapter 9, modern hard-peg exchange rate arrangements that have been adopted unilaterally by various countries are essentially designed to mimic the characteristics of the gold standard that we have just discussed. In the next chapter we will examine what it is about the macroeconomic implications of the gold standard and other hard pegs that some people find attractive.

---

## Empirical Study 5.1    Credibility of the Gold Standard

This chapter has argued that the organic evolution of the gold standard contributed to gold standard countries' commitment to make their paper money "as good as gold" by maintaining convertibility into gold (the first of the "rules of the game"). But were there other reasons for countries to maintain gold convertibility?

We will explore this question in more detail in the next chapter, but one hypothesis that has been proposed by macroeconomic historians is that adherence to the gold standard functioned as a "good housekeeping seal of approval" in the eyes of the international capital market. That is, countries that adhered to the gold standard were more likely to follow prudent policies that would make it possible to service their debts, and markets rewarded such countries with lower borrowing costs, creating an incentive for them to respect the "rules of the game." But is there any evidence that this was so?

A classic study of this issue was by Bordo and Rockoff (1995). They examined the experience of nine countries (Canada, Australia, the United States, Italy, Spain, Portugal, Argentina, Brazil, and Chile) with varying experiences with the gold standard during 1880–1914 (i.e., with varying degrees of adherence to the gold standard). They expected that countries that adhered to the standard more faithfully would face lower international borrowing costs (as measured by the interest rate on long-term government bonds) than those that deviated from it more frequently and for less justifiable reasons. Australia and Canada remained on the standard throughout the period, the United States and Italy left it during wartime, but returned afterward, Spain and Portugal did not always adhere, but followed policies (including fairly stable exchange rates) similar to those that they would have followed under the standard, and the remaining three countries only adopted the standard intermittently, and at different parities.

To test the effect of gold standard adherence on borrowing costs, Bordo and Rockoff estimated annual regressions of the form:

$$R_t^i - R_t^{UK} = a_0 + a_1(\bar{R}_t - R_t^{UK}) + a_2 dum_t^i + a_3\, EMG_t^i + a_4 DEF_t^i + u_t^i$$

where $R_t^i$ is the long-term government bond interest rate for the $i$th country in year $t$, $R_t^{UK}$ is the corresponding rate for the United Kingdom (so $R_t^i - R_t^{UK}$) is the risk premium paid by the $i$th country), $\bar{R}_t$ is the average rate for all the countries in the sample in year $t$, $dum_t^i$ is a dummy variable indicating whether the $i$th country was on the gold standard in year $t$, $EMG_t^i$ is a measure of "excess money growth," the difference between the growth rate of the money supply and that of GDP, $DEF_t^i$ is the ratio of the fiscal deficit to GDP, and $u_t^i$ is a random variable. The average differential paid by all countries is a measure of worldwide risk factors which may affect any individual country's borrowing costs regardless of whether it is on the gold standard or not, and the monetary and fiscal policy variables are indicators of the extent to which countries followed responsible policies (i.e., avoided excessive money growth and large fiscal deficits) that would have earned them lower borrowing costs independently of their adherence to the gold standard.

The key parameter in this regression is the coefficient $a_2$. If the "good housekeeping" phenomenon is operative, $a_2$ should be negative and statistically significant. This is indeed what Bordo and Rockoff found. They concluded that adherence to the gold standard indeed conferred a "good housekeeping seal of approval" on the participating countries, representing an economic incentive for countries to remain on gold.

## 5.3  Summary

The international gold standard was the most important historical example of a hard exchange rate peg. The immutability of the price of gold (except in times of war), was a key factor in making the gold standard a hard peg. As we have seen, the reverence accorded by policymakers to the prevailing gold parity emerged as the result of a long historical process of monetary evolution. This process, and especially the repeated returns to previously prevailing gold parities by Britain after exceptional circumstances resulted in the suspension of convertibility of paper money into gold, imbued the gold parities prevailing during the gold standard era with exceptional credibility.

Coupled with an immutable price of gold, the freedom to ship gold across international boundaries fixed the value of the exchange rate between any two participating currencies. Thus, the process of arbitrage transformed the immutability of gold parities into immutability of exchange rates. The third of the "rules of the game," which guided central bank behavior under the gold standard, tied changes in the money supply to changes in the central bank's stock of foreign exchange reserves (the overall balance of payments), thus satisfying the second of the two requirements specified in this chapter for a fixed exchange rate to become a hard peg.

Our next task is to examine what these characteristics imply for macroeconomic behavior. That is the subject of Chapter 6.

## Questions

1   An economist who was a prisoner of war during World War II once wrote a paper about the use of cigarettes as money in the prisoner of war camp. What attributes of cigarettes would make them likely candidates to be used as money in this setting?

2    Assume that all cows are homogeneous. Explain how the international monetary system would operate if all central banks undertook to fix the price of cows in terms of each country's currency. Would you expect large fluctuations in exchange rates under this system?

3    Why might convertibility be important for the establishment of paper money? Would you expect it to remain as important if the paper money has the status of legal tender? Explain why or why not.

4    What determined movements of gold between countries under the gold standard, and why? Under the gold standard "rules of the game" would such movements be likely to continue until a country's gold stock was depleted? Why or why not?

5    What effect would you expect an innovation in transportation technology that made it cheaper to ship gold from one country to another to have had on the volatility of market exchange rates between countries on the gold standard? Explain why.

## Further Reading and References

### On the history of money

Williams, Jonathan, ed. (1997), *Money: A History* (London: British Museum Press).

### On the history of the gold standard

Bernstein, Peter L. (2000), *The Power of Gold: The History of an Obsession* (New York: John Wiley and Sons).

Bordo, Michael D. (1981), "The Classical Gold Standard: Some Lessons for Today," Federal Reserve Bank of St. Louis *Review* (May), pp. 2–17.

Bordo, Michael D. (1993), "The Gold Standard, Bretton Woods, and Other Monetary Regimes: A Historical Appraisal," Federal Reserve Bank of St. Louis *Review* (March/April), pp. 123–99.

Bordo, Michael D. and Hugh Rockoff (1995), "The Gold Standard as a 'Good Housekeeping Seal of Approval,' " NBER Working Paper 5340 (November).

### On the history of money in the United States

Friedman, Milton (1990), "Bimetallism Revisited," *Journal of Economic Perspectives* Volume 4, Number 4 (Fall), pp. 85–104.

Russell, Steven (1991), "The U.S. Currency System: A Historical Perspective," Federal Reserve Bank of St. Louis *Review* (September/October), pp. 34–61.

# 6

# Gold Standard Macroeconomics

......................................................................................................................

In the last chapter, we examined the institutional features that rendered the gold standard a hard peg. The key characteristics were that the prevailing exchange rate, which was based on the existing gold parities, was perceived as immutable, and that under the gold standard "rules of the game" the central bank was essentially required to surrender monetary autonomy. Monetary policy was instead determined by the outcome of the balance of payments.

In this chapter we will examine the implications of these characteristics for macroeconomic behavior. We will proceed as follows. Our first step will be to apply the results of Chapter 5 to the analytical framework of Chapter 4 to derive a model that we can use to investigate how an economy operating under gold standard conditions works in the short run. We will then apply the model to see how such an economy responds to a variety of macroeconomic shocks. Because this analysis will represent the first application of the analytical framework of Chapter 4, and because we will use that framework repeatedly in future chapters, we will take the time to carefully develop the tools that will be used to solve our short-run model. We will then extend our investigation to the long run by applying a version of the model that describes macroeconomic equilibrium when enough time is allowed to pass for the price level to fully adjust to shocks. Having explored how gold standard macroeconomics works from the perspective of a single country, we will then turn to consider briefly how the world economy as a whole would tend to operate under gold standard conditions. The chapter concludes with an evaluation of the gold standard as an international monetary system and an explanation of why it was eventually abandoned.

## 6.1   Short-Run Macroeconomics under the Gold Standard

The gold standard era was characterized by more than the "rules of the game" for central banks described in Chapter 5. Specifically, the period from about 1880 to 1914 was also one during which barriers to trade in both goods and financial assets – indeed, to the movement of labor – among the major trading countries were relatively few, so these countries were highly integrated – "globalized," using today's terminology – in both goods and financial markets compared to the 70 years or so after 1914. Indeed, in many ways, the world may have been more globalized then than it has become in recent years. In this and the following sections we will explore the macroeconomics of intensive financial integration under hard pegs. We will do so by adapting the analytical framework of Chapter 4 to this particular set of conditions and investigating what the resulting model implies about the behavior of the economy. We will begin by exploring short-run behavior in this section, and will turn to long-run behavior in the section that follows.

### Adapting the Analytical Framework

To see how a small open economy behaves with fixed exchange rates and under conditions of high economic integration, we need to adapt the framework developed in the last chapter to reflect those circumstances. To do so, we can begin by making three observations:

1   Under conditions of *high capital mobility*, we can assume that uncovered interest parity (UIP) holds. This means that we will need to use equation (4.3b), rather than (4.3a).
2   Because we are considering a *fixed exchange rate regime*, we have to use equations (4.9a) and (4.9b). Note in particular that if the exchange rate is assumed to be credibly fixed in the economy that we will be studying, that is, if no exchange rate changes are anticipated in the future, as we might expect to be the case under a credibly fixed peg, we would have:

$$S^e_{+1} = S = \bar{S}$$

In that case, equation (4.3b) would take the form:

$$R = R^*$$

This is an important feature of hard exchange rate pegs.
3   Finally, since we will begin by analyzing how the economy works in the short run, we will use equation (4.7a) rather than (4.7b), and (4.8a) rather than (4.8b), which means that the Fisher equation will take the form:

$$r = R$$

(As mentioned before, we will examine what happens in long-run equilibrium in the following section.)

Solving the Short-Run Model

The short-run gold standard model implied by these observations is summarized in Box 6.1. The first step in solving the model is to identify which variables are exogenous and which are endogenous. Recalling the assumptions that we made in Chapter 4, since we are working with a small open economy, $P^*$, $R^*$, and $\theta$ are exogenous. In addition, $G$ and $T$ are policy variables. Finally, under the gold standard, the exchange rate is given by its mint parity value:

$$S = P_G/P_G^*$$

Since $P_G$ and $P_G^*$ are exogenous policy variables, we can also treat $S$ as exogenous in the model.

---

### Box 6.1    The Gold Standard Model in the Short Run

**Central bank balance sheet**

$$P_G Au + B_C = M \tag{6.1}$$

**Money market equilibrium**

$$M = PL(R, Y) \tag{6.2}$$

**Bond market equilibrium**

$$R = R^* \tag{6.3}$$

**Goods market equilibrium**

$$Y = \varphi(Q)A(Y-T, r) + G + X(Q, \theta) \tag{6.4}$$

**Definition of the real exchange rate**

$$Q = SP^*/P \tag{6.5}$$

**Fisher equation**

$$r = R \tag{6.6}$$

**Aggregate supply**

$$P = \bar{P} \tag{6.7}$$

## Box 6.2    The Short-run Gold Standard Model in Compact Form

**Money market equilibrium (MM)**

$$M = \bar{P}L(R, Y) \tag{6.2}$$

**Bond market equilibrium (UIP)**

$$R = R^* \tag{6.3}$$

**Goods market equilibrium (GM)**

$$Y = \varphi(SP^*/\bar{P})A(Y - T, R) + G + X(SP^*/\bar{P}, \theta) \tag{6.4}$$

This leaves us with eight endogenous variables ($Au$, $B_C$, $M$, $R$, $Y$, $r$, $Q$, and $P$) but only seven equations. Note, though, that $Au$ and $B_C$ only appear in equation (6.1). The rest of the model consists of six equations in the six endogenous variables ($M, R, Y, r, Q$, and $P$). Thus, we should be able to solve this part of the model first, and then come back to see what we can do about equation (6.1).

As a first step, we can write the model in a much more compact form by substituting equation (6.7) into (6.5), and equations (6.5), (6.3), and (6.6) into (6.4). This leaves us with a much simpler model consisting of the three equations listed in Box 6.2 in the three endogenous variables $M$, $R$, and $Y$.

How do we solve this more compact version? The first thing to check is that our compact model is internally consistent and can actually be used to solve for the variables of interest. To see that, notice that the endogenous variable $M$ does not appear in equations (6.3) and (6.4). Thus, these two equations only contain two endogenous variables, $R$ and $Y$. Since these are two independent equations in two unknowns, we should be able to solve them for the equilibrium values of $R$ and $Y$. This is easy to do in the present case because, as you can see, equation (6.3) by itself determines the domestic interest rate, which has to be equal to the world rate $R^*$. Substituting $R^*$ for $R$ in equation (6.4) leaves $Y$ as the only endogenous variable in (6.4). Thus the equilibrium value of $Y$ is that which clears the goods market. Once the equilibrium values of $R$ and $Y$ are known, we can substitute their solved values into equation (6.2), which then becomes one equation in one unknown, and that equation can therefore be used to determine the equilibrium value of $M$.

We will adopt a graphical solution procedure that basically implements the solution process just described. To do so, notice that since equations (6.3) and (6.4) contain only two endogenous variables ($R$ and $Y$), we can find the values of $R$ and $Y$ that simultaneously satisfy these two equations by using a familiar procedure from intermediate macroeconomics: putting the two endogenous variables $R$ and $Y$ on a pair of coordinate axes, plotting the set of combinations of $R$ and $Y$ that satisfy each of equations (6.3) and (6.4) in that space as separate curves, and looking for a combination of $R$ and $Y$ that satisfies these two relationships simultaneously by finding the point of intersection of those two curves.

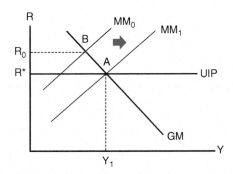

**Figure 6.1**    Short-run equilibrium under a "hard" peg

*The UIP Curve*    A good place to begin is with the uncovered interest parity condition (6.3), which is the bond market equilibrium condition in our current model. Notice that under UIP, the equilibrium value of the domestic interest rate depends only on the foreign interest rate, and not on $Y$. Thus, the set of all combinations of $R$ and $Y$ that satisfy equation (6.3), labeled UIP (for uncovered interest parity) in Figure 6.1, must be parallel to the horizontal $Y$-axis, reflecting the fact that there is a unique value of $R$ that satisfies equation (6.3) no matter what value $Y$ takes on. Because the equilibrium value of $R$ is that which is equal to the foreign interest rate $R^*$, the height of the UIP curve is determined by $R^*$. An increase in $R^*$ shifts the UIP curve upward by an exactly equal amount, while a decrease in $R^*$ shifts it downward by an equal amount. Notice that at any point above the UIP curve, the domestic interest rate would exceed the foreign interest rate. Since domestic and foreign bonds are perfect substitutes, this situation would induce both domestic and foreign residents to try to switch from holding foreign to holding domestic bonds. Thus, the economy would experience a massive capital *inflow*. Below the UIP curve the relationship between the domestic and foreign interest rate is reversed, and the domestic economy would experience a massive capital *outflow* as both domestic and foreign residents switch from domestic to foreign bonds.

*The GM Curve*    Consider next the goods market equilibrium condition (6.4). The set of all combinations of $R$ and $Y$ that are consistent with equilibrium in the market for domestic goods – that is, that satisfy equation (6.4) – is depicted in the form of the curve labeled GM (for "goods market") in Figure 6.1. This curve is drawn with a negative slope. To see why, and to explore other properties of this curve, let us explore the equilibrium in the goods market in more detail.

The determination of equilibrium in the goods market is depicted in Figure 6.2, which is adapted from Figure 4.4 in Chapter 4.[1] With aggregate demand measured on the vertical axis and real output (income) on the horizontal axis, the goods market equilibrium condition $Y = AD$ can be plotted as a 45-degree line (that is, a line with slope equal to one) from the origin. The aggregate demand curve $AD = AD(Y, R, \ldots)$ illustrates how aggregate demand depends on income and the domestic interest rate. This curve has a positive slope which is

---

[1]    The main change from Figure 4.4 is that the goods market equilibrium condition $Y = AD$ has been inserted in the figure in the form of the solid 45-degree line from the origin, and that the determinants of aggregate demand other than income and the domestic interest rate are not explicitly indicated, to avoid clutter.

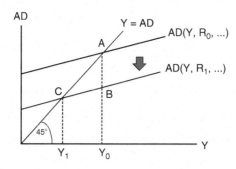

**Figure 6.2**    Goods market equilibrium

less than unity, because each additional unit of income leads to less than one unit of spending on domestic goods.[2] Because changes in the domestic interest rate affect aggregate demand, the position of the aggregate demand curve depends on the domestic interest rate. Since higher values of the domestic interest rate reduce absorption and thus aggregate demand, the AD curve shifts down (reflecting a reduced demand for domestic goods at any given level of income) when the domestic interest rate rises, and shifts up (showing an increased demand for domestic goods at each income level) when the domestic interest rate decreases. Goods market equilibrium must lie along the $Y = AD$ line, because only along this line does the aggregate demand for domestic goods equal the aggregate supply of such goods, but it must also lie on the $AD = AD(Y, R, ...)$ curve, because only points on this curve capture the dependence of aggregate demand for domestic goods on domestic income. Thus, goods market equilibrium will be determined by the point where the two curves intersect. This point is labeled A in Figure 6.2, and implies an equilibrium level of real GDP equal to $Y_0$.

Now consider what would happen to the equilibrium level of real GDP if the domestic interest rate were to rise. For concreteness, suppose that the domestic interest rate takes on the value $R_1$, with $R_1 > R_0$. The increase in the domestic interest rate would cause the AD curve to shift down, as shown in Figure 6.2. At the initial level of output $Y_0$, aggregate demand would now fall short of $Y_0$ by the amount AB and domestic real GDP would thus fall, until a new equilibrium level is established at a point such as C where $Y = AD$ once again. The upshot is that a higher domestic interest rate causes the equilibrium level of real GDP to fall. The negative slope of the GM curve captures this effect.

What determines the steepness or shallowness of the GM curve? The curve is flatter the stronger the effect of the domestic interest rate on the level of absorption, since the stronger this effect is the larger is the shift of the AD curve in Figure 6.2 when the interest rate changes, and therefore the larger the impact of the interest rate change on the equilibrium level of GDP.[3] Similarly, you can see from Figure 6.2 that the steeper the AD curve the larger the impact that a change in the domestic interest rate will have on the equilibrium level of real GDP. This is so because when the AD curve is very steep, a given downward

---

[2]    The slope of the AD line is given by $\varphi A_Y$, where $A_Y$ is the marginal propensity to absorb and $\varphi$ is the share of absorption devoted to spending on domestic goods. Since both of these are less than one, their product must also be less than one.

[3]    You can verify by looking at Figure 6.1 that when small changes in R have large impacts on Y the GM curve is flat.

shift in the curve will be associated with a larger reduction in the equilibrium value of $Y$ than when the curve is shallow. The economic reasoning is the following: since the slope of the AD curve is equal to the marginal propensity to spend on domestic goods, given by $\varphi A_Y$, the curve will be steep when the marginal propensity to spend on domestic goods is high. But the larger this propensity is, the larger the "multiplier" effect of changes in autonomous expenditures on equilibrium real GDP. Under these circumstances, a change in the domestic interest rate will have a large effect on equilibrium real GDP, making the GM curve flat.

Next, let's examine what determines the position of the GM curve. You can readily see that anything that causes the equilibrium level of real GDP to change *at a given level of the domestic interest rate* must cause the GM curve to shift horizontally – to the right when the equilibrium level of real GDP increases, and to the left when it decreases. In turn, changes in the equilibrium level of real GDP will be triggered by changes in the variables that affect the position of the aggregate demand curve in Figure 6.2, including the real exchange rate, fiscal policy (in the form of $G$ and $T$), exogenous shocks to export demand, and shocks to domestic absorption. Changes in any of these variables that tend to *increase* aggregate demand (real exchange rate depreciation, increases in government spending, tax cuts, increases in export demand, and positive shocks to domestic absorption) will shift the AD curve *up* in Figure 6.2 and will therefore cause the GM curve to shift to the *right*, while changes that *reduce* aggregate demand (real exchange rate appreciation, decreases in government spending, tax increases, decreases in export demand, and negative shocks to domestic absorption) cause the AD curve to shift *down* and the GM curve to shift *left*. These shifts in GM are larger the larger the marginal propensity to spend on domestic goods.

Finally, consider what happens when the economy is not on the GM curve. To the right (left) of the GM curve, the equilibrium level of real GDP is too high (low) at the prevailing value of the domestic interest rate. That means that an excess supply of domestic goods must exist to the right of the GM curve and an excess demand for such goods to the left of the curve. Thus, when the economy is to the right of the GM curve real GDP must be falling, and when it is to the left of the GM curve real GDP must be rising.

Having derived the UIP and GM curves, we can now put them together. Uncovered interest parity and goods market equilibrium can both hold simultaneously only at the intersection of UIP and GM. Only at such a point will there be no arbitrage pressures for domestic and foreign residents to switch into or out of domestic bonds, and no pressure for domestic real output to either rise or fall. The intersection of UIP and GM is labeled A in Figure 6.1, and this point therefore determines the economy's short-run equilibrium interest rate $R^*$ and level of real output $Y_0$.

*The MM Curve*    To complete our description of the economy's short-run macroeconomic equilibrium, consider next equation (6.2), which imposes equilibrium in the domestic money market. This equilibrium is depicted in Figure 6.3. For a *given* value of $M$, such as $M_0$ in Figure 6.3, the set of combinations of $R$ and $Y$ that are consistent with equilibrium in the domestic money market can be plotted as the positively sloped curve labeled MM (for "money market") in Figure 6.1. To see why the MM curve in Figure 6.1 has a positive slope, go to the money market equilibrium depicted in Figure 6.3, and consider what happens to this equilibrium if $Y$ rises. If real income increases, the increased demand for money associated with the additional transactions that are undertaken at higher levels of income causes the demand for money curve in Figure 6.3 to shift to the right. This means that equilibrium in the domestic money market moves from point A to point B – that is, a

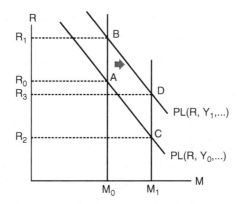

**Figure 6.3**    Money market equilibrium

higher domestic interest rate is required to maintain money market equilibrium. You can see that lower values of $Y$ would be associated with leftward shifts in the demand for money curve, and thus with lower equilibrium interest rates. These effects of changes in real output on the equilibrium interest rate in the money market are what give the MM curve its positive slope.

Note that the exercise we just conducted was carried out for a specific value of the money supply $M$. The value of $M$ for which the MM curve is drawn determines the position of the MM curve in $R$-$Y$ space. To see this, note that if the money supply were larger, such as $M_1$ in Figure 6.3, for example, the equilibrium interest rate that would prevail for the *same* value of $Y$ would have to be lower (compare the interest rates prevailing at points A and C, and at points B and D in the figure), since at a given level of income only a lower interest rate could persuade domestic residents to voluntarily hold the higher money supply. Thus the MM curve must shift downward when $M$ is increased. Conversely, the curve would shift upward when $M$ is decreased.

*General Macroeconomic Equilibrium*    Now we can consider how short-run equilibrium is simultaneously achieved in the goods, bond, and money markets. Assume that we begin with some arbitrary value of $M$. To be concrete, suppose that the value of $M$ is initially sufficiently low that the MM curve originally passes to the left of the point A, and intersects the GM curve at point B in Figure 6.1. This means that the domestic interest rate that would prevail for the given value of the money supply corresponding to this curve, labeled $R_1$ in the figure (and given by the point of intersection of the GM and MM curves) would be higher than the interest rate that would satisfy UIP. As we have seen, however, since the UIP condition is violated in that case, bond-market arbitrage would trigger a massive capital inflow into the domestic economy as both domestic and foreign residents seek to switch from low-return foreign bonds to high-return domestic bonds.

The result of such an inflow would be an incipient appreciation of the domestic currency, because to bring capital into the domestic economy foreign residents would have to purchase the domestic currency in the foreign exchange market. But the domestic and foreign central banks' commitments to sell gold at a fixed price means that this potential appreciation would never take place. Instead, as soon as the price of the domestic currency in the foreign exchange market begins to exceed its mint parity, individuals who wish to acquire the currency would find it cheaper to do so by buying gold from the foreign central bank, shipping it to the domestic economy, and selling it to the domestic central bank in exchange for domestic currency that the central bank prints for the purpose. The effect of these transactions on the domestic central bank's balance sheet is to increase $Au$ and the domestic money supply.

The interesting question is what happens next. The answer depends on how domestic monetary policy responds to this situation. Since the response of monetary policy is one of the distinguishing characteristics of "hard" pegs, it is worth spending some time on this. We will consider three possibilities, each of which solves the problem of the "extra" endogenous variable in equation (6.1) in a different way.

First, suppose that the central bank does *not* adhere to the third of the gold standard "rules of the game," so that it actually retains discretion over its domestic monetary policy, that is, over the value of $B_C$. In that case, we would have to treat $B_C$ as an exogenous policy variable.[4] Now consider two ways that the central bank could manage $B_C$ in response to capital inflows:

1   The simplest case is that in which the central bank makes no change in monetary policy, that is, it keeps $B_C$ unchanged. In that case, the capital inflows into the domestic economy would expand the central bank's stock of gold and the domestic money supply dollar for dollar. The monetary expansion will continue as long as the incentives that give rise to capital inflows remain in place. Pressure for capital to come into the country will persist as long as the domestic interest rate determined by the intersection of GM and MM exceeds the foreign rate $R^*$. As the domestic money supply increases, the MM curve must shift to the right. This reduces the domestic interest rate relative to the foreign interest rate. As long as any gap remains at all, however, there is an incentive for capital to be brought into the country. Thus, the total size of the capital inflow has to be exactly sufficient to increase $M$ so that MM passes through A, completely eliminating the gap between domestic and foreign interest rates.
2   The central bank tries to keep the money supply fixed at a certain value. That would make $M$ an exogenous variable in equation (6.1). But in that case $B_C$ must be endogenous, because to fix the value of $M$, the central bank will have to try to resist the pressure for money supply expansion caused by capital inflows by *selling* \$1 worth of domestic bonds for every \$1 worth of gold that it is forced to buy. That is, it must set:

$$\Delta B_C = -P_G \Delta Au$$

where the symbol $\Delta$ denotes a change in a variable. In this process, called **sterilization**, the central bank tries to prevent the domestic money supply from being affected by central bank gold operations by buying or selling domestic securities to offset the effects of reserve flows on the domestic money supply.[5] But could the central bank successfully fix the value of the money supply under the circumstances we have been analyzing? The answer is *no*, because as long as the central bank's actions keep the money supply from expanding, the domestic interest rate must remain above the foreign rate, and the pressures for capital inflows would continue to be felt. In principle, there would be no limit to the amount of gold that the central bank would have to buy and the number of bonds that it would have to sell. At some point,

---

4   Doing so removes $B_C$ as an endogenous variable in equation (6.1).
5   We will see later in this chapter why the central bank might try to do this.

the central bank would have to give up its attempt to keep the money supply from rising.[6] In other words, *with a fixed exchange rate and perfect capital mobility, the money supply must be an endogenous variable.* The only effect of central bank sales of domestic bonds would be to make the total amount of capital inflows bigger, but the end result must still be for the domestic money supply to increase by enough for the MM curve to pass through A and the domestic interest rate to fall into equality with the foreign rate.

Finally, suppose that instead of trying to contravene them, the central bank actually plays by the gold standard "rules of the game," that is, as its reserves increase, it actually *reinforces* the expansionary effects of capital inflows on the money supply by *buying* (rather than selling) domestic bonds. As we saw in the last section, under these circumstances $B_C$ is endogenous and is given by:

$$B_C = (1/\sigma - 1)P_G A u$$

while the money supply is related to the reserve stock by:

$$M = P_G A u / \sigma^7 \qquad (6.8)$$

The final change in the money supply still has to be the same in this case as in the previous ones – $M$ has to increase by exactly the amount required to cause the MM curve to shift to a position that causes it to pass through the point A. But the total inflow of gold required to achieve this monetary expansion is smaller – possibly much smaller – in this case because the expansionary effects of the capital inflow on the domestic money supply are magnified by an expansionary monetary policy. While the money supply increase is the same, only a fraction $\sigma$ of the increase in the domestic money supply would be backed by the increase in the stock of gold and convertible currencies held by the central bank. A fraction $(1 - \sigma)$ is instead backed by an increase in central bank's stock of government securities. In this case, the increase in the domestic money supply would be a multiple $(1/\sigma)$ of the increase in the central bank's gold stock.

The bottom line is that in our model the domestic money supply must be an endogenous variable. Whatever the central bank does, the money supply must increase by enough for the MM curve to adjust so that it passes through the point of intersection of the UIP and GM curves. How the central bank actually behaves in this situation will affect only the composition of its own balance sheet. The more closely it plays by the gold standard rules of the game in setting its monetary policy, the smaller the inflow of gold. The more it departs from the rules of the game, the larger the inflows of gold. Thus, *playing by the rules of the game tends to stabilize reserve flows, while contravening the rules destabilizes them.* This result is a general one that we will return to at several points in this book.

Before moving on, though, it is worth noting that the mechanisms just described also work in reverse: if the MM curve initially passes to the right of point A, then the domestic interest rate determined by the intersection of GM and MM would be below the world rate, and a capital *outflow* would ensue, shifting MM leftward. The process would once again

---

[6]    Why would it have to give up? Notice that, while $R > R^*$, the domestic bonds that the central bank is selling yield a higher return than the reserves that it is acquiring, so the central bank incurs increasingly large losses of income when it tries to sterilize.

[7]    This solves the problem of the "extra" endogenous variable in equation (6.1) by adding a new equation, equation (6.8), to the model.

continue until MM passes through A. The point is that MM is passive through all this, adapting endogenously to the equilibrium determined by GM and UIP. In short, in this model, the equilibrium values of $R$ and $Y$ are determined by the intersection of UIP and GM, and the role of MM is only to determine the value of the domestic money supply. The role of monetary policy, in turn, is only to determine the size of the central bank's gold stock.

## 6.2  Short-Run Comparative Statics

To gain a deeper understanding of how the economy works under a hard peg such as the gold standard, it is useful to analyze how it adjusts in response to changes in exogenous variables, a method called **comparative statics**. This is a technique that we will use throughout this book. In general we will classify these exogenous shocks into three types: shocks that have their primary impact on domestic asset markets, those that have their primary impact on domestic goods markets, and external financial shocks, which operate through both markets. We will refer to shocks that have their primary impacts on asset markets as **monetary shocks**, which could include shocks to the demand for money or supply of money. Shocks that have their primary impact on the goods market will be referred to as **aggregate demand shocks**. These could include changes in fiscal policy, in the exogenous component of export demand $\theta$, unexplained shocks to private absorption, or unexplained changes in private preferences between domestic and foreign goods. We will not consider shocks to aggregate supply, which operate through both asset and goods markets, until Chapter 13. Finally, **external financial shocks** will consist of changes in world interest rates, in expected future exchange rates, or in private preferences between domestic and foreign bonds.

In analyzing how the economy adjusts to such shocks, we will work with our graphical model. To sort out the effects of a particular shock on the economy's short-run equilibrium, you will find it useful to ask these three questions:

1  What markets (or curves) are affected by the shock?
2  How do the affected markets adjust, that is, in what direction do the affected curves shift?
3  What is the process that drives the economy to a new equilibrium determined by the new positions of the affected curves?

To analyze macroeconomic behavior under the gold standard, we will now consider how the economy reacts to each of the types of shocks that we identified above.

### Monetary Shocks

As we have seen, under a hard exchange rate peg, the domestic central bank cannot conduct an independent monetary policy. However, monetary shocks can nevertheless arise in the form of unexplained changes in domestic residents' preference for holding money instead of bonds.

Suppose, for example, that domestic residents' preferences for holding domestic money change in such a way that, given domestic incomes and the prevailing interest rate, they would like to hold more cash in their financial portfolios than they did before. For given values of the domestic money supply $M$ and domestic real GDP $Y$, this increase in the demand for money would require the domestic interest rate to increase in order to sustain equilibrium in the domestic money market – i.e., the MM curve would have to shift upward, to a position such as $MM_0$ in Figure 6.1. But as we have already seen, this would cause the domestic interest rate to rise above the UIP rate, and that would induce capital to flow into the country. The capital inflow would cause the money supply to rise, shifting the MM curve to the right until the interest rate differential is eliminated, that is, until the MM curve returns to its original position $MM_1$. The sequence of events is:

Demand for money↑ → Domestic interest rates ↑ → Capital inflows ↑ → Money supply ↑

The upshot is that the economy's original macroeconomic equilibrium would tend to be restored in this case, with one difference: the money supply would have increased to satisfy the larger demand for money, and if the central bank follows the gold standard rules of the game, the larger stock of money would be backed by larger stocks of both gold and government bonds in the central bank's coffers. Thus, this particular exchange rate-monetary policy regime perfectly insulates the economy's real equilibrium from the effects of money demand shocks.

As you will see, other shocks to the economy will not have the property that the original equilibrium is restored after the economy has adjusted to the shock. This example thus conveys an important lesson that will carry through to other exchange rate and monetary policy regimes that we will examine in this book: each regime will have different properties in protecting domestic macroeconomic stability when the economy is subjected to shocks. Each regime will be more effective in insulating against some types of shocks than against other types, and no single regime can insulate against all conceivable types. In general, designing exchange rate and monetary policies to preserve macroeconomic stability in open economies necessarily involves making tradeoffs.

## Aggregate Demand Shocks

Let's now turn to the effects of shocks that take the form of exogenous changes in the aggregate demand for domestic goods, with no direct effects on financial markets. As we have seen, these could take several forms in our model. For concreteness, consider the effects of changes in the level of government spending, $G$, or exogenous changes in exports, $\theta$. Such shocks would affect only the GM curve. In the case of increases in either of these variables, since the aggregate demand for domestic goods increases at any given value of the domestic interest rate, the GM curve would shift to the right, to a position such as $GM_1$ in Figure 6.4.

At the intersection of the new GM curve and the original MM, labeled B in the figure, the domestic interest rate would tend to be higher than the foreign rate. As described previously, this would attract massive capital inflows into the economy, which would tend to appreciate the domestic currency, setting in motion an adjustment process operating through gold inflows. If it follows the rules of the game, the domestic central bank purchases both gold and domestic bonds by printing new money, which has the effect of increasing the domestic money supply and thus shifting the MM curve to the right. The incentives for this process to

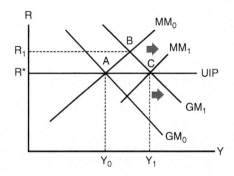

**Figure 6.4**  Aggregate demand shocks in the gold standard model

continue remain in place as long as the domestic interest rate exceeds $R^*$, so the MM curve must keep shifting to the right until it passes through the intersection of GM and UIP, at the point C. At this new equilibrium, the economy achieves a higher level of output $Y_1$ with an unchanged domestic interest rate. In this case we thus have:

Government spending↑ → Output ↑ → Demand for money↑ → Domestic interest rates ↑ →
Capital inflows ↑ → Money supply ↑

Note the following aspects of this result:

1  There is no conventional "crowding out" of private absorption. Indeed, private absorption is in fact "crowded in" because domestic output rises while the domestic interest rate remains unchanged. As we shall see, this makes fiscal policy relatively powerful when the exchange rate is fixed compared to what happens under floating exchange rates, where – at least under some circumstances – fiscal policy can become completely powerless to affect the level of domestic economic activity. But the relatively powerful effects of fiscal policy under a fixed exchange rate also apply to other real shocks that may hit the economy randomly, such as shocks to domestic absorption. Such shocks may thus substantially destabilize the macroeconomic equilibrium under gold standard conditions. This explains why a central bank may be tempted to depart from the rules of the game in setting its monetary policy. If the money supply could be kept from expanding, the effects of crowding out would serve to stabilize domestic real GDP in the face of real shocks. As we have seen, however, this attempt would be useless as long as the central bank continues to fix the price of gold and capital mobility remains high.
2  Recall that $\theta$ is a catch-all variable that reflects the effects on exports of exogenous foreign factors that affect the rest of the world's demand for domestic goods. Foreign real incomes are one of these factors. Because a change in $\theta$ affects the economy in the same way as a change in $G$, national business cycles are directly transmitted across national boundaries under fixed exchange rates.[8] The strength of the transmission depends on foreigners' "marginal propensity" to consume domestic goods. It will be larger the more trade there is between the domestic economy and the rest of the world, that is, the more integrated the domestic economy is with the rest of the world in the market for goods and services.

---

[8]  Again, this result will not always hold under floating exchange rates.

So far, we have only examined the effects of aggregate demand shocks on the equilibrium level of real GDP. But what effects do these shocks have on other macroeconomic variables?

First, since the domestic interest rate is determined by UIP and the world rate $R^*$, it is easy to see that changes in $G$ and $\theta$ can have no effect on the domestic interest rate under fixed exchange rates and perfect capital mobility. Now consider the effects of the shock on the balance of payments accounts. We have already seen that a large capital inflow is associated with the transition from A to C. But what do the balance of payments accounts look like once the point C is reached? In the case of an increase in $G$, the resulting increase in $Y$ increases imports, while the other determinants of net exports – the real exchange rate, real interest rate, and $\theta$ – do not change. Thus, net exports must be lower at C than at A. What happens to the *overall* balance of payments at the new equilibrium, however? We have just seen that net exports (and thus the current account) must deteriorate (become more negative). We also know that the money supply reaches a new stable value at a point like C, *after* the initial capital inflow that causes the MM curve to shift its position. To see what must happen to the overall balance of payments at the new equilibrium, recall that the central bank's balance sheet implies that $M = P_G Au + B_C$. Assuming that the central bank follows the gold standard rules of the game, $P_G Au = \sigma M$, so $M = P_G Au/\sigma$. Taking the first difference of this expression produces:

$$\Delta M = P_G \Delta Au/\sigma$$

It follows that $\Delta M = 0$ implies $\Delta Au = 0$. However, we know that $\Delta M = 0$ at the point C, because the money supply is stable at the new equilibrium. Thus it must be that $\Delta Au = 0$ as well, that is, that the overall balance of payments is in equilibrium. How can this be, with an ongoing current account deficit? The answer is that a capital inflow must exactly offset the current account deficit. If that weren't the case, foreign exchange reserves would fall, the money supply would also fall, and the domestic interest rate would rise, which would *create* a capital inflow sufficient to offset the current account deficit.

In contrast with what happens when government spending increases, in the case of an increase in $\theta$ net exports must *increase* at the point C, despite the induced increase in domestic income. To see why this must be so, recall from Chapter 4 (equation 4.4') that goods market equilibrium can be written as:

$$Y = A + G + N$$

The increase in domestic income $Y$ must induce an increase in private absorption $A$. However, because the marginal propensity to absorb is less than unity, and neither taxes nor the domestic interest rate change under this shock, it follows that the increase in $Y$ must exceed that in $A$. Since $G$ is unchanged in the case of a shock to $\theta$, you can see that goods market equilibrium can only hold if $N$ increases: only a larger level of net exports can provide the additional aggregate demand required to sustain the higher level of $Y$. It follows that, once a new equilibrium is reached after an increase in $\theta$, an ongoing current account *surplus* is exactly offset by a *deficit* in the nonreserve financial account.

Thus, under both types of expansionary shock, the overall balance of payments must move into surplus *temporarily* (while the capital is flowing in that causes the MM curve to shift to the right from one equilibrium to the next) and then settle into a position of equilibrium at the intersection of the new GM curve with the UIP line. But the composition

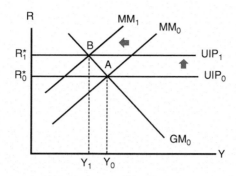

**Figure 6.5**   Effects of world financial shocks

of the balance of payments (that is, the current and nonreserve financial accounts) at the new equilibrium will be quite different in the two cases.

## External Financial Shocks

*Changes in World Interest Rates*   Next, let's consider the effect on the economy of a foreign financial shock in the form of a change in the world interest rate $R^*$. Suppose, for example, that the world interest rate increases. As we have seen, this shifts the UIP curve upward, as in Figure 6.5. The original domestic interest rate, given by the intersection of GM and MM, is now lower than the UIP rate, causing capital to flow out of the country. The resulting demand for foreign exchange would tend to depreciate the value of the domestic currency in the foreign exchange market. As it becomes increasingly expensive to buy the foreign currency in the foreign exchange market, market participants would tend to make payments by shipping gold out of the domestic economy instead. Since they buy this gold from the central bank in exchange for domestic currency, the supply of such currency held by the public contracts, causing the MM curve to shift to the left. As before, this process continues until the MM curve passes through the intersection of $R^*$ and the stationary GM curve. The sequence of events is:

Foreign interest rate$\uparrow$ $\rightarrow$ Capital outflows $\uparrow$ $\rightarrow$ Money supply$\downarrow$ $\rightarrow$ Domestic interest rates $\uparrow$ $\rightarrow$ Output $\downarrow$

The upshot is that this shock to the economy causes $Y$ to fall and results in a capital outflow and loss of reserves. We shall see that this is exactly the opposite of the result that occurs under floating exchange rates. In this case net exports must improve in the new equilibrium at point B, because of the lower value of $Y$ and higher value of $R$.

In sum, under conditions of high capital mobility and fixed exchange rates, world financial conditions (measured by $R^*$) tend to be fully reflected in domestic financial markets and to be transmitted through those markets to the domestic real economy.

*An Unanticipated Change in the Price of Gold*   To gain some insight into the costs and benefits that policymakers may have perceived in deciding whether to adhere to the gold standard, it is useful to ask what would happen in the economy if the domestic central bank unexpectedly increased $P_G$. Note first, from equation (6.1), that an increase in $P_G$ would tend to increase the domestic-currency value of the central bank's gold stock. Since the central bank's assets (in the form of $P_G Au + B_C$) would rise in value while its liabilities (in the form of $M$) would remain unchanged, the central bank's wealth would tend to increase. Moreover, since the value of the gold stock would rise relative to that of currency outstanding, the ratio $\sigma$ would increase as well, allowing the central bank to expand the domestic money supply without violating the monetary policy "rules of the game."

But let us assume that the central bank does not take advantage of this opportunity, that is, that rather than increase the money supply in proportion with the increase in the value of its gold stock (through expansionary open-market operations), it keeps its stock of government bonds unchanged, thus essentially adopting the new higher value of $\sigma$ as its targeted ratio of gold backing for the currency. What would happen to the economy in this case?

Remember that the "mint parity" $\bar{S}$ is given by $\bar{S} = P_G / P_G^*$, so an increase in $P_G$ is equivalent to a devaluation of the mint parity. The implication is that the increase in the price of gold would increase $Q$. The resulting reduction in the relative price of domestic goods causes domestic and foreign residents to switch their spending from foreign to domestic goods. This expenditure-switching effect in favor of domestic goods would cause the GM curve to shift to the right. Because the effects on the curves that we are using to solve our model graphically are the same, the effects of this shock can be analyzed graphically using the diagram that we used to analyze real shocks, Figure 6.4. As in the case of the expansionary real shock, the increase in demand for domestic goods increases domestic real output. Thus, the demand for money increases and the domestic interest rate tends to rise. This triggers a capital inflow that shifts MM to the right, until it passes through the new equilibrium point determined by the intersection of UIP and the new GM curve. The domestic interest rate would be unaffected in the new macroeconomic equilibrium.

It is worth noticing here that the size of the rightward shift in the GM curve will be larger, and thus the effects of this shock on domestic economic activity will be magnified, the stronger the expenditure-switching effect of the devaluation of the mint parity – that is, the closer the degree of substitutability between domestic and foreign goods. Thus an increase in the price of gold is more expansionary the more open the economy.

Notice that net exports must increase in this case despite the fact that the increase in $Y$ causes them to decrease, because the offset to the initial improvement cannot eliminate it, or there would be insufficient aggregate demand to support the higher level of $Y$. The argument is exactly the same as the one that we went through in the case of an increase in $\theta$. As in that case, when the economy reaches the new equilibrium, the country will be running a current account surplus matched by a nonreserve financial account deficit, with the overall balance of payments in equilibrium.

An increase in the price of gold is thus expansionary and tends at the same time to increase net exports. This would suggest that for countries to abstain from frequently increasing the price of gold, there must have been important benefits to maintaining a stable gold price. As we shall now see, these benefits came in the form of credibility. Indeed, this perceived benefit was so great as to cause countries to endure substantial macroeconomic pain to avoid raising the price of gold.

*An Anticipated Future Change in the Price of Gold*    To see why the credibility of the announced gold parity was important, consider the effects on the economy if domestic agents come to expect that the government may indeed increase the price of gold sometime in the near future. As we have just seen, an increase in the price of gold would alter the mint parity and would be equivalent to a nominal exchange rate depreciation. But an expected *future* depreciation would not shift the GM curve in the present, since the relative prices of domestic and foreign goods would not yet have changed. However, recall the general version of the uncovered interest parity (UIP) relationship, equation (4.3b), repeated below for convenience:

$$R = (1 + R^*)S^e_{+1}/S - 1$$

An anticipated future nominal devaluation is reflected in this equation in the form of an increase in $S^e_{+1}$. This *increases* the value of the domestic interest rate consistent with UIP, and thus shifts the UIP curve upward, as in Figure 6.5. As we have already seen, such an upward shift has a contractionary effect on the domestic economy and results in a loss of reserves for the central bank. These are not typically macroeconomic outcomes that policy-makers welcome. Thus, preserving the credibility of the gold parity had important benefits for policymakers during the gold standard era in the form of preserving macroeconomic stability.

*Summary*   We can summarize the short-run properties of our model as follows. With high capital mobility and a credible commitment to a fixed exchange rate on the part of the central bank:

1   Individual countries have no monetary autonomy, in the sense that their central banks cannot determine the size of the domestic money supply.
2   The economy would be relatively well insulated against the effects of shocks to domestic money demand.
3   This endogeneity of the money supply eliminates any crowding-out effects associated with real (goods market) shocks.
4   Real shocks are transmitted directly across international boundaries with no crowding out and with effects that are larger the more integrated are the goods markets of the relevant countries.
5   With world financial markets highly integrated as well, domestic financial markets would tend to mirror world financial conditions.
6   While central banks would retain some power to affect domestic economic activity by changing the price of gold, they would be deterred from doing so by the fact that domestic financial markets would become highly sensitive to expectations of expected future changes in the gold price.

## 6.3   The Long-run Model

The analysis we have just completed was predicated on the assumption that the domestic price level was fixed. As discussed in Chapter 4, this assumption is a standard one in the analysis of the short-run effects of shocks to the economy, because in fact the aggregate price level tends to be "sticky," that is, not literally fixed, but slow to adjust in response to

## Box 6.3    The Gold Standard Model in the Long Run

**Money market equilibrium**

$$M = PL(R, \bar{Y}) \tag{6.2'}$$

**Bond market equilibrium**

$$R = R^* \tag{6.3}$$

**Goods market equilibrium**

$$\bar{Y} = \varphi(SP^*/P)A(\bar{Y} - T, R) + G + X(SP^*/P, \theta) \tag{6.4'}$$

shocks. Over a sufficiently long time frame, however, as labor contracts are revised and firms' pricing policies are adjusted to reflect changes in their costs, the price level can be expected to adjust so as to restore the economy to a condition of full employment. In this section we will complete our analysis of the gold standard model by examining what happens in long-run equilibrium.

Analysis of long-run equilibrium under the conditions assumed in this chapter is straightforward. All we need to do is to treat the level of real GDP as an exogenous variable and the domestic price level as an endogenous one, reversing their roles in the short-run model. If we restrict our attention to a long-run equilibrium in which all of the exogenous variables take on fixed values, the endogenous variables will also be unchanging in the long run, so while the price level $P$ is endogenous, it will not change over time. That means that we can set $P^e_{+1} = P$ as in equation (4.8b), and make no distinction between nominal and real interest rates.

The resulting long-run model is summarized in Box 6.3. Notice that it looks very similar to the short-run model in Box 6.2. All that we have done is replaced the symbol $\bar{P}$ in Box 6.2, which identified the price level as an exogenous variable by the symbol $P$ and the symbol $Y$ by $\bar{Y}$, which identifies real GDP as an exogenous variable in the long-run model.

Diagrammatically, we can depict the economy's equilibrium in the form of UIP, GM, and MM curves that look similar to the previous ones except that, since $P$ is now endogenous while $Y$ is exogenous, they are drawn in $R$-$P$ space, instead of $R$-$Y$ space, as in Figure 6.6. The factors driving the shapes of the GM and MM curves are also somewhat different. The GM curve has a negative slope because a reduction in the domestic interest rate leads to an excess demand for domestic goods, just as in the short-run model. However, the excess demand is now eliminated by an increase in the domestic price level, rather than an increase in domestic output, thus giving the curve a negative slope in $R$-$P$ space. The increase in the domestic price level eliminates the excess demand by causing the real exchange rate to appreciate, thus making domestic goods more expensive. This means that the GM curve will be steeper the more open the economy, because openness increases the sensitivity of demand to the real exchange rate, requiring smaller increases in the domestic price level to eliminate a given amount of excess demand. The MM curve has a positive slope because an increase in the

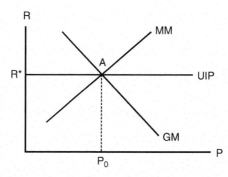

**Figure 6.6** Long-run equilibrium in the gold standard model

domestic price level creates an excess demand for money (remember that the nominal demand for money is proportional to the price level), which requires an increase in the domestic interest rate to restore money market equilibrium.

In contrast with the results of the last section, the economy's long-run equilibrium determines the domestic price level, instead of the level of real output. However, the analysis of the effects of various shocks is similar to what we have already done. The difference is only in interpretation: excess demand and supply of domestic goods are eliminated through adjustments in their relative price (the real exchange rate), rather than through variations in domestic output.[9] The main conclusions that emerge from the analysis are the following:

1  Equations (6.3) and (6.4′) (that is, the UIP and GM curves) together determine the equilibrium value of the domestic price level and thus the equilibrium value of the real exchange rate. The value of the equilibrium real exchange rate depends on the long-run values of "real" variables such as $G$, $\theta$, and $R^*$ that affect the relative price of foreign goods in terms of domestic goods. Thus, in general, PPP will not hold.
2  In the absence of real shocks (that is, shocks that alter the equilibrium real exchange rate), or once adjustment to such shocks is completed, the stability of the real exchange rate in the long run means that the domestic price level is determined by the world price level $P^*$ and the fixed exchange rate chosen by the domestic country. Thus, in this fixed exchange rate model, *the inflation rate in the domestic economy ultimately equals the world rate of inflation.*

This last point is an important one. The variable that determines an economy's average long-run price level is referred to as the economy's **nominal anchor**. What we have just shown is that in a small open economy with a fixed exchange rate and perfect capital

---

[9]  An alternative and useful way to illustrate the determination of long-run equilibrium is to do so in the $R$-$Y$ space that we used to explore short-run equilibrium. Under this approach, the economy's long-run equilibrium combination $(R, Y)$ is determined by the intersection of the horizontal $R = R^*$ (UIP) curve and a *vertical* $Y = \bar{Y}$(full employment) curve. In this case, both the MM and GM curves must adjust passively to pass through this point. The GM curve does so through adjustments in the domestic price level that alter the real exchange rate. Such adjustments cause the GM curve to shift until it passes through $(R^*, \bar{Y})$. The MM curve does so through changes in both the money supply and the domestic price level, which similarly cause the curve to shift until it too passes through $(R^*, \bar{Y})$.

mobility, the exchange rate provides the economy with its nominal anchor and the domestic rate of inflation will in the long run be equal to that of the country's trading partners. As we will see, these conclusions do *not* hold under floating exchange rates. In fact, the desire to maintain a stable domestic price level has historically provided an important motivation for countries to adopt a regime of fixed exchange rates relative to the currency of a stable-price trading partner. This is sometimes referred to as "importing" price stability. This also explains why, in countries that are seeking to emerge from a bout of high inflation, fixing the exchange rate has often been an important component of policy packages designed to bring inflation under control. Inflation-stabilization programs that feature an important role for exchange rate policy are referred to as **exchange rate-based stabilization programs**.

## 6.4    The Gold Standard as an International Monetary System

In previous sections we have examined how the gold standard worked from the perspective of a single economy. We now take a broader perspective and consider the gold standard as an international monetary system. The interesting questions here are why individual countries adhered to the system as long as they did and how the existence of the gold standard system affected the performance of the world economy. We conclude by considering the demise of the gold standard as an international monetary system.

### Why didn't Countries Change the Price of Gold?

An interesting question on which the comparative static results that we have just derived may shed some light is why countries adhered to the gold standard as long as they did. Notice that under the gold standard if a country was faced with a recession and was unable or unwilling to use fiscal policy as a countercyclical tool, it could try to achieve full employment by increasing the price of gold. As we have seen, this would effectively devalue the mint parity. Why didn't countries regularly do that?

The simplest explanation concerns the power of conventional wisdom about what constituted good economic policy. As we saw in Chapter 5, making the currency "as good as gold" and balancing government budgets were the hallmark of financial orthodoxy during the gold standard era. The government's responsibility for economic policy was interpreted as consisting of upholding these two principles, which had the effect of "hardening" the peg. Britain's return to gold at an overvalued parity in 1925, described in Box 5.1, is often cited as an example of the power that financial orthodoxy had over the formulation of economic policy. However, such an explanation actually begs the question of *why* these principles became the reigning orthodoxy.

One explanation is that, like the goldsmiths who preceded them, governments valued the opportunity to gain command over real resources by printing paper money. This would, however, only be feasible as long as people considered this money to be "as good as gold." To maintain that belief, it was important for governments to nurture a reputation for exchanging paper money for gold at a fixed price. Occasionally increasing the price of gold for stabilization purposes would certainly have undermined that confidence and reduced the public's demand for paper money.

The comparative static results that we derived previously in the chapter suggest that a commitment to keep the price of gold fixed may also have been based on economic performance. If the possibility of increasing the price of gold had been perceived as a valid option whenever the economy fell into periods of high unemployment, the credibility of any announced gold parity would have been impaired. To see why the credibility of the announced gold parity may have been perceived as important, recall that an increase in the price of gold would alter the mint parity and would be equivalent to a nominal exchange rate devaluation. But as we also saw previously, an expected *future* increase in the price of gold increases the value of the domestic interest rate consistent with UIP, and thus shifts the UIP curve upward, exerting a contractionary effect on the domestic economy, and resulting in a loss of reserves for the central bank. Thus, it may be easy to see why preserving the credibility of the gold parity would become an important objective for policymakers during the gold standard era.

Political factors must also have been at work to enable these principles to be sustained. Some observers have argued that a higher degree of price-wage flexibility reduced pressures for governments to depart from gold-standard principles, since it meant that real exchange rate adjustment could be achieved without altering the nominal exchange rate, thereby reducing the severity and duration of periods of unemployment. Thus the price of gold would not have been raised during prolonged periods of high unemployment simply because wage-price flexibility ensured that such periods did not tend to emerge, or that if they did, they would be relatively short-lived and mild. Also, the relative weakness of labor-based political parties during this time meant that whatever pressures to stabilize the economy may have existed at the grass-roots level were not effectively transmitted through the political system. The rise of labor unions and labor-based political parties during the early part of the 20th century acted to change all this.

## The Gold Standard and the International Price Level

Some international macroeconomists occasionally argue for the restoration of the gold standard as an international monetary system. One attractive feature of the gold standard as a system claimed by such economists was that it contained a built-in mechanism to stabilize the international price level. To see why this might have been so, we can use a modified version of our model. First, since we want to explain price level determination, we need to use the flexible-price version of the model that we described in the previous section. Second, note that since the world as a whole is a closed economy, we have to adapt our flexible-price gold standard model to the case of a closed economy. We can do so by assuming that there is no trade in either financial assets or in goods and services between residents of the economy being modeled and residents of any other economy. This means that uncovered interest parity (UIP) no longer affects the determination of the domestic interest rate (so we can eliminate the UIP condition from the model), and that both exports and imports of goods and services must be equal to zero (so $X = 0$ and $\varphi = 1$). The resulting modified gold standard model can be written as summarized in Box 6.4.

This very classical model has two endogenous variables: the world interest rate $R$ and world price level $P$. But it has a rather special structure: the world interest rate $R$ affects the world goods market equilibrium (equation 6.6), but the world price level $P$ does not.

**Box 6.4    A Long-run Model for the World under
the Gold Standard**

**World money market equilibrium**

$$P_GAu + B_C = PL(R, \bar{Y}) \tag{6.5}$$

**World goods market equilibrium**

$$\bar{Y} = A(\bar{Y} - T, R) + G \tag{6.6}$$

However, both the world interest rate and world price level affect the world money market equilibrium (equation 6.5). This means that the world interest rate must be determined by the world goods market equilibrium condition (if we disaggregate absorption into consumption and investment, we can show that this is equivalent to a world equality of saving and investment) and, given the equilibrium value of the world interest rate, the world price level is determined by equilibrium between the world money supply and demand, as given by equation (6.5).

To see how the gold standard would have tended to stabilize the world price level, notice that the world price level would have fallen if the gold standard countries reduced $B_C$ and would have risen if they increased it. But if world prices rose, there would have been upward pressure on the market price of gold as well, since the costs of production in the gold industry would have increased. Since the **demand price** of gold (the price the market was willing to pay for gold) was fixed by central banks, an increase in its **supply price** (the price at which producers are willing to sell it) would have caused private citizens to satisfy their demand for gold by buying it from central banks. This would have reduced the amount of gold held by central banks ($Au$), thereby (under the third rule) reducing $B_C$ as well. The effect would be to offset the initial money supply expansion, thus tending to stabilize the world price level. On the other hand, if contractionary monetary policies caused world prices to fall, this would have reduced the cost of mining gold and thus increased the supply of gold to central banks, tending to increase their gold reserves and the world money supply, thereby increasing the world price level. Thus, the gold standard included an automatic mechanism for protecting the world price level from irresponsible behavior by the monetary authorities. This explains some of the appeal of the classical gold standard for some observers today.

However, there is one problem with this scenario: it depends on stable conditions of supply and demand for gold. Under the gold standard, the predictable effects of shocks to world gold supply conditions, for example, such as through new gold discoveries or through technological innovations in gold mining, would have been to destabilize the world price level, since reductions in the supply price of gold would have increased $Au$ in equation (6.5).

## Experience Under the Gold Standard

How do the predictions of the previous scenario square with reality under the gold standard? In reality, governments did not always adhere closely to the third rule of the game – they did not always maintain a fixed ratio between the notes issued by the central bank and the bank's

---

### Box 6.5 The Cross of Gold

As discussed in the text, under the international gold standard the average world price level tended to fluctuate with shocks to the demand and supply of gold. A deflationary shock was associated with an increased world demand for gold following the accessions of several important countries to the gold standard after 1880.

This deflationary shock had important political repercussions in the United States. The period after 1880 was associated with the completion of the country's westward expansion, and economic activity in the new Western states was dominated by agriculture. Farmers traditionally are heavily dependent on credit for the purchase of land and intermediate goods such as seed and fertilizers, and many Western farmers held substantial amounts of debt. When the aggregate price level fell in the United States this debt, which was denominated in nominal dollars, tended to increase in real value, placing a substantial financial hardship on the farmers. Farmers' financial hardships contributed to the power of the populist movement in the United States during the last two decades of the 19th century.

A fascinating aspect of this movement was the role that monetary issues played in the Populist platform. In particular, Populists agitated strongly for the remonetization of silver in the United States. This essentially means that they wanted the government to declare an official price of silver. Williams Jennings Bryan, a congressman from Nebraska and a dynamic orator who ran for President as the candidate of the Democratic and Populist parties in 1896, famously declared at the 1896 nominating convention in Chicago: "We will answer their demand for a gold standard by saying to them: You shall not press down upon the brow of labor this crown of thorns, you shall not crucify mankind upon a cross of gold!" This is one of the few times that the arcane details of international finance played such a strong role in domestic political debate in the United States.

Why was the monetization of silver so important to the Populists? The flexible-price version of our model suggests that under the gold standard the domestic price level is determined by the price of gold, since that determines the nominal exchange rate. If the United States monetized silver at its prevailing market price, this would have had no effect on the domestic price level, since it would have implied no change in the official price of monetary metal. What the populists were interested in, however, was monetizing silver at a price *above* its prevailing market price. As we saw in Chapter 5, this would have driven gold out of circulation and placed the United States on a silver standard. More importantly, it would have been associated with an *increase* in the price of the monetary metal. The result would have been an increase in the domestic price level, and relief for Western farmers in the form of a reduction in the real value of their debts.

stock of gold. However, as we have seen, adherence by central banks to the basic rules of behavior under the gold standard was sufficiently close that the system prevailed among the major trading countries of the world for nearly 35 years. It turns out that the gold standard was much better at keeping the international price level from drifting over long periods of time than it was at maintaining either stability of the price level or of real output over shorter periods.

*Effects on Inflation*    As predicted by the model, the gold standard period was one of low average inflation in the United Kingdom and the United States, with little long-run trend in the price level in either country. During this time, however, inflation tended to be highly variable. The first part of the gold standard period (roughly 1880–96) was one of falling international prices. This was associated with the adoption of the gold standard in the United States and France, which increased the world demand for gold and therefore required an increase in its real price. Given its nominal price as set by the world's central banks, an increase in the real price of gold could only be brought about by a reduction in the nominal prices of other goods and services. On the other hand, the second half of the period was associated with rising international price levels, associated with new gold discoveries in South Africa and the development of the cyanide process for the mining of gold (see Neeley and Wood 1995). As discussed in Box 6.5, these price level fluctuations sometimes had important domestic political repercussions in the gold standard countries.

*Effects on Real Output*    Real output and unemployment tended to be relatively unstable during this period. As we have seen, the gold standard provided no mechanism for stabilizing real economic activity (recall the absence of ''crowding out'') and prevented the use of domestic monetary policy for stabilizing output.

## The Demise of the Gold Standard

As described in Box 5.1 of Chapter 5, convertibility into gold was suspended worldwide among major trading nations with the outbreak of World War I, and exchange rates floated internationally after the war until 1925. It was taken for granted that the gold standard would eventually be restored after the war, but the question was when and at what parities.

Because of wartime inflation, after World War I the real price of gold would have been too low at anything close to the prewar gold parities.[10] Under the classical gold standard, as we have seen, automatic forces would have resulted in a lowering of the money supplies of the gold standard countries, as official (reserve) gold became diverted into nonmonetary uses because of its low price. This monetary contraction would have lowered the world price level, restoring the equilibrium real price of gold. But, as we have seen, conditions changed both in domestic labor markets as well as in the political sphere during this time. The increasing power of labor unions in the workplace tended to make wages and prices less flexible downward than they had been before the war, meaning that worldwide monetary contraction would have resulted in economic contraction, rather than just lower prices. Moreover, the advent of universal male suffrage (which increased democratic pressure on countries'

---

[10]    In 1916, Swedish economist Gustav Cassell actually developed the theory of purchasing power parity (PPP, which we studied in Chapter 3) to argue against restoration of the gold standard at the prewar parities.

## Box 6.6   The Gold Standard and the Great Depression

What role did the gold standard play in creating, aggravating, and/or transmitting the Great Depression? It is clear that the Depression was an international event, affecting countries both at the center as well as on the periphery of the world economy during the early 1930s. Was the gold standard responsible in some way for this cataclysmic macroeconomic event?

While the Depression was indeed international in scope, most observers agree that it was not only especially severe in the United States, but that it started in and was transmitted from the United States (see, for example, Romer 1993). Thus, to understand the role of the gold standard in the evolution of the Great Depression, it is useful to consider how it affected events in the United States.

The US economy actually began to slow down in the summer of 1929, before the stock market crashed in October of that year. This slowdown was associated with a tightening of monetary policy that had begun in 1928. While it has been argued that this monetary tightening was in response to an outflow of gold (specifically to France, which had returned to the gold standard in 1928 at an undervalued parity), the United States actually held ample stocks of gold at the time, and was not compelled to tighten monetary policy by the gold standard "rules of the game." Instead, many observers have concluded that the monetary tightening was more likely due to the Fed's concern about a rapid increase in stock prices that occurred in the late 1920s. (However, this stock market "bubble" may itself have been triggered by loose Federal Reserve monetary policies in the preceding years, which in turn were partially driven by an attempt to help the United Kingdom maintain the overvalued gold parity it had established in 1925. The low interest rates that expansionary policies created in the United States would have driven capital, and therefore gold, to the United Kingdom, increasing the Bank of England's gold reserves.)

However, the increase in US interest rates associated with the monetary tightening was influential in spreading the economic slowdown to other countries, because rising US interest rates attracted capital flows from other countries, forcing foreign monetary authorities to tighten monetary policy as well in order to maintain their gold parities.

The Depression was substantially aggravated in the United States both by the famous stock market collapse of October 1929 as well as by a series of banking panics that began in the fall of 1930. These panics led to a sharp endogenous contraction of the US money supply that the Fed could have countered through a policy-induced monetary expansion. Its unwillingness to do so may well have been related to the gold standard as well – i.e., a fear that a monetary expansion would have triggered gold outflows, threatening the gold backing of the US dollar. This fear was heightened by capital outflows from the United States that began after Britain abandoned the gold standard in 1931, creating the concern that the United States may have done the same. The result was a very severe contraction in economic activity and an increase in the unemployment rate, to a peak of 24 percent of the labor force in 1933.

The gold standard also played a role in the recovery from the Depression, both in the United States as well as elsewhere. In the United States, recovery was associated with

*(Continued)*

**Box 6.6**    *(Continued)*

a sharp expansion of the money supply after 1933. This monetary expansion was partly fueled by rising capital outflows from Europe, triggered by the growing political uncertainty there, but was also facilitated by a devaluation of the dollar parity by newly elected President Roosevelt in January 1934. Internationally, a strong pattern emerged in the 1930s: countries that abandoned the gold standard and expanded their money supplies tended to recover quickly, while those that adhered to the gold standard and tightened monetary policies to prevent falling prices elsewhere from draining their gold stocks through current account deficits, did not.

In short, the jury is still out on the role that the gold standard may have had in causing the Great Depression. But economists are in agreement that the gold standard played a key role in transmitting the depression across the world, as well as in deepening and prolonging it, both in the United States as well as elsewhere.

financial authorities) and the increasing power in the political arena of political parties backed by labor would have tended to make the associated unemployment politically intolerable.

After the outbreak of the Great Depression in 1929, the new gold standard started to give way. The United Kingdom abandoned it after only six years, in 1931. The United States also did so – albeit only briefly – in 1933, and sharply increased the official price of gold in early 1934. By 1936, all of the major trading countries had abandoned their post-World War I gold parities. The role of the gold standard in triggering, propagating, and increasing the depth of the Great Depression has long been a topic of debate among international macroeconomists. The issues are reviewed in Box 6.6.

During the Great Depression international macroeconomic relations deteriorated into a series of competitive devaluations among trading blocs (recall that increases in the price of gold are expansionary in our model) and substantial intervention with trade and capital flows for macroeconomic reasons. The result was a collapse of international trade and finance that effectively ended the great pre-World War I era of globalization. Floating exchange rates prevailed among the major currencies during the immediate post-World War I years 1919 to 1925, and then again after 1936.

## Empirical Study 6.1    How the Gold Standard Worked

An early interpretation of how the gold standard worked in terms of a small open economy model with high integration in both goods and capital markets was by McCloskey and Zecher (1976). McCloskey and Zecher disputed an interpretation of how the gold standard worked in terms of Hume's price specie flow mechanism (see Appendix 6.1), which relies on imperfect goods market integration and gradual adjustment through the current account of the balance of payments as the result of real exchange rate changes. They argued for an alternative interpretation that took both goods and financial markets to be highly integrated, at least for the major gold standard countries, with capital flows providing the primary adjustment mechanism to eliminate balance of payments deficits or surpluses, as in the model of this chapter.

Their empirical argument consisted of two parts:

a    They maintained that goods markets were highly integrated, so domestic and foreign prices tended to move together in the main gold standard countries. This suggested to them that relative price changes could not have been a major part of the adjustment mechanism. A regression of annual changes in British wheat prices on American wheat prices during 1880–1913 yielded a coefficient of 0.646, which McCloskey and Zecher interpreted as sufficiently close to unity, in light of likely errors in measurement, as to suggest a unified, closely arbitraged market. Moreover, correlations among US, British, and German wheat prices during this period were as high as those among pairs of German cities, again suggesting a unified market for wheat among these countries. Such correlations were not restricted to goods such as wheat, however, since correlations between broader wholesale price indices between the United States and Britain were also found to be high during this period. Finally, though wholesale price indices tend to weigh goods exposed to international competition relatively heavily, bilateral correlations did not diminish significantly when more comprehensive indices, such as GDP deflators, were considered. They concluded that arbitrage was highly effective, and therefore that relative price changes were probably not an important part of the adjustment mechanism.

b    To propose an alternative adjustment mechanism through the capital account, McCloskey and Zecher derived an expression for the balance of payments under the gold standard which, in terms of our model, essentially constituted of substituting equation (6.1) into (6.2) and taking first differences of the resulting equation (i.e., subtracting last period's value of the equation from the current period's value). This yields an expression for the change in the central bank's gold stock given by:

$$P_G \Delta Au = \Delta(PL[R, Y]) - \Delta B_C$$

where $\Delta X = X - X_{-1}$. By estimating the money demand function $PL(R, Y)$ for the United States and Britain during 1880–1913 and subtracting changes in the domestic component of the money supply $\Delta B_C$ from changes in the fitted values of this equation, they generated annual estimates of the balance of payments for the two countries under the assumptions of their model. They found that the predicted values of the balance of payments for both countries matched the actual values quite closely, and concluded that a model featuring high degrees of integration in both goods and financial markets, with balance of payments adjustment occurring through the effects of capital flows on the domestic money supply, provided a better description of how the gold standard worked than Hume's price specie flow mechanism.

## 6.5    Summary

In this chapter we have developed our first open-economy macroeconomic model and used it to analyze how small open economies behave both in the short run as well as in the long run under conditions of high capital mobility and a fixed exchange rate. We were particularly interested in understanding the workings of a hard exchange rate peg. This refers to an exchange rate regime in which the central bank has no discretion over the exchange rate and in which changes in monetary policy depend only on balance of payments outcomes.

The gold standard era was a period in which the financial markets of the participating countries were highly integrated. Thus, we analyzed gold standard macroeconomics under the assumptions of credibly fixed exchange rates and high capital mobility. We saw that under these conditions, real shocks to the economy had large effects on domestic economic activity, and both international business cycles as well as changes in international economic conditions were strongly transmitted to the participating economies. As we shall see in Chapter 9, modern versions of hard pegs, in the form of currency boards and dollarization, tend to have similar properties.

The gold standard effectively ended during the period between the two world wars of the 20th century, a period during which the highly ''globalized'' conditions prevailing among the major trading economies also came to an end. The international monetary system that succeeded the gold standard was similarly characterized by fixed exchange rates, but as we shall see in the next chapter, it did not feature hard pegs and mobility of capital among countries was highly imperfect. In Chapters 7 and 8 we will explore how these changes in circumstances affected macroeconomic behavior.

## Questions

1   Consider the case of a gold-standard economy.
   a   What effect would you expect an increase in thee price of gold to have on the level of domestic real GDP, and why?
   b   What effect would you expect the change in real GDP to have on net exports?
   c   What is the net effect of the increase in the price of gold and the change in real GDP on net exports, and why?
2   In ''The Economic Consequences of Mr. Churchill'' John Maynard Keynes lambasted Winston Churchill for returning the United Kingdom to its prewar gold parity after World War I despite the much higher inflation experienced by the United Kingdom than by the United States during the war years.
   a   Based on what you have learned in this chapter, explain what consequences you would have expected Mr Churchill's actions to have had on the following UK macro variables:
      i   Net exports
      ii   The nonreserve financial account of the balance of payments
      iii   Domestic nominal interest rates
      iv   Domestic real GDP.
   b   Based on the information given, would you characterize Mr Keynes or Mr Churchill as a believer in purchasing power parity? Explain.
3   While in theory the process of adjusting the overall balance of payments from one position of equilibrium to another after a shock during the gold standard era involved the shipping of gold between central banks, many observers have noted that despite the prevalence of a variety of macroeconomic shocks during that time, gold flows between countries tended to be relatively small. Can you explain why this might have been?
4   Consider a country that was debating whether to adopt the gold standard during the heyday of that international monetary arrangement. What difference would the level at

which the price of gold was set by the central bank make for the level of economic activity in the country? Explain.

5 During the gold standard era, London was the world's financial center and the Bank of England the most important financial institution in the world. Suppose that the financial prominence of the United Kingdom implied that that country could be considered as a financial "large" country, which you can take to mean that the Bank of England could set the domestic interest rate for the United Kingdom as a policy variable, rather than taking it as given from the UIP condition. What factors should have guided the Bank of England's interest rate policy for the gold standard system as a whole to have promoted international price stability?

## Further Reading and References

### On how the gold standard worked

McCloskey, Donald N., and J. Richard Zecher (1976), "How the Gold Standard Worked," in J. Frenkel and H. Johnson, eds., *The Monetary Approach to the Balance of Payments* (Surrey, George Allen & Unwin), pp. 357–85.

### On economic performance under the gold standard

Neely, Christopher J., and Geoffrey E. Wood (1995), "Deflation and Real Economic Activity under the Gold Standard," Federal Reserve Bank of St. Louis *Review* (September/October), pp. 27–37.

### On the role of the gold standard in the great depression

Eichengreen, Barry (1995), *Golden Fetters: The Gold Standard and the Great Depression, 1919–1939* (Oxford: Oxford University Press).
Eichengreen, Barry and Peter Temin (1997), "The Gold Standard and the Great Depression," NBER Working Paper 6060 (June).
Hall, Thomas E. and J. David Ferguson (1998), *The Great Depression* (Ann Arbor: University of Michigan Press).
Romer, Christina (1993), "The Nation in Depression," *Journal of Economic Perspectives* Vol. 7, No. 2 (Spring), pp. 19–39.
Temin, Peter (1993), "Transmission of the Great Depression," *Journal of Economic Perspectives* Vol. 7, No. 2 (Spring), pp. 87–102.

## Appendix 6.1   The Gold Standard with Zero Capital Mobility

How would the gold standard have worked if there had been no capital movements? In the absence of links between the domestic and international capital markets, there would have been no UIP curve, and after a shock such as those examined in this chapter, the temporary equilibrium determined by the intersection between the domestic GM and MM curves would not have been disturbed by capital inflows and outflows. However, that equilibrium would nonetheless have been unsustainable to the extent that it was associated with a surplus or deficit in net exports, because that deficit or surplus would have resulted in gold outflows (or inflows) that would have affected the domestic money supply, and thus shifted the MM curve.

To see the implications of this mechanism (called the **specie flow mechanism** under the gold standard) consider the effect of a fiscal shock. In the figure below, the GM and MM

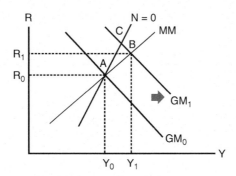

**Figure A6.1**   Effects of real shocks with no capital mobility

curves are reproduced as before, but now instead of containing a UIP line, the figure contains a line labeled $N = 0$. This line describes the set of all combinations of $R$ and $Y$ consistent with a zero value of net exports. It is drawn with a positive slope, because an increase in domestic output increases imports, and thus requires an increase in the domestic interest rate to restore a zero value of net exports.

Suppose the economy starts from a balanced-trade position such as the point A. As shown earlier in Chapter 6, an increase in $G$ causes the GM curve to shift to the right, resulting in a new temporary equilibrium where the GM and MM curves intersect at the point B. But at B, the economy will not generally find itself on the $N = 0$ curve. It may be to the right or to the left of it, depending on whether the $N = 0$ curve is steeper or shallower than the MM curve. If the new equilibrium is to the right of the $N = 0$ line, $Y$ is too high for trade to remain balanced, that is, net exports must be negative. Since there are no capital movements, the overall balance of payments must be in deficit as well, implying gold outflows. But, under the rules of the game, this means that the domestic money supply must be decreasing, that is, the MM curve must be shifting to the left. This must continue as long as trade remains unbalanced, meaning until the MM curve has shifted leftward enough to cause it to pass through the intersection of the GM and $N = 0$ curves. As this point the economy will reach a new equilibrium with a higher value of $Y$ and a higher domestic interest rate than at A. Similarly, if the point B lies to the left of the $N = 0$ curve, net exports will be positive, and in that case reserve inflows will expand the money supply, causing the MM curve to shift to the *right* until it passes through the intersection of GM and $N = 0$. The end result is the same in either case: a higher equilibrium level of output and higher domestic interest rate. Notice what closing the capital account has done: whereas fiscal policy was relatively powerful with an open capital account, because of the absence of crowding out caused by UIP, now fiscal policy has much weaker effects on the economy.

The original analysis of this mechanism dates back to the Scottish philosopher David Hume, who described it in the 18th century. Hume's adjustment mechanism was formulated in a flexible-price context, rather than the sticky-price version considered above. In Hume's formulation, therefore, expansionary domestic policies would have triggered a deterioration in the current account by causing an increase in the domestic price level, thus resulting in an appreciation of the real exchange rate. The resulting deterioration of the current account would cause gold to flow out of the domestic economy, contracting the money supply. Contractionary domestic policies would have produced the opposite effect. Because it operated through changes in the domestic price level rather than real output, this original formulation of the adjustment mechanism under the gold standard is referred to as the **price specie flow mechanism**.

# 7

# The Bretton Woods System

.......................................................................................................................................

As we saw in Chapter 6, the international gold standard prevailed during a period of time when the major trading economies were highly integrated with each other, both in markets for goods and services as well as in markets for financial assets. But this high degree of economic integration did not turn out to be permanent. As discussed in Chapter 6, after the gold standard collapsed the leading economies tended to turn inward. Barriers to trade in goods and services, as well as to capital flows between countries, proliferated throughout the world economy.

In this chapter we will examine the macroeconomics of imperfect international integration, specifically under the international monetary system that emerged after World War II. This new system, known as the **Bretton Woods system** after the small town in New Hampshire that hosted the conference at which the structure of the system was agreed upon, was characterized by fixed exchange rates, just as the gold standard had been. But during most of the time that the Bretton Woods system was in place, approximately 1946 to 1973, the vast majority of the economies that participated in the system had restrictions in place both on trade in goods and services as well as on capital movements. While restrictions on trade in goods and services were gradually eased during this period, capital account restrictions remained in place much longer. These restrictions did not make it impossible for capital to flow between countries, but greatly reduced the ease with which it could do so. Thus, the Bretton Woods system was characterized by *fixed exchange rates* and *imperfect capital mobility*.

As we will see in the next part of this book, for industrial countries and for many middle-income countries, neither of these conditions remains true today. Most such economies operate floating exchange rates and are characterized by a high degree of capital mobility. Why, then, should we study the Bretton Woods system? As in the case of the gold standard, there are several reasons to do so.

First, the design of the international monetary system remains on the international policy agenda today, and in designing future international monetary arrangements, it is important to understand the experience of the world economy with past arrangements.

Second, the option of adopting fixed exchange rates and imposing restrictions on capital movements remains very much open to individual countries today.[1] Thus, it is important to understand how macroeconomic behavior would be affected under such a policy regime.

Third, as we saw in Chapter 3, the majority of countries in the world still operate with traditional fixed exchange rates, and most of those countries are at best only imperfectly integrated with world financial markets.[2] Indeed, as Empirical Study 7.1 indicates, some economists have suggested that fixed exchange rates are even more prevalent in the world than the official exchange rate regime classifications would indicate.

Finally, and perhaps most importantly, the set of contemporary economies that operate under officially determined exchange rates and are only imperfectly integrated into international financial markets includes two of the world's largest countries, which also happen to possess two of the world's most rapidly growing economies: China and India. Accordingly, a macroeconomic environment characterized by fixed exchange rates and imperfect capital mobility aptly describes the situation in which most of the world's people live today.

We begin this chapter by examining the evolution of the Bretton Woods system. We then explore how the benchmark model that we developed in Chapter 4 can be adapted to investigate the macroeconomics of fixed exchange rates and imperfect capital mobility. Finally, we will look more closely at how bond market equilibrium is determined when capital mobility is imperfect, since that is one of the most important differences between the analysis of this chapter and that of Chapter 6.

## 7.1 Evolution of the Bretton Woods System

### Historical Background

In Chapter 5, we saw how the international gold standard arose spontaneously as the result of individual countries' use of gold as the standard of value for their currencies. By contrast, an important characteristic of the post-World War II international monetary system was that it was a *planned* arrangement, reflecting the prevailing views and experiences of the economic thinkers of the time. The new system was created in July 1944, as the product of an agreement among the Allied countries in anticipation of the end of the war. As mentioned above, it is usually referred to as the Bretton Woods system, named for the small town in New Hampshire where the conference establishing the arrangement took place. The conference was attended by 730 delegates representing 44 Allied nations. The agreements reached at this conference were ratified shortly thereafter by those countries, and the new system came into effect in 1946.

---

[1]   Indeed, Malaysia adopted just such a set of policies in 1998, in response to the 1997 Asian financial crisis.

[2]   Isard (2005), for example, judges that 130 of the IMF's 184 member countries are not extensively involved in international capital markets and notes that pegged exchange rates remain an attractive option for these countries.

As we saw in Chapter 6, the gold standard as an international monetary system collapsed during the depression decade of the 1930s. The decade of the 1930s was characterized by competitive devaluations intended to stimulate the depressed economies of the major trading nations, by trade barriers intended to bottle up aggregate demand in those countries (that is, orient demand toward domestic goods), and by capital controls intended to prevent capital outflows when domestic monetary policy turned expansionary. This experience, combined with the implications of the emergence of a new Keynesian perspective on macroeconomics that accorded the government a major role in preserving macroeconomic stability (John Maynard Keynes' *General Theory of Employment, Interest, and Money* was published in 1936), had a major impact on the international monetary system that emerged after World War II.

Given this background, the design of the Bretton Woods system reflected two prevailing views of its framers:

1  The system was designed to contain features that would help it avoid the cycles of competitive devaluation and trade restrictions that prevailed before the war.
2  Since in the new Keynesian perspective, governments bore an important responsibility for the performance of their domestic economies, and since price-wage flexibility could not be relied upon to keep economies at full employment, the system needed to allow for an appropriate preoccupation with "internal balance" (noninflationary full employment) as a policy objective on the part of all governments, rather than simply assume that the maintenance of the value of the currency would constitute an overriding objective for government policy.

## Structure of the System

The new system was asymmetric, treating the United States differently from the rest of the participating economies. The United States undertook the obligation to exchange dollars for gold, in gold-standard fashion, at the fixed price of $35/ounce that the United States government had established domestically in 1934. Other countries, however, fixed an exchange rate (known as a **par value**) against the US dollar, rather than against gold, with narrow fluctuation bands of 1 percent on either side of the rate.[3]

Note that the United States would need to hold gold reserves in order to defend the $35/ounce price of gold, but that other countries would not necessarily need to do so, since their central banks were committed to intervening directly in the foreign exchange market rather than in the market for gold. They could choose to hold their reserves in the form of either gold or US dollars. The dollars could be used directly to intervene in the foreign exchange market, while gold could always be turned into dollars for the purpose of intervention simply by selling it to the United States at the official price. This asymmetric arrangement reflected two important characteristics of the postwar international economy: first, at the end of World War II, the United States held a disproportionate share of the world's monetary gold (about 75 percent of the total in 1949); second, the size and relative health

---

[3]  Because of this asymmetric obligation (the United States kept reserves in gold, while other countries did so largely in dollars), the system was known as a **gold exchange standard**.

of the American economy, as well as its large and relatively highly developed financial system, had combined to make the US dollar the international vehicle currency (recall from Chapter 2 that this is the currency in which most foreign exchange transactions take place) at this time.[4]

The system was monitored through a newly created supranational organization called the **International Monetary Fund** (IMF). The IMF was a fund into which governments deposited money according to assigned quotas determined by country size and trading weight in the world economy. One-quarter of the quota was paid in the form of reserves (gold or dollars), and the rest in domestic currency. The IMF was governed by an Executive Board consisting of representatives of all member countries, whose voting rights were apportioned according to quota size.

The IMF was essentially designed to prevent the emergence in the future of the destructive policies that had undermined the international trading system during the interwar period. It was intended to do so in two ways:

1    Countries that were losing reserves (that is, those that were experiencing balance of payments deficits) could borrow from the IMF if those deficits were perceived by the IMF to be temporary. Small amounts of borrowing (up to one-half of their quotas) were essentially automatic, but larger amounts required the countries to demonstrate that the deficits were indeed temporary, if necessary by promising to undertake policy measures that would make them so (these measures were referred to as **policy conditionality**).

2    At the same time, countries with balance of payments problems that were not perceived to be temporary (that is, whose problems reflected a **fundamental disequilibrium**) could devalue their currencies, under certain conditions. Devaluations of up to 10 percent of the currency's par value did not require consultation with the IMF. But countries could not devalue by more than 10 percent without the IMF's permission (granted through its Executive Board). Because par values relative to the US dollar could be changed, the system was actually an **adjustable peg** system.

The ability of countries to borrow from the IMF and inability to undertake large unilateral devaluations were measures intended to prevent competitive devaluations such as those that became common during the interwar period. The options of borrowing and/or devaluing were also intended to prevent such countries from resorting to trade restrictions by giving them alternative ways to cope with deficits in their balance of payments. The fact that exchange rate pegs were regarded as adjustable, on the other hand, respected countries' concerns with domestic macroeconomic objectives, since countries did not have to follow the gold standard ''rules of the game'' to restore balance of payments equilibrium when they made use of this instrument. The system did not establish clear rules for when a par value should change, however. It is worth noting that under this system, the United States could not devalue or revalue against other currencies by itself.

---

[4]    It is worth noting that this arrangement had the important advantage, relative to the international gold standard, that, to the extent that countries were induced to hold dollars as reserves instead of gold, it economized on the sterile use as international reserves of a valuable commodity (gold), just as the earlier development of paper money had done domestically.

## Implications for Central Bank Behavior

The design of the new system had important implications for central bank behavior. First, the Bretton Woods system, like the gold standard, was a fixed exchange rate system. However, unlike the gold standard, under the Bretton Woods system central banks were obliged to participate in the foreign exchange market directly. Their obligation was essentially to offer a perfectly elastic demand/supply of their own currencies at the officially determined exchange rate (the par value of the currency). This meant that, as under the gold standard, central banks had no discretion over their accumulation of reserves. Their reserve accumulation was the passive response to overall balance of payments surpluses or deficits generated by other agents in their transactions with the rest of the world. Thus, under the Bretton Woods system the nominal exchange rate $S$ was an exogenous policy variable, while the central bank's stock of international reserves $F_C^*$ was endogenous.

Finally, unlike under the gold standard, central banks retained monetary discretion under the Bretton Woods system. That is, there was not even the presumption that a rigid tie would exist between their money supplies and their stocks of foreign exchange reserves, as in the third of the gold standard "rules of the game," leaving them free to alter their amount of domestic bonds, $B_C$, as they saw fit. Thus, unlike the case under the gold standard, $B_C$ became a policy variable. Since under Bretton Woods, countries retained the discretion to dedicate monetary policy to domestic economic objectives (rather than tying changes in the money supply to changes in foreign exchange reserves), and since exchange rates were explicitly adjustable, according to the definition given in Chapter 5, this type of arrangement can be characterized as a soft exchange-rate peg.

We saw in Chapter 6 that the link between monetary policy and changes in reserves that is created under hard pegs tends to stabilize reserves when the economy adjusts to shocks. This automatic stabilization cannot be taken for granted under soft exchange rate pegs such as those that existed under the Bretton Woods system. How, then, did countries assure that they would always have enough reserves to meet their fixed-exchange rate obligations under the Bretton Woods system?

One possibility would have been for central banks to be judicious in their pursuit of domestic objectives at the expense of external objectives, that is, that central banks would have used their discretion over monetary policy to expand the money supply when the balance of payments was in surplus and contract it when it was in deficit, thereby tending to stabilize reserve flows and in that way protect the par values of their currencies, essentially *choosing* to do what a hard peg would *compel* them to do. As we will see in the next chapter, however, such behavior was certainly not general under Bretton Woods.

Another possibility would have been for the problem to be solved through the lending and policy conditionality of the IMF, which were explicitly designed to address this issue by providing additional reserves when needed and inducing policy adjustments that would tend to rectify payments imbalances. The IMF certainly played a role in facilitating balance of payments adjustment under the Bretton Woods system. However, though there were some prominent exceptions (such as loans to the United Kingdom during the Suez crisis in 1958 and to France in 1968), the IMF was much more involved in lending to smaller developing countries than to major industrial countries.

Instead, a third factor was probably more important. Besides the fact that the option to devalue was explicitly retained, another important difference between the gold standard and Bretton Woods was that, whereas the gold standard involved unrestricted convertibility of domestic currencies into gold, whether for current or capital account transactions, *restrictions on capital account convertibility were explicitly allowed under Bretton Woods*. As we have seen, many countries had implemented capital account restrictions before World War II. Some of these countries intensified restrictions during the war, and others introduced them. These restrictions were explicitly permitted under the Bretton Woods agreement and remained in place for much of the Bretton Woods period.

The implication of the fact that the Bretton Woods system constituted a soft peg and that capital account restrictions were a policy option was that portfolio managers had to contend both with exchange rate risk as well as political risk when comparing assets issued in different political jurisdictions (see Chapter 3). Such asymmetric risks tended to make assets issued in different political jurisdictions imperfect substitutes for each other. Thus, the Bretton Woods system can best be described as one characterized by a soft peg under conditions of imperfect capital mobility.

## 7.2    Modeling Soft Pegs with Imperfect Capital Mobility

In analyzing the macroeconomics of the gold standard, we employed a fixed exchange rate model with perfect capital mobility. We have just seen that the Bretton Woods system was also one with fixed exchange rates, but one in which the fixed exchange rate was soft and imperfect capital mobility was the rule. How do these modifications affect our previous analysis of the macroeconomics of fixed exchange rates?

The most important change we have to make to our model is that imperfect capital mobility requires us to use the bond market equilibrium condition (4.3a), rather than the uncovered interest parity equation (4.3b). Recall that the bond market equilibrium condition set the total supply of domestic bonds available to the private sector $B$-$B_C$ equal to the total demand for such bonds by domestic residents, given by $H[R, (1 + R^*) S^e_{+1}/S - 1](W_P - PL)$, and by foreign residents, given by $H^*[R, (1 + R^*)S^e_{+1}/S - 1]S(W_F^* - P^*L^*)$. We thus wrote the bond market equilibrium condition as:

$$B - B_C = H\left[R,(1 + R^*)S^e_{+1}/S - 1\right](W_P - PL) + H^*\left[R,(1 + R^*)S^e_{+1}/S - 1\right]$$
$$\times S\left(W_F^* - P^*L^*\right)$$

Assuming that the exchange rate is credibly fixed, we can set $S^e_{+1} = S$. Doing so allows us to simplify the equation above to:

$$B - B_C = H[R, R^*](W_P - PL) + H^*[R, R^*]S\left(W_F^* - P^*L^*\right)$$

The other change we need to make to the model of Chapter 6 concerns the central bank's balance sheet. Since under the Bretton Woods system central banks' official reserves were primarily held in foreign exchange rather than gold (at least by countries other than the United States), we can write the central bank's balance sheet in the form that we originally did in Chapter 4, with the central bank's assets consisting of foreign exchange $F_C^*$ and domestic bonds $B_C$:

$$SF_C^* + B_C = M$$

## Box 7.1    A Fixed-Exchange Rate Model with Imperfect Capital Mobility

**Central bank balance sheet**

$$SF_C^* + B_C = M \tag{7.1}$$

**Money market equilibrium**

$$M = PL(R, Y) \tag{7.2}$$

**Domestic bond market equilibrium**

$$B - B_C = H[R, R^*](W_P - PL(R, Y)) + H^*[R, R^*]S\big(W_F^* - P^*L^*(R^*, Y^*)\big) \tag{7.3}$$

**Domestic goods market equilibrium**

$$Y = \varphi(Q)A(Y - T, r) + G + X(Q, \theta) \tag{7.4}$$

**Real exchange rate**

$$Q = SP^*/P \tag{7.5}$$

**Fisher equation**

$$r = R \tag{7.6}$$

**Short-run aggregate supply**

$$P = \bar{P} \tag{7.7}$$

Our revised model is thus as described in Box 7.1 (for a list of variable definitions, see Box 4.1). Recall from Chapter 4 that the wealth variables $W_P$ and $W_F^*$ in equation (7.3) are predetermined, though they are affected by exchange rate changes. As before, $G$ and $T$ are fiscal policy variables determined by the government's budget, while $S$ and $B_C$ are the exchange rate and monetary policy variables controlled by the central bank. Since we are considering fixed exchange rates at present, $S$ will be exogenous in our model. The treatment of $B_C$, however, requires a little more discussion.

In Chapter 6, where we analyzed a hard peg with perfect capital mobility, we treated $B_C$ as endogenous and were able to solve our model with both $M$ and $B_C$ as endogenous variables by adding an equation that linked the two of them (the third of the three "rules of the game" under the gold standard). However, in the model we are analyzing now, while we retain the assumption of fixed exchange rates, we have abandoned that of perfect capital mobility. We will see shortly that under these circumstances, the domestic interest rate becomes

## Box 7.2   The Compact Version of the Bretton Woods Model

**Central bank balance sheet**

$$SF_C^* + B_C = M \tag{7.1'}$$

**Money market equilibrium**

$$M = \bar{P}L(R, Y) \tag{7.2'}$$

**Domestic bond market equilibrium**

$$B - B_C = H[R, R^*](W_P - \bar{P}L(R, Y)) + H^*[R, R^*]S\big(W_F^* - P^*L^*(R^*, Y^*)\big) \tag{7.3'}$$

**Goods market equilibrium**

$$Y = \varphi(SP^*/\bar{P})A(Y - T, R) + G + X(SP^*/\bar{P}, \theta) \tag{7.4'}$$

endogenous, with its behavior depending on the monetary policy pursued by the central bank. Since $B_C$ is the policy variable controlled by the central bank, we will treat it as exogenous, and examine how alternative monetary policy "regimes" (rules for setting $B_C$) affect the behavior of the domestic interest rate. Under these conditions, we are left with seven equations that we can use to solve for seven endogenous variables ($F_C$, $R$, $Y$, $r$, $Q$, $P$, and $M$).

To solve the model, we will proceed as we did in Chapter 6. The first step is to write it in more compact form. Using equations (7.4) to (7.7) in equations (7.2) and (7.3), as we did with the gold standard model, we can summarize our new model more compactly as in Box 7.2. This means that, just as with the perfect capital mobility model of the previous chapter, this new model becomes a system of four equations in the four unknowns $R$, $Y$, $F_C^*$, and $M$.

How do we solve this compact version of our model? Suppose that the central bank sets the value of $B_C$ exogenously. You can see that neither $M$ nor $F_C^*$ appear in the domestic bond market equilibrium and goods market equilibrium equations (7.3') and (7.4'). That means that we can use the bond market and goods market equilibrium conditions to solve for the domestic interest rate and level of output and then, given the equilibrium values of these two variables, we can determine the domestic money supply from the money-market equilibrium condition (7.2) and the central bank's stock of foreign exchange reserves from the central bank balance sheet (7.1).

As we did in Chapter 6, however, we will proceed graphically, drawing three curves:

- One that corresponds to equation (7.2), drawn for a fixed value of $M$, which we will call MM, since it is identical to the closed-economy MM curve.
- One that is the graphical representation of equation (7.3'), that is, that corresponds to equilibrium between the supply and demand for bonds, which we will call *BB*.
- One depicting the goods market equilibrium shown in equation (7.4), denoted GM just as before.

By comparing the expressions for the MM and GM curves in Boxes 6.2 and 7.2, you can verify that the MM and GM curves are unchanged from those of Chapter 6. However, the *BB* curve in Box 7.2 replaces the UIP curve in Box 6.2. Before we solve the model, therefore, we need to derive the BB curve.

## 7.3    The Bond Market Equilibrium (BB) Curve

To do so, consider the bond market equilibrium diagram shown in Figure 7.1, which illustrates the two sides of equation (7.3'). The supply of domestic bonds available to the private sector, given by $B - B_C$, is depicted as a vertical straight line in Figure 7.1, since it is independent of the bond interest rate $R$. The upward-sloping curve labeled $B^D$, on the other hand, represents the aggregate demand for domestic bonds by both the domestic and the foreign private sectors together.

To see that the curve depicting the demand for domestic bonds must have a positive slope, consider what happens to the demand for domestic bonds when the domestic interest rate rises. Foreigners will switch their bond portfolios from foreign to domestic bonds, so the foreign component of demand for domestic bonds increases. What about demand by domestic residents? In their case there are two influences at work: an increase in $R$ causes domestic residents to switch from foreign to domestic bonds just as foreign residents do, increasing their demand for domestic bonds. At the same time, though, the increase in $R$ also induces them to switch from holding domestic money to holding more of both domestic and foreign bonds. Because both of these effects work to increase the demand for domestic bonds by domestic residents, their demand for domestic bonds must also increase when the domestic interest rate rises. Thus the aggregate demand for domestic bonds $B^D$, which includes both foreign and domestic demand, must increase when the domestic interest rate increases.

As you will soon see, the flatness or steepness of the $B^D$ curve will turn out to be an important issue. This curve will be flatter the more responsive the demand for domestic bonds is to the domestic interest rate. Responsiveness, in turn, is determined by the degree of substitutability between domestic and foreign bonds. The more similar domestic and foreign

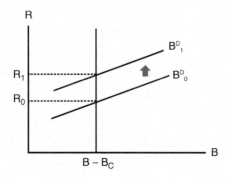

**Figure 7.1**    Domestic bond market equilibrium

bonds are to each other, the more the demand for domestic bonds by both domestic and foreign residents will be affected when the domestic interest rate changes. Thus, the greater the degree of substitutability between domestic and foreign bonds, the flatter the $B^D$ curve will be.

The equilibrium value of the domestic interest rate is determined by the intersection of $B^D$ and $B - B_C$, and is labeled $R_0$ in Figure 7.1. This essentially determines the value of the domestic interest rate required for the domestic and foreign private sectors to willingly hold the supply of domestic bonds that the domestic central bank makes available to them.

Next we will explore what happens to this equilibrium interest rate as domestic output $Y$ changes. For concreteness, consider the effects of an increase in $Y$. As we have seen, an increase in $Y$ causes domestic residents to increase their demand for money. Since their total financial wealth is fixed, this means that they must reduce their demand for bonds of all types, including domestic bonds. Suppose a one-unit increase in $Y$ causes domestic residents to increase their demand for money by the amount $L_Y$. This means that domestic residents wish to increase their monetary wealth by $L_Y$ and decrease their nonmonetary wealth by $L_Y$. Since a fraction $H$ of domestic residents' nonmonetary wealth is allocated to domestic bonds and a fraction $1 - H$ to foreign bonds, the demand for domestic bonds will fall by a fraction $H$ of the increase in the demand for money – that is, by $HL_Y$. This reduction in the demand for domestic bonds must cause the bond demand curve $B^D$ to shift to the left by the amount $HL_Y$, to a position such as $B_1^D$ in Figure 7.1. Since the supply of domestic bonds is unchanged, at the original domestic interest rate $R_0$ there is now an excess supply of domestic bonds. The domestic interest rate must therefore rise to make domestic bonds more attractive to hold. The new equilibrium value of the domestic interest rate is $R_1$. The implication of this analysis is that increases in $Y$ result in increases in the interest rate that clear the domestic bond market.

By repeating this exercise for alternative values of $Y$, we can identify the set of all combinations of $Y$ and $R$ that are consistent with equilibrium in the domestic bond market. Figure 7.2 traces out this set of points in $R$-$Y$ space. Based on the analysis just completed, the resulting curve must have a positive slope. We will refer to it as the BB curve. It is the analogue of the UIP curve under imperfect capital mobility. The BB curve will be an important tool in our analysis of open economies that maintain a fixed exchange rate under conditions of imperfect capital mobility. Thus our next task will be to explore the properties of the BB curve.

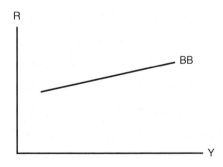

**Figure 7.2**   The bond-market equilibrium (BB) curve

## 7.4 Properties of the BB Curve

Just as we did for the GM and MM curves in Chapter 6, we will now explore several properties of the BB curve. First, we will be interested in investigating what determines the shape (flatness or steepness) of the curve. Since both the MM and BB curves have positive slopes, we also need to investigate the relative slopes of the two curves. Finally, we will examine the factors that determine the position of the curve, as well as what happens when the economy is off the BB curve.

### Shape of the BB Curve

The first question is what determines how flat or how steep the BB curve is. It is easy to see that the BB curve will be flatter the smaller the change in $R$ that is required to offset the effects of a given change in $Y$ on the domestic bond market – in other words, when changes in $Y$ have relatively weak effects on the bond market and changes in $R$ have relatively strong ones. Changes in $Y$ will have weak effects on the domestic bond market when the demand for money is not very sensitive to changes in $Y$ and when domestic residents hold a relatively small share of their nonmonetary wealth in the form of domestic bonds. Under these conditions, changes in $Y$ will cause relatively small shifts in domestic residents' preferences between domestic bonds and money. Together these factors make $HL_Y$ small and thus reduce the size of the leftward shift in the $B^D$ curve in Figure 7.1 when $Y$ rises. Changes in $R$, on the other hand, will have stronger effects on the domestic bond market the more responsive the demand for domestic bonds is to the domestic interest rate (that is, the *flatter* the $B^D$ curve), which in turn will be true when domestic and foreign bonds are close substitutes – i.e. when the domestic economy is closely integrated with the international economy financially. Under this set of conditions, the BB curve will be relatively flat, since a given change in $Y$ would require only a small change in $R$ for the domestic bond market to remain in equilibrium. Note that in the extreme case when domestic and foreign bonds are *perfect* substitutes for each other, the $B^D$ of Figure 7.1 becomes completely flat and is unresponsive to changes in $Y$. In that case, the BB curve is also completely flat, and we are back to the UIP curve of Chapter 6.

### BB and MM

Recall that in the last chapter we plotted the domestic money market equilibrium condition (7.2′) in the form of a positively sloped MM curve. A second important question to ask about the BB curve is whether it is steeper or flatter than the MM curve. It turns out that the MM curve must be steeper as long as there is *any* substitutability between domestic and foreign bonds in the portfolios of private agents.

To see why, notice that the question of which curve is steeper boils down to the following: for a given increase in $Y$, is the increase in the domestic interest rate required to restore equilibrium in the money market greater or less than that required to restore equilibrium in the bond market? If it is greater, then the MM curve must be steeper, and if it is less, then the BB curve must be steeper.

To answer this question, recall that an increase in $Y$ increases the demand for money by $L_Y$ and reduces the demand for domestic bonds by $HL_Y$. Because $H$ is a fraction, the impact of the increase in $Y$ on the domestic bond market must be *smaller* (in absolute value) than on the money market. Because both curves have positive slopes, an increase in $R$ is required to restore equilibrium in both markets. You can now see that if an increase in $R$ has a more powerful effect in restoring equilibrium in the bond market than in the money market, the BB curve must be flatter than the MM curve. This is so because a smaller change in $R$ is required to maintain equilibrium in the bond market than in the money market when $Y$ changes for *two* reasons: because changes in $Y$ have weaker effects on the bond market and because changes in $R$ are more effective in restoring equilibrium in that market. But changes in $R$ must indeed have more powerful effects on the domestic bond market than on the money market, because when $R$ rises, the increase in the demand for domestic bonds that this induces is the sum of the induced reduction in the demand for money *and* the induced reduction in the demand for foreign bonds by both domestic as well as by foreign residents. Thus, changes in $Y$ have *smaller* impacts, and changes in $R$ much *larger* impacts, on the bond market than on the money market. The implication is that smaller increments in $R$ are required to restore equilibrium after a given change in $Y$ in the bond market than in the money market, which means that the BB curve must be *flatter* than the MM curve.

## Bond Market Disequilibrium

Next, consider what happens when the economy is *not* on the BB curve. Notice that, by definition, the BB curve plots the value of the domestic interest rate that is consistent with equilibrium in the domestic bond market for different values of $Y$. Consequently, above the curve the interest rate on domestic bonds must be *too high* to clear the domestic bond market. Since bonds are more attractive when the interest rate that they pay is high, this must mean that above BB there must be an *excess demand* for domestic bonds. Below BB, therefore, where the interest rate is too low to clear the market, there must be an *excess supply* of domestic bonds. Since domestic and foreign residents will both be trying to acquire more domestic bonds when there is an excess demand for them, and to sell them when there is an excess supply of them, points above BB must be associated with *capital inflows* into the domestic economy, and points below it with *capital outflows*. Recall that this is exactly what happened in the case of the UIP curve of Chapter 6 (see p. 000 in Chapter 6).

## Position of BB

The final issue that we need to investigate is what determines the position of the BB curve. In general, the position of the curve will be affected by a change in any variable that alters the equilibrium interest rate in the bond market for a given value of $Y$. The set of factors that can have this effect includes changes in $B_C$, changes in the world interest rate, changes in foreign income, and changes in the exchange rate.

*Changes in $B_C$*    An open-market purchase of bonds by the central bank results in an increase in $B_C$ and thus a *decrease* in the supply of bonds held by the public, given by $B - B_C$. With an upward-sloping bond demand curve, this leftward shift in bond supply means that the

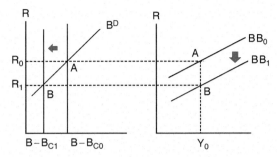

**Figure 7.3** Effect of expansionary monetary policy on the BB curve

equilibrium interest rate must fall in the bond-market equilibrium diagram, as shown in the left-hand panel of Figure 7.3. This reduction in the interest rate that domestic bonds pay creates a reduced demand for domestic bonds to match the reduced supply of such bonds available to the public. Since the equilibrium interest rate must fall for any given value of domestic real GDP, the BB curve must shift downward, as shown in the right-hand panel.

It is worth noting that this open-market purchase increases the supply of money in the hands of the public at the same time – and by exactly the same amount – that it decreases the supply of bonds. Thus it shifts *both* the MM and BB curves downward, or to the right. How do the shifts in the two curves compare? The size of the *downward* shift in the two curves is determined by the change in the interest rate required to restore equilibrium in each market after an increase in $B_C$. But we have already seen that changes in interest rates are more effective in restoring bond market equilibrium than in restoring money market equilibrium, so it must be the case that a smaller interest rate change is required to restore equilibrium in the bond market than in the money market – that is, the downward shift in BB must be *smaller* than that in MM. In Figure 7.4, for example, the MM curve shifts downward by the amount AC, while the BB curve shifts only by AB. Because interest rate changes have more powerful effects on the bond market the greater the degree of substitutability between domestic and foreign bonds, the downward shift in the BB curve will be smaller the higher the degree of capital mobility.

At the same time, the size of the *rightward* shift in the two curves is determined by the change in domestic output that would be required to restore equilibrium in each market after

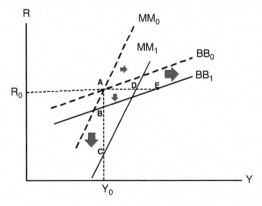

**Figure 7.4** Effects of expansionary monetary policy on the positions of the BB and MM curves

an increase in $B_C$, at a given value of $R$. Since we have seen that changes in $Y$ have a larger impact on the money market than on the market for domestic bonds (because only a fraction $H$ of the effect of a change in $Y$ on the demand for money is transmitted to the market for domestic bonds), it follows that a smaller increase in $Y$ is required to restore equilibrium in the money market than in the bond market. Thus the BB curve must shift to the right by more than the MM curve. The shift in the BB curve is by the amount AE in Figure 7.4, compared to AD for the MM curve.

*Changes in the World Interest Rate*    An increase in $R^*$ causes both domestic and foreign residents to switch away from domestic bonds and into foreign bonds. In the case of domestic residents, this change in portfolio composition results in an unambiguous decrease in their demand for domestic bonds. For foreign residents, however, two effects are at work in opposite directions.

While they too seek to switch from foreign to domestic bonds, the higher foreign interest rate induces them to hold less money and *more* bonds, both foreign as well as domestic. Thus, the increase in the nonmonetary component of their portfolio (the **portfolio scale effect**) and the desire to switch the composition of this portfolio away from domestic bonds (the **substitution effect**) have offsetting effects on their total demand for domestic bonds. To pin down the net effect of these countervailing influences, we will assume that domestic and foreign bonds are **gross substitutes** in the portfolios of foreign residents, that is, that the substitution effect dominates the portfolio scale effect, so that foreigners' demand for domestic bonds *decreases* when $R^*$ rises. Under this assumption, an increase in $R^*$ reduces the demand for domestic bonds (shifts the $B^D$ curve to the left, as in the left-hand panel of Figure 7.5), thus causing the equilibrium value of the domestic interest rate to rise. The upshot is that the BB curve must shift upward, as in the right-hand panel of Figure 7.5.

How large will this shift be? The answer is that *the upward shift in BB must be smaller than the increase in $R^*$*. To see why, suppose that BB shifts up by exactly as much as the change in $R^*$. In that case, since the *relative* returns on domestic and foreign bonds would be unchanged, it would be reasonable to suppose that people's preferences between the two types of bonds would remain unchanged as well, but since the opportunity cost of holding money would have risen in both the domestic and foreign economies, both domestic and foreign residents would want to hold more bonds, so there must exist an excess demand for domestic bonds. This means that an increase in $R$ equal to that in $R^*$ would be too large to restore equilibrium in the bond market, since it would *more* than eliminate the excess supply of domestic bonds, replacing it instead with an excess demand. The implication is that BB must shift upward when $R^*$ rises, but not by as much as the change in $R^*$.

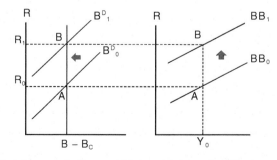

**Figure 7.5**    Effect of an increase in the world interest rate on the BB curve

*Changes in Foreign Income*    An increase in foreign real GDP ($Y^*$) causes foreigners to increase their demand for money, which means that they must reduce their demands for both domestic and foreign bonds. Since the aggregate demand for domestic bonds thus decreases, the $B^D$ curve must shift leftward. As we have already seen, a leftward shift in $B^D$ is associated with an upward shift in BB.

*Changes in the Exchange Rate*    Finally, suppose that there is a change in the exchange rate – for concreteness, assume a devaluation of the domestic currency (an increase in $S$). The key to understanding the effects of this shock on the domestic bond market is to note that as long as domestic and foreign residents both hold bonds denominated in each other's currencies, the **valuation effects** on these bonds (that is, the changes in their values when expressed in the portfolio managers' home currency) that are caused by the devaluation will result in portfolio imbalances for both domestic and foreign residents that will affect their demand for domestic bonds.

Specifically, the devaluation will give domestic residents a capital *gain* on the value of their foreign bonds (because these bonds will be worth more in domestic-currency terms). This increase in their financial wealth will cause domestic residents to want to hold more domestic bonds – that is, their demand for domestic bonds will rise. At the same time, foreign residents will suffer a capital *loss* on their domestic bonds (their foreign-currency value will fall). Consequently, they will find themselves with fewer of these bonds than they would like, despite the fact that their financial wealth has fallen. The reason is that their financial wealth goes down by an amount exactly equal to the reduction in the foreign-currency value of the domestic bonds that they hold, but for every \$1 loss in financial wealth their demand for domestic bonds goes down by only $1 - H^*$, so the supply of domestic bonds that they hold decreases more than their demand for such bonds, leaving them with an unsatisfied demand for domestic bonds. As a result, they also will try to acquire more of them. Since both domestic and foreign residents have an increased demand for domestic bonds, the $B^D$ curve shifts to the right, and thus a devaluation of the domestic currency must cause the BB curve to shift downward.

This concludes our investigation of the properties of the BB curve. Notice that it is substantially more complicated than the simple UIP curve: it has a positive slope that depends on the degree of capital mobility, and can be shifted by domestic monetary and exchange rate policies, as well as by foreign interest rate and income shocks. Moreover, even in the case of foreign interest rate shocks, which also affected the UIP curve, the effect on the BB curve is different – specifically, it is weaker since the vertical shift in the BB curve is less than one-for-one. However, like the UIP curve the BB curve has the property that points above it are associated with capital inflows into the domestic economy, and points below it with capital outflows.

---

## Empirical Study 7.1    Fear of Floating?

While the model introduced in this chapter is of historical interest, how great is its contemporary relevance? Figure 3.5 examined the official exchange rate arrangements of 188 countries. Of these, 23 maintained a hard peg, 82 some form of "soft" officially determined exchange rate consistent with the model of this chapter, and

*(Continued)*

**Empirical Study 7.1**    *(Continued)*

83 declared themselves as floating. But it is not clear that the *actual* exchange rate policies of these floaters have indeed been consistent with their official exchange rate regime, suggesting that there may be many more ''soft'' pegs in the world than the official declarations of the countries themselves would suggest.

This point was made in a well-known paper by Calvo and Reinhart (2002), who dubbed a *de facto* policy of pegging in the face of a *de jure* policy of floating ''fear of floating.'' Based on an analytical model, Calvo and Reinhart argued that if declared floaters actually intervened extensively to stabilize their exchange rates, we should observe less volatile exchange rates, and more volatile interest rates and monetary aggregates, in countries that engage in such intervention than in true floaters, assuming that both types of countries experience similar shocks. For small countries that can have no effect on the prices of their export commodities, fluctuations in the relative price of their exports in terms of their imports (known as their **terms of trade**) is a major source of macroeconomic shocks, driving business cycles in those economies. For such countries, Calvo and Reinhart argued that fear of floating should show up in the form of procyclical monetary policies – i.e., an expansion of the money supply when the country's terms of trade improve, and contraction when they deteriorate.

Calvo and Reinhart examined monthly data on a variety of financial and macroeconomic variables for 39 countries from January 1970 to April 1999. They calculated the absolute values of monthly percentage changes in exchange rates, reserves, and interest rates for each country, compiled the frequency distribution of such changes for each country, and then estimated the probability that changes would fall into specific bands. To classify countries' exchange rate regimes, they compared such probabilities with those of a reference group of ''pure'' floaters (the United States, Germany, and Japan). They found a large number of declared floaters whose exchange rate volatility was significantly less than that of the reference group, and whose reserve, interest rate, and money supply volatility was much greater. For the small commodity-exporting countries, the terms of trade turned out to be much more volatile than exchange rates, consistent with a preference on the part of these countries to stabilize the exchange rate, rather than allow it to respond to terms of trade shocks. The authors conclude that ''because countries that are classified as having a managed float mostly resemble noncredible pegs, the so-

## 7.5  Summary

This chapter has introduced the macroeconomics of imperfect financial integration under fixed exchange rates. We have seen that the first wave of globalization during the gold standard period ended with the imposition of barriers to trade in goods and financial assets during the Great Depression. The post-World War II international monetary system

---

[5]    For the case of Asia, see McKinnon (1999) and (2000).

designed at Bretton Woods featured fixed exchange rates, but endorsed the restrictions on capital movements that had been put in place before the war. The resulting international monetary system thus featured fixed exchange rates and imperfect capital mobility. This set of circumstances still characterizes many emerging and developing economies today, including some of the most important economies in the world.

The introduction of imperfect capital mobility requires us to modify the analytical framework that we use to understand how open economies work. The main modification to our previous analysis came in the form of an upward-sloping bond-market equilibrium (BB) curve that replaced the UIP curve of Chapter 6. We saw that the slope of this curve became flatter as the degree of a country's integration with world financial markets increased, and that the position of this curve could be affected by a variety of variables in addition to the world interest rate. Most importantly, the BB curve can be shifted by domestic monetary policy. In the next chapter we will explore the implications for macroeconomic behavior of replacing the UIP curve with the BB curve in our model.

## Questions

1  Suppose that you had been a foreign exchange dealer under the Bretton Woods system. How do you think that the officially determined parities would have affected your day-to-day operations?
2  Many economists claim that in a small open economy operating under a fixed exchange rate regime, the domestic central bank is powerless to control the money supply, and monetary policy is thus powerless as a tool to stabilize domestic output. Do you agree or disagree? Explain.
3  Many economies impose restrictions on international capital flows. Assuming that such restrictions limit the scope for arbitrage between domestic and foreign bonds, thereby effectively making such bonds poorer substitutes for each other, explain how the intensification of capital flow restrictions would affect the BB curve.
4  What would you expect to happen to the domestic money supply as $R$ and $Y$ both increase along a stable BB curve? Explain in intuitive terms what forces would tend to bring about such a change in the money supply.
5  What would you expect to happen to the stock of domestic bonds in the hands of the public as $R$ and $Y$ both increase along a stable MM curve? Explain in intuitive terms how such a change in the stock of domestic bonds in the hands of the public could be brought about.

## Further Reading and References

### On the Keynesian Revolution

Keynes, J.M. (1936), *The General Theory of Employment, Interest and Money* (London: Macmillan).

### On the history of the Bretton Woods System

Solomon, Robert (1977), *The International Monetary System, 1945–1976* (New York: Harper & Row).

Tew, Brian (1977), *The Evolution of the International Monetary System, 1945–77* (New York: Halsted Press).

## On the prevalence of imperfect financial integration among developing countries

Isard, Peter (2005), *Globalization and the International Financial System: What's Wrong? What Should Be Done?* (Cambridge: Cambridge University Press).

## On the prevalence of officially determined exchange rates among developing countries

Calvo, Guillermo, and Carmen Reinhart (2002), "Fear of Floating," *Quarterly Journal of Economics* Vol. CXVII, Issue 2 (May 2002), pp. 379–408.

McKinnon, Ronald I. (1999), "The East Asian Dollar Standard: Life after Death?" mimeo, World Bank (February).

McKinnon, Ronald I. (2000), "After the Crisis, the East Asian Dollar Standard Resurrected: An Interpretation of High-Frequency Exchange Rate Pegging," mimeo, Stanford University.

Reinhart, Carmen (2000), "The Mirage of Floating Exchange Rates," *American Economic Review Papers and Proceedings*, Vol. 90, No. 2 (May), pp. 65–70.

## On the Capital-Inflow Problem

Calvo, Gullermo, Leonrdo Leiderman, and Carmen Reinhart (1996), "Inflows of Capital to Developing Countries in the 1990s," *Journal of Economic Perspectives*, Vol. 10, Number 2 (Spring), pp. 123–39.

# 8

# Macroeconomics under "Soft" Pegs and Imperfect Capital Mobility

························································································································

In the last chapter we saw that the international monetary system that prevailed after World War II was quite different from the classical gold standard that preceded it. The two most important differences were that the degree of capital mobility among countries was greatly reduced, and that the officially determined exchange rates among currencies were no longer regarded as immutable. Instead, exchange rates were regarded as "fixed but adjustable" – that is, they became an instrument of economic policy. As mentioned in the last chapter, a situation in which capital mobility is less than perfect, and exchange rates are officially determined but subject to being altered as an instrument of macroeconomic policy, continues to characterize many developing countries today.[1]

These changes in the characteristics of the macroeconomic environment relative to those that prevailed under the gold standard require a change in the analytical framework that we use to analyze open-economy macroeconomic behavior. The key change is that the BB curve derived in Chapter 7 replaces the UIP curve of Chapter 6. Our next task is to examine how this change in our model affects the analysis of macroeconomic behavior in open economies. That is the task that we will undertake in this chapter. We will solve the new model in the next section, and will then turn to investigating how the economy adjusts to shocks under imperfect financial integration. The chapter concludes with an investigation of the demise of the Bretton Woods system and how the current international monetary system came to be.

---

[1]    Empirical Study 8.1 at the end of this chapter examines some evidence on both of these issues for the cases of Korea and Taiwan.

## Box 8.1   The Compact Version of the Bretton Woods Model

**Central bank balance sheet**

$$SF_C^* + B_C = M \tag{8.1}$$

**Money market equilibrium (MM)**

$$M = \bar{P}L(R, Y) \tag{8.2}$$

**Domestic bond market equilibrium (BB)**

$$B - B_C = H[R, R^*](W_P - \bar{P}L(R, Y)) + H^*[R, R^*]S\big(W_F^* - P^*L^*(R^*, Y^*)\big) \tag{8.3}$$

**Goods market equilibrium (GM)**

$$Y = \varphi(SP^*/\bar{P})A(Y - T, R) + G + X(SP^*/\bar{P}, \theta) \tag{8.4}$$

## 8.1   Solving the Model

Box 8.1 reproduces the compact version of the Bretton Woods model that we derived in Chapter 7. As with the gold standard model of Chapter 5, the model consists of four independent equations in five endogenous variables ($F_C^*$, $B_C$, $M$, $R$, and $Y$). Thus, before we can solve the model we need to make an assumption about the way that the central bank conducts monetary policy – i.e. about which variable is taken to be the exogenous monetary policy variable. Once we specify the exogenous monetary policy variable, the model will contain four independent equations in four endogenous variables. There are three possibilities, depending on whether the central bank targets $B_C$, $M$, or $R$ as its policy variable. These three options correspond to three different **monetary policy regimes**. We will refer to them as **domestic credit targeting**, **monetary targeting**, and **interest rate targeting** respectively.[2] Because domestic credit targeting is in many ways the most revealing of these alternatives for understanding how the model works, we will analyze the model under that assumption in the main body of the chapter, leaving monetary and interest targeting for an appendix.

As in Chapter 6, we will solve the model graphically. As indicated in Box 8.1, equations (8.2), (8.3), and (8.4) can be represented in the form of MM, BB, and GM curves in $R$-$Y$ space. These curves are dawn in Figure 8.1. Since all three equations have to hold simultaneously,

[2]   The term ''domestic credit'' comes from the traditional application of this model to developing countries. Since many of these countries lacked functioning securities markets until recently, the central bank provided loanable resources to the government by extending direct nonmarketable loans, rather than by buying government securities in an open market. The loans were entered in the central bank's books as ''domestic credit.''

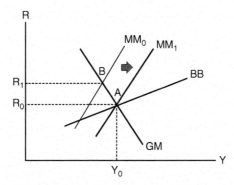

**Figure 8.1**  Macroeconomic equilibrium with imperfect capital mobility

the economy will be in equilibrium only where all three curves intersect – that is, at point A in Figure 8.1.

It is worth noting that, in contrast with the analysis in Chapter 6, the equilibrium value of the domestic interest rate does *not* have to coincide with the foreign interest rate $R^*$ under imperfect capital mobility, even if no future exchange rate changes are expected. The reason is that when domestic and foreign bonds are imperfect substitutes, the interest rate required for domestic bonds to be willingly held depends on the amount of such bonds that are in private hands. People may be willing to hold domestic bonds, for example, even if they pay an interest rate lower than what they can receive on foreign bonds simply because by doing so they can diversify their portfolios and decrease their overall portfolio risk.[3]

As in the case of the perfect capital mobility model, the equilibrium is determined by the intersection of two curves, with the third curve adjusting passively to that equilibrium. A key difference between the model of this chapter and that of Chapter 6, however, is that which curves pin down the macroeconomic equilibrium and which one adjusts passively depends on the monetary policy followed by the central bank. When the central bank targets $B_C$, the money supply becomes an endogenous variable, just as in the gold-standard model. It is demand-determined by equation (8.2), and given that $B_C$ is exogenously fixed, the quantity of money adjusts through a change in $F_C^*$, the magnitude of which is determined by equation (8.1). Thus, in terms of the equations of the model, equations (8.3) and (8.4) together determine $R$ and $Y$, while the roles of equations (8.2) and (8.1) are respectively to determine the money supply and the stock of foreign exchange reserves $F_C^*$. Graphically, the economy's equilibrium is determined by the intersection of GM and BB, as at the point A in Figure 8.1, and MM must adjust passively to this point.

To see the economics of the situation, suppose that the MM curve initially passes through a point on the GM curve that lies above the BB curve, as the curve $MM_0$ does at point B in Figure 8.1. At B the domestic interest rate is too high to sustain bond market equilibrium – that is, there is an excess demand for domestic bonds. As we saw in the last chapter, this situation would give rise to capital inflows, as both domestic and foreign residents seek to acquire additional domestic bonds. Since the assumption that the central bank fixes $B_C$ – and therefore does not *sterilize* the effects of capital flows on the domestic money supply – implies that the resulting increase in its foreign exchange reserves is allowed by the central

---

[3]  These diversification benefits decrease as domestic bonds become a larger and larger part of financial portfolios, that is, as the supply of domestic bonds increases.

bank to increase the money supply, the MM curve must shift to the right. This process must continue as long as the point of intersection of GM and MM lies above BB, so it continues until the MM curve intersects GM and BB at a point like A. The mechanism would work in reverse, shifting MM to the left, if the initial intersection of GM and MM lies below BB.

## 8.2    Comparative Statics

To understand how the economy works with fixed exchange rates under conditions of imperfect capital mobility, we can examine how it adjusts to a variety of exogenous shocks. Since central banks have discretion over monetary policy under soft pegs such as those prevailing under Bretton Woods, a useful point of departure is to investigate how this policy instrument works. Next, we will examine how imperfect capital mobility affects the consequences of aggregate demand shocks. Finally, we will examine the domestic macro-economic effects of external financial shocks, including both changes in world interest rates and in the exchange rate.

### Monetary Shocks

Because central banks have no discretion over monetary policy under hard pegs, when we examined the effects of monetary shocks under the gold standard in Chapter 6 we considered only money demand shocks. We saw that such shocks had no effects on the economy's short-run equilibrium other than to change the money supply and the central bank's stock of foreign exchange reserves. As mentioned above, central banks can employ an active monetary policy under soft pegs, so it is useful to begin by examining how this policy works under conditions of imperfect capital mobility.

Consider, then, how the economy is affected by an expansionary monetary policy shock in the form of an open market purchase of bonds by the central bank. An open market purchase is captured in our model in the form of an increase in $B_C$. As we saw in the last chapter, this causes both the MM and BB curves to shift down and to the right, and we have already seen that the MM curve must shift downward by more than the BB curve, but rightward by less. The impact of the increase in $B_C$ on the MM and BB curves is illustrated in Figure 8.2a.

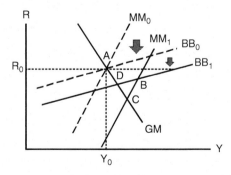

**Figure 8.2a**    Effects of a monetary expansion with high capital mobility

How is the economy's equilibrium affected by this shock? In the absence of capital flows (that is, if the capital account were completely closed), the new equilibrium would be at a point such as C in Figure 8.2a, corresponding to the intersection of the new MM curve with the GM curve. Now let's see what happens in the case of imperfect capital mobility.

A crucial issue in understanding how the new equilibrium is attained is whether there is an excess demand for or supply of domestic bonds at C, and thus whether the expansionary monetary policy triggers a capital inflow or outflow. In principle the outcome could go either way. While the lower domestic interest rate that prevails at C than at A would tend to trigger a capital *outflow* because it induces switching from domestic to foreign bonds, the higher level of domestic real GDP at C causes domestic residents to hold more money and fewer bonds. Since this means that domestic residents wish to hold fewer foreign bonds, they would tend to repatriate capital, thus inducing a capital *inflow*.

Recall from Chapter 7 that points above the BB curve are associated with capital inflows and those below it with capital outflows. Since the monetary expansion shifts the BB curve, whether it triggers a capital inflow or outflow therefore depends geometrically on whether the point C lies above or below the new BB curve. In Figure 8.2a, the point C is drawn below the new BB curve, implying an excess supply of domestic bonds and thus a capital outflow. But is this necessarily the case? The answer is no: whether the monetary expansion creates pressures for capital inflows or outflows depends on the degree of capital mobility in the economy.

To see why, notice that since the monetary expansion causes BB shifts to the right by *more* than the MM curve, but to shift downward by *less* than the MM curve, the new MM and BB curves must intersect somewhere to the southeast of the original equilibrium point A, at a point such as B. If this point of intersection lies to the northeast of C along the MM curve, then C must be below the BB curve, as in Figure 8.2a. But if it lies to the southeast of C, then C must lie *above* BB, as in Figure 8.2b. In the latter case, the monetary expansion would create pressures for capital *inflows*, rather than outflows.

What determines where the point B is located? Because the new BB curve will have a smaller downward shift (and will be flatter) the greater the degree of substitutability between domestic and foreign bonds (i.e., the higher the degree of capital mobility), the point of intersection of the new MM and BB curves will lie further to the northeast along the MM curve (as in Figure 8.2a) the higher the degree of capital mobility. This means that, given the slope of the GM curve, the point C is more likely to be *below* the BB curve the higher the degree of capital mobility. In other words, the higher the degree of financial

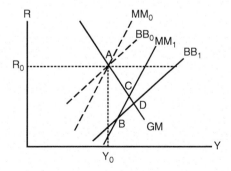

**Figure 8.2b**   Effects of a monetary expansion with low capital mobility

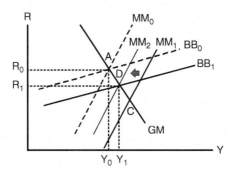

**Figure 8.3**    Effects of a monetary expansion with high capital mobility

integration between the domestic economy and the rest of the world, the more likely it is that the monetary expansion will be associated with pressures for capital *outflows*.

With this important observation in hand, we can now explore the macroeconomic effects of the monetary expansion.

As already noted, in Figure 8.2a the point C lies below the BB curve. As a result, capital flows out of the country. This reduces foreign exchange reserves, and in the absence of sterilization the loss of reserves means that the money supply must contract. The implication is that the MM curve must shift to the *left* from its original post-shock location passing through C. This leftward shift of MM is illustrated in Figure 8.3.

Unlike in the perfect capital mobility case, however, the shift in the MM curve must cease before the curve returns to its original position passing through point A. In fact, the MM curve must stop shifting when it passes through point D where the GM and BB curves intersect, as in Figure 8.3. How do we know this? The reason is that, since the GM curve intersects the BB curve at D, this must be the point where goods market and bond market equilibrium hold simultaneously. Once the MM curve passes through this point, money market equilibrium must hold as well, and the economy must be back in general macroeconomic equilibrium. In particular, because the bond market is in equilibrium at D, there are no longer any pressures generating capital inflows, and therefore nothing to drive further shifts in MM.

The effect of the expansionary monetary policy is that $R$ falls from $R_0$ to $R_1$, and $Y$ rises from $Y_0$ to $Y_1$. The reduction in the equilibrium domestic interest rate $R_1$ contrasts with the perfect capital mobility case, in which monetary expansion left the domestic interest rate unchanged. What is the difference here? The answer is that the central bank's purchase of domestic bonds leaves fewer domestic bonds for the private sector to hold, and *because these are imperfect substitutes for foreign bonds*, the private sector requires an interest-rate inducement to switch from domestic to foreign bonds. The important point to take note of is that domestic monetary policy retains some power to affect real economic activity under these circumstances, despite the fact that a capital outflow offsets some of the effects of the monetary expansion. We will come back to this observation in the next chapter.

What would have happened if a lower degree of capital mobility had made BB steeper, causing the point C to lie *above* BB? Once again the new equilibrium would have been at the point of intersection of GM and BB, and once again it would have been associated with a lower domestic interest rate and a higher level of domestic output. But now the MM curve would have had to shift to the *right* in moving to the point of intersection of GM and BB, as in Figure 8.4. In other words, the initial monetary expansion would actually have been

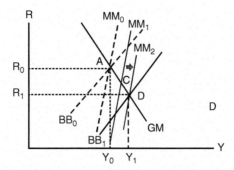

**Figure 8.4**   Effects of a monetary expansion with low capital mobility

reinforced by a capital *inflow*. A capital inflow would have arisen in this case because, with capital mobility relatively low, the effect of a higher domestic level of real income in attracting capital to the domestic economy would have dominated the effect of a lower domestic interest rate in repelling it. In summary, the effects of the monetary expansion are:

Capital inflows $\uparrow \rightarrow$ Domestic interest rate $\downarrow$

Nominal exchange rate $\uparrow \rightarrow$ $\rightarrow$ Real output $\uparrow$

Real exchange rate $\uparrow$

*Effects on Net Exports*   What effects does the monetary expansion have on the country's net exports? From Chapter 4, net exports are given by:

$$N(Q, Y - T, R, \theta) = X(Q, \theta) - (1 - \varphi(Q))A(Y - T, R) \qquad (8.5)$$
$$\;\;\;\;\;+\;\;\;\;\;\;-\;\;\;\;\;+\;\;+$$

A monetary expansion affects net exports in two ways: through higher domestic output and a lower domestic interest rate. Both effects tend to decrease net exports, so expansionary monetary policy must reduce net exports.

## Aggregate Demand Shocks

Next, let's examine how the effects of aggregate demand shocks on the economy differ when capital mobility is imperfect from those that we derived in Chapter 6. For concreteness, consider the case of an increase in government spending.

The effects of an increase in domestic government spending can be depicted graphically as in Figure 8.5. As in Chapter 6, the increase in $G$ shifts the GM curve to the right, to a position such as $GM_1$ in the figure. The MM and BB curves are unaffected by this shock. With no capital flows, and thus no change in $M$, the new equilibrium would be at B. With perfect capital mobility, as in Chapter 6, it would be at point C, where the domestic interest rate would remain equal to $R^*$ (assuming that initially $R_0 = R^*$).

With imperfect capital mobility and domestic credit targeting, the new equilibrium is at D, where the new GM curve intersects the BB curve. The new equilibrium is brought about through monetary expansion caused by capital inflows, since at B the domestic interest rate

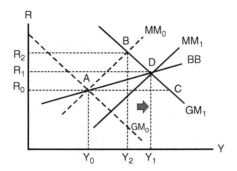

**Figure 8.5**    Macroeconomic effects of an expansionary real shock

lies above BB and thus corresponds to a situation of excess demand for domestic bonds. As described before, the induced capital inflows result in reserve accumulation, since the fixed exchange rate means that the central bank has to buy the foreign currency that portfolio managers sell in order to buy domestic bonds. The monetary emission associated with this foreign exchange market intervention shifts MM to the new position $MM_1$. The monetary expansion caused by capital inflows dampens the increase in domestic interest rates caused by the expansionary fiscal policy and thus mitigates the extent of crowding out. We thus have:

Government spending $\uparrow \rightarrow$ Real output $\uparrow \rightarrow$ Domestic interest rate $\uparrow \rightarrow$ Capital inflows $\uparrow \rightarrow$ Money supply $\uparrow$

## External Financial Shocks

*Changes in World Interest Rates*    We begin by investigating how the domestic economy responds to a change in world financial conditions. Suppose, to be concrete, that the foreign interest rate increases. For the sake of comparison with the case of perfect capital mobility, assume that initially the domestic and world interest rates are equal to each other, and that the world interest rate increases from $R_0^*$ to $R_1^*$, as in Figure 8.6. In Chapter 6, we saw that

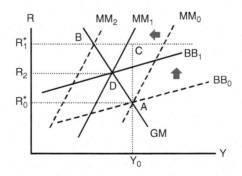

**Figure 8.6**    Effects of an increase in the world interest rate

under conditions of perfect capital mobility the new domestic macroeconomic equilibrium would be at a point such as B, corresponding to a shift of the UIP curve equal to the increase in the world interest rate, and a new domestic interest rate would prevail that would be exactly equal to the new external interest rate $R_1^*$. The MM curve would shift up to this point as the result of capital outflows, to a position such as $MM_2$.

To see where the economy actually ends up under imperfect capital mobility, as in our current model, notice first that a change in $R^*$ affects only the BB curve on impact, and not GM or MM. As we have seen, the increase in $R^*$ must cause BB to shift up, since with foreign bonds paying a higher return, domestic bonds would have to do so as well for people to want to continue to hold them, under the gross substitutes assumption that we discussed previously. However, as shown in Chapter 7, *under imperfect capital mobility the shift in BB is smaller in magnitude than the increase in the world interest rate*, so BB shifts up to a position like $BB_1$, passing below the point C that would correspond to an upward shift equal to the increase in $R^*$.

Because at the initial point A the domestic interest rate is below the new bond market equilibrium rate associated with the higher world interest rate, the increase in the foreign interest rate induces a capital outflow. If the central bank does not sterilize this outflow, the domestic money supply falls, thus causing the MM curve to shift leftward. This money supply contraction must continue until the MM curve intersects the GM curve on the BB curve – that is, until the MM curve has shifted to $MM_1$. Thus the effect of the increase in the foreign interest rate is to induce a capital outflow in this case, just as in the case of perfect capital mobility. But the outflow must be smaller than would be observed under perfect capital mobility (because the shift in MM is smaller than what would be required to get to $MM_2$), so although the domestic interest rate rises in this case just as it would under perfect capital mobility, it does not increase by as much as the foreign interest rate. The effects on the economy are:

$R^* \uparrow \rightarrow$ Capital outflows $\uparrow \rightarrow$ Money supply $\downarrow \rightarrow$ Domestic interest rate $\uparrow \rightarrow$ Real output $\downarrow$

Note that the increase in foreign interest rate is contractionary, but less so than it would have been under perfect capital mobility, precisely because the domestic interest rate does not rise by as much as it would have in that case. Thus imperfect capital mobility plays the role of insulating the domestic economy from changes in world financial conditions.

*Unanticipated Exchange Rate Changes* As in the perfect capital mobility case, a devaluation (remember that in Chapter 6 this was brought about by an increase in the price of gold) shifts the GM curve to the right, because it induces expenditure-switching effects that increase the demand for domestic goods at a given level of the domestic interest rate. We saw in the discussion of the BB curve in Chapter 7 that valuation effects on private financial portfolios would create an excess demand for domestic bonds, causing the BB curve to shift down and to the right.

What happens to the MM curve? As in Chapter 6 when we examined the effects of an increase in the price of gold, there is a slight complication here, because as you can see from equation (8.1), devaluation increases the domestic-currency value of the central bank's stock of foreign exchange reserves, and that would require an offsetting change in either $B_C$ or $M$ for equation (8.1) to continue to hold. If the offsetting change were in $M$, then the money supply would increase and the MM curve would shift to the right. However, as we

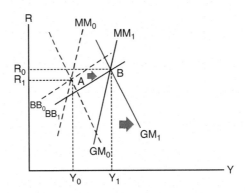

**Figure 8.7**    Effects of an exchange rate devaluation

did in Chapter 6, we will assume that the central bank does not allow the increase in the domestic-currency value of its foreign exchange reserves to affect the domestic money supply. The simplest way to achieve that in the present case is to assume that the offsetting change involves a contraction in $B_C$.[4]

As we have just seen, a devaluation shifts both the GM and BB curves to the right, as in Figure 8.7. Under domestic credit targeting the new equilibrium will be at the intersection of the new GM and BB curves at a point such as B, and capital inflows will cause the MM curve to shift rightward until it passes through this intersection. Domestic output will rise and foreign exchange reserves will increase, but the domestic interest rate may rise or fall, depending on which of the GM or BB curves undergoes the larger horizontal shift. If the BB curve shifts to the right by more than the GM curve does, the domestic interest rate will fall. If the GM curve shifts to the right more than the BB curve does, as in the case depicted in Figure 8.7, the rate will rise. Since the domestic interest rate does not change in response to a devaluation when capital mobility is perfect (Chapter 6), you can readily see that whether the expansionary effect on real output of an unanticipated devaluation is larger or smaller under imperfect capital mobility than under perfect capital mobility depends precisely on how the domestic interest rate responds. The expansionary effect will be larger if the domestic interest rate falls, but smaller if it rises.

The channels of transmission are:

$$\text{Capital inflows} \uparrow \rightarrow \text{Domestic interest rate} \downarrow$$

Nominal exchange rate $\uparrow \rightarrow$ $\rightarrow$ Real output $\uparrow$

$$\text{Real exchange rate} \uparrow$$

It is interesting to note that the effect of the devaluation on net exports is actually ambiguous in this case. Going back to equation (8.5), notice that the devaluation itself improves net

---

[4]    We can imagine that the central bank transfers the capital gains on its holdings of foreign exchange reserves to the government, canceling out some of the government's debt with the central bank (in the form of government bonds held by the central bank). Notice that in this case $B$ and $B_C$ both fall by equal amounts, implying no change in the stock of government bonds held by the public $B - B_C$. Thus this operation has no separate effects on the BB curve. Alternatively, the central bank can avoid a monetary expansion by simply accumulating its capital gains as part of its net worth. In that case the central bank's net worth, which we called $W_C$ in Chapter 4, would no longer be equal to zero and equation (8.1) would need to be modified accordingly.

exports, but the associated increase in real GDP has the opposite effect. Since the domestic interest rate may rise or fall, this further adds to the ambiguity of the result. As we have noted before, an alternative way to investigate the effects on net exports is to use the absorption approach. Writing the goods market equilibrium condition as:

$$Y = A + G + N$$

we can see that since $G$ is unchanged, the effect of a devaluation on $N$ must depend on whether $A$ increases by more or less than $Y$. Since the marginal propensity to absorb is less than one, $A$ will increase by less than $Y$ and net exports will therefore rise, unless other factors cause $A$ to increase. The only other variable affecting private absorption that changes in this case is the domestic interest rate $R$. It follows that if $R$ rises, as it does in Figure 8.7, private absorption $A$ cannot increase by as much as $Y$ (because the marginal propensity to absorb is less than unity and the increase in the domestic interest rate reduces absorption), so goods market equilibrium requires an increase in net exports $N$. If $R$ falls, however, the effect on net exports is ambiguous.

## Summary

Based on the analysis of this section, we can draw the following conclusions about macroeconomic behavior under fixed exchange rates and imperfect capital mobility:

1  Monetary policy retains the power to affect the domestic economy, and sterilization of balance of payments flows is feasible. But the power of a given (unsterilized) change in monetary policy to affect real output is weaker the higher the degree of capital mobility.
2  Unlike what happens under perfect capital mobility, aggregate demand (real) shocks, such as changes in fiscal policy, are potentially susceptible to crowding out. The degree of crowding out induced by such shocks depends on the degree of capital mobility: it is high when capital mobility is low, and low when capital mobility is high.
3  Foreign financial ($R^*$) shocks are transmitted directly to the domestic economy, but their effects are more muted than under perfect capital mobility. The effects of such shocks on the domestic economy are greater the greater the degree of capital mobility.
4  The effects of an unanticipated exchange rate devaluation are somewhat more complicated when capital mobility is imperfect than when it is perfect, because in addition to the effects of this policy on the domestic goods markets, it also affects the economy's financial markets through portfolio effects (effects on the BB curve). These effects may temper or even reverse the increase in the domestic interest rate that a devaluation would tend to produce under conditions of imperfect capital mobility.

## 8.3   Bretton Woods as an International Monetary System

The model that we have just analyzed describes macroeconomic behavior in most of the world's economies during the Bretton Woods era – that is, from 1946 to 1973. Remember that the Bretton Woods system was a soft exchange rate peg, which meant that, in principle, the domestic central bank retained discretion over both exchange rate and monetary policy.

While exchange rates tended to remain fixed over long periods of time for most countries during this period and changes in official parities were newsworthy events, discretion over monetary policy was exercised fairly continuously, as countries used activist monetary policy and sterilization of the monetary effects of real and financial shocks to achieve domestic economic objectives. The comparative static analysis of the last section suggests that when capital mobility was very low, the effects on foreign exchange reserves of using monetary policy in this way tended to be rather muted, but that variability in international reserves tended to increase as capital mobility increased, as it gradually did during the Bretton Woods period.

This provides a clue to the factors underlying the eventual demise of the Bretton Woods system. To understand how the major currencies of the world arrived at the current system of floating exchange rates that we will study in Part 3 of this book, as well as to learn some cautionary lessons about the design of international monetary arrangements, in this section we will review how the Bretton Woods system met its end. We begin by examining the properties of Bretton Woods as an international monetary system, and will then turn to the series of events that brought about its demise.

## Design of Bretton Woods as a System

The framers of the Bretton Woods system designed it to resemble the gold standard in several important ways. For example, since the system fixed an official price of gold, the mechanism governing the growth of international reserves under the Bretton Woods system should have been similar to that which operated under the gold standard. If the world began to run short of reserves, the implied international monetary tightness would cause world nongold prices to fall, which would make it more attractive for gold production to increase and for gold to be sold out of nonmonetary uses to central banks, thus expanding international reserves. If the world had excessive reserves, on the other hand, this would tend to make the world money supply expand and cause world nongold prices to rise. The demand for gold for nonmonetary uses would thus increase and world gold production would drop, thus draining gold from the central banks' coffers.[5]

Fixing the price of gold should also have stabilized the international price level, again through a mechanism similar to that of the gold standard system. If central banks pursued excessively expansionary monetary policies, world nongold prices would rise. The resulting decrease in the relative price of gold would deter gold production and encourage individuals to buy gold from central banks, thereby decreasing international reserves and putting corrective downward pressure on the world money supply. Similarly, if policies were excessively contractionary, prices would fall and gold would flow into central banks, expanding the world money supply.

However, these self-regulating features designed into the system relied on two important assumptions: (1) the flexibility of world nongold prices and (2) the willingness of the world's central banks to tie money growth to reserve growth, that is, to play by what

---

[5]   However, this mechanism would have had to operate through central banks other than the Federal Reserve System, since the US government did not trade gold with private citizens after 1934. In fact, the Articles of Agreement of the International Monetary Fund allowed central banks to buy and sell gold at the official price in private gold markets.

amounted to the third of the gold standard "rules of the game." The second of these assumptions is worth examining more closely.

## Incentives Facing Individual Countries Under Bretton Woods

We have already seen that political and economic developments after World War I increased pressures on governments to give more importance to domestic macroeconomic performance as compared to external objectives. This would make it less likely that governments would play by the rules of the game, when doing so would have prevented them from undertaking policies that they perceived as addressing domestic macroeconomic problems. The question is: What incentives did the Bretton Woods system create for countries to sacrifice domestic macroeconomic objectives in order to promote international adjustment? The answer depended on the country and its circumstances.

As we have seen, under Bretton Woods one country (the United States) was effectively entrusted with fixing the nominal price of gold, since the United States was the only country that fixed the value of its currency relative to gold. The responsibility of the United States was to stand ready to exchange gold for dollars with central banks at the official price of $35/ounce. To preserve its ability to do so, on average it would have had to run balance of payments deficits when its gold stock expanded (thus increasing world reserves) and surpluses when its gold stock contracted (thereby reducing world reserves). If the United States did not play by these rules, then the world supply of US dollar reserves would not be tied to the world stock of gold reserves. This would short-circuit both of the automatic adjustment mechanisms described above (for the world supply of reserves and world price level) and would jeopardize the ability of the United States to fix the price of gold in terms of dollars, which was the linchpin of the system. Thus, the United States was essentially entrusted with the preservation of the system, and its incentives to perform its role depended on the importance that it attached to that goal.

Similarly, countries other than the United States were expected to adopt expansionary policies when running balance of payments surpluses and contractionary ones when running deficits, to support the official values of their currencies. The implications for them of their failure to do so, however, depended on whether they were running balance of payments deficits or surpluses.

For countries running balance of payments *deficits*, failure to abide by the rules (e.g., by sterilizing the monetary contraction associated with reserve depletion) would mean that deficits would be prolonged, eventually causing the country to run out of reserves and thus jeopardizing its ability to sustain the value of its currency. Under the Bretton Woods system this would cause the country to have to appeal to the IMF for permission to devalue its currency or for funds with which to sustain its official parity. The latter would be available only if the country promised to mend its ways and indeed agree to adjust its policies so as to remove the deficit in its balance of payments. Thus, for these countries, incentives came in the form of the stigma attached to devaluation or to accepting policy conditionality in exchange for loans from the IMF.

For countries running balance of payments *surpluses*, on the other hand, there was no such constraint in operation. Such countries could continue to accumulate reserves indefinitely as long as they were willing to hold the additional dollars. For these countries, incentives to modify their behavior came in the form of having to hold potentially large stocks of dollar reserves.

Thus, the incentives for countries to behave in such a way as to make the automatic adjustment mechanisms under Bretton Woods work correctly – that is, to give precedence to following the "rules of the game" over pursuing domestic macroeconomic objectives if the two were in conflict – were very different for the reserve-currency country, for non-reserve currency deficit countries, and for non-reserve currency surplus countries. As we will see later on, these incentives did not prove to be strong enough to hold the Bretton Woods system together, especially when capital began to flow more freely across international borders.

## Problems with the Bretton Woods System

Why didn't the Bretton Woods system survive? There are two views, which we will examine in this section. One perceives the system as intrinsically flawed and bound to break down eventually. The other takes the view that the breakdown of the system was the result of a failure to reconcile conflicting macroeconomic objectives among the major countries in the world economy.

*The Triffin Dilemma*    Some international macroeconomists have argued that the Bretton Woods system was intrinsically flawed in the context of a growing world in which governments cared about domestic economic performance and wages and prices were sticky downwards. One way to state the problem is that, like the gold standard, the system was too vulnerable to developments in the gold industry.

The argument goes as follows: generalized growth during the world's postwar recovery would have meant an increased demand for monetary gold (since it would have implied an increased demand for money, and thus for foreign exchange reserves, in each country). As long as productivity growth in the gold industry allows the increased demand for monetary gold to be met without a change in the relative price of gold, the international monetary system would not provide an obstacle to the growth of the world economy. But now suppose that productivity growth in the gold industry does not keep up with that in other industries.[6] Since the supply of gold would then not keep pace with that of other goods, a rise in the relative price of gold would be required to supply the increased demand for gold. This could come about either through an increase in the nominal price of gold or through a decrease in the prices of other goods. But the system did not readily allow the former to happen, and downward price stickiness would have prevented the latter.[7] This would have created a **liquidity problem**, that is, an insufficient supply of reserves to facilitate the expansion of the world economy.

Under these circumstances, world growth would only be sustainable through reserve growth in the form of US balance of payments deficits that increased world dollar reserves more than in proportion to the increase in the US stock of gold reserves. But since such

---

[6]    Productivity growth was actually very high by historical standards in the industrial countries during the years 1946 to 1973.

[7]    An increase in the price of gold had to be approved by a majority of the Fund's voting members and also had to have the approval of all members with at least 10 percent of the total quotas.

deficits would increase US dollar liabilities relative to the size of the US gold stock, this would create a **confidence problem**, in the form of doubts that the United States would be able to continue to fulfill its obligation to convert dollars into gold without limit.

Thus the system would be caught on the horns of a dilemma known as the **Triffin dilemma**, after Robert Triffin, the Belgian-born Yale economist who brought attention to it. A solution to the confidence problem would have created a liquidity problem, and a solution to the liquidity problem would have exacerbated a confidence problem. In short, the system was inherently inconsistent in the face of economic growth and downward price stickiness. Under such circumstances, it did not provide a systematic means for increasing aggregate reserves in a growing world economy.

Given downward price stickiness, the dilemma could have been resolved essentially by changing the metal gold/dollar reserve ratio. There were two ways of doing so: by increasing the price of gold or by creating a new type of reserve asset with superior properties to those of gold. As we have seen (n. 6) changing the dollar price of gold required a substantial degree of consensus among the Fund's member countries. Such consensus, however, was difficult to generate for several reasons:

- Increasing the price of gold would have reduced the pressure on the United States to tighten monetary policy when excessively expansionary policy in that country created excessive international reserves, and thus was perceived as potentially inflationary.
- Changing the official gold price could also have destabilized the system by inducing central banks to speculate on gold. For example, expected increases in the price of gold when reserves are scarce might have encouraged more countries to hold their foreign currency reserves in the form of gold rather than dollars, which would undermine the benefits to be expected from the higher price of gold.
- Finally, increasing the price of gold was perceived as potentially benefiting the wrong people. This would have included countries that had hoarded gold in anticipation of such increases, as well as the two major gold-producing countries (the USSR and South Africa). Because of Cold War tensions with the USSR and the apartheid regime in South Africa, the governments of these countries were not favored by many Western countries.

The preferred alternative to changes in gold prices turned out to be the creation of a new reserve asset in the form of a claim not on the United States, but on the International Monetary Fund itself. In 1967 the IMF created a new asset called a **special drawing right (SDR)**, also known as "paper gold." The SDR was essentially an artificial liability of the IMF that the central banks of member countries agreed to accept in exchange for their own currencies. Thus SDRs functioned as international reserves. Since SDRs were essentially bookkeeping entries, with value initially set as 1 SDR = $1, they could be created whenever and in whatever amounts were desired. What this innovation was designed to do was to make it possible to regulate the growth of the official "gold" stock (gold plus SDRs), taking into account the growth of dollar reserves determined by the US balance of payments. The effect would have been to keep the total (metal plus paper) gold backing of the dollar constant if the United States behaved responsibly, even as the stock of dollars increased and the stock of metallic gold did not keep pace.

However, the SDR did not prove to be a successful innovation. Not many were issued, essentially because of disagreements about how many SDRs to create and how to allocate them among countries. Countries such as Germany, with strong preferences for price stability, preferred to restrict the creation of SDRs, while developing countries, which perceived the creation of SDRs as a potentially important form of external financial assistance, favored a more generous expansion of SDRs. In one view, then, the political stalemate over SDRs and changes in the price of gold essentially left the system impaled on the horns of Triffin's dilemma and doomed it to an eventual breakdown.

*Conflicting Macroeconomic Priorities*   While the Bretton Woods system may have been inherently vulnerable to Triffin's dilemma, many economists believe that the system was brought down not by this inherent contradiction, but rather by conflicting economic priorities between the United States and several other important countries in the system, especially France and Germany.

Notice that the Triffin dilemma would have arisen even if all countries in the world agreed on the desirable rate of international reserve growth and the United States, as the center country, behaved so as to produce that rate of reserve growth. The problem would have arisen because the failure of the monetary gold stock to keep pace with the generally desired pace of reserve growth would in any case have resulted in an increase in the ratio of dollar reserves to the stock of monetary gold. But what if the United States behaved so as to run larger balance of payments deficits, and thus produced a higher rate of reserve growth, than desired by other countries? As we will see next, this is exactly what happened, and its effect was to sharply intensify the confidence problem.

Policies in the United States turned relatively expansionary during the mid-1960s, a time during which the country was simultaneously fighting a war in Vietnam and the War on Poverty – an ambitious federal effort to combat poverty in the United States – at home. The expansionary stimulus associated with these policies at times resulted in large overall US balance of payment deficits that fueled an acceleration of reserve growth in other countries.[8] The implication of this situation was that, unless foreign central banks sterilized the monetary expansion associated with their reserve accumulation, the world money supply would expand and foreign countries would import the expansionary US policies. On the other hand, if they did sterilize, they would be able to protect themselves from the US stimulus, but at the cost of having to hold very large foreign exchange reserves. This situation was aggravated by the fact that technological and institutional developments, in the form of improved transportation, communication, and information-processing technologies, as well as reduced official barriers to capital movements, had the effect of increasing the degree of capital mobility among industrial countries.[9]

The growth of international reserves undoubtedly facilitated world growth, but it also contributed to inflationary pressures around the world as incomplete sterilization of balance of payments surpluses by countries other than the United States caused their money supplies

---

[8]   The United States actually had small current account surpluses during most of this period, but during the first half of the 1960s, those surpluses were more than offset by deficits in the nonreserve financial account, resulting in overall balance of payments deficits. Though the US balance of payments was in approximate balance during most of the second half of the decade, deficits grew dramatically in 1970–2.

[9]   From the perspective of other countries, expansionary monetary policies in the United States would have been transmitted to them in the form of higher values of $\theta$ and lower values of $R^*$. As we saw in the last section, both of these would have resulted in increases in the stocks of reserves held by their central banks, and as capital mobility increased, this reserve accumulation would have been magnified if these countries chose to sterilize the reserve accumulation (see the appendix to this chapter).

to expand. As world prices increased, not only did US dollar liabilities grow, but the stock of US gold reserves was also gradually depleted, for two reasons.

First, the rise in nongold prices meant a reduction in the real price of gold, which contributed to sluggish gold production and strong demand for gold from the private sector, as the intended working of the automatic adjustment mechanism would suggest. The excess private demand for gold thus contributed to the gradual depletion of official gold stocks.

Second, foreign central banks had a strong incentive to convert dollar reserves into gold in order to put pressure on the United States to modify its macroeconomic policies. They had two different reasons to seek such a modification of US policies.

One reason arose from an **equity problem** that was built into the Bretton Woods system. The problem was the following: Under the system, since US paper liabilities were held by foreign central banks as reserves, the United States was able to acquire real assets from foreigners in exchange for paper liabilities that were not expected to be redeemed, since countries needed to hold them as reserves. Recall from Chapter 5 that this benefit, which accrues to any issuer of fiat money, is known as **seignorage**. Under the Bretton Woods system, the United States was the only recipient of the seignorage associated with the issuance of international liquidity. The United States increased its seignorage revenue at the expense of the rest of the world when world inflation was high. To exert pressure on the United States to refrain from collecting high seignorage revenues, the main recourse available to other countries was to convert dollars into gold.[10]

A second reason was more fundamental. It stemmed from basic incompatibilities among national economic objectives, known as the **adjustment problem**. As we have seen, surplus countries with a strong preference for price stability tended to sterilize reserve growth in order to resist excessive expansion of aggregate demand. But to do so, they had to issue domestic government bonds at the higher domestic interest rates that these countries required in order to keep aggregate demand under control. This created a fiscal burden for these countries, since they in effect issued high-interest rate domestic bonds in order to acquire low-interest rate reserves. Countries in this situation, of which Germany was a prominent example, also had an incentive to put pressure on the United States by converting dollars into gold.

The implication of large private and official demands for gold was that US gold reserves dwindled while US dollar liabilities to foreign central banks increased. Thus US gold reserves began to seem inadequate, imperiling the convertibility of dollars into gold on which the system was built.

The framers of the Bretton Woods system foresaw such a situation, as indicated previously. The solution envisioned under the system was for the United States to be induced to undertake a corrective monetary contraction by the pressure to maintain the dollar's convertibility into gold. However, this would have required the United States to sacrifice its domestic macroeconomic priorities to preserve the Bretton Woods system, and the United States was unwilling to do this. The inducement offered by the opportunity to preserve the system (and the special role of the United States within it) was simply not sufficiently strong to compel the United States to sacrifice its domestic priorities (fighting

---

[10] Note that the issuance of SDRs could have coped with the seignorage problem, but the problem of distributing the seignorage that arose from the issuance of SDRs was another source of political stalemate in implementing this innovation.

the war in Vietnam as well as the domestic War on Poverty without resorting to substantial additional taxation or monetary contraction) for the sake of international ones.

Instead, responses to the potential US dollar convertibility problem consisted of the creation of a two-tier gold market and of SDRs:

1   *Creation of a two-tier gold market.* The private price of gold was set in the London gold market, where the Bank of England bought or sold gold at the official price, replenishing its stocks as needed by acquiring it from the United States. But when in October 1960 it appeared that the US treasury might be reluctant to provide gold to the Bank of England, the Bank withdrew from the market and the private price of gold rose above its official price.[11] To prevent such a situation from arising in the future, the United States and seven other industrial countries formed the London Gold Pool in 1961, an arrangement to intervene in the private gold market by buying or selling monetary gold jointly so as to keep the price in that market close to the official price. As the Bretton Woods system came under strain, however, private agents began to speculate on an increase in the price of gold; stabilizing the price of gold thus began to drain large amounts of monetary gold from the central banks of the countries that participated in the Gold Pool. Rather than respond to this situation by tightening monetary policy, the attempt to stabilize the private price of gold was finally given up in 1968, when central banks stopped intervening in the private gold market. As a result, a two-tier gold market was created. Central banks continued to trade gold among themselves at $35/ounce, but no longer traded with the private market. It is easy to see, though, that since this measure was designed to stop the drain of gold into nonmonetary uses, it essentially implied abandoning the automatic adjustment mechanism that would have counteracted an excessive expansion of world reserves.

2   *Creation of SDRs.* As noted previously, the creation of SDRs was designed to help with the problem of insufficient international reserves. It could also have helped deal with the problem that actually emerged – that of a dollar glut – by essentially creating "paper gold" to back US dollars. But this would have amounted to ratifying the expansionary policies that the United States was imposing on the rest of the world and removing the only constraint that the rest of the world could impose on US policies. This was unacceptable to countries, such as France and Germany, that valued this constraint for domestic political reasons. Thus, solving the dollar convertibility problem by creating SDRs was a political nonstarter.

The continued pressure of excessive US balance of payments deficits relative to the preferences of other key countries ultimately had two effects. First, despite sterilization in several major countries, the associated rapid growth of international reserves and expansion of the world economy triggered a burst of worldwide inflation and ran up commodity prices in the early 1970s, including that of oil (this increase in the worldwide demand for oil set the stage for the emergence of OPEC). Second, as US liabilities grew relative to the country's gold reserves, markets became increasingly convinced that a devaluation of the dollar was in the offing. The year 1964 was important, not only because for the first time US dollar liabilities to foreign central banks exceeded the US gold stock in that year, but also because after that time the rising aggregate demand pressures driven by the war in Vietnam and the

---

[11]   See Meltzer (1991).

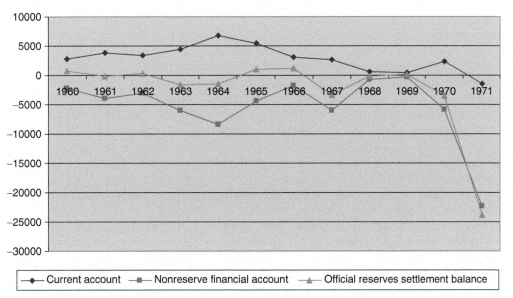

**Figure 8.8**    US balance of payments accounts, 1960–71
*Source*: US Department of Commerce, Bureau of Economic Analysis.

domestic War on Poverty caused inflation in the United States to begin to exceed that in the country's main trading partners, causing the dollar to appreciate in real terms and the US current account surplus to begin to decline (Figure 8.8).

In particular, as it became likely that the system would break down because European countries would refuse to continue accumulating dollars, pressures on the system increased in the form of capital flows from the United States to Germany in anticipation of a revaluation of the Deutschmark relative to the dollar. As shown in Figure 8.8, these pressures eventually led to a huge speculative run on the dollar, manifesting itself in the form of dramatic capital outflows from the United States in 1971. In the face of such speculative pressures, Germany dropped out of the Bretton Woods system in May 1971, floating the Deutschmark against the dollar. Some small European countries followed. President Nixon finally closed the US "gold window" for foreign central banks – that is, he announced that the United States would no longer be willing to exchange dollars held by foreign central banks for gold – on August 15, 1971, effectively ending the Bretton Woods system as it had existed since the end of World War II.

Floating exchange rates prevailed temporarily among the major industrial countries until the Smithsonian Agreement in December 1971, which set a new price of gold at $38.02/ ounce, but did not reopen the US gold window. The European currencies and the Japanese yen were revalued, and fluctuation margins were set at 2.25 percent on each side of the par value. However, since US dollars were no longer redeemable into gold, even by central banks, the Smithsonian Agreement essentially placed the world on a **pure exchange standard** in which exchange rates were fixed among the major currencies, but the system as a whole was no longer anchored to gold through the fixing of the price of gold in terms of any individual currency.

While this step eliminated the Triffin dilemma (since there was no longer even the pretense that the US dollar would be convertible into gold), it did nothing to reconcile conflicting macroeconomic priorities among the key industrial countries. Not surprisingly, therefore, speculative flows resumed in 1972, and in June the United Kingdom abandoned the revised system. Switzerland did so as well in January 1973, followed by Japan and Italy in February. The dollar was devalued again in that month, this time to $42.22/ounce. By March 1973, speculative flows had become too great, and several other major currencies were allowed to float. In view of these basic international disagreements about international monetary arrangements, the IMF Articles of Agreement were amended to legalize floating in 1978, and ever since then, exchange rates among the major industrial countries have floated.

Box 8.2 reviews the performance of the major industrial countries under the Bretton Woods system, as compared to its gold standard predecessor and the floating exchange rate system that followed it. Overall, the system was associated with relatively favorable economic performance among the major industrial countries, especially after 1958, when many such countries finally removed a variety of restrictions that they had imposed on current account transactions during and after World War II. However, the extent to which such performance was facilitated by the Bretton Woods system, or emerged for independent reasons, remains a debated topic among international macroeconomists.

## Box 8.2    Industrial Country Economic Performance under Alternative International Exchange Rate Regimes

How did the performance of the major countries compare under the gold standard, Bretton Woods, and the floating exchange rate system that emerged after 1973? A comprehensive study by Bordo (1993) sheds some light on this question. Bordo looked at a large number of measures for macro performance for seven large industrial countries under these three regimes, subdividing the period from 1881 to 1989 into the gold standard period (1881–1913), the interwar period (1919–39), Bretton Woods (1946–70), and the floating rate period (1971–89). He further subdivided the Bretton Woods regime into a "preconvertible" phase from 1946 to 1958, and the convertible phase from 1959 to 1970. His findings can be summarized briefly as follows:

1  Inflation was lowest during the gold standard era, and lower during Bretton Woods than during the floating rate period. Inflation rates showed the highest cross-country convergence during the gold standard and the Bretton Woods convertible subperiod, compared to the interwar period and the floating rate period.
2  Output growth was highest during Bretton Woods and lowest during the interwar period. It was most stable during the convertible Bretton Woods subperiod, and least stable in the preconvertible subperiod. The Bretton Woods period as a whole had the highest degree of convergence in output variability across countries. Overall, output variability was higher during both the gold standard era and the interwar years than during the floating rate period.
3  The degree of convergence of short-term interest rates among countries was highest in the convertible Bretton Woods subperiod, while both nominal and real long-term rates were most stable as well as most convergent under the gold standard, followed by the convertible Bretton Woods subperiod.

4    The lowest and most convergent mean rates of change of nominal and real exchange rates were found during the gold standard and convertible Bretton Woods regimes.

Overall, Bordo concludes:

In summary, the Bretton Woods regime exhibited the best overall macroeconomic performance of any regime. This is especially so for the convertible period (1959–70) ... both nominal and real variables were most stable in this period. The floating exchange rate regime, on most criteria, was not far behind ... whereas the classical gold standard exhibited the most stability and the closest convergence of financial variables. (p. 143).

---

## Empirical Study 8.1    Monetary Autonomy in Emerging Economies

In the introduction to this chapter, one motivation given for studying a model with fixed exchange rates and imperfect capital mobility was that such a model describes the situation in which many emerging and developing countries currently find themselves. As we saw in the last chapter, many such countries indeed either maintain some form of soft exchange rate peg, or manage their floating exchange rates in such a way as to stabilize the nominal rate, effectively managing *de facto* soft pegs. But are such economies imperfectly integrated with international capital markets?

This question is not easy to answer, because imperfect capital market integration has many macroeconomic implications, and there are consequently many ways in which financial integration can be tested empirically. This note provides an example of one such test: a test for monetary autonomy. As we have seen in this chapter, a country that maintains an officially determined exchange rate can retain control over its domestic money supply – and thus enjoy monetary autonomy – only if it is characterized by imperfect capital mobility. Thus, under officially determined exchange rates, tests of monetary autonomy are informative about capital mobility.

A particularly revealing context in which to conduct such tests is in countries that have received large private capital inflows. Such countries have to have at least some degree of integration with world capital markets to become capital-inflow recipients. Moreno (1996) conducted such tests for two such countries, Korea and Taiwan, over the period 1981–94, during which both countries received large capital inflows.

Moreno estimated a four-variable vector autoregression (VAR) for both countries, using monthly data. An *n*-variable VAR is simply a set of *n* regressions in which each variable in the system is regressed on a given number of its own lagged values as well as the same number of lagged values of the other variables. The estimation is intended to reveal the dynamic interactions that exist among the variables in the data without specifying the structural channels through which those interactions may operate. Once the equations are estimated, the fitted values of the regressions can be used to examine the response over time of each of the variables in the system to an independent shock in one of the others (called **impulse responses**). However, because the residuals of the

*(Continued)*

**Empirical Study 8.1**    *(Continued)*

estimated system are likely to be correlated across equations, the residual in any given equation cannot be interpreted simply as a shock to the dependent variable in that equation. The reason is that if a shock to any variable in the system affects other variables contemporaneously, the residual in each equation would tend to reflect the combined effects of shocks to other variables, as well as to the dependent variable in that equation. Thus, it is necessary to stipulate a set of assumptions about how independent shocks to each variable affect each other contemporaneously (called **identifying restrictions**). A simple form of such restrictions is a **recursive causal ordering** – i.e., the assumption that the residual in the equation ordered first is an independent shock to that variable, the residual in the equation ordered second reflects the combined effects of the contemporaneous effect of the first variable on the second plus an independent shock to the second variable, and so on.

The four variables in Moreno's system were (the logs of) the central bank's stock of foreign exchange reserves $F_C$, its stock of domestic credit $B_C$, the nominal exchange rate $S$, and the domestic price level $P$ (measured by the consumer price index). To identify independent shocks, he placed the variables in the order $S$, $P$, $F_C$, and $B_C$. He found that in Korea, but not in Taiwan, positive shocks to the exchange rate (i.e., nominal *depreciations*) were associated with *reductions* in foreign exchange reserves in the impulse responses, suggesting that the central bank sold reserves to stabilize the exchange rate, consistent with ''fear of floating.'' However, in both countries shocks to foreign assets were associated with offsetting shocks in domestic credit, indicating that sterilization was pursued actively in both cases. In Korea, such sterilization appeared to be complete, so that shocks to foreign exchange reserves had no effect on the money supply. The implication is that Korea retained a very high degree of monetary autonomy. In Taiwan, a shock to foreign exchange reserves tended to be only partially sterilized. In both countries, however, shocks to domestic credit were not offset by changes in foreign exchange reserves, indicating that changes in domestic credit had persistent effects on the domestic money supply, again consistent with the retention of monetary autonomy by both countries. Further reinforcement of this conclusion was provided by the fact that lagged domestic credit did not help predict future changes in foreign exchange reserves, while lagged changes in foreign exchange reserves did help predict future changes in domestic credit. The interpretation of this last finding is that in both countries changes in domestic credit were not offset by capital outflows (monetary autonomy) while changes in foreign exchange reserves did trigger offsetting monetary policy responses (sterilization).

**Empirical Study 8.2    Determinants of Capital Inflows
                         to Developing Countries**

As indicated in Box 8.3, capital inflows to developing countries have been episodic in nature, and the relative importance of alternative factors that may have been driving such flows has not often been clear. In particular, as discussed in Box 8.3, the relative importance of external ("push") factors and internal ("pull") factors in driving the inflows of the early 1990s proved to be controversial. This distinction mattered, among other things, because if capital flows to developing were "pushed" to such countries by temporarily lower interest rates in the industrial countries, such flows were likely to be less sustainable than if they were "pulled" to such countries by a permanently improved policy environment there.

Taylor and Sarno (1997) conducted a recent careful empirical study of this issue. They examined monthly data for US portfolio flows to nine Latin American countries (Argentina, Brazil, Chile, Colombia, Ecuador, Jamaica, Mexico, Uruguay, and Venezuela) and nine Asian countries (China, India, Indonesia, Korea, Malaysia, Pakistan, the Philippines, Taiwan, and Thailand) over the period January 1988 to September 1992. To investigate the determinants of capital flows to those countries over this period, they considered a set of country-specific "pull" factors $x$ (the country credit rating and the black market exchange rate premium), as well as global "push" factors $w$ (the US Treasury bill rate, the US government bond rate, and an index of US industrial production). Their estimation of the determinants of portfolio capital inflows to these countries from the United States $f_{it}$ was based on panel (combined cross-section and time-series) as well as country-by-country estimation of an equation of the form:

$$f_{it} = \psi_i - \rho_i(f - \beta'x - \gamma'w)_{i,\,t-1} + \theta_i \Delta f_{it-1} + \Sigma \lambda'_{ij} \Delta x_{i,\,t-1} + \Sigma \delta'_{ij} \Delta w_{i,\,t-1} + u_{i\,t}$$

where the symbol $\Delta$ indicates a change in a variable. In this specification, the change in capital flows is taken to be a function of the previous month's difference between actual capital flows and the "normal" level of such flows, conditional on the values of the driving variables $x$ and $w$ (this difference is given by the **error-correction** term $f - \beta'x - \gamma'w$), as well as of lagged values of capital flows and both "pull" and "push" factors. The latter allow for a potentially rich pattern of dynamic adjustment in capital flows in response to changes in their determinants.

Taylor and Sarno found that *both* domestic as well as global variables were important in driving portfolio capital flows from the United States to these countries. As might be expected, the coefficient $\rho_i$ was not only positive and statistically significant, but also large in magnitude, indicating rapid adjustment of capital flows to the equilibrium value determined by the combined operation of "push" and "pull" factors. Portfolio bond flows were more affected by global factors, while portfolio equity flows were more affected by domestic factors. Latin American flows were found to be as responsive as Asian flows to interest rates in the United States, but less responsive to all other factors.

## 8.4  Summary

We investigated the macroeconomics of imperfect integration under the assumption that a soft exchange rate peg is maintained in which the central bank retains discretion over exchange rate and monetary policies, as was true under the international monetary system designed at Bretton Woods. We saw that under this system central banks retained monetary autonomy, in the sense that they could determine domestic money supplies.

This autonomy could be implemented via the use of monetary policy as an instrument to control aggregate demand or to modify the effects of other shocks on aggregate demand (through sterilization). The use of monetary policy in this way, however, tended to insulate domestic economic activity at the cost of destabilizing the central bank's international reserves, and the effects of shocks on reserves under a policy of sterilization were greater the greater the degree of a country's integration with world financial markets.

The Bretton Woods system prevailed during a period of rapid growth in the world economy, but it eventually came to an end as the result of conflicting domestic macroeconomic objectives between the United States, on the one hand, and several major industrial economies, on the other. What followed was a system of floating exchange rates among the currencies of the main industrial countries, the analysis of which will be the subject of Part 3 of this book.

As emphasized at the beginning of this chapter, the demise of the Bretton Woods system did not mean that the world as a whole converted to floating exchange rates. While this was indeed the case for the major industrial countries, most developing countries retained their fixed exchange rates after the demise of the Bretton Woods system, and since many of these countries remain imperfectly – at best – integrated with international financial markets, the analysis of soft pegs under imperfect capital mobility remains highly relevant for them. However, as more and more of these countries have become increasingly integrated with world financial markets, thereby becoming **emerging economies**, the survival of these soft pegs has become problematic for them, as it did for the industrial countries. Indeed, in several important ''emerging market'' economies, the transition to floating exchange rates was associated with severe macroeconomic crises. In the next chapter we will examine why this has been the case.

## Questions

1   The IMF frequently prescribes devaluation and contractionary fiscal policy for developing countries operating fixed exchange rates and facing problems with excessive deficits in the current account of their balance of payments. These policies are frequently quite controversial. Based on what you learned in this chapter, can you provide a rationale for this particular combination of policies, as opposed to using a single policy to achieve the current account target? [Hint: what other macroeconomic outcomes might both the country and the Fund care about?]

2   As described in Box 8.2, many emerging economies had their domestic macroeconomic equilibria disrupted by sharp decreases in world interest rates in the early 1990s. Assuming that such countries maintained fixed exchange rates at the onset of the interest rate shock:

   a   Explain what effect the fall in the foreign interest rate would have had on capital flows to/from such countries, on domestic real GDP, and on the current account of their balance of payments.

   b   Describe three domestic policy instruments that these countries could have used to offset the effects of the shock on domestic real GDP, and explain how each would have worked (i.e., using diagrams).

3   Economists sometimes refer to the attempt by countries to fix their exchange rates, control their money supplies, and operate with open capital accounts in their balance of

payments (that is, to have no restrictions on capital movements) as the "impossible trinity" of international macroeconomics. Based on what you have learned so far, would you agree that this combination of policies is impossible to achieve? Explain.

4 Under fixed exchange rates and with imperfect capital mobility, why would the central bank choose to sterilize the effects of balance of payments surpluses or deficits on the domestic money supply? Explain your answer using graphs and in the context of a concrete example.

5 Would you expect the international transmission to business cycles (think of a change in $\theta$) to have been more extensive under the gold standard or under the Bretton Woods system? Explain.

6 Consider two small open economies that maintain fixed exchange rates and are linked to world capital markets under conditions of imperfect capital mobility. Suppose that the two economies are otherwise identical, except that capital flows (portfolio allocations between domestic and foreign bonds) are more sensitive to interest rate differentials in economy A than in economy B. How would you expect the effectiveness of fiscal policy (its ability to affect real GDP) in the two countries to be influenced by this difference between them? Explain.

7 Assume that an economic expansion in the United States that is driven by expansionary monetary policy tends to be accompanied by low interest rates, while one that is driven by expansionary fiscal policies tends to be accompanied by high interest rates. From the perspective of a small developing country that maintains a fixed exchange rate against the US dollar and whose bonds are imperfect substitutes for US bonds, show – using diagrams – what difference it makes for the impact on the small country's GDP whether an expansion in the United States is driven by monetary or fiscal policy.

8 Consider a small open economy that maintains a fixed exchange rate and is characterized by imperfect capital mobility. Suppose that its domestic goods market is continually afflicted by unpredictable changes in private absorption. In such an environment, will the level of domestic real GDP tend to be more stable if the central bank follows a policy of sterilizing or of not sterilizing capital flows in and out of the domestic economy? Explain.

9 Consider a small open economy that maintains a fixed exchange rate. Explain what effects a reduction in the interest rate that prevails in world financial markets would have on each of the following domestic variables after the economy has adjusted to a new equilibrium:
a Real GDP.
b The domestic interest rate.
c The central bank's stock of foreign exchange reserves.
d The real exchange rate.
e The current and nonreserve financial accounts of the balance of payments.

10 Using graphs, show how you would establish the following proposition: "In a small open economy operating a fixed exchange rate, in which domestic and foreign bonds are imperfect substitutes, in the absence of sterilization the effects of an increase in the world interest rate on the domestic interest rate will be larger the closer the degree of substitutability between domestic and foreign bonds."

11 Discuss three advantages that SDRs would have had over US dollars as international reserves under the Bretton Woods system.

## Further Reading and References

### On the Bretton Woods system

Bordo, Michael D. (1993), "The Gold Standard, Bretton Woods and Other Monetary Regimes: A Historical Appraisal," Federal Reserve Bank of St. Louis *Review* (March/April), pp. 123–91.

Hetzel, Robert L. (1996), "Sterilized Foreign Exchange Intervention: The Fed Debate in the 1960s," Federal Reserve Bank of Richmond *Economic Quarterly*, Volume 82/2 (Spring), pp. 21–46.

Meltzer, Allan H. (1991), "U.S. Policy in the Bretton Woods Era," Federal Reserve Bank of St. Louis *Review* (May/June), pp. 54–83.

Solomon, Robert (1977), *The International Monetary System, 1945–1976* (New York: Harper & Row).

### On contemporary applications of the model

Alfaro, Laura, Sebnem Kalemli-Ozcan, and Vadym Volosovych (2005), "Capital Flows in a Globalized World: The Role of Policies and Institutions," NBER Working Paper 11696 (October).

Kaminsky, Graciela, Carmen Reinhart, and Carlos Vegh (2004), "When It Rains, It Pours: Procyclical Capital Flows and Macroeconomic Policies," NBER Working Paper No. 10780 (September).

Lothian, James R. (2006), "Institutions, Capital Flows, and Financial Integration," *Journal of International Money and Finance* 25, pp. 358–69.

Montiel, Peter J. (1996), Managing Economic Policy in the Face of Large Capital Inflows: What Have We Learned?" in G. Calvo and M. Goldstein, eds., *Private Capital Flows to Emerging Markets After the Mexican Crisis* (Washington: Institute for International Economics).

Moreno, Ramon (1996), "Intervention, Sterilization, and Monetary Control in Korea and Taiwan," Federal Reserve Bank of San Francisco *Economic Review*, Number 3, pp. 23–33.

Portes, Richard, and Helene Rey (2005), "The Determinants of Cross-Border Equity Flows," *Journal of International Economics* 65, pp. 269–96.

Taylor, Mark P., and Lucio Sarno (1997), "Capital Flows to Developing Countries: Long- and Short-Run Determinants," *World Bank Economic Review* Vol. 11 (September), pp. 451–70.

## Appendix 8.1    Alternative Monetary Policy Regimes

In the text, we assumed that the central bank adopted a monetary policy regime consisting of domestic credit targeting. This meant that our model treated $B_C$ as the exogenous policy variable. Alternatively, we could have analyzed the model under two different monetary policy regimes: interest rate targeting, which involves treating the domestic interest rate $R$ as the central bank's exogenously determined policy variable, or monetary targeting, which takes $M$ as the exogenous policy variable.

The analysis of how the economy works under interest rate targeting is a straightforward extension of the domestic credit targeting regime examined in the chapter. The only difference is that, instead of keeping the BB curve fixed in response to shocks, the central bank alters $B_C$ so as to shift the BB curve in such a way that it always intersects the GM curve at the bank's desired interest rate target. Suppose, for example, that the central bank targets the interest rate $R_0$ in Figure A8.1, but that, as the result of some unspecified shock, the economy finds itself at a point like A, with an interest rate that exceeds the central bank's target. Then to ensure that $R_0$ becomes the equilibrium rate, the central bank needs to shift the BB curve from its initial location $BB_0$ to $BB_1$, such that the GM and BB curves intersect at the targeted interest rate $R_0$. Because the domestic interest rate was initially above $R_0$ at point A, this requires expansionary monetary policy – i.e., an increase in $B_C$ through central-bank purchases of government bonds. As described in the chapter, the MM curve will then adjust passively through capital flows to pass through the intersection of BB and GM at B.

Since the analysis of interest rate targeting is thus a straightforward extension of domestic credit targeting, in this appendix we will focus on how the model works under the alternative of monetary targeting. We will begin by describing how the economy adjusts to equilibrium, and then consider the effects of the same shocks analyzed in the chapter under domestic credit targeting.

### Adjustment to Equilibrium

From equation 8.1, if the central bank chooses $M$ as its policy variable, it must adjust $B_C$ to offset the effects of any balance of payments-induced changes in its foreign exchange reserves, $SF_C^*$, on the money supply. As we saw in Chapter 6, this is referred to as *sterilizing* the effects of the balance of payments on the money supply. When the central bank sterilizes, the money supply becomes the exogenous policy variable, so the economy's equilibrium is determined by the intersection of GM and MM, just as in the closed-economy case. In this case, equations (8.2) and (8.3) determine $R$ and $Y$, and the role of equation (8.3) is to determine $B_C$ endogenously. Going back to Figure 8.1, in this case the economy's equilibrium would be at point B, rather than A.

The adjustment process is as follows: As before, the domestic interest rate is higher than required for equilibrium in the domestic bond market at point B. Consequently, capital inflows are attracted to the economy, which would tend to increase the domestic money supply in the absence of sterilization, as we saw just above. When the central bank sterilizes, however, it has to sell bonds (reduce $B_C$) to offset the effects of these inflows on the money supply. Because the selling of bonds by the central bank puts more domestic bonds into private portfolios, and for private agents to willingly absorb them requires an increase in their rate of return, a higher interest rate is required to clear the domestic bond market (Chapter 7). Thus the BB curve must shift upward as the result of the central bank's bond sales. Notice that MM would not move in this case even though $B_C$ is falling, because $F_C^*$ is rising at the same time, and this offsets the effects of open market bond sales on the money supply.

This process continues as long as BB lies below point B, because as long as it does so, the domestic interest rate is higher than that required to clear the bond market. This means that capital inflows and sterilization must continue, and sterilization is what causes BB to move. Once BB passes through point B, capital inflows stop (since the domestic bond market is in

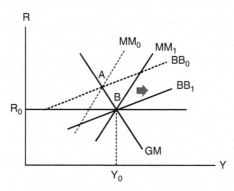

**Figure A8.1**   Adjustment to equilibrium under interest rate targeting

equilibrium, people are satisfied with the compositions of their portfolios). When sterilization stops, $B_C$ stops falling and BB stops moving.

Note that sterilization can work only because the central bank's monetary policy is able to move BB. If it couldn't, then the central bank would have to live with whatever the intersection of GM and BB implied for the domestic economy. That was indeed the case under perfect capital mobility, because the central bank had no influence over the UIP curve. What is the difference here? As we have seen, under imperfect substitutability, the rate of return on domestic bonds depends on the supply of such bonds in private portfolios, which is something the central bank does have control over. By contrast, under perfect substitutability, the rate of return on domestic bonds does *not* depend on the supply of such bonds outstanding, so the central bank's ability to alter the supply of domestic bonds does not give it any influence over the domestic interest rate.

### Monetary Expansion

Next, consider the effect of a monetary expansion. In particular, suppose from an initial point A in Figures 8.3 or 8.4, the domestic central bank wants to attain a new domestic equilibrium at a point like C, rather than D. Can it achieve this? The answer is that it can do so by undertaking the initial monetary expansion described in the chapter, but then offsetting the effects of any induced capital flows on the money supply by either buying or selling bonds. For example, when the point C lies below BB as in Figure 8.3, so that capital is induced to flow out of the country, thereby tending to shift the MM curve to the left, the central bank would have to buy even *more* bonds than it did in its original intervention in order to counteract the balance of payments-induced contraction of the money supply, and thus keep the MM curve stable at C. The additional purchase of bonds would cause BB to shift further down, doing so continuously until it intersects GM and MM at C. The process stops there, as it did under domestic credit targeting, because all of the economy's markets clear and pressures for additional capital outflows are eliminated.

This raises the interesting question of how the effects of a given monetary policy action on the domestic economy depend on whether the central bank sterilizes the monetary effects of the capital flows that its action induces. Intuitively, the answer depends on whether, say, a monetary expansion would have triggered capital inflows or outflows in the absence of sterilization. If it would have triggered capital *inflows*, then the sterilization of such inflows prevents the further monetary expansion that the inflows would have caused. In this case sterilization would tend to *weaken* the effects of monetary policy. If it would have triggered capital *outflows*, on the other hand, then sterilization prevents the monetary *contraction* that those outflows would otherwise have caused, and thus it would tend to *strengthen* the effects of monetary policy. Thus, whether sterilization strengthens or weakens monetary policy depends on the degree of capital mobility. It is more likely to strengthen the effects of monetary policy when capital is highly mobile than when it is not.

### Aggregate Demand Shocks

Turning to the effects of shocks under monetary targeting, consider first the case of aggregate demand shocks, such as a fiscal expansion. This was analyzed in the chapter under domestic credit targeting in Figure 8.5.

If the central bank sterilizes the monetary effects of the capital inflows caused by a fiscal expansion, leaving the money supply unchanged, the economy's new equilibrium would be at B, rather than D in Figure 8.5. The bank would still buy the foreign currency generated by capital inflows, as in the domestic credit-targeting case, but would offset the monetary impact of the operation by selling bonds. Since sterilization involves a reduction in $B_C$, it would cause BB to shift to the left until it intersects $MM_0$ and $GM_1$ at point B in Figure 8.5. The central bank may be motivated to sterilize to prevent the real shock from causing an excessive expansion in aggregate demand – that is, to mitigate the effect of the fiscal expansion on aggregate demand. Alternatively, the central bank may be forced to sterilize if it is committed to a publicly announced money supply target, which would be violated by the monetary expansion associated with the capital inflows triggered by higher domestic interest rates.

Since private absorption depends positively on income and negatively on the domestic interest rate, it is easy to see that the effects of a fiscal expansion on imports in the new equilibrium would tend to be ambiguous. Since exports do not change in this case, effects on net exports would tend to be ambiguous as well. However, imports would be more likely to increase, and net exports to fall, when the central bank does not sterilize capital inflows than when it does, since the domestic interest rate is lower in this case, increasing domestic absorption relative to income. On the other hand, it is easy to show, as we did in Chapter 6, that if the real shock takes the form of an exogenous increase in export demand, net exports must increase in the new equilibrium. In any case, the overall balance of payments will experience a temporary surplus driven by capital inflows while the economy makes the transition from A in Figure 8.5 to either B or D.

### Changes in World Interest Rates

The domestic effects of changes in world interest rates were considered in Figure 8.6. Recall that under domestic credit targeting, imperfect capital mobility partly insulated the domestic economy from the effects of changes in world interest rates. Through its monetary policy, the domestic central bank can further insulate domestic economic activity from the effects of changes in world interest rates, something that was impossible to do under perfect capital mobility. It can do so by sterilizing the capital outflows through open market bond purchases that prevent the contraction in the domestic money supply that shifted the MM curve leftward in Figure 8.6. The effect of these open market purchases is to reduce the supply of domestic bonds in private hands, thus shifting the BB curve back down. Through these means the central bank can actually return the equilibrium to A in Figure 8.6, leaving the domestic interest rate and level of output unchanged.

However, though the domestic interest rate and level of real output would remain undisturbed in this case despite the shock, the central bank's balance sheet would nevertheless reflect the effects of this policy. Specifically, the central bank must own fewer foreign exchange reserves and more domestic bonds than it would have in the absence of the shock. Thus, the shock is associated with a reserve loss. This is easy to see, since, with $R$ and $Y$ unchanged, the demand for domestic bonds must fall with the increase in the world interest rate. This means that the central bank has to absorb more domestic bonds to maintain equilibrium in the domestic bond market. But with the domestic money supply unchanged and the central bank's stock of domestic bonds increased, its stock of foreign exchange reserves must have fallen. Box 8.3 describes an important recent application of this policy in response to a *reduction* in world interest rates. An interesting issue arises in this context. We saw that if the central bank did *not* sterilize, it would also lose reserves. It was this reserve loss that caused the domestic money supply to contract. Is the loss of reserves when sterilization keeps the economy at A in Figure 8.6 larger than it would have been in the absence of sterilization when the economy moved to D?

## Box 8.3    The Capital-Inflow Problem

Capital inflows to developing countries have been episodic in nature. During certain periods these countries receive a substantial amount of capital from industrial countries (in various forms, including official loans, foreign direct investment, portfolio flows, and bank loans), while at other times such flows tend to dry up. Figure A8.2, for example, shows the patterns of net debt (loans plus portfolio bond flows) and portfolio equity flows to developing countries over the period 1970 to 2005. Notice how these flows accelerated during the 1970s, tailed off sharply during the debt crisis years 1982 to 1989 (see Chapter 2), resumed strongly in the first half of the 1990s, fell again after 1998, and boomed after 2002.

Many factors have been offered to explain this pattern. For the particular episode of the early 1990s several economists have found that sharp reductions in international interest rates were responsible for "pushing" capital to emerging-market economies. This is precisely what the analysis of world interest rate shocks in our model would suggest would happen when international interest rates fall, rather than increase (just the reverse of the analysis that we conducted in the section "Changes in world interest rates"). However, others have argued that improvements in the domestic policy environment in many developing countries during the early 1990s were more important, by attracting ("pulling") capital flows to the recipient countries. We can capture this phenomenon in our model in the form of a positive shock to the world demand for domestic bonds; the effects on the domestic economy would be qualitatively similar to those of a reduction in foreign interest rates. Empirical Study 8.2 describes some recent evidence on the relative importance of "push" and "pull" factors during the early 1990s.

The acceleration of capital inflows during those years actually created a serious macroeconomic policy problem for the countries that received the flows, because as our model suggests, the arrival of capital inflows driven by a reduction in world interest rates or by an increase in world demand for domestic bonds would tend to be expansionary. This represented an unwelcome shock to macroeconomic stability in countries such as Chile, Colombia, and Mexico that were trying to stabilize the domestic price level.

Our model suggests that the policy choices that these countries could have made to prevent an undesired expansion in aggregate demand included sterilization, fiscal contraction, and/or exchange rate revaluation. In fact, capital-inflow recipients tended to do all three (see Montiel 1999), although perhaps not surprisingly in view of the relatively greater flexibility of monetary policy as a stabilization instrument, most countries at least initially relied on a heavy dose of sterilization.

Given the slopes of the GM and MM curves, the answer turns out to depend on the degree of capital mobility. To see why, note that in the absence of sterilization, the economy would have achieved a new equilibrium at D in Figure 8.6, with a lower level of output and higher domestic interest rate than at A. Thus the alternative policy of sterilization can be thought of as a monetary expansion that moves the economy back from D to A. Therefore, if monetary expansion results in capital outflows, a policy that keeps the economy at A will result in

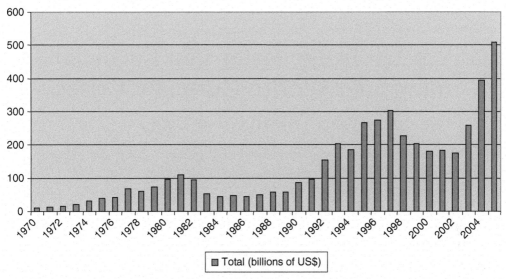

**Figure A8.2**   Developing countries: total capital inflows, 1970–2005

larger capital outflows and more extensive reserve losses than the alternative of allowing the money supply to contract. But as we saw in our examination of monetary policy, this must indeed be what happens when capital mobility is high.

**Unanticipated Exchange Rate Changes**

In the chapter, the effects of an unanticipated devaluation of the exchange rate under domestic credit targeting were analyzed in Figure 8.7. In the alternative case, that of monetary targeting, the MM curve is unaffected by the devaluation and the new equilibrium is at the intersection of the new GM with the old (pre-devaluation) MM, resulting in a higher level of domestic real output as well as a higher domestic interest rate. Since the intersection of MM with the new GM curve must lie above the new BB curve, the devaluation will be accompanied by capital inflows that increase the central bank's stock of foreign exchange reserves. As the central bank sells domestic bonds to sterilize these capital inflows the BB curve must shift up, and it will continue to do so until it passes through the intersection of the MM curve with the new GM curve. Net exports must rise in this case, because since the domestic interest rate is unambiguously higher, the increase in domestic real GDP must exceed any increase in absorption.

**Summary**

1   Under monetary targeting, the size of the open market operation required to achieve a given money supply target will be larger the greater the degree of capital mobility.
2   Sterilization tends to magnify the effects of real shocks on the country's stock of foreign exchange reserves when capital mobility is high.
3   The domestic economy can protect itself from foreign financial ($R^*$) shocks by sterilizing their monetary effects. However, sterilization magnifies the effects of foreign financial shocks on the country's stock of foreign exchange reserves when capital mobility is high.

# 9

# Fixed Exchange Rates in a Financially Integrated World: Currency Crises and ''Hard'' Pegs

..........................................................................................................................

We learned in Chapter 8 that international capital mobility gradually increased as the result of technological and institutional developments during the Bretton Woods period. Improvements in transportation and communications technologies, rapid financial development in the form of new institutions and instruments, and the gradual easing of restrictions on international capital movements among industrial countries, all contributed to a process of increased financial integration. This process actually accelerated after the Bretton Woods system collapsed, as many countries completed the process of removing official restrictions on capital flows.[1] During recent years, just as during the Bretton Woods era, the process of financial integration has been accelerated worldwide by technological and institutional developments that have facilitated cross-border flows of information and reduced the costs of making financial transactions with residents of other countries. We noted in Chapter 5 that the major trading countries were highly integrated in both goods and financial markets at the end of the 19th century. Most observers would agree that by the end of the 20th century a high level of financial integration had once again been attained among industrial countries. Consequently, Part 3 of the book is devoted to an analysis of how floating exchange rates work when the economy is highly integrated with world financial markets.

---

[1]   The United States removed most of its restrictions on international capital movements in the 1970s and early 1980s, followed in the later 1980s and early 1990s by Japan and Western Europe.

However, the process of financial integration has affected not only industrial countries, but also developing ones. Though the vast majority of today's developing countries – especially those at very low levels of income per capita – still have very imperfect links with world capital markets, a group of relatively large middle-income developing economies, including countries such as Argentina, Brazil, Chile, Indonesia, Korea, Mexico, and South Africa, has also become highly integrated with world capital markets in recent years. These are often referred to as **emerging market** economies. The vast majority of these countries retained some form of fixed exchange rate regime after the collapse of the Bretton Woods system, but as their degree of integration with world financial markets has increased, many of them have engaged in repeated changes of their official parities, have adopted hard pegs, or have switched to floating exchange rates, often in the wake of dramatic sell offs of their currencies in a crisis atmosphere. We will discuss some of these crises over the course of this chapter.

Why should financial integration have made exchange rate policies in emerging-market economies so unstable? To answer this question, in this chapter we will investigate the macroeconomics of fixed exchange rates in a financially integrated world. Since the gold standard system featured fixed exchange rates in a context of a high degree of international financial integration, we already did much of this work when we analyzed how the gold standard worked in Chapter 6. However, we have yet to analyze the macroeconomics of soft exchange rate pegs under conditions of high capital mobility. We undertake this analysis in the first section of this chapter. We will follow up that analysis by looking at the factors that cause currency crises (dramatic movements in nominal exchange rates), focusing especially on how the likelihood of such a crisis for a country with a fixed exchange rate may be influenced by its degree of integration with world capital markets. This discussion reveals that soft pegs are indeed likely to prove very fragile when capital mobility is high, explaining the transitions in exchange rate regimes that have been undergone by many emerging economies in recent years. We then explore one possible response to the fragility of soft pegs: moving to modern versions of hard pegs. Finally, as our first foray into the issue of optimal exchange rate regimes (a topic we will return to in Chapter 15), we analyze some of the considerations that influence the choice between soft and hard pegs for countries choosing to fix their exchange rates in a context of high capital mobility. That discussion will set the stage for an analysis of the alternative response to the fragility of soft pegs in a financially integrated world: moving to a floating exchange rate.

## 9.1    Soft Pegs with High Capital Mobility

The defining characteristic of a soft peg is that both the official exchange rate, $S$, and the central bank's stock of domestic assets, $B_C$, are policy variables chosen by the central bank *at its discretion*. This means, in particular, that the exchange rate is taken to be fixed but adjustable, as in the Bretton Woods system. Similarly, the central bank is free to conduct domestic monetary policy as it sees fit, with no external restrictions on the value that it chooses for $B_C$ and no compelling reason to link changes in $B_C$ to changes in its stock of foreign exchange reserves. In this section, we use our model to explore how monetary and exchange rate policies work under conditions of high capital mobility.

Solving the Model

Since we previously analyzed the macroeconomics of fixed exchange rates with perfect capital mobility in Chapter 6, we can begin the analysis of soft pegs by reproducing the compact version of the fixed exchange rate model of that chapter in Box 9.1. Since $S$ and $B_C$ are now very explicitly taken to be policy variables, our model consists of four equations in five potentially endogenous variables $F_C^*$, $M$, $B_C$, $R$, and $Y$.

*The Impossible Trinity*    When analyzing soft pegs under imperfect capital mobility in the last chapter, we addressed the problem of having an extra endogenous variable by specifying the central bank's monetary policy regime, noting that the central bank could choose to target $B_C$, $M$, or $R$. Once the monetary policy variable was chosen, that variable became exogenous, leaving the model consisting of four equations in four unknowns. However, that option is no longer available to us when capital mobility is high and the imperfect-substitutes bond-market equilibrium condition of the last chapter is replaced by the UIP condition in Box 9.1. To see why, notice first that the UIP condition (9.3) now determines the domestic interest rate, so the central bank cannot engage in interest rate targeting. But second, notice that if the UIP condition is substituted into the goods market equilibrium condition (9.4), that condition is sufficient to determine the equilibrium level of GDP. With the domestic interest rate and equilibrium level of GDP pinned down in this way, the money market equilibrium condition (9.2) determines the equilibrium value of the domestic money supply, so the central bank cannot engage in monetary targeting (sterilization) either. It follows that $B_C$ is the only candidate for the exogenous monetary policy variable under fixed exchange rates and perfect financial integration – i.e., the central bank can only engage in domestic credit targeting.

What we have just derived is an extremely important result, called the ***impossible trinity of international macroeconomics***. This proposition states that there are three things that

---

**Box 9.1    A Model with a Soft Peg and Perfect Capital Mobility**

**Central bank balance sheet**

$$SF_C^* + B_C = M \tag{9.1}$$

**Money market equilibrium (MM)**

$$M = \bar{P}L(R, Y) \tag{9.2}$$

**Bond market equilibrium (UIP)**

$$R = R^* \tag{9.3}$$

**Goods market equilibrium (GM)**

$$Y = \varphi(SP^*/\bar{P})A(Y - T, R) + G + X(SP^*/\bar{P}, \theta) \tag{9.4}$$

open economies cannot have at the same time: a fixed exchange rate, perfect capital mobility, and **monetary autonomy** (the ability to engage in monetary targeting). We have just shown that fixed exchange rates and perfect capital mobility make it impossible for the domestic central bank to target the money supply as a policy variable. We saw in the appendix to Chapter 8, however, that if capital mobility is imperfect a fixed exchange rate is compatible with monetary autonomy. As you will see in the next chapter, monetary autonomy is compatible with perfect capital mobility under a floating exchange rate. The impossible trinity is one of the most important principles in international macroeconomics, and we will encounter it repeatedly in the rest of this book.

*Model Solution*    In light of the impossible trinity, we will take $B_C$ to be the exogenous monetary policy variable. With this assumption, the procedure for solving the model should be familiar. We proceed as suggested in the derivation of the impossible trinity result above: as in Chapter 6, the uncovered interest parity (UIP) relationship ensures that the domestic interest rate must be equal to the foreign rate $R^*$. Substituting $R^*$ for $R$ in the goods market equilibrium condition (equation 9.4) determines the equilibrium level of output. With the equilibrium values of $R$ and $Y$ known, the next step is to substitute these into the money market equilibrium condition (equation 9.2) to determine the equilibrium value of the domestic money supply. Finally, using this equilibrium value of $M$ in the central bank's balance sheet (equation 9.1) we can determine the equilibrium level of the country's stock of foreign exchange reserves $F_C^*$.

The solution of the model is depicted graphically in Figure 9.1. As in Chapter 6, the UIP relationship is plotted as the horizontal line at height $R^*$, while the goods market equilibrium condition is drawn as the downward sloping GM curve. The equilibrium values of $R$ and $Y$ are determined at the intersection of UIP and GM, at point B. The money market equilibrium condition is depicted as the upward sloping MM curve. As noted in previous chapters, the position of the MM curve is determined by the value of the money supply. Given an arbitrary initial value of the money supply, the MM curve may intersect the GM curve either above or below the UIP line. In Figure 9.1, the initial intersection happens to occur at a point A that lies below the UIP line. The economy contains an automatic adjustment mechanism that causes the MM curve to shift from any arbitrary initial position so that it passes through the intersection of UIP and GM. This adjustment mechanism takes the form of capital flows that cause adjustments in the money supply. From point A, for example, capital outflows caused by a domestic interest rate such as $R_0$ that is lower than the foreign rate cause the

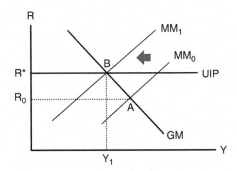

**Figure 9.1**    Short-run equilibrium under a soft peg with high capital mobility

money supply to decrease, shifting the MM curve to the left from its initial position at $MM_0$ until it shifts to a new position such as $MM_1$ passing through B. If the arbitrarily chosen initial position of the MM curve was such that it intersected the GM curve above UIP, a similar adjustment process would be driven by capital *inflows* triggered by a high domestic interest rate. In this case, unlike in the gold standard model of Chapter 6, $B_C$ is an exogenous variable. Thus changes in $B_C$ do not contribute to the automatic adjustment in the money supply under soft exchange rate pegs. All of the adjustment in the money supply comes about through changes in the central bank's stock of foreign exchange reserves $F_C^*$ caused by capital outflows or inflows.

We can now see the role of the central bank's balance sheet (equation 9.1) in our model. Given the equilibrium value of the domestic money supply (which appears on the right-hand side of the equation), and since both $S$ and $B_C$ are exogenous, equation (9.1) simply tells us the size of the central bank's stock of foreign exchange reserves $F_C^*$ – that is, just how large the capital flows are that are required to lower the domestic interest rate to $R^*$.

## Monetary and Exchange Rate Policies

Though we previously analyzed how the economy adjusts to shocks when the central bank maintains a fixed exchange rate under conditions of high capital mobility, we did so only in the context of a hard peg in which the central bank had no control over monetary and exchange rate policies. Since we are now considering a soft peg, we can complete our analysis by examining the effects of monetary and exchange rate policies. We will begin by examining how monetary policy works in this environment and will then consider the effects of actual and anticipated future exchange rate changes.

*Monetary Policy*    Figure 9.2 shows the effects of a monetary expansion. Given the central bank's stock of foreign exchange reserves, the effect of an increase in $B_C$ is to shift MM to the right from a position such as $MM_0$ to $MM_1$, since the central bank can only acquire more domestic bonds by printing new money. The intersection of $MM_1$ with the stationary GM curve, at a point such as B, would thus occur at a lower level of the domestic interest rate (labeled $R_1$) than that which prevails in world capital markets. As we have seen, this interest rate differential triggers capital outflows from the domestic economy that reduce the central

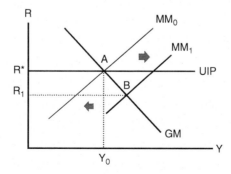

**Figure 9.2**    Effects of a monetary expansion

bank's foreign exchange reserves and cause the domestic money supply to contract, shifting MM back to the left. This process continues until MM has returned to its initial point, leaving $Y$ unaffected.

At the final equilibrium the impact of the policy would be felt only in the central bank's balance sheet. Since in the restored equilibrium there would be no change in the money supply despite the increase in the stock of domestic bonds held by the central bank, equation (9.1) confirms that the only effect of the monetary expansion must have been to reduce the foreign exchange "backing" of the domestic money supply dollar for dollar with the increase in bonds held by the central bank. The change in the stock of foreign exchange reserves ($SF_C^*$) associated with each unit of change in the central bank's stock of domestic assets ($B_C$) is sometimes referred to as the **offset coefficient** associated with monetary policy. Since under current circumstances the change in $B_C$ has no effect on the equilibrium value of the domestic money supply, and is simply offset dollar-for-dollar by a change in the central bank's stock of foreign exchange reserves, the offset coefficient in this case is $-1$.

An important question that arises at this point is why the central bank would engage in a monetary expansion if such an expansion in the end has no effect on the domestic macro-economic equilibrium. The answer is that the central bank may do so in order to finance a **fiscal deficit** – that is, an excess of government spending over government revenues. If the government has an excess of spending over revenue, it can cover the difference only by issuing bonds. To the extent that the central bank buys some of those bonds they do not have to be sold to the public, and the fiscal deficit is effectively financed by printing money. As we have seen, however, under fixed exchange rates and perfect capital mobility, no new money is actually created by this process in equilibrium. Instead, the deficit is in reality financed by drawing down the central bank's stock of foreign exchange reserves. This will have important implications for the sustainability of the fixed exchange rate, as we will see in the next section.

*Exchange Rate Policy*    An important defining characteristic of soft pegs is that the central bank retains the option to alter the exchange rate. As we have seen, under fixed exchange rates, a discrete change in $S$ is called a devaluation if the currency depreciates ($S$ increases), and a revaluation if the currency appreciates ($S$ decreases). What would happen, then, if the domestic central bank unexpectedly devalues the currency (increases $S$), for example?

Notice first, from equation 9.1, that an increase in $S$ would increase the domestic-currency value of the central bank's foreign exchange reserves. Since the central bank's assets (in the form of $SF_C^* + B_C$) would rise in value while its liabilities (in the form of $M$) would remain unchanged, the central bank's wealth would increase. We will assume, as in Chapter 8, that the central bank simply transfers this capital gain to the government, which uses it to buy back some of its bonds from the central bank, leaving the money supply $M$ unchanged on impact. What would happen to the economy in this case?

The answer is given in Figure 9.3. Since the domestic price level is fixed in the short run, a nominal devaluation would result in a depreciation of the real exchange rate, that is, an increase in $Q$. The resulting expenditure-switching effect in favor of domestic goods and services would cause the GM curve to shift to the right, to a position such as $GM_1$. This shift is larger the stronger the expenditure-switching effect of the devaluation, that is, the closer the degree of substitutability between domestic and foreign goods. At the point B, where the new GM curve intersects the MM curve, the domestic interest rate $R_1$ would exceed the foreign rate $R^*$, triggering a capital inflow that shifts MM to the right until it passes through

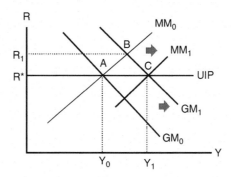

**Figure 9.3**    Effects of an exchange rate devaluation

the intersection of UIP and the new GM. At the new equilibrium (labeled C in the figure) the level of real output would increase, but the domestic interest rate would be unaffected.

*Expected Exchange Rate Changes*    We have implicitly assumed so far in this chapter that the exchange rate peg is fully credible, that is, even though the central bank *could* in principle change the exchange rate peg, no one actually expects the exchange rate to change. But under a soft peg, this may not always be reasonable, since the central bank retains the option to alter the peg at its discretion. Moreover, as we shall see later in this chapter, sometimes the central bank may be *forced* to alter the peg. What happens to the economy if, say, a devaluation of the exchange rate is expected to take place in the next period?

If such an expectation were to materialize, it would no longer be true that $S_{+1}^e = \bar{S}$. In that case, the UIP condition reverts to its original form:

$$R = (1 + R^*)S_{+1}^e/\bar{S} - 1$$

An expected devaluation then represents an increase in $S_{+1}^e$. The effect of this expectation is exactly the same as that of an increase in the expected future price of gold that we considered in Chapter 6, the analysis of which is reproduced in Figure 9.4. The increase in $S_{+1}^e$ would cause the UIP curve to shift upward, to a position such as $UIP_1$. This upward shift leaves the domestic interest rate at the original point A below the level that would be required to satisfy UIP. The result is to trigger a massive capital outflow from the domestic

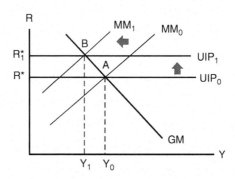

**Figure 9.4**    Effects of an expected exchange rate devaluation

economy, which causes the MM curve to shift to the left until it passes through the intersection of the GM curve with the new UIP curve (point B). Domestic interest rates rise to compensate for the expected loss of value of the domestic currency, and as a result of the increase in the domestic interest rate, the level of real output falls. Box 9.2 illustrates the powerful effect that expected exchange rate changes can have on a small open economy by reviewing the Argentine recession of 1995.

In summary, we have seen that under conditions of high capital mobility, countries that maintain soft pegs have no monetary autonomy, in the sense that they cannot determine the size of the domestic money supply, despite their retention of control over monetary policy. In this context, monetary policy remains effective only in that it can alter the central bank's stock of foreign exchange reserves. On the other hand, central banks do retain some power to affect domestic economic activity: specifically, they can do so by changing the exchange

## Box 9.2    How the Mexican Crisis Caused a Recession in Argentina

Mexico and Argentina shared some similarities in macroeconomic experience during the mid-1990s. Both countries had been heavily affected by the Latin American debt crisis of 1982, an episode during which many countries in their region defaulted on their international debts. For both countries the decade of the 1980s had been a period of high inflation and low growth (though inflation was much higher in Argentina than in Mexico during this period). During the late 1980s and early 1990s both countries attempted to reduce the rate of inflation by using a fixed exchange rate as a nominal anchor. Mexico did so under a soft peg regime, while Argentina did so using a currency board, a form of hard peg that we will examine later in this chapter. In both countries the inflation rate came down gradually during the early 1990s, but for a period of time the domestic inflation rates in both countries exceeded those of the countries' trading partners, so that in both countries the real exchange rate (recall that this is given by $Q = SP^*/P$) appreciated substantially.

The appreciation of the real exchange rate in Mexico resulted in a loss of competitiveness for the Mexican economy that eventually caused an exchange rate crisis in December 1994, during the course of which Mexico was forced to give up its fixed exchange rate (see Box 9.4). The Mexican peso depreciated sharply after the fixed exchange rate was abandoned. The experience of the Mexican peso led financial markets to suspect that Argentina was preparing to undergo a similar fate in early 1995, which created the expectation of a sharp depreciation of the Argentine peso. As our model predicts, this caused a sharp increase in interest rates in Argentina in the first quarter of 1995, together with very substantial capital outflows from the country and a strong monetary contraction. The result was a severe recession in Argentina and a sharp increase in unemployment. In the event, however, the Argentine peso held firm, and when expectations of devaluation eventually subsided in mid-1995, capital returned to the country, domestic interest rates fell, and real economic activity recovered.

rate peg. However, under these circumstances financial markets would tend to be highly sensitive to expectations of expected future exchange rate changes.

## 9.2    Currency Crises

In recent years, many economists have formed the opinion that a soft peg is not a viable exchange rate regime in the context of high capital mobility. The argument is that such regimes are vulnerable to **speculative attacks** – situations in which domestic and foreign residents switch such a large volume of resources from domestic currency-denominated assets to foreign currency-denominated ones that they either threaten to exhaust the central bank's stock of foreign exchange reserves or otherwise to compel the central bank to abandon its announced exchange rate parity. The abandonment of the fixed parity makes for a dramatic event known as a **currency crisis**, similar to other types of financial crises in which some economic entity is unable to fulfill its financial commitments.

Currency crises have been frequent occurrences over the past several decades, as shown in Figure 9.5. Crises have affected both industrial and developing economies. They have increasingly occupied the attention of international macroeconomists, because in some highly visible cases – especially in Mexico in 1994–5, in several Asian countries in 1997–8 and in Argentina in 2001–2, these crises have been very disruptive to the economies that have undergone them.

Why do currency crises happen? They arise when the central bank's commitment to defend the value of the currency conflicts with some other economic objective. There are

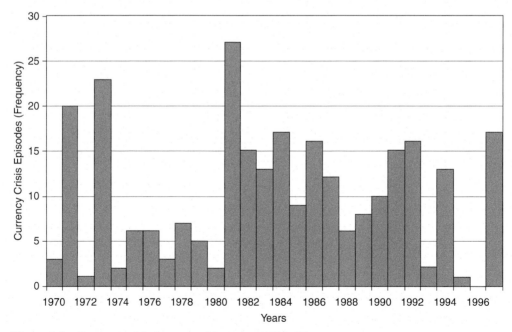

**Figure 9.5**    Currency crisis frequency histogram (1970–97)

two types of crisis models. In "first-generation" models the competing objective is a fiscal one. In these models, the central bank is mechanically committed to the objective of financing an ongoing government fiscal deficit by buying the bonds that the government issues to raise funds. The central bank is assumed to be willing to fulfill its commitment to fix the exchange rate only as long as doing so is compatible with the fiscal objective. Notice that since the instrument that the bank uses to satisfy its fiscal objective consists of open-market purchases of government bonds, this type of crisis is only possible under fixed exchange rate regimes that leave the central bank with discretion about when to make such purchases – that is, under soft pegs.

In "second generation" crisis models, the set of potential competing objectives can be much broader. It may include a fiscal objective, but may alternatively refer to the level of economic activity, the health of the domestic financial system, and so on. In these models, the central bank weighs the benefits of adhering to its announced exchange rate peg against the costs of sacrificing one of these other objectives. It sacrifices the exchange rate peg when it perceives the costs of maintaining it to be greater than the benefits of doing so, even if it would be feasible for the peg to be maintained. Notice once again that this kind of tradeoff is only possible when the exchange rate is fixed but adjustable, that is, under soft pegs.

In this section we will examine how both types of crisis may arise, and will consider the possibility that currency crises may be self-fulfilling, that is, that they may happen primarily because they are expected to happen, which makes soft pegs potentially very brittle creatures indeed.

## "First-Generation" Crises

The model that we examined in the previous section describes the behavior of an economy under soft peg conditions, in which the domestic monetary authorities are free to set $B_C$ in a discretionary fashion. As already mentioned, this allows them to use $B_C$ in order to achieve other economic objectives and creates the possibility that these other objectives could conflict with the objective of maintaining a fixed exchange rate.

To illustrate the potential problem, consider the "first generation" case. Suppose, in particular, that a country fixes the value of its currency against a foreign currency, but that its central bank adopts as its alternative objective the continual financing of a fiscal deficit by buying a given amount of government bonds each period. Suppose that the central bank is completely committed to the financing objective and will maintain the fixed exchange rate only as long as it does not conflict with the central bank's overriding fiscal role.

What would happen in such an economy? The answer can be inferred from what we have already done in this chapter. This policy essentially involves a continuous increase in $B_C$ each period. Notice that, since changes in $B_C$ have no impact on the real economy, the domestic interest rate, level of real output, and price level are not affected by this policy, so the demand for money, given by $PL(R, Y)$, is unchanged. Consequently, the nominal money supply $M$ must remain unchanged as well. As we saw in the previous section this happens because increases in $B_C$ are offset by decreases in $SF_C^*$ on a one-for-one basis.

Figure 9.6 shows the evolution of the economy over time. The domestic money supply is shown in the figure as a constant value $M_0$. On the other hand, the stock of domestic bonds $B_C$ is shown as increasing by a constant amount each period. The central bank's stock of foreign exchange reserves can be seen in the figure as the vertical distance between

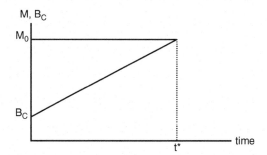

**Figure 9.6**    Reserve depletion in a ''first-generation'' currency crisis

$M$ and $B_C$. Over time, as $B_C$ increases, the stock of reserves must be falling continuously – indeed, dollar for dollar with the increase in $B_C$. When the central bank's stock of foreign exchange reserves is depleted at time $t^*$, it can no longer continue to support the value of the currency, and the fixed exchange rate regime must be abandoned. The moment when the central bank abandons its currency peg is typically called a currency crisis because, as we will see in the discussion of the monetary approach to the exchange rate in Chapter 14, currency pegs tend to be abandoned with a bang, not a whimper.

A currency crisis is not a necessary outcome under a soft exchange rate peg. It arises in this case because the central bank devotes its domestic monetary policy to the financing of fiscal deficits and is unwilling to compromise on this goal. In other words, it arises because of the way that the central bank uses its discretion over $B_C$. Some economists have argued that to avoid such crises, it is necessary to remove the central bank's discretion over domestic monetary policy. As we will explore later in this chapter, this involves replacing a soft peg with a modern hard currency peg.

### ''Second-Generation'' Crises

The model we have just examined does not describe the only way that a currency peg may be abandoned under a soft peg arrangement. It is also possible for a central bank to decide to alter the exchange rate peg simply to improve domestic economic performance, and the mere anticipation of such a decision could give rise to speculative attacks and large capital outflows. For example, suppose that an economy that operates a soft peg under conditions of perfect capital mobility finds itself in a deep recession. What measures could the authorities take to revive economic activity?

One possibility, of course, is to administer a fiscal stimulus. We saw in Chapter 6 that fiscal policy can be very powerful when capital mobility is high and a country maintains a fixed exchange rate. But fiscal policy has rarely proven to be a very flexible stabilization instrument, because changes in government spending and taxes tend to create winners and losers, and it is not unusual for the political process to produce a stalemate that makes it impossible to legislate appropriate fiscal measures. In this context, the burden of responding to the recession falls to the central bank.

As we have also seen, however, monetary policy is powerless to affect real economic activity under fixed exchange rates and high capital mobility. Hence the only instrument that the central bank can use effectively is an adjustment in the exchange rate parity. As we saw in the last section, under recession circumstances, this would call for a nominal devaluation. Thus, the objective of maintaining the exchange rate peg conflicts with that of stabilizing domestic real GDP around its full employment level. This is a familiar quandary under fixed exchange rates. Box 9.3 provides one example in which the dilemma was resolved in favor of the domestic macroeconomic objective. It describes the events surrounding the ERM (European Exchange Rate Mechanism) crisis of 1992, showing how a conflict between internal and external economic objectives caused several countries to drop out of the ERM in the fall of that year and float their currencies.

## Self-Fulfilling Currency Crises

This analysis suggests that currency crises could happen as the result of welfare-maximizing behavior by central banks when an economy operating a soft exchange rate peg under conditions of high capital mobility falls into recession. But matters may actually be worse than this. Recall the analysis of the macroeconomic effects of an expected future devaluation in the last section. Suppose that the economy is in equilibrium at full employment, but that for no apparent reason, financial markets begin to expect that the exchange rate could be devalued. As we have seen, such an expectation could itself cause a recession (as the case of Argentina in Box 9.2 shows). If the central bank attempts to combat the recession by devaluing the currency, as in the previous case that we examined, then the seemingly arbitrary expectations of devaluation in the market would actually have been correct! International macroeconomists refer to such a situation as a **self-fulfilling currency crisis**. The problem is that as long as central banks care about the performance of the economy, and as long as they are willing and able to use the exchange rate as an instrument of macroeconomic policy (as under a soft peg), such an outcome cannot be ruled out in general. This has led some economists to refer to soft pegs under conditions of high capital mobility as a mirage – they are only there as long as they are not tested, but when they are tested they disappear.[2]

We conclude that soft pegs are potentially highly vulnerable to currency crises when capital mobility is very high. This is the case if the central bank persistently finances a fiscal deficit by monetizing it (a "first-generation" crisis), but it can also happen even if there is no ongoing monetization of fiscal deficits, through a variety of second-generation crisis mechanisms, including the possibility of a self-fulfilling speculative attack.

## 9.3    Financial Integration and Crises

What is the role of perfect capital mobility in affecting the likelihood that a fixed exchange rate will collapse, that is, that the central bank will either be forced to or will choose to abandon its exchange rate peg? In this section, we will show that if capital mobility is imperfect, each of the mechanisms reviewed in the last section through which a currency crisis could be triggered would tend to operate more weakly, thus making a fixed exchange rate easier to sustain under imperfect capital mobility. As a country's degree of financial

---

[2]  See Obstfeld and Rogoff (1995).

## Box 9.3    The ERM Crisis of 1992

In Chapter 18 we will study in some detail the process of European monetary unification, which culminated in the creation of a new currency, the euro. The euro began to circulate as notes and coins throughout most of Western Europe in January 2002, replacing the national currencies that had existed until that time. As we will see there, that process was not without some bumps along the way. A very large bump was encountered in the fall of 1992, in the form of a severe exchange rate crisis.

The process of adopting the euro involved some intermediate steps in which countries that were prospective participants in the single-currency arrangement – that is, members of the European Union such as France, Germany, and Italy – fixed the values of their currencies against each other. This was done by fixing the value of each currency against a synthetic basket of currencies called the **European Currency Unit (ECU)** as part of the **European Exchange Rate Mechanism (ERM)**. The latter was an arrangement among participating countries that committed their central banks to intervene in foreign exchange markets under stipulated conditions in order to sustain the agreed-upon parities. The ECU, in turn, floated against the other major currencies of the world. In practice, pegging the value of the currency against the ECU amounted to pegging against the German Deutschmark, since Germany had both the largest economy and the strongest currency in the arrangement.

The stability of this arrangement was disturbed by two events that took place at the end of the 1980s: the abolition of capital controls within Europe, which created a situation tantamount to perfect capital mobility among the participating countries, and the reunification of East and West Germany. For reasons that we will explore in Chapter 10, the latter gave rise to an increase in interest rates in Germany as well as to a strong tendency for the Deutschmark to appreciate against major currencies such as the US dollar and Japanese yen. As we have seen, the countries that effectively pegged their currencies to the Deutschmark and were financially integrated with Germany would have been forced not only to follow the appreciation of the Deutschmark against the major currencies, but also to import the high German interest rates.

This was a problem for countries within the ERM mechanism that found themselves in a recession at the time, since high interest rates and an appreciating currency against trading partners outside the ERM would both have tended to reduce aggregate demand in their economies, thus magnifying the severity of the recession. Such countries – the most important of which were the United Kingdom and Italy – thus found themselves in a position where their *external* economic objectives (maintaining their exchange rate parities against the Deutschmark) conflicted with their *internal* ones (sustaining domestic prosperity). They thus were forced to weigh the benefits of continuing to participate in the ERM against the cost of foregoing the opportunity to devalue their currencies and give a boost to their economies.

Matters came to a head in June 1992, when a referendum in Denmark rejected the Maastricht Treaty – a treaty that had to be approved in order to move to the next step in monetary unification (Chapter 18 will explore this further). A similar referendum was due to be held in France in September, and preliminary polls indicated that the vote would be close. This situation called the future of monetary unification in Europe into question and tended to undermine the perceived benefits to individual countries of remaining within the ERM.

Markets began to speculate on a devaluation in countries such as the United Kingdom and Italy, leading to massive capital flows from these countries into Germany. By mid-September the pressure was too much to bear, and on September 13 the Italian lira was devalued by 7 percent. Germany responded with interest rate cuts, but by amounts that were perceived as too small by financial markets. Comments by the president of the Bundesbank appeared to question the central parity of the British pound, and speculative pressures on the pound intensified. Interest rate increases in the United Kingdom did little to stem capital outflows, and the Bank of England was forced into massive intervention in the foreign exchange markets to sustain the currency's parity. In the evening of September 16, the United Kingdom dropped out of the arrangement.

integration with the rest of the world increases, however, these mechanisms gradually become stronger.

To see why this is so, consider first the effects of monetary financing of fiscal deficits. In our model, we can think of this as a continued increase in $B_C$. For simplicity, suppose that there is no attempt on the part of the central bank to sterilize the effects of the monetary expansion on capital flows. As we saw in Chapter 8, under imperfect capital mobility a monetary expansion results in a reduction in the domestic interest rate and increase in real GDP. But both of these effects tend to increase the demand for money. Since the expansion in $B_C$ is therefore at least partially absorbed by an increase in the domestic demand for money, the implication is that the induced loss of reserves (the "offset coefficient") will be less than one-for-one. Because a given amount of monetary expansion is associated with a smaller reserve loss, this prolongs the period of time until the central bank's stock of reserves are exhausted. In short, imperfect capital mobility makes it possible to prolong the life of the fixed exchange rate under first-generation crisis conditions.

Next, consider a second-generation crisis in which a domestic recession gives rise to the expectation of a devaluation, simply because the central bank has no other instrument with which to stimulate the domestic economy. Since monetary policy is no longer impotent when capital mobility is imperfect, private agents would have less reason to anticipate a devaluation under recessionary conditions, because the option of adopting a more expansionary monetary policy would remain an effective anti-recessionary alternative for the central bank. Thus, one might expect devaluation to be likely only when monetary expansion is ruled out on other grounds, say, when the stock of foreign exchange reserves is inadequate and is likely to be depleted by the capital outflows that may be associated with a monetary expansion.

Finally, consider the potential for "self-fulfilling" speculative attacks. When the exchange rate is expected to be devalued, the equation for the BB curve of Chapter 8 reverts to:

$$B - B_C = H[R,(1 + R^*)S^e_{+1}/S - 1](W_P - PL) + H^*$$
$$[R,(1 + R^*)S^e_{+1}/S - 1]S(W^*_F - P^*L^*)$$

That is, we can no longer make the simplifying assumption that $S^e_{+1}/S = 1$. Notice that the expected future value of the exchange rate enters this equation only in the form $(1 + R^*)$ $S^e_{+1}/S - 1$, that is, only as part of the expression for the expected domestic-currency return from investing in foreign bonds. Thus, the effect of an increase in $S^e_{+1}$ in this model is exactly the same as that of an increase in $R^*$. As we saw in Chapter 8, the BB curve will shift up, but not by as much as the increase in the domestic-currency rate of return on foreign bonds, and the domestic interest rate will therefore rise, but not by as much as the magnitude of the upward shift in the BB curve.

The upshot is that expectations of devaluation put much less upward pressure on the domestic interest rate under conditions of imperfect capital mobility than when capital mobility is very high. Thus, such expectations do much less harm to the domestic economy, and the domestic monetary authorities are under much less pressure to give in to them. The implication is that soft pegs are likely to prove more robust to speculative pressures under imperfect capital mobility than under perfect capital mobility, making self-fulfilling speculative attacks less likely the less integrated an economy is with international financial markets.

## Box 9.4    Emerging Market Crises in the 1990s

Although the period from 1989 to 1994 was marked by the return of large amounts of international capital to the major emerging-market economies in Asia and Latin America, the remainder of the decade of the 1990s was punctuated by a series of severe financial crises in some of these economies. This box reviews the causes of some of the major episodes.

### Mexico 1994

The Mexican currency crisis that broke out in December 1994 followed a major effort at market-oriented reform that the country undertook in the mid- to late 1980s, featuring a fixed exchange rate, a major fiscal contraction, greatly increased openness to international trade, domestic financial liberalization, and enhanced openness in the capital account of the balance of payments. Unfortunately, the institutional framework for the domestic banking sector was weak when the domestic financial sector was liberalized (that is, banks were poorly supervised and regulated), and the liberalization led to a rapid expansion of bank credit, partly fueled by large capital inflows in the early 1990s. At the same time, the exchange rate-based stabilization resulted in a substantial appreciation of the real exchange rate. The weakness of the banking system and the appreciated currency made it more likely that the government would devalue rather than raise interest rates in the event of a speculative attack. In this fragile context, a series of internal and external political and economic shocks in 1994 resulted in capital outflows which, to prevent pressures on the financial system, the central bank attempted to sterilize. Given Mexico's financial openness, the magnified loss of reserves caused by this policy culminated in a collapse of the currency in December. In addition to the sterilization, the government attempted to reduce its borrowing costs by switching its liabilities to short-maturity dollar-denominated debt in mid-1994, making it vulnerable to a public sector liquidity crisis in early 1995, which raised domestic interest rates dramatically and caused a collapse of the financial system, with severe effects on real output. The country's relatively solid fiscal performance in the period leading up to the crisis suggests that this was not a first-generation crisis.

## Asia 1997

As in Mexico, the Asian crisis – which had its most severe effects on Indonesia, Korea, Malaysia, the Philippines, and Thailand – emerged in a context in which the countries' fundamental macroeconomic performance appeared to be sound. Fiscal deficits and public sector debt were relatively small relative to GDP, and inflation was low, again suggesting that first-generation factors were not critical in these crises. As in Mexico, however, domestic and external financial liberalization had been implemented in the late 1980s and early 1990s under questionable domestic institutional conditions. Real exchange rate overvaluation was probably not as important as in Mexico, but there are some indications that real exchange rates may have been overvalued in at least some of these countries before the outbreak of the crisis in July of 1997, when Thailand abandoned its exchange rate peg. Though observers still disagree about the ultimate causes of the crisis (for example, some argue that though fiscal performance appeared to be strong in these countries, their governments had hidden financial obligations that called their solvency into question), it was immediately preceded by a growth slow-down in some of these economies (especially in Thailand) and featured rapid conta-gion from Thailand to the other affected countries, suggesting that pre-existing domestic economic problems made these economies vulnerable.

## Russia 1998

Unlike the two previous crises, the Russian crisis in August 1998 played out in a context in which almost all macroeconomic factors were weak. Because of a combin-ation of political instability, weak fiscal institutions, and poor tax administration, Russia had been unable to achieve a sustainable fiscal position and had relied heavily on borrowing and printing money to finance fiscal deficits. Russian inflation had been high in the early part of the 1990s, but an exchange rate based stabilization helped to reduce it substantially by mid-decade. As in the other crises described above, the domestic financial sector was extremely weak. Moreover, the Russian macroeconomic situation was adversely affected by the reduction in world oil prices that followed the outbreak of the Asian crisis. Not only is oil Russia's major export, but oil revenues have a large impact on the government's fiscal position, making the fiscal situation even worse. The crisis, which broke out in August of 1998, was triggered when it became evident that the country's external creditors were unwilling, in the absence of a major fiscal adjustment by Russia, to finance the fiscal gap that emerged under these circumstances. This event led to a sharp reduction in the willingness by financial markets around the world to accept risk, raising interest rates for many other emer-ging-market economies.

*(Continued)*

**Box 9.4**    *(Continued)*

**Brazil 1999**

Brazil emerged from a succession of bouts with high inflation through the implementation of the *real* plan, an exchange rate-based stabilization, in 1994. Though the plan was very successful in bringing down inflation and a substantial fiscal effort was made in Brazil during the second half of the 1990s, the durability of the fiscal adjustment remained questionable as a result of the fiscal pressures created by a generous public pension system and the government's continuing difficulties in reining in provincial finances. Continuing fiscal uncertainties, coupled with the real exchange rate appreciation that accompanied the *real* plan, contributed to the persistence of high real interest rates in Brazil. The short-term maturity of much of Brazil's public debt meant that this increase in real interest rates magnified fiscal deficits. This situation was aggravated by the sharp increase in international risk premia that followed the 1998 Russian crisis. The increased fiscal pressures faced by Brazil as a result of the adverse effects of higher real interest rates on the economy, as well as directly on the fiscal accounts, increased capital outflows in the fall of 1998, which ultimately resulted in the abandonment of the exchange rate peg in mid-January 1999. Unlike the other crises discussed above, the financial sector in Brazil, which had been in a strong position prior to the crisis and did not face serious currency-mismatch problems, withstood the crisis rather well, and the contraction of economic activity that followed the currency crisis in the country was rather mild.

**Argentina 2002**

Like Brazil, Argentina had struggled with episodes of high inflation throughout the decade of the 1980s. But Argentina's inflation problems were both more long-lasting and more severe than those of Brazil, and a drastic cure was implemented in 1991 in the form of the imposition of a currency board (see Section 9.4), which pegged the Argentine peso to the US dollar under the *Convertibility Plan*. As in Mexico, this attempt at stabilization was accompanied by a number of reform measures that were intended to boost economic growth. The plan was immensely successful along both the stabilization and growth dimensions up until 1995, as the Argentine economy simultaneously recorded rapid increases in economic activity and single-digit inflation, albeit in the presence of a severely appreciated real exchange rate. However, fiscal adjustments were limited, and the true state of the public finances was somewhat hidden by the positive impact of rapid growth on tax revenues and the government's receipts from the sale of public enterprises. After a temporary contraction in 1995 due to spillover effects from the Mexican crisis (see Box 9.2), the Argentine government took measures to strengthen the domestic financial system, but little was done with respect to the fiscal accounts. Growth resumed in 1996, but public sector debt began to rise. In the latter half of the 1990s, Argentina suffered from a variety of shocks, including adverse changes in the prices of its exports as a result of the effects of the Asian crisis on world commodity markets, the higher risk premia associated with the Russian crisis, the appreciation of the US dollar relative to the currencies of Argentina's major trading partners, and finally the depreciation of the Brazilian *real* after January 1999. All of these events combined to push the economy into recession after 1998, which increased the fiscal pressures facing the government. Argentina's inability to make the fiscal adjustments required to preserve its solvency resulted in a solvency crisis in early 2002, which became a banking crisis as a result of measures previously taken by the government to induce the banks to hold its debt. The anticipation of these events had caused capital outflows during 2001 that eventually forced a rather chaotic abandonment of the currency board in early 2002.

The combination of soft pegs and high capital mobility has been implicated in many emerging-market economy currency crises during the 1990s. Box 9.4 provides a brief overview of the factors underlying the most prominent of these crises during the decade, and Empirical Study 9.1 examines what international macroeconomists know about the predictability of such events.

## 9.4 Modern Versions of Hard Pegs

The potential vulnerability of soft pegs to currency crises under conditions of high capital mobility has led many international macroeconomists to conclude that such exchange rate regimes will become increasingly difficult to sustain as countries around the world become more closely integrated with world capital markets. This has led many economists to the conclusion that under conditions of high capital mobility the only feasible exchange rate regimes are floating exchange rates or fixed exchange rate regimes featuring hard pegs. This has come to be known as the **bipolar view** of exchange rate regimes.

As we have seen, hard pegs are fixed exchange rate regimes containing institutional features that deprive central banks of discretion over both exchange rate policy and monetary policy. The gold standard system was a hard peg because the "rules of the game" had the effect of removing such discretion. However, this feature of hard pegs continues to make them attractive for some countries today, and modern versions of hard pegs are designed to mimic the gold standard in this respect. In this section we will examine some of the modern versions of hard pegs, before discussing some of the considerations that may influence a country's willingness to adopt this type of exchange rate regime.

As we saw in Chapter 3, modern versions of hard pegs can take the form of currency boards, dollarization, or monetary unification. Among these, currency boards and dollarization can be adopted unilaterally, while monetary unification requires an international agreement among the participating countries. In the rest of this section we will discuss currency boards and dollarization briefly, deferring consideration of monetary unification until Chapter 18.

### Currency Boards

The least extreme version of a unilateral hard peg retains an independent domestic currency, but ties its value to that of a foreign currency through an institutional arrangement known as a **currency board**. A currency board is simply a redefined central bank with sharply limited powers. Under a currency board regime, a country commits itself to a hard peg by adopting institutional arrangements that make the fixed exchange rate very difficult to change (e.g., the exchange rate is sometimes enshrined in the country's constitution, or a parliamentary supermajority is required to change the official parity). Similar arrangements compel the central bank to tie changes in the money supply to changes in foreign exchange reserves. Thus currency boards have the following components:

1    The value of the domestic currency is fixed relative to that of a foreign currency, usually that of a major trading partner, by requiring the central bank (either constitutionally or through some other legal means) to buy and sell that currency on demand at a fixed price, leaving it no discretion to alter the exchange rate.
2    The central bank (currency board) is required to maintain foreign exchange (not gold) reserves proportional to the value of the domestic monetary base (that is, it has to set $SF_C^* = \sigma M$, where $\sigma$ is a positive number, as in the case of the gold standard). The textbook version of a currency board is one in which $\sigma = 1$, so the central bank simply cannot hold domestic assets such as government bonds.
3    Domestic residents are free to borrow and lend abroad.

Currency boards exist today in Bosnia and Herzegovina, Brunei, Bulgaria, Hong Kong, Djibouti, Estonia, Lithuania, and the Eastern Caribbean Currency Union, as well as in a number of smaller countries and territories. A currency board existed in Argentina from 1991 until 2002. Currency boards have been proposed in the aftermath of currency crises for Mexico, Indonesia, and Russia, among other countries. Figure 9.7 illustrates the tight link that exists between reserve growth and money growth under a currency board, focusing on the case of Estonia. Notice that while the correspondence is not perfect, in most quarters base money growth and reserve growth move in the same direction and by similar magnitudes.

## Dollarization

Dollarization is a more extreme form of hard peg. **Dollarization** is simply the name given to the abandonment of the national currency in favor of a previously existing foreign currency as legal tender, whether the foreign currency happens to be the US dollar or not. We can represent this case in our model by setting $S = 1$, $\sigma = 1$, and $B_C = 0$. Panama and Liberia have traditionally used the US dollar as legal tender (though Liberia has begun to use its own currency recently), and in recent years, both Ecuador and El Salvador have adopted the dollar. Botswana, Lesotho, and Swaziland all used the South African rand as their currency after they became independent.

Why would countries do this? The reasons can be various. As we will see in the next section, the expected advantages of hard pegs are in the form of gains in credibility and improved discipline on the government's budget. Yet these gains may be available through a currency board. Why go further and abandon the domestic currency altogether?

There are two reasons. First, while the adoption of a currency board makes it much less likely that the exchange rate can be changed, it does not make it impossible for that to happen. Thus, currency boards are not altogether invulnerable to expected exchange rate

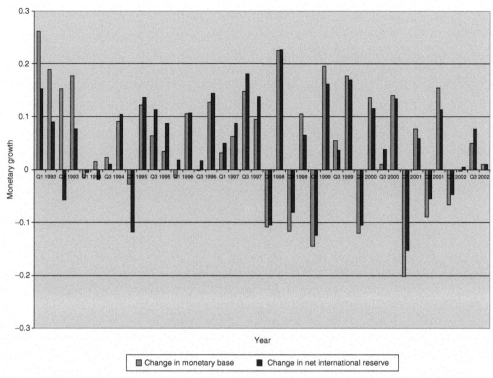

**Figure 9.7**    Estonia: monetary growth under currency board, 1993–2002

changes, as illustrated by the case of Argentina in Box 9.2. Under dollarization, on the other hand, the possibility of future exchange rate changes is entirely removed. This was an important consideration in the case of Ecuador in 1999, for example, where the government's previous default on its international debts created a need for unusually strong measures to restore credibility. Second, adopting a foreign currency may be desirable if the country's external trade is dominated by the country that issues that currency, and the domestic authorities want to facilitate that trade by reducing the transaction costs that arise from currency exchange and from the need to protect against the risk of future exchange rate changes. Indeed, some economists have found that sharing a common currency substantially increases trade among the countries sharing the currency.[3] We will come back to these issues in Chapter 18.

On the other hand, relative to the adoption of a currency board, dollarization involves the loss of the seignorage revenue that a country receives from the power to print its own legal tender. In many cases, this may not be insignificant. For example, Fischer (1992) estimated this loss at between 0.3 and 1.8 percent of GDP for various countries from 1960 to 1978, and Chang (2000) estimated it at about 0.4 percent of GDP for Argentina, 0.9 percent for Mexico, and 1.3 percent for Brazil during the 1990s.

---

[3]    See Rose (2000).

## 9.5    Soft Versus Hard Pegs: Some Policy Issues

We have seen that hard pegs differ from soft pegs in that the former entail a loss of discretion on the part of the central bank over monetary and exchange rate policies. We have also seen that it is precisely this loss of discretion that makes modern versions of hard pegs attractive to some countries today. This may seem somewhat puzzling. Why should the loss of discretion over such policy instruments be perceived to be a good thing? In this section we will address this issue, which will help us identify the potential benefits from the adoption of hard pegs, and then will turn to some potential costs. The consideration of benefits and costs will shed some light on the question of why modern fixed exchange rate regimes tend to come in both forms.

### Credibility and Discipline Under Hard Pegs

The expected gains from the loss of discretion under a hard peg come in the form of credibility and discipline. We have seen that the expectation of a future exchange rate change has the potential to be macroeconomically disruptive under a soft peg, because it implies sharp changes in domestic interest rates as well as in capital flows. This means that enhancing the credibility of the exchange rate can be extremely valuable, because it helps preserve macroeconomic stability. Hard pegs do this in two ways. First, as we have seen, the institutional arrangements associated with hard pegs make the exchange rate very difficult to change. Second, these institutional arrangements also tend to force monetary policy to be conducted in a way that reduces the variability of reserves. This protects the resources that the central bank needs in order to fulfill its exchange rate commitment.

Hard pegs can also help to impose discipline on the government's budget, when the government is unable to do so itself. As we saw in our examination of first-generation currency crises, by buying bonds issued by the government, central banks make it possible for the government to finance spending without raising taxes or borrowing directly from the public. However, since central banks have no discretion over monetary policy under hard pegs, they cannot print money when the government needs it (such as when fiscal deficits are high), but only when the balance of payments allows it. This provides an external source of discipline on the government.[4,5] Since under such an arrangement the government is not able to count on the central bank to print money to cover its deficits, it is only able to run deficits when it can convince the private sector to finance them, that is, when it proves itself creditworthy.

### Macroeconomic Adjustment Under Hard and Soft Pegs

Despite the advantages of increased credibility and discipline, hard pegs are not always preferred over soft pegs. While the loss of discretion that the central bank suffers under

---

[4]    As we saw in Chapter 6, this is why the gold standard tended to be abandoned during wartime.

[5]    For example, states in the United States, which operate under a (literally) dollarized exchange rate regime, cannot print their own currencies to finance deficits in state budgets.

hard pegs may enhance the credibility of the exchange rate and impose discipline on the government, these benefits come at a price: the inability to use the exchange rate as a policy instrument.

Suppose that domestic macroeconomic policymakers want to achieve full employment in the short run, while maintaining a desired value of net exports (for concreteness, say zero). The first of these targets is sometimes referred to as **internal balance**, while the second is referred to as **external balance**. How can they use the policy instruments at their disposal to achieve both objectives simultaneously?

A first requirement is to identify the relevant policy instruments under their control. In principle these consist of fiscal policy (in the form of $G$ or $T$), monetary policy (in the form of $B_C$), and exchange rate policy. But as we have seen, the impossible trinity of international macroeconomics implies that monetary policy is ineffective in influencing either net exports or the level of real GDP under perfect capital mobility and fixed exchange rates, either under a soft peg or a hard one, so the policy instruments potentially available are really only two: fiscal policy and exchange rate policy. How can these be deployed to achieve the government's macroeconomic objectives?

To address this question, consider Figure 9.8. This figure essentially represents the economy's short-run equilibrium in the same form as in Figure 9.1, but with two new curves added. The first, denoted $Y = \bar{Y}$, identifies the value of potential (or full employment) real GDP in this economy. The second, labeled $N = 0$, depicts the set of all combinations of $R$ and $Y$ that are consistent with a zero value of net exports, given by $N = X$ $(Q, \theta) - (1 - \varphi(Q))A(Y - T, R^*) = 0$, for given values of the exogenous variables in this equation. The curve $N = 0$ has a positive slope, because the higher $Y$ is, the larger imports must be and the higher the domestic interest rate will therefore have to be to discourage domestic absorption and keep net exports in balance. To the right of $N = 0$, net exports are negative (since the higher value of $Y$ implies more imports than would be consistent with a zero balance), while to the left of $N = 0$, net exports are positive.

Under the circumstances depicted in this figure, the economy is in short-run equilibrium at point A, with output below full employment and a negative value of net exports. Ideally, the authorities would like to shift the GM curve to a position such as $GM_1$, so that it passes through point B, and shift the $N = 0$ curve so that it passes through the point B as well, as

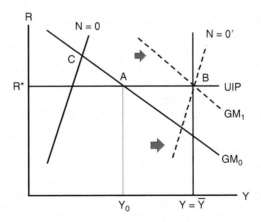

**Figure 9.8**    Macroeconomic stabilization with hard and soft pegs

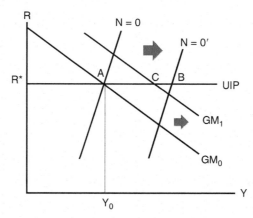

**Figure 9.9**    Real devaluation, net exports, and goods market equilibrium

shown in the figure. This would allow them to achieve both of their policy goals simultaneously. Can they do so with the instruments at their disposal?

To answer this question, we need to consider as a preliminary matter the effects of changes in $Q$ on the $N = 0$ and GM curves (Figure 9.9). Because a more depreciated value of $Q$ tends to increase net exports, making it possible to sustain a zero value of net exports with a higher level of $Y$, an increase in $Q$ would cause the $N = 0$ curve to shift to the right, to a position such as $N = 0'$ in Figure 9.9. Precisely because it tends to increase net exports, and thus to increase the demand for domestic goods, an increase in $Q$ shifts the GM curve to the right as well, to a position like $GM_1$. But which curve shifts the most? To answer this question, what we need to know is: what is the situation in the goods market at a point such as B? Since there is an excess demand for goods to the left of the GM curve and an excess supply to the right of it, answering this question will tell us whether point B is to the left or to the right of the new GM curve, that is, whether the GM curve has shifted more or less than the $N = 0$ curve.

Note that since $Y$ is higher at B than at A, for the goods market to be in equilibrium at B there would have to be a source of added demand at B other than the increase in $Y$ itself. Since at B net exports are once again zero, there is no additional demand for domestic goods coming from net exports – or from any other source – at that point. This means that the goods market must be in a situation of excess supply at B. Since conditions of excess supply are always found to the right of the GM curve, this means that the GM curve must pass to the *left* of B, through a point such as C. In other words, the shift in $N = 0$ caused by an increase in $Q$ must be *larger* than the shift in GM.

Looking back at Figure 9.6, we can now examine what policymakers can do if the economy finds itself at a point such as A. Their simplest option is to do nothing. As we saw in Chapter 6 when we examined long-run equilibrium under the gold standard, over time changes in the domestic price level will restore the economy to full employment. In the present context, this would happen through reductions in the domestic price level. As the domestic price level falls, given the nominal exchange rate, the real exchange rate $Q$ must rise (depreciate). The effect is to cause the GM curve to shift to the right. This rightward shift in GM must continue until the GM curve passes through B, restoring full employment.

This option has the disadvantage, however, of subjecting the economy to what may be a sustained period of underemployment during the transition from A to B.[6]

In addition, since the shift in GM is brought about by an increase in $Q$, the N = 0 curve will shift as well, and as we have just shown, a given change in $Q$ will shift N = 0 further to the right than the GM curve. Thus, when GM has shifted to $GM_1$, the N = 0 curve must pass to the right of point B at $R = R^*$. This means that at point B net exports will be *positive*. Consequently, policymakers cannot achieve both of their macroeconomic objectives simultaneously by doing nothing.

Alternatively, consider the use of fiscal policy. Recall that changes in $G$ cause shifts in the GM curve; however, since $G$ does not affect net exports directly, they have no effect on the N = 0 curve. Thus, increases in $G$ could in principle move the economy to full employment without a possibly lengthy intervening period of underemployment, but in doing so the economy would be moving further from the stationary N = 0 curve, thus *aggravating* the previously existing negative value of net exports. Changes in $T$ are even less helpful. To shift the GM curve to the right, the government would find it necessary to reduce $T$. But reducing $T$, precisely because it would tend to increase the level of absorption, would increase imports and thus would shift the N = 0 curve to the *left* (a lower value of $Y$ would be required to maintain a zero value of the trade balance with a lower level of $T$).

The problem with the "do nothing" and fiscal options is that they bring into play only one of the instruments at policymakers' disposal at any one time, and the authorities cannot hit two independent macroeconomic targets by deploying only one instrument. To hit both targets simultaneously, they must use both of the instruments at their disposal. What is required, in brief, is a depreciation of the real exchange rate that causes N = 0 to intersect $Y = \bar{Y}$ at B. This will also cause GM to shift, but will not in general cause it to pass through point B. Thus, the real depreciation must be supplemented by a fiscal policy action that shifts the GM curve the rest of the way to point B.

Notice that the required change in the real exchange rate can take the form of a change in the nominal exchange rate or in the domestic price level. The authorities thus have two options:

1   If they wait until gradual adjustment of the domestic price level has depreciated the real exchange rate sufficiently so as to bring the N = 0 curve into a position that intersects $Y = \bar{Y}$ at B, they can then shift the GM curve the rest of the way by implementing an expansionary fiscal policy (for example, an increase in government spending). This allows them to hit both targets without adjusting the nominal exchange rate by instead relying on the endogenous adjustment of the *real* exchange rate. This in essence captures the only strategy that is feasible under a hard peg.
2   They can achieve the same adjustment of the real exchange rate by devaluing the *nominal* exchange rate and supplementing this with the same fiscal expansion as in the first option. This option is available only if the fixed exchange rate is a soft peg.

The positions of the GM and N = 0 curves will be the same under both options, but the performance of the economy will be characterized by two important differences: under the first option, the new equilibrium is reached gradually after a prolonged period of

---

[6]   This is precisely the situation that Argentina's currency board encountered during 1998–2001, when a shortfall in aggregate demand arising from external events led to a slow reduction in the aggregate price level in the context of a prolonged recession.

underemployment, but at the new equilibrium the domestic price level is permanently lower. In contrast, under the second option underemployed resources are avoided and the transition is immediate, but the domestic price level is permanently higher than in the first case.

What does this say about the relative desirability of hard versus soft pegs? It suggests that the reduced fragility of hard pegs is purchased at a cost, with the cost being that real exchange rate adjustments can be brought about only by changes in the price level. How large this cost turns out to be depends on how much transitory unemployment it takes in a particular economy to achieve a permanent reduction in the price level.

The specific combinations of fiscal and exchange rate policies required to achieve internal and external balance will depend in general on the economy's initial position. For example, if the GM curve had intersected the $R = R^*$ line to the *right* of $Y = \bar{Y}$ in Figure 9.6, then a fiscal contraction would have been called for, while if $N = 0$ had been located to the right of $Y = \bar{Y}$, a real exchange rate appreciation would have been required. But the general points made in this section carry over to all of these cases: two instruments have to be deployed to hit two macroeconomic targets, and while real exchange rate adjustment can be achieved through nominal exchange rate adjustments or adjustments in the domestic price level, the latter may turn out to be a painful process. It is no wonder that despite their advantages in promoting credibility and discipline, relatively few countries have opted for hard pegs.

---

## Empirical Study 9.1    Are Currency Crises Predictable?

One interesting feature of the currency crises of the 1990s is that many of them seem to have taken international financial markets by surprise. For example, as we have seen, our model predicts that when capital mobility is high, an anticipated devaluation of the domestic currency should be associated with the emergence of a large spread between domestic and foreign interest rates. Yet interest rate differentials did not widen dramatically before the ERM crisis, or either the Mexican or Asian crises. This is somewhat puzzling, because both first- and second-generation crisis models suggest that the likelihood of a crisis in a particular country should be systematically related to specific features of the economy (referred to as **fundamentals**), such as large fiscal deficits associated with rapid domestic credit growth and systematic losses of foreign exchange reserves, a severely appreciated real exchange rate, an ongoing recession, or a host of factors that might make central banks unwilling to live with high domestic interest rates for very long, such as a weak domestic financial system or a large stock of government debt. The emergence of such factors should be readily observable by financial markets, and should therefore serve as **early-warning signals** of the likely unsustainability of a ''soft'' exchange rate peg.

The problem is, of course, that the exchange rate regime is an important determinant of how an open economy functions, and the decision to abandon a soft peg is therefore a very complicated one, depending on many factors other than those listed above. This means that even when early-warning signals are flashing, a crisis does not always happen. Moreover, the possibility of self-fulfilling crises implies that crises may happen even when no early-warning signals are flashing at all.

Research by international macroeconomists has tried to identify systematic predictors of currency crises. Berg and Pattillo (2000) examined several such efforts. The research that they reviewed identified several systematic predictors of currency crises, including severe real exchange rate appreciation, rapid domestic credit growth, a large ratio of the money supply to foreign exchange reserves, large current account deficits, rapid reserve losses, high ratios of short-term external debt to foreign exchange reserves, slow export growth, and a large government budget deficit. Overall, statistical models for crisis prediction were able to predict about half of the crises that occurred during the sample period over which the statistical prediction equations were estimated, but only about one-third of crises that occurred post-sample. ''False alarms'' – crisis predictions that did not come true – occurred about half the time. That is, in half of the cases in which the statistical models predicted a crisis, no crisis occurred.

Overall, then, while our models clearly identify some key determinants of currency crises, these important phenomena are still imperfectly understood. It is not so surprising, then, that financial markets have not always been very successful at predicting them.

## 9.6   Summary

This chapter took up the question of how economies behave with fixed exchange rates under conditions of high capital mobility. We saw that even if the fixed exchange rate arrangement that is adopted by a country in such circumstances is of the soft peg variety, in which the central bank retains discretion over monetary and exchange rate policy, the country will not enjoy monetary autonomy under these circumstances, as a consequence of the impossible trinity of international macroeconomics. Monetary policy is effective only in altering the central bank's stock of foreign exchange reserves, and this implies that when monetary policy is driven by the need to finance a sustained fiscal deficit, the fixed exchange rate must eventually collapse in a ''first-generation'' currency crisis.

Exchange rate policy, on the other hand, remains available as a macroeconomic policy instrument under soft pegs. However, this turns out to be something of a double-edged sword. While the government can use exchange rate policy together with fiscal policy to hit internal and external balance targets simultaneously without putting the economy through what may be a long and painful period of price level adjustment, financial markets' awareness of the potential for exchange rate changes to be implemented leaves the fixed exchange rate vulnerable to ''second-generation'' currency crises. Indeed, some economists have argued that the potential for self-fulfilling crises renders soft pegs little more than a mirage under conditions of high capital mobility, making the relevant choice of exchange rate regimes for countries that are highly integrated with world capital markets one between hard pegs and floating exchange rates.

We have seen in this chapter that, in the search for credibility and discipline, some countries have indeed opted for modern forms of hard pegs such as currency boards and dollarization. However, the other pole of the bipolar view of exchange rate regimes, floating exchange rates, is much more common in the modern world. In the next part of the book, we turn to the analysis of macroeconomics under floating exchange rates.

## Questions

1  Many economists claim that in a small open economy operating under a fixed exchange rate regime, the domestic central bank is powerless to control the money supply, and monetary policy is thus powerless as a tool to stabilize domestic output. Do you agree or disagree? Explain.

2  Consider a small open economy operating a fixed exchange rate. Compare the effects on domestic real GDP of an increase in government spending under each of the following circumstances:
   a  Imperfect capital mobility with *sterilized* intervention.
   b  Imperfect capital mobility and *unsterilized* intervention.
   c  Perfect capital mobility.

3  What is a currency board? Based on what you learned in this chapter, what are the benefits and costs a country should consider in deciding whether to adopt a currency board?

4  In the wake of the financial crises that afflicted many developing countries during the 1990s, many participants in international financial markets at times came to fear that the exchange rates underpinning the currency boards maintained by Hong Kong and Argentina might be devalued. Based on what you learned in this chapter, explain what effects you would expect such fears to have on domestic interest rates and on real economic activity in those two countries. Be sure to use the appropriate diagrams in developing your answer.

5  During the 1980s, Chile imposed several restrictions on capital movements. One rationale given for such restrictions was that fiscal policy was too inflexible to be used as a stabilization policy in that country, and the authorities wanted to preserve the power of monetary policy to affect the domestic economy under Chile's fixed exchange rate. Using what you have learned in this chapter, explain how the power of monetary policy under fixed exchange rates may be affected by the presence of capital account restrictions.

6  Consider a country that is operating with a fixed exchange rate under conditions of perfect capital mobility.
   a  Explain what effects you would expect an increase in world interest rates to have on the equilibrium values of the following domestic macroeconomic variables in such an economy, assuming no domestic policy response: the level of real GDP, the domestic interest rate, the current and nonreserve financial of the balance of payments, and the central bank's stock of foreign exchange reserves.
   b  Describe two policy responses that the domestic economy could implement to restore the original level of real GDP, and show how they would work.

7  Identify two factors that determine how long the currency peg can be sustained in a "first generation" currency crisis model.

8  Consider a small open economy that operates a fixed exchange rate under conditions of perfect capital mobility. What tradeoffs does it face in choosing between a "soft" and "hard" peg for its currency?

9  In 1995, following the currency crisis that hit Mexico at the end of 1994, many individuals both inside and outside of Argentina formed the expectation that the Argentine peso would be permanently devalued. Explain what effects this expectation would have on the following macroeconomic variables in Argentina:

a  The domestic interest rate.

b  Real GDP.

c  The current and capital accounts of the balance of payments.

d  Domestic absorption.

10  As you learned in Chapter 2, a well-known macroeconomic open-economy identity expresses the surplus in the current account of the balance of payments as equal to the sum of the excess of private saving over investment and the fiscal surplus (the excess of tax revenues over government spending). As you know, some people have interpreted this as implying that a $1 increase in government spending (resulting in a $1 *decrease* in the fiscal surplus) would result in a $1 decrease in the current account surplus. Does this relationship hold true under fixed exchange rates and perfect capital mobility? Explain why or why not.

11  In the wake of the currency crises that afflicted several Asian economies, many open-economy macroeconomists have expressed the view that emerging economies that have become highly integrated with world capital markets have to choose between the extreme exchange rate regimes of floating rates or ''hard'' fixed exchange rate pegs, because ''soft'' pegs are too vulnerable to speculative attacks. Explain:

a  Why the degree of capital mobility might affect the sustainability of ''soft'' currency pegs.

b  Why a ''hard'' peg might be more sustainable.

12  Why have some economists referred to fixed exchange rates as a ''mirage''? Using the tools that you have learned in this chapter, describe the analysis that led them to this conclusion.

13  What determines what monetary policy can and cannot do in an open economy that operates under a fixed exchange rate regime?

14  Compare the effectiveness of fiscal policy in affecting the equilibrium level of real GDP in a closed economy and in an open economy with fixed exchange rates and perfect capital mobility.

## Further Reading and References

### On second-generation crisis models

Obstfeld, Maurice, and Kenneth Rogoff (1995), ''The Mirage of Fixed Exchange Rates,'' *Journal of Economic Perspectives* (Fall), Vol. 9, No. 4, pp. 73–96.

### On the ERM crisis

Higgins, Bryan (1993), ''Was the ERM Crisis Inevitable?'' Federal Reserve Bank of Kansas City *Quarterly Review* (Fourth Quarter), pp. 27–40.

Zurlinden, Mathias (1993), ''The Vulnerability of Pegged Exchange Rates: The British Pound in the ERM,'' Federal Reserve Bank of St. Louis *Review* (September/October), pp. 41–56.

### On predicting currency crises

Berg, Andrew and Catherine Pattillo (2000), ''The Challenge of Predicting Economic Crises,'' International Monetary Fund, *Economic Issues No. 22*, pp. 1–11.

### On currency boards

Fieleke, Norman S. (1992), "The Quest for Sound Money: Currency Boards to the Rescue?" Federal Reserve Bank of Boston, *New England Economic Review* (November/December), pp. 13–24.
Kopke, Richard W. (1999), "Currency Boards: Once and Future Monetary Regimes?" Federal Reserve Bank of Boston *New England Economic Review* (May/June), pp. 21–37.
Zarazaga, Carlos (1995), "Argentina, Mexico, and Currency Boards: Another Case of Rules versus Discretion," Federal Reserve Bank of Dallas *Economic Review* (Fourth Quarter), pp. 14–24.

### On dollarization

Antinolfi, Gaetano and Todd Keiser (2001), "Dollarization as a Monetary Arrangement for Emerging Economies," Federal Reserve Bank of St. Louis *Review* (November/December), pp. 29–39.
Berg, Andrew and Eduardo Borensztein (2000), "Full Dollarization: The Pros and Cons," International Monetary Fund, *Economic Issues*, No. 24, pp. 1–17.
Chang, Roberto (2000), "Dollarization: A Scorecard," Federal Reserve Bank of Atlanta *Economic Review* (Third Quarter), pp. 1–11.
Fischer, Stanley (1992), "Seignorage and the Case for a National Money," *Journal of Political Economy*, Vol. 90 (April), pp. 295–313.

### On the trade effects of common currencies

Rose, Andrew (2000), "One Money, One Market: The Effects of Common Currencies on Trade," *Economic Policy* 30 (April), pp. 7–46.

# Appendix 9.1   The Monetary Approach to the Balance of Payments (MABP)

A specific application of the basic fixed exchange rate model with perfect capital mobility that was very influential in the 1970s and early 1980s is called the "monetary approach to the balance of payments" (MABP). This model provided the analytical underpinnings for a set of important macroeconomic policy experiments that were undertaken in the Southern Cone of Latin America in the late 1970s, and it remains the model underlying the policy conditionality associated with balance of payments loans extended by the International Monetary Fund.

The MABP makes two changes to the fixed exchange rate-perfect capital mobility model of Section 9.1:

a   Domestic prices are perfectly flexible, even in the short run.
b   The price of foreign goods in terms of domestic goods (the real exchange rate) does not change.

Note that, based on the analysis of this chapter, the second assumption requires either that domestic and foreign goods markets are highly integrated, so that domestic and foreign goods are perfect substitutes for each other and *absolute* PPP holds, or that domestic and foreign goods are imperfect substitutes, but there are no "real" shocks (requiring changes in relative prices of goods) to the economy during the period in question, meaning that *relative* PPP is an appropriate theory of real exchange rate determination.

To see the implications of these changes, and thus derive the MABP, we can use the log-linear version of the model derived in the appendix to Chapter 4. Substituting the UIP condition and the vertical aggregate supply curve into the money-market equilibrium condition we have:

$$m - p = a_0 - a_1\left(R^* + s^e_{+1} - s\right) + a_2\bar{y} + \epsilon$$

where $\epsilon$ is a random term that captures the effects of money-demand shocks. As we have seen, under credibly fixed exchange rates, $s^e_{+1} - s = 0$, so this becomes:

$$m - p = a_0 - a_1 R^* + a_2\bar{y} + \epsilon$$

or equivalently, given relative PPP:

$$m = a_0 + s + p^* - a_1 R^* + a_2\bar{y} + \epsilon$$

Taking first differences, and assuming that the world interest rate is not changing over time:

$$\Delta m = (\Delta s + \Delta p^*) + a_2\Delta\bar{y} + \Delta\epsilon$$

Now, using the log-linear version of the central bank's balance sheet from Appendix 4.1 we can show:

$$\Delta m = (1 - \mu)s\Delta f^*_C + \Delta b_C$$

where $\mu$ is the ratio of government bonds held by the central bank (referred to by the IMF as "domestic credit") to the money supply $M$. Substituting this back into the previous equation:

$$s\Delta f_C = [1/(1 - \mu)]\Delta p) + [a_2/(1 - \mu)]\Delta\bar{y} - [\mu/(1 - \mu)]\Delta b_C$$

This model has the following implication: given a desired balance of payments outcome $\Delta f^*_C$, as well as projections for domestic inflation $\Delta p$ (derived from projections about foreign inflation $\Delta^* p$ and projected devaluation of the domestic currency, $\Delta s$) and growth of the economy's productive capacity $\Delta\bar{y}$, this equation determines the rate of growth of domestic credit ($\Delta b_C$) that is compatible with the desired balance of payments outcome.

Note, however, that if the projections or domestic inflation or capacity growth are incorrect, if external interest rates change unexpectedly, or if there is an unexpected money demand shock, the desired balance of payments outcome will not be attained, even if the credit condition is met. Note also that this model breaks down if capital mobility is less than perfect, because in that case the domestic interest rate will not be equal to the foreign rate, and will in general change when the growth of domestic credit changes.

# Part 3
# Floating Exchange Rates

# 10

# Floating Exchange Rates I:
# Transitory Shocks

The abandonment of the Bretton Woods system after the demise of the Smithsonian Agreement in 1973 meant that central banks no longer had an international commitment to follow particular rules in their foreign exchange market intervention. Though most developing countries chose to maintain some type of exchange rate parity, industrial countries – with the exception of those within the European Union, which we will discuss in Chapter 18 – typically adopted floating exchange rates, a situation which has persisted until the present. Floating rates can thus be defined as an international *nonsystem*, in the sense that central bank behavior is not constrained either by long-established international norms (as under the gold standard) or by formal international agreements, as under Bretton Woods. To the extent that there is a "system" that constrains industrial country macroeconomic policies under floating exchange rates, it operates in the form of informal arrangements for international policy coordination among the major industrial countries (known as the G-8), which we will discuss in Chapter 17.

For now, we will concentrate our attention on the macroeconomics of floating exchange rates, continuing to rely on the small country case. In the first five chapters of Part 3, we will examine how small open economies work when they operate under conditions of high capital mobility and allow their exchange rates to float. In the present chapter we will introduce the floating exchange rate model, and use it to analyze how the economy responds to transitory shocks. We will consider the effects of longer-lasting shocks in the chapter that follows. Chapter 12 will take up the issue of exchange rate dynamics – i.e., how the path over time of the response of the exchange rate (and the rest of the economy) to macroeconomic shocks is affected when the markets for goods and financial assets clear at different speeds. In all three of these chapters we will retain a short-run perspective. We will turn to the analysis of the economy's long-run equilibrium under floating exchange rates in Chapter 13, and then in Chapter 14 will explore how short-run macroeconomics under floating rates differs when one adopts a "classical" perspective in which prices are assumed to adjust to clear markets continuously. The final chapter in this part of the book will take up the question of optimal exchange rate regimes, examining the considerations that come into play when countries decide whether to fix or float the exchange rate.

This chapter provides an introduction to the macroeconomics of floating exchange rates. It is divided into three sections. We begin by exploring how to adapt the benchmark analytical framework of Chapter 4 to a situation in which the exchange rate is allowed to float. We then solve the resulting model and study how the economy adjusts to changes in the macroeconomic environment under these circumstances. As mentioned above, for now we will focus on transitory shocks, which we will take to mean shocks that last for only one period.

## 10.1    Analytical Framework

To analyze how floating exchange rates work, let us go back to our analytical framework and extract from it a floating exchange rate model. An important initial step is to recall that, while the early years of the postwar period were characterized by the presence of capital account restrictions among industrial countries, by the latter part of the decade of the 1990s these restrictions had largely been eliminated. Thus the only major source of risk that differentiated the bonds issued by industrial country governments was exchange rate risk. We will assume that economic agents are risk neutral – that is, that they care about the expected returns on bonds, not the uncertainty associated with those returns. As we saw in Chapter 3, under these conditions we should expect uncovered interest parity to hold. Thus, we will build our floating exchange rate models with the assumption of perfect capital mobility and UIP. This is indeed the standard practice in international macroeconomics.

As we did for fixed exchange rates, we will begin by using our framework to analyze how floating exchange rates operate in the short run. This means that we will use the short-run supply curve, so the price level will be given (this means that we will use equation (4.7a), rather than (4.7b) from Chapter 4). In addition, just as in the fixed exchange rate case, it also means that $P^e_{+1} = \bar{P}$, so we will use Chapter 4's equation (4.8a) rather than (4.8b). As we saw in Chapter 4, if we take the central bank's stock of government bonds $B_C$ to be the exogenous monetary policy variable in our model, this leaves us with ten unknowns and eight equations, listed in Box 10.1.

Under fixed exchange rates, our next step was to set $S = S^e_{+1} = \bar{S}$, thereby eliminating two unknowns and leaving us with a model that we could actually solve. However, under floating exchange rates both the current and expected future exchange rates must be considered to be endogenous variables, since they are freely determined in the foreign exchange market. This is the key analytical difference in moving from fixed to floating rates. On the other hand, the stock of foreign exchange reserves $F^*_C$, which was endogenous under fixed exchange rates (since central banks had no control over $ORS$), will become a policy variable in our model under floating exchange rates. The reason is that, since the central bank is no longer committed to buying or selling foreign exchange in unlimited amounts at an officially announced price, it can engage in foreign exchange market

## Box 10.1   A Floating Exchange Rate Model

**Central bank balance sheet**

$$SF_C^* + B_C = M \tag{10.1}$$

**Money market equilibrium**

$$M = PL(R, Y) \tag{10.2}$$

**Domestic bond market equilibrium**

$$R = R' = (1 + R^*)S_{+1}^e/S - 1 \tag{10.3}$$

**Domestic goods market equilibrium**

$$Y = \varphi(Q)A(Y - T, r) + G + X(Q, \theta) \tag{10.4}$$

**Definition of the real exchange rate**

$$Q = SP^*/P \tag{10.5}$$

**Definition of the real interest rate**

$$r = P(1 + R)\left(1/P_{+1}^e\right) - 1 \tag{10.6}$$

**Short-run aggregate supply**

$$P = \bar{P} \tag{10.7}$$

$$P_{+1}^e = \bar{P} \tag{10.8}$$

intervention at its discretion, rather than at the private sector's initiative. This removes an endogenous variable, leaving us with nine endogenous variables and eight equations.

We can move to a more compact version of our model by eliminating four of these equations. This can be done by using equations (10.7) and (10.8) to replace the actual and expected future price levels $P$ and $P_{+1}^e$ by their known value $\bar{P}$, as well as by using the definitions of the real exchange rate and real interest rate (equations 10.5 and 10.6) to substitute these two variables out of our model, as we did in Chapters 5 to 9. But this still leaves us with four equations in five unknowns.

We can make a little more progress in simplifying things by noticing that, since both $F_C^*$ and $B_C$ are policy variables under floating exchange rates, the money supply identity $M = SF_C^* + B_C$ indicates that the money supply itself is also a policy variable, at least as long

## Box 10.2    The Compact Version of the Floating Exchange Rate Model

**Money-market equilibrium**

$$M = PL(R, Y) \tag{10.2}$$

**Domestic bond market equilibrium**

$$R = (1 + R^*)S^e_{+1}/S - 1 \tag{10.3}$$

**Goods market equilibrium**

$$Y = \varphi(SP^*/\bar{P})A(Y - T, R) + G + X(SP^*/\bar{P}, \theta) \tag{10.4}$$

as the central bank does not "monetize" the capital gains and losses on its foreign exchange reserves that arise from exchange rate changes.[1] All that the identity (10.1) now tells us is that the central bank can alter the money supply by intervening either in the domestic bond market or in the foreign exchange market – that is, it simply tells us how changes in $M$ are brought about. But since $F^*_C$ and $B_C$ do not appear anywhere else in our model while $M$ does, what ultimately matters for macroeconomic performance is the change in $M$, not how it is brought about. Thus, we can focus on what actually matters by treating $M$ as the exogenous variable ultimately controlled by the central bank, and doing without the central bank balance sheet altogether.[2] This leaves us with three equations in four unknowns. The resulting compact form of our floating rate model appears in Box 10.2. As noted above, this model contains four endogenous variables ($R$, $Y$, $S^e_{+1}$, and $S$), but only three equations. How do we deal with this problem in solving the model?

Since one of the endogenous variables measures exchange rate expectations, we will do so by adding to the model a story about how people form expectations. We will assume that expectations are formed **rationally**. What this means is that whenever people have to form expectations about the endogenous variables in the model, we will assume that they use the solutions for those variables given by the model itself to form those expectations. Since the required expectation in our case is about the *future* value of the exchange rate, we will basically be assuming that people use the model's solution for the exchange rate next period to form the expectation $S^e_{+1}$. In turn, to find the model's solution for the exchange rate next period, they simply solve the model using the expected values of the next period's exogenous variables.

---

[1]    That is, as long as changes in $S$ are not allowed to affect $M$. Under this condition, since $M = SF^*_C + B_C$ and both $B_C$ and $F^*_C$ are policy variables, $M$ must be a policy variable as well.

[2]    There is actually some useful economics in these observations. We will come back to it when we analyze central bank intervention in the foreign exchange market under floating exchange rates later in this chapter.

This means that it will make a big difference how long any shocks experienced by the economy today are expected to last, because that is what will determine whether those shocks will affect the model's solution for the exchange rate next period. We will begin in this chapter with the assumption that shocks are expected to be *transitory*, meaning that people expect that they will last only one period and then go away. In the next chapter we will explore what happens when shocks are expected to last more than one period, including when they are expected to be permanent.

To see the significance of our assumption of transitory shocks, suppose that the economy is initially in a short-run equilibrium with $S = \bar{S}$, and is then affected by a shock that everyone expects to be transitory. This means that the shock is expected to be gone next period, which in turn implies that the economy's equilibrium next period *will be expected to be the same as it was before the shock arrived*. More specifically, that means that everyone expects that next period's exchange rate will return to its original value $S = \bar{S}$. In that case, we can set $S_{+1}^e = \bar{S}$. In other words, since any shocks experienced by the economy in the present will not affect the exchange rate that is expected to prevail one period ahead, *it is appropriate to treat $S_{+1}^e$ as exogenous*. Since this eliminates the extra unknown variable, it gives us a complete and well-specified floating exchange rate model.

## 10.2 Solving the Floating Exchange Rate Model

With the problem of too many endogenous variables solved, we are now ready to analyze our model. To make more transparent how the model works, it is useful to do so in stages. We will begin with the determination of the exchange rate.

### The Asset Market Approach to the Exchange Rate

Under the maintained assumption about the expected future exchange rate $S_{+1}^e$, the domestic interest rate determines the unique current-period nominal exchange rate (sometimes called the **spot** exchange rate) that is consistent with equilibrium in asset markets through uncovered interest parity (UIP). To see how, notice that UIP is given by:

$$R = (1 + R^*)S_{+1}^e/S - 1$$

This can be solved for the spot exchange rate $S$ to yield:

$$S = (1 + R^*)S_{+1}^e/(1 + R)$$

Since both $R^*$ and $S_{+1}^e$ are exogenous, $(1 + R^*) S_{+1}^e$ is exogenous too. This means the equilibrium exchange rate is determined by the domestic interest rate $R$. What is the intuition for this? With the expected future exchange rate $S_{+1}^e$ given, the current level of the spot exchange rate $S$ relative to $S_{+1}^e$ determines the expected rate of nominal depreciation or appreciation of the exchange rate between the current period and the next. Recall that if domestic and foreign bonds are perfect substitutes (which is what UIP assumes), they must

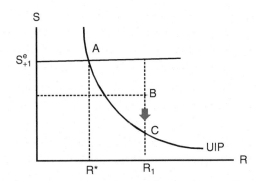

**Figure 10.1**    The asset-market approach to the exchange rate

yield the same return when expressed in the same currency. Given the domestic interest rate, *the role of the spot exchange rate S is to equalize nominal returns on the domestic and foreign assets by causing the expected rate of depreciation to equal the interest rate differential.* We can explore how this works by plotting the relationship above in *S-R* space, as in Figure 10.1.

The curve that plots *S* as a function of *R*, labeled UIP in Figure 10.1, has a negative slope and must pass through the point $(R^*, S^e_{+1})$, labeled A. The reason for this is that if domestic and foreign interest rates are equal, there can be no expected exchange rate change in equilibrium, meaning that if the expected future exchange rate is $S^e_{+1}$, the current (spot) exchange rate *S* must be equal to $S^e_{+1}$ as well. Since the curve must always pass through the point $(R^*, S^e_{+1})$, it follows that changes in $R^*$ must shift the curve *horizontally* by an amount that is exactly equal to the change in $R^*$, while changes in $S^e_{+1}$ must shift it *vertically* by the same amount as the change in $S^e_{+1}$.

The UIP curve tells us that, given $R^*$ and $S^e_{+1}$, changes in *R* and *S* must be inversely related. Why should this be? Note first that, at any given value of the domestic interest rate, the vertical distance between $S^e_{+1}$ and the value of *S* corresponding to that interest rate on the UIP curve is the expected depreciation of the exchange rate between the present period and the next. This vertical distance is *negative* (that is, $S^e_{+1} < S$) when $R < R^*$, it becomes smaller as *R* approaches $R^*$ from the left, is zero when $R = R^*$, and becomes increasingly positive as $R > R^*$. This means that:

1   A low domestic interest rate must be associated with an *expected appreciation* of the domestic currency for UIP to hold, so it must imply a current exchange rate that is relatively *depreciated* (high) compared to the expected future exchange rate.
2   A high domestic interest rate, on the other hand, must be associated with an expected *depreciation* of the domestic currency for UIP to hold, so it requires a current exchange rate that is relatively *appreciated* (low) compared to the expected future exchange rate.

What mechanism brings these outcomes about? Suppose that, at a given value of the domestic interest rate, say $R_1$, the exchange rate is above the UIP curve, say at point B. At points like B that are above the UIP curve the spot exchange rate is closer to the expected future exchange rate $S^e_{+1}$ than it would be at a point like C that actually lies on the curve. Since the expected future depreciation of the currency is given by the vertical distance between the prevailing value of $S$ and that of $S_{+1}^e$, a value of $S$ that is above the UIP curve means that a *smaller* future depreciation is expected than would be required to offset the higher interest rate paid by domestic assets and thus maintain the expected rate of return on domestic assets equal to that on foreign assets. This means that at B, domestic assets yield a *higher* return than foreign assets (this can be verified by looking at the UIP expression). Under perfect capital mobility, this state of affairs triggers massive capital inflows. These inflows create an excess demand for the domestic currency in the foreign exchange market, which – now that the central bank is no longer supplying the domestic currency at a fixed price – must cause the exchange rate to appreciate. The appreciation of the exchange rate represents a downward movement from B toward point C in Figure 10.1. The mechanism just described must continue to operate until the spot exchange rate is brought all the way back down to its UIP value at point C, since until that happens domestic assets will be expected to yield a higher return than foreign assets, leaving the incentives in place for capital inflows to continue.

Similarly, if the spot exchange rate lies *below* the UIP curve, the vertical distance between $S$ and $S_{+1}^e$ will be *greater* than is required to maintain UIP. In this case, the domestic currency is expected to depreciate *more* (not less) than it would take to make up for the higher value of the domestic interest rate, meaning that domestic assets pay *lower* returns than foreign assets. This differential causes massive capital *outflows* that cause the currency to depreciate until $S$ rises to the value required to restore UIP. The upshot is that above UIP we have massive capital inflows that drive the exchange rate down to the UIP curve, while below the curve we have massive outflows that drive it up to the curve.

Notice that, given the value of the domestic interest rate, the equilibrium value of the exchange rate does not at all depend on what is happening to the current account of the balance of payments. This might seem puzzling, since foreign exchange trades are also motivated by transactions in international markets for goods and services. *The basic reason that this can be so is that capital flows are potentially so large in response to deviations of the exchange rate from the value implied by UIP, that they would tend to swamp any excess demand or supply of foreign exchange arising from commercial transactions.* The implication is that the foreign exchange market cannot be in equilibrium at any exchange rate other than that which satisfies UIP.

So the foreign exchange market should be thought of as working in the following way: the UIP condition determines the equilibrium value of the exchange rate. Based on this value, there will be an excess supply or demand for foreign exchange arising from commercial (current) transactions. Since at the equilibrium exchange rate capital flows are indeterminate (because domestic and foreign assets yield the same return), net capital flows will be whatever they have to be to offset the excess demand or supply for foreign exchange arising from current transactions. If they were not exactly equal to this amount, the exchange rate would tend to move, and this would immediately trigger the required adjustment in net capital flows. Appendix 10.1 explains how all of this happens in more detail. The bottom line is that the equilibrium exchange rate is determined in asset markets.

## Domestic Asset Market Equilibrium

We have now told a story about the determination of the exchange rate, but that story was conditioned on given values of the domestic interest rate $R$, the expected future exchange rate $S_{+1}^e$, and the foreign interest rate $R^*$. The latter is exogenous by the small country assumption, and for now we are taking $S^e_{+1}$ as given. The next step is thus to explain what determines the domestic interest rate.

The answer is that, *for a given value of domestic income Y*, the domestic interest rate must be determined by the money-market equilibrium condition $M = PL(R, Y)$ (equation 10.2). This must be so, because once we hold $Y$ at a given value the interest rate is the only remaining endogenous variable in this equation.

Asset-market equilibrium requires both that UIP hold and that the domestic money market be in equilibrium. Thus we must simultaneously have:

$$R = (1 + R^*)S^e_{+1}/S - 1 \tag{10.3}$$

and:

$$M = PL(R, Y) \tag{10.2}$$

Putting these two relationships together, we can examine the effects of a wide variety of asset market variables on the equilibrium exchange rate. To see how, we can proceed in two steps: first, we determine the effects of each of the variables that we are interested in on the domestic interest rate $R$ using (10.2), and then, using our previous analysis of (10.3), we examine what effect they have, through the domestic interest rate, on the exchange rate $S$.

Consider first the effects of changes in either the world interest rate $R^*$ or the expected future exchange rate $S^e_{+1}$. Notice that when we change either of these variables we are implicitly holding the money supply $M$, the price level $P$, and real GDP $Y$ constant. Consequently, by the money-market equilibrium condition (10.2), the domestic interest rate $R$ must be constant as well. This makes the analysis of changes in these variables exactly what it was before we took the money market into consideration – an increase in the expected future exchange rate $S^e_{+1}$ must increase the current exchange rate $S$ by the same amount in order to keep rates of return on domestic and foreign bonds equal to each other, while an increase in the foreign interest rate $R^*$ must result in a depreciation in the current exchange rate (an increase in $S$), as it induces capital to flow out of the domestic economy.

The analysis of the effects on the equilibrium exchange rate of changes in the remaining variables, however, requires us first to investigate what effect such changes have on the domestic interest rate before we can determine their effect on the exchange rate. The results are as follows:

1    From equation (10.2), an increase in real GDP requires an increase in the domestic interest rate to maintain money market equilibrium. Thus from (10.3), everything else being equal, an increase in real GDP must cause the exchange rate to *appreciate* (that is, $S$ must fall).

2    From (10.2), increases in the money supply and/or reductions in the domestic price level imply a reduction in the domestic interest rate. Thus, from (10.3), such changes must cause the exchange rate to *depreciate* ($S$ must rise).

These properties of asset-market equilibrium can be summarized conveniently by combining equations (10.2) and (10.3) into a single asset market equilibrium condition and plotting that equation in $S$-$Y$ space (since $Y$ is the endogenous variable that we were provisionally holding constant in explaining the determination of the exchange rate in asset markets).

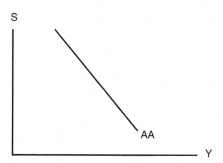

**Figure 10.2**   The AA curve

We can derive this asset market equilibrium condition by using equation (10.3) to replace the domestic interest rate in (10.2). This yields:

$$M = PL[(1+\underset{-}{R^*})S^e_{+1}/S - 1, \underset{+}{Y}] \tag{10.2'}$$

The effects on the exchange rate of changes in $R^*$, $S^e_{+1}$, $Y$, $M$, and $P$ that we just derived in two steps can also be derived directly just be examining (10.2') itself. You should confirm that you are able to do that. We can summarize these results in the form of the AA (**asset market equilibrium**) curve drawn in Figure 10.2 below. This curve describes the set of all combinations of $S$ and $Y$ that satisfy equation (10.2') – that is, that are consistent with equilibrium in domestic asset markets.

The properties of the AA curve can be summarized as follows:

1   Changes in real GDP $Y$ correspond to *movements along* the AA curve. An increase in real GDP requires an appreciation of the exchange rate to maintain equilibrium in domestic asset markets because a higher value of real GDP increases the demand for money, causing the domestic interest rate to rise to maintain money market equilibrium. The increase in the domestic interest rate attracts capital inflows into the domestic economy, and these inflows cause the exchange rate to appreciate. The size of the appreciation has to be large enough so as to induce an expected future *depreciation* that just offsets the interest differential in favor of the domestic economy.

2   For a given value of real GDP, increases in $1 + R^*$ and $S^e_{+1}$ must *shift AA upward* by an equal proportionate amount, because *at a given value of Y* these shocks must leave the domestic interest rate unchanged. With an unchanged domestic interest rate, these shocks create a return differential in favor of the *foreign* economy, giving rise to a capital outflow that causes the exchange rate to depreciate. The size of this depreciation has to be large enough so as to induce an expected future *appreciation* that just offsets the return differential in favor of the foreign economy.

3   Increases in the real money supply $M/P$ must cause *AA to shift upward* as well. In this case, the reason is that, for a given value of $Y$, the increase in the real money supply must lead to a reduction in the domestic interest rate to clear the domestic money market. Just as in the previous case, this reduction in the domestic interest rate leads to the emergence of a return rate differential in favor of the foreign economy, which triggers the same set of responses that we have just reviewed.

To complete the analysis of our model, we now need to pin down the determination of real GDP.

## Domestic Goods Market Equilibrium

To do so, we can substitute equation (10.3) for the nominal (and real) interest rate into the goods market equilibrium condition. This yields:

$$Y = \varphi(SP^*/\bar{P})A\left(Y - T, \ (1 + R^*)S^e_{+1}/S - 1\right) + G + X(SP^*/\bar{P}, \ \theta) \tag{10.4'}$$

This equation describes goods market equilibrium under floating exchange rates. It is similar to what you have seen before, except for the determination of the domestic interest rate.

Notice that the nominal exchange rate enters this equation twice. This reflects the fact that changes in the exchange rate affect aggregate demand through two channels:

1    A depreciation of the exchange rate (increase in $S$) lowers the nominal interest rate, because with the expected future exchange rate $S^e_{+1}$ fixed, a more depreciated exchange rate today means that the exchange rate is expected to depreciate *less* between now and the future (after all, the larger $S$ is today the more the exchange rate has *already* depreciated, leaving less depreciation to take place in the future). By UIP, the smaller expected depreciation allows the domestic interest rate to fall. Since the lower nominal interest rate is also a lower real interest rate in the present model, this stimulates spending by domestic residents. This is referred to as the **expenditure increasing** effect.
2    A more depreciated nominal exchange rate (higher $S$) is associated with a depreciation of the *real* exchange rate, and since this makes domestic goods relatively cheaper, it causes both domestic and foreign residents to switch from buying foreign to buying domestic goods. As we have seen previously, this is referred to as the **expenditure switching** effect.

Since an increase in $S$ increases demand for domestic goods through both of these channels, it requires an increase in output to maintain goods market equilibrium, and consequently if we plot this relationship in $S$-$Y$ space, it would appear as a curve with a positive slope. We will call it the **YY curve**. It is depicted in Figure 10.3.

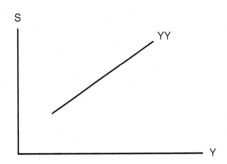

**Figure 10.3**  The YY curve

We have already seen that this curve has a positive slope because an increase in $S$ exerts expenditure-increasing and expenditure-switching effects on the aggregate demand for domestic goods, requiring an increase in output to maintain equilibrium in the market for those goods. It is easy to see that the stronger the expenditure increasing and switching effects are, the flatter the YY curve will be, since a given change in $S$ will trigger a larger increase in the equilibrium value of $Y$ when these effects are strong.

The next question is: what determines the position of the YY curve? The answer is that the curve will shift whenever there are changes in the exogenous variables that affect the market for domestic goods. In particular:

1   Increases in government spending $G$ or reductions in the level of taxation $T$ (the two components of fiscal policy in our model), as well as increases in the price of foreign goods $P^*$, and in the exogenous component of the demand for exports $\theta$ (both of which are external exogenous variables) are expansionary (that is, they tend to increase the demand for domestic goods). Consequently to maintain goods market equilibrium when any of these variables change in the directions indicated, either the supply of domestic goods would have to increase or the increase in demand for domestic goods would have to be offset by an appreciation of the exchange rate that increases their relative price. Thus the YY curve would have to shift *down and/or to the right*.
2   Increases in the world interest rate $R^*$ or in the expected future exchange rate $S^e_{+1}$ are contractionary, because they cause the domestic interest rate to rise. Thus they call for an *increase* in $S$ and/or a reduction in $Y$ to restore equilibrium in the goods market – i.e. the YY curve has to shift *up and/or to the left*.

In the latter case, it is worth investigating just how large the vertical displacement of the YY curve would have to be. The important point is that the upward shift in YY must be *smaller* than the upward shift in AA that would be caused by the same shocks. Why? Because when $R^*$ or $S^e_{+1}$ rise, the exchange rate depreciation required to restore equilibrium in financial markets has to be large enough actually to restore the nominal interest rate to its original value. That is *not* true in the case of the goods market. The increase must actually be *smaller* in this case, because the nominal exchange rate affects aggregate demand not just through its effects on the domestic interest rate, but through another channel as well (the expenditure-switching effect associated with changes in the real exchange rate). This means that even if the magnitude of the exchange rate depreciation falls short of what would be required to restore the interest rate to its original value (i.e., even if it leaves the nominal interest rate higher than it was before the shock), the additional impetus to demand arising from real exchange rate depreciation may be sufficient for domestic demand to be restored to its original level.

As a final observation about the YY curve, it is interesting to ask what happens to net exports as we move along this curve. The answer to this question will be useful in the next section when we analyze how the economy responds to transitory macroeconomic shocks under floating exchange rates. Suppose, then, that from some arbitrary point on the YY curve we move, say, to the northeast – that is, to a goods market equilibrium with a more depreciated exchange rate and a higher level of output. What happens to net exports as we do so?

The answer is: it depends. As we move to the northeast along YY, real output increases and the exchange rate depreciates. The increase in real output is associated with an increase in demand for imports, and thus with a reduction in net exports. The expenditure-switching effects associated with the depreciation of the exchange rate, on the other hand, would tend to induce an *increase* in net exports. Finally, since the depreciation of the exchange rate implies that the domestic currency must be expected to *appreciate* in the future, it must be associated with a reduction in the domestic interest rate. This reduction in the domestic interest rate, by increasing domestic absorption, increases demand for imports and thus reduces net exports.

Which effects dominate? In general, we just can't tell. But we can identify the conditions under which net exports would tend to increase or decrease. In particular, the stronger the expenditure-switching effects associated with an exchange rate change relative to its expenditure-increasing effects, the more likely it is that net exports will increase. Thus, when domestic and foreign goods are relatively close substitutes and when the interest elasticity of domestic absorption is relatively small, net exports will increase as we move to the northeast along the YY curve.

### General Macroeconomic Equilibrium

The economy as a whole will be in equilibrium when both the asset market and the goods market are in equilibrium. The exchange rate and the level of output will adjust until this is the case. Thus, the determination of the level of production and the exchange rate can be shown by the intersection of the AA and YY curves, as in Figure 10.4. The economy is in general macroeconomic equilibrium at point A, where both the asset and goods market clear, and the equilibrium values of the exchange rate and real output are given by $S_0$ and $Y_0$ respectively.

## 10.3   Comparative Statics

How does the model work? Before answering this question, we have to specify how the central bank conducts monetary policy. Recall that when we analyzed fixed exchange rates under conditions of imperfect capital mobility, we considered three possibilities for the economy's monetary policy regime: domestic credit targeting, interest rate targeting, and monetary targeting. With fixed exchange rates and perfect capital mobility, however, the impossible trinity ruled out both interest rate targeting and monetary targeting. Now that we

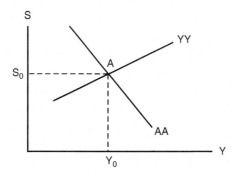

**Figure 10.4**   General equilibrium

are considering floating exchange rates, the implication of the impossible trinity is that even under perfect capital mobility the central bank retains monetary autonomy, so it is again possible to consider alternative monetary policy regimes. In this case, however, there is essentially no distinction between domestic credit and monetary targeting, because both essentially affect the economy only through their effects on the domestic money supply, as we saw previously. Interest rate targeting, however, is potentially different. Because monetary targeting allows for a richer set of macroeconomic interactions, and thus is more revealing about how the model works, we will focus on monetary targeting in this section, and consider the case of interest rate targeting in Appendix 10.3.

To see what our model tells about how key macroeconomic endogenous variables are determined under floating exchange rates, we will consider our usual range of potential shocks to the economy. In each case we will investigate effects on four endogenous variables: the exchange rate, the domestic interest rate, real GDP, and net exports. As in previous chapters, to analyze the effects of these shocks in each case we ask first which market is affected, then how it is affected, to know how the curves shift. From the new positions of the curves, we infer what happens to the exchange rate and the level of output, and then from that we infer the effects on the other endogenous variables that interest us.

## Monetary Shocks

It is useful to begin by looking at the effects of monetary policy under floating exchange rates, since this will facilitate a clear comparison with the somewhat dramatic results that we derived about the effects of monetary policy under fixed exchange rates and perfect capital mobility in Chapter 9. Consider, then, the macroeconomic effects of a monetary expansion. Since changes in the money supply only affect the money market equilibrium condition, an increase in the domestic money supply only affects the position of the AA curve, and not that of the YY curve. As we saw previously, the curve shifts up vertically, as shown in Figure 10.5, to a new position such as $AA_1$. The economy's new equilibrium is at point B. You can see from the figure that at this new equilibrium, the domestic currency must have depreciated and domestic output must have risen. Since $S$ has risen, we can infer from the UIP condition that the domestic interest rate must have fallen.

How do these outcomes come about? Answering this question involves examining the **transmission mechanism** for monetary policy (the channels through which monetary

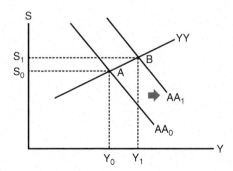

**Figure 10.5**   Effects of a monetary expansion

policy affects the economy) under floating exchange rates. This mechanism works as follows: a monetary expansion creates an excess supply of money, which causes the domestic interest rate to fall in order to maintain equilibrium in the domestic money market. But the reduction in the domestic interest rate relative to the foreign interest rate creates an incipient capital outflow, which immediately depreciates the exchange rate, *since the central bank does not intervene to sustain its value*. Together the depreciated exchange rate and lower interest rate increase aggregate demand, both by stimulating private absorption (expenditure increasing) as well as by switching demand from foreign to domestic goods (expenditure switching). Thus, unlike in the closed-economy or fixed exchange rate cases, where monetary policy works only through interest-sensitive components of aggregate demand, under floating rates monetary transmission operates *both* through the domestic interest rate as well as the real exchange rate. As noted, expansionary monetary policy induces both expenditure increases as well as expenditure switching in favor of domestic goods.

Notice the contrast in the power of monetary policy in this case compared to what happens under fixed exchange rates and perfect capital mobility. The model of Chapter 9 described an identical economy to the one we are examining here, except for the exchange rate regime. However, monetary policy was rendered completely powerless under fixed exchange rates when capital mobility was high, essentially because the central bank's commitment to defend the currency under conditions of perfect capital mobility meant that it could not control the domestic money supply. There is no such commitment under floating rates, so the central bank is able to control the money supply in that case, making it a policy variable.

This analysis enables us to call attention once again to the important principle that ties together the models that we have studied so far: the ''impossible trinity'' of international macroeconomics. Remember that the ''impossible trinity'' states that three things can never be observed at the same time: perfect capital mobility, a fixed exchange rate, and effective monetary policy (monetary autonomy). Recall that in the models of Chapter 6 and 9 we had a fixed exchange rate and perfect capital mobility, but ineffective monetary policy. In the model of Chapter 8, on the other hand, we had a fixed exchange rate and effective monetary policy, but imperfect capital mobility. Under floating rates, as we have now seen, we have perfect capital mobility and effective monetary policy, but of course, the exchange rate is no longer fixed.

To fix ideas a little more, it is worth calling attention so some other properties of the exercise that we have just conducted. Notice that at point B in Figure 10.5 the domestic currency has indeed depreciated, as we have noted, but this depreciation is smaller than it would have been at a fixed value of $Y$, that is, less than it would have been at a point on $AA_1$ directly above $Y_0$. In other words, the depreciation is smaller than we would have predicted just by looking at the requirements for equilibrium in asset markets. Why is this so? The answer is that when we looked at the asset markets in isolation from the goods market, we held real output fixed. But in a general equilibrium, we have seen that real output must rise as a result of the monetary expansion. Since the increase in real GDP increases the demand for money, the domestic interest rate does not have to fall by as much to clear the money market as it would have had to with a fixed level of real GDP, and since higher values of the domestic interest rate are associated with a more appreciated exchange rate in asset markets, this means that asset market equilibrium is compatible with a smaller value of $S$ when $Y$ increases.

Finally, consider the effects of the monetary expansion on net exports. Since the point B represents a movement to the northeast along YY, the properties of YY that we derived previously indicate that the effects of a monetary expansion on net exports must be ambiguous: the depreciation of the exchange rate tends to increase net exports, while the increase in real output and the reduction in the domestic interest rate tends to reduce them. We cannot resolve the ambiguity by examining the equilibrium in the goods market (that is, by using the "absorption" approach) in this case, as we have in previous chapters, because here the level of output rises at the same time that the domestic interest rate falls, meaning that both output and absorption increase, and the increase in absorption does not have to be smaller than that of real output. The implication is that we cannot unambiguously infer whether net exports must make a positive or negative contribution to aggregate demand. As we saw in the previous section, net exports are more likely to increase the stronger are the expenditure-switching relative to the expenditure-increasing effects of monetary policy.

Box 10.3 provides an application of the analysis we have just conducted, by looking at the effects of the sharp monetary expansion that took place in Japan during the first half of 1995 on interest rates and exchange rates in that country.

## Aggregate Demand Shocks

Let's turn now to the effects of aggregate demand shocks under floating exchange rates. As under fixed exchange rates, such shocks could take the form of changes in government spending and taxation, in exogenous variables that affect the demand for the country's exports or in unexplained factors affecting private absorption and its composition. For concreteness, we again consider the case of an increase in government spending. As a point of reference, recall that with perfect capital mobility, under fixed exchange rates fiscal policy was potentially very powerful, because there was no crowding out effect on private spending.

To examine the effects of an increase in government spending in this case, note that since government spending only directly affects the goods market, an increase in $G$ shifts YY to the right, leaving AA unaffected, as in Figure 10.7. The effects on the economy are the following:

1   The currency appreciates ($S$ falls).
2   From UIP, the appreciation of the spot exchange rate means that the domestic interest rate has to rise. Notice that this means that crowding out takes place, even with perfect capital mobility, in contrast to what happened under fixed exchange rates.
3   Output of domestic goods increases ($Y$ rises).

How do these results come about? The expansionary real shock tends to increase output, which increases the demand for money, putting upward pressure on domestic interest rates. As domestic interest rates rise, capital is attracted into the country, which causes the exchange rate to appreciate. The increase in the domestic interest rate and exchange rate appreciation partly offset the expansionary effects on aggregate demand of the increase in government spending (this is the crowding out effect mentioned previously), but they cannot fully offset it, because with an unchanged money supply, equilibrium in the domestic money

## Box 10.3   Monetary Policy in Japan in 1995–6

A useful application of the analysis in the text of the effects of monetary policy under floating exchange rates is to events in Japan in 1995. The Japanese yen has been floating since the collapse of the Bretton Woods system in 1973. For most of the post-World War II period until the late 1980s, the performance of the Japanese economy was little short of spectacular, with extremely rapid growth that substantially improved the living standards of the Japanese people. But in the 1990s, following the collapse of an **asset-price bubble** (a series of increases in stock and real estate prices that were driven largely by the expectation of future price increases), Japan entered a period of very slow growth – so slow, in fact, that it took on the character of a prolonged recession. The Japanese authorities tried to stimulate their economy through a variety of means during the 1990s, in particular by successively launching a series of expansionary fiscal programs financed by government borrowing. By the end of the decade these fiscal programs had left Japan with the highest ratio of public debt to GDP of any industrial country.

But in the mid-1990s, the tool of choice to promote a revival of economic growth in Japan was monetary expansion. Figure 10.6 shows what happened. The rate of growth of the money supply increased dramatically in the second and third quarters of 1995, and was very high on average during the period 1995:II to 1996:I. Impacts on interest rates in Japan and the yen-dollar exchange rate were exactly as our model would predict: interest rates fell sharply during 1995, and the yen-dollar exchange rate, which had been appreciating steadily until that point, depreciated strongly after the second quarter of the year.

It may be worth noting that this abrupt change in Japanese monetary policy had important repercussions beyond Japan, as often happens in international macroeconomics. The depreciation of the yen against the US dollar resulted in the real appreciation of the currencies of several Southeast Asian countries that had kept their exchange rates pegged against the US dollar, but that traded extensively with Japan. The resulting real effective appreciation of these currencies (Chapter 3), and the consequent loss of competitiveness of the countries involved, was an important factor behind the Asian financial crisis that broke out in the region in the summer of 1997, described in Chapter 9.

market can only be sustained with a higher domestic interest rate if a higher level of income sustains an unchanged level of money demand.

If the expansionary real shock takes the form of a fiscal expansion, as we have been supposing, effects on net exports are ambiguous, just as in the case of an expansionary monetary shock. This time, the increase in the domestic interest rate tends to increase net exports by reducing domestic absorption, while the increase in real output and appreciation of the exchange rate cause net exports to fall. Both of these changes increase imports, while the exchange rate appreciation reduces exports. Thus, if the expenditure switching effects of exchange rate changes are relatively powerful compared to their expenditure increasing (or in this case, decreasing) effects, then net exports will deteriorate.

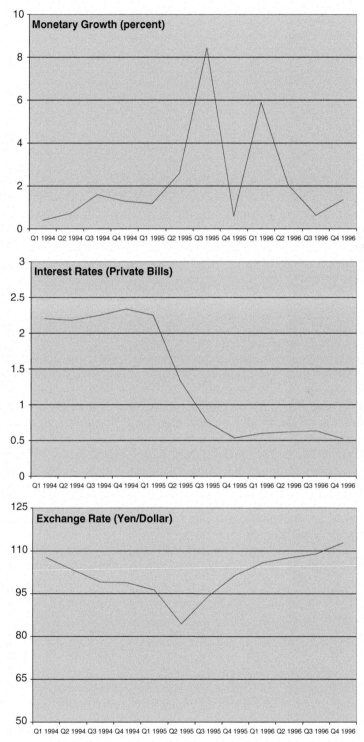

**Figure 10.6** Japanese monetary policy, 1994–96
*Source*: IFS, International Monetary Fund.

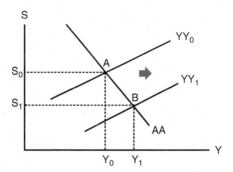

**Figure 10.7**    Effects of an expansionary real shock

However, if the expansionary shock arises from an exogenous increase in the demand for the country's exports, the ambiguity in the effects on net exports disappears. We can rely on the absorption approach to see why. Recall that the goods market equilibrium condition can be written as:

$$Y = A + G + N$$

We know from Figure 10.7 that $Y$ has to rise, and since the marginal propensity to absorb is less than one and the domestic interest rate rises, either absorption must actually fall or the increase in absorption must fall short of that in output. Since $G$ is unchanged in this case, it follows that the goods market can clear only if the net effect of the shock on $N$ is positive. In this case, then, net exports must increase.

Remember that one potential source of increased demand for the home country's exports would be an increase in partner-country incomes. Under fixed exchange rates and perfect capital mobility, we found that such changes had powerful effects on the domestic economy – that is, there was strong international transmission of business cycles – because real shocks were not subject to crowding out. With floating exchange rates, however, because the real exchange rate appreciates and the domestic interest rate rises, the expansionary impacts on domestic aggregate demand caused by increases in partner-country incomes are dampened. The implication is that international transmission of business cycles is weaker under floating rates than under fixed rates.[3]

Now that we have considered both monetary and real shocks, we can analyze the implications of changes in the fiscal-monetary "mix" – that is, the combinations of fiscal and monetary policies that are consistent with a given level of output. Boxes 10.4 and 10.5 consider two important applications.

## External Financial Shocks

Having examined the effects of shocks originating in the domestic money market and the market for domestic goods, consider next the macroeconomic effects of disturbances in the external financial conditions facing the country. We can describe these as shocks to the

[3]    Actually, this is true as long as the domestic central bank is targeting the money supply. If it targets the interest rate instead, the transmission of business cycles is just as strong as under fixed rates, as shown in Appendix 10.3.

## Box 10.4    The Reagan–Volcker Disinflation in the United States

The period after the final collapse of the Bretton Woods system and the first oil price shock, both of which occurred in 1973, was characterized by high inflation and relatively slow growth in the United States. Under Chairman Paul Volcker, the Federal Reserve System undertook a very tight monetary policy during the early 1980s that was intended to wring inflation out of the American economy. At the same time, the new government of President Ronald Reagan, elected in 1980, launched a very expansionary fiscal policy featuring tax cuts of historic magnitudes and substantial increases in defense spending that were not fully compensated for by expenditure cuts elsewhere in the US government budget. The result was that during the early part of the 1980s, the macroeconomic stance in the United States was one that combined a very tight monetary policy with an extremely loose fiscal policy.

What macroeconomic effects would our model predict from such a policy combination? The answer is given in Figure 10.7. The dashed lines in the figure represent the YY and AA curves before the fiscal expansion and monetary contraction, while the solid ones are the corresponding curves under the early-1980s' loose fiscal–tight monetary policy mix. To keep things simple, the figure has been drawn with the two new curves crossing at the same level of output as the old. The strong prediction of the model is that the currency would appreciate, and therefore that domestic interest rates would rise. In general, the exchange rate appreciation and high interest rates would be associated with some combination of crowding out of domestic absorption and a deterioration in net exports. Check back to Figure 3.2 (Chapter 3) and you will see that the nominal effective exchange rate of the United States did indeed appreciate strongly during the early 1980s. Figure 2.3 (Chapter 2) shows the substantial deterioration of the US current account balance that took place during the same years. In fact, the association of the substantial fiscal deficits that characterized those years with the large current account deficits seen in Figure 2.2 gave rise to the phrase "twin deficits."

It is worth noting that the Reagan–Volcker disinflation did succeed in wringing inflation out of the American economy, though at substantial costs. These took the form of a severe recession in the United States in 1982 and the Latin American debt crisis that broke out in August of that same year. Though the latter had deeper underlying causes (see Box 2.6 in Chapter 2), its immediate trigger was the combination of slow growth, high real interest rates, and a sharply appreciating dollar that resulted from the monetary-fiscal policy mix adopted by the United States. As happened to Southeast Asian countries during the period of yen depreciation (and thus dollar appreciation) in the second half of the 1990s, the Latin American countries that were affected by the debt crisis of the 1980s had maintained fixed exchange rates against the US dollar, and the strong appreciation of the dollar in the early 1980s contributed to an appreciation of the real exchange rates of these countries.

world interest rate $R^*$ or to the expected future exchange rate $S^e_{+1}$. Since the foreign interest rate and expected future exchange rate enter the model only as the product $(1 + R^*) S^e_{+1}$, the effects of changes in either of them are qualitatively the same.

## Box 10.5    The Macroeconomics of German Reunification

Another important application of the analysis of the macroeconomic effects of the tight monetary–loose fiscal policy mix concerns the unification of West Germany with the former East Germany in 1990. To facilitate the unification process politically, the then West German Chancellor Helmut Kohl promised a substantial amount of West German government spending in the former East Germany (in a variety of forms) that would be undertaken without unduly raising the tax burden on West Germans. This signified that German reunification would be accompanied by a very expansionary fiscal policy in the united Germany. This large fiscal expansion had the potential to create inflationary pressures in Germany, a prospect of which the German central bank, the Bundesbank, was no more enamored in the early 1990s than it had been in the late 1960s and early 1970s, when the Bundesbank resisted the inflationary pressures coming from the United States under the Bretton Woods system (Chapter 8). Consequently, the Bundesbank responded to the unification-induced fiscal expansion by maintaining a very tight monetary policy. Thus, the process of unification left Germany in the early 1990s with a tight monetary–loose fiscal policy mix reminiscent of that of the United States in the early 1980s.

The outcome was also similar to that which occurred in the United States nearly a decade earlier. As our model predicts and as illustrated in Figure 10.7, this particular policy mix was associated with very high interest rates in Germany and a sharp appreciation of the deutschmark against the US dollar.

Like the earlier American episode, the policy mix followed by Germany also had strong effects on third countries. As we saw in Box 9.3 (Chapter 9), the countries that belonged to the European Union and participated in the European Exchange Rate Mechanism (ERM) at the time essentially maintained a fixed exchange rate against the deutschmark, under conditions of what amounted to perfect capital mobility within the European Union. This meant that these countries had to import the higher German interest rates and also had to follow the deutschmark in its appreciation against the US dollar. The combination of higher interest rates and an appreciated real exchange rate had a strong contractionary effect on these economies, and since some of them (especially the United Kingdom and Italy) were already in recession, it created strong pressures for them to give up their fixed exchange rates by abandoning the ERM mechanism. The result was the second-generation ERM crisis described in Box 9.3.

To be concrete, consider, then, an increase in the expected future exchange rate $S_{+1}^e$. Unlike the previous two shocks we have considered, which affected one of the two curves in our model at a time, this one affects both curves simultaneously, since the uncovered interest parity interest rate $(1 + R^*) S_{+1}^e / S - 1$ affects equilibrium in both asset markets (equation 10.2′) as well as the goods market (equation 10.4′). Specifically, an increase in $S_{+1}^e$ causes both the AA and YY curves to shift upward, as in Figure 10.9.

As indicated before, the upward displacement in AA must be proportionately the same as the increase in $S_{+1}^e$. However, the upward displacement in YY must be *less than* proportional to the increase in $S_{+1}^e$. Since AA shifts up more than YY does, the new equilibrium must

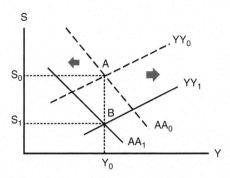

**Figure 10.8**  Effects of a tight monetary–loose fiscal policy mix

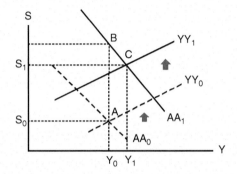

**Figure 10.9**  Effects of a depreciation of the expected future exchange rate

be found at a more depreciated value of the exchange rate and higher level of output than prevailed previously, as in Figure 10.9, but the depreciation of the spot exchange rate must be less than proportional to the depreciation in the expected future exchange rate, implying (from the UIP condition) that the domestic interest rate must have risen.

Intuitively, when the expectation of a more depreciated future exchange rate emerges, foreign bonds (which are denominated in foreign currency) become more attractive than domestic bonds and capital tends to flow out of the country, causing the spot exchange rate to depreciate. But the depreciation of the spot exchange rate must fall short of that of the expected *future* exchange rate, for if it did not, the domestic interest rate would return to its original level, and with an unchanged interest rate and more depreciated exchange rate the goods market could not be in equilibrium; there would be an excess demand for domestic goods. This incipient excess demand would cause output to rise, making it necessary for the money market to be cleared with a *higher* domestic interest rate than prevailed before the shock, and for a higher domestic interest rate to be consistent with UIP, the depreciation of the spot exchange rate would have to fall short of that in the expected future exchange rate.

It is worth making two observations at this point. First, notice that the analysis of an increase in the world interest rate $R^*$ would be conducted in exactly the same fashion as we have just done for a depreciation of the expected future exchange rate. But this must mean that a higher foreign interest rate must actually have an *expansionary* effect on the domestic economy, despite the fact that an increase in $R^*$ by itself has a contractionary effect on the goods market. The contrast to what happened under fixed exchange rates and perfect capital mobility in Chapter 6 is stark. We saw there that an increase in $(1 + R^*) S^e_{+1}$ had an unambiguously contractionary effect on the domestic economy.[4] Why the difference?

There are two reasons, both related to the general-equilibrium effects of the depreciation of the nominal exchange rate: the resulting depreciation of the *real* exchange rate switches spending to domestic goods, and the expected future appreciation of the currency causes the rise in the domestic interest rate to be smaller than it would have been without the exchange rate change. Notice that the domestic interest rate increases in both cases, and this effect is indeed contractionary. But the increase must be *smaller* under floating rates, and the combination of this with the favorable expenditure-switching effects of an exchange rate depreciation is enough to reverse the effects of the shock on domestic GDP.

Second, you should mark carefully the important result derived in this section: an expected future exchange rate depreciation leads to a *less than proportionate depreciation in the current exchange rate*. As we shall see, this result plays an important role in the analysis of longer-lived transitory shocks in Chapter 11.

Shocks to the uncovered interest parity relationship can take forms other than changes in world interest rates and expected future exchange rate changes. In particular, the effects of foreign financial shocks that we have just examined provide us with a good opportunity to explore the effects on the domestic economy of having a particularly ''strong'' or ''weak'' currency under floating exchange rates. Box 10.6 takes up this issue.

## Central Bank Intervention in the Foreign Exchange Market

Up until now we have been assuming that the central bank operates a ''clean'' float – that is, one in which it does not intervene in the foreign exchange market, allowing the exchange rate to be determined purely as the outcome of interactions among private agents. But recall that the stock of foreign exchange reserves $F_C^*$ is a policy variable under floating rates, so the central bank retains the option to intervene if it chooses to.

What happens if it does? There are two possibilities:

1   *Unsterilized intervention.* Suppose the central bank buys foreign exchange. This represents an increase in its stock of foreign exchange reserves $F_C^*$. If this increase in $F_C^*$ is not offset by a reduction in the bank's holdings of domestic bonds $B_C$ – that is, if the intervention is not sterilized – then it results in an increase in the money supply, and is equivalent to expansionary monetary policy. As we have seen, the exchange rate depreciates and output increases in this case. All the other results derived for expansionary monetary policy follow as well.

2   *Sterilized intervention.* If, on the other hand, the intervention is sterilized (so that central bank holdings of domestic bonds decrease by \$1 through an open-market sale of such bonds for every \$1 increase in its stock of foreign exchange reserves, leaving the money supply unchanged), then the intervention has no effect whatsoever except to change the composition of the central bank's balance sheet.

Why is this so? Because with sterilized intervention all that the central bank has done has been to withdraw foreign bonds from private portfolios (its original foreign exchange

---

[4]   Indeed, the result here is directly opposite to what happened in the case of fixed exchange rates, whether with perfect or imperfect capital mobility.

## Box 10.6 Is a Strong Currency Good for the Economy?

Policymakers often make pronouncements about the economic consequences of the domestic currency being "strong" or "weak" under floating exchange rates. Your first reaction to any such statement should be to wonder what it means, since under floating exchange rates the nominal exchange rate is an endogenous variable, so the economic consequences of the currency being "strong" (relatively appreciated) or "weak" (relatively depreciated) should depend on the type of shock that caused it to be one thing or the other.

To make sense of such a statement in isolation from other types of shocks, we might interpret what the politicians are talking about as implicitly referring to the strength of an exogenous "taste" for acquiring domestic assets instead of foreign assets. How could we capture such a phenomenon in our model?

A more general form of the uncovered parity relationship can be written as $1 + R = (1 + R^*)(S_{+1}^e/S)(1 + \delta)$, where $\delta$ is a premium that captures the effects of unspecified factors affecting investors' "taste" for domestic as opposed to foreign assets. In this case, when $\delta$ increases, peoples' "taste" for domestic assets *decreases*, so they have to be compensated by higher domestic interest rates in order to hold them. Thus, the domestic currency would be "strong" when $\delta$ is *small* and it would be "weak" when $\delta$ is large. Now consider an economy such as the one that we have been studying in this chapter. What would happen to the equilibrium level of real GDP in that economy if there was a transitory *increase* in peoples' "taste" for its assets – that is, if the domestic currency became temporarily strong?

The answer is, of course, that a reduction in $\delta$ would affect the economy in exactly the same way as a reduction in the foreign interest rate or an expected future exchange rate *appreciation* (a reduction in $S_{+1}^e$): the domestic currency would appreciate and equilibrium real GDP would contract. Thus, a strong currency is at best a mixed blessing: while buyers of foreign goods would benefit by being able to purchase them more cheaply, the economy would find it more difficult to attain high levels of employment and output.

market intervention), while putting more domestic bonds into private portfolios (its open market sale). But since domestic and foreign bonds are by assumption perfect substitutes in private portfolios, no one cares about this transaction and no one alters their behavior because of it, leaving the macroeconomic equilibrium unchanged. The bottom line is that in our model only unsterilized foreign exchange market intervention has any effect on the exchange rate, and that effect only comes about through its influence on the money supply.

## Empirical Study 10.1 Monetary Shocks and the Real Exchange Rate

The model of floating exchange rate that we have developed in this chapter assumes that the domestic price level is "sticky" in the short run. In that context, monetary

*(Continued)*

## Empirical Study 10.1    *(Continued)*

shocks (shocks to money supply or demand) that affect the nominal exchange rate would also tend to affect the real exchange rate, since domestic prices cannot adjust on impact to offset the effect of a change in the nominal exchange rate on the real exchange rate. In a competing view of the world, however, in which domestic prices are fully flexible, monetary shocks affect the nominal exchange rate, but not the real exchange rate. With fully flexible domestic prices, real exchange rate changes would tend to arise only from changes in "real" (goods market) variables. We will explore a version of our analytical framework that has this property in Chapter 14.

What does the evidence say regarding the effects of nominal shocks on the real exchange rate? A classic reference on this question is a study by Clarida and Gali (1994). Clarida and Gali explored the issue by estimating a three-variable VAR in which the endogenous variables were (changes in the logs of) real GDP, the real exchange rate, and the price level.[5] Recall from Empirical Study 8.1 that the error terms in such a VAR are "reduced form" errors that reflect the combined influence of unobserved structural shocks. Clarida and Gali interpreted the structural shocks underlying the reduced-form shocks in the VAR as aggregate supply shocks, aggregate demand shocks, and monetary shocks. They were able to identify these (i.e., to infer them from the estimated values of the reduced-form VAR error terms) by imposing three long-run restrictions on the structural shocks: in the long run real output is only affected by aggregate supply shocks, the real exchange rate is affected by both aggregate supply and demand shocks, and the price level can potentially be affected by all three types of shocks. They estimated VARs for each of four industrial countries (Britain, Canada, Germany, and Japan) using quarterly data from 1973 to 1992.

Clarida and Gali found that nominal shocks were indeed quite important in driving real exchange rate movements in Germany and Japan during their sample period. Not only did monetary shocks explain a large proportion of the variance in real exchange rate changes for these two countries during 1973–92, but simulations using the estimated VARs indicated that a large share of the systematic variation of the bilateral real exchange rate of these two countries relative to the United States (i.e., appreciation in the late 1970s, and depreciation during the early 1980s) could be explained by monetary shocks. By contrast, for Britain and Canada, most of the variation in the bilateral real exchange rate against the dollar arose as the result of demand shocks.

More interestingly, Clarida and Gali computed impulse responses for their system, to gauge the extent to which the response of several macro variables to a variety of shocks accorded with the predictions of a simple sticky-price model such as that developed in this chapter. They found that dynamic responses to nominal shocks for all four countries matched those of the sticky price model quite closely, with a positive monetary shock resulting in a real exchange rate depreciation and an expansion in domestic output. If the shock is permanent, both effects eventually die out as the domestic price level adjusts. As we will see in the next two chapters, this is also a prediction of our model.

---

[5]    Their VAR actually used *differentials* between domestic and foreign real output and inflation rates. For a description of the VAR methodology, see Empirical Study 8.1.

## 10.4   Summary

In this chapter we have made the transition from fixed to floating exchange rates, in a context in which the domestic economy is highly integrated with world financial markets. We have examined how our basic model has to be adjusted to incorporate the change in exchange rate regimes, and found in particular that the exchange rate now becomes an endogenous variable while the central bank's stock of foreign exchange reserves is a policy variable, in an exact reversal of their roles under fixed exchange rates. An additional change is that the expected future exchange rate also becomes an endogenous variable under floating rates. This adds a complication to our analysis, because the compact version of our model now contains more endogenous variables than it does equations with which to solve for them.

We handled that problem in this chapter by assuming that expectations about the future value of the exchange rate are formed rationally (that is, using the model itself), and that shocks to the economy are expected to be transitory. The latter means that, in response to a shock to the economy, the expected future value of the exchange rate remains what it would have been without the shock. Based on this assumption, we derived the asset market approach to the exchange rate and embedded it in a complete floating exchange rate model of the economy.

This model told us that economies behave very differently under floating exchange rates than they do under fixed exchange rates. In particular, monetary policy remains an effective tool to affect aggregate demand, even under conditions of perfect capital mobility (an application of the ''impossible trinity''), fiscal policy is weakened by ''crowding out'' phenomena, and external financial shocks have effects on the domestic economy that are the reverse of what we found them to be under fixed exchange rates.[6]

But of course, not all shocks to the economy last as briefly as those that we have examined in this chapter. In the next chapter we will extend our analysis of macroeconomics under floating exchange rates by considering how the economy reacts to longer-lasting shocks. We will discover that the contrast between fixed and floating rates becomes even more dramatic when shocks to the economy are expected to be permanent.

### Questions

1   In the early 1980s, under the Reagan administration, macroeconomic policies in the United States were characterized by relatively expansionary fiscal policy (fueled by increased defense spending and tax cuts) and very tight monetary policy. Compared to an alternative policy mix which produced the same level of Y using more expansionary monetary policy and more contractionary fiscal policy, explain what effects you would expect such a policy mix to have on each of the following:
   a  Interest rates in the United States.
   b  The effective exchange rate of the US dollar.
   c  The current account of the US balance of payments.
   d  The nonreserve financial account of the US balance of payments.

---

[6]   These properties emerge under the ''sticky price'' assumption that the aggregate price level is fixed in the short run. Empirical Study 10.1 examines some evidence on the empirical relevance of this assumption for four industrial countries.

2    Explain why the money supply could not be considered a policy variable in our open-economy macro model under fixed exchange rates, but it can under floating exchange rates.

3    After its financial crisis in December 1994, Mexico has operated under a system of floating exchange rates relative to the United States. Explain how, under such a system, the Mexican economy (specifically, real output, the real exchange rate, and the domestic interest rate) would be affected, in both the short run and the long run, by:
    a   an increase in US real GDP.
    b   an increase in US interest rates.

4    Under what conditions would a temporary monetary expansion cause the current account of the balance of payments to improve (i.e., move into a smaller deficit or larger surplus)? Explain.

5    Though uncovered interest parity is a reasonable approximation for industrial countries much of the time, in times of crisis a "risk premium" sometimes emerges that creates a gap between the domestic interest rate and the expected rate of return on foreign interest-bearing assets. Suppose that, because of a domestic political problem, such a risk premium suddenly emerges for some country, but is expected to be a temporary phenomenon. Explain what effect you would expect it to have while present on the affected economy's nominal exchange rate, level of output, and interest rate.

6    For a small country that maintains a floating exchange rate, describe the effects of a temporary increase in foreign GDP (interpreted as an increase in $\theta$) on each of the following domestic variables:
    a   The nominal exchange rate.
    b   The nominal interest rate.
    c   The level of real GDP.
    d   The current account of the balance of payments.
    e   The nonreserve financial account of the balance of payments.

7    The European Central Bank (ECB) has occasionally intervened heavily in support of the euro. If their objective is to cause an appreciation of the euro:
    a   Explain exactly what actions the ECB must have been taking in the foreign exchange market, and how this would have affected the ECB's balance sheet.
    b   Explain what specific actions the ECB can take to prevent its intervention from affecting the domestic money supply in Euroland.
    c   Explain how the effectiveness of the ECB's intervention in affecting the value of the euro would be influenced by whether it undertook the actions in (b) or not, and why this is so.

8    What is the "asset market" approach to the exchange rate? Under what circumstances can this approach be applied?

9    Under the Exchange Rate Mechanism of the European Monetary System that prevailed until 1992, the British pound was essentially fixed against the German mark. When Germany adopted a tight monetary policy in association with the reunification of the country in the early 1990s, Britain was thrown into recession. After the British switched to a floating exchange rate system in the fall of 1992, the economy of the UK began to grow briskly. Using models you have learned in this chapter, can you explain why tight money in Germany was associated with recession in the United Kingdom under a fixed exchange rate, but with economic expansion under floating exchange rates? (For the purposes of this question, you should assume that the United Kingdom is a small open economy.)

10   Consider a small open economy that maintains a floating exchange rate and is characterized by perfect capital mobility. Suppose that the interest rate prevailing in the international capital market falls, and that this decrease is expected to be temporary. Explain what effects you would expect this shock to have on the following domestic macroeconomic variables:

a  The nominal exchange rate.

b  Real GDP.

c  The domestic interest rate.

d  The domestic money supply.

e  The current and nonreserve financial accounts of the country's balance of payments.

11   What is the ''impossible trinity'' of open-economy macroeconomics? Use three of the models you have studied in this book to illustrate its application.

12   Consider a small open economy with a floating exchange rate in which the government undertakes an increase in spending that is regarded as being transitory. Suppose that the central bank decides to prevent the fiscal expansion from affecting the domestic interest rate.

a  What would the central bank have to do to prevent the domestic interest rate from changing? Show the effects of the government and central bank actions on the economy using diagrams.

b  In this situation, what effect would the fiscal expansion have on the current and nonreserve financial accounts of the country's balance of payments?

## Further Reading and References

### On modeling floating exchange rates

Taylor, Mark (1995), ''The Economics of Exchange Rates,'' *Journal of Economic Literature* XXXIII (March), pp. 13–47.

### On fiscal policy and the exchange rate

Fieleke, Norman S. (1984), ''The Budget Deficit: Are the International Consequences Unfavorable?'' Federal Reserve Bank of Boston, *New England Economic Review* (May/June), pp. 5–10.

### On nominal shocks and the real exchange rate

Clarida, Richard and Jordi Gali (1994), ''Sources of Real Exchange Rate Fluctuations: How Important Are Nominal Shocks?'' *Carnegie-Rochester Conference Series on Public Policy*, Vol. 41, pp. 1–56.

Eichenbaum, Martin and Charles Evans (1995), ''Some Empirical Evidence on the Effects of Monetary Policy on Exchange Rates,'' *Quarterly Journal of Economics*, Vol. 110, No. 4 (November), pp. 975–1009.

### On international experience with floating exchange rates

Obstfeld, Maurice (1985), ''Floating Exchange Rates: Experience and Prospects,'' *Brookings Papers on Economic Activity*, Vol. 2, pp. 369–450.

Obstfeld, Maurice (1995), ''International Currency Experience: New Lessons and Lessons Relearned,'' *Brookings Papers on Economic Activity,* Vol. 1, pp. 119–91.

## Appendix 10.1    The Asset Market Approach to the Exchange Rate

How can the exchange rate be determined in asset markets, since we know that transactions in goods and services are also being conducted in the foreign exchange market? To answer this question, assume that exports of goods and services, measured in foreign currency terms, are an increasing – and imports a decreasing – function of the real exchange rate (as they actually are in our model). With the domestic price level $P$ and foreign price level $P^*$ given to us, we can write:

$$EX = X\,(\underset{+}{S},\ \ldots)$$

$$IM = Z\,(\underset{-}{S},\ \ldots)$$

Similarly, suppose that capital outflows are a decreasing, and capital inflows an increasing, function of the exchange rate:

$$KO = KO\,(\underset{-}{S},\ \ldots)$$

$$KI = KI\,(\underset{+}{S},\ \ldots)$$

This would be true, for example, if capital inflows were a positive function and capital outflows a negative function of the interest rate differential:

$$R - \left[(1 + R^*)S^e_{+1}/S - 1\right]$$

How could we use this information to find the equilibrium value of the exchange rate? One way would be to set the demand for foreign exchange equal to its supply:

$$IM + KO = X + KI$$

But notice that this is equivalent to:

$$IM - X = KI - KO$$

The left-hand side is the *excess demand* for foreign exchange arising from the current account of the balance of payments, while the right-hand side is the *excess supply* arising from the nonreserve financial account. Graphically, the excess demand for foreign exchange can be derived as in Figure A10.1 (where EDF stands for "excess demand for foreign exchange," measured in foreign currency).

A similar diagram could be derived for the nonreserve financial account of the balance of payments. The equilibrium exchange rate would then be the value of the exchange rate for which excess demand equals excess supply, as is true at $S_0$ in Figure A10.2. Notice that the more elastic one of the curves is, the closer the equilibrium value of the exchange rate $S_0$ will be to the value of the exchange rate where that curve crosses the vertical axis – that is, to the equilibrium exchange rate for that curve (you can verify this by mentally rotating one of the curves). In the limit, if one of the excess demand curves is perfectly elastic, the equilibrium exchange rate for the market as a whole must coincide with the relevant equilibrium exchange rate for that curve. *But under UIP and the assumption that $S^e_{+1}$ is exogenous,*

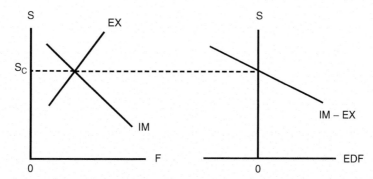

**Figure A10.1** Excess demand for foreign exchange arising from trade in goods and services

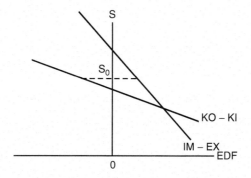

**Figure A10.2** The foreign exchange market and the equilibrium exchange rate

*KO − KI is indeed perfectly elastic. Thus the equilibrium value of the exchange rate will be determined in the asset market. This is what is meant by the asset-market approach to the exchange rate.*

## Appendix 10.2 Algebraic Solution of the Log-linear Model

Written in log-linear form, the two equations of our model, representing asset market equilibrium and goods market equilibrium, are:

$$\text{AA}: m - p = c_0 - c_1\left[R^* + \left(s^e_{+1} - s\right)\right] + c_2 y$$
$$\text{YY}: y = b_0 - b_1\left[R^* + \left(s^e_{+1} - s\right)\right] + b_2(s + p^* - p) + b_3\, g + b_4\, \theta$$

To solve for the (log of the) exchange rate $s$, substitute YY into AA. The result is:

$$
\begin{aligned}
m - p &= c_0 - c_1\left[R^* + \left(s^e_{+1} - s\right)\right] + c_2\left(b_0 - b_1\left[R^* + \left(s^e_{+1} - s\right)\right] +\right) + b_3\, g + b_4\, \theta) \\
&= (c_0 + c_2 b_0) - (c_1 + c_2 b_1)\left[R^* + \left(s^e_{+1} - s\right)\right] + c_2 b_2(s + p^* - p) + c_2(b_3\, g + b_4\, \theta) \\
&= (c_0 + c_2 b_0) - (c_1 + c_2 b_1)\left(R^* + s^e_{+1}\right) + c_2 b_2(p^* - p) + c_2(b_3\, g + b_4\, \theta) \\
&\quad + (c_1 + c_2 b_1 + c_2 b_2)s
\end{aligned}
$$

Dividing both sides by $(c_1 + c_2 b_1 + c_2 b_2)$ and solving for $s$ yields:

$$s = \frac{(m-p) - (c_0 + c_2 b_0) + (c_1 + c_2 b_1)(R^* + s^e_{+1}) - c_2 b_2(p^* - p) - c_2(b_3\, g + b_4\theta)}{c_1 + c_2 b_1 + c_2 b_2}$$

The results derived in the text for the effects of various shocks on the exchange rate can be confirmed directly from this equation. For example, a 1 percent increase in the money supply will cause the exchange rate to depreciate by $1/(c_1 + c_2 b_1 + c_2 b_2)$ percent, while a 1 percent increase in government spending causes it to appreciate by $c_2 b_3/(c_1 + c_2 b_1 + c_2 b_2)$ percent.

## Appendix 10.3    Interest Rate Targeting under Floating Exchange Rates

In this appendix we will investigate how the adoption of interest rate targeting would affect our floating rate model.

To answer this question, go back to the three equations of the compact version of the floating exchange rate model in Box 10.2. Under interest rate targeting, the domestic interest rate $R$ becomes an exogenous policy variable, so we can write the UIP condition as:

$$R = (1 + R^*)S^e_{+1}/S - 1 \tag{10.3$'$}$$

where $\bar{R}$ is the policy-determined value of the domestic interest rate. The goods market equilibrium condition becomes:

$$Y = \varphi(S\bar{P}^*/\bar{P})A(Y-T, \bar{R}) + G + X(S\bar{P}^*/\bar{P}, \theta) \tag{10.4$'$}$$

Finally, we can write the money market equilibrium condition as:

$$M = PL(\bar{R}, Y) \tag{10.2$'$}$$

Notice that equation (10.3$'$) now contains a single endogenous variable: the nominal exchange rate $S$. This equation therefore determines the equilibrium value of the exchange rate as a function of the policy-determined domestic interest rate. It therefore represents the AA curve under interest rate targeting, and can be plotted as a horizontal straight line, as in Figure A10.3. The goods market equilibrium condition (10.4$'$) differs from that in the chapter in that the exchange rate no longer affects aggregate demand through expenditure increasing or decreasing, but only through expenditure switching. The reason is that expenditure increasing or decreasing effects arise through the effects of the exchange rate on the domestic interest rate, and such effects are not present when the domestic interest rate is treated as a policy variable by the central bank. The implication is that the YY curve still has a positive slope, but is steeper (i.e., the exchange rate has a weaker effect on the goods market) under interest rate targeting. The YY curve is also depicted in Figure A10.3. What about the money market equilibrium condition (10.2$'$)? The only role of this condition is to determine where the central bank must set the money supply $M$ in order to hit its interest rate target. The equation plays no role in determining the equilibrium values of the exchange rate, the interest rate, or real output under interest rate targeting.

How does the model work? Consider first the effects of monetary policy. Expansionary monetary policy now takes the form of a reduction in the central bank's interest rate target.

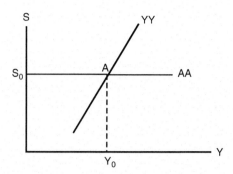

**Figure A10.3** General equilibrium under interest rate targeting

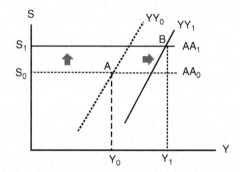

**Figure A10.4** Expansionary monetary policy under interest rate targeting

With a lower domestic interest rate, capital will flow out of the country and the exchange rate will depreciate, so the AA curve will shift upward, as in Figure A10.4. At the same time, the lower domestic interest rate will increase domestic absorption, causing the demand for domestic goods to increase and thus shifting the YY curve to the right. As shown in Figure A10.4, the combined effects of the two shifts is to increase output and depreciate the exchange rate. As you can easily see from equation (10.2′), the lower domestic interest rate and higher domestic output will both increase the demand for money, so to enforce its lower interest rate target the central bank must expand the money supply.

Shocks to aggregate demand will shift the YY curve horizontally in this case in the same way (and by the same amounts) as in the text, causing output to change but leaving the exchange rate unchanged. The effect on the equilibrium level of real output of a given-size aggregate demand shock will be larger under interest rate targeting than under monetary targeting, because there will be no crowding-out effects in this case. In this case, the central bank must adjust the money supply to offset any changes in the demand for money caused by changes in equilibrium real GDP. Finally, external financial shocks will affect only the AA curve and not the YY curve under interest rate targeting. Increases in $R^*$ or $S^e_{+1}$ will trigger capital outflows that cause the nominal exchange rate to depreciate, shifting AA vertically upward, while decreases in either of these variables shift it downward. The former will be expansionary and the latter contractionary, as in the text, but their impact on real GDP is larger under interest rate targeting than under monetary targeting, because there is no dampening impact arising from changes in the domestic interest rate. Again, since the domestic interest rate is unchanged, effects on the money supply depend on impacts on equilibrium real GDP.

# 11

# Floating Exchange Rates II: Intermediate and Permanent Shocks

The floating exchange rate model that we studied in Chapter 10 focused on the effects of transitory shocks to the economy. The shocks we analyzed were assumed to arrive unexpectedly, to last for only one period and then to go away, and everyone was assumed to know that that was exactly what would happen. It is useful to begin the study of floating exchange rates with shocks of that type, because such shocks do not affect the expected future value of the exchange rate in our framework.

In the real world, however, shocks to the economy do not always behave in that fashion. For example, sometimes changes in the economic environment are anticipated before they actually materialize. Moreover, when such changes do materialize they often last for several periods, and may even be permanent. In this chapter we will generalize our analysis to consider all of these possibilities. We will examine how the economy reacts *on impact* to shocks that are anticipated before they arrive, as well as to those that are expected to last longer than a single period, including shocks that are expected to be permanent. As we will see, shocks that are anticipated before they happen will generally begin to affect the economy *before* they actually materialize, and the length of time that a shock is expected to last will be a key determinant of its macroeconomic effects on impact.

In the first section of this chapter, we will consider how the anticipation of a future shock may affect the economy before the shock actually appears. As you will see, this is an important analytical building block for understanding the impact effects of transitory shocks that are expected to last more than a single period. The next section of the chapter will apply this analysis to examine the impact effects of shocks that are expected to last for multiple periods. We then extend the analysis to consider the impact effects of shocks that are expected to be permanent. Interestingly, you will find that this case creates rather dramatic contrasts between the way the economy behaves under fixed and floating exchange rate regimes. Finally, the chapter concludes with a comparison of the short-run effects of transitory and permanent shocks. In analyzing multi-period shocks in this chapter, we will retain the assumption that the domestic price level is expected to remain fixed. We will relax this assumption in Chapter 14.

## 11.1    Anticipated Future Shocks

The compact version of our short-run floating exchange rate model is reproduced in Box 11.1. As we saw in Chapter 10, this model contains four endogenous variables: the domestic interest rate $R$, domestic real output $Y$, the spot exchange rate $S$, and the expected future exchange rate $S^e_{+1}$. However, we noted that under rational expectations, when the shocks affecting the economy were taken to be only one period in duration, $S^e_{+1}$ could be treated as an exogenous variable. Since this eliminated the extra endogenous variable, it left us with three endogenous variables (consisting of $Y$, $R$, and $S$) and three equations, representing a complete, well-specified floating exchange rate model that we could solve.

However, that is obviously a very special case. In general, macroeconomic shocks may last several periods, and may even be expected to be permanent. To see how the effects of shocks depend on their expected duration, we will break up the analysis into three parts. In this section, we will consider the effects on the economy in the *current* period of shocks that last only one period, but are not expected to arrive until some point in the future. We will refer to this as an **anticipated future shock**. Since a shock that is expected to last for two periods is just a one-period shock plus an expected recurrence of the same shock one period from now, our second step will be to put the analysis of anticipated future shocks together with that of the last chapter to establish what the effects on the economy would be if some unspecified shock were expected to last for two periods, instead of just one. Then we will

---

### Box 11.1    The Compact Version of the Floating Exchange Rate Model

**Money-market equilibrium**

$$M = PL(R, Y) \tag{11.1}$$

**Bond market equilibrium**

$$R = (1 + R^*)S^e_{+1}/S - 1 \tag{11.2}$$

**Goods market equilibrium**

$$Y = \varphi(SP^*/\bar{P})A(Y - T, R) + G + X(SP^*/\bar{P}, \theta) \tag{11.3}$$

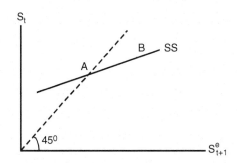

**Figure 11.1**   Effect of the expected future exchange rate on the current exchange rate

discuss how the analysis can be extended in a straightforward way to shocks of multi-period (but finite) duration.

Why should a shock that is not expected to arrive until tomorrow have any effect at all on the economy today? The answer is that today's macroeconomic equilibrium is linked to tomorrow's equilibrium in our model through the role of exchange rate expectations. Since we are assuming that people form their expectations rationally (that they base their expect-ations of the effects of shocks on what the model itself predicts will happen), any event that can be foreseen to disturb the economy tomorrow will affect the expectations that people form today about the exchange rate that will prevail tomorrow. In turn, a change in the expectation formed today about what the exchange rate will be tomorrow will affect the economy today, because of its effects on financial markets. Specifically, we saw in the last chapter that a depreciation in the expected future exchange rate $S_{t+1}^e$ would result in capital outflows that would cause the *current* exchange rate to depreciate and the domestic interest rate to rise. In the new macroeconomic equilibrium induced by the expected future depre-ciation there would be a less-than-proportionate depreciation in the current exchange rate $S$ and an expansionary effect on domestic real output.

Figure 11.1 illustrates the relationship between the expected future exchange rate and the current exchange rate that we derived in Chapter 10. The curve SS depicts the equilibrium value of the exchange rate in the current period, now labeled $S_t$ (indicated on the vertical axis) as a function of the exchange rate expected to prevail in the next period, now labeled $S_{t+1}^e$ (indicated on the horizontal axis), holding constant the current-period values of all the other exogenous variables that may affect the economy.[1] For the reasons discussed in the last paragraph, in the vicinity of $S_t = S_{t+1}^e$ (shown in the figure as a 45-degree line from the origin) this curve has a positive slope that is less than unity. In other words, changes in the expected future exchange rate move the current exchange rate in the same direction, but by a smaller amount than the change in the expected future exchange rate.

What determines the position of the SS curve? Anything that affects the equilibrium value of the spot exchange rate $S_t$, for a *given* value of the expected future exchange rate $S_{t+1}^e$ would affect the height of the curve. Thus, any shock to the economy in the present period that alters the equilibrium exchange rate would cause this curve to shift up (for a

---

[1]   We will use the subscript $t$ in graphs like Figure 11.1 to indicate that the relationship shown there links the exchange rate prevailing in *any* given period to the one that is expected to prevail one period ahead, regardless of whether the two adjacent periods refer to the current period and the next one or to two other adjacent periods at some point in the future.

depreciation) or down (for an appreciation). By contrast, any shock to the economy that is expected to occur in the *next* period does not shift the curve but only results in a movement along it, since such shocks would affect the current exchange rate only through their effects on the expected future exchange rate $S_{t+1}^e$.

How do we determine the effect that an unspecified shock that is not expected to arrive until tomorrow would have on the economy today? Based on what has just been said, there are two steps to the process: first we determine the effect of the anticipated future shock on the future exchange rate, and then we determine the effect of the change in the expected future exchange rate on the economy today. As we have just discussed and as summarized in Figure 11.1, the second step was already taken in the last chapter. What remains for us to do now is to link expected future shocks to future exchange rate changes.

To do so, let's call "today" period 1, "tomorrow" period 2, and the future that prevails after tomorrow period 3. Suppose that a shock is expected to hit the economy tomorrow (that is, in period 2), and to last for only a single period, so it is expected to be gone by period 3. Then the key observation to make is that, since the shock will be gone by period 3, in that period the economy will revert to the same equilibrium in which it would have been if the shock had never happened. In other words, the shock will have no effect on the exchange rate that prevails in period 3. But that means that, looking forward from period 2, the shock influencing the economy at that time is in effect only a one-period shock arriving in period 2. That being so, the conditions assumed in the model of Chapter 10 must prevail in period 2 – that is, in period 2 the economy is subjected to a transitory (one-period) shock. Thus, the model of Chapter 10 can be used to solve for the exchange rate that will prevail in period 2. Under rational expectations, that is precisely the exchange rate that people who are forming their expectations in period 1 should expect to prevail one period ahead.

What all of this means is that by solving the transitory shock model of the last chapter from the perspective of the *next* period, we essentially derive the solution for $S_{+1}$, and this solution therefore provides us with the expectation $S_{+1}^e$. But once we have the solution for $S_{+1}^e$, we can substitute that value of $S_{+1}^e$ into the model above and solve the model as we did in the last chapter – that is, for $S$, $Y$, and $R$ as functions of the given value of $S_{+1}^e$. Box 11.2 describes how an analysis of this type can be used to understand why good economic news – portending favorable future economic performance – tends to be associated with an appreciation of the exchange rate.

To be concrete, consider the case of an increase in the money supply that is expected to materialize one period from now and to last for exactly one period. How should we expect this anticipated future increase in the money supply to affect the economy today? Since the shock is only expected to last one period, its effects on the economy when it arrives will be those that we identified in the last chapter: the nominal exchange rate will depreciate, the domestic interest rate will fall, and output will rise. Thus, from the perspective of the current period, the anticipated future monetary expansion implies an increase in $S_{+1}^e$ – that is, a movement to the right away from A along SS in Figure 11.1, to a position such as B. But we saw in the last chapter that an increase in $S_{+1}^e$ would result in a less than proportionate depreciation in S, an increase in the domestic interest rate, and an expansion in domestic output. We conclude, therefore, that an anticipated future monetary expansion will actually increase output *before* the expansion itself takes place, even though it is actually associated with an increase in the domestic interest rate before the expansion materializes. The stimulus to the economy in this case comes from the expenditure-switching effects of an exchange rate depreciation. Box 11.3 provides an example of how

## Box 11.2    Why Do Good Economic News Cause the Exchange Rate to Appreciate?

You will often have encountered press reports about changes in the value of the US dollar, and will have noticed that such reports are usually accompanied by an interpretation of why those changes happened. They may be linked to domestic economic developments in the United States or to economic developments overseas. When currency movements are linked to domestic economic performance, a common pattern is that a strengthening of the dollar (a dollar appreciation) is linked to positive news about economic activity in the United States, and a weakening of the dollar (a dollar depreciation) to negative news about domestic economic activity.

Why should that be? It may not have occurred to you to raise that question, because it seems somehow intuitive that if the domestic economy strengthens, the domestic currency should be stronger as well. But not so fast. Isn't it also true that if the strengthening of the domestic economy is caused by an unexpected increase in aggregate demand, that increase in demand will result in an increased demand for imports, and therefore in more sales of US dollars in foreign exchange markets by individuals who are trying to buy foreign currency in order to pay for those imports? The answer is yes, but the dollar will appreciate anyway, because those transactions are likely to be dominated in their effects on the exchange rate by capital inflows.

Where do those capital inflows come from? The answer is that good news about the economy means that aggregate demand is likely to be stronger in the future than it was previously expected to be. If the central bank is expected to keep the money supply constant when that happens, or even to tighten monetary policy to prevent the economy from expanding too fast, then the domestic interest rate will be expected to rise in the future when the anticipated increase in aggregate demand materializes. If that is so, then as we saw in the last chapter, the exchange rate will appreciate. It is that anticipated future exchange rate appreciation caused by a higher expected future interest rate that induces people to try to acquire the domestic currency *today* in the hope of reaping a capital gain, and that is the source of the capital inflows that drive the appreciation of the currency in the present. Thus good economic news is linked to dollar appreciation through the expectation of higher future domestic interest rates.

This mechanism also works in reverse: if the economic news is bad, suggesting weaker aggregate demand in the future, future domestic interest rates will be expected to fall, particularly if the central bank is expected to expand the money supply in response to a contraction in aggregate demand. In that case the exchange rate will be expected to weaken (depreciate) in the future, and that will create capital outflows that will cause the exchange rate to depreciate in the present.

central banks may try to affect the economy in the present by signaling their future monetary policy intentions.

The effects just described are not specific to the case of an anticipated future monetary expansion. Any anticipated future shock that is expected to depreciate the exchange rate when it arrives would have the same set of effects on the economy in the present. Similarly,

## Box 11.3    Foreign Exchange Market Intervention as a Signal of Monetary Policy

According to the model in Chapter 10, intervention by central banks in the foreign exchange market would affect the exchange rate only to the extent that such intervention affects the money supply. This means that *sterilized* intervention – i.e., purchases or sales of foreign exchange by the central bank accompanied by exactly offsetting sales of purchases of domestic bonds, thereby leaving the money supply unchanged – should have no effect on the exchange rate. Yet many countries with floating exchange rates have often done just that. For example, as we will see in Chapter 17, the major industrial countries have at times engaged in **concerted** (joint) intervention in foreign exchange markets, with a view to affect the paths of the major-currency exchange rates, while simultaneously sterilizing the monetary impacts of such intervention. Why would central banks engage in such seemingly fruitless behavior?

One answer is that by publicly intervening in the foreign exchange market – even if such intervention is sterilized – a central bank may be sending a signal to the market that it is concerned with the value of the exchange rate, and therefore may be willing to engage in nonsterilized intervention in the *future*. If the foreign exchange market perceives that the central bank is committed to altering the value of the exchange rate in the future, and this changes the market's expectation of the future value of the exchange rate, this would in turn affect the equilibrium value of the exchange rate in the present. Thus intervention would affect the exchange rate indirectly through expectations, rather than directly by affecting the money supply.

Is there any evidence that sterilized intervention has actually worked in this way? Klein and Rosengren (1991) consider this possibility for the United States and Germany over the two-year period following the Plaza Accord in September 1985, during which the central banks of the major industrial countries had agreed jointly to intervene to influence the exchange rate of the US dollar (see Chapter 17). They first examine whether foreign exchange market intervention was indeed used as a signal of future changes in monetary policy by testing whether discernible changes in monetary policies during the period tended to be preceded by unusual amounts of foreign exchange market intervention, and whether unusual levels of foreign exchange market intervention tended to be followed by changes in monetary policy. They found that neither was true, either for the United States or Germany, suggesting that sterilized intervention was not a particularly good signal of future changes in monetary policy.

But this leaves the possibility that sterilized intervention may nevertheless have been (wrongly) *interpreted* by the foreign exchange market as providing useful information about future monetary policy anyway. To test this possibility, they examined whether intervention tended to be systematically associated with exchange rate changes over the same period of time by running regression of daily changes in the exchange rates on dummy variables capturing whether news about foreign exchange rate intervention by either the Fed or the German central bank, the Bundesbank, appeared in the financial press during the day, as well as the direction of that intervention. The regression also contained dummy variables capturing changes in

*(Continued)*

**Box 11.3** *(Continued)*

monetary policy announced during the day in the United States and Germany. The results suggest that *joint* intervention to weaken the dollar was indeed perceived by the market as a signal from September 1985 to May 1986, but unilateral intervention by either bank was not. From May 1986 to February 1987 the results were mixed, but after February 1987 the authors found no effect of any type of intervention on the dollar-mark exchange rate. They interpret these results as suggesting that the market learned only gradually that central banks were not indeed using intervention as a signal of future monetary policy.

any shock that is anticipated to appreciate the exchange rate when it arrives would have the opposite set of effects in the present: the exchange rate would appreciate less than proportionately, the domestic interest rate would fall, and output would contract.

It is worth emphasizing one important implication of these results: while we saw in the last chapter that a transitory fiscal expansion could be expected to be expansionary, an anticipated future fiscal expansion would tend to have the opposite effect on the economy before it happens – it would actually be *contractionary*. The reason is that the anticipation of a fiscal expansion implies that the exchange rate will be expected to *appreciate* in the future. The anticipation of a future appreciation of the domestic currency would induce a capital inflow that would cause the currency to appreciate in the present, making domestic goods more expensive and reducing aggregate demand as the result of expenditure-switching effects. More generally, as illustrated in Empirical Study 11.1, the effects even of a current change in fiscal policy are likely to depend on what that change signifies about *future* fiscal policies.

Finally, consider what happens if the anticipated future shock is expected to materialize not in the next period, but 2, 3, or $N$ periods in the future. Suppose, for example, that when the term of the current governor of the central bank expires in a few years, the government is expected to appoint a new governor who will pursue a much more expansionary monetary policy. What effects would that expectation have on the economy today? We can show that the effects of changes in the economic environment that are expected to happen in the more distant future will be *qualitatively* the same as those of a shock expected to take place next period, but will be *quantitatively* weaker the further in the future the change is expected to happen.

To see why, consider the example of a monetary expansion that is expected to emerge two periods from now. Again, such a shock will affect the economy in the present only through $S^e_{+1}$, the exchange rate that is expected to prevail next period. Since the shock is not expected to happen until the period *after* next, however, how do we determine its effects on $S^e_{+1}$? Figure 11.2 shows how this can be done. Since the monetary expansion is expected to take place in period 3, the economy will revert back to its original situation in period 4. Thus, the expected effect of the monetary expansion on the exchange rate in period 3 can once again be determined from the transitory shock model of Chapter 10. We will call the new period 3 exchange rate $S_{+2}$. Locating $S_{+2}$ along the SS curve in Figure 11.2 determines what the equilibrium exchange rate must be in the previous period, period 2. The value of the period 2 exchange rate, $S_{+1}$, is determined by the height of the point B on SS. This is the exchange rate that will be expected to prevail in period 2. The next step is to locate $S_{+1}$ on

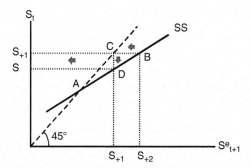

**Figure 11.2** Effect of a monetary expansion two periods from now on the current exchange rate

the *horizontal* axis. We can do this by using the 45-degree line. Since the slope of this line is one, the point on the horizontal axis directly below point C, where a line from $S_{+1}$ on the *vertical* axis intersects the 45-degree line, must correspond to $S_{+1}$. Once we have determined the expected value of next period's exchange rate $S_{+1}$ in this fashion, we can use the SS curve as before to determine the current exchange rate $S$, which must be given by the height of the point D. Notice that $S$ is relatively *less* depreciated than $S_{+1}$ – that is, *the anticipated monetary expansion has a larger effect on the economy in the period just before it is expected to materialize than in the period before that.*

This exercise can be repeated for a monetary expansion – or any other shock – that is expected to occur more than two periods in the future. Because the effect of future exchange rate changes on the exchange rate in each period is less than proportional, the further in the future the shock is expected to occur, the weaker will its effects be in the present. Box 11.4 shows how the analysis of the macroeconomic effects of anticipated future shocks can be used to explain the weakness of the US dollar during 2002–4.

## 11.2  Multi-period Shocks

### Two-period Shocks

A shock that is expected to last for two periods would affect the economy on impact – i.e., when it arrives. The key insight on which we will rely in analyzing the impact effects of such shocks is that a shock that is expected to last for two periods can be thought of as a combination of a one-period shock arriving today and an anticipated one-period shock of the same direction and magnitude arriving tomorrow.

*Effects on the exchange rate of a two-period monetary expansion*  Consider, for example, the monetary shock that we just analyzed. If the central bank undertakes a monetary expansion that is assumed to be preserved for two periods before the money supply reverts to its original value, the effects on the economy in the second period of the shock are those described in Chapter 10, as we have just seen. In the first period, the effects are a combination of two of the effects that we investigated there: those of an expected exchange rate depreciation (to take into account what is expected to happen in period 2) and a monetary expansion (to take into account what actually *does* happen in period 1).

## Box 11.4   US Dollar Weakness in 2002–7

As shown in Figure 3.2, the US dollar underwent a period of substantial weakness during 2002–7, depreciating by about 16 percent in real effective terms from early 2002 to the end of 2007. What might have caused this depreciation?

Many observers blame these movements in the dollar on the US current account deficit. We saw in Chapter 2 that the US current account deficit indeed reached historically high values during those years, peaking at over 6 percent of GDP by 2006. But what exactly is the relationship between the current account deficit and the value of the dollar? We can use our model to try to get a handle on this question.

The first observation that we need to make is that current account deficits cannot grow indefinitely relative to the size of the domestic economy. Since a current account deficit implies net international borrowing by the residents of a country (recall our discussion of this issue in Chapter 2), to service its accumulated debt a country will eventually have to run surpluses on the balance on goods and services (net exports) of sufficient size to cover the interest on its debt. Thus, the United States faces a foreseeable future need to achieve a large increase in its net exports. The questions are when the increase in net exports will take place and how it will be brought about.

Consider the expression for net exports that we derived in Chapter 4:

$$N(Q, Y - T, r, \theta) = X(Q, \theta) - (1 - \varphi(Q))A(Y - T, r).$$

Assuming that the United States will seek to achieve the required adjustment in net exports under conditions of full employment and without excessively high domestic interest rates that could stifle investment and growth, the adjustment in net exports will require some combination of real exchange rate depreciation (a higher value of $Q$) and tighter fiscal policy (a higher value of $T$). As you can see, the looser fiscal policy is (the lower $T$), the more depreciated the real exchange rate will have to be to achieve the required adjustment in net exports.

We can now provide an interpretation of dollar weakness in 2002–7. As you saw in Chapter 2, these years were characterized by growing fiscal deficits in the United States. During this time, the US government displayed no clear intention to achieve a dramatic future fiscal adjustment. In the absence of such an adjustment, the implication of our analysis is that the eventual reduction in net exports will have to feature a substantial real exchange rate depreciation. As we have seen in this chapter, the anticipation of such a future depreciation will tend to cause the US dollar to depreciate in the present. Thus, the weakening of the US dollar in 2002–7 can be interpreted as arising from ''news'' about the US government's future fiscal stance in the presence of an unsustainable current account deficit.

We can illustrate the effects of such a shock on the exchange rate using Figure 11.3. The economy starts out at point A where the curve $SS_0$ intersects a 45-degree line from the origin, and consequently where the actual and expected future exchange rates are both equal to S. A two-period monetary expansion affects the economy by changing *two* of the

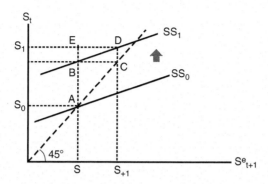

**Figure 11.3** Effect of a two-period monetary expansion on the current exchange rate

variables that we took to be exogenous in the last chapter: the money supply and the expected future exchange rate. Since – holding the expected future exchange rate constant – this period's monetary expansion would tend to cause this period's exchange rate to depreciate, this period's monetary expansion must cause the SS curve to shift upward, to a position such as $SS_1$. The vertical size of this shift, given by the distance AB in Figure 11.3, is equal to the magnitude of the exchange rate depreciation that would be induced by a *transitory* (one-period) monetary expansion equal to the one we are considering. To determine where the economy winds up on this new SS curve – and thus what the new value of today's exchange rate will be – we need to determine what happens to $S^e_{+1}$ as the result of this shock. The answer is straightforward. From the standpoint of the next period, the monetary expansion is a one-period shock, since the shock will go away after the next period is over. Thus $S_{+1}$ must exceed $S$ by precisely the amount that a one-period monetary expansion would tend to depreciate the exchange rate – that is, by the amount AB. To locate $S_{+1}$ on the horizontal axis we can therefore move horizontally to the right from point B until we cross the 45-degree line at point C and then drop straight down to the horizontal axis, as shown in Figure 11.3. Once we have identified $S_{+1}$ we can read off the new value of the current period's exchange rate from the point on $SS_1$ above $S_{+1}$ – that is, from the point D. The current period's exchange rate is identified as $S_1$ in Figure 11.3.

Notice that the total depreciation of the exchange rate in this case is given by the distance AE (which is equal to the distance between $S_0$ and $S_1$) in Figure 11.3, rather than just AB. That is, the exchange rate depreciation *on impact* is larger when the monetary expansion is expected to be sustained for two periods than when it is expected to go away after only a single period. As is evident from the figure, this is because the total depreciation of the exchange rate is the result of two different factors in this case: the current period's monetary expansion (which accounts for a portion AB of the total depreciation) and the depreciation of the expected future exchange rate (which accounts for the remaining portion BE).

*Effects on other macroeconomic variables*   It is interesting to consider how the impact effects on other domestic macroeconomic variables of a two-period monetary expansion differ from those of a one-period expansion. Recall that both a monetary expansion and an expected future exchange rate depreciation tended to expand real output in the last chapter. But as we have just seen, the macroeconomic effects of a two-period monetary expansion can be interpreted as arising from a combination of these two shocks. Thus, just as was shown to be true for exchange rate depreciation, the *expansion of real output must be larger in this case than when the monetary expansion is expected to be reversed after only one period*. Be careful to note that this is not because the monetary expansion is *larger*, but instead because it is preserved *longer*.

What happens to the domestic interest rate on impact in this case? The answer falls out directly from the UIP condition. Recall that in the second period the depreciation of the exchange rate is that which is associated with a one-period monetary expansion, while in the first period the depreciation is that associated with a one-period monetary expansion *plus* an expected future exchange rate depreciation. Thus, the exchange rate must depreciate by more in the first period (relative to its pre-shock value) than in the second period. It follows that the exchange rate must be expected to *appreciate* between the first and second periods of the shock's duration, and the direct implication of uncovered interest parity (UIP) is therefore that the interest rate must fall on impact, just as is true for a one-period monetary expansion. However, since the effect on the money supply in the first period is the same whether the expansion is expected to last for one period or two, while the effect on real output is larger for the two-period expansion, money-market equilibrium implies that the reduction in the domestic interest rate must be smaller on impact when the expansion is expected to be sustained for two periods than when it is expected to be reversed after a single period.

*Nonmonetary shocks*    We have found that the effects of a monetary shock on the exchange rate and the level of output are larger when the shock is expected to last two periods than when it is expected to last for just one, while effects on the domestic interest rate are smaller. Do these results generalize to other types of shocks? In other words, do the effects of all shocks on the exchange rate and level of output get magnified, while those on interest rates get reduced, when they last for two periods instead of just one?

The answer turns out to be no. The effects on the exchange rate must indeed always be magnified the longer the shock is expected to last. The reason is the following. Remember that the exchange rate effect of a two-period shock is just the sum of the effect of a one-period transitory shock and those of an anticipated transitory shock in the second period shock (AB plus BE in Figure 11.3). Because the effect of an anticipated future shock on the future exchange rate must be the same as that of a current shock on the current exchange rate and because changes in the expected future exchange rate always move the current exchange rate in the same direction, it must be true that exchange rate movements are larger when shocks are expected to last two periods than when they are expected to last for only one. This means that the conclusions we drew above about the effects on the exchange rate of prolonging the duration of the monetary shock to two periods must generalize to all other types of shocks as well.

But are output effects always larger too? The answer is no. Whether prolonging the shock to two periods magnifies its impact effect on real output turns out to depend on whether the shock in question causes the exchange rate and the level of output to move in the same direction or not (that is, whether the shock causes an exchange rate depreciation or appreciation to be associated with an increase in the level of output).

To illustrate this point, consider an expansionary real shock such as an increase in the level of government spending that is expected to last for two periods. Proceeding as before, if we solve the model for the last period that the shock is in place (period 2 in this case), the analysis of Chapter 10 tells us that the exchange rate will appreciate and real output will increase in that period. Thus the exchange rate and real output will move in *opposite* directions in period 2, compared to their no-shock levels. What happens to the economy in the first period? Though the increase in government spending that is initially implemented in that period is expansionary in its effect on the level of real output, the expected exchange rate appreciation in the next period is actually contractionary. This contractionary effect will partly offset the expansionary effect of the increase in government spending, so in this case the effect of the shock is actually *weaker* in its impact effects on real output when it is expected to last for two periods than for just one. On the other hand, since the increase in government spending and expected future appreciation both tend to appreciate the exchange rate on impact, the exchange rate appreciation is indeed larger in the first period than in the second, when only the increase in government spending affects the exchange rate.

Can the expected exchange rate appreciation actually more than offset the expansionary effects of the increase in government spending, rendering that shock actually contractionary on impact when it is expected to last for two periods? The answer is no. Since the exchange rate appreciates more relative to its original value in the first period than in the second, it follows that it must actually be expected to depreciate from the first period to the second. That means that the fiscal expansion must cause the domestic interest rate to increase on impact. But with a higher domestic interest rate, and an unchanged money supply, the money market cannot remain in equilibrium in the first period unless real output increases. We conclude that a two-period real shock has greater effects on the exchange rate than a one-period shock, but weaker effects on real output.

Since the effect on real output is weaker, the increase in the demand for money will be smaller in this case, and therefore the domestic interest rate will increase less when the fiscal shock is expected to last for two periods than when it is expected to be reversed after a single period, as was true for the monetary shock. Finally, with a more appreciated exchange rate, a smaller increase in output, and a smaller increase in the domestic interest rate, it follows that negative effects on net exports will be larger for two-period fiscal expansions than for one-period expansions.

## Shocks Lasting more than Two Periods

Now consider a shock that is expected to last for $N$ periods. If the shock lasts for exactly $N$ periods, the shock will be expected to have gone away in period $N + 1$. That means that in the $N$th period, it is essentially a one-period shock and, just as we did before, we can apply the analysis of Chapter 10 to assess its macroeconomic effects in period $N$. In the $N$th $- 1$ period, it will be a two-period shock, and the analysis that we just completed will apply. The key point is that effects on the exchange rate in that period will have been magnified relative to what they were in the $N$th period. But that means that the change in the exchange rate expected to prevail in the next period will be even larger in period $N - 2$ than it was in $N - 1$, which in turn was larger than it was in the $N$th period. In terms of Figure 11.3, the impact effect of a three-period shock, for example ($N = 3$), can be determined by extending the segment ED at height $S_1$ to the 45-degree line, then moving vertically up from that point to the $SS_1$ curve. The exchange rate that results on impact from a shock that is expected to last three periods can be read off from the height of the $SS_1$ curve at this point, say $S_2$. You can see that $S_2$ will be larger than $S_1$. This procedure can be repeated for four-period and longer shocks, with the impact effect of a permanent shock converging to the point where the $SS_1$ curve intersects the 45-degree line. You can see what this process implies: for monetary shocks, this cascading exchange rate effect will magnify in period $N - 2$ the effects of the shock in $N - 1$, while for real shocks, the cascading exchange rate effect will further weaken the effects on real output.

This reasoning can be repeated for every previous period, leading to the following general conclusion: *On impact, the effects of both monetary and real shocks on the exchange rate will be larger the longer that the shocks are expected to last; however, the impact effects of shocks on real output are larger the longer the shock lasts in the case of monetary shocks and smaller in the case of real shocks.*

## 11.3  Permanent Shocks

What happens when shocks are expected to be permanent? Fortunately, to answer this question we do not have to simply keep making $N$ larger and larger. In fact, we cannot really do that, because with permanent shocks there is no period after the shock is gone during which the expected exchange rate can be expected to revert to what it was before the shock arrived. Thus, the analysis of the previous section cannot be extended directly to the case of permanent shocks. We need to develop a different approach.

### A Permanent-shock Model

Let's return to our three-equation model, as laid out in Box 11.1. Recall that the basic problem that we faced under floating exchange rates was that we had four unknowns and only three equations in that model. In Chapter 10 we solved this problem by noting that with a one-period shock, we could assume that $S^e_{+1}$ would be the same after the shock arrived as it would have been in the absence of the shock. In the last section we essentially did the same thing to solve for the exchange rate in the last period of the shock and then worked backward from that solution to pin down $S^e_{+1}$ in all previous periods. With a permanent shock, however, we have no such anchor from which to solve backwards, because the economy will be different not only in the present, but also in *every period* of the future. That means, in effect, that $S^e_{+1}$ must be endogenous with respect to the shock.

The key to understanding what happens when $S^e_{+1}$ is endogenous is to notice that in response to a permanent shock, there is no reason to believe that the economy's equilibrium configuration will look any different tomorrow from what it does today. Once the shock has arrived and today's economy has reached a new equilibrium, no additional disturbances to that equilibrium are expected to emerge in the future. *Specifically, there is no reason to believe the exchange rate would be any different tomorrow from what it is today.* That means that for a permanent shock, rational economic agents should expect that $S_{+1} = S$. In other words, for permanent shocks we should have:

$$S^e_{+1} = S$$

In words, the expected future exchange rate should be equal to the current (spot) exchange rate. The implication is that in the permanent-shock case we need to add this equation to our model. Thus, whereas for transitory shocks we solved the problem of one too many

## Box 11.5 Modeling Permanent Shocks under Floating Exchange Rates

**Money-market equilibrium**

$$M = PL(R, Y) \tag{11.1}$$

**Bond market equilibrium**

$$R = R^* \tag{11.2'}$$

**Goods market equilibrium**

$$Y = \varphi(SP^*/\bar{P})A(Y - T, R) + G + X(SP^*/\bar{P}, \theta) \tag{11.3}$$

endogenous variables by making $S^e_{+1}$ exogenous, in the case of permanent shocks we solve it by adding an equation to the model.

Imposing $S^e_{+1} = S$ in the model of Box 11.1, we derive the permanent shock model described in Box 11.5. Notice that $S$ drops out completely from the UIP condition. The reason is that when shocks are expected to be permanent, the current and expected future exchange rates are the same, so UIP implies that the domestic interest rate cannot deviate from the world rate. The nominal exchange rate, however, remains in the goods market equilibrium condition through its influence on the real exchange rate.

This version of the model consists of three equations in the three unknowns $R$, $S$, and $Y$. To solve it, we proceed as before to write it in more compact form by substituting (11.2′) into (11.1) and (11.3), as we did in the transitory shock case. This produces a compact model consisting of two equations corresponding to asset market and goods market equilibrium, in the two endogenous variables $S$ and $Y$. The model is summarized in Box 11.6.

This model is depicted graphically in Figure 11.4. As before, the AA curve depicts the asset market equilibrium condition, now given by equation (11.1′). Notice that this curve is

## Box 11.6 A Compact Permanent Shock Model

**Money-market equilibrium (AA)**

$$M = PL(R^*, Y) \tag{11.1'}$$

**Goods market equilibrium (YY)**

$$Y = \varphi(SP^*/\bar{P})A(Y - T, R^*) + G + X(SP^*/\bar{P}, \theta) \tag{11.3'}$$

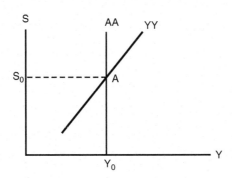

**Figure 11.4**   General equilibrium with permanent shocks

now a vertical straight line, since the value of real output that is consistent with financial-market equilibrium does not depend on the exchange rate. The curve YY depicts the set of all combinations of the exchange rate and real output that are consistent with equilibrium in the market for goods, given by equation (11.3′). As before, it has a positive slope, arising from the fact that a depreciation of the exchange rate switches spending by both domestic and foreign residents toward domestic goods, thus necessitating an increase in real output to restore equilibrium in the goods market.

The new YY curve corresponding to permanent shocks must be *steeper* than the one that we derived in Chapter 10 to analyze the effects of transitory shocks. The reason is because aggregate demand for domestic goods is less responsive to changes in the exchange rate when shocks are permanent than when they are transitory. This is due to the fact that, since the domestic interest rate cannot deviate from the world rate, the effect of exchange rate changes on aggregate demand operating though the domestic interest rate (the expenditure increasing effect) is absent when shocks are permanent. When shocks are permanent, therefore, the YY curve incorporates only expenditure switching effects.

## Comparative Statics

It is useful to put our new model through the same paces that we did the transitory shock model in Chapter 10, to compare the impact effects on the economy of transitory and permanent shocks. We will see that the economy's macroeconomic properties are significantly affected by the expected duration of shocks.

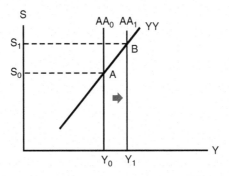

**Figure 11.5**   Macroeconomic effects of a permanent monetary expansion

*Monetary shocks*   Consider first the effects of a permanent expansion in the money supply. As in Chapter 10, an expansionary monetary policy causes AA to shift to the right, to a position such as $AA_1$ in Figure 11.5, with no effect on YY. The reason is that at a given domestic interest rate, an increase in the money supply requires a higher level of output to increase the demand for money by an amount sufficient to maintain equilibrium in the money market. As shown in Figure 11.5, the equilibrium value of the exchange rate depreciates and the equilibrium level of output rises, as the economy moves from A to B.

Notice that the domestic interest rate must remain unchanged, according to UIP, since the current and expected future exchange rates depreciate by the same amounts. An immediate implication is that when the monetary shock is permanent, monetary policy transmission does not occur through interest rates. Recall that in a closed economy, as well as in the version of our model with fixed exchange rates and imperfect capital mobility that we analyzed in Chapter 8, monetary transmission operated through the domestic interest rate. Under floating exchange rates, by contrast, we saw in Chapter 10 that when shocks are expected to be transitory, monetary transmission occurred through *both* the interest rate and the exchange rate. However, we now see that when the exchange rate floats and monetary shocks are perceived to be permanent, monetary transmission operates only through the exchange rate and its effects on net exports.

As a second point of contrast, note that unlike in the case of a transitory increase in the money supply, where we found that the effect on net exports was ambiguous, net exports must increase when the monetary expansion is permanent, despite the conflicting effects of a more depreciated exchange rate and a higher of domestic income. The absorption approach tells us that the higher value of domestic output can only be sustained with a higher value of net exports, since the constancy of the domestic interest rate means that absorption must rise less than output.

How does the process of adjustment to a permanent monetary expansion work out in practice? An increase in the money supply causes an incipient reduction in the domestic interest rate, which results in a depreciation of the exchange rate.[2] This increases net exports and thus increases real output. This process must continue until net exports have risen enough to increase domestic output by an amount that is sufficiently large for the resulting increase in the demand for money to absorb the higher money supply, thereby removing the downward pressure on the domestic interest rate.

In addition to the contrasts that emerge with the case of transitory shocks, it is also worth noting the contrast between these results for monetary policy and those that we derived under fixed exchange rates and perfect capital mobility in Chapter 9. Recall that we found that under those circumstances monetary policy was totally ineffectual, because the effects of open market operations on the money supply would be fully offset by capital inflows or outflows. It is important to emphasize that the only difference between the results of this chapter and those of Chapter 9 is in the assumed exchange rate regime, not the structure of the economy. In each case we were examining the effects of monetary policy in the context of perfect capital mobility and in the short run. The contrast between the power of monetary policy in this chapter and its ineffectiveness in Chapter 9 makes it clear that the policies that the central bank pursues in the foreign exchange market can have an enormous impact on

---

[2]   The use of the term "incipient" in this context refers to something that would tend to happen in the absence of countervailing forces.

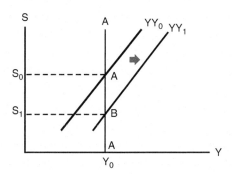

**Figure 11.6**   Macroeconomic effects of a permanent fiscal expansion

the effects that its other policy instrument – intervention in the market for domestic securities – can have on the domestic economy.

*Aggregate demand shocks*   To investigate the effects on the economy of permanent aggregate demand shocks, consider once again the case of a fiscal expansion. An expansionary fiscal policy causes the YY curve to shift to the right with no effect on AA, as in Figure 11.6. We can immediately see that the equilibrium value of the exchange rate must appreciate, and that there is no effect on the equilibrium value of real GDP. This complete powerlessness of fiscal policy to affect the equilibrium level of real output is a rather surprising result. To understand it, it is useful to first consider why it must be so in the context of our model, and then interpret what it means for the use of fiscal policy as a macroeconomic stabilization tool.

Why is output unchanged in this case? First note that our model implies that the domestic interest rate must remain unchanged under present circumstances, as it did in the case of a permanent monetary shock. The reason is that the expected future exchange rate appreciates as much as the current exchange rate does, and with an unchanged foreign interest rate UIP implies that the domestic interest rate must remain at its original value. With an unchanged money supply and an unchanged domestic interest rate, however, money market equilibrium requires that domestic output cannot deviate from its original equilibrium value. Thus, the inability of fiscal policy to affect the level of economic activity in this case is a direct consequence of UIP and the requirements of money market equilibrium.

How does this outcome get brought about? An expansionary fiscal policy – say an increase in government spending – causes an incipient increase in real output, which in turn causes an incipient increase in the demand for money. This would tend to make the domestic interest rate rise, given the fixed money supply. With capital mobility being very high, such an increase in the domestic interest rate would generate capital inflows that cause the exchange rate to appreciate. The question is how large this exchange rate appreciation must be. The answer is that for the economy to return to equilibrium, it must be large enough to cause net exports to decrease to the point where the contraction in net exports exactly offsets the effects on aggregate demand of the fiscal expansion, thus restoring real output to its original value and permitting the pressure on the money market to be eased.

This discussion emphasizes that the inability of the fiscal expansion to affect real output has as its counterpart a complete, dollar-for-dollar crowding out of external demand, in

## Box 11.7   The "Twin Deficits"

Recall the current account identity that we examined in Chapter 2,

$$CA = (S_P - I) + S_G$$

where $CA$ is the current account, $I$ is domestic investment and $S_P$ and $S_G$ are respectively private and public saving. In Chapter 2 you were cautioned against a naive interpretation of this identity in which reductions in public saving (that is, increases in the fiscal deficit) had a one-for-one effect on the current account.

However, the result derived in the text about the effect of an increase in government spending on net exports is precisely a case where a $1 reduction in $S_G$ indeed leads to a $1 reduction in $CA$, as a naive interpretation of the identity would suggest. We saw in the text that with floating exchange rates and perfect capital mobility, net exports must fall dollar for dollar with an increase in government spending that is expected to be permanent. This is the only way that output can remain unchanged despite the increase in $G$.

The reason that the naive reading of the identity turns out to be correct in this case is that, if private saving and investment depend only on real output $Y$, taxes $T$, and the domestic interest rate $R$, as we have assumed in our model, the fact that both $Y$ and $R$ remain unchanged in the face of a permanent increase in $G$ must mean that private saving $S_P$ and domestic investment $I$ have to remain unchanged as well. This is the first of the four versions of our model that we have studied so far that actually has this property, however. The association between fiscal and current account deficits that emerges under these circumstances has led some people to refer to the fiscal and current account deficits as the "twin deficits."

the form of a reduction in net exports that exactly offsets the aggregate demand effects of the fiscal expansion. This close link between fiscal and current account outcomes under the circumstances that we are considering in this section is discussed further in Box 11.7.

The contrast with the results that we derived for fiscal policy under fixed exchange rates is instructive. We noted in that context that fiscal policy could become very powerful indeed, because of the absence of crowding out of the type familiar from the closed economy context. Here, however, fiscal policy has no effect on output at all. Again, the difference between the two cases is neither the structure of the economy nor the particular policy being considered. The only difference is the exchange rate regime, once again suggesting the policies pursued by the central bank in the foreign exchange market matter a great deal for macroeconomic performance.

Finally, though we have taken as our example of an aggregate demand shock up to this point that of a fiscal expansion, the analysis of the effects on the economy arising from an increase in $\theta$, the exogenous component of demand for the domestic economy's exports, is very similar. As in the case of a fiscal expansion, the YY curve shifts to the right, the exchange rate appreciates and real output remains unchanged. The reasons for these outcomes are the same as those just discussed.

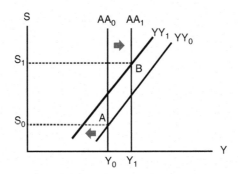

**Figure 11.7**   Macroeconomic effects of a permanent increase in international interest rates

A difference in this case is that there are no "twin deficits" (similar fiscal and current account deficits). The increase in $\theta$ would tend to increase net exports, but this would create pressure on aggregate demand and output that would cause the domestic interest rate to rise, which, as we have seen, is not possible under current assumptions.

Thus what happens is that the appreciation of the currency offsets the positive effects of the increase in foreign demand on net exports, leaving them unchanged in the new equilibrium. Notice the implication of this: *there is no spillover of international business cycles through direct demand effects.* A change in partner-country incomes that affects $\theta$ has no effect on domestic output unless it is accompanied by a change in the world interest rate $R^*$. In other words, in contrast with the fixed exchange rate model under conditions of high capital mobility, where business cycles were strongly transmitted internationally, a floating exchange rate completely insulates the domestic economy from foreign business cycles.

Changes in fiscal policy or in the exogenous component of export demand are examples of *real* aggregate demand shocks. A change in the foreign price level $P^*$, on the other hand, is a *nominal* aggregate demand shock. You can readily see that a change in $P^*$ that is expected to be permanent would have no real effects on the economy. By looking back at the goods market equilibrium condition (11.3') you can see that $P^*$ only enters our model multiplied by the nominal exchange rate $S$ – that is, in the form $SP^*$, and that neither the exchange rate $S$ not the foreign price level $P^*$ appear anywhere else in the model. Thus a permanent increase in $P^*$, say, would simply lead to an exactly offsetting reduction in $S$, such that the product $SP^*$ remains unchanged.[3] The important implication is that the floating exchange rate not only insulates the domestic economy from the effects of changes in foreign income, but also from changes in the world price level.

*External financial shocks*   In examining the effects on the economy of changes in international financial conditions that are expected to be permanent, we can no longer analyze the effects of shocks to the expected future exchange rate $S_{+1}^e$, as we have previously, since $S_{+1}^e$ is now an endogenous variable that is determined by the model. However, we can still consider the effects of changes in the world interest rate $R^*$.

---

[3]   Graphically, an increase in $P^*$ would simply shift the YY curve upward in the same proportion, causing the equilibrium value of the nominal exchange rate $S$ to depreciate by that proportion, with no change in the equilibrium value of real output.

An increase in the world interest rate that is perceived to be permanent shifts the AA curve to the *right*, because at a given value of the spot exchange rate, the associated increase in the domestic interest rate (required to sustain uncovered interest parity) would create an excess supply of money, requiring an increase in real output to clear the money market. At the same time, the YY curve shifts to the *left*, because in this case the increase in the domestic interest rate required to maintain UIP reduces domestic aggregate demand, requiring a reduction in real output to maintain goods market equilibrium. The new equilibrium is depicted at point B in Figure 11.7.

The effects on the economy are as follows. First, as is evident from the figure, the exchange rate must depreciate and domestic real output must increase. Next, since UIP takes the form $R = R^*$ in this case, it follows that the domestic interest rate must rise one for one with the foreign interest rate – that is, the change in the domestic interest rate must be exactly the same as that in the foreign rate. Using the absorption approach you can see that net exports must increase, since real output has risen while the domestic interest rate has risen as well, which together imply that the increase in domestic absorption must fall short of the increase in real output. This leaves only an increase in net exports to provide the higher aggregate demand required to sustain the higher level of domestic output.

The key result is that an increase in the foreign interest rate that is expected to be permanent actually has an expansionary effect on the domestic economy, in contrast with the contraction induced under fixed exchange rates. We derived the same result in the case of transitory shocks under floating exchange rates. As we saw in Chapter 10, the reason that the effects on domestic real output of changes in the foreign interest rate are reversed under floating exchange rates is that a higher foreign interest rate would tend to generate an incipient capital outflow from the domestic economy, which causes the exchange rate to depreciate, increasing net exports and domestic aggregate demand.

As mentioned above, in contrast with the transitory shock case, when the increase in the foreign interest rate is expected to be permanent, the domestic interest rate must actually increase by the full amount of the increase in the foreign interest rate. This indeed has a contractionary effect on domestic aggregate demand. However, unless the expansionary effect of a depreciating exchange rate dominates this contractionary effect of a higher domestic interest rate, the domestic money market cannot be in equilibrium, because with a fixed money supply equilibrium cannot be restored with both higher interest rates and lower output. As long as output remains below its original value, therefore, there is an excess supply of money in the domestic economy, which lowers domestic relative to foreign interest rates and sustains a capital outflow, which in turn causes the exchange rate to depreciate further.

## 11.4   Comparing Permanent and Transitory Shocks

We have now analyzed the impact effects of a variety of macroeconomic shocks on an economy that maintains a floating exchange rate under the assumptions that these shocks are expected to be transitory (they are expected to disappear after a single period), of intermediate duration (they are expected to last N periods), or permanent (they are never expected to go away). Obviously, an economy can experience shocks with expected duration ranging along this entire spectrum. We have already seen how the macroeconomic effects of shocks

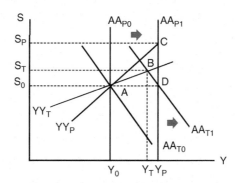

**Figure 11.8**    Comparing the effects of transitory and permanent monetary expansions

may depend on whether they are expected to last for a single or for multiple periods. To conclude our analysis of the difference that the expected duration of shocks can make, it is useful to compare shocks at each end of the spectrum: purely transitory shocks versus permanent shocks. In doing so, we will show that the effects of shocks of expected intermediate duration are also intermediate between those of transitory and permanent shocks.

To compare the effects of transitory and permanent shocks, we will consider the three distinct types of shocks that we analyzed in the last section: monetary shocks, real shocks, and external financial shocks.

## Monetary Shocks

Consider the effects of an increase in the money supply, $M$. How do the effects of that increase today depend on whether it is expected to be transitory or permanent? The contrast is illustrated in Figure 11.8. The figure contains two sets of AA and YY curves. Those labeled with the subscript T correspond to asset and goods market equilibrium under transitory shocks, while those labeled with the subscript P depict asset and goods market equilibrium when shocks are expected to be permanent. As shown in Chapter 10, an increase in the money supply $M$ that is expected to be transitory shifts the asset-market equilibrium curve $AA_T$ to the right, while as shown in the last section, if the same shock is expected to be permanent, $AA_P$ would shift to the right. Which curve shifts by more?

Suppose the $AA_T$ curve shifts, say, from a position passing through point A in Figure 11.8 to one passing through D. Note that the only difference between the $AA_T$ and $AA_P$ curves is that the asset market equilibrium condition underlying the former depends on $S$ (giving it a negative slope), while that underlying the latter does not (making it vertical). This means that *the increase in Y required to restore equilibrium in domestic asset markets after an increase in M, holding S constant, must be exactly the same whether the increase in M is expected to be transitory or permanent.* The implication of this observation is that $AA_P$ must shift to the right by exactly the same amount as $AA_T$ does in response to a given money supply increase in the current period – that is, the new $AA_P$ must pass through point D as well. The two curves shift horizontally by the same amount.

Recall that the goods market equilibrium curve, labeled $YY_T$ for transitory shocks and $YY_P$ for permanent ones, is unaffected by monetary shocks. If the monetary shock is expected to be transitory, the new equilibrium must therefore be at point B, where $AA_T$ intersects $YY_T$. If the shock is perceived to be permanent, on the other hand, the new equilibrium is at C, where $AA_P$ intersects $YY_P$. Notice that a permanent increase in the money supply thus has a larger impact (on both real output and the exchange rate) than a transitory one. Why should this be? With a permanent increase, the change in real output is that which is required to clear the money market at an unchanged nominal interest rate, and the change in the exchange rate is that required to generate a sufficiently large real depreciation so as to support the larger value of real output in the goods market. If the increase is transitory, the domestic interest rate can fall, thereby picking up some of the burden of absorbing the excess supply of money and meaning that the level of real output does not have to increase as much to restore money market equilibrium. Thus the key difference is the role of the domestic interest rate when the change in the money supply is perceived to be transitory.

Recall from section 11.2 that lengthening the expected duration of a monetary expansion tended to magnify its effects on the exchange rate and on the level of real output, while weakening its effects on the domestic interest rate. We now see that lengthening the shock's expected duration to the extent of making it permanent takes these effects to their logical conclusion: when the monetary shocks are expected to be permanent, exchange rate and output effects are maximized, and the domestic interest rate remains completely unchanged.

## Aggregate Demand Shocks

Consider now the effects of an increase in government spending $G$, shown in Figure 11.9. In this case, the YY curves shift, while the AA curves remain stable. Since the difference between $YY_T$ and $YY_P$ again involves only the role of the exchange rate $S$, the magnitude of the rightward shifts of the $YY_T$ and $YY_P$ curves must be the same, since they reflect the adjustment in real output required to restore goods market equilibrium after an increase in government spending at a given value of the exchange rate. Thus the new $YY_T$ and $YY_P$ curves, labeled $YY_{T1}$ and $YY_{P1}$ in the figure, must both pass through a common point like D. For a transitory shock, the new equilibrium is at B, where $YY_{T1}$ intersects $AA_T$, while for a permanent shock, the new equilibrium is at C, where $YY_{P1}$ intersects $AA_P$. At C the exchange rate is more appreciated than at B, and there is no change in real output.

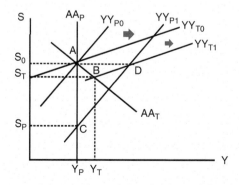

**Figure 11.9**   Comparing the effects of transitory and permanent fiscal expansions

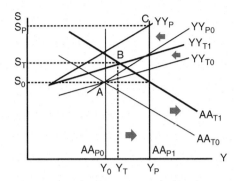

**Figure 11.10**   Comparing the effects of transitory and permanent increases in the foreign interest rate

Again, the reason that the transitory shock has a different effect on real output from that of the permanent one has to do with the role of the domestic interest rate in the two cases. Since the real money supply has not changed, if the domestic interest rate does not change, real output has to remain unchanged in order to maintain equilibrium in the money market. This is what happens in the case of the permanent shock because, as we have seen, once the exchange rate has changed it is not expected to change further, and this pins the domestic interest rate down to equal the (unchanged) world interest rate $R^*$. In the case of the transitory shock, on the other hand, the domestic interest rate can (and does) rise, because the shock gives rise to an appreciation that is only transitory – that is, it gives rise to an expected future depreciation. This reduces the demand for money, allowing real output to rise without creating an excess demand for money.

Recall that as the expected duration of a fiscal expansion became longer, the impact effect of a given change in government spending on the exchange rate became more pronounced, while those on real output and the domestic interest rate became weaker. We have now seen that when the fiscal expansion is perceived to be permanent, the effect on the exchange rate is maximized, while those on real output and the domestic interest rate dwindle to zero.

## External Financial Shocks

Finally, consider the contrast between the domestic macroeconomic effects that emerge when external financial shocks are expected to be transitory and when they are expected to be permanent. Note that the relevant graph in this case (Figure 11.10) is somewhat more complicated than the previous ones, because external financial shocks affect both the asset and goods market equilibrium conditions. Let us once again consider the concrete case of an increase in the foreign interest rate. As in the case of the monetary shock, it is possible to show that the impacts of such an increase are smaller when it is expected to be transitory than when it is expected to be permanent.

The economy begins at point A in Figure 11.10. The increase in the foreign interest rate shifts $AA_T$ and $AA_P$ to the right by the same amount, because the reduction in the demand for money caused by the higher interest rate has to be offset by an increase in money demand arising from higher real output for the money market to remain in equilibrium. $YY_T$ and

$YY_P$ both shift to the left, because the increase in the interest rate reduces aggregate demand at a given value of the exchange rate, so real output has to fall to maintain goods market equilibrium. Because the reduction in aggregate demand for a given value of the exchange rate is the same in both cases, the leftward shift in $YY_P$ must be the same as the leftward shift in $YY_T$.

When the shock is expected to be permanent, the expansion of real output must be greater than when it is expected to be transitory, because the full brunt of restoring money market equilibrium falls on output in this case, rather than on a combination of higher output and lower domestic interest rates. Given that output is higher, the exchange rate depreciation must be higher as well, to sustain higher demand in the goods market.

The outcome in this case is thus similar to that in the case of a monetary shock. The common element is that, because the full brunt of adjustment in the money market falls on real output when shocks are permanent, shocks that affect the money market directly – such as changes in the money supply and in the world interest rate – have much larger effects on real output (and thus on the exchange rate) when they are expected to be permanent than when they are expected to be transitory.

---

## Empirical Study 11.1   Deficit Reduction and the Exchange Rate

As shown in Chapter 10, our floating-rate model predicts that tight fiscal policy should be associated with a depreciating exchange rate. The mechanism operates through the domestic interest rate: as tighter fiscal policy reduces real GDP and thus the demand for money, under monetary targeting the domestic interest rate has to fall. This creates a capital outflow that causes the exchange rate to depreciate. Despite this seemingly clear-cut conclusion from the theory, however, as noted by Hakkio (1996), the effect of fiscal tightening on the exchange rate has actually proven to be a controversial topic in the United States. Why should this be?

One possibility is that the effect of fiscal contraction on the exchange rate may depend on how monetary policy responds to the fiscal contraction. This is undoubtedly true, but is unlikely to reverse the predicted effect on the exchange rate. As shown in Appendix 10.3, under interest rate targeting, a fiscal contraction would tend to leave the exchange rate unchanged. If the central bank responds to tighter fiscal policy with a *looser* monetary policy, so as to leave equilibrium real GDP unchanged, the AA curve would shift upward by the same amount as the YY curve, and the effect would be to cause the exchange rate to depreciate even more. In fact, this switch to a tight fiscal–loose monetary mix is exactly the opposite of the US case in the early 1980s and German case in the early 1990s that we examined in Chapter 10, and as we saw there the opposite mix was associated with a strong exchange rate appreciation. Thus, to reverse the depreciation of the exchange rate that would ordinarily accompany a fiscal contraction, monetary policy would have to become much more *restrictive*, aggravating the effect of tight fiscal policy on GDP. But in this case, of course, the effect on the exchange rate would be due to the tight monetary, not fiscal policy.

So how else could fiscal tightening be associated with exchange rate appreciation? Hakkio discusses several possibilities. For example, the fiscal tightening may reduce

*(Continued)*

**Empirical Study 11.1**    *(Continued)*

the risk premium on domestic bonds. As we have seen, such an increased ''taste'' for domestic bonds would cause the AA curve to shift to the left, causing the exchange rate to appreciate. An alternative story has to do with the variable that we are focusing on in this chapter: the expected *future* exchange rate. If fiscal tightening were to be associated with the expectation of an appreciated future exchange rate, then the exchange rate could indeed appreciate when fiscal policy is tightened. In this case an upward shift in the YY curve could be more than offset by a downward shift in the AA curve. But why should such a change in the expected future exchange rate happen?

A plausible scenario is that the current fiscal tightening may be perceived as reducing the likelihood that the central bank will print money in the future to purchase government debt. Such a monetary expansion would tend to depreciate the exchange rate in the future, by shifting the future AA curve to the right. Hakkio argues that the risk premium on domestic bonds is most likely to fall as the result of a fiscal contraction when the government has a large stock of debt and when a reduction in the fiscal deficit is brought about through reduced spending rather than higher taxation, and that the risk of future **monetization** (central bank purchase of government debt) is higher in countries that tolerate high rates of inflation.

To test these propositions, Hakkio estimated the effect of budget deficit reduction on the real exchange rate for 18 Organization for Economic Cooperation and Development (OECD) member countries over the period 1979 to 1994, using a regression in which the real exchange rate was taken to depend on interactions between the budget deficit and the inflation rate, the outstanding stock of government debt, and the change in the share of government spending in GDP. He found that, while the effects of deficit reduction on the real exchange rate were small in magnitude, the qualitative effects were consistent with the arguments above: a reduction in the deficit was more likely to lead to an appreciated real exchange rate the higher the country's inflation rate, the higher its stock of government debt, and the more its deficit was reduced by cutting government spending rather than raising government revenue. Since different OECD countries found themselves in different circumstances with respect to these variables during the sample period, deficit reduction was predicted to have different effects on the exchange rate in different OECD countries.

## 11.5   Summary

In this chapter we extended the analysis of Chapter 10 to examine the effects on a floating rate economy of shocks that are expected to affect it in the future as well as of shocks that arrive unexpectedly and are expected to last longer than a single period. We learned that, because current macroeconomic outcomes are affected by expectations regarding the future exchange rate, expected future shocks can affect the economy even before they happen. However, the effects of such shocks will be weaker the further in the future they are expected to appear.

We also learned that the effects of multi-period shocks on the exchange rate tend to be larger the longer that shocks are expected to last, while the consequences of the duration of shocks for their impact effects on real output are different for different types of shocks.

When shocks are expected to be permanent, the contrasts that we observed in the last chapter between their effects on the economy under floating and fixed exchange rates become magnified: monetary policy has even larger effects on real output, fiscal policy generates even stronger crowding-out effects, and external financial shocks have even larger effects on real output in a direction opposite to those observed under fixed rates. Thus, increasing the expected duration of shocks to the economy sharpens the contrast between fixed and floating exchange rates.

Up until this point, however, we have not allowed for any factors that would cause the effects of permanent shocks on a floating exchange rate economy to evolve over time – that is, that would induce any *dynamics* in the response of the economy to a permanent shock. There is indeed a variety of factors in the real world that may induce an economy's response to shocks to evolve endogenously over time, so that impact effects are only part of the story. In the next chapter we will examine the role of one of these factors: the gradual adjustment of production to changes in aggregate demand.

## Questions

1 Explain in intuitive terms why the expectation of a depreciated future exchange rate would tend to result in a less-than-proportionate exchange rate depreciation in the present.

2 Explain why the effects of an expected future depreciation of the home currency has a smaller effect on the current value of that currency the further in the future that depreciation is expected to materialize.

3 Assuming that the domestic price level is fixed, compare the effects on net exports of a monetary expansion that is expected to be transitory to one that is expected to be permanent.

4 Consider an open economy in which the aggregate price level can be taken to be fixed in the short run. Explain how the short-run effect of a monetary expansion on real GDP in such an economy depends on whether it is expected to be temporary or permanent, and provide the economic intuition that lies behind your conclusion.

5 Compare the effects on Mexico of a permanent increase in US interest rates prior to December 1994, when Mexico maintained a fixed exchange rate, and after that date, when the country adopted a floating exchange rate regime. What is the macroeconomic explanation for the contrast between the two effects?

6 In Chapter 2, we derived an identity that linked a country's current account surplus to the sum of two terms: the excess of private saving over investment and the excess of tax revenues over government spending (the budget surplus). We indicated that, because private saving and investment are endogenous variables, this identity did not imply that a \$1 increase in government spending would necessarily reduce the current account surplus by \$1. Describe a model under which this result would hold and one in which it would not do so.

7 "The direction of the effects of an expected future depreciation of the currency on domestic real GDP depends on whether a country is maintaining fixed or floating exchange rates." Do you agree or disagree? Explain.

8 Describe the effects of a fiscal expansion that is expected to be permanent on real GDP in a small open economy with a floating exchange rate. Explain in *intuitive* terms (i.e., without diagrams) why you get the result that you do.

9  Suppose that, in a small open economy that maintains a floating exchange rate, the central bank intervenes in the foreign exchange market by buying foreign currency. Explain how the effects of this shock on the equilibrium values of the exchange rate and real GDP depend on:

a  whether the purchase of foreign exchange is sterilized or not

b  whether the purchase is perceived by the public as being temporary or permanent.

10  Consider a small open economy that maintains a floating exchange rate and whose domestic price level is sticky in the short run. Suppose that the central bank of this economy implements an increase in the domestic money supply. Explain what difference the expected duration of this shock (i.e., whether it is perceived as transitory or long-lasting) makes for its effects on:

a  the small country's exchange rate

b  its level of real GDP

c  its domestic interest rate

d  the current account of its balance of payments

e  its domestic level of absorption.

11  Compare how the transmission mechanism for monetary policy works under: (a) fixed exchange rates with imperfect capital mobility; (b) floating exchange rates with monetary shocks that are expected to be transitory; (c) floating exchange rates with monetary shocks that are expected to be permanent.

12  Suppose that the uncovered parity relationship can be written as:

$$1 + R = (1 + R^*)\left(S^e_{+1}/S\right)(1 + \delta)$$

where $\delta$ is a "premium" that captures the effects of unspecified factors affecting investors' "taste" for domestic as opposed to foreign assets (when $\delta$ increases people's "taste" for domestic assets *decreases*, so they have to be compensated by higher domestic interest rates in order to hold them). Now consider a small open economy operating a floating exchange rate and characterized by perfect capital mobility. What would happen to the equilibrium level of real GDP in that economy if there was a permanent *increase* in people's "taste" for its assets?

## Further Reading and References

### On sterilized intervention as a signal of future monetary policy

Klein, Michael W. and Eric S. Rosengren (1991), "Foreign Exchange Intervention as a Signal of Monetary Policy," Federal Reserve Bank of Boston, *New England Economic Review* (May/June), pp. 39–50.

### On fiscal policy and the expected future exchange rate

Hakkio, Craig S. (1996), "The Effect of Budget Deficit Reduction on the Exchange Rate," Federal Reserve Bank of Kansas City *Economic Review* (Third Quarter), pp. 21–38.

# 12

# Floating Exchange Rates III:
# Exchange Rate Dynamics

........................................................................................................................

In Chapters 10 and 11 we studied a model that describes how economies with floating exchange rates are affected on impact by a variety of macroeconomic shocks. We found that the effects of shocks on the economy depended not just on the type of shock involved, but also on how long the shock was expected to last. In the case of purely transitory (one-period) shocks, the economy simply returns to its initial equilibrium after the period in which the shock occurs. However, for longer-lasting shocks, the response of the economy is pro-longed, with macroeconomic equilibrium being affected in every period that the shock persists. The **dynamic** effects on the economy (that is, the effects on the economy over time) are different depending on whether the shocks that it experiences are truly permanent (they never go away) or simply long lasting (they go away after $N$ periods).

All of the dynamics that we studied in Chapter 11 were driven by changing exchange rate expectations. In other words, the reason that the economy's equilibrium changed from one period to the next in the case of the $N$-period shocks that we examined there was because the exchange rate expected to prevail in the *subsequent* period was changing over time. These changes were ultimately driven by the fact that a substantial exchange rate adjustment would eventually have to take place between period $N$, the last period in which the shock would be in place, and period $N + 1$, when the shock would disappear.

Tracing out even the relatively simple dynamics arising from these changes in expect-ations may seem complicated enough, but in fact the real world contains other potential sources of dynamics that tend to further complicate how an economy adjusts to shocks over time. In this chapter we will explore one such source, arising from the possibility that the level of production in an economy may not adjust instantaneously to fluctuations in aggregate demand for domestic goods. We will see that slow adjustment in the goods market can induce interesting dynamics in the way that the economy responds to shocks even in the case of permanent shocks, where changes in exchange rate expectations would not otherwise play a role. This is important, because one surprise that emerged upon the widespread adoption of floating exchange rates among industrial countries after the collapse of the Bretton Woods system was that floating rates tended to be much more volatile than many economists had expected them to be. Understanding the potential sources of this volatility is a key step in evaluating the macroeconomic performance of floating exchange rate regimes.

This chapter will explore a particular interpretation of exchange rate volatility: one that attributes it to asymmetric speeds of adjustment in goods markets and financial markets. We will begin by exploring why speeds of adjustment may differ in the markets for goods and those for financial assets, and will then construct a simple illustrative model to explore the implications of such asymmetries. We will see that the striking results of the illustrative model carry through to more realistic settings, suggesting that asymmetric speeds of adjustment may be empirically important in explaining exchange rate volatility.

## 12.1  Asymmetric Adjustment in Goods and Asset Markets

The models that we have been analyzing up to this point in the book all have the property that all markets in the economies that they represent – both asset markets and goods markets – adjust immediately to changes in the exogenous variables that affect them. In the real world, though, not all markets may adjust so quickly, and this has implications for how the economy as a whole responds to macroeconomic shocks.

One reason that adjustment takes time, familiar from intermediate macroeconomics, is that changing the level of production is much more difficult for firms than adjusting the composition of their financial portfolios is for individuals. Because changing the composition of financial portfolios is relatively costless, financial markets tend to adjust very quickly to shocks. But because changing the level of production is costly, the goods market will tend to adjust only gradually to a new equilibrium after a shock. For example, in order to increase production in response to an increase in demand, producers of manufactured goods will need to set up new contracts with their suppliers, to hire and train more workers, to refurbish machinery that had not been in use, and so on. Not only do all of these processes take time, but because they are all costly, producers are likely to want to wait to make sure that any increase that they encounter in demand for their products can be expected to be long-lasting before they undertake such activities. In this chapter we will develop a new version of our model, called the **Dornbusch overshooting model** (after the MIT economist Rudiger Dornbusch, who developed it) that builds on this insight to describe how the economy adjusts to shocks over time. The model thus explains the *dynamics* of adjustment to shocks.[1]

To keep matters simple and provide a clear contrast with what we have done up to this point, we will restrict our attention to the dynamics of adjustment to permanent

---

[1]  The version of the Dornbusch model that we will develop in this chapter retains the assumption of a fixed domestic price level for the entire time frame of the analysis, so its dynamics are driven not by gradual adjustment of the price level to its long-run value, but by gradual adjustment of output to its demand-determined equilibrium value.

shocks only. Recall that the analysis of Chapter 11 suggested that adjustment would be instantaneous, with the economy immediately adjusting to its new equilibrium in the period during which the shock arrived, and remaining at that new equilibrium from that moment on. As we will see, with slow adjustment in the goods market, we will need to draw a distinction between the impact effects of a permanent shock and the new short-run equilibrium to which the economy converges. We have already explored the properties of that equilibrium in the last chapter. Our task now is to investigate the impact effects of permanent shocks under slow goods-market adjustment, as well as to explore how the economy makes the transition between these impact effects and its new short-run equilibrium.

Dornbusch devised this model to explain a very important real-world puzzle: specifically, why floating exchange rates turned out to be so much more volatile than most observers had expected them to be before the collapse of the Bretton Woods system. Before the Bretton Woods system collapsed, opponents of moving to floating exchange rates among the industrialized countries argued that floating rates would tend to be very volatile and that this volatility would prove disruptive to international trade and capital flows. Advocates of floating exchange rates, on the other hand, argued that floating exchange rates would prove to be only as volatile as the *fundamentals* – the exogenous variables – that drove them, so that if policymakers could maintain a stable policy environment there would be no reason to expect floating exchange rates to exhibit excessive volatility. In the event, the switch to floating was indeed associated with increased volatility of both nominal and real exchange rates. But this fact does not establish either that the increase in volatility was *caused* by the switch to floating exchange rates nor that the resulting volatility was "excessive." These two issues are addressed in Boxes 12.1 and 12.2.

Dornbusch essentially showed that the opponents of floating exchange rates had a point: for certain types of macroeconomic shocks, the induced movements in exchange rates would tend to be both larger and more prolonged than would be predicted by models such as the ones that we analyzed in the last two chapters. We will see that the crux of the explanation is precisely that the kind of equilibrium described by our short-run model is only reached gradually and that in response to certain types of shocks (specifically, monetary and external financial ones), the path followed by the exchange rate from its initial value to the new short-run equilibrium involves an initial adjustment that is *larger* than the eventual short-run adjustment. This is what is meant by the term **overshooting**.

## 12.2 The Dornbusch Overshooting Model

It is useful to begin by analyzing a very simple version of the Dornbusch overshooting model. Specifically, we will assume that, rather than moving immediately to its new equilibrium after a shock, the level of real output in the economy adjusts with a one-period lag, as illustrated in Figure 12.1. Thus, when a shock arrives, say at time $t$ in the figure, the economy's level of output does not adjust in the first period, but remains at its initial pre-shock level $Y_0$, determined by the economy's past history. Only in the next period (period $t + 1$) does the level of output adjust to its new equilibrium value $Y_1$. Because lagged adjustment in the goods market means that real output $Y$ is not free to adjust to shocks when

## Box 12.1  Floating Exchange Rates and Volatility of the Real Exchange Rate: What Causes What?

As indicated in the text, the behavior of floating exchange rates among the currencies of the major industrial countries turned out to be quite different after the dissolution of the Bretton Woods regime than had been anticipated by many proponents of floating exchange rates. Proponents of floating rates had not necessarily expected exchange rates to be stable, but believed that nominal exchange rates would move to offset differences in inflation rates between countries, thus keeping *real* exchange rates relatively stable, in keeping with PPP (Purchasing Power Parity; see Chapter 3). The reality proved to be otherwise: whether measured by average monthly percentage changes or by the standard deviation of average monthly percentage changes, nominal exchange rates proved to be much more volatile than national price levels. Real exchange rates thus proved to be much more volatile than the proponents of floating exchange rates had anticipated (see Mussa, 1979). But did the switch to floating exchange rates make the real exchange rate more volatile, or did the major industrial countries switch to floating exchange rates because the underlying "fundamental" determinants of the real exchange rate (we will discuss these in Chapter 13) became more volatile in the 1970s?

One way to get a handle on this issue is to consider the experience of countries that switched back and forth between the different types of systems, for reasons that can plausibly be claimed to be independent of changes in the volatility of real "fundamentals" in the international economy. Leduc (2001) considers the cases of Canada and Ireland.

Canada had a floating exchange rate from 1950 to 1962, a fixed exchange rate against the dollar until the collapse of the Bretton Woods system in 1971, and a floating exchange rate once again since that time. The volatility of the Canadian bilateral real exchange rate against the United States was significantly higher during the two floating rate periods than it was during the period when the Canadian dollar was fixed relative to the US dollar (the standard deviation of quarterly changes in the log of the Canadian real exchange rate was 1.5, 0.54, and 1.83 respectively in the three periods).

Similarly, the Irish pound was fixed relative to the UK pound, which floated against the German mark, from 1973–8. However, it was fixed against the mark – and thus floating against the UK pound – when Ireland joined the European Monetary System (EMS; see Chapter 18) in 1979. The standard deviation of quarterly changes in the log of the Irish real exchange rate against the United Kingdom rose from 1.69 to 4.21 from 1973–8 to 1979–99, but fell from 4.87 to 2.77 against Germany during the same time.

These examples do not clinch the case for causation from floating exchange rates to increased real exchange rate volatility, of course (since in switching between regimes, Canada and Ireland may have been responding to changes in the volatility of their own, country-specific fundamentals), but they are strongly suggestive of the proposition that the exchange rate regime indeed matters.

## Box 12.2    Assessing Exchange Rate Volatility

How do we know whether the volatility of floating exchange rates is in some sense "excessive"? To answer this question, we would have to ask: compared to what? In other words, what criterion should be used to judge whether exchange rate volatility is excessive? There are several possibilities. One approach is to focus on the fact that under floating exchange rates the equilibrium value of the exchange rate is determined in asset markets, as we saw in Chapter 10. Since financial assets are traded in well-informed, well-organized and competitive exchanges, prices of financial assets constantly fluctuate in response to new information. Using the behavior of other asset prices as the standard, the question then is whether there is something about foreign exchange markets that makes the exchange rate behave differently from other asset prices – i.e., that makes the exchange rate more volatile than other asset prices.

Bergstrand (1983) addressed this issue after the first decade of floating. He compared the volatility (measured by the average absolute monthly percentage changes and standard deviation of monthly percentage changes) of exchange rates relative to the US dollar to that of a variety of other financial asset prices (short-term interest rates, long-term bond yield, and stock market price index) for seven large industrial countries during 1973–83. He found that, except for the long-term bond yield in France and Italy, exchange rates proved to be *less* volatile than the prices of these other financial assets during this period. Bergstrand also compared the volatility of exchange rates to that of the prices of individual primary commodities (which also tend to be traded in organized exchanges), as well as to that of price indexes of baskets of such commodities, finding exchange rates less volatile than both.

However, knowing that exchange rates are no more volatile than other asset prices is not very reassuring from another perspective on the issue of "excessive" volatility. Suppose that what one cares about is the choice of exchange rate regime, and one wants to ask whether the adoption of floating exchange rates makes the underlying equilibrium real exchange rate (a concept that we will define more precisely in Chapter 13) more difficult to observe than it would be under fixed exchange rates.

From this perspective the standard of comparison is different: even if the exchange rate is no more volatile than other asset prices, its volatility may nevertheless be "excessive" if it makes the observed real exchange rate a more "noisy" (less reliable) indicator of the true underlying real exchange rate than would be the case under an alternative exchange rate regime in which the exchange rate does *not* behave like an asset price. This is an important consideration in the choice of optimal exchange rate regimes, so we will defer discussion of this issue until we address that topic in Chapter 15.

they arrive, real output is no longer an endogenous variable in our model. Since it is inherited from the past, it is a **predetermined** or **state** variable. It is neither endogenous (in the sense that it responds to shocks when they arrive) nor exogenous (in the sense that we are free to consider changing it independently).

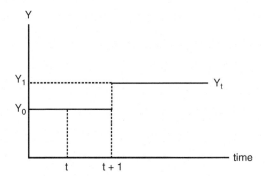

**Figure 12.1**  Output dynamics in the simple Dornbusch model

## Solving the Model

What happens to our previous model under these circumstances? Consider the compact version of the floating exchange rate model that we derived in Chapter 10, reproduced in Box 12.3 for convenience. When we analyzed this model in Chapter 10, we described it as containing two equations in three unknowns, consisting of the expected future exchange rate $S_{+1}^e$, the spot exchange rate $S$, and the level of real output $Y$. But now we are taking $Y$ to be a predetermined variable, with its value given to us as the result of the economy's past history, say at $Y = Y_0$. Because $Y$ will not change in the first period, we no longer have to solve for $Y$ when we analyze the model to determine the impact effects of shocks. This would seem to leave us with two equations with which to solve for the two endogenous variables $S_{+1}^e$ and $S$.

Remember, though, that we have assumed that people form their expectations rationally. That means that the expected future exchange rate $S_{+1}^e$ must be equal to what the model predicts that the exchange rate will be next period. Suppose that the economy is subjected to a permanent shock, and let's examine what the economy's equilibrium will look like next period. Since real output $Y$ will be free to adjust endogenously to the shock by then, the next period's exchange rate and level of real output must be those predicted by the permanent-shock version of our model developed in the last chapter. We will call these $\bar{S}$ and $\bar{Y}$, respectively. Thus we must have:

$$S_{+1}^e = \bar{S}, \; Y_{+1} = \bar{Y}$$

That means that $S_{+1}^e = \bar{S}$, and therefore $S_{+1}^e$ cannot be treated as an endogenous variable in the model above. We are now in an unfamiliar situation: we have more equations (two) than endogenous variables (one: $S$). When we have more equations than endogenous variables, our model is said to be **overdetermined**.

How do we solve this problem? The answer is that one of the equations cannot hold. In this case, it must be the goods market equilibrium condition, equation (12.2). To see why, notice that to say that the economy's level of output does not immediately adjust to the level determined by the aggregate demand for domestic goods, but does so only one period later, is precisely to say that equation (12.2) does not hold, since the right-hand side of (12.2) is the level of aggregate demand for domestic goods, while the left-hand side is the level of output of such goods. This means that in the period when a shock that

> ### Box 12.3    The Compact Version of the Floating Exchange Rate Model
>
> **Asset-market equilibrium (AA)**
>
> $$M = PL\big((1 + R^*)S^e_{+1}/S - 1, Y\big) \tag{12.1}$$
>
> **Goods market equilibrium (YY)**
>
> $$Y = \varphi(SP^*/\bar{P})A(Y - T, R) + G + X(SP^*/\bar{P}, \theta) \tag{12.2}$$

would tend to change the equilibrium level of output hits the economy, equation (12.2) must become an inequality, with an excess demand for domestic goods prevailing when the right-hand side exceeds the left-hand side, and excess supply prevailing when the opposite is true.

Thus we are left with one equation (equation 12.1), and one unknown (the exchange rate $S$). Once we have determined $\bar{S}$ by solving the permanent-shock version of our model for next period's equilibrium values of the exchange rate and real output, we can solve for the current period's exchange rate following a shock by using (12.1).

The solution of our model thus proceeds as follows:

1   The first step is to determine what the equilibrium will look like in the *next* period, that is, after the adjustment in the goods market has taken place. To do that, we simply need to solve the permanent-shock model of Chapter 11. That will determine $\bar{S}$, $\bar{Y}$, and all of the economy's other endogenous variables in the next period.

2   The next step is to solve the model for the first period – the period when the shock arises – to determine its impact effects. To do that, we replace $Y$ in equation (12.1) by $Y_0$ (the level of output prevailing in the economy before the shock hits), and $S^e_{+1}$ by $\bar{S}$ (the value of the exchange rate expected to prevail in the next period after goods-market adjustment is complete). With these two values of $S^e_{+1}$ and $Y$ in place, we then solve equation (12.1) for the post-shock equilibrium value of $S$. This permits us to proceed to solve for all of the model's other endogenous variables in the first period.

3   The dynamics of the economy's adjustment to shocks can then be determined by comparing the first-period solution of the model in step 2 with its second-period solution in step 1.

### The DD Curve

We indicated above that we would use equation (12.1) to solve for $S$, after replacing $S^e_{+1}$ by the rationally expected next-period value of the exchange rate $\bar{S}$. After substituting $\bar{S}$ for $S^e_{+1}$, equation (12.1) becomes:

$$M = P\, L[\underset{+}{(1 + R^*)\bar{S}}/S - 1, \underset{+}{\bar{Y}}] \tag{12.1'}$$

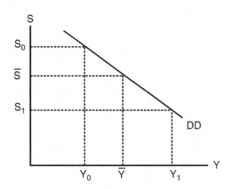

**Figure 12.2**   The DD curve

Notice that, for a given value of real output $Y_0$ this equation contains a single endogenous variable, the exchange rate $S$. To show how changes in real output affect the equilibrium value of the exchange rate, we can plot this equation in $S$-$Y$ space. To do this, we rely on two observations:

1   Given $\bar{S}$, equation (12.1′) must trace out a curve with a negative slope, since increases in $Y$ will have to be offset by increases in the domestic interest rate (given by $(1 + R^*)\bar{S}/S - 1$) – and thus by *decreases* in $S$ – in order to maintain equilibrium in domestic asset markets.
2   The curve traced out by (12.1′) must pass through the point $(\bar{S}, \bar{Y})$ corresponding to the permanent equilibrium values of the exchange rate and the level of output. To see why this must be so, recall from Chapter 11 that $\bar{Y}$ is precisely the value of $Y$ that satisfies:

$$M = PL[R^*, \bar{Y}]$$

By examining (12.1′), you can see that this means that (12.1′) must be satisfied when $S = \bar{S}$ and $Y = \bar{Y}$.

With these two properties in hand, we can draw the set of combinations of $S$ and $Y$ that satisfy (12.1′) in the form of the curve labeled DD in Figure 12.2.[2] Since asset-market equilibrium must hold continuously, equation (12.1′) must always be satisfied.

Thus the economy must always be on the DD curve: whatever the level of real output $Y$ happens to be, the equilibrium value of the exchange rate must be the value of $S$ that corresponds to that level of $Y$ on the DD curve. Thus if the level of output is $Y_0$, the exchange rate must be $S_0$, while if the level of output is $Y_1$, the exchange rate must be $S_1$.

## 12.3   Comparative Statics

To see how the economy responds to shocks with slow goods market adjustment, in this section we will analyze the macroeconomic effects of the three types of macroeconomic

[2]   What is the difference between DD and the downward-sloping AA curve in Chapter 10? They are both derived from the asset market equilibrium condition (12.1), but the difference between them is how they model the expected future exchange rate $S^e_{+1}$. In the AA curve of Chapter 10, which was used to analyze the effects of transitory (one-period) shocks, $S^e_{+1} = S_0$, the pre-shock exchange rate, while in the DD curve of this chapter $S^e_{+1} = S$, the new *post-shock* exchange rate.

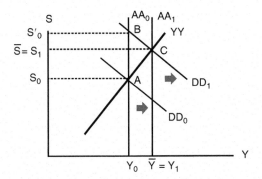

**Figure 12.3**    A permanent monetary expansion in the Dornbusch model

shocks that we have considered in other contexts: monetary shocks, aggregate demand shocks, and external financial shocks. As we have done before, we will conduct the analysis graphically.

## Monetary Shocks

Suppose that the economy that we have just described is subjected to a monetary shock in the form of a permanent expansion in the domestic money supply. How does this shock affect the economy over time? This question is answered in Figure 12.3. Before the money supply increases, the economy is in equilibrium at point A where the asset market equilibrium curve $AA_0$ and the goods market equilibrium curve YY intersect. Since the monetary expansion is permanent, our analysis in the last chapter indicates that its effect is to shift the vertical AA curve to the right, from $AA_0$ to $AA_1$. If the goods market could adjust within the first period, the economy would immediately move from A to C – where $AA_1$ intersects YY – and stay there, as it did in Chapter 11. However, that would require an immediate increase in output, and by the assumption of slow goods market adjustment that we have made in this chapter, this adjustment in the level of output cannot take place until the next period. Since the exogenous variables will not change from the first period to the next, point C therefore indicates where the economy will be in the *second*, not the first, period.

What happens to it in the meantime? Since the DD curve must always pass through the point $(\bar{S}, \bar{Y})$, which moves from A to C as a result of the permanent monetary expansion, the DD curve must immediately shift from $DD_0$ to $DD_1$, as indicated in the figure. Since Y must remain equal to $Y_0$ on impact, the exchange rate must jump to a point like B above $Y_0$, but located on the $DD_1$ curve. Thus, the exchange rate jumps from $S_0$ to $S'_0$, initially overshooting its new short-run equilibrium value $\bar{S}$.

Why does this happen? The economics are the following: with real output unchanged on impact, the increase in the money supply requires a drop in the domestic interest rate to maintain money-market equilibrium. This means, by uncovered interest parity (UIP), that the domestic currency has to be expected to appreciate over time. But this in turn means that the exchange rate must depreciate *more* on impact than it does in the new short-run equilibrium (that is, it must overshoot). Given that the exchange rate depreciates in the new short run equilibrium, therefore, it must depreciate *even more* on impact, and this is the mechanism that accounts for magnified fluctuations in the exchange rate.

Thus the dynamics induced by the monetary expansion are the following: when the expansion takes place, the exchange rate initially depreciates sharply and output does not change (point B). Because the exchange rate overshoots its second-period value, it will be expected to appreciate from the first period to the second, and this will imply, through UIP, that the domestic interest rate must fall. It is this reduction in the domestic interest rate that enables the domestic money market to clear in the first period with a larger money supply and no higher level of output to increase money demand.

What happens next? Since at point B the economy is located above the YY curve, an excess demand for domestic output must exist at this point. The excess demand arises from the sharply depreciated exchange rate and reduction in the domestic interest rate. For both expenditure-switching and expenditure-increasing reasons, therefore, the demand for domestic goods has increased, while the supply has not. The resulting excess demand for domestic goods is what causes a subsequent increase in production. When real output rises, the economy must continuously remain on DD (because asset markets always clear), so the transition involves a movement along DD from B to C. The output expansion in the next period increases the next period's demand for money by an amount that is exactly sufficient for the pre-shock domestic interest rate to be restored in the next period. This higher level of output is itself sustained by a depreciated exchange rate that increases aggregate demand through expenditure-switching effects.

Notice that, unlike in Chapter 11, the economy's response to a permanent monetary expansion is different in the first period from what it is in the second period – that is, the shock has induced dynamic adjustment effects that were not present in the previous version of our model. Notice also, however, that both in the first period as well as in all subsequent periods the expected next-period exchange rate is $\bar{S}$. Thus, the adjustment dynamics are not caused by changing exchange rate expectations in this case, as they were in the finite-duration shocks explored in Chapter 11. Instead, the source of dynamics is the one-period lag in the adjustment of the level of production.

## Aggregate Demand Shocks

Do all shocks to the economy induce this type of dynamics under the assumption of slow goods-market adjustment? The answer is no. Since the source of the dynamics is the slow adjustment in the goods market, shocks that do not require the level of production to adjust will not induce a dynamic response from the economy. Instead, the economy will immediately adjust to its new equilibrium.

To illustrate, consider the effects of an aggregate demand shock, in the form of a permanent fiscal expansion. As shown in Figure 12.4, the effect of the fiscal expansion is to shift the YY curve to the right from $YY_0$ to $YY_1$, leaving AA unchanged. When all markets have been allowed to adjust, the economy will settle at the new short-run equilibrium determined by the intersection of $YY_1$ with AA, given by the point B. As explained in the last chapter, at this new equilibrium the exchange rate will have appreciated, but the economy's level of output will not have changed, the effects on aggregate demand of the fiscal expansion being exactly offset by a lower value of net exports.

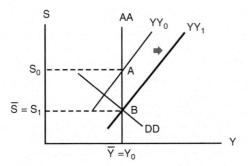

**Figure 12.4** A permanent fiscal expansion in the Dornbusch model

To solve the model with slow goods-market adjustment, we once again need to introduce the curve DD, which as we saw in the previous section, must pass through $(\bar{S}, \bar{Y})$, given in this case by the intersection of AA and $YY_1$. On impact, the exchange rate must jump to a point on DD directly above $Y_0$. This point is, of course, B itself. This means that the economy adjusts to its new short-run equilibrium immediately in the first period, without any intervening dynamics. The reason is obvious: since this type of shock does not call for any changes in production, slow goods-market adjustment plays no role in the economy's response to the shock.

### External Financial Shocks

To complete our analysis of permanent shocks in the Dornbusch model, consider the effects of an external financial shock that takes the form of an increase in the foreign interest rate (Figure 12.5). The economy begins at A. The increase in the foreign interest rate shifts the AA curve to the right and the YY curve to the left, as in the last chapter. If all markets could adjust immediately, the new short-run equilibrium would be at C. Instead, since goods-market adjustment is delayed by one period, point C identifies the equilibrium to which the economy will move in the next period, and therefore the DD curve passes through C. On impact, the economy will move to point B on the DD curve above $Y_0$. As in the case of a domestic monetary shock, the exchange rate will once again overshoot its eventual short-run equilibrium level. The reason is the same: the disturbance affects the economy's

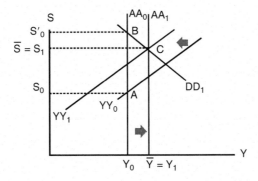

**Figure 12.5** A permanent increase in the foreign interest rate in the Dornbusch model

asset-market equilibrium, and the burden of restoring equilibrium in that market would ordinarily be shared by interest rate movements as well as changes in the level of real output. Thus, when the level of real output cannot change, all of the burden of adjustment falls on the interest rate, which must move by a correspondingly larger amount. As it does so, UIP requires that the exchange rate also move by a larger amount relative to its expected next-period level. Thus, the exchange rate must overshoot that level.

What you should take away from this is that overshooting will be triggered by any shock to the economy that calls for a change in real output to restore equilibrium, because when real output is slow to adjust, financial variables will carry more of the adjustment burden. Once output has had time to adjust, the burden on financial variables is eased.

## 12.4    Generalizing the Model

Recall that the dynamics in the economy's adjustment to shocks in the previous section were driven entirely by the lag in the adjustment of real output, since exchange rate expectations were identical in every post-shock period. This property of our model is not general, however, and holds only because we modeled the slow adjustment of output in a relatively simple way: in the form of a one-period lag. The purpose of doing so was essentially to make the mechanics of the model more transparent. Now that we have seen how the model works, however, we can generalize it somewhat to allow output adjustment to take longer than a single period.

There are two reasons to do so. First, in the real world output does not adjust discretely one period after a shock, as we have been supposing and as illustrated in Figure 12.1. Instead, adjustment is more gradual, with production moving more smoothly to its equilibrium value, as in Figure 12.6. Second, once we allow output to be different in all future periods, the exchange rate will have to be different in those periods as well, implying that changing exchange rate expectations will also play a role in the economy's dynamic process of adjustment. Both of these features more closely represent the real world than the model of the last section.

### Gradual Adjustment in the Goods Market

Suppose that instead of completing its adjustment to its new equilibrium level in one period, the level of output adjusts gradually to that level over time, with the speed of adjustment

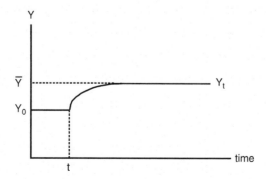

**Figure 12.6**   Output dynamics in the generalized Dornbusch model

depending on the size of the gap that remains to be closed between the actual and equilibrium levels of output. We can write this as:

$$Y_{t+1}/Y_t = (\bar{Y}/Y_t)^\lambda \qquad (12.3)$$

where, as before, $\bar{Y}$ is the model's solution for real output when all markets are free to adjust instantaneously, and $\lambda$ is a positive fraction. This specification simply states that the change in output from this period to the next is proportional to the gap between this period's output and its equilibrium level, with the factor of proportionality given by $\lambda$. Thus, whenever real output is not equal to its equilibrium value $\bar{Y}$, a fraction $\lambda$ of the gap is closed each period. This mechanism captures gradual adjustment of production in the goods market. Notice that if $\lambda = 0$, real output would never adjust at all, while if $\lambda = 1$, output adjusts to $\bar{Y}$ in a single period, as in the last section.

It can be shown (see Appendix 12.1) that when real output behaves in this fashion, if agents form expectations of the future value of the exchange rate rationally, then $S$ itself must behave according to:

$$S_{t+1}/S_t = (\bar{S}/S_t)^\lambda \qquad (12.4)$$

where $\bar{S}$ is the solution for the exchange rate derived from the model under the assumption of instantaneous adjustment. To get some intuition into why $S$ must behave in this way, suppose there is some shock to the economy that is expected to be permanent, such as a monetary expansion. People know that both real output and the exchange rate will be affected by this shock, in accordance with our model. They also know that real output will not adjust immediately to its new value, because goods-market adjustment takes time. Since real output does not adjust immediately, the demand for money will not adjust immediately to a new level consistent with an unchanged value of the domestic interest rate. That means that the interest rate must do the adjusting, and must change by a larger amount the further real output is from $\bar{Y}$. Because of uncovered interest parity (UIP) and rational expectations, the larger the initial movement in $R$, the larger the movement in $S_{t+1}/S_t$ must be as well. As real output gradually approaches $\bar{Y}$, the interest rate $R$ will gradually return to its original level, and $S_{t+1}/S_t$ must therefore gradually converge toward unity. This means that the exchange rate must appreciate continuously, and at a decreasing rate, as real output approaches $\bar{Y}$ from below, and depreciate continuously, also at a decreasing rate, when it approaches $\bar{Y}$ from above.

## Model Specification

This more general version of the Dornbusch overshooting model can be written as follows. First, we need the two equations of our former model to tell us how the new equilibrium values of $\bar{S}$ and $\bar{Y}$ will be determined after the arrival of a permanent shock:

$$M = PL(R^*, \bar{Y}) \qquad (12.1'')$$

$$\bar{Y} = \varphi(\bar{S}P^*/\bar{P})A(\bar{Y} - T, R^*) + G + X(\bar{S}P^*/\bar{P}, \theta) \qquad (12.2')$$

Next, we need to specify that during the process of transition, domestic asset markets, in the form of the money and bonds markets, will be in equilibrium continuously:

$$M = P\,L[(1+R^*)S_{+1}/S - 1,\, Y) \tag{12.1}$$

where $S$ and $Y$ are now the *actual* values of the exchange rate and real output that prevail at each instant during the transition, and where $S_{+1}^e$ in the original version of equation (12.1) from Box 12.1 has been replaced in the uncovered interest parity condition by $S_{+1}$ under the assumption of rational expectations. Notice that we are not adding an equation for goods market equilibrium during the transition, because gradual adjustment to equilibrium in this market means that equilibrium does *not* have to hold in every period. Finally, we incorporate the two Dornbusch gradual adjustment equations:

$$Y_{+1}/Y = \left(\bar{Y}/Y\right)^{\lambda} \tag{12.3}$$

$$S_{+1}/S = \left(\bar{S}/S\right)^{\lambda} \tag{12.4}$$

The $t$ subscripts have been deleted for notational simplicity. This completes our extended model. Recalling that $Y$ is a predetermined variable, this version of the model, summarized in Box 12.4, contains five equations in the five endogenous variables $\bar{S}$, $\bar{Y}$, $S$, $Y_{+1}$, and $S_{+1}$.

---

## Box 12.4    The Generalized Dornbusch Model

**Steady-state asset market equilibrium**

$$M = PL\left(R^*,\, \bar{Y}\right) \tag{12.1''}$$

**Steady-state goods market equilibrium**

$$\bar{Y} = \varphi\left(\bar{S}P^*/\bar{P}\right)A\left(\bar{Y} - T,\, R^*\right) + G + X\left(\bar{S}P^*/\bar{P},\, \theta\right) \tag{12.2'}$$

**Asset market equilibrium**

$$M = PL[(1+R^*)S_{+1}/S - 1,\, Y) \tag{12.1}$$

**Goods market adjustment**

$$Y_{+1}/Y = \left(\bar{Y}/Y\right)^{\lambda} \tag{12.3}$$

**Exchange rate adjustment**

$$S_{+1}/S = \left(\bar{S}/S\right)^{\lambda} \tag{12.4}$$

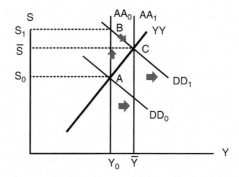

**Figure 12.7**    A permanent monetary expansion in the generalized Dornbusch model

## Solving the General Model

To see how the model is solved, suppose the Dornbusch economy is hit by some permanent shock. We can immediately solve for the new values of $\bar{Y}$ and $\bar{S}$ using equations 12.1″ and 12.2′, which correspond to the AA and YY curves in the model of the last chapter. Then, substituting (12.4) into (12.1), the rest of the model reduces to:

$$M = P\,L\left[(1+R^*)(\bar{S}/S)^{\lambda}-1,\,Y\right] \qquad (12.5)$$

and

$$Y_{+1}/Y = (\bar{Y}/Y)^{\lambda} \qquad (12.3)$$

The basic strategy for solving this more general version of the Dornbusch overshooting model is thus exactly the same as it was for the simpler version of the last section:

1   Solve the short-run model to determine the values of $\bar{S}$ and $\bar{Y}$.
2   Substitute the solution for $\bar{S}$ into the financial market equilibrium condition (12.5) at the *original* value of real output. This gives the *initial* value of the exchange rate in response to the shock.
3   From the dynamic equation for real output, determine what happens to $Y$ over time. As this equation determines new values of real output, substitute these successively into (12.5) to determine the path of $S$ over time.

Geometrically, the solution of this slightly more general model proceeds in exactly the same fashion as the simpler model of the last section. It is illustrated in Figure 12.7 for the case of a monetary expansion. Equations (12.1″) and (12.2′) represent the AA and YY curves respectively. Their intersection in $S$-$Y$ space at C determines the values of $\bar{S}$ and $\bar{Y}$, just as before.

In turn, equation (12.5) represents the DD curve in the more general model. Like the DD curve of the last section, it will have a negative slope and must pass through the point

$(\bar{S}, \bar{Y})$. However, the slope of the DD curve will be steeper in this case than it was in the last section. The reason is that the ratio $(\bar{S}/S)$ enters equation (12.5) raised to the power $\lambda$. The model of the last section represented the special case when $\lambda$ was equal to unity, and goods market adjustment took place within a single period. When goods market adjustment is more sluggish, as indicated above, $\lambda$ will be less than one, and that means that a given change in $S$ will have a smaller impact on $S_{+1}/S$, and thus on the domestic interest rate as well as the demand for money. Because changes in $S$ will have weaker effects on asset market equilibrium in this case, *larger* changes in $S$ are required to maintain asset market equilibrium for a given change in $Y$, which makes the DD curve steeper.

The level of output during any given period is determined by equation (12.3). Given this value of $Y$ on the horizontal axis, we can use the fact that the economy must always be on DD to determine the equilibrium value of the exchange rate. Thus at the initial level of output $Y_0$, the immediate post-shock value of the exchange rate will be $S_1$.

Notice several important implications of this analysis that were obscured by the simpler output adjustment mechanism in the model of the last section:

1   Since the slower the speed of adjustment in the goods market the steeper the DD curve, it follows that the slower is the speed of adjustment in the goods market, the greater the degree of exchange rate overshooting in the economy in response to permanent financial shocks. This could not be established in the last section, since that model did not allow us to consider alternative speeds of adjustment in the goods market.
2   Adjustment to permanent shocks need not be complete within two periods. The dynamics of adjustment may play themselves out over a significantly more prolonged period of time, which will depend essentially on the speed of adjustment in the goods market. The slower the speed of adjustment, the longer the transition dynamics.
3   In contrast with the previous section, the expected future exchange rate is different along each period of the transition toward the new short-run equilibrium. In the permanent monetary expansion example, the expected future exchange rate will in fact be more appreciated the closer the economy moves to its new short-run equilibrium.

---

## Empirical Study 12.1    Testing the Dornbusch Model

The Dornbusch model predicts that a monetary tightening should cause an exchange rate appreciation, followed by a monotonic depreciation, all the while satisfying UIP. Despite the theoretical popularity of the model and its enormous impact on international macroeconomics (see Rogoff, 2002), these predictions have actually proved difficult to verify empirically. A recent attempt to do so by Bjornland (2006) builds on the Clarida and Gali (1994) structural VAR methodology described in Empirical Study 10.1.

Bjornland examines the dynamic response of the exchange rate to monetary policy in five small industrial countries that maintained floating exchange rates during the period 1983 to 2004: Australia, Canada, New Zealand, Sweden, and the United Kingdom. Her VAR system includes five variables: the log of real GDP, the rate of inflation, the domestic and foreign interest rates, and the real exchange rate. She considers a set of structural shocks consisting of monetary policy shocks, real exchange rate shocks, cost-push inflation shocks, output shocks, and foreign interest rate shocks.

Previous research on this issue using the VAR methodology had relied on a procedure to extract the structural shocks from the reduced-form VAR shocks that had essentially made it impossible for the data to yield the results of the Dornbusch model: previous authors imposed the restriction that monetary policy had no contemporaneous effect on the exchange rate. Bjornland noted that such an assumption is inconsistent with the asset market approach to the exchange rate. She replaced the restriction with the more reasonable one that monetary policy does not affect the real exchange rate in the long run, as in Clarida and Gali (1994). Bjornland's restrictions thus allow monetary policy to affect the real exchange rate contemporaneously, as is required to identify the full dynamic response of the exchange rate to monetary policy. Among her other restrictions were two others implied by the Dornbusch model: that monetary policy affects domestic output and the price level only with a lag.[3]

Bjornland found that contractionary monetary policy shocks in these countries behaved empirically just as the Dornbusch model predicts: it induced a strong exchange rate appreciation on impact, with the maximum impact on the exchange rate occurring immediately. This was followed by a gradual depreciation, consistent with the Dornbusch overshooting mechanism. Real output and the rate of inflation both decreased in the short run in response to a monetary contraction.

## 12.5   Summary

In this chapter we have examined the dynamics of the economy's adjustment to shocks under the realistic assumption that financial markets adjust to equilibrium more rapidly than do the markets for goods and services. An important implication of this asymmetry in the speed of adjustment is that for certain types of shocks – specifically, shocks that call for a change in the level of real output – the economy's response is characterized by an overshooting of the exchange rate – that is, on impact the exchange rate would move beyond its eventual equilibrium value, only gradually returning to that value.

Recall that Dornbusch developed this model to help explain the substantial amount of volatility that nominal exchange rates tended to display when the industrial countries abandoned the Bretton Woods system. Based on the results of this chapter, the interpretation for nominal exchange rate volatility in the post-Bretton Woods period suggested by the Dornbusch model has two parts:

1   Goods-market adjustment is not instantaneous.
2   The post-Bretton Woods period has been characterized by frequent financial-market shocks (changes in $M$, $R^*$, and perhaps in portfolio preferences as well).

---

[3]   In the version of the Dornbusch model that we examined in this chapter monetary policy does affect the real exchange rate, but this only applies over a time period for which the domestic price level can be taken as fixed. Once we allow for long-run price flexibility, as in the two chapters that follow, this will no longer be true.

This concludes our analysis of short-run macroeconomics with sticky (in our model, fixed) prices and floating exchange rates. In the next chapter, we will examine long-run equilibrium in this economy.

## Questions

1   Floating exchange rates have proven to be much more volatile in the post-Bretton Woods period than was anticipated prior to their widespread adoption. Based on what you have learned in this chapter, can you offer an explanation for the post-1973 volatility of exchange rates among the currencies of the major industrial countries?
2   Explain in intuitive terms why, in a floating exchange rate economy with short-run price stickiness, an increase in the money supply that is expected to be permanent would tend to have a larger effect on the exchange rate on impact if the economy's level of real GDP reacts to changes in aggregate demand with a lag than if it does so immediately.
3   Explain why monetary and external financial shocks lead to overshooting in the Dornbusch model, while aggregate demand shocks do not.
4   What determines the extent of exchange rate overshooting in response to a permanent monetary shock in the Dornbusch model? Explain intuitively why your answer makes sense.
5   What would happen to the degree of overshooting in response to a permanent monetary expansion in the simple version of the Dornbusch model that we developed in Section 12.2 if the adjustment in real output occurs after two periods, rather than one? Explain why.

## Further Reading and References

### On exchange rate volatility under floating exchange rates

Bergstrand, Jeffrey H. (1983), "Is Exchange Rate Volatility 'Excessive'?" Federal Reserve Bank of Boston, *New England Economic Review* (September/October), pp. 5–14.
Engel, Charles and Craig S. Hakkio (1993), "Exchange Rate Regimes and Volatility," Federal Reserve Bank of Kansas City *Economic Review* (Third Quarter), pp. 43–58.
Leduc, Sylvan (2001), "Who Cares about Volatility? A Tale of Two Exchange-Rate Systems," Federal Reserve Bank of Philadelphia *Business Review* (First Quarter), pp. 16–25.
Meese, Richard (1990), "Currency Fluctuations in the Post-Bretton Woods Era," *Journal of Economic Perspectives* Vol. 4, No. 1 (Winter), pp. 117–34.
Mussa, Michael (1979), "Empirical Regularities in the Behavior of Exchange Rates and Theories of the Foreign Exchange Market," *Carnegie-Rochester Conference Series on Public Policy*, Vol. 11, pp. 9–57.

### On the Dornbusch model

Rogoff, Kenneth (2002), "Dornbusch's Overshooting Model after Twenty-Five Years," International Monetary Fund Working Paper WP/02/39 (February).

**Testing the Dornbusch model**

Bjornland, Hilde C. (2006), "Monetary Policy and Exchange Rate Overshooting: Dornbusch was Right after All," University of Oslo and Norges Bank, mimeo.

Clarida, Richard and Jordi Gali (1994), "Sources of Real Exchange Rate Fluctuations: How Important Are Nominal Shocks?" *Carnegie-Rochester Conference Series on Public Policy*, Vol. 41, pp. 1–56.

Driskill, Robert A. (1981), "Exchange Rate Dynamics: An Empirical Investigation," *Journal of Political Economy* Vol. 89, No. 21, pp. 357–71.

# Appendix 12.1  Proof that $(S_{t+1} / S_t) = \lambda \, (\bar{S}/S_t)$

To see that the nominal exchange rate must behave as claimed in Section 12.4 in the generalized Dornbusch model, we can work with the log-linear version of our model. In log-linear form, the money market equilibrium condition (the AA curve) becomes:

$$m - p = c_0 - c_1 \left[ R^* + \left( s^{e}_{+1} - s \right) \right] + c_2 y$$

As we saw in this chapter, this equation must hold throughout the economy's adjustment path. When the economy reaches its new equilibrium, however, we must have:

$$m - p = c_0 - c_1 R^* + c_2 \bar{y}$$

Subtracting the second of these equations from the first yields:

$$0 = -c_1 \left[ \left( s^{e}_{+1} - s \right) \right] + c_2 (y - \bar{y})$$

which implies:

$$s^{e}_{+1} - s = (c_2/c_1)(y - \bar{y}) \tag{A12.1}$$

In log-linear terms, the gradual adjustment mechanism for the level of real output is:

$$(y_{t+1} - y) = \lambda(\bar{y} - y)$$

Substituting this in (A12.1) produces:

$$s^{e}_{+1} - s = -(c_2/\lambda c_1)(y_{t+1} - y)$$

Under rational expectations, $s^{e}_{+1} = s_{+1}$, so we can get rid of the expectations superscript:

$$s_{+1} - s = -(c_2/\lambda c_1)(y_{t+1} - y)$$

Now the total change in $s$ from the moment a shock hits to the new equilibrium must be given by:

$$s - \bar{s} = \sum_{t=0}^{\infty} (s_{++1} - s_t)$$

$$- - \sum_{t=0}^{\infty} (c_2/\lambda c_1)(y_{t+1} - y)$$

$$= -(c_2/\lambda c_1) \sum_{t=0}^{\infty} (y_{t+1} - y)$$

$$= -(c_2/\lambda c_1)(\bar{y} - y)$$

Substituting this back into equation (A12.1), we finally get:

$$s_{+1} - s = -(c_2/c_1)(\lambda c_1/c_2)(s - \bar{s})$$
$$s_{+1} - s = \lambda(\bar{s} - s)$$

which is what we set out to show.

# 13

# Long-run Equilibrium under Floating Exchange Rates

......................................................................................................................

Up until this point in the book, we have been analyzing how open economies adjust to macroeconomic shocks over a short-run time frame, where "short-run" means a period of time brief enough that the economy's average price level does not have time to change appreciably. This means that other macroeconomic variables have to bear the brunt of adjustment to changes in the economy's circumstances. In the last three chapters, we have studied how an economy that operates with floating exchange rates responds to a variety of shocks under these conditions, we have examined how that response depends on how long the shocks are expected to last, and we have also considered the implications for the adjustment process of asymmetries in the speed with which markets return to equilibrium after a macroeconomic disturbance.

Macroeconomists of almost all persuasions are agreed, however, that while the economy's average price level may be "sticky" (that is, may not change very rapidly) in the short run, over a long enough time frame it will eventually adjust, causing the economy to revert to a "natural" (or "full employment," or "potential") level of output.[1] This means that we cannot consider the price level to be exogenous in the long run, as we have in the short run. Instead, since the level of real output to which the economy will return in the long run is the

---

[1]   Those who dissent from this view believe that prices adjust much more quickly – so much so, in fact, that they should be treated as endogenous in the short run. We will examine the implications of this assumption in Chapter 14.

one determined by the economy's productive capacity when its resources are fully employed, in the long run we can treat real GDP as exogenous, but must consider the domestic price level to be endogenous.

Why worry about the long run at all?[2] The answer is that once the price level is allowed to adjust fully, the effects of shocks and policies may turn out to be very different from those that we have examined so far. This means that some of the effects of the permanent shocks that we have analyzed in the last two chapters may themselves be transitory and that after enough time elapses, other effects may arise that were not apparent when we examined the economy's response in the short run. Thus, to gain a fuller understanding about how open economies work under floating exchange rates, we need to examine not only the short-run effects of permanent shocks, but also their long-lasting implications after all of the economy's various adjustment mechanisms have worked themselves out.

That is our task for this chapter. In the first section, we will build a long-run model of the economy under floating exchange rates. In the next section, we will solve the model and explore how the economy responds in the long run to the familiar set of shocks that we have been studying. We then will compare short-run and long-run adjustment, linking the results of this chapter to those of the preceding ones. Finally, we will take up an issue that can only be addressed when prices are free to change: the determinants of ongoing inflation in the economy.

## 13.1    A Long-run Model

To examine the long-run effects of shocks to the economy, we need to go back to our model and analyze how it behaves in long-run equilibrium. We will derive the compact form of the long-run model in this section and will examine how it behaves in the section that follows.

### Model Specification

Recall from Chapter 4 that the short-run model included the aggregate supply relationship:

$$P = \bar{P}$$

In other words, in the short run the price level was exogenous, reflecting the assumption that, over the time frame of the analysis, there was not enough time for the price level to adjust to shocks to the economy. In this setup, adjustment in the goods market consisted entirely of changes in the level of real output – i.e., $Y$ was endogenous.[3]

Now we move to the opposite extreme: we ask what happens in the economy when all price-level adjustments have been completed and the economy has reverted to its natural level of output. Since this natural level of output is given, we will treat it as exogenous. What becomes endogenous in this case is the price level, since in the long run (by definition) we

---

[2]    No macroeconomist can raise this question without recalling John Maynard Keynes's famous dismissive quip about the long run: "In the long run we are all dead."

[3]    In the Dornbusch version of the model, on the other hand, this adjustment in $Y$ was itself gradual, making it a predetermined variable.

have allowed enough time for price-level adjustments to be completed. Thus the previous equation is replaced by:

$$Y = \bar{Y}.$$

The long-run version of our model is given in Box 13.1. It is identical to the model we have been using in this part of the book except for the description of aggregate supply. In the model described in Box 13.1, real GDP has been set equal to the exogenous level of productive capacity $\bar{Y}$, and the domestic price level is endogenous.

### Deriving the Compact Form

How does the behavior of our new model differ from that of the short-run version that we solved before? To answer this question, let's begin by simplifying it, as we have done before, by consolidating it into two equations representing equilibrium in the asset and goods markets. Before we do so, however, we have to decide which endogenous variables we want to leave in these equations and which we want to substitute out. In previous chapters in which we analyzed macroeconomic performance under floating exchange rates, we expressed the compact version of our model in terms of the level of real GDP ($Y$) and the nominal exchange rate ($S$), having eliminated the other endogenous variables. By analogy

---

**Box 13.1   The Long-run Model**

**Money market equilibrium**

$$M = PL(R, \bar{Y}) \tag{13.1}$$

**Domestic bond market equilibrium**

$$R = (1 + R^*)S^e_{+1}/S - 1 \tag{13.2}$$

**Domestic goods market equilibrium**

$$\bar{Y} = \varphi(Q)A(\bar{Y} - T, r) + G + X(Q, \theta) \tag{13.3}$$

**Definition of the real exchange rate**

$$Q = SP^*/P \tag{13.4}$$

**Definition of the real interest rate**

$$r = P(1 + R)(1/P^e_{+1}) - 1 \tag{13.5}$$

with this procedure, it would be natural to express the financial and goods market equilibrium conditions in terms of endogenous variables consisting of the nominal exchange rate $S$ and the domestic price level $P$, since the new endogenous variable $P$ would then just replace the former endogenous variable $Y$. We could indeed proceed in that manner. It is simpler, however, to solve the model for $S$ and $Q$ instead, that is, for the nominal and real exchange rates. You can easily see that solving the model for the real exchange rate is equivalent to solving it for the domestic price level. The reason is that the real exchange rate and domestic price level are related to each other by equation (13.4), which defines the real exchange rate. By solving equation (13.4) for $P$, we can write:

$$P = SP^*/Q \tag{13.4'}$$

Since $P^*$ is exogenous under the small country assumption that we have maintained throughout the book, this tells us that if we can succeed in solving the model for $S$ and $Q$, then simply by substituting the solved values of $S$ and $Q$ into this equation, we can derive the model's solution for the domestic price level $P$.

Having decided which endogenous variables to focus on, we can now proceed to describe the model in the compact form that we will need to use in order to solve it graphically. First, to derive the asset market equilibrium condition, we can begin by substituting the uncovered interest parity (UIP) condition (13.2) into the money-market equilibrium condition (13.1), as we did in deriving the AA curve in Chapter 10 (Figure 10.2). This gives us:

$$M = PL\big[(1 + R^*)S_{+1}^e/S - 1, \bar{Y}\big]$$

You can easily verify that if we hold the expected future exchange rate $S_{+1}^e$ constant, this equation can be used to derive the downward-sloping AA curve of Chapter 10, while if we set $S_{+1}^e = S$ we get the vertical AA curve corresponding to permanent shocks, as in Chapter 11 (Figure 11.4).

Next, we need to eliminate the endogenous variable $P$ from this equation. Using the expression for the domestic price level that we derived from the definition of the real exchange rate (equation 13.4'), we can write the asset market equilibrium condition as:

$$M = (SP^*/Q)L\big[(1 + R^*)S_{+1}^e/S - 1, \bar{Y}\big] \tag{13.6}$$

This is the form of the asset market equilibrium condition that we will use in this chapter (the counterpart of the AA curve).

To derive the condition for equilibrium in the goods market in terms of the endogenous variables that we are interested in, we need to do some preliminary work. First, we need to derive a new expression for the real interest rate. Substituting equation (13.2) into (13.5) we can express the domestic real interest rate as:

$$r = (1 + R^*)\big(S_{+1}^e/S\big)\big(P/P_{+1}^e\big) - 1$$

It will simplify matters below to express the foreign interest rate $R^*$ in this equation in real rather than nominal terms. To do that, we can use the foreign counterpart to equation (13.5) to write the foreign real interest rate $r^*$ as $r^* = P^*\,(1 + R^*)(1/P_{+1}^{*e}) - 1$, which implies that $1 + R^* = (1 + r^*)(P_{+1}^{*e}/P^*)$. Using this to substitute for $1 + R^*$ in the equation above, we have:

$$r = (1 + r^*)\left(S_{+1}^e/S\right)\left(P_{+1}^{*e}/P^*\right)\left(P/P_{+1}^e\right) - 1$$
$$= (1 + r^*)\left(S_{+1}^e P_{+1}^{*e}/P_{+1}^e\right)/(SP^*/P) - 1$$

Using the definition of the real exchange rate, this can be written in the much simpler form:

$$r = (1 + r^*)\left(Q_{+1}^e/Q\right) - 1$$

where $Q_{+1}^e$ is the value of the real exchange rate that is expected to prevail next period, given by $Q_{+1}^e = S_{+1}^e P_{+1}^{*e}/P_{+1}^e$.

The relationship that we just derived is referred to as **real interest parity** (RIP). It simply states that when domestic and foreign bonds are perfect substitutes, the return from investing the equivalent of one domestic good must be the same whether that good is invested at home or abroad. Notice that this is very similar to the uncovered interest parity (UIP) condition that we have been using throughout the book, except that it is written in real terms.

Substituting this expression into the goods market equilibrium condition (13.3) we have:

$$\bar{Y} = \varphi(Q)A\left[\bar{Y} - T, (1 + r^*)\left(Q_{+1}^e/Q\right) - 1\right] + G + X(Q, \theta) \tag{13.7}$$

This is the version of the goods market equilibrium condition that we will use in solving our model. An interesting application of this equation is described in Box 13.2, "Overvaluation and the Mexican Recession."

As we have done in previous chapters, we have collapsed our model into two equations, the asset market equilibrium condition (13.6) and the goods market equilibrium condition (13.7). These equations determine the two endogenous variables in the model, the nominal exchange rate $S$ and the real exchange rate $Q$. As usual, the equilibrium values of the nominal and real exchange rates depend on the exogenous variables in the model. These consist of two types of variables: (1) characteristics of the economy's external environment, consisting of the world real interest rate $r^*$, the world nominal interest rate $R^*$, the world price level $P^*$, the exogenous component of demand for domestic exports $\theta$, and (2) domestic policy variables, consisting of government spending $G$, the level of taxes $T$, and the money supply $M$.

Notice, however, that the two equations of our model actually contain four unknowns: not just $Q$ and $S$, but also $S_{+1}^e$ and $Q_{+1}^e$. How do we deal with this indeterminacy? The answer is similar to that given in the permanent shock model of Chapter 11: in a long-run equilibrium in which none of the exogenous variables are changing over time, there would be no reason to expect any of the endogenous variables to be changing continuously either. Thus, with unchanging exogenous variables, we can impose the long-run equilibrium conditions:

$$0 = Q_{+1}^e - Q = S_{+1}^e - S$$

This essentially adds two equations to our model and removes the indeterminacy. Substituting these two conditions in equations (13.6) and (13.7) we can now rewrite the model in the much simpler form given in Box 13.3.

## Box 13.2   Overvaluation and the Mexican Recession

Economists Rudiger Dornbusch and Alejandro Werner used equation (13.7) to analyze the events that led to the Mexican crisis of December 1994 (see Box 9.4). They argued in a forum at the Brookings Institution in Washington, DC in early 1994 that the Mexican pcso had become substantially overvalued. According to Dornbusch and Werner, the currency overvaluation was reducing demand for Mexican goods and had created a recession in Mexico. They maintained that a devaluation of the exchange rate was required to reactivate the Mexican economy.

To understand the Dornbusch–Werner argument, suppose that there is some stable equilibrium value of the real exchange rate $Q$ – say $Q_0$ – that satisfies equation (13.7) with $Q_{+1}^e - Q = 0$, so the real exchange rate is not expected to change in the future. $Q_0$ is then the **equilibrium value** of the real exchange rate. If the *actual* real exchange rate $Q$ is below this value, the currency is said to be overvalued. If the actual real exchange rate is above $Q_0$, on the other hand, the currency is said to be undervalued (recall our discussion of this issue in the context of the "Big Mac" index in Chapter 3). If the actual real exchange rate temporarily falls below its equilibrium value for whatever reason (making the currency overvalued), the very meaning of equilibrium suggests that it must eventually be expected to return to its equilibrium value. If the process of return to equilibrium is **monotonic** – that is, if the real exchange rate always moves in the same direction as it approaches its equilibrium value, then $Q_{+1}^e - Q$ must be positive. In that case, real interest parity suggests that the domestic real interest rate must be temporarily high. It is easy to see that the higher domestic real interest rate and appreciated real exchange rate would both tend to cause the demand for domestic goods to fall below its natural level $\bar{Y}$.

Dornbusch and Werner essentially argued that by depreciating its officially determined exchange rate at rates below the domestic rate of inflation during previous years, Mexico had allowed the real exchange rate to fall too far below its equilibrium value by 1994, and this situation created the deficient-demand recession that the country was experiencing at the time. They argued in April 1994 that unless the currency was devalued to bring the real exchange rate back to its equilibrium value, output would remain depressed in Mexico and a foreign exchange crisis would eventually ensue, since speculators would know that a devaluation was inevitable (recall the "second-generation" currency crisis mechanism that we discussed in Chapter 9).

The Mexican peso was not devalued in response to the Dornbusch–Werner argument, the Mexican economy remained depressed, and the crisis predicted by the economists happened even sooner than most observers expected: in December of that year, when speculation about an upcoming devaluation depleted the foreign exchange reserves of the Bank of Mexico. As we saw in Box 9.4, the very sharp depreciation of the Mexican peso that ensued made it difficult for the Mexican government to service its foreign currency-denominated debt, causing interest rates to rise sharply in Mexico and sending the Mexican economy into a very severe recession. This was one of the few times in recent memory that a macroeconomic event of this magnitude was accurately foretold in a public prediction by prominent macroeconomists.

> ### Box 13.3 The Compact Version of the Long-run Model
>
> **Asset market equilibrium**
>
> $$M = (SP^*/Q)L[R^*, \bar{Y}] \tag{13.6'}$$
>
> **Goods market equilibrium**
>
> $$\bar{Y} = \varphi(Q)A(\bar{Y} - T, r^*) + G + X(Q, \theta) \tag{13.7'}$$

## 13.2 Solving the Long-run Model

As we have done previously, we will solve this model graphically. Notice first that the nominal exchange rate $S$ does not appear in the goods market equilibrium condition (13.7′), while the asset market equilibrium condition (13.6′) contains both the nominal exchange rate $S$ and the real exchange rate $Q$. Moreover, if we are interested in solving for the domestic price level $P$ as well, and thus add the rewritten real exchange rate definition (equation 13.4′) to our model, that equation contains *all three* endogenous variables. This means that the entire three-equation model used to explain the determination of $S$, $Q$, and $P$ is **recursive** – that is, its equations are not interdependent, and we can therefore solve them sequentially. This makes our long-run model very easy to solve.

To see how the solution is found, let's plot the asset market equilibrium condition (13.6′) and the goods market equilibrium condition (13.7′) in $S$-$Q$ space, since $S$ and $Q$ are the two endogenous variables that we are trying to explain. Consider the goods-market equilibrium condition (13.7′) first. Since this equation only contains the single endogenous variable $Q$, it can be plotted as a vertical straight line in $S$-$Q$ space, as shown by the curve labeled QQ in Figure 13.1. As this curve suggests, the value of $Q$ that is consistent with long-run equilibrium in the market for domestic goods, which we will call the **long-run equilibrium real exchange rate** (labeled $Q_0$ in Figure 13.1) does not depend on the nominal exchange rate, because the nominal exchange rate does not affect the goods market in the long run.

What does $Q_0$ depend on? The answer is that it depends on all of the exogenous variables in our model that affect the goods market in the long run. These include foreign variables such as the world real interest rate $r^*$ and the exogenous component of export demand $\theta$, domestic fiscal policy variables in the form of the level of domestic government spending $G$ and taxation $T$, and the economy's level of productive capacity $\bar{Y}$. The long-run equilibrium real exchange rate will appreciate ($Q$ will fall and the QQ curve in Figure 13.1 will shift to the left), when changes in any of these variables create an excess demand for domestic goods, while the long-run equilibrium real exchange rate will depreciate ($Q$ will rise and the QQ curve will shift to the right), when changes in any of these variables create an excess supply of domestic goods. When this happens, since the level of capacity output cannot change in the long run, the market for domestic goods can be brought back into equilibrium only by a change in the relative price of domestic goods in terms of foreign goods – that is, by changes in the real exchange rate. When government spending $G$ or the exogenous

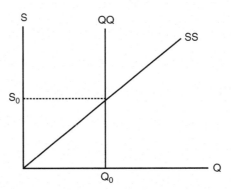

**Figure 13.1**    Long-run equilibrium

component of export demand $\theta$ increases, the demand for domestic goods increases, so their relative price has to rise ($Q$ has to appreciate). On the other hand, when the world real interest rate $r^*$ or the level of taxation $T$ increases, domestic spending falls, so the demand for domestic goods falls as well, and the price of the domestic good must fall ($Q$ must depreciate). Finally, when the supply of the domestic good ($\bar{Y}$) increases, this also must cause its relative price to fall. As shown in Box 13.4, "Why Purchasing Power Parity Fails," this equation helps to explain why the purchasing power parity (PPP) hypothesis, which we examined in Chapter 3, tends to fail empirically.

Now turn to the asset market equilibrium condition (13.6′). To plot this equation in Figure 13.1, we can simply solve it for $S$. The answer is:

$$S = [(M/P^*)/L(\underset{-}{R^*}, \underset{+}{\bar{Y}})]Q \tag{13.6''}$$

## Box 13.4    Why Purchasing Power Parity Fails

Recall that in Chapter 3 we described purchasing power parity (PPP) and concluded that it could not be expected to hold when the baskets of goods consumed (or produced, depending on the price index used) in the domestic economy and in its trading partners were different, even if the process of arbitrage equalized the prices of individual goods (when expressed in the same currency). The reason was that if the domestic and foreign baskets contained different goods, changes in the relative prices of these goods would alter the equilibrium value of the real exchange rate.

In our model, the real exchange rate is based on the prices of the goods produced at home and abroad (so you can think of it as a real exchange rate based on GDP deflators). Since the domestic and foreign economies produce different baskets of goods, the real exchange rate will change whenever the relative price of these baskets changes. We now see how these changes in relative goods prices can be brought about. Permanent changes in the real demand for or supply of the domestic good must alter its relative price to maintain goods market equilibrium, so $Q$ cannot permanently be equal to unity. This result essentially explains why PPP fails.

You can see that this is the equation of a straight line in $S$-$Q$ space starting from the origin and with positive slope equal to $(M/P^*)/L(R^*, \bar{Y})$. The asset market equilibrium curve (13.6″) is labeled SS in Figure 13.1. The slope of this curve is affected by changes in the exogenous variables that affect the domestic money market equilibrium, consisting of the domestic money supply $M$, the world price level $P^*$, the world interest rate $R^*$, and the domestic level of capacity output $\bar{Y}$. The slope of the curve changes in direct proportion with changes in $M$, and in inverse proportion to changes in $P^*L(\,)$. For example, a doubling of the domestic money supply would double the slope of the SS curve (make it twice as steep), while a doubling of $P^*L(\,)$ would cut the slope of the SS curve in half (make it half as steep). Changes in $R^*$ or $\bar{Y}$ affect the shape of the curve through their effects on $P^*L(\,)$.

It is easiest to interpret the determination of the nominal exchange rate in our model if we first rewrite equation (13.6″) slightly. If we substitute this equation into the rewritten definition of the real exchange rate (13.4′) and solve the resulting expression for the domestic price level $P$, we have:

$$P = M/L(R^*, \bar{Y}) \tag{13.8}$$

This is the model's solution for the long-run value of the domestic price level. The price level is simply determined by the ratio of the nominal supply of money to the real demand for money. Thus, the role of the price level in the long run is to set the real supply of money equal to the real demand for money. Again, this is a fairly intuitive result. Based on this insight, we can now rewrite the solution of the nominal exchange rate as:

$$S = Q\left[M/L(R^*, \bar{Y})\right]/P^* \tag{13.9}$$

Since, as we have just seen, the term in square brackets is the domestic price level, this equation tells us that in the long run the nominal exchange rate must be equal to the real exchange rate times the ratio of the domestic price level to the foreign price level. If the equilibrium real exchange rate remains unchanged, then any change in the domestic price level relative to the foreign price level must be offset by a change in the nominal exchange rate. On the other hand, if the relationship between the domestic and foreign price levels remains unchanged, then any change in the equilibrium real exchange rate can be brought about only by a change in the nominal exchange rate.

The determination of the equilibrium value of the nominal exchange rate is illustrated in Figure 13.1. The equilibrium value of the nominal exchange rate, given by $S_0$, is determined at point A, where the SS curve intersects the vertical QQ curve. Changes in $Q$, holding the ratio of domestic to foreign prices constant, represent a movement along the SS curve and cause $S_0$ to change in proportion to changes in $Q$, while changes in $P/P^*$ ($= [M/L(R^*, \bar{Y})/P^*]$) cause the SS curve to rotate around the origin, again causing $S_0$ to change in proportion to changes in $P/P^*$.

## 13.3 Comparative Statics

To understand more generally how our model works in the long run we will now examine some of its properties by exploring how the economy responds in the long run to the types of shocks that we have analyzed previously.

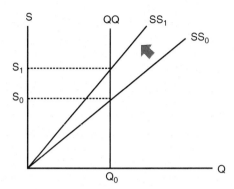

**Figure 13.2**    Effects of a permanent increase in the money supply

## Monetary Shocks

In the long run, permanent changes in the money supply cause the domestic price level and nominal exchange rate to change in the same proportion, leaving all of the economy's real variables unchanged.

We can see that this must be so, because the domestic price level is determined by the ratio of the nominal supply of money to the real demand for money (equation 13.8), and the real demand for money is unaffected by a change in the nominal money supply. Thus an increase in the nominal money supply, holding the real demand for money constant, must increase the domestic price level in the same proportion. From equation (13.7′), we can see that changes in the money supply have no effect on the goods market and therefore on the real exchange rate, so the effect of the monetary expansion in equation (13.9) is to increase the ratio of $P$ to $P^*$ in the same proportion as the increase in the money supply – that is, to rotate the SS curve upward, increasing its height in the same proportion as the increase in the money supply, as shown in Figure 13.2. The implication, as we have seen, is that the nominal exchange rate must depreciate in proportion to the increase in the domestic price level, from $S_0$ to $S_1$.

The property of the model that we have just established is called **monetary neutrality**. The term "neutrality" refers to the fact that changes in the money supply are neutral in their effects on real variables – i.e., they neither cause them to increase nor decrease in magnitude. Since this means that the domestic price level will be determined by the money supply, the money supply is said to be the **nominal anchor** in this economy – the exogenous variable that is responsible for determining the economy's average price level in the long run – just as the price of gold was in the gold standard model of Chapter 6.[4] Empirical Study 13.1 examines some evidence on long-run monetary neutrality.

## Foreign Nominal Shocks

In the long run, changes in the foreign price level give rise to changes in the nominal exchange rate that are equal in magnitude but opposite in sign, leaving the domestic price level unchanged.

[4]    Appendix 13.2 derives the long-run version of the model that we analyzed in Chapter 9, featuring a fixed exchange rate and a high degree of capital mobility. As shown there, under fixed exchange rates the exchange rate serves as the economy's nominal anchor.

To see why this must be so, notice from equation (13.7′) that like changes in the domestic money supply, changes in $P^*$, a nominal variable, have no effect on the domestic goods market and thus on the equilibrium real exchange rate $Q_0$. Since they also have no effect on the ratio of the nominal supply of money to the real demand for money, equation (13.8) tells us that they do not affect the domestic price level. Thus, their only effect must be to *decrease* the ratio of $P$ to $P^*$. It follows that such changes must rotate the SS curve in a direction *opposite* to that of the change in $P^*$ (that is, the curve rotates upward if $P^*$ falls and downward if $P^*$ rises). This means that permanent changes in $P^*$ will cause the nominal exchange rate to change in the same proportion, but in the opposite direction.

The implication of this result is that in the long run, the domestic economy is insulated from changes in the foreign price level. Changes in the foreign price level do not affect the domestic-currency prices of domestic goods, because the nominal exchange rate changes so as to offset the effects of changes in the foreign-currency prices of such goods. We will verify in Section 13.5 that this result applies not just to the *level* of foreign prices $P^*$, but also to the foreign *rate of inflation*, given by $\Delta P^*/P^*$.

## Aggregate Demand Shocks

Changes in the long-run equilibrium real exchange rate brought about by permanent changes in government spending and/or the exogenous component of demand for domestic exports $\theta$ will be effected through changes in the nominal exchange rate, rather than through changes in the domestic price level.

As we have already seen, and as you can infer from equation (13.7′), permanent changes in $G$ and/or $\theta$ change the long-run equilibrium real exchange rate $Q_0$. Such shocks do not affect either the nominal supply of money nor the real demand for money, so they must leave the domestic price level unchanged. It follows that the change in the long-run equilibrium real exchange rate must be brought about by changes in the nominal exchange rate only. Figure 13.3 illustrates what happens in the case of a permanent reduction in government spending: the QQ curve shifts to the right, since the reduced demand for domestic goods requires its relative price to fall in order for the goods market to clear. The economy's equilibrium thus moves along the SS curve from point A to point B, causing the nominal and real exchange rates to depreciate in the same proportion, from $S_0$ to $S_1$ and from $Q_0$ to $Q_1$ respectively.

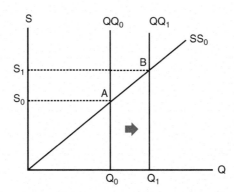

**Figure 13.3**  Effects of a permanent reduction in government spending

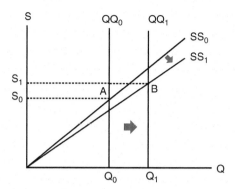

**Figure 13.4**   Effects of a positive aggregate supply shock

## Aggregate Supply Shocks

If changes in the long-run equilibrium real exchange rate are caused by permanent changes in the natural level of output $\bar{Y}$, the long-run values of *both* the nominal exchange rate and the domestic price level will be affected.

The effects of an aggregate supply shock, in the form of an increase in the economy's natural level of output, are illustrated in Figure 13.4. An increase in $\bar{Y}$, for example, will lower the domestic price level (because it increases the real demand for money) at the same time that it causes the real exchange rate to depreciate (because it increases the supply of domestic goods). Thus the SS curve rotates downward at the same time that the QQ curve shifts to the right, as in Figure 13.4. In general the nominal exchange rate will change, but the long-run effect on the nominal exchange rate is ambiguous in sign. It could depreciate as shown in Figure 13.4 (if the reduction in the domestic price level is insufficient to produce the required increase in the equilibrium real exchange rate) or appreciate (if the reduction in the domestic price level is more than sufficient to produce the required change in the equilibrium real exchange rate), or stay the same (if the change in the domestic price level happens to be exactly enough to bring about the required change in the equilibrium real exchange rate).

## External Financial Shocks

Permanent changes in the world (nominal and real) interest rate $R^*$ will also in general affect the long-run values of the domestic price level as well as the real exchange rate.[5] The direction of change in the nominal exchange rate is unambiguous.

A permanent change in the world interest rate affects the long-run value of the domestic price level because it alters the domestic demand for money. Thus, for a given money supply, a change in the domestic price level is required to clear the money market. It also affects the real exchange rate because it alters the demand for domestic goods.

Consider, for example, an increase in the world interest rate. This would have the effects of reducing both the demand for money as well as the demand for domestic goods. Since the nominal money supply and the supply of domestic goods are unchanged, the domestic price

---

[5]   World nominal and real interest rates are the same in this case, because we have not yet allowed for world inflation.

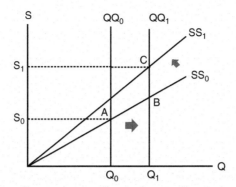

**Figure 13.5** Effects of an increase in the world interest rate

level must rise and the equilibrium real exchange rate must depreciate. But for this to happen, the nominal exchange rate must depreciate *more* than in proportion to the increase in the domestic price level. This can be verified from Figure 13.5. Because it reduces demand for domestic goods, the increase in the world interest rate causes the QQ curve to shift to the right, from $QQ_0$ to $QQ_1$. Thus the equilibrium real exchange rate must depreciate from $Q_0$ to $Q_1$. Because it reduces the demand for domestic money, it also causes the SS curve to rotate in a counterclockwise direction, from $SS_0$ to $SS_1$. Notice that at point B on the original SS curve, the nominal and real exchange rates would have increased in the same proportion. But the rotation of SS implies that the new long-run equilibrium is at C, rather than B. This means that the nominal exchange rate must depreciate more than in proportion to the depreciation in the real exchange rate.

## 13.4  Comparing the Short-run and Long-run Responses to Permanent Shocks

Now that we have examined how the economy behaves in the long run, we can compare our results with those that we derived in previous chapters. In particular, suppose that from an initial position of long-run equilibrium, the economy experiences a permanent shock of one of the types that we have been studying throughout this book. How do its short-run and long-run responses to the shock differ? As we shall see, the answer depends on the type of shock involved.

It is easy to see that for certain types of shocks the short-run and long-run responses of the economy must be exactly the same, because the economy never deviates from its full employment level of output $\bar{Y}$ in response to these shocks. This is true for permanent aggregate demand shocks and for shocks to the foreign price level. Recall that aggregate demand shocks that are perceived to be permanent when they arrive simply cause the nominal exchange rate to adjust immediately on impact, causing the relative price of domestic goods to adjust immediately, with no change in domestic output. Since the change in the nominal exchange rate is sufficient to keep the economy at its natural level of output $\bar{Y}$ continuously, there is nothing to disturb the money market in the long run and thus no long-run change in the domestic price level.

The same is true with respect to permanent shocks to the foreign price level. The nominal exchange rate adjusts immediately so as to offset exactly the change in the foreign price level, keeping the real exchange rate unchanged at its equilibrium level and leaving the economy at $\bar{Y}$ in the short run. Moreover, the domestic price level does not change in the long run in this case either, since the change in the foreign price level does not disturb the equilibrium in the domestic money market.

For financial shocks – whether domestic or foreign – things work out differently. As we have seen, increases in the money supply and in the world interest rate increase real output in the short run, but not in the long run. The price level is not affected in the short run, but in both cases it increases in the long run. Thus, both shocks are expansionary, but the expansion takes the form of higher real output in the short run, and only a higher price level in the long run. In the case of the monetary shock, the real exchange rate depreciates temporarily, but in the long run it does not change. In the case of the foreign interest rate shock, there is real depreciation both in the short run as well as in the long run.

To illustrate how adjustment happens, consider the case of a monetary shock, such as a permanent monetary expansion. In Figure 13.6, the economy begins in a short-run (and long-run) equilibrium at point A. A permanent expansion of the money supply by $x$ percent shifts the AA curve to the right from $AA_0$ to $AA_1$, producing an increase in real output and a nominal exchange rate depreciation from $S_0$ to $S_1$, as we've seen before. The new short-run equilibrium is at B. The higher value of real output at point B, however, puts upward pressure on the domestic price level. As the price level rises, the AA curve begins to shift back to the left, because higher prices increase the nominal demand for money, thus requiring a lower level of output to clear the money market. At the same time, higher prices shift the YY curve upward, because the increase in the price level tends to appreciate the real exchange rate. This means that a nominal depreciation (an upward shift in YY) would be necessary to keep the real exchange rate constant at the level required to clear the goods market for a given value of $Y$.

The implication of these two shifts is that real output begins to fall from its short-run equilibrium level, and the nominal exchange rate depreciates further than it did on impact. It is easy to see that the leftward shifts in AA and upward shifts in YY must continue until the price level has increased by a proportionate amount that is exactly equal to the increase in the money supply (i.e., by $x$ percent). That is so because when this has happened, the AA

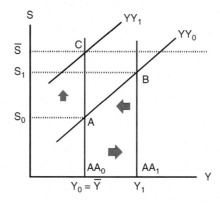

**Figure 13.6**   Permanent monetary expansion in the short run and long run

curve will have returned to its original position (since the real supply of money will be back to its pre-shock value), and the YY curve will have shifted up by exactly $x$ percent (since the price level has risen by $x$ percent, the nominal exchange rate would have to depreciate by $x$ percent to restore the original value of the real exchange rate and thus maintain goods market equilibrium). The new long-run equilibrium is thus at point C, where real output has returned to its original value $\bar{Y}$ and the nominal exchange rate $S$ has depreciated by $x$ percent.[6]

## 13.5   The Role of Long-run Inflation

Notice that, while the analysis in the previous section considered the effects on the economy of changes in the two exogenous nominal variables $M$ and $P^*$, these were *one*-time changes – that is, the analysis assumed that the values of both of these variables did not change *repeatedly* over time. But since these variables are exogenous, we can't count on their remaining fixed, and since they are nominal variables, they can in principle increase without limit. What happens to the economy if they do?

To answer this question, suppose that the money supply is indeed increasing repeatedly over time. To make things concrete, assume that the money supply grows at a constant rate per year, say x percent, so that:

$$M/M_{-1} = (1 + x)$$

What does this do to our long-run equilibrium? Notice first that, since $M$ does not enter the goods-market equilibrium condition, it has no effect on the long-run equilibrium real exchange rate. This is important because, as we shall see, continuous monetary growth will affect the economy's long-run inflation rate, and this result thus implies that the presence of ongoing inflation has no long-run real effects on our economy.

Now let's turn to the money-market equilibrium condition. We can show that if $M/M_{-1} = (1 + x)$, then the nominal exchange rate must also depreciate at the rate $x$ – that is, that $S/S_{-1} = (1 + x)$ as well. How do we show this? We simply have to demonstrate that *with the money supply increasing by x percent, a simultaneous x percent increase in the nominal exchange rate is consistent with money market equilibrium*. To show this, take the money market equilibrium condition (equation 13.6):

$$M = (SP^*/Q)L\left[(1 + R^*)S^e_{+1}/S - 1, \bar{Y}\right]$$

lag it by one period and divide the result into the equation above. Since $P^*$, $R^*$, $\bar{Y}$ and $Q$ are constant over time, the result is:

$$M/M_{-1} = (S/S_{-1})L\left[(1 + R^*)S_{+1}/S - 1, \bar{Y}\right]/L\left[(1 + R^*)S/S_{-1} - 1, \bar{Y}\right]$$

[6]   The value of the nominal exchange rate at B may be more or less depreciated than at C. In general, we can't tell. The answer depends on the slope of the YY curve, which depends on the degree of substitutability between domestic and foreign goods.

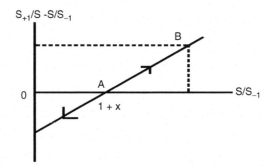

**Figure 13.7**   Exchange rate dynamics in response to continuous monetary expansion

Dividing both sides of this equation by $S/S_{-1}$, we get:

$$(M/M_{-1})/(S/S_{-1}) = L[(1 + R^*)S_{+1}/S - 1, \bar{Y}]/L[(1 + R^*)S/S_{-1} - 1, \bar{Y}]$$

To see what this implies, consider Figure 13.7. In this figure, we have plotted the relationship between $(S_{+1}/S - S/S_{-1})$ – that is, the *change* in the rate of nominal exchange rate depreciation from the last period to the current one – and $S/S_{-1}$ – the *level* of nominal exchange rate depreciation – that is implied by the equation that we have just derived. This relationship must take the form of a curve with positive slope that crosses the horizontal axis at $S/S_{-1} = 1 + x$. To see why, notice that the larger $S/S_{-1}$ is, the smaller the left-hand side of the equation above must be, since $M/M_{-1}$ is always equal to $1 + x$, and therefore constant. But that means that the right-hand side of the equation must be smaller as well – that is, the ratio of this period's real demand for money to last period's real demand for money must be falling. But that can only be true if the gap between this period's domestic interest rate and last period's domestic interest rate is increasing, which in turn requires that $(S_{+1}/S - S/S_{-1})$ be increasing. Thus, higher values of $S/S_{-1}$ are associated with higher values of $S_{+1}/S - S/S_{-1}$. Where the curve cuts the horizontal axis, however, we have $S/S_{-1} = 1 + x$, so both sides of the equation above must be equal to unity, implying that $S_{+1}/S = S/S_{-1}$, so $(S_{+1}/S - S/S_{-1}) = 0$.

Now consider the dynamics of the economy along the curve depicted in Figure 13.7. If the rate of exchange rate depreciation is greater than $x$, the economy must be to the right of point A where this curve crosses the horizontal axis, at a point such as B. But this means that the gap between $S_{+1}/S$ and $S/S_{-1}$ must be increasing, so in the next period, the rate of depreciation must be even higher, moving the economy further to the right along the positively sloped curve, which would in turn imply an even larger rate of depreciation in the period after that, and so on. In other words, the rate of nominal exchange rate depreciation must be *accelerating*. On the other hand, for values of $S/S_{-1}$ that are *smaller* than (to the *left* of) $1 + x$, the gap between $S_{+1}/S$ and $S/S_{-1}$ must be falling, so in the next period the rate of depreciation must be lower, moving the economy further to the left along the curve in Figure 13.7, which would in turn imply an even smaller rate of depreciation in the period after that, and so on. In other words, the economy will exhibit explosive behavior (continuous movement to the right or left, as shown by the arrows in the figure) if $S/S_{-1}$ does not equal $1 + x$. It follows that the economy can be in a stable long-run equilibrium only if $S/S_{-1} = 1 + x$.

What this says is that, if the money supply increases by $x$ percent every period, actual and expected nominal exchange rate depreciation by $x$ percent in every period is consistent with money market equilibrium in every period. Thus if the money supply grows at the rate $x$, the nominal exchange rate must depreciate at the rate $x$. Since the real exchange rate $Q$ is constant and we are assuming that the foreign price level is unchanged, this means that the domestic rate of inflation must be $x$ as well, that is, $P / P_{-1} = 1 + x$.

What if the foreign price level $P^*$ is also changing, say by $z$ percent per period? Notice that, as we established in Section 13.3, $P^*$ does not affect our model's solution either for the long-run real exchange rate or for the domestic price level. Thus, the domestic rate of inflation would continue to be $x$ in this case – determined by the rate of growth of the money supply only – regardless of what foreign inflation happens to be. What about the rate of depreciation of the exchange rate? Since the equilibrium real exchange rate is unchanged and the domestic rate of inflation is given by the rate of growth of the money supply at $x$ percent, the rate of depreciation would have to be exactly what is required to keep the real exchange constant at its equilibrium value. It follows that the rate of depreciation of the currency must be equal to the difference between the domestic and foreign inflation rates. As mentioned in Section 13.3, the implication is that a floating exchange rate insulates the economy from foreign inflation in the long run. This property of floating rates was emphasized by some of the advocates of floating exchange rates in the period before the collapse of the Bretton Woods system, as described in Box 13.5, "The Insulation Property of Floating Exchange Rates."

## Box 13.5   The Insulation Property of Floating Exchange Rates

The Nobel prize-winning monetary economist Milton Friedman argued strongly for the adoption of floating exchange rates prior to the collapse of the Bretton Woods system, partly on grounds that this would permit different countries to have different long-run inflation rates. This was one of the key virtues that he cited for floating exchange rates as an alternative to Bretton Woods. Our model supports the contention that floating exchange rates would indeed achieve the result that Friedman claimed (since domestic inflation is determined by the rate of growth of the domestic money stock, rather than by the foreign inflation rate), at least in the long run. According to our model, moving to floating rates allows each country to choose its own price level in the long run by choosing the growth rate of its money supply. Nominal exchange rate adjustments reconcile the choices made by individual countries with the long-run equilibrium real exchange rate.

We will see an example of this when we discuss European monetary unification in Chapter 18. While their intention was ultimately to adopt the fixed exchange rate regime required for eventual admission to the euro zone, several high-inflation European Union countries in Southern Europe maintained floating exchange rates while they tried to lower their domestic inflation rates, so that depreciation of their nominal exchange rates could accommodate their high domestic inflation rates without causing their real exchange rates to appreciate away from their equilibrium levels.

## Box 13.6    Real Exchange Rate Targeting

The result we have just derived about the determination of the long-run inflation rate has led many countries to adopt an exchange rate system known as a **crawling peg**, or a system of **real exchange rate targeting**. It consists of an officially determined exchange rate regime in which the exchange rate is not literally fixed, but is actually depreciated by an amount equal to the difference between domestic and foreign inflation, keeping the real exchange rate stable. The domestic inflation rate is determined by the long-run rate of growth of the money supply, and this regime essentially mimics what a floating exchange rate would do in the long run under these circumstances, without allowing the exchange rate to change in response to transitory shocks, as a floating exchange rate would do. Many developing countries are still following this type of exchange rate policy. Indonesia conducted its exchange rate policy in this manner prior to the 1997 Asian crisis (Chapter 9), and Chile did so as well until fairly recently.

Figure 13.8 illustrates how the implementation of real exchange rate targeting in Costa Rica during the period 1983–2000 has affected the real effective exchange rate (REER), the nominal effective exchange rate (NEER), and the ratio of trading-partner price levels to the domestic price level relative to (RELPRICE) in that country. As you can see, faster inflation in Costa Rica than in its trading partners resulted in a continuous decline in RELPRICE during this period, but this was offset by continuous nominal effective exchange rate depreciation, leaving the country's real effective exchange rate essentially constant over the entire period.

Countries that have abandoned crawling peg regimes have typically fixed the exchange rate to use it as a nominal anchor (see Appendix 13.2) or to adopt a floating exchange rate. We will analyze the factors that influence exchange regime choice in Chapter 15.

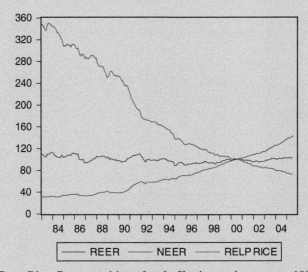

**Figure 13.8**    Costa Rica: Decomposition of real effective exchange rate, 1983–2000

The result that under floating exchange rates the nominal exchange rate depreciates in the long run by an amount equal to the difference between the domestic and foreign inflation rates has also induced some countries that maintain officially determined exchange rates to mimic this outcome by continuously depreciating their official exchange rates by an amount equal to the domestic-foreign inflation differential. This practice, which is referred to as **real exchange rate targeting**, is discussed further in Box 13.6.

## Empirical Study 13.1    Testing Long-run Monetary Neutrality

This chapter introduced the notion of **long-run monetary neutrality**, the view that unexpected, permanent changes in an exogenous nominal variable such as the money supply or the nominal exchange rate would have no real effects on the economy in the long run – i.e., after enough time has been allowed to pass for the economy to adjust fully to the shock. This is a view that is widely adhered to by macroeconomists, because it is based on the perspective that what people ultimately care about are real variables. That being so, what must be determined in an economy's long-run equilibrium are real magnitudes, including the real magnitude of whatever nominal variable is determined exogenously in that economy. If this is the case, a permanent change in such a variable must ultimately result only in a proportionate change in the price level.

But is there evidence to support long-run monetary neutrality? Bullard (1999) recently provided a readable overview of such evidence, covering studies employing a variety of empirical methodologies applied to several different countries and time periods. He concluded that the weight of the international evidence supported the proposition of monetary neutrality.

One particularly interesting approach discussed by Bullard was by King and Watson (1997), who looked specifically at the relationship between the money stock and real output. In this context, money is neutral in the long run if a permanent change in the money stock has no long-run effect on the level of real output. King and Watson examined long-run neutrality by estimating bivariate (two-variable) vector autoregressions (VARs, see Empirical Study 8.1) using quarterly data on these two variables for the United States from 1949:1 to 1990:4.

A key challenge in testing the neutrality proposition with this method is identifying an exogenous change in the money supply in the VAR (recall from Empirical Study 8.1 that the error terms in the VAR are in general combinations of exogenous shocks to the variables in the VAR). One of the important contributions of the King and Watson study is that they considered the robustness of their tests for monetary neutrality to several alternative ways of identifying the exogenous monetary policy shock. They identified the exogenous money supply change both by imposing restrictions on the contemporaneous relationship between money and real output as well as by imposing long-run restrictions on the relationships between the two variables. In every case their results were consistent with long-run monetary neutrality in the United States during the post-World War II period. The robustness of this result in the face of several different methods of identification provides strong support for monetary neutrality.

## 13.6    Summary

This chapter has extended our analysis of floating exchange rate macroeconomics to the long run, which is characterized by a flexible domestic price level and full employment. In this context, shocks that affect the domestic goods market help to determine the long-run equilibrium real exchange rate. Such shocks include domestic fiscal policies, exogenous determinants of demand for the country's exports, and international financial conditions. Given the long-run equilibrium real exchange rate, the domestic price level is determined by the money market equilibrium condition – that is, it adjusts so as to equate the real supply of money with the real demand for money. Finally, the nominal exchange rate reconciles the equilibrium value of the real exchange rate with that of the domestic price level.

In this context, we also explored the determinants of the economy's long-run inflation rate. We saw that under a floating exchange rate, the money supply became the economy's nominal anchor, and the long-run inflation rate was determined by the rate of growth of the money supply, irrespective of the rate of inflation in the country's trading partners. In the long run, the floating exchange rate depreciates or appreciates at a rate that is just sufficient to reconcile domestic-foreign inflation differentials with a stable value of the long-run equilibrium real exchange rate.

We have now concluded our analysis of macroeconomics under floating exchange rates in a world in which prices are sticky in the short run, but flexible in the long run. However, as indicated in the introduction to this chapter, some economists believe that price level adjustment is much more rapid in practice than this framework suggests, so that a perspective in which prices are taken to be flexible even in the short run provides a better approximation to reality than the sticky-price view that we have developed so far. The next chapter explores the macroeconomics of floating exchange rates in this flexible-price context.

## Questions

1    In a floating exchange rate model in which the domestic price level is endogenous and output can deviate from its long-run full-employment value, explain what effect a permanent increase in the money supply would have on each of the following in both the short run and the long run:
    a  Domestic output.
    b  The domestic price level.
    c  The real exchange rate.
    d  The nominal exchange rate.
    e  The domestic interest rate.
2    Under what conditions would you expect the theory of purchasing power parity to provide a good approximation to the long-run equilibrium real exchange rate in a particular country?
3    During the 1990s the United States frequently exerted strong pressure on Japan to stimulate its economy. Japan is the largest trading partner of several countries in Southeast Asia. Assuming that the Japanese do succeed in expanding their economy, and do so with unchanged domestic interest rates, what effect would you expect this to have on the long-run equilibrium real exchange rates of their Southeast Asian trading

partners? Would you expect this effect to materialize through a change in the nominal exchange rate or the domestic price level in those countries? Why?

4   Consider an economy that is in long-run equilibrium with zero monetary growth. Now suppose that its rate of monetary growth increases to a new permanent value of 5 percent per year. After things have settled down and a new long-run equilibrium has been reached, explain how each of the following macro variables would be affected:

a   The real exchange rate.

b   The rate of depreciation of the nominal exchange rate.

c   The domestic rate of inflation.

d   The domestic nominal interest rate.

e   The domestic real interest rate.

5   In sorting out the reasons for Southeast Asia's financial crisis in 1997–8, analysts have been divided over the role that may have been played by real exchange rate overvaluation in the crisis countries – i.e., a value of the *actual* real exchange rate exchange rate that was significantly below the *long-run equilibrium* value of the real exchange rate. Suppose that you knew that the real exchange rate of Southeast Asian country X was equal to its long-run equilibrium value in 1990. Based on what you have learned in this chapter, how would you assess whether an overvaluation may have emerged by 1997?

6   Consider a small open economy that is highly averse to inflation, but whose trading partners all have relatively high rates of inflation. Would that economy be better off operating with a fixed or with a floating exchange rate regime? Explain.

7   "Uncovered interest parity implies that in long-run equilibrium expected *real* interest rates are equalized across countries, though *nominal* interest rates need not be." Comment.


## Further Reading and References

### On an empirical application of the long-run model to Canada

Bordo, Michael D. and Efsan U. Choudhri (1982), "The Link between Money and Prices in an Open Economy: The Canadian Evidence from 1971 to 1980," Federal Reserve Bank of St. Louis *Review* (August/September), pp. 13–23.

### On exchange rate depreciation and the domestic price level

Chang, Roberto (1995), "Is a Weak Dollar Inflationary?" Federal Reserve Bank of Atlanta *Economic Review* (September/October), pp. 1–14.

### On testing for long-run monetary neutrality

Bullard, James (1999), "Testing Long-Run Monetary Neutrality Propositions: Lessons from the Recent Research," Federal Reserve Bank of St. Louis *Review* (November/December), pp. 57–77.

King, Robert G. and Mark W. Watson (1997), "Testing Long-Run Neutrality," Federal Reserve Bank of Richmond *Economic Quarterly* (Summer), pp. 69–101.

## Box A13.1   The Log-linear Version of the Long-run Floating Rate Model

**Money market equilibrium**

$$m - p = c_0 - c_1 R + c_2 \bar{y} \qquad (A13.1)$$

**Domestic bond market equilibrium**

$$R = R^* + \left( s_{+1}^e - s \right) \qquad (A13.2)$$

**Goods market equilibrium**

$$\bar{y} = b_0 - b_1 r + b_2 g - b_3 t + b_4 q + b_5 \theta \qquad (A13.3)$$

**Definition of the real exchange rate**

$$q = s + p^* - p \qquad (A13.4)$$

**Definition of the real interest rate**

$$r = R - \left( p_{+1}^e - p \right) \qquad (A13.5)$$

## Appendix 13.1   The Long-run Floating Rate Model in Log-linear Form

In the text, the long-run floating rate model was solved graphically. To solve it algebraically, we need to work with the log-linear version of our model.[7] Recall that we derived the log-linear version of our analytical framework in Appendix (4.1). Box A13.1 derives the special case of this framework that is applicable to floating exchange rates in the long run, corresponding to Box 13.1 in the text.

To derive the compact form of the model, we begin by solving equation (A13.4) for $p$:

$$p = s + p^* - q \qquad (A13.4')$$

Next, to derive the asset market equilibrium condition, we substitute the UIP condition (A13.2) into the money-market equilibrium condition (A13.1). This gives us:

$$m - p = c_0 - c_1 \left[ R^* + \left( s_{+1}^e - s \right) \right] + c_2 \bar{y}$$

Using the definition of the real exchange rate (equation A13.4), we can write the asset market equilibrium condition as:

$$m - (s + p^* - q) = c_0 - c_1 \left[ R^* + \left( s_{+1}^e - s \right) \right] + c_2 \bar{y}$$

---

[7] Remember that we use lowercase letters to denote the logs of the corresponding ''level'' variables (e.g., $x = \log (X)$).

or:

$$m - (s + p^*) = c_0 - c_1[R^* + (s^e_{+1} - s)] + c_2\bar{y} - q \tag{A13.6}$$

This is the log-linear version of the asset market equilibrium condition that we used in the chapter.

To derive the goods market equilibrium condition, we begin by rewriting our equation for the real interest rate. Substituting equation (A13.2) into (A13.5):

$$r = R - (p^e_{+1} - p)$$
$$= \{R^* + (s^e_{+1} - s)\} - (p^e_{+1} - p)$$

Adding and subtracting $p^{*e}_{+1} - p^*$ from $R^*$ on the right-hand side yields:

$$r = \{R^* - (p^{*e}_{+1} - p^*)\} + (s^e_{+1} + p^{*e}_{+1} - p^e_{+1}) - (s + p^* - p)$$
$$= r^* + (q^e_{+1} - q)$$

where $r^*$ is the foreign real interest rate, given by $r^* = R^* - (p^{*e}_{+1} - p^*)$, and $q^e_{+1}$ is the (log of) the expected future real exchange rate, given by $q^e_{+1} = s^e_{+1} + p^{*e}_{+1} - p^e_{+1}$.

Substituting this expression into the goods market equilibrium condition (A13.3) produces the log-linear version of the goods market equilibrium condition:

$$\bar{y} = b_0 - b_1[r^* + (q^e_{+1} - q)] + b_2 g - b_3 t + b_4 q + b_5 \theta \tag{A13.7}$$

By imposing the long-run equilibrium conditions $q^e_{+1} - q = 0$ and $s^e_{+1} - s = 0$ we obtain the compact version of our log-linear model, shown in Box A13.2.

To solve the model, consider the goods-market equilibrium condition (A13.7′) first. Solving this equation for $q$, we have:

$$\bar{q} = (\bar{y} - b_0 + b_1 r^* - b_2 g + b_3 t - b_5 \theta)/b_4 \tag{A13.8}$$

This equation derives algebraically the results that we derived graphically in the text. Specifically, the long-run equilibrium real exchange rate appreciates when either domestic government spending or foreign demand for exports rises, and depreciates when the

---

## Box A13.2  Compact Version of the Log-linear Model

**Long-run asset market equilibrium**

$$m - (s + p^*) = c_0 - c_1 R^* + c_2 \bar{y} - q \tag{A13.6′}$$

**Long-run goods market equilibrium**

$$\bar{y} = b_0 - b_1 r^* + b_2 g - b_3 t + b_4 q + b_5 \theta \tag{A13.7′}$$

domestic natural level of output, the level of taxation, or the foreign (and domestic) real interest rate increases.

Now turn to the money market equilibrium condition. Notice that since we have already solved for $q$ in terms of the exogenous variables, we can treat $\bar{q}$ as exogenous in this equation. Solving it for $s$, given $\bar{q}$, we have:

$$s = m - p^* + \bar{q} - c_0 + c_1 R^* - c_2 \bar{y} \tag{A13.9}$$

based on equations (A13.8) and (A13.9), we can now derive the comparative static results of section 13.3:

1   Because $m$ does not appear in equation (A13.8) and appears in equation (A13.9) with a coefficient of 1, permanent changes in the money supply cause the domestic price level and nominal exchange rate to change in the same proportion, leaving all of the economy's real variables unchanged.

2   Because $p^*$ does not appear in equation (A13.8) and appears in equation (A13.9) with a coefficient of $-1$, permanent changes in the foreign price level give rise to changes in the nominal exchange rate that are equal in magnitude but opposite in sign, leaving the domestic price level and all domestic real variables unchanged.

3   Because $g$ and $\theta$ have negative coefficients in equation (A13.8), while $t$ has a positive coefficient, because none of these variables enter equation (A13.9) directly, and because $\bar{q}$ has a coefficient of 1 in equation (13.9), permanent increases in $g$ or $\theta$ will be associated with an appreciation, and permanent increases in $t$ with a depreciation, of the long-run equilibrium real exchange rate that is effected through changes in the nominal exchange rate, rather than through changes in the domestic price level.

4   Because $\bar{y}$ enters equation (A13.8) with a positive sign and equation (A13.9) with a negative one, a permanent increase in $\bar{y}$ will lower the domestic price level and cause the long-run equilibrium real exchange rate to depreciate, but its effect on the nominal exchange rate will be ambiguous (notice that $\bar{y}$ enters (A13.9) both directly as well as indirectly through $\bar{q}$).

5   Because $R^* = r^*$ enters both (A13.8) and (A13.9) with a positive sign, a permanent increase in the world interest rate will cause the long-run equilibrium real exchange rate to depreciate and the nominal exchange rate to depreciate more than proportionately, implying an increase in the domestic price level.

## Appendix 13.2   Fixed Exchange Rates in the Long Run

As we have seen in this chapter, our long-run floating-exchange rate model, expressed in log-linear form, could be summarized in the form of three equations:

$$\bar{y} = b_0 - b_1 \left[ r^* + \left( q^e_{+1} - q \right) \right] + b_2 g + b_3 t + b_4 q + b_5 \theta$$
$$m - (s + p^*) = c_0 - c_1 \left[ R^* + \left( s^e_{+1} - s \right) \right] + c_2 \bar{y} - \bar{q}$$
$$p = s + p^* - \bar{q}$$

How would the economy's long-run equilibrium differ if it maintained *fixed* exchange rates instead? Note first that since these equations were derived from our general analytical framework *before* imposing an exchange rate regime, they apply for fixed as well as for floating rates. The difference arises in the interpretation of the variables.

Consider what is exogenous and what is endogenous under fixed rates. Under fixed rates, we know that $s^e_{+1}$ and $s$ are exogenous, because $s$ is policy-determined, and under rational expectations we also know that $s^e_{+1} = s_{+1}$. On the other hand, as we have seen, the money supply becomes an endogenous variable under fixed rates. Finally, notice that unlike what is true in the short run, the real exchange rate $q$ is endogenous in the long run under fixed rates, because it depends on the domestic price level $p$, which we have seen to be endogenous in the long run.

Suppose, initially, that $s_{+1} = s$ – that is, the nominal exchange rate is literally kept fixed (unchanging) over time. Then the economy's long-run equilibrium under fixed exchange rates can be described by the equations:

$$\bar{y} = b_0 - b_1 R^* + b_2 g + b_3 t + b_4 q + b_5 \theta$$
$$m - (s + p^*) = c_0 - c_1 R^* + c_2 \bar{y} - \bar{q}$$
$$p = s + p^* - \bar{q}$$

with $\bar{q}$, $m$, and $p$ the endogenous variables. As with the floating rate model, this system is recursive. The goods market equilibrium condition determines the long-run equilibrium real exchange $\bar{q}$. Using the solution for $\bar{q}$, the money market equilibrium condition determines the long-run value of the domestic money supply $m$, and the third equation determines the price level.

Notice, however, that to solve for the price level in this model, we do not have to have previously solved the money market equilibrium condition, as we did in the floating-rate model. Instead, all we need to know to solve for the price level is the value of the long-run equilibrium real exchange rate $\bar{q}$. That, plus the policy-determined value of the nominal exchange rate and the exogenous foreign price level determine the domestic price level. Notice what this means:

1  Changes in the nominal exchange rate result in changes in the domestic price level in the same proportion – that is, the *nominal exchange rate* becomes the economy's nominal anchor under fixed exchange rates. This result underlies the common view that nominal exchange rate depreciation is inflationary. Box A13.3 explores this issue in more detail.
2  Changes in the foreign price level result in changes in the domestic price level in the same proportion. Thus, under fixed exchange rates there is no insulation from foreign price-level changes.

This has an important implication: under an exchange rate that is literally fixed, the long-run domestic inflation rate is given by:

$$\Delta p = \Delta p^*$$

In other words, the domestic economy imports the world rate of inflation.

The determination of the long-run equilibrium value of the domestic money supply is illustrated in Figure A13.1. The money market equilibrium condition can be depicted as a

## Box A13.3    Is Exchange Rate Depreciation Inflationary?

The analysis of the determinants of the long-run inflation rate in this chapter gives us the tools with which to analyze an issue that often concerns policymakers: whether a depreciation of the nominal exchange rate results in higher domestic inflation.

A first observation to make about this issue is that the question is not well posed. Under floating exchange rates and in the long run, both the exchange rate and the domestic price level are endogenous variables. Thus, movements in the nominal exchange rate and the price level both respond to changes in exogenous variables – i.e. to the variety of shocks the effects of which we have been analyzing in this chapter. Consequently, whether the nominal exchange rate and the price level move together in the long run (whether exchange rate depreciation is associated with a higher domestic price level) depends on the specific shock that is driving the changes in the two variables. For example, if exchange rate depreciation is driven by an increase in the domestic money supply, our model implies that we should expect to observe a depreciation of the nominal exchange rate and a higher domestic price level, leaving the real exchange rate unchanged. But if the shock driving exchange rate depreciation is a permanent contraction in world demand for the domestic good (that is, a decrease in $\theta$), then we would expect that the depreciation of the nominal exchange rate would *not* be associated with an increase in the domestic price level. In this case, the required depreciation of the real exchange rate is brought about by a nominal depreciation only.

An alternative way to pose the question under floating exchange rate is whether shocks originating in the foreign exchange market that result in nominal exchange rate depreciation (e.g., an exogenous increase in the risk premium on domestic assets, as considered in Chapter 6) tend to be associated with an increase in the domestic price level. Since this is equivalent to a positive $R^*$ shock, the analysis in Section 13.3 suggests an affirmative answer, but this is a far cry from saying that exchange rate depreciation is *in general* associated with an increase in domestic prices.

The question becomes more meaningful when applied to a fixed exchange rate economy, because in that case the nominal exchange rate is a policy variable, so it is at least possible to imagine an exogenous policy decision to devalue the exchange rate, possibly, say, to secure a competitive advantage for domestic exporters. But decisions to depreciate the currency are not always made in this way. Sometimes they are driven by a desire to adjust the real exchange rate in response to a real shock that causes the *equilibrium* value of the real exchange rate to depreciate. In this case, we also would not expect the domestic price level to increase, since under these circumstances the fixed exchange rate is simply mimicking what a floating exchange rate would do. It is only when a country undertakes an exogenous depreciation of a fixed nominal exchange rate by an amount that exceeds any change in the equilibrium real exchange rate that we would expect the domestic price level to increase as a *result* of the exchange rate policy, as shown in Appendix 13.2.

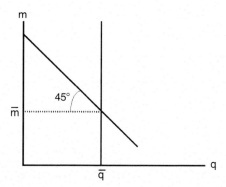

**Figure A13.1**   Long-run determination of the money supply under fixed exchange rates

straight line with slope equal to $-1$ in $m$-$q$ space, and the solution for $\bar{q}$ determined from the goods market picks out a point on this line that determines the long-run equilibrium value of $m$. Changes in variables that affect the demand for money shift the negatively sloped line vertically, thus altering the equilibrium value of the money supply at a given value of $\bar{q}$, while changes in $\bar{q}$ change the equilibrium value of $m$ by inducing movements along the negatively-sloped line.

    Based on what has been said so far, it is easy to see what would happen if, instead of being held constant, the exchange rate were to be depreciated by a constant proportional amount, say $x$ percent, each year. This is sometimes referred to as a *crawling peg*, as indicated in Box 13.6. This is analogous, under fixed exchange rates, to a constant proportionate change in the money supply under floating rates. As is true under floating rates, the long-run equilibrium real exchange rate $\bar{q}$ is unaffected, since the nominal exchange rate has no effect on the goods-market equilibrium condition. Taking first differences in the third equation above, we get:

$$\Delta p = \Delta s + \Delta p^*$$

It is easy to see from this expression that if the nominal exchange rate depreciates by $x$ percent per period, the domestic price level must increase by $x$ percent, as long as the foreign price level is constant. On the other hand, if the foreign price level is rising by $z$ percent simultaneously, the domestic price level will rise each period by $x + z$ percent. Thus, under a crawling peg the long-run domestic rate of inflation is equal to the sum of the rate of crawl of the exchange rate and the foreign rate of inflation. Finally, by taking first differences in the money-market equilibrium condition, we can verify that the money supply must also grow by $x + z$ percent under these circumstances.

# 14

# Floating Exchange Rates with Short-run Price Flexibility

..............................................................................................................................

Up until this point in the book, we have been working in a traditional Keynesian macroeconomic framework in which the price level is fixed in the short run, but flexible in the long run. Because the aggregate price level does not change in the short run, changes in the level of real output play an important role in the process through which the economy adjusts to shocks in such a framework. However, the economy's adjustment process changes over time. As time passes, the aggregate price level slowly begins to adjust, and the level of real output gradually returns to its natural level.

Just how long does the "short run" last in the real world, however? Over what time frame does it make sense to assume that changes in the aggregate price level do not play a part in the economy's initial adjustment to shocks? Unfortunately, this is a question to which there is no generally accepted answer. The speed with which the average price level responds to shocks in any given economy – that economy's **degree of short-run price flexibility** – is likely to depend on a wide variety of institutional factors and will thus be different across different economies and even for the same economy at different points in time. We have already seen, for example, that the degree of short-run price flexibility within the major trading economies that formed the core of the international gold standard during the late 19th century probably diminished substantially after World War I (Chapter 6). Moreover, the role that changes in the aggregate price level plays in short-run macroeconomic adjustment in industrial economies such as those of the United States and United Kingdom has been one of the key unresolved issues in macroeconomics for a very long time. For example, many economists believe, contrary to what we have been assuming so far, that price flexibility holds in the American economy not just in the long run, but in the short run as well.

If this is so, then the process through which the economy adjusts to shocks in the short run would be very different from what we have described so far. To see how, in this chapter we will revise the analysis of macroeconomic adjustment under floating exchange rates on the assumption that the price level can exhibit some short-run flexibility. We will begin by examining the implications of assuming that the price level is fully flexible in the short run. To do so, we will develop a flexible-price ("flexprice") model, and then study how the economy reacts to shocks under these circumstances. Rather than follow the step-by-step approach that has guided us so far in this part of the book, we will consider the effects of transitory, intermediate, and permanent shocks simultaneously. Next, as an application of our "flexprice" model, we will use the analytical tools developed in this chapter to study the dynamics of the transition from fixed to floating exchange rates in the context of a first-generation currency crisis. Finally, we will consider the more general case in which the price level is neither fixed nor fully flexible in the short run, but adjusts partially each period to its long-run equilibrium value. As you will see, the resulting analysis has much in common with the Dornbusch model of Chapter 12, even though we will not assume slow goods-market adjustment. In effect, gradual price-level adjustment will play the same role in driving the economy's dynamics.

You should be advised at this point that the material in this chapter is somewhat more technical that that in the chapters that precede this one. Specifically, in order to perform our analysis algebraically, in this chapter we will proceed as we did in Appendix 13.1, by focusing on the log-linear version of our model, and will do most of the analysis algebraically, rather than graphically. Thus, before proceeding you may want to review the properties of logs in Appendix 3.1 and the analysis of the log-linear version of the long-run floating exchange rate model in Appendix 13.1.

## 14.1   A "Flexprice" Model

Let us begin by adopting the assumption that prices are completely flexible in the short run and that output is exogenous. How would the analysis that we developed in previous chapters change? As just indicated, in order to combine the study of transitory, long-lasting, and permanent shocks into a single piece of analysis, we will use the log-linear version of our analytical framework to answer this question. In particular, we will rely on the floating exchange rate model with flexible prices that we derived in Appendix 13.1. The compact version of this model is presented in Box 14.1.

In the last chapter we noted that although this model consisted of only three equations, it contained five endogenous variables (the nominal exchange rate $s$, the real exchange rate $q$, the domestic price level $p$, the expected future nominal exchange rate $s_{+1}^e$, and the expected future real exchange rate $q_{+1}^e$). We thus needed additional restrictions to be able to solve the model. Because in Chapter 13 we were concerned with long-run equilibrium, we addressed this problem by imposing the conditions $s_{+1}^e = s$ and $q_{+1}^e = q$, which ensured that the economy was in a stable long-run equilibrium. Since the model of Chapter 13 is already a flexible-price model of the economy, the only difference between what we will be doing in this chapter and what we did in Chapter 13 concerns the additional restrictions that we will be imposing so that we can solve the model.

Before turning to these, note that the structure of the economy described in equations (14.1)–(14.3) is rather special, in the sense that the goods market equilibrium condition (14.2) contains a single endogenous variable (the real exchange rate $q$), the asset market

## Box 14.1    Compact Version of the Log-Linear Model

**Asset market equilibrium**

$$m - s = c_0 - c_1\left(R^* + s_{+1}^e - s\right) + c_2\bar{y} + p^* - q \tag{14.1}$$

**Goods market equilibrium**

$$\bar{y} = b_0 - b_1\left(r^* + q_{+1}^e - q\right) + b_2 g - b_3 t + b_4 q + b_5\theta \tag{14.2}$$

**Relationship between the price level and the real exchange rate**

$$p = s + p^* - q \tag{14.3}$$

equilibrium condition (14.1) contains two endogenous variables (the real and nominal exchange rates $q$ and $s$) and only the equation that links the price level to the real exchange rate (14.3) contains all three endogenous variables. This means that we can solve for the real exchange rate by using the goods market equilibrium condition, then use this result in the asset market equilibrium condition to find the equilibrium value of the nominal exchange rate, and finally use these equilibrium values of the real and nominal exchange rates to determine the price level from equation (14.3).

## 14.2    Real Exchange Rate Dynamics

Let us consider what goods market equilibrium implies about the equilibrium value of the real exchange rate $q$. Notice that though equation (14.2) contains neither $p$ nor $s$, it does contain both current and expected future $q$, that is, two unknowns in only one equation. How do we use the goods market equilibrium condition to solve for the real exchange rate under such circumstances? As indicated above, when we were interpreting the model above as a long-run model, we could do so by simply imposing the long-run equilibrium condition $q_{+1} - q = 0$. However, we can no longer do that automatically, because in the short run there is no presumption that the equilibrium value of $q$ must be unchanging from one period to the next.

We can begin by seeing what goods market equilibrium tells us about the factors that influence $q$. To find this out, we solve the goods market equilibrium condition for $q$:

$$q = [b_1/\ (b_1 + b_4)]q_{+1}^e + [\bar{y} - (b_0 - b_1 r^* + b_2 g - b_3\ t + b_5\theta)]/(b_1 + b_4)$$

You can see that not imposing $q_{+1}^e = q$ makes a difference. Since the expected future real exchange rate $q_{+1}^e$ is one of several variables that affect the current real exchange rate $q$ according to this equation, the model now implies that the current value of the real exchange rate will depend on its expected future value $q^e_{+1}$. This is a familiar situation that we encountered in the floating exchange rate models that we analyzed in Chapters 10–12. Just as in those chapters, to pin down the value of current real exchange rate under these circumstances we have to begin by taking a position about how people form their expectations of the future real exchange rate. As we have been doing throughout the book, we will solve the model under the familiar assumption of rational expectations, that is, that people use the model itself to form their expectations about the future value of the exchange rate. However, rather than deal with expectations of the future exchange rate as we did before – by distinguishing among transitory, intermediate, and permanent shocks and then analyzing the separate cases – this log-linear model is sufficiently simple that it is possible to solve for the general case in which shocks can be of any length and then analyze shocks of different duration as special cases.

To see how this is done, note that under the rational expectations assumption $q^e_{+1} = q_{+1}$, the previous equation can be written as:

$$q = [b_1/(b_1 + b_4)]q_{+1} + [b_4/(b_1 + b_4)]\Omega \tag{14.4}$$

where in addition to setting $q^e_{+1} = q_{+1}$, the notation $\Omega = [\bar{y} - (b_0 - b_1 r^* + b_2 g - b_3 t + b_5 \theta)]/b_4$ has been used to capture the joint influence on the real exchange rate of all of the variables that affect it other than its own expected future value. These are referred to as the real exchange rate's **fundamental determinants**, and we can simply refer to $\Omega$ as "the fundamentals." Notice that because all of the determinants of $\Omega$ are exogenous, $\Omega$ must be exogenous as well. Notice also that $\Omega$ looks very similar to the long-run equilibrium real exchange rate $\bar{q}$ that we derived in Chapter 13. But it is not the same, because in the present short-run context the components of $\Omega$ – that is, the natural level of output $\bar{y}$, the world real interest rate $r^*$, the levels of government spending and taxation $g$ and $t$, and the exogenous component of foreign demand for domestic goods $\theta$ – could be changing over time. Notice, though, that if we held these variables constant and set $q_{+1} = q$, then we would indeed get $q = \bar{q} = \Omega$, as you can easily verify for yourself.

As we have just seen, equation (14.4) tells us that in order to know the equilibrium value of this period's real exchange rate we have to know the value of next period's real exchange rate – that is, of $q_{+1}$. But under rational expectations, it also tells us how to find $q_{+1}$. If $q$ must satisfy equation (14.4), then it follows that $q_{+1}$ must satisfy the next-period value of the same equation. That is, $q_{+1}$ must be given by:

$$q_{+1} = [b_1/(b_1 + b_4)]q_{+2} + [b_4/(b_1 + b_4)]\Omega_{+1} \tag{14.5}$$

Unfortunately, while this does tell us what determines $q_{+1}$, it does so only by introducing a new endogenous variable, $q_{+2}$. You can see what the pattern is: what happened in the first period must happen in every future period, so in order to know each period's value of the real exchange rate, we have to know that of the next period.

How do we deal with this problem? Suppose that we repeat the exercise for $q_{+2}$. Our model implies:

$$q_{+2} = [b_1/(b_1 + b_4)]q_{+3} + [b_4/(b_1 + b_4)]\Omega_{+2}$$

Now let's substitute this value of $q_{+2}$ into our solution for $q_{+1}$ in equation (14.5). This gives us:

$$q_{+1} = [b_1/(b_1 + b_4)]^2 q_{+3} + [b_4/(b_1 + b_4)]\{\Omega_{+1} + [b_1/(b_1 + b_4)]\Omega_{+2}\} \qquad (14.6)$$

We could then proceed to solve for $q_{+3}$ and substitute the result in (14.6), but you can probably see what would happen if we kept doing this over and over again. After substituting $N - 1$ times we would have:

$$q_{+1} = [b_1/(b_1 + b_4)]^N q_{N+1} + [b_4/(b_1 + b_4)] \sum_{j=1}^{N} [b_1/(b_1 + b_4)]^{j-1} \Omega_{+j}\}$$

Finally, if we did this an *infinite* number of times, we would have:

$$q_{+1} = [b_4/(b_1 + b_4)] \sum_{j=1}^{\infty} [b_1/(b_1 + b_4)]^{j-1} \Omega_j + \lim_{N \to \infty} [b_1/(b_1 + b_4)]^N q_{N+1}.$$

Thus, next period's value of the real exchange rate depends on *all* of the expected future values of the fundamentals, as well as on a future real exchange rate expectation. But the effects on the real exchange rate of the future fundamentals, as well as of the future exchange rate expectation, become weaker the further ahead we go in time. The reason is that in each period changes in the expected future real exchange rate have a less-than-proportionate effect on the current real exchange rate, as shown in equation (14.4).

The last term in the previous equation is referred to as the **bubble** term. It captures the possible influence of "rational bubbles" on the real exchange rate – that is, it reflects the fact that the real exchange rate may be relatively depreciated today simply because it is expected to depreciate further in the future. But remember that the influence of future real exchange rate expectations becomes weaker the further ahead they are in time. That means that, for the real exchange rate that is expected to prevail very far in the future to have an important effect on the *current* value of the real exchange rate, the real exchange rate would have to be expected to depreciate at a very fast rate indeed – at least by $(b_1 + b_4)/b_1$ percent per period. Otherwise the bubble term would eventually approach zero and have an imperceptible effect on the current real exchange rate. Though we cannot rule out that such explosive behavior of expectations would happen, we shall proceed by ruling out rational bubbles.[1] In that case, the bubble term must be zero and we must have:

$$q_{+1} = [b_4/(b_1 + b_4)] \sum_{j=1}^{\infty} [b_1/(b_1 + b_4)]^{j-1} \Omega_j$$
$$= \sum_{j=1}^{\infty} [b_1/(b_1 + b_4)]^{j-1} \{[b_4/(b_1 + b_4)]\Omega_j\}$$

To complete our analysis of the determinants of the equilibrium real exchange rate, we can now substitute this expression for the expected future value of the real exchange rate into (14.4):

---

[1]    This is essentially the short-run counterpart of the long-run assumption that $q^e_{+1} = q$. It rules out self-fulfilling explosive behavior.

$$q = [b_4/(b_1 + b_4)]\Omega + [b_1/(b_1 + b_4)] \sum_{j=1}^{\infty} [b_1/(b_1 + b_4)]^{j-1} \{[b_4/(b_1 + b_4)]\Omega_j\}$$

$$= [b_4/(b_1 + b_4)]\Omega + \sum_{j=1}^{\infty} [b_1/(b_1 + b_4)]^{j} \{[b_4/(b_1 + b_4)]\Omega_j\}$$

$$= \sum_{j=0}^{\infty} [b_1/(b_1 + b_4)]^{j} \{[b_4/(b_1 + b_4)]\Omega_j$$

$$= [b_4/(b_1 + b_4)] \sum_{j=0}^{\infty} [b_1/(b_1 + b_4)]^{j} \Omega_j \tag{14.8}$$

Thus, in our flexible-price model, the equilibrium real exchange rate depends on the current and all of the expected future values of the fundamentals. To gain some intuition for this solution, let us consider what our model implies about how the real exchange rate responds to the three types of shocks that we have previously considered: permanent shocks, transitory shocks, and shocks of intermediate duration. Since only shocks that affect the goods market will affect the real exchange rate, we will continue to refer to these as "real" shocks.

## Permanent Real Shocks

Suppose that $\Omega$ is constant over time, so that any shocks affecting the goods market, such as a change in the economy's natural level of output $\bar{y}$, are permanent. In this situation, we must have $\Omega_j = \Omega'$, where $\Omega'$, is the "shocked" value of the fundamentals, for all values of $j$ (that is, for the current period as well as for all future periods) and (14.8) would then become:

$$q = [b_4/(b_1 + b_4)] \sum_{j=0}^{\infty} [b_1/(b_1 + b_4)]^{j} \Omega'$$

$$= [b_4/(b_1 + b_4)]\Omega' \sum_{j=0}^{\infty} [b_1/(b_1 + b_4)]^{j}$$

$$= [b_4/(b_1 + b_4)]\Omega'(b_1 + b_4)/b_4$$

$$= \Omega' = \bar{q}.$$

Thus, when the fundamentals take on their permanent values from the initial period on, the solution for the real exchange rate is exactly what we would expect: it is equal to the long-run equilibrium real exchange rate from Chapter 13. In this case, the properties of the long-run equilibrium real exchange rate that we investigated in Chapter 13 apply in the short run as well.

*Transitory real shocks* Now suppose that shocks to the goods market last for a single period, as in the "transitory shock" model of Chapter 10. For example, suppose there is a transitory change in the world real interest rate. In that case we will have $\Omega_0 = \Omega'$, but $\Omega_j = \Omega$ for all $j > 0$. That is, only the current period's value of the fundamentals is affected by the shock. The fundamentals are unchanged in all future periods. Because this means that the long-run equilibrium real exchange rate will be attained in the next period, we must have $q_{+1} = \bar{q} = \Omega$. Thus, from equation (14.4):

$$q = [b_4/(b_1 + b_4)]\Omega' + [b_1/(b_1 + b_4)]\Omega \tag{14.9}$$

Notice what this implies: this period's real exchange rate $q$ is a weighted average of the long-run equilibrium real exchange rate $\bar{q} = \Omega$ and this period's value of the fundamentals $\Omega'$. Thus, transitory real shocks captured in $\Omega'$ will in general have *weaker* effects (because $b_4/(b_1 + b_4) < 1$) on the short-run equilibrium value of the real exchange rate than will permanent ones. As you will recall, this is consistent with what we found for the fixed-price model in Chapter 11.

*Intermediate real shocks*    Finally, let us consider the case of real shocks that are expected to be of intermediate duration. For concreteness, suppose that the shock, say an increase in government spending, arrives in the first period (period zero) and is expected to last for $T$ periods. In this case, we have $\Omega_j = \Omega'$ for $j = 0 \ldots T$, but $\Omega_j = \Omega$ for $j = T + 1$ on.

As a first step in investigating what happens in this case, notice that we can write (14.8) as:

$$q = [b_4/(b_1 + b_4)]\left\{\sum_{j=0}^{T} [b_1/(b_1 + b_4)]^j \Omega_j + \sum_{j=T+1}^{\infty} [b_1/(b_1 + b_4)]^j \Omega_j\right\}$$

That is, we have split up the infinite sum that captures the effects of current and all future fundamentals on the current real exchange rate into the effects of fundamentals from the present until time $T$ and the effects of those from time $T + 1$ on. Using $\Omega_j = \Omega'$ for $j = 1 \ldots T$, and $\Omega_j = \Omega$ for $j = T + 1$ to infinity, we have:

$$q = [b_4/(b_1 + b_4)]\left\{\Omega' \sum_{j=0}^{T} [b_1/(b_1 + b_4)]^j + \Omega \sum_{j=T+1}^{\infty} [b_1/(b_1 + b_4)]^j\right\}$$

Next, we can factor out $[b_1/(b_1 + b_4)]^{T+1}$ from the second summation. This leaves:

$$q = [b_4/(b_1 + b_4)]\left\{\Omega' \sum_{j=0}^{T} [b_1/(b_1 + b_4)]^j + [b_1/(b_1 + b_4)]^{T+1} \Omega \sum_{j=0}^{\infty} [b_1/(b_1 + b_4)]^j\right\}$$

which is equivalent to:

$$q = [b_4/(b_1 + b_4)]\{[(1 - [b_1/(b_1 + b_4)]^{T+1})\, (b_1 + b_4)/b_4)\Omega'.$$
$$+ [b_1/(b_1 + b_4)]^{T+1}(b_1 + b_4/b_4)\Omega\}^2$$
$$= [(1 - [b_1/(b_1 + b_4)]^{T+1}\Omega' + [b_1/(b_1 + b_4)]^{T+1}\Omega \qquad (14.10)$$

Notice what this means. The equilibrium real exchange rate in period zero is a weighted average of the fundamentals that prevail from period zero to period $T$ and those that prevail from period $T + 1$ on. If the shock is a transitory one, so $T = 0$ (the shock is only in place in period zero, the initial period), then equation (14.10) becomes:

$$q = [1 - b_1/(b_1 + b_4)]\Omega' + [b_1/(b_1 + b_4)]\Omega$$
$$q = [b_4/(b_1 + b_4)]\Omega' + [b_1/(b_1 + b_4)]\Omega$$

[2]    Recall that the infinite series $1 + a^2 + a^3 + \ldots$, where $a$ is a fraction, sums to $1/(1 - a)$, and the first $N$ terms of the series sum to $(1 - a^{N+1})/(1 - a)$.

which is identical to equation (14.9). On the other hand, if the shock is permanent, so $T$ goes to infinity, we can see from equation (14.10) that the equilibrium value of the real exchange rate must be $q = \Omega'$, as we found previously. For shocks of intermediate duration, the impact of the "shocked" fundamentals $\Omega'$ on the real exchange rate will be larger the longer the shock is expected to last. Again, this is consistent with our results under fixed prices in Chapter 11.

## 14.3   The Monetary Approach to the Exchange Rate

Having explained the behavior of the real exchange rate, we can now turn to explaining that of the nominal exchange rate. As it turns out, the approach to explaining nominal exchange rate behavior that we will develop in this section happens to be a venerable one in international monetary economics. It is called the **monetary approach to the exchange rate**.

Just as in the last chapter, the first step in solving for the exchange rate in our flexible-price model is to substitute the solution for the real exchange rate $q$ into the money market equilibrium condition to derive:

$$m - s = c_0 - c_1\left[R^* + \left(s^e_{+1} - s\right)\right] + c_2\bar{y} + p^* - q$$

To keep the notation simple, we can write this as:

$$m - s = \gamma - c_1\left(s^e_{+1} - s\right)$$

where $\gamma = c_0 - c_1 R^* + c_2\bar{y} + p^* - q$ is a catch-all exogenous variable (remember that the behavior of the real exchange rate $q$ is determined independently of what happens in the money market) that captures the influences of the constant and the exogenous variables on the asset market. In other words, it is the counterpart in the money market of the variable $\Omega$ that we previously introduced in the goods market. We can rewrite this equation as:

$$m = s + \gamma - c_1\left(s^e_{+1} - s\right)$$

The left-hand side of this new equation is just the nominal supply of money, while the right-hand side is the nominal demand for money. Notice that the exchange rate $s$ affects the nominal demand for money in two ways: an increase in $s$ increases the price level, and thus increases the demand for money through that channel (the first term on the right-hand side of the equation) while, given $s^e_{+1}$, it also reduces the expected rate of depreciation of the domestic currency, thus lowering the domestic interest rate and increasing the demand for money through that channel as well (the third term on the right-hand side).[3] A 1 percent increase in $s$ increases the demand for money by $1 + c_1$ percent, the sum of both effects.

---

[3]   How do we know that an increase in $s$ increases the price level? Remember that the real exchange rate is determined in the goods market, so it is not affected by a change in $s$. Since $p^*$ is exogenous, equation (14.3) tells us that a 1 percent change in $s$ leads to a 1 percent change in the domestic price level.

## Solving for the nominal exchange rate

The previous equation can be solved for the nominal exchange rate $s$ as follows:

$$s = [c_1/(1+c_1)]s^e_{+1} + [1/(1+c_1)](m-\gamma) \tag{14.11}$$

Notice that, just as we discovered when we were solving for the real exchange rate, this is not a full-fledged solution for the nominal exchange rate, because this equation contains the endogenous variable $s^e_{+1}$ on the right-hand side. Again, we need to assume something about what determines $s^e_{+1}$. Proceeding as before, note that under our usual assumption of rational expectations, $s^e_{+1} = s_{+1}$, where the value of $s_{+1}$ is that predicted by the model itself. According to the model (that is, using equation 14.11) the future value of $s$ must be given by:

$$s_{+1} = [c_1/(1+c_1)]s_{+2} + [1/(1+c_1)](m_{+1} - \gamma_{+1}) \tag{14.12}$$

To remove the expected value of the exchange rate two periods ahead, we can "lead" this equation forward one period, giving:

$$s_{+2} = [c_1/(1+c_1)]s_{+3} + [1/(1+c_1)](m_{+2} - \gamma_{+2})$$

which can be substituted for $s_{+2}$ in equation (14.12). The result is:

$$s_{+1} = [c_1/(1+c_1)]^2 s_{+3} + [1/(1+c_1)]\{(m_{+1} - \gamma_{+1}) + [c_1/(1+c_1)](m_{+2} - \gamma_{+2})\}$$

Repeating this procedure an infinite number of times, as in the last section, we finally come up with:

$$s_{+1} = [1/(1+c_1)] \sum_{j=0}^{\infty} [c_1/(1+c_1)]^j \{(m_{j+1} - \gamma_{\varphi+1}) + \lim_{N \to \infty} [c_1/(1+c_1)]^N s_{N+1}$$

$$= [1/(1+c_1)] \sum_{j=0}^{\infty} [c_1/(1+c_1)]^j \{(m_{j+1} - \gamma_{j+1})\}$$

if we rule out "rational bubbles," as we did before.

By substituting this result into equation (14.11), we can write down the complete solution for the nominal exchange rate as:

$$s = [1/(1+c_1)](m-\gamma) + [c_1/(1+c_1)]\{[1/(1+c_1)] \sum_{j=0}^{\infty} [c_1/(1+c_1)]^j$$

$$\times \{(m_{j+1} - \gamma_{j+1})\}$$

where the expression in curly brackets represents the expected future exchange rate.

Some Special Cases

The solution for the exchange rate that we just derived is a general one, but it is one that is hard to interpret directly and compare with our previous results. To gain some insight into how floating exchange rates work under flexible prices, therefore, it is useful to consider some special cases that allow us to simplify the solution for the nominal exchange rate.

*Constant future money supply*   Suppose, for example, that the paths of the money supply and $\gamma$ are expected to be constant over time at the value that they are expected to take on *next* period – that is, $m_{j+1} = m_{+1}$ and $\gamma_{j+1} = \gamma_{+1}$. The solution for $s_{+1}$ then becomes:

$$s_{+1} = [1/(1 + c_1)] \sum_{j=0}^{\infty} [c_1/(1 + c_1)]^j (m_{+1} - \gamma_{+1})$$

which, since the $(m_{+1} - \gamma_{+1})$ term can be factored out of the summation sign, can be written as:

$$s_{+1} = (m_{+1} - \gamma_{+1})/(1 + c_1)\{1/[1 - c_1/(1 + c_1)]\}$$

or:

$$s_{+1} = (m_{+1} - \gamma_{+1})$$

Substituting this solution for the expected future value of $s$ in equation (14.11), we thus have:

$$s = [c_1/(1 + c_1)](m_{+1} - \gamma_{+1}) + [1/(1 + c_1)](m - \gamma)$$

This has the following implications:

1   *Permanent changes in the money supply change the exchange rate in the same proportion as the change in the money supply.*
   Notice that this must be so because $m_{+1}$ and $m$ are both changed by the same amount in the equation above and everything else is held constant, so that the change in $s$ is given by:

$$\Delta s = [c_1/(1 + c_1)]\Delta m + [1/(1 + c_1)]\Delta m$$
$$= \Delta m$$

where the symbol $\Delta$ denotes a change in a variable from one period to the next.

2   *Transitory changes in the money supply cause the exchange rate to depreciate* less than in proportion *to the change in the money supply.*
   This is so because only $m$, and not $m_{j+1}$ changes in this case. Thus the change in the exchange rate is given by:

$$\Delta s = [1/(1 + c_1)]\Delta m$$

3   *Expected* future *changes in the money supply change the exchange rate less than in proportion to the change in the money supply.*

In this case, only $m_{+1}$ changes, and not $m$, so the change in the exchange rate is:

$$\Delta s = [c_1/(1 + c_1)]\Delta m_{+1}$$

What is the rationale behind these results? Notice first that changes in $m - \gamma$ do not cause one-for-one changes in the exchange rate because, as we saw above, an increase in $s$ reduces the excess supply of money in two ways: First, an increase in $s$ increases the price level, and thus lowers the real supply of money. Second, for a given value of $s_{+1}$, an increase in $s$ lowers the domestic interest rate (which depends on $s_{+1} - s$), thereby increasing the demand for money by the amount $c_1$. Thus, the total effect of an increase in $s$ is to lower the excess supply of money by $1 + c_1$.

An increase in the money supply that is expected to be permanent increases the excess supply of money today by an amount equal to the change in $m$, and also increases $s_{+1}$ by the same amount. The excess supply of money thus increases by $1 + c_1$ times the increase in $m$. Since an exactly equal increase in $s$ reduces the excess supply by exactly $1 + c_1$ per unit, an equal increase in $s$ is what is required. On the other hand, in the case of a transitory increase in $m$, there is no change in $s_{+1}^e$ (since the change in money demand is by assumption transitory), so all that is required is a reduction in $s$ equal to $1/1 + c_1$ times the change in $m$.

What about the expected *future* increase in $m$? All effects operate through $s_{+1}$, which increases one for one with the expected future change in $m$. Thus, an excess supply of money equal to $c_1 \Delta m$ is created, where $\Delta m$ is the expected future increase in $m$. What is happening is that with the money supply expected to be larger in the future, $s$ is expected to depreciate in the future. This raises the domestic nominal interest rate by $\Delta m$ today, lowering the demand for money today by $c_1 \Delta m$ and thus creating an excess supply of money of the same magnitude. The necessary change in $s$ is $1/1 + c_1$ times this, so the change in $s$ today is:

$$\Delta s = (c_1/1 + c_1)\Delta m$$

as derived above.

*Constant money supply growth*   Let us assume that instead of being constant over time from the next period on, the money supply is expected to grow by $x$ percent each period, and let us hold the factors determining $\gamma$ constant at their current period values. What happens to the exchange rate in this case?

Recall first that:

$$s_{+1} = [1/(1 + c_1)] \sum_{j=0}^{\infty} [c_1/(1 + c_1)]^j (m_{j+1} - \gamma_{j+1})$$

With $\gamma$ constant over time, this becomes:

$$s_{+1} = [1/(1 + c_1)] \sum_{j=0}^{\infty} [c_1/(1 + c_1)]^j (m_{j+1} - \gamma)$$

which simplifies to:

$$s_{+1} = \left\{ [1/(1+c_1)] \sum_{j=0}^{\infty} [c_1/(1+c_1)]^j m_{j+1} \right\} - \gamma$$

By analogy with this expression, it is easy to see that the exchange rate expected to prevail *two* periods ahead must be given by:

$$s_{+2} = \left\{ [1/(1+c_1)] \sum_{j=0}^{\infty} [c_1/(1+c_1)]^j m_{j+2} \right\} - \gamma$$

The expected rate of depreciation of the currency from period 1 to period 2 must therefore be:

$$
\begin{aligned}
s_{+2} - s_{+1} &= [1/(1+c_1)] \left\{ \sum_{j=0}^{\infty} [c_1/(1+c_1)]^j m_{j+2} - \sum_{j=0}^{\infty} [c_1/(1+c_1)]^j m_{j+1} \right\} \\
&= [1/(1+c_1)] \left\{ m_{+2} + [c_1/(1+c_1)]m_{j+3} + [c_1/(1+c_1)]^2 m_{j+4} + \ldots \right. \\
&\quad - m_{+1} - [c_1/(1+c_1)]m_{j+2} - [c_1/(1+c_1)]^2 m_{j+3} - \ldots \left. \right\} \\
&= [1/(1+c_1)] \left\{ (m_{+2} - m_{+1}) + [c_1/(1+c_1)](m_{j+3} - m_{j+2}) \right. \\
&\quad + [c_1/(1+c_1)]^2 (m_{j+4} - m_{j+3}) + \ldots \left. \right\} \\
&= x[1/(1+c_1)] \sum_{j=0}^{\infty} [c_1/(1+c_1)]^j = x
\end{aligned}
$$

Thus, from period 1 to period 2, the currency is expected to depreciate by $x$. Note that since the same exercise could be conducted from period 2 to period 3 and for all subsequent future periods, the currency must be expected to depreciate by $x$ percent per period for all future periods as well.

Now consider what this means about the exchange rate in period 1. Recall the money market equilibrium condition:

$$m = s + \gamma - c_1 \left( s_{+1}^e - s \right)$$

In period 1, this must take the form:

$$m_{+1} = s_{+1} + \gamma - c_1 (s_{+2} - s_{+1})$$

or:

$$m_{+1} = s_{+1} + \gamma - c_1 x$$

using what we just learned about the expected rate of depreciation of the currency from period 1 to period 2. This means that the expected value of the exchange rate next period must be:

$$s_{+1} = m_{+1} - \gamma + c_1 x$$

Finally, remember the expression that we previously derived for $s$ (equation 14.12):

$$s = [c_1/(1 + c_1)]s^e_{+1} + [1/(1 + c_1)](m - \gamma)$$

Substituting for $s^e_{+1}$ in this expression, we have:

$$s = [c_1/(1 + c_1)](m_{+1} - \gamma + c_1 x) + [1/(1 + c_1)](m - \gamma)$$

But since $m_{+1} = m + x$, this can be simplified to:

$$\begin{aligned} s &= [c_1/(1 + c_1)][m - \gamma + (1 + c_1)x] + [1/(1 + c_1)](m - \gamma) \\ &= m - \gamma + c_1 x \end{aligned} \tag{14.13}$$

What this expression says is that, relative to a situation in which $m$ and $\gamma$ are always at their permanent values, a constant rate of future monetary growth of $x$ percent causes today's exchange rate to depreciate by $c_1 x$ percent.

What are the economics underlying this result? The answer is that if the money supply grows by $x$ percent each period, an $x$ percent rate of depreciation of the currency would maintain equilibrium in the money market because, given that the real exchange rate is constant, it would cause the price level to rise by $x$ percent each period and thus keep the real money supply constant. Since the exchange rate is depreciating by $x$ percent per year, the domestic nominal interest rate must be equal to $(R^* + x)$ percent. This would reduce the equilibrium value of the real money supply by $c_1 x$ percent relative to a zero money growth situation. Given the initial nominal money stock, to achieve a reduction in the real money supply by $c_1 x$ percent requires the exchange rate to depreciate by $c_1 x$ percent. Thus, from a position of zero money supply growth and thus zero inflation, a change in monetary policy to one of constant $x$ percent money supply growth would cause the domestic nominal interest rate to jump from $R^*$ to $R^* + x$ percent, and would cause the nominal exchange rate to immediately depreciate by $c_1 x$ percent.

## 14.4   Currency Crises Revisited

What we have learned about how floating exchange rates work under flexible prices permits us to shed a different light on the mechanics of currency crises under soft pegs that we reviewed in Chapter 9. Recall the basic situation in "first-generation" crisis models: with fixed exchange rates and perfect capital mobility, the domestic interest rate is equal to the foreign rate $R^*$. Monetary policy is powerless to affect the real economy, since any expansion of the money supply caused by an open market bond purchase by the central bank is immediately offset by an exactly equal capital outflow. Suppose that the central bank, in order to finance a fiscal deficit, expands its holding of government bonds at a constant rate of $x$ percent per period. We saw in Chapter 9 that such a monetary policy is inconsistent with the maintenance of a fixed exchange rate, and would eventually mean the end of the exchange rate peg, because the central bank must eventually run out of reserves.

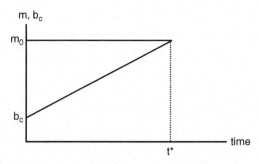

**Figure 14.1**   "Slow death" of an exchange rate peg in a "first-generation" currency crisis model

The dynamics as we described them were as shown in Figure 14.1, which reproduces Figure 9.5.[4] The stock of bonds in the central bank's hands, $b_C$, increases steadily at the rate $x$. The stock of foreign exchange reserves is the vertical distance between $b_C$ and the money supply $m$. As $b_C$ increases, reserves fall, until at time $t^*$, the stock of reserves is depleted and the fixed exchange rate can no longer be sustained.

In reality, however, fixed exchange rate regimes do not tend to end in this way. Rather than a slow, gradual depletion of reserves, it is more likely that the reserve stock would be depleted all at once by a sudden speculative attack that would immediately force the adoption of a floating exchange rate. In other words, fixed exchange rates in first-generation currency crisis models tend to end with a bang rather than a whimper. The analysis of why this might be so was first formulated by Krugman (1979), and it is useful to examine it here because it relates the analysis of continuous monetary expansion under fixed exchange rates in Chapter 9 to that of the same monetary policy under floating exchange rates that we have conducted in this chapter.

Consider first what would happen in the "slow death" scenario once the economy reaches $t^*$. At that point, since there are no more foreign exchange reserves in the central bank's coffers, three things must happen:

1   Because it can no longer defend an officially announced exchange rate, the central bank must abandon the fixed exchange rate and allow the exchange rate to be determined by the market, that is, it must adopt a floating exchange rate. This means that at time $t^*$ the economy must suddenly switch from behaving like a fixed exchange rate economy such as that described in Chapter 9 to behaving like the floating exchange rate economy described in this chapter.
2   When the central bank's stock of foreign exchange reserves is depleted, the money supply must equal the stock of domestic bonds, that is, $m = b_C$. Moreover, from that moment on, the money supply must always equal the central bank's stock of domestic bonds, since under the floating exchange rate the central bank does not hold any foreign exchange reserves.
3   Recall that what actually doomed the fixed exchange rate in the first generation crisis model of Chapter 9 was the central bank's exercising its monetary policy discretion by increasing its bond holdings by $x$ percent each period so as to finance its fiscal deficit.

[4]   The money supply and stock of bonds held by the central bank are written in lowercase letters in Figure 14.5, because in this chapter we are working with these variables in log form.

Presumably it would continue to do so after the switch to a floating exchange rate. That means that from the instant the reserve stock is depleted onward, the money supply must begin to grow at the rate of $x$ percent per period, because under floating exchange rates there is no reserve-depletion offset to the accumulation of domestic bonds in the central bank's balance sheet.

The bottom line is that at the instant that the central bank is forced to adopt a floating exchange rate by the depletion of its reserves, the economy immediately switches to a floating exchange rate with constant money supply growth of $x$ percent per year – that is, to a situation described by the model that we analyzed in the last section.

What happens to the exchange rate at this point, compared to the fixed exchange rate that prevailed before the switch in exchange rate regimes? To answer this question, notice that, since the money market was in equilibrium under fixed exchange rates, the fixed exchange rate (call it $\bar{s}$) must have satisfied the asset market equilibrium condition:

$$m = \bar{s} + \gamma - c_1(s_{+1} - s)$$

Notice also that, as long as the fixed exchange rate was expected to persist, we must also have had $s_{+1} - \bar{s} = 0$, which means that $\bar{s}$ must have been given by:

$$\bar{s} = \bar{m} - \gamma$$

where $\bar{m}$ is the unchanging money supply from Figure 14.1. (Recall that the money supply was unchanging under fixed rates because reserve depletion caused by capital outflows offset bond accumulation in the central bank's balance sheet.) As soon as the switch to a floating rate happens, the result of the last section tells us that the new floating exchange rate must be given by:

$$s = \bar{m} - \gamma + c_1 x$$
$$= \bar{s} + c_1 x$$

What this means is that if the fixed rate lasts until time $t^*$, at the instant when it is abandoned, the new floating rate must jump up (depreciate discontinuously) by the amount $c_1 x$. In other words, if the depletion of reserves takes place through the "slow death" route at time $t^*$, it will be accompanied by a sudden and sharp depreciation of the currency by the amount $c_1 x$ relative to its old fixed level.

Is such an outcome consistent with rational, profit-maximizing behavior on the part of informed economic agents? The answer must be no, because the anticipated depreciation of the currency means that anyone who is holding assets denominated in domestic currency (money or bonds) at time $t^*$ will incur a capital loss that they could easily have avoided (if they understood the model!) by simply selling those assets just before $t^*$. The important implication is this: the anticipation of a sudden, discrete change in the exchange rate creates an incentive for informed economic agents to switch out of domestic-currency bonds and into foreign-currency bonds just before that discrete change takes place. Such sudden switches in portfolios away from domestic and into foreign assets are called speculative attacks, as we saw in Chapter 9, and what we have just seen is that any time that an upward jump in the exchange rate is anticipated, a speculative attack can be expected to precede it.

## Box 14.2    The 1997 Speculative Attack on the Thai Baht and the Asian Crisis

Speculative attacks on fixed exchange rates are not uncommon events. When such attacks are sufficiently strong, they can force the country's central bank to stop defending the exchange rate peg, and cause a transition to a floating exchange rate, as in the model described in this section. Such an attack took place in Thailand during the first half of 1997, triggering a series of events that resulted in widespread currency crises throughout East and Southeast Asia, commonly referred to as the Asian financial crisis (Box 9.4).

For the decade and a half before 1997, Thailand had gone through a period of very rapid economic growth, fueled by a rapid expansion of exports that was facilitated by a relatively depreciated real exchange rate. The latter was in part achieved by keeping the nominal exchange rate of the Thai currency, the baht, stable against the US dollar, which had been depreciating against the currencies of Thailand's other trading partners. But a series of events in the mid-1990s, featuring especially an appreciation of the US dollar against the Japanese yen, caused Thailand's real exchange rate to begin to appreciate, contributing to a sharp slowdown in the growth of the country's exports. This caused international capital markets to begin to expect a devaluation of the baht against the US dollar, triggering capital outflows from Thailand.

As these outflows began to take their toll on Thai foreign exchange reserves during late 1996, devaluation expectations strengthened and capital outflows became a full-blown speculative attack in the spring of 1997. Figure 14.2 provides a crude indication of how a speculative attack can cause a sharp break in the time series of a country's foreign exchange reserves. It shows the *gross* foreign exchange reserves of the Bank of Thailand (the bank's US dollar assets), which fell by more than a quarter from 1996 to 1997. The collapse in the Bank's *net* foreign exchange reserves (US dollar assets less US dollar liabilities) was even more dramatic. Indeed, by July 2, 1997, the Bank of Thailand had essentially exhausted its net foreign exchange reserves, so it abandoned the attempt to stabilize the baht-dollar rate and allowed the currency to float. As we saw in Box 9.4, this triggered a series of speculative attacks on other countries in the region, initially including Indonesia, Malaysia and the Philippines, but subsequently spreading to Taiwan, Singapore, Hong Kong, and Korea. By the end of 1997, not only Thailand, but also Indonesia, Korea, Malaysia, and the Philippines had all floated their currencies.

Box 14.2 describes such an attack on the foreign exchange reserves of Thailand during the 1997–8 Asian financial crisis.

How large must such a speculative attack be? The answer is that if an attack takes place – that is, if the exchange rate would undergo a discrete devaluation in the absence of an attack – then the attack must be large enough to take away all of the central bank's reserves. The reason is that if this weren't so, someone would be passing up the opportunity to buy foreign exchange from the central bank at the cheap price that prevails under the fixed exchange rate and later sell it in the market at the more expensive price that will prevail after the exchange rate floats. Thus, there is always an incentive to sell domestic bonds and buy

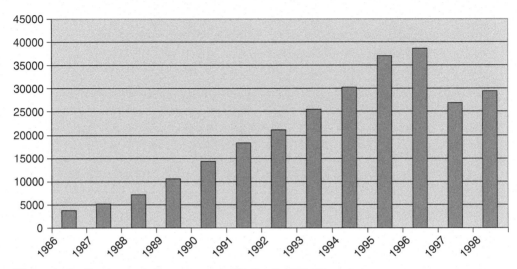

**Figure 14.2**   Foreign exchange reserves in Thailand, 1986–98

foreign ones as long as the exchange rate is expected to jump and the central bank still has any reserves left. Since this means that the speculative attack must completely deplete the central bank's reserves, it must also mean that the fixed exchange rate must end through a speculative attack that takes place before $t^*$ – that is, the fixed exchange rate must end with a bang, not a whimper. As we saw in Chapter 7, this sudden ending of the fixed exchange rate as the result of a speculative attack is usually referred to as a **currency crisis**.

So far we have established that if the central bank persists in the policy of increasing its stock of domestic bonds at a constant rate, the fixed exchange rate will end in dramatic fashion – in a speculative attack culminating in a currency crisis – sometime before the time $t^*$ at which the regime would have died a natural death. Does this mean that a crisis could happen at any time before $t^*$? The answer is no. What triggers the attack is the expectation of a sudden devaluation in the event that the fixed exchange rate is abandoned. It is not necessarily the case that if an attack happens and a switch to a floating exchange rate is forced by the market, the ensuing floating exchange rate will be sharply depreciated relative to the previously prevailing fixed rate.

To see the conditions under which this would indeed happen, consider equation (14.13), which determines the value of the floating exchange rate that will prevail at the instant that the regime switch takes place. Because the stock of domestic bonds held by the central bank $b_C$ is increasing over time, the money supply that would be in existence at the instant of the switch to a floating rate will tend to be higher the more time elapses before the attack takes place that forces the regime switch. That means that $m$ in equation (14.13) is a function of time, that is, $m = m(t)$. If $m$ is a function of time, the floating exchange rate that would prevail at the instant when the floating exchange regime starts, given by equation (14.13), must be a function of time as well. This is sometimes called the **shadow exchange rate**. What has just been said suggests that we can write it as:

$$s(t) = m(t) - \gamma + c_1 x$$

We can use the shadow exchange rate to tell us when an attack will happen. An attack cannot happen at a moment in time during which the shadow exchange rate is more depreciated than the fixed exchange rate, because if an attack were to happen at that moment the new floating rate would experience a discrete depreciation relative to the previous fixed rate, implying that speculators would reap a large and foreseeable capital gain on their holdings of foreign currency. As we have previously seen, this implies that an attack must occur *before* that time. On the other hand, at any moment in time during which the shadow exchange rate would be more appreciated than the official rate, the exchange rate would actually *appreciate* discretely if an attack were to take place that wiped out the central bank's foreign exchange reserves and forced it to move to a floating exchange rate regime. That means that speculators who switch to foreign currency would actually *lose* money if they successfully attacked the currency (they would buy foreign exchange at a more expensive price from the central bank than the price at which they would subsequently have to sell it in the market). Under those conditions, there is no incentive for anyone to speculate. The conclusion is that the attack must take place at the time $t_C$ that satisfies:

$$s(t_C) = \bar{s}$$

When this condition is met, the exchange rate neither appreciates nor depreciates discretely on impact. Attacking before that time would mean that speculators would lose money, while attacking after that time would require at least some individuals to pass up the opportunity to enjoy riskless profits by reaping easily anticipated capital gains.

The dynamics of a currency crisis of this type are illustrated in Figure 14.3. The intersection of the shadow exchange rate $s(t)$ with the fixed exchange rate $\bar{s}$ in the top panel determines the timing of the crisis $t_C$. At that time, the stock of foreign exchange

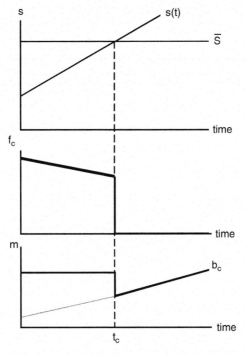

**Figure 14.3**  Dynamics of ''first generation'' currency crises

reserves $f_C$ is suddenly depleted by a speculative attack, as shown in the middle panel. The bottom panel shows that the depletion of reserves at the time of the attack will cause the money supply, which had been constant under fixed exchange rates, to contract at the time of the attack, but from that moment on the money supply will begin to grow at the rate of growth of the central bank's stock of domestic bonds.

## 14.5    Gradual Price Adjustment

Up to this point in this chapter we have assumed that the domestic price level is completely flexible. To conclude the chapter, we now examine exchange rate dynamics in response to permanent shocks under a more general case: one in which the domestic price level is ''sticky'' – that is, while not fixed in the short run, it adjusts only gradually to the long-run equilibrium value that we studied in Chapter 13. Specifically, suppose that the (log of the) domestic price level is given by:

$$p = (1 - v)p_{-1} + vp_{LR}. \tag{14.14}$$

Thus, the current price level $p$ is a weighted average of the previous period's price level $p_{-1}$ and the long-run price level $p_{LR}$ determined in Chapter 13, where $(1 - v)$ is the weight that applies to last period's price level and $v$ is that applied to the long-run price level to which the economy must eventually adjust. If $v = 0$, this equation reproduces the permanent-shock case of Chapter 12 in which the price level was taken to be constant, and if $v = 1$ it reproduces the long-run equilibrium analysis of Chapter 13.

With this new assumption about price-adjustment behavior, our monetary model is summarized in Box 14.3. Since it is determined from an analysis of the economy's long-run equilibrium such as that in Appendix 13.1, the long-run price level $p_{LR}$ is exogenous to this model. Consequently, in contrast to the flexprice monetary model that we considered in the first four sections of this chapter, the domestic price level is a predetermined variable in this model. From equation (14.14), its evolution over time is given by:

$$\Delta p = v(p_{LR} - p_{-1}) \tag{14.15}$$

Thus the domestic price level will be increasing over time if it initially falls short of the long-run equilibrium price level, and will be falling over time if it initially exceeds the long-run equilibrium price level. Also in contrast to the flexprice model, the domestic level of real output is now once again an endogenous variable.

To solve this model, notice that the goods market equilibrium condition (14.2) can be written as:

$$y = \Lambda_0 - b_1 \, \Delta q^e_{+1} + b_4 q \tag{14.2'}$$

where $\Lambda_0 = b_0 - b_1 r^* + b_2 g - b_3 t + b_5 \theta$ is a constant and $\Delta q^e_{+1} = q^e_{+1} - q$. Similarly, using equations (14.3) and (14.15), we have:

$$s = q - p^* + p$$

## Box 14.3  A Monetary Model with Gradual Price Adjustment

**Asset market equilibrium**

$$m - s = c_0 - c_1\left(R^* + s_{+1}^e - s\right) + c_2 y + p^* - q \tag{14.1}$$

**Goods market equilibrium**

$$y = b_0 - b_1\left(r^* + q_{+1}^e - q\right) + b_2 g - b_3 t + b_4 q + b_5 \theta \tag{14.2}$$

**Relationship between the price level and the real exchange rate**

$$p = s + p^* - q \tag{14.3}$$

**Price adjustment equation**

$$p = (1 - v)p_{-1} + v p_{LR} \tag{14.4}$$

and:

$$
\begin{aligned}
s_{+1} - s &= (q_{+1} - q) - \left(p_{+1}^* - p^*\right) + (p_{+1} - p) \\
&= \Delta q_{+1} - \Delta p_{+1}^* - \Delta p_{+1} \\
&= \Delta q_{+1} - \Delta p_{+1}^* - v(p_{LR} - p)
\end{aligned}
$$

Imposing the rational expectations condition $s_{+1}^e = s_{+1}$ in the asset market equilibrium condition (14.1) and substituting into this condition from the relationships above yields:

$$m - (q - p^* + p) = c_0 - c_1\left[R^* + \Delta q_{+1} - \Delta p_{+1}^* - v(p_{LR} - p)\right] + c_2 y + p^* - q$$

Solving this equation for $y$:

$$y = \Lambda_1 + (c_1/c_2)\Delta q_{+1} - (c_1/c_2)v p_{LR} - [(1 + c_1 v)/c_2]p$$

where $\Lambda_1 = c_2^{-1}\left[m - c_0 + c_1\left(R^* - \Delta p_{+1}^*\right)\right]$ is a constant. Finally, using this equation to substitute for $y$ in (14.2′) and solving for $\Delta q_{+1}$, we have:

$$\Delta q_{+1} = \frac{(\Lambda_0 - \Lambda_1) + (c_1/c_2)v p_{LR} + [(1 + c_1\,v)/c_2]p + b_4\,q}{b_1 + (c_1/c_2)} \tag{14.16}$$

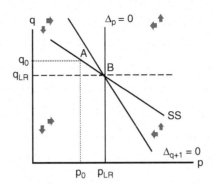

**Figure 14.4**   Dynamics with gradual price adjustment

This equation describes the (actual and expected) change in the real exchange rate from this period to the next as a function of this period's price level, this period's real exchange rate, and a set of "fundamentals," consisting of $(\Lambda_0 - \Lambda_1) + (c_1/c_2)\, v\, p_{LR}$.

Our model thus boils down to the two equations (14.15) and (14.16), consisting of equations that determine the change in the price level and real exchange rate as functions of the levels of these two variables and some constants.

To solve the model we can proceed as follows. Notice first, from equation (14.15), that the change in the price level from the previous period to the current one depends only on the past period's price level and the long-run price level, both of which are known – the former because it is inherited from the past and the latter because it can be determined from the long-run model of Chapter 13. Since the change in the price level is therefore known, so is this period's price level. It remains to solve for this period's real exchange rate $q$ and the change in the real exchange rate from the current period to the next $\Delta q_{+1}$.

We can solve for these two variables graphically using a **phase diagram**, as in Figure 14.4. Consider the set of all combinations of $q$ and $p$ that are consistent with an unchanging level of $q$ – i.e., with $\Delta q_{+1} = 0$. Since both $p$ and $q$ have positive coefficients in equation (14.16), from any arbitrary initial combination of $p$ and $q$ that satisfies $\Delta q_{+1} = 0$, an increase in $p$ requires a *reduction* in $q$ to keep the condition $\Delta q_{+1} = 0$ satisfied. Thus the set of all combinations of $p$ and $q$ that satisfy this condition must have a negative slope, as indicated by the curve $\Delta q_{+1} = 0$ in Figure 14.4. Above and to the right of this curve $q$ must be increasing, whereas below and to the left of it $q$ must be decreasing, as indicated by the arrows in the figure. We can also plot the locus of points that satisfy $\Delta p = 0$ in the same diagram. From equation (14.15) this locus must be vertical, since $\Delta p$ does not depend on $q$. It must cross the horizontal axis at $p = p_{LR}$, since the condition $\Delta p = 0$ only holds when $p = p_{LR}$. To the right of this vertical locus $p$ must be falling, while to the left it must be increasing.

The economy's long-run equilibrium must be at the point of intersection of the $\Delta q_{+1} = 0$ and $\Delta p = 0$ curves. But what happens when the initial price level does not equal $p_{LR}$ – say when the initial price level is below its long-run equilibrium, at a value such as $p_0$? Notice that, given $p_0$, the initial value of $q$ will determine the path that the economy will follow from that point on, since $p$ and $q$ must move in the directions indicated by the arrows in Figure 14.4. The question is whether there is some initial value of $q$ that will allow the

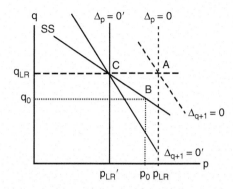

**Figure 14.5**   Adjustment to a permanent monetary contraction

economy eventually to move to its long-run equilibrium. If we can find such a value of $q$, we will have solved the model, since from that initial combination of $p$ and $q$ the economy's dynamics (i.e., its future values of $p$ and $q$) are fully determined by equations (14.15) and (14.16).

Since $p_0$ is given, the initial value of $q$ must lie somewhere on the vertical dotted line through $p_0$. But notice that the initial value of $q$ cannot lie either below the dashed line in Figure (14.4) or above the $\Delta q_{+1} = 0$ curve, because if it did, the arrows would subsequently drive the economy *away* from its long-run equilibrium. It follows that if the economy is to converge to its long-run equilibrium with an initial price level of $p_0$, the initial value of $q$ must be found on the dotted line through $p_0$, but above the dashed line and below the $\Delta q_{+1} = 0$ curve, at a point like A. From this initial combination $(p_0, q_0)$, the economy gradually moves to the southeast, with the domestic price level $p$ rising and the real exchange rate $q$ appreciating, until it reaches its long-run equilibrium at B, along a path such as SS. A similar argument could have been made if the price level had initially been *higher* than its long-run equilibrium value $p_{LR}$. In that case the initial value of $q$ would have been on the path SS to the southeast of B, and the economy would have reached its long-run equilibrium by moving to the northwest, with the price level gradually falling and the real exchange rate depreciating.

We can now consider how the economy would respond to shocks. Let us restrict our attention to a simple shock: a permanent decrease in the money supply. The analysis is given in Figure 14.5.

As you have already seen, in the long run, a permanent monetary contraction causes the domestic price level to fall in the same proportion as the decrease in the money supply, but leaves the real exchange rate unchanged. In Figure 14.5, these results are produced through a leftward shift of both the $\Delta p = 0$ and $\Delta q_{+1} = 0$ curves in the same proportion as the decrease in the money supply, say from $\Delta p = 0$ to $\Delta p = 0'$ and $\Delta q_{+1} = 0$ to $\Delta q_{+1} = 0'$ in the figure. As a result, the long-run equilibrium moves from A to C, with the long-run equilibrium value of the price level falling from $p_{LR}$ to $p_{LR}'$, and the long-run equilibrium value of the real exchange rate remaining at $q_{LR}$.

What happens on impact? Since the long-run price level has fallen, equation (14.15) indicates that the price level will also fall on impact, though not by the full amount required to attain its long-run equilibrium value. In Figure 14.5 the new short-run price level is $p_0$, which is smaller than $p_{LR}$, but larger than $p_{LR}'$. Since the economy must move to its new long-run equilibrium along the path SS, the real exchange rate appreciates on impact, to a new value $q_0$, then gradually depreciates as the economy moves to the northwest to the point C. Since the real exchange rate is expected to depreciate over time, the domestic real interest rate must increase on impact. Coupled with an appreciated real exchange rate, this means that the monetary contraction must reduce aggregate demand, and thus domestic real output.

---

## Empirical Study 14.1    Testing Exchange Rate Models

The flexprice monetary model and the 'sticky-price' version of the Dornbusch model that we studied in this chapter are two of the most widely accepted and used macroeconomic exchange rate models. But how useful are such models in understanding actual exchange rate movements?

For quite some time this has been a discouraging question for international macro-economists to ask. An extremely influential study by Meese and Rogoff (1983) suggested that our existing exchange rate models may actually not be very useful at all. Meese and Rogoff used empirical estimates of the parameters of exchange rate models such as those described in this chapter to examine how well such models could do at explaining out-of-sample exchange rate movements over relatively short horizons. As a standard of comparison they used a **random walk** – a simple model assuming that period-to-period changes in exchange rates are driven by unpredictable random shocks, so that the best guess about tomorrow's exchange rate is just today's exchange rate. To much professional surprise and consternation, they found that the profession's favorite exchange rate models could not outperform the relatively unsophisticated random walk alternative in predicting future exchange rate movements, even when actual future values of the ''fundamentals'' assumed to be driving the exchange rate in such models were used to generate the forecasts. This surprising result was subsequently verified by many other researchers, leaving the profession in the uncomfortable position of possessing some rather elegant models of exchange rate behavior that nevertheless appeared not to have much empirical usefulness.

More recently, however, Engel and West (2007) have shown that this interpretation of Meese and Rogoff's results may have been too pessimistic. They noted that asset market models of the exchange rate (which include all the models that we have examined in this book) consider the exchange rate to be a discounted sum of expected future values of a set of fundamentals (the specific fundamentals involved depend on the model). If changes in these fundamentals tend to be permanent (such as would be the case if the fundamentals were themselves random walks) and if the discount factors applied to the expected future values of the fundamentals are relatively large, Engel and West showed that exchange rates would indeed tend to behave like random walks. This means that using ''simple'' random walk behavior as a standard for evaluating model-based exchange rate forecasts actually sets a very difficult standard for empirical exchange rate models to meet. They also noted that if asset-market exchange rate models are correct, current exchange rates should help to predict future movements in the fundamentals. They found this property to be confirmed by the evidence, though they emphasized that this finding provides relatively weak support for the asset market view of the exchange rate, since other mechanisms could also generate this result.

Overall, then, our exchange rate models may not be as poor as we previously thought. Additional research is called for to evaluate the empirical usefulness of standard exchange rate models in explaining exchange rate movements.

## 14.6   Summary

To complete our analysis of floating exchange rates, in this chapter we have examined how a floating-exchange rate economy behaves under the "classical" assumption that the price level is flexible in the short run as well as under the more general assumption that it is "sticky" – i.e., that the short-run price level adjustment is only partial.

The analytical framework for the case of full flexibility is very similar to that used in the last chapter, except that in the short-run context it is no longer possible to assume that the real and nominal exchange rates are constant over time. The implication is that both exchange rates become functions of current and all expected future values of separate sets of "fundamental" determinants, with the influence of future fundamentals on the current real and nominal exchange rates becoming weaker the further in the future those fundamentals are. In this context we examined several special cases, showing that the long-run results of the last chapters correspond to the special case in which the fundamentals are constant over time and that the effects of shocks to the economy in general tend to be larger the longer such shocks are expected to last, consistent with the results we derived under sticky-price conditions.

The case of partial short-run price adjustment represents the most common version of the Dornbusch model. In this version the economy's dynamic response to shocks is driven by gradual price level adjustment, rather than gradual adjustment in the level of production.

The "flexprice" and "sticky-price" versions of the monetary model that we have analyzed in this chapter are among the most widely used exchange rate models among international macroeconomists. Empirical testing of these models, however, has provided some surprises for international macroeconomists. The state of play on this issue is summarized in Empirical Study 14.1.

With this chapter, we complete our descriptive analysis of the behavior of small open economies under floating exchange rates. In the next part of the book, we will turn to normative (prescriptive) issues concerning exchange rate management. In particular, now that we have separately considered how small open economies work under both fixed and floating exchange rates, it is natural to ask what conditions determine which type of regime is likely to be optimal for a particular economy. We will address that question in Chapter 15.

### Questions

1   In a simple "monetary approach to the exchange rate" world, explain what effect the expectation of a permanent future monetary *contraction* (reduction in $m$) would have on the nominal exchange rate today.

2   Using the flexible-price monetary approach to the exchange rate, explain what effects you would expect each of the following shocks to have on today's equilibrium exchange rate:

   a  A permanent decrease in the demand for money triggered by domestic financial innovations.

   b  The election of a conservative government likely to appoint a central bank governor in the future who would follow a more restrictive monetary policy than the current governor.

   c  A bond-financed fiscal expansion.

   d  A reduction in the external interest rate that is expected to be temporary.

   e  A permanent improvement in the productivity of the domestic economy caused by economic reforms.

3   Using the flexible-price monetary model of the exchange rate developed in this chapter, explain what predictions you would make about the behavior of the nominal exchange rate in response to each of the following shocks:

   a  An anticipated permanent future monetary expansion.

   b  A permanent reduction in the world nominal interest rate.

   c  An anticipated future increase in domestic real GDP, say because of the discovery of a large oil deposit.

   d  A temporary decrease in the demand for money.

   e  A permanent reduction in the world nominal interest rate to which the domestic government responds with a fiscal policy change designed to keep the domestic real exchange rate from changing.

   Be sure to explain in each case *why* you answer the way you do – i.e., how the shock in question gets transmitted to the nominal exchange rate.

4   In early 2002, Argentina abandoned its currency board and replaced it by a floating exchange rate. Given Argentina's history of hard-to-tame fiscal deficits, and assuming that its economy fits the classical assumption of flexible short-run prices, can you explain why the Argentine peso would have depreciated abruptly when the floating exchange rate regime was implemented?

5   Consider a small open economy that operates with a floating exchange rate and perfect capital mobility. Compare the effects on that country's real and nominal exchange rates, as well as on its domestic price level, of each of the following shocks:

   a  A monetary expansion that is expected to be transitory.

   b  A monetary expansion that is expected to be permanent.

   c  A permanent monetary expansion that is not expected to be implemented until next period.

6   Explain why, in the flexible-price model developed in this chapter, a permanent monetary shock has a larger effect on the nominal exchange rate than a transitory shock of the same magnitude. How do the effects of these two shocks on the **real** exchange rate compare?

7   Suppose that a permanent increase in the money supply in the present period is accompanied by the expectation that money supply growth will be greater in all future periods. Under these circumstances, what would be the relationship between the size of the induced change in the exchange rate and that of the change in the money supply? Explain.

## Further Reading and References

### On the development of the monetary model

Frankel, Jacob A. (1976), "A Monetary Approach to the Exchange Rate: Doctrinal Aspects and Empirical Evidence," *Scandinavian Journal of Economics*, Vol. 78, No. 2, pp. 200–24.

### On the monetary model in the context of other models of exchange rate determination

Bergstrand, Jeffrey H. (1983), "Selected Views of Exchange Rate Determination after a Decade of 'Floating,'" Federal Reserve Bank of Boston *New England Economic Review* (May/June), pp. 14–29.

Macdonald, Ronald and Mark P. Taylor (1992), "Exchange Rate Economics," *IMF Staff Papers*, Vol. 39, No. 1, pp. 1–57.

Marriman, Jane (1989), "Exchange Rate determination: Sorting Out Thoery and Evidence," Federal Reserve Bank of Boston *New England Economic Review* (November/December), pp. 39–51.

### On the empirical performance of the monetary model

Neely, Christopher J. and Lucio Sarno (2001), "How Well Do Monetary Fundamentals Forecast Exchange Rates?" Federal Reserve Bank of St. Louis *Economic Review* (September/October), pp. 51–74.

### On the mechanics of "first generation" currency crises

Agenor, Pierre-Richard, and Robert Flood (1994), "Macroeconomic Policy, Speculative Attacks, and Balance of Payments Crises," in F. Van der Ploeg, ed., *The Handbook of International Macroeconomics* (Cambridge MA: Blackwell), pp. 224–50.

Flood, Robert, and Peter M. Garber (1984), "Collapsing Exchange Rate Regimes: Some Linear Examples," *Journal of International Economics*, Vol. 17, pp. 1–13.

Krugman, Paul (1979), "A Model of Balance of Payments Crises," *Journal of Money, Credit, and Banking* (August), pp. 311–25.

### On testing exchange rate models

Engel, Charles, and Kenneth D. West (2007), "Exchange Rates and Fundamentals," *Journal of Political Economy*, Vol. 113, No. 3, pp. 485–517.

Meese, Richard A. and Kenneth Rogoff (1983), "Empirical Exchange Rate Models of the Seventies: Do They Fit Out of Sample?" *Journal of International Economics*, Vol. 14, pp. 3–24.

# 15

# Choosing an Exchange Rate Regime

.....................................................................................................................................................

At this point, we have analyzed the consequences of macroeconomic openness under both fixed and floating exchange rate regimes. We now want to address the important and controversial question of what exchange rate regime a country *should* choose. This is an old question in international macroeconomics, and one that is continually re-evaluated as the world economy changes and as our state of knowledge about international macroeconomics evolves. It is a question that every country has to answer for itself and that each country has continually to reconsider in light of its own changing circumstances.

As we saw in Chapter 3, countries have a wide range of exchange regime options from which to choose. The spectrum of exchange rate regimes runs from adopting the currency of a trading partner (dollarization), as has been done by countries such as Ecuador and El Salvador, to allowing the domestic currency's value to be determined in the foreign exchange market with little or no central bank intervention (a clean float), as the United States did during the early 1980s and as countries such as New Zealand have done more recently. In this chapter, we will not consider where exactly along the spectrum of exchange regimes a country should wind up, but will instead explore the broader question of the circumstances that might determine whether a fixed or a floating exchange rate would be more suitable for a particular country.[1]

If you were called upon to give advice to a country's policymakers about the exchange rate policies that the country should follow, you would presumably advocate the exchange rate regime that you would expect to promote the most successful macroeconomic

---

[1] Recall that in Chapter 9 we considered some of the factors that may influence the optimal choice between the hard- and soft-peg versions of fixed exchange rates.

performance for that country. But what exactly does that mean? To answer this question we have to specify a set of criteria that we can use to evaluate macroeconomic performance. We will see that three types of criteria have traditionally been employed for this purpose: (1) the minimization of transactions costs in international commerce, (2) the promotion of long-run domestic price stability, and (3) the facilitation of macroeconomic adjustment to the exogenous shocks that inevitably affect the economy. Our main task in this chapter will be to evaluate how fixed and floating exchange rate regimes perform with respect to each of these criteria.

One important implication of using several criteria to evaluate exchange rate regimes immediately arises: if different regimes promise to deliver superior performance according to different criteria, then the exchange rate regime that is likely to be optimal for a particular country will depend on the relative importance that it attaches to those criteria. Countries are likely to weigh these multiple objectives very differently, depending on their circumstances. Because a large share of its economic transactions are international, a small and highly open economy such as that of Hong Kong, for example, may give more weight to the minimization of transactions costs in international commerce than a large, diversified and relatively closed economy such as that of Brazil. Similarly, a historically high-inflation economy such as Argentina is likely to be more concerned with the price-stabilization properties of an exchange rate regime than a historically low-inflation country like India. This means that different exchange rate regimes are likely to be optimal for different countries, and that different regimes may even be optimal for the *same* country at different points in time. We will indeed find that in choosing between fixed and floating exchange rates, the type of exchange rate regime that is optimal for a country will depend on its circumstances. The trick is to understand exactly which set of circumstances make it optimal to adopt which exchange rate regime.

In this chapter we will attempt to shed light on this issue by considering how fixed and floating exchange rates perform with respect to each of our three optimality criteria and exploring the conditions under which a country would tend to give high priority to particular criteria. We will begin with the criterion of minimizing the costs of international transactions, and move from there to that of securing price stability and of reducing the costs of adjustment to macroeconomic shocks. The chapter will conclude with an analysis of the implications for exchange regime choice of the dilemma faced by countries whose circumstances force them to simultaneously care about multiple criteria that have potentially conflicting implications for the choice of an optimal exchange rate regime.

## 15.1    Optimality Criterion I: Minimizing the Costs of Making International Transactions

Aside from what is given up in exchange, there are always costs of one type or another associated with undertaking economic transactions. Economists refer to these costs as **transactions costs**. The transactions costs associated with international commerce can take several forms, which we previously considered in Chapter 3. In the rest of this section we will examine some transactions costs – specifically brokerage costs and costs associated with exchange rate risk – whose magnitudes are likely to depend on a country's exchange rate regime.

## Brokerage Costs

As anyone who has traveled abroad knows, the financial institutions that manage the foreign exchange market (typically commercial banks) tend to buy foreign exchange at a slightly lower price than that for which they are willing to sell it (this is known at the **bid-ask spread**). This spread arises from the need by these institutions to cover their costs of doing business. The presence of such **brokerage costs** implies that buyers of foreign exchange typically pay a little more than the quoted market price, while sellers typically receive a little less than that price. This is, of course, what always happens in the presence of a specific tax on a commodity (except that in the case of a tax, the difference between what the buyer pays and what the seller receives accrues as revenue to the government). Brokerage costs thus act in the same way as a small tax on transactions between residents and nonresidents, and as with any other tax, they would tend to have the effect of discouraging such transactions.

Brokerage costs are relevant for both capital flows as well as for current account transactions. We saw in Chapter 3, for example, that investing funds abroad involves undertaking three separate transactions: a domestic resident has to purchase foreign currency in the foreign exchange market, use that currency to buy a foreign financial asset, and then sell the proceeds of holding that asset in the foreign exchange market when the asset matures in order to repatriate domestic currency. Each of those transactions will involve incurring a brokerage cost, and if those costs are sufficiently large, an investment opportunity that would look attractive in the absence of brokerage costs may not look profitable once such costs are taken into account.

It is easy to see how the incidence of such costs can be affected by a country's foreign exchange regime. In particular, some of these costs – the costs of exchanging currencies – can obviously be avoided if an economy were to use the same currency as that of its main trading partners. Thus, in a dollarized economy, or in economies participating in a monetary union, the transactions costs associated with currency exchanges would be eliminated between the home country and the foreign country with which it shares a common currency. The elimination of such costs would act like the removal of a tax and thus would be expected to promote trade between the two economies.

## Costs Associated with Exchange Rate Risk

However, brokerage costs are not the costs that figure most prominently in our first criterion. Much more important are the costs associated with exchange rate uncertainty. These costs also arise from the fact that the two parties in an international transaction typically tend to conduct their business in different currencies, but the separate influence of this factor arises from the fact that transactions are not typically concluded until some time after they are initially negotiated. Goods and services sold to foreigners, for example, are typically invoiced in the currency of the exporter, to be paid for on delivery. During the time that elapses between the moment when the price for a transaction is agreed upon and the moment when payment is made, the exchange rate between the two currencies may change. If the transaction is invoiced in the currency of the exporter, that means that the importer is subjected to **exchange rate risk**, the risk that his or her own currency may depreciate relative to the currency in which the payment has to be made, thus making the transaction potentially much more expensive in domestic currency than the importer had bargained for. Since people tend to be risk averse, they typically are willing to pay to avoid such a risk, and the amount that they are willing to pay to do so can also be considered as the equivalent of a differential tax on international transactions (since no such payment would be required to be made in order to avoid exchange rate risk on a similar transaction with a domestic agent who uses the same currency).

We already saw in Chapter 3 that a similar risk prevails in capital account transactions, arising from potential exchange rate changes between the time when a domestic resident either lends or borrows abroad in foreign currency and the time when the loan is repaid. When the exchange rate between two currencies is not anchored to any particular value in the long run, this risk would tend to be greater the longer the maturity of the asset, since the longer the life of the asset, the more opportunities there are for the exchange rate to deviate from the value that prevailed at the time that money initially changed hands. Thus, exchange rate risk may tend to be particularly important when, say, a domestic resident is considering acquiring a long-term financial asset or a physical asset in a foreign country (as in the case of foreign direct investment).[2]

Thus, exchange rate risk may create potentially important disincentives for international commerce, both in goods and services as well as in financial and physical assets. Analytically, exchange rate risk is the equivalent of a differential tax on international, as opposed to domestic, commerce. The risk to which potential exchange rate changes can subject economic agents is important enough as to significantly affect behavior. Even central banks are not immune to being influenced by exchange rate risk. A dramatic recent example of exchange rate risk for central banks is described in Box 15.1.

Such risks can be exaggerated, however, because markets exist in which individuals can pay relatively small amounts to protect themselves from exchange rate risks. To see how this is possible, suppose that a domestic importer expects to have to make a payment in foreign exchange in 6 months' time, while a foreign importer expects to have to make a similar payment at the same time in domestic currency. The two parties could completely eliminate the exchange rate risk to which each of them is vulnerable by simply agreeing to exchange domestic for foreign currency in 6 months' time at a price that they agree on today. Markets in which such future currency trades can be arranged at predetermined prices are available for many currencies. They are called **forward**, or **futures**, markets, and the currently negotiated price at which the future currency trade is carried out is called the **forward exchange rate**.[3] Notice that, if both parties agree on the value that they expect the exchange rate to attain in six months' time, if there is no commercial risk (i.e., if both parties fully expect the other to carry out its commitments), and if we ignore brokerage costs, then each party in this transaction can effectively ''lock in'' the exchange rate that they expected to prevail at the time that they agreed to purchase the foreign good – and thus completely protect themselves from foreign exchange risk – without incurring a cost.

If it were always possible to do this, then exchange rate risk would cease to be a factor discouraging international commerce. Unfortunately this situation does not prevail in the

---

[2]  Even though such assets can, of course, be sold, exchange rate risk continues to be important because the domestic-currency value of the sale proceeds is subject to exchange rate risk.

[3]  The forward market is a market administered by commercial banks all around the world in which individuals can contract to buy or sell currencies in amounts and at future dates that are set by the contracting parties, while futures markets are markets in which contracts to buy or sell (a limited number of) currencies in bundles of standard sizes and at standard future dates are traded on specific organized exchanges.

## Box 15.1    Exchange Rate Risk for Central Banks

Like any other economic agent, central banks are subject to exchange rate risk when they have assets or liabilities denominated in foreign currency. Since central banks typically hold a substantial amount of foreign exchange reserves, they are exposed to exchange rate risk on the asset side of their balance sheets – that is, they are vulnerable to the possibility that the currency in which their foreign exchange reserves are denominated will lose value

As you learned in Chapter 2, the US dollar is the world's most commonly used reserve currency. Thus, many central banks hold a substantial amount of US dollar assets. During the first part of the 21st century many emerging market economies – particularly in East and Southeast Asia, but also elsewhere – accumulated very large foreign exchange reserves through foreign exchange market intervention designed to prevent their currencies from appreciating. But as we have noted in various places in this book, the first years of the 21st century have been characterized by very large current account deficits in the United States, deficits so large that they are widely regarded as unsustainable, because the rest of the world is unlikely to continue to acquire financial claims on the United States on the scale required to finance these deficits indefinitely. The reduction of these deficits, however, is likely to require a depreciation of the US dollar. The problem is that nobody knows when the dollar depreciation will happen or how large it will need to be.

Where does this leave the emerging-economy central banks that have accumulated large US dollar reserves? The answer is that it leaves them exposed to very large potential exchange rate risk, no different from that faced by private residents of foreign countries who hold assets denominated in US dollars. But because individual central banks hold such large amounts of US dollars (the central bank of China, for example, was estimated to hold some $700 billion in US dollar-denominated assets in mid-2006) they are caught in a quandary not faced by private individuals: if they try to avoid exchange rate risk by diversifying their reserve holdings into other currencies or by ceasing to accumulate dollars, they may precipitate the dollar depreciation that would saddle them with huge capital losses on their foreign exchange reserves, but if they don't, their foreign exchange risk just increases. Thus foreign exchange risk complicates life not just for private agents engaged in international transactions, but for central banks as well.

real world. Individuals who have to make payments in foreign currency often have to pay a substantial premium for foreign exchange relative to what they might expect the future spot exchange rate to be. Thus, the elimination of exchange rate risk comes at a price, and this price itself then functions as a tax on international transactions. Moreover, forward markets do not exist for transactions in many currencies, and even for those that do, they tend to cover only relatively short maturities.

Why would forward markets not exist for every currency? Brokerage costs and commercial risk obviously play a role in determining the currency coverage of such markets. These are likely to be more important (per unit traded) for the currencies of smaller economies that are not traded in large amounts. But that is not all that is involved. Go back to our domestic importer who has to make a foreign-currency payment in 6 months' time. Suppose that everyone agrees on what the future value of the spot exchange rate is likely to be at that time. A transaction that completely eliminates risk for our importer will be possible if there is someone with an offsetting currency obligation on the other side of the market, as in our example. If that is not the case, then someone somewhere would have to be induced to absorb exchange rate risk in order for our importer to be able to buy **forward cover**, that is, to buy foreign currency in the future at a price that is known today. This may be someone with an offsetting obligation of approximately the same maturity as our importer, who would have to be induced to take on a risk of shorter maturity than that originally confronting him, or someone *without* an offsetting exposure who is simply less risk averse. In either case, our importer would have to pay a premium over and above the commonly expected future spot exchange rate in order to compensate others for bearing risk. It is easy to see that this premium would tend to be greater the greater the uncertainty about the future exchange rate over a given time horizon, or the longer the maturity of the forward contract. It is also likely to be greater in the case of currencies that are potentially subject to future capital controls. If the premium required by potential future sellers of foreign exchange is sufficiently large, it may exceed what any potential future buyer is willing to pay, and a forward market will therefore not exist.

In short, the possibility of **hedging**, or covering exchange rate risk by trading in forward markets, may reduce the implicit tax that such risks impose on international transactions in many cases, but it does not eliminate such risk for all currencies or over all maturities. Thus exchange rate risk may often act as an important disincentive to international transactions.

The implications for optimal exchange rate arrangements are clear. If such risks could be eliminated without cost (that is, without sacrificing other important economic objectives), then mutually advantageous trades would be fostered between domestic and foreign residents that would not otherwise take place. The adoption of a common currency would eliminate exchange rate risk, and the evidence indeed suggests that the use of common currencies can have enormous effects on the volume of trade between countries.[4] This first criterion, then, provides an argument for exchange rate regimes that restrict the uncertainty associated with future exchange rate changes. It suggests that a credibly fixed exchange rate may have at least one important advantage over floating rates. Notice, though, that the need to credibly fix the exchange rate is fairly restrictive in this case. It suggests that the benefits of reduced transactions costs may be available only when countries use common currencies, since any other fixed exchange rate arrangement may be susceptible to exchange rate changes on short notice.

## 15.2 Optimality Criterion II: Long-run Inflation Stabilization

We saw in Chapter 13 that adopting fixed or floating exchange rates involved a choice of alternative long-run nominal anchors for the domestic economy.[5] Under a fixed exchange

---

[4]  Rose (2000), for example, found that the adoption of a common currency tended to increase trade between the countries involved by a factor of 300 percent.
[5]  Recall that an economy's nominal anchor is a nominal policy variable that determines that economy's average price level in the long run.

rate regime, the economy's long-run inflation rate was determined by the sum of the rate of depreciation of the domestic currency against the currencies of the country's trading partners and the rate of inflation in the trading partners. Under floating exchange rates, by contrast, the domestic rate of inflation was determined by the rate of change in the domestic money supply. The contrasting results reflected the fact that under fixed exchange rates the nominal policy variable determined by the central bank (the economy's nominal anchor) was the exchange rate, while under floating exchange rates it was the money supply.

The second traditional criterion that has been used to evaluate the performance of exchange rate regimes is the economy's long-run inflation rate. Since economists agree that high rates of inflation have harmful effects on the real economy, a desirable feature of an exchange rate regime is that it should be conducive to a low and stable long-run rate of inflation. From this perspective, then, the question is whether a fixed or a floating exchange rate is more likely to facilitate such an outcome.

It should be puzzling to you that the choice of nominal anchor could potentially make a difference to the economy's long-run inflation rate. Suppose that a country's partner countries maintain a completely stable price level (that is, suppose that the foreign inflation rate is zero) and that a rate of inflation of 2 percent per year is perfectly satisfactory from the perspective of the domestic economy. Then wouldn't the long-run domestic rate of inflation be 2 percent whether the central bank adopts an officially determined exchange rate that it depreciates by 2 percent per year or allows the exchange rate to float while setting the rate of growth of the domestic money supply at 2 percent per year? Our analysis in Chapter 13 suggests that the answer is yes. But if that is true – that is, if the same inflation rate can be achieved with different nominal anchors – then why should it make a difference which exchange rate regime the central bank actually adopts?

The answer is that if we think of the central bank as simply independently choosing the rate of inflation that it wants the domestic economy to achieve, and then relentlessly pursuing that objective without regard to the economy's circumstances, indeed it would make no difference for the long-run rate of inflation whether it pursues that objective by depreciating the currency at the desired rate or by instead causing the money supply to grow at that rate.

Suppose, however, that we treat the central bank's inflation objective as an endogenous variable – that is, a variable that is subject to being influenced by macroeconomic events. In particular, suppose that in making its decision about its inflation objective the central bank actually chooses as its target the rate of inflation that it perceives as maximizing social welfare in light of the economy's current circumstances. As we shall see, in this case it may indeed make a difference which policy instrument the central bank chooses to control in order to achieve its objective, and the economy's inflation performance may then depend on whether the central bank chooses the exchange rate as its instrument (as it would under a fixed exchange rate system) or the money supply (as it could under floating exchange rates).

## The Barro–Gordon Model

To see why this is so, we can work out a simple model proposed by Barro and Gordon (1983). Barro and Gordon describe the economy's aggregate supply curve in log-linear form as follows:

$$y = \bar{y} + a(p - p^e) \tag{15.1}$$

where $y$ is the log of the economy's real GDP; $\bar{y}$ is the log of natural, or full employment, GDP; $p$ is the log of the price level; $p^e$ is the expectation of $p$ that was formed last period; and $a$ is a positive parameter. This specification states that the economy's actual level of real GDP will deviate from its natural level $\bar{y}$ to the extent that this period's actual price level turns out to be higher than it was expected to be.[6] As in Chapter 14, this period's price level is assumed to be flexible, that is, $p$ is an endogenous variable. Now suppose that, after the public (rationally) forms its expectation of the next period's price level, the central bank sets its policy instrument (either the exchange rate or the money supply) so as to determine the current period's price level. What price level should the central bank choose to implement?

The answer depends on what the central bank is trying to achieve when it determines its desired value of $p$. As noted previously, suppose that the central bank wants to maximize social welfare, which in turn depends on two components:

1   Social welfare is higher the higher the level of output.
2   Social welfare is lower the higher the rate of inflation (higher inflation is equivalent to a higher value of $p$ in this context, because a higher value of $p$ this period means a larger increase in the price level relative to last period's value, which is what we mean by a higher rate of inflation).

The first effect is assumed to be linear, meaning that social welfare improves by a fixed amount whenever the log of real GDP goes up by one unit, whether real GDP is initially high or low. The second effect is nonlinear: while the first unit of inflation has essentially zero social cost, the social cost of an additional unit of inflation becomes higher the higher the rate of inflation.

What rate of inflation does the central bank choose under these circumstances? Suppose that the central bank can exercise discretion in its choice of the price level. That is, suppose that in deciding where to set the price level, it is not bound by any commitments it may have made in the past. Now suppose that the central bank announces that it will set the rate of inflation equal to zero – that is, that it will set this period's price level equal to last period's price level. If the public believes that this is indeed what will happen, would the central bank be likely to do what it said it was going to do?

The interesting insight of the Barro–Gordon model is that the answer is actually no. The reasoning is as follows: once the public has formed its expectation about what the price level will be, the central bank chooses where to actually set the price level based on a comparison of the marginal social benefits and marginal social costs of increasing the price level, taking the public's expectation as given. In other words, it chooses where to set $p$, taking $p^e$ as given. If the central bank sets the price level a little higher than what it was last period, the public will be taken by surprise, since it expected the price level to be the same as last period. According to equation (15.1), the effect will be to increase the level of output in the economy. As we have seen, this has a positive marginal social benefit. At the same time, the small increase in inflation required to achieve this result has essentially no marginal

[6]   The microeconomic rationale for this specification is that workers cannot observe the actual price level, so they base their nominal wage demands for this period on their expectation of this period's price level, in order to achieve a desired real wage objective. When the price level turns out to be higher, firms are able to offer a higher nominal wage, and since workers perceive this as an increase in their *real* wage, they increase their supply of labor, which in turn allows firms to offer a higher level of output.

social cost. A comparison of marginal benefits and costs will therefore induce the central bank to increase the price level – that is, *not* to follow through on its previous commitment to keep the price level constant. Thus, the central bank's optimal price level decision after the public has formed its expectations is different from what it was before such expectations were formed. Macroeconomists refer to this situation as one in which the bank's optimal plans are **time-inconsistent**.

The problem is that, because the public expected zero inflation while the bank actually produced positive inflation, the situation just described cannot be a rational expectations equilibrium – that is, an equilibrium in which expectations are equal to the outcomes predicted by the model. If the public is aware of the incentives faced by the central bank, and thus knows what the central bank is likely to do, it would never have been gullible enough to have expected zero inflation in the first place. This means that the situation just described cannot be the final outcome when the public forms its expectations rationally.

If that is so, how do we find an equilibrium rate of inflation in this situation? The answer is that the public has to expect the central bank to choose a price level that is high enough so that at the margin the central bank will have no further incentive to deviate from the public's expectation. To see what this means, notice that as the price level that the public expects to prevail increases, the marginal social benefit of a given amount of "surprise" inflation – of a price level that is higher than what the public expected – does not change. However, the marginal social cost associated with such an inflation surprise becomes increasingly larger, because it entails a progressively larger increase in the price level relative to its actual value in the previous period. Thus, for some sufficiently large increase in the price level, the marginal social benefit of a further increase will exactly equal the marginal social cost. That is the price level increase that the public will expect and that the central bank will actually deliver.

However, this rational expectations equilibrium is not a very satisfactory one from society's point of view. The reason is that, since the high rate of inflation that emerges in this situation is fully anticipated by the public, there is actually no *unanticipated* inflation. By equation (15.1), that means that output must remain equal to its natural level $\bar{y}$. Since the economy suffers from a high rate of inflation with no compensation in the form of a higher level of output, it would certainly have been preferable from society's perspective if the central bank could have credibly promised to keep the price level constant, since in that case the level of real output would have been the same, but the inflation rate would have been zero. However, the central bank's initial promise would have been credible only if the public perceived at the time that the bank would not have an incentive after the fact to deviate from what it said it would do. What is required to avoid the undesirable high-inflation outcome, therefore, is some mechanism that will make it optimal for the central bank to do after the fact what it said it would do beforehand. This is referred to as a **pre-commitment mechanism**.

## Credibility and the Exchange Rate Regime

What does any of this have to do with the exchange rate regime? As you know, the central bank does not control the price level directly, but affects it only through its choice of a nominal policy instrument. Thus the central bank we have been describing would have announced its price level objective by way of a specific announcement about what it intends to do with the exchange rate or the money supply, depending on whether it was pursuing a fixed or floating exchange rate. The key point is that the credibility of the bank's initial promise to maintain a stable price level (and thus the price level that ultimately materializes) may depend on which nominal policy instrument the central bank uses to set the price level. In other words, the two alternative policy instruments may have different characteristics as pre-commitment mechanisms.

Why should the choice of nominal anchor affect the central bank's credibility? To answer this, consider first what characteristics a good pre-commitment mechanism should have. Recall the sequence of events in the exercise that we worked out above: the central bank announced a policy; then the public formed its expectations of inflation; finally, the central bank chose the actual policy that it would follow. This suggests that a good pre-commitment mechanism, that is, one that actually makes it more likely that the central bank does what it said it would do, should have the following characteristics:

First, the public should believe that if the central bank announces a value for its nominal policy instrument that it claims will produce low inflation and it acts in good faith, inflation will in fact turn out to be low. For this to be the case, the policy instrument should in fact be something that the central bank can effectively control, that is tightly linked to the behavior of the price level, and that is linked to the price level in a way that is transparent enough for the public to understand.

Second, the public should believe that once its expectations are formed, the central bank will have few incentives to deviate from its policy announcement. This depends on the perceived benefits versus the perceived costs of doing so from the perspective of the central bank. The benefits depend in part on how large an impact the instrument used by the central bank can have on aggregate demand (and thus on real output), while the costs depend on how easy it is for the public to detect any tendency for the central bank to renege on its commitments, as well as on how much damage reneging would do to the central bank.

How well do the alternative nominal policy instruments that we have been considering satisfy these criteria? Notice that fixing an official value for the exchange rate is a simple announcement that everyone can understand, it is a variable that the central bank can control directly, and it is tied directly to the price level as long as the real exchange rate is unchanged. Moreover, the exchange rate can be observed directly, so everyone knows whether the central bank is complying with its announcement or not, and it lends itself to formal or informal international agreements, in the form of common exchange rate regimes adopted by groups of countries. The latter two observations imply that breaking promises with respect to the nominal exchange rate may have high political costs for the central bank, and these costs may negate the benefit that the central bank may perceive from inflationary surprises. This would leave the bank with reduced incentives to generate such surprises, and consequently may help to make policy announcements more credible.

On the other hand, the exchange rate may have several disadvantages as a nominal anchor. First, the relationship of the nominal exchange rate to the price level may not be stable if there are large changes in the short-run equilibrium real exchange rate. Thus, even if the central bank acts in good faith, the public may have a reason not to expect the price level to be low. Second, as we saw in Part 2, fixed exchange rates are vulnerable to speculative attacks. Thus, the central bank may have reasons not to follow through on an exchange rate other than those highlighted in the analysis above. You can think of these additional motives as being captured by a higher value of the parameter $a$, which captures the central bank's incentive to deviate from its policy announcement after the fact.

Despite these shortcomings, fixing the exchange rate may be a more effective pre-commitment mechanism than targeting the money supply. The reasons are several. First, the link between the money supply and the price level may be less transparent to the public than that between the exchange rate and the price level, since the exchange rate has a direct impact on the domestic-currency prices of foreign goods, while the influence of the money supply on the price level is an indirect one, operating through the effects of money supply changes on aggregate demand. Second, the money supply concept that the central bank can control closely may not be tightly linked to the price level. As we shall see in the next section, the central bank can directly control the **monetary base** (consisting of currency in the hands of the public plus bank reserves), but broader concepts of money may actually be more tightly linked to the price level than the monetary base. Third, even the links with the price level of the money supply concepts that are most closely associated with the price level may not be very reliable. In particular, these links break down when the real demand for money is unstable (that is, when the function $L(\ )$ that we have used in previous chapters is subject to frequent unexplained shocks). Finally, information about the money supply, which is published by the central bank, is not as easily available to the public as is that about the exchange rate, which can be observed directly in the marketplace. Thus, while theory does not provide a clear-cut verdict as to whether nominal exchange rate targeting (fixed exchange rates) or money supply targeting (floating exchange rates) is more effective as a pre-commitment device, there seems to be a stronger case for the former than for the latter. Some evidence on this issue is reviewed in Empirical Study 15.1.

## 15.3   Optimality Criterion III: Short-run Macroeconomic Stability

The previous section considered the advantages and disadvantages of alternative exchange rate systems from the point of view of imposing discipline on the monetary authorities and thus promoting long-run inflation stabilization. However, the choice of exchange rate regime has other macroeconomic implications of concern to policymakers. As we have seen throughout this book, economies are typically afflicted by a variety of shocks to which they have to adjust. The short-run stickiness of nominal wages and prices means that the arrival of such shocks has the potential to destabilize domestic real GDP. Because the extent to which this happens depends (among other things) on the exchange rate regime maintained by the central bank, the third criterion that we will consider for evaluating the choice between fixed and floating exchange rate regimes concerns the consequences of the exchange rate regime for the short-run stability of domestic economic activity in response to exogenous shocks.

We have seen that shocks can be classified along two important dimensions: their duration (that is, whether they are expected to be temporary or permanent), and their origin. Specifically, shocks to the domestic economy can originate in the domestic goods market, in domestic asset markets, and in the international economic environment. To see how the exchange rate regime can play a role in the economy's adjustment to macroeconomic shocks, in this section we will focus on how adjustment would work in response to permanent shocks, since that is the only case in which we have analyzed how the economy behaves under both fixed and floating exchange rates.

Suppose that the country's authorities have a single policy objective – to stabilize real GDP around its natural level – and that they are constrained from undertaking a discretionary policy response when shocks arrive that may cause GDP to deviate from that level. In this case, the superior exchange rate regime will be the one that proves to be the best "automatic stabilizer" for the economy – that is, the one that is most successful in stabilizing real output automatically (without explicit countervailing policy actions) around its natural level in response to shocks.

As we will see, from the standpoint of this stabilization objective, the choice of optimal exchange rate regime depends on what the typical sources of disturbances are for the domestic economy. We will analyze the effects of the three types of disturbances that we have been considering throughout this book:

1   Aggregate demand shocks. These are unavoidable changes in the factors that affect the equilibrium in the goods market. They include exogenous shocks to the function $A(Y - T, r)$ that determines domestic private absorption, to the function $\varphi(sP^*/P)$ that determines the composition of domestic private demand between foreign and domestic goods, to the parameter $\theta$ in the function $X(sP^*/P, \theta)$ that determines foreign demand for domestic goods, and to the fiscal policy variables $G$ and $T$.
2   Monetary shocks. This refers to unavoidable changes in the money demand function $L(R, Y)$ for given values of $R$ and $Y$, as well as to the supply of money, originating either in policy decisions or private behavior. We will explore how private behavior can affect the money supply below.
3   External financial shocks. In the present context, this refers to changes in international financial conditions, as captured by the world interest rate, $R^*$.

In our analysis, we will first consider what the economy's short-run equilibrium looks like under conditions of perfect capital mobility under fixed and floating exchange rates, respectively. We can actually depict both types of equilibrium in the same diagram, to facilitate comparison of how the economy responds to given shocks under both types of regime. Then we will subject the economy to three different types of shocks and compare the outcomes for equilibrium real GDP under the two regimes.

As we saw in Chapter 6, under fixed exchange rates the short-run equilibrium value of real GDP is determined in the goods market, given the values of the domestic interest rate determined by uncovered interest parity (UIP) and of the exchange rate as set by the central bank. Holding constant the domestic interest rate at the value consistent with UIP (that is, at $R = R^*$), the relationship between the exchange rate set by the central bank and the equilibrium level of real GDP is depicted as the positively sloped curve YY in $(S, Y)$ space in Figure 15.1.[7] This curve has a positive slope because the expenditure-switching

---

[7]   Note that we are using the label YY to denote the goods market equilibrium condition, instead of the label GM that we actually used for the analysis of fixed exchange rates in Part 2. The reason is that the GM curve was drawn in $R$-$Y$ space, whereas the analysis we are now undertaking will be carried out in $S$-$Y$ space to facilitate comparison with the floating-rate equilibrium. For the same reason, we will use the AA terminology of Part 3 to label the asset-market equilibrium curve, rather than the label MM that we used in Part 2.

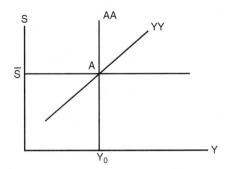

**Figure 15.1**    Short-run equilibrium with perfect capital mobility

effects of a devaluation of the exchange rate would tend to increase demand for domestic goods, and thus induce an increase in the equilibrium level of output. Given the domestic interest rate determined by UIP, the equilibrium level of real GDP is determined from the YY curve at the point where the official exchange rate $\bar{S}$ intersects it, labeled A in the figure. The asset market equilibrium curve AA, which is vertical under credibly fixed exchange rates (because the value of the official exchange rate does not affect the economy's asset-market equilibrium), adjusts passively as the result of capital inflows and outflows so as to pass through the intersection of $\bar{S}$ and YY.

Under floating exchange rates, on the other hand, in the case of permanent shocks, the economy's equilibrium configuration can be depicted using exactly the same curves, but with a different interpretation. In this case, as shown in Chapter 10, short-run macroeconomic equilibrium is determined by the intersection of the AA and YY curves. We can now interpret the horizontal line that determines the exchange rate as being the one that moves passively to the point of intersection of the other two.

With this analytical apparatus in hand, we can now consider each potential type of shock, and examine how it affects the economy under each of the two regimes. For a particular type of shock the regime to be judged superior is the one that keeps real output closest to its natural level in response to the shock. We will consider each type of shock in turn.

## Aggregate Demand Shocks

The effect of a shock that affects the aggregate demand for the domestic good is to shift the YY curve to the right or left, depending on whether the shock is an expansionary or contractionary one, respectively. Figure 15.2 illustrates the case of an expansionary shock. We will now consider how the economy would adjust to such a shock under the two alternative exchange rate regimes, remembering that under fixed rates the new equilibrium must lie along the unchanged $\bar{S}$ line, while under floating rates it must lie along the unchanging AA curve.

You can easily see that under floating exchange rates, shocks of this type would have no effect on real GDP. Because AA is vertical and its position is unaffected by such shocks, the economy moves from the point A to the point B in the figure, and the equilibrium level of real GDP does not change. Why not? The reason is that the exchange rate adjusts to affect expenditure switching in such a way as to exactly offset the effects of the shock on aggregate

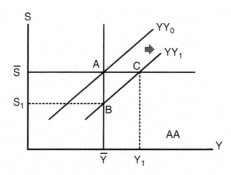

**Figure 15.2**   Real shocks and macroeconomic stability

demand for domestic goods. For example, if the shock is an expansionary one, as in the figure, under floating exchange rates the exchange rate will appreciate from $\bar{S}$ to $S_1$, switching spending away from domestic goods and exerting a contractionary effect on aggregate demand that exactly offsets the expansionary effects of the shock, leaving the equilibrium value of real GDP unchanged. Thus, exchange rate movements act as automatic stabilizers in response to aggregate demand shocks.

No such automatic stabilizer comes into play if the central bank maintains a fixed exchange rate. Indeed, since the $\bar{S}$ curve is unchanged in response to aggregate demand shocks, the equilibrium level of real GDP changes by the full amount of the horizontal shift in YY, and the economy's new equilibrium is at the point C in Figure 15.2. In other words, there is no mechanism in the economy that even partially dampens the effect of the shock on real economic activity, as there would be in a closed economy (through the standard crowding-out effects). We can therefore draw the following conclusion: *When domestic aggregate demand shocks are the dominant type of shock, floating exchange rates make the economy more stable than fixed rates and are thus preferable from the perspective of the stability criterion.*

## Monetary Shocks

Monetary shocks can come in the form of money demand shocks or money supply shocks. The latter may be hard to conceive, since up to this point in the book we have been assuming that there are no commercial banks in the economy and that money simply takes the form of currency, the supply of which is directly controlled by the central bank and is held directly by the public. If so, then a money supply shock would have to be the outcome of a policy decision by the central bank. To inject some realism into our stability criterion, however, it is useful to now expand our standard model slightly to allow a very simple role for commercial banks, since a world in which the decisions of commercial banks and the public can influence the (domestic component of) the money supply greatly enriches the possible sources of domestic financial shocks.

In such a world, the central bank only directly controls the monetary base, consisting of its own liabilities, which are held by the public in the form of currency and by commercial banks in the form of reserves. Using the symbol $H$ to denote the monetary base (because another term for the base is **high-powered money**), $CU$ the currency held by the public, and

*RES* the reserves held by commercial banks (remember that commercial banks hold reserves to meet the potential withdrawal requests of their customers), we can therefore write the monetary base as:

$$H = CU + RES \tag{15.2}$$

In a world with commercial banks, the money supply consists of the currency held by the public and the checking account balances, or **demand deposits** ($D$) that they hold at commercial banks:

$$M = CU + D \tag{15.3}$$

The public chooses the composition of the money supply by simply maintaining a constant ratio $c$ of currency in its hands to the demand deposits that it holds at commercial banks:

$$CU = cD \tag{15.4}$$

Finally, commercial banks hold reserves equal to a fraction $\sigma$ of their checking-account liabilities outstanding:

$$RES = \sigma D \tag{15.5}$$

In this model, the money supply is determined by the joint decisions of the central bank, the public, and the commercial banks. We can derive a convenient expression that shows how the actions of all three agents interact to determine the money supply by dividing (15.2) by (15.3), and then substituting from (15.4) and (15.5). The result is:

$$M/H = (CU + D)/(CU + RES) = (1 + c)/(c + \sigma)$$

This implies:

$$M = [(1 + c)/(c + \sigma)]H \tag{15.6}$$

The expression in square brackets in equation (15.6) is called the **money multiplier**. You can see that, since $0 < \sigma < 1$, the money multiplier is greater than one, so that \$1 in base money is typically transformed into more than \$1 of money supply by the actions of commercial banks (that is why the term *high-powered* money is used synonymously with monetary *base*).

For our purposes, however, what is important is that the actions of the public and the commercial banks can alter the size of the money multiplier, and thus of the total money supply, for a given value of the monetary base. You can easily see from equation (15.6) that if the public were to increase its desired ratio of currency to demand deposits $c$, or if commercial banks were to increase their desired reserve ratio $\sigma$, the money multiplier would decrease in value and the money supply would therefore contract, unless the central bank offsets these actions by increasing the monetary base $H$. Thus changes in the behavioral parameters $c$ and $\sigma$ can affect the money supply, and thus can generate money supply shocks.

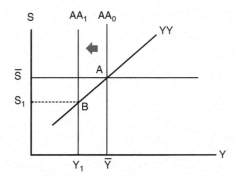

**Figure 15.3** Domestic financial shocks and macroeconomic stability

With this new perspective on money supply determination in hand, we can now see that monetary shocks can arise from money-supply shocks originating in changes in $c$ and/or $\sigma$ or money-demand shocks in the form of changes in the function $L(R,Y)$ that determines the public's total demand for money. Increases in $c$ or $\sigma$ that tend to contract the supply of money, as well as increases in the demand for money, would reduce the level of output that is consistent with equilibrium in the domestic money market for a given value of the domestic interest rate (which is pinned down by UIP in this setting). Thus, such shocks would tend to shift AA to the left. We can therefore refer to these as contractionary shocks. The opposite changes in each of these variables would obviously shift AA to the right, and these would therefore be characterized as expansionary monetary shocks.

How does the economy react to shocks of this type under the exchange regime alternatives that we are considering? Figure 15.3 considers the case of contractionary monetary shocks. As we have seen, such shocks have the effect of shifting the AA curve to the left. Under floating exchange rates, the economy's new equilibrium would once again be at the point of intersection of AA and YY – at a point like B – with reduced domestic output and an appreciated exchange rate. What happens in this case is that the contractionary monetary shock gives rise to an incipient excess demand for money, causing the domestic interest rate to rise, which attracts capital inflows that cause the exchange rate to appreciate. The negative expenditure-shifting effects of the exchange rate appreciation reduce the demand for domestic goods, thus lowering the level of income. The decrease in income must be sufficient to reduce the domestic demand for money by an amount that is just enough to restore equilibrium in the money market at an unchanged domestic interest rate. Thus, under floating rates monetary shocks affect the equilibrium value of domestic real GDP.

Under fixed rates, the contractionary shock would similarly cause an incipient rise in the domestic interest rate that would trigger capital inflows. But in this case, the central bank is forced to intervene in the foreign exchange market to prevent an appreciation of the domestic currency. To do so, it will have to buy foreign currency and sell domestic currency, thereby increasing the monetary base. If the contractionary shock takes the form of a reduction in the money multiplier, the expansion of the base would have to continue until it exactly offsets the reduction in the multiplier, restoring the money supply to its original value and thus allowing the money market to clear with an unchanged domestic interest rate and level of real output. If instead it takes the form of an increase in money demand, the base would expand to the point where the total money supply increases by just enough to satisfy the increased demand for money at the original levels of the domestic interest rate and real

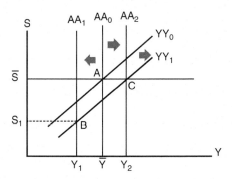

**Figure 15.4**   Foreign financial shocks and macroeconomic stability

output. In either case, the endogenous response of the money supply under fixed exchange rates acts as automatic stabilizer that returns the AA curve to its original position $AA_0$ in Figure 15.3, keeping the economy at the point A and thus preventing the shock from destabilizing real GDP. It follows that *when monetary shocks are the preponderant type of shock, fixed exchange rates make the economy more stable than floating rates, and are thus preferable on the basis of the stability criterion.*

### External Financial Shocks

For our purposes, external financial shocks take the form of changes in the world interest rate $R^*$. The effects of shocks of this type are slightly more complicated to illustrate, because both the YY and AA curves are drawn for given values of $R^*$, so a change in $R^*$ would tend to shift both curves. A reduction in $R^*$ would cause the YY curve to shift to the right, because a lower value of $R^*$ gives rise to a corresponding reduction in the domestic interest rate, which stimulates aggregate demand and thus calls for an increase in real GDP to maintain equilibrium in the goods market. Since a horizontal shift reflects a change in the equilibrium value of real output at a *given* value of the exchange rate, YY shifts to the right by the same amount under both floating and fixed exchange rate regimes. This is shown as a shift from $YY_0$ to $YY_1$ in Figure 15.4. On the other hand, Figure 15.4 shows that AA must shift to the left when the world interest rate falls, say from $AA_0$ to $AA_1$, because the associated reduction in the domestic interest increases the demand for money, and for a given value of the domestic money supply, this would require a lower value of $Y$ to maintain equilibrium in the money market.

Under floating exchange rates, the new equilibrium is at B, with an appreciated currency and a reduced level of domestic output. This happens because the reduced value of $R^*$ causes an incipient capital inflow at the original level of the domestic interest rate, which in turn causes the currency to appreciate and reduces the level of output by switching demand to foreign goods. The reduction in domestic output reduces the demand for money and causes the domestic interest rate to fall. This process must proceed to the point at which output has fallen sufficiently so as to allow the domestic money market to clear with an unchanged money supply but with a domestic interest rate that has fallen by enough to match the decline in the foreign rate. Thus the reduction in $R^*$ is contractionary under floating exchange rates, as we saw in Part 3.

Under fixed rates, by contrast, the central bank must intervene in the foreign exchange market by buying the additional foreign currency generated by capital inflows, so as to prevent the exchange rate from appreciating. As a result, the domestic money supply increases, which causes the domestic interest rate to fall and stimulates demand for domestic output, increasing the equilibrium value of real GDP in the goods market. This process must continue until the money supply has increased by enough (thus shifting the AA curve to the right) to satisfy the additional domestic money demand created by a higher level of domestic real GDP and a domestic interest rate that has fallen by an amount that matches the decrease in the foreign rate. Thus the shift must be from $AA_0$ to $AA_2$ in Figure 15.4, and the fixed-rate equilibrium will be at point C, with a higher level of output and an unchanged exchange rate. It is clear that the reduction in the foreign interest rate is expansionary in this case.

Thus, in response to a foreign financial shock, unlike in the other cases we have examined, domestic GDP will deviate from its initial equilibrium level under *both* exchange rate regimes, albeit in opposite directions. Neither regime provides complete insulation for the level of domestic economic activity. The question in this case is how large the deviation will be in the two cases, that is, which regime is most successful in insulating the domestic economy from the destabilizing effects of the shock.

Unfortunately, the answer is that no general conclusion can be drawn about this. Which regime is most successful in maintaining domestic macroeconomic stability will depend on the structure of the economy, that is:

- If the domestic demand for money is very sensitive to the interest rate, and not very sensitive to real income, then the initial (and final, under floating rates) leftward shift in AA will be large. If at the same time aggregate demand is not very sensitive to the interest rate, then the shift in YY will be small. Since the changes in equilibrium real GDP under floating and fixed rates are determined by the magnitudes of these two shifts respectively, under these circumstances C will be closer to $Y_0$ than B, and fixed rates will be preferable.
- Under the opposite circumstances (when the demand for money is very sensitive to real income, and not very sensitive to the interest rate, and when aggregate demand is very sensitive to the interest rate) B will be closer to $\bar{Y}$ than C, and floating rates will be preferable.

Thus when external financial shocks predominate, the choice of optimal regime is not unambiguous. In general, it will depend on the structure of the economy.

## 15.4   Weighing Optimality Criteria

We have now examined three independent optimality criteria for evaluating exchange rate regimes. It is worth reiterating the point made at the beginning of this chapter: the multiplicity of criteria has the important implication that considering all three criteria to be valid implies that the choice of exchange rate regime must be made by weighing multiple objectives. This means that even if we can come to the conclusion that a particular regime is best for meeting each objective, unless a single regime dominates for *all* objectives we will face the need to make a tradeoff among competing objectives. As we have seen, an extreme form of fixed exchange rate regime (dollarization or monetary unification) may have advantages from the perspective of reducing transactions costs in international commerce, but the choice between more conventional fixed exchange rates and floating rates is not clear in this case. On the other hand, theory and evidence weakly support the proposition that fixed rates may be a more effective pre-commitment device for central banks, thus resulting in lower rates of inflation. Finally, from the perspective of automatic short-run stabilization, which regime is superior depends on the sources of shocks to the economy.

To weigh the objectives in making the choice of optimal regime for a particular country, then, we would have to ask questions such as the following:

1 How important is it for the country to reduce transaction costs with a particular trading partner?
2 How costly is high inflation to the country, and how large a gain in the form of lower inflation might it expect when it switches from one regime to another?
3 How large are shocks to the economy, where do they tend to originate, and how much of an adjustment to such shocks can be achieved by flexible domestic wages and prices without an explicit policy response?

The important point is that, in light of considerations such as these, countries with different preferences or facing different circumstances may choose different exchange rate regimes, and the same country may choose different regimes at different points in time as its circumstances change.

What do these considerations suggest about the conditions under which the adoption of an extreme fixed exchange rate regime, in the form of some type of hard peg, would make sense? The answer is that there are indeed circumstances that favor the adoption of such a regime, but these circumstances are far from universal. They would include situations in which:

1 A hard fixed exchange rate is perceived to be useful because a country is very open and its trade is dominated by a single trading partner with stable prices.
2 The domestic central bank suffers from a time inconsistency problem, so gaining anti-inflationary credibility is very important.
3 Either domestic wages and prices are very flexible or, if they are not, the types of shocks to which the economy is typically vulnerable are such that a fixed exchange rate does a reasonably good job in providing some automatic stabilization. This would be the case if shocks to the economy are dominated by monetary shocks or if external financial shocks are very important and the structure of the economy is such that a fixed exchange rate provides the best insulation from such shocks.

By contrast, under what conditions might countries prefer to adopt floating exchange rate regimes? Several such conditions are suggested by the preceding discussion:

1 When the economy is relatively closed, so transactions costs in international commerce are not very important.
2 When long-run price stability is not a problem, because the country possesses an independent central bank with a well-established anti-inflationary reputation.

3 When aggregate demand shocks are important and domestic wages and prices are sticky in nominal terms.

---

**Empirical Study 15.1    Exchange Rate Regimes**
                            **and Inflation Performance**

In the real world, countries that have maintained fixed exchange rates have indeed tended on average to have experienced lower inflation rates than those with floating rates. Unfortunately, interpreting this evidence is trickier than you might think.

The problem is that it is hard to tell the direction of causation between exchange regime choice and inflation performance. It is not clear whether the relatively higher inflation experienced by countries with floating exchange rates arises because floating exchange rates cause higher inflation or because countries that have trouble keeping inflation low are forced to float their exchange rates.

Nonetheless, the existing evidence is indeed weakly supportive of the proposition that fixed exchange rates are more effective than floating rates as a commitment device for central banks. For example, a careful study by Ghosh et al. (1997), using a sample of 140 countries with data over the years 1960 to 1990, found that the rate of inflation tended to be lower in countries that maintained a fixed exchange rate, even after using statistical methods to control for the possibility that exchange regime choice is caused by inflation performance rather than vice versa.

Thus fixed exchange rates may indeed be more effective in promoting long-run price stability than floating exchange rates. However, because of the empirical problems just mentioned and the scarcity of studies that have addressed them, it is most accurate to say that the evidence we have on this issue is suggestive rather than conclusive.

---

## 15.5  Summary

Having separately analyzed, in Parts 2 and 3 of this book respectively, how small open economies operate under fixed and floating exchange rates, it is only natural to ask which exchange rate regime is best. In this chapter we have seen that the definition of "best" depends on the criterion by which one chooses to evaluate exchange rate regimes. Traditionally, three criteria have been used: the reduction of costs in international commerce, the stabilization of the domestic price level, and short-run stabilization of the economy in response to exogenous shocks.

We have analyzed how fixed and floating exchange rates perform with respect to each of these criteria and concluded that an extreme form of hard peg in which a country shares the same currency with at least one major trading partner may be desirable from the perspective of reducing transactions costs in international commerce. However, this criterion has little to say about the choice between other forms of fixed exchange rates and floating rates. We reviewed arguments (and some evidence) suggesting that fixed rates may be superior from the standpoint of inflation stabilization, though there is room for disputing this view.

Finally, for the purpose of automatically stabilizing the economy in response to exogenous shocks, which regime is superior depends on where those shocks originate.

All of this means that, as one well-known international macroeconomist has put it, "no single exchange rate regime is best for all countries at all times."[8] Since no exchange rate regime dominates with respect to all of the criteria that countries may use in making the choice between regimes, the choice of optimal regime will invariably require the weighing of objectives. Since the weight to be placed on each objective depends on the circumstances in which the country finds itself, and since these circumstances tend to be different both across countries as well as for a single country at different points in time, different countries may find different regimes to be optimal, and the optimal regime for a given country may be different at different points in time.

## Questions

1   In the wake of the Mexican crisis at the end of 1994, many observers formed the opinion that the international financial environment in which developing countries were likely to be operating over the next few years was likely to be a very unstable one (Read: $R^*$ would be bouncing around a lot). If you accept this view, how would it influence the advice you would give any particular developing country regarding whether it would be best for it to fix its exchange rate or allow it to float?

2   Many developing countries had their domestic macroeconomic equilibria disrupted by sharp decreases in US interest rates in the early 1990s. Assuming that such countries maintained fixed exchange rates at the onset of the interest rate shock:

   a  Explain what effect the fall in the foreign interest rate would have had on capital flows to/from such countries, on domestic real GDP, and on the current account of their balance of payments.

   b  Holding the foreign exchange regime unchanged, describe one domestic policy instrument that these countries could have used to offset the effects of the shock on domestic real GDP, and explain how it would have worked (i.e., using diagrams).

   c  How would domestic macroeconomic outcomes (real GDP) have differed if the countries had responded to the shock by switching to a floating exchange rate regime?

3   One lesson that seems to have emerged from recent experiences with financial reform around the world is that emerging market economies may have to face significant instability in domestic money demand and/or the domestic money supply function. How should this observation influence the choice that such countries might make between operating with fixed or floating exchange rate regimes?

4   Consider a small open economy that is highly integrated with world financial markets. As we have seen in this book, the exchange rate regime adopted by such a country has important effects on its macroeconomic performance. Explain how you would decide whether to advise such an economy to float or fix its exchange rate.

5   Consider the effects of a permanent external "real" shock (a change in $\theta$) on an economy that maintains a floating exchange rate. Would those effects differ if that

8    See Frankel (1999).

economy had no financial links with the rest of the world (**financial autarky**) from what they would be under perfect capital mobility? Explain why or why not.

6   Consider a small open economy that maintains a fixed exchange rate. Compare the stability of real output in response to monetary shocks for such an economy in the cases of financial autarky and perfect capital mobility.

## Further Reading and References

### On the effects of shared currencies on trade

Rose, Andrew (2000), "One Money, One Market: The Effects of Common Currencies on Trade," *Economic Policy*, Vol. 30 (April), pp. 7–46.

### On credibility and monetary policy

Barro, Robert J., and David B. Gordon (1983), "Rules, Discretion, and Reputation in a Model of Monetary Policy," *Journal of Monetary Economics*, Vol. 12, pp. 101–21.

### On the effects of the exchange rate regime on macroeconomic performance

Ghosh, Atish R., Anne-Marie Gulde, Jonathan Ostry and Holger Wolf (1997), *Exchange Rate regimes: Choices and Consequences* (Cambridge, MA: MIT Press).

Husain, Asim, Ashoka Mody and Kenneth Rogoff (2005), "Exchange Rate Regime Durability and Performance in Developing versus Advanced Economies," *Journal of Monetary Economics*, Vol. 52, No. 1, pp. 35–64.

Levy-Yeyati, Eduardo, and Federico Sturzenegger (2001), "Exchange Rate Regimes and Economic Performance," IMF *Staff Papers*, Vol. 47, pp. 62–98.

Levy-Yeyati, Eduardo, and Federico Sturzenegger (2003), "To Float or to Trail: Evidence on the Impacts of Exchange Rate Regimes," *American Economic Review*, Vol. 94, No. 4, pp. 1173–93.

### On exchange regime optimality

Frankel, Jeffery A. (1999), "No Single Currency Regime Is Right for All Countries or At All Times," Graham Lecture, Princeton University.

# Part 4
# International Monetary Cooperation

# 16

# The International Financial Architecture

...................................................................................................................

Previous chapters have largely considered international macroeconomics from the perspective of a single country, taking the world economic environment as given. We have implicitly been assuming that countries can choose their domestic macroeconomic policies (fiscal, monetary, and exchange rate policies) in an unconstrained fashion – that is, without any specific limitations arising from international agreements on the choices available to them. This assumption was partly motivated by the observation that most countries in the world are too small to perceptibly influence the external economic environment in which they operate, so the international community would have no reason to concern itself with policy formulation by individual countries.

As we have seen, however, at various times in history open economies have voluntarily participated in international monetary systems that specified certain "rules of the game." Such rules indeed imposed specific restraints on the formulation of domestic macroeconomic policies. We saw in Chapters 5 and 6 that under the hard exchange rate pegs characteristic of the international gold standard (1880–1913), these constraints affected both exchange rate and monetary policies. Under the soft pegs associated with the Bretton Woods system (1945–73), which we examined in Chapters 7 and 8, they primarily affected exchange rate policies.

Since the demise of the Bretton Woods system in 1973, countries have formulated macroeconomic policies by and large without internationally agreed upon or even tacitly accepted constraints of these types. Yet the International Monetary Fund (IMF), which provided the institutional foundation of the Bretton Woods system, has remained in operation, and other forms of international macroeconomic cooperation have emerged during this period. In Part 5 of this book, we will examine why and how countries have voluntarily decided to undertake international cooperation of a sort that constrains the domestic macroeconomic choices that they can make. The next three chapters will examine three forms that such cooperation has taken. They are arranged in increasing order of the severity of constraints that each type of cooperation tends to place on the formulation of domestic macroeconomic policies.

In this chapter, we will examine the evolution of the international "rules of the game" after the demise of Bretton Woods, with a specific focus on recent discussions, driven by a spate of currency crises during the decade of the 1990s, of several proposals for reforming the prevailing international monetary system (or non-system, as some have called it). These discussions, often described as a rethinking of the **international financial architecture**, would potentially affect all countries engaged in international commerce in one way or another. They do not, however, primarily concern the formulation of traditional macroeconomic policies at the national level. Instead, their focus is on the rules governing international capital flows as well as the behavior of the IMF and other prospective international financial institutions. Their primary impact on national macroeconomic policies would operate through the terms on which countries would access foreign private capital as well as on the conditions under which they would have access to an international "lender of last resort." Thus, proposals for reforming the international monetary system along these dimensions are the least constraining form of international macroeconomic cooperation that we will consider in this part of the book from the perspective of policymakers in individual countries.

A somewhat more intrusive form of cooperation has been the policy coordination process among the G-8 (a group of seven industrial countries plus Russia). This is an ongoing process of policy discussions among industrial countries that are of sufficient size so as to create the potential for their policies to exert macroeconomic spillover effects on other countries in the international system. As we will see in Chapter 17, such spillovers among large countries give each individual country an interest in the policies formulated by the others, and the G-8 policy coordination process is essentially a forum in which individual countries try to exert "peer pressure" on the others to induce them to modify their policies in ways that are perceived as beneficial to the group. Because this form of coordination, unlike the previous one, directly addresses the formulation of traditional macroeconomic policies, and because informal pressure is imposed on participating countries to behave in ways that they would not choose to do otherwise, this type of policy coordination is at least potentially more constraining on the individual countries that participate in it than a mere redesign of the rules of the game pertaining to private international capital flows and to official crisis lending.

Finally, a third form of coordination that has come to be extremely important in the post-Bretton Woods era has taken the form of monetary unification. As we discover in Chapter 18, this is by far the most constraining and intrusive form of international macroeconomic cooperation, since it effectively eliminates independent national exchange rate and monetary policies, and places – either implicit or even quite explicit – constraints on the formulation of fiscal policy. The best-known example of monetary unification is, of course the adoption of the euro as a new currency by 15 of the 27 (as of the time of writing) member states of the European Union. We shall see that other experiments in monetary unification are also under way elsewhere and are being actively considered, or at least have been proposed, for adoption in other parts of the world.

In this chapter, we take up the weakest form of international monetary cooperation that we will consider in this part of the book: the redesign of the international financial architecture. We begin by reviewing the evolution of exchange rate arrangements and the role of the IMF after the collapse of the Bretton Woods system. We then consider why changes in the international financial environment have created an interest in a new set of rules to govern international capital flows. Finally, we examine a set of specific proposals that have been offered of late for revising the international financial architecture.

## 16.1 The International Monetary System after Bretton Woods

To understand the proposals for reform of the international monetary system, it is important to establish a point of departure by examining the evolution of the system after the collapse of the Bretton Woods fixed exchange rate arrangement in 1973. As indicated in Chapter 8, the collapse of the arrangement left individual counties free to establish their own exchange rate policies, and this discretion was formalized in the form of the Jamaica Agreement in 1978, which modified the IMF's original Articles of Agreement to legalize the discretion of individual countries over exchange rate regimes.

### Exchange Rate Regimes and Capital Flows after Bretton Woods

The initial outcome, as shown in Table 16.1, was that most of the major industrial countries chose to float their currencies relative to each other, while most developing countries retained some form of fixed exchange rate, pegging the values of their currencies against that of a single major trading partner (usually an industrial country, with the US dollar being the most common ''anchor'' for exchange rate pegs), or to a basket of trading-partner currencies. It is worth noting that, since most developing countries trade much more with industrial countries than with each other, floating exchange rates among industrial countries meant that the *effective* nominal exchange rate (see Chapter 3) of a developing country that pegs its currency to that of a single industrial country would tend to fluctuate when the bilateral exchange rate among its trading partners does so. But that does not mean that the developing country has a floating exchange rate, of course, since those fluctuations in its effective exchange rate are exogenous to events in the developing country. At the same time,

**Table 16.1**  Exchange rate regimes in 1978

| Exchange rate regimes | Developing | Industrial |
|---|---|---|
| Exchange rate maintained within a relatively narrow margin | 61 | 0 |
| Cooperative exchange arrangements (under mutual intervention system) | 2 | 5 |
| Pegged to a composite of currencies | 31 | 5 |
| Adjusted according to a set of indicators | 7 | 1 |
| Exchange rate not maintained within narrow margins, or otherwise determined | 16 | 11 |

*Notes*: Classification of countries is from the World Bank, 2003.
''Industrial'' refers to high-income countries that are members of the Organization for Economic Cooperation and Development (OECD).

certain sub-groups of both industrial and developing countries participated in international arrangements that limited the fluctuations among their currencies. We will return to some of these experiences in Chapter 18.

A second feature of the post-Bretton Woods era is that the restrictions on capital movements that the Bretton Woods system had allowed to remain in place after World War II (see Chapter 7) were retained by most countries after the system collapsed. Thus, industrial country "floaters" maintained regimes of floating exchange rates with limited capital mobility, while developing-country "fixers" maintained fixed rates either with imperfect capital mobility or with capital accounts that were essentially closed. This situation began to change in the late 1970s, when the United States, the United Kingdom, and some other industrial countries began to open up their capital accounts, but for developing countries very little changed in this respect (except episodically) until the late 1980s.

What was the role of the International Monetary Fund in this environment? The IMF remained in existence, newly independent countries joined it, and the sizes of individual-member quotas were occasionally increased, albeit at a significantly slower pace than the growth in world trade during these years. It collected and published macroeconomic data, offered technical advice, and through a process referred to as **surveillance**, it provided (until recently, unpublished) periodic reports on the state of the economies of its member countries. These reports were discussed by the IMF's governing body, which offered nonbinding policy advice to member countries. Taking advantage of its international expertise, the IMF also published periodic reports and analyses on the state of the world economy.

Most importantly, the IMF continued to engage in lending activities. Not surprisingly, in view of the IMF's mandate to lend to countries facing a "temporary balance of payments need," the IMF's lending activities focused increasingly on developing countries, whose fixed exchange rates continued to make the overall balance of payments outcome an important policy objective.[1] Most of the countries that the IMF loaned money to during the early post-Bretton Woods years tended to have limited access at best to international capital markets, and to the extent that they did, it was only the public sectors of these countries that tended to be able to borrow from foreigners. The private sector was shut out of international borrowing by domestic capital controls, by poor availability of information about private borrowers in developing countries, or simply by the scarcity of creditworthy borrowers in such countries.

## 16.2    The International Debt Crisis

### Background

The end of the Bretton Woods regime in 1973 coincided with another important change in the international economic environment. Prior to 1973, most capital flows to developing countries had taken the form of subsidized loans from bilateral or multilateral aid agencies or foreign direct investment. A substantial increase in international oil prices in 1973, however, left oil-exporting countries flush with funds (recall the example of Kuwait in

---

[1]   The last IMF lending program involving an industrialized country was in 1983.

Box 2.2 in Chapter 2), a substantial portion of which they chose to invest overseas, mainly in large commercial banks in industrial countries. These banks, in turn, "recycled" these funds by lending them to the governments of several relatively large middle-income oil-importing developing countries, in the form of **syndicated loans** (loans funded jointly by several banks) with interest rates indexed to those prevailing in major financial centers. The availability of these funds enabled the borrowing countries to run larger current account deficits than they otherwise could have done, and consequently caused their international net creditor positions to deteriorate. By the end of the 1970s, some of these countries had become large net international debtors.

In part because the borrowing governments did not always allocate these funds properly, and in part because international financial conditions deteriorated for these countries at the beginning of the decade of the 1980s (in the form of the high interest rates and the industrial-country recession caused by the Reagan–Volcker disinflation described in Box 10.4 of Chapter 10), many of the heavily indebted developing countries, especially in Latin America, found themselves unable to service their debts. Since this created an obvious balance of payments need, the IMF, together with some of the major industrial countries, became heavily involved in lending to the heavily indebted developing countries as well as in designing policies to restore the viability of their balance of payments during the decade of the 1980s. During that decade, voluntary lending to the countries that were having difficulty servicing their debts essentially stopped. This episode became known as the **international debt crisis**.

The debt crisis faced the IMF with a set of circumstances not well anticipated by the framers of the Bretton Woods agreement that created the institution (see Chapter 7). Recall that the original mandate of the IMF was to extend loans to countries in temporary balance of payments difficulties (even if these difficulties would not have been "temporary" without major changes in macroeconomic policies), so that they could preserve their official exchange rate parities. In addition, the IMF could approve adjustments of a country's official exchange rate in the event of a "fundamental" disequilibrium. The implicit assumption was that a country's balance of payments troubles could be remedied through some feasible combination of fiscal, monetary, and exchange rate policies, as in the "internal and external balance" policy problem analyzed in Section 9.5 of Chapter 9. But the problem faced by the heavily indebted developing countries during the 1980s was quite different: these countries' governments had borrowed so much from international capital markets that no feasible combination of fiscal, monetary, and exchange rate policies would have enabled them to raise the resources to service their debts on the terms to which they had originally agreed. That is, these governments were technically **insolvent**.

Unfortunately, it took the international community a long time to recognize this fact, because there was an alternative interpretation of the heavily indebted countries' difficulties. That interpretation was that rather than being permanently unable to service their debts, these countries were just temporarily unable to do so – i.e., rather than being insolvent, these countries were perceived as simply **illiquid** (being unable to convert their resources into cash in order to make payments). This view was based on the fact that the international economic environment was particularly unfavorable during the early 1980s (particularly because of low demand for developing-country exports and high international real interest rates) and this, together with a "bunching" of principal repayments during the early 1980s on debt that developing countries had contracted in the 1970s, accounted for these countries' difficulties in meeting their debt obligations.

From this perspective, the solution to these countries' debt problems was that, together with adjustments in fiscal, monetary, and exchange rate policy in the indebted countries to increase net exports, the international community should provide these countries with emergency loans to tide them over until the situation improved. These loans came in the form of IMF lending, plus additional funds from industrial-country governments and from large banks that already had extended large syndicated loans to developing-country borrowers. The latter was referred to as **"concerted" lending**, because the banks were not eager to extend these loans voluntarily. They did so only as the result of "moral suasion" (direct pressure) by the IMF and industrial-country governments, who made the argument that providing new loans under these circumstances was the only way to prevent the existing loans from going into default. This explicit engagement of the private sector in providing funding for countries in balance of payments difficulties was a new role for the IMF, and not one directly envisioned by its framers.

Unfortunately, the "illiquidity" diagnosis of these countries' troubles proved not to be accurate, as recovery of the world economy, lower international real interest rates, and macroeconomic policy adjustments in the indebted countries did not prove to be sufficient to restore their capacity to service their debts, and voluntary private capital flows did not resume to the countries facing debt difficulties during the 1980s. The absence of capital flows, together with the macroeconomic uncertainties created by a large "overhang" of debt that could not be repaid, made the decade of the 1980s one of very poor macroeconomic performance in the heavily indebted developing countries. In fact, this period of time is referred to in Latin America as the "lost" decade, because of the reduced living standards that the macroeconomic difficulties associated with debt problems produced for many countries in the region. As Figure 16.1 illustrates, real living standards, measured by real GDP per person, barely changed over the decade of the 1980s for the heavily indebted countries that faced serious debt difficulties during the decade, both in Latin America and elsewhere.

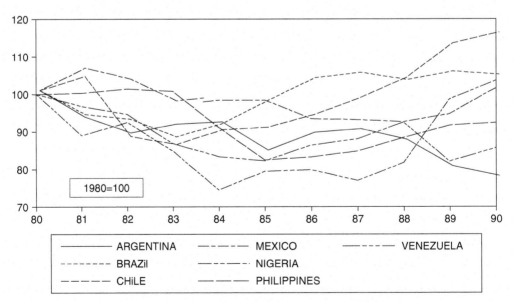

**Figure 16.1**  GDP per person in seven heavily indebted countries, 1980–9

The Brady Plan

The resolution of the international debt crisis, at least for the middle-income heavily indebted countries, finally came at the end of the decade when it became widely recognized that the debt problem was one of insolvency, rather than of illiquidity. Once it became clear that many countries were not going to be able to repay their debts, even under relatively favorable international circumstances and after making whatever domestic policy adjustments were feasible, the international community was faced with the need to resolve the issue of the debt that would remain unpaid. A plan to do so was developed under the leadership of US Treasury Secretary Nicholas Brady – therefore making it known as the Brady Plan – that involved the participation of the lending banks, the indebted countries, the IMF, and the industrial countries.

Under the Brady Plan, the lending banks agreed to write down a portion of their outstanding claims on the indebted countries. The remainder was converted into marketable bonds, in some cases with partial guarantees of interest payments provided through resources contributed by industrial countries. In return, the indebted countries undertook additional policy adjustments under the supervision of the IMF. The majority of the middle-income developing countries that had encountered debt-servicing difficulties during the 1980s agreed to Brady Plan restructuring of their outstanding debt over a short period of time after the inception of the Brady Plan, and by the early 1990s the way was once again clear for private capital to resume flowing to these countries.

## Implications of the Experience of the 1980s

The international debt crisis marked an important point in the evolution of the international monetary system. Recall that the International Monetary Fund had been founded as an institution to supervise the fixed exchange rate arrangement that had been designed for the post-World War II international monetary system. As we saw in Chapter 7, that system had been characterized by limited, but gradually increasing mobility of capital among countries, and especially among industrial countries. The collapse of the international fixed exchange rate system coincided with the advent of large private capital flows to developing countries, even if these flows were initially largely to the official sectors of these countries. But this new financial openness created the possibility of a new kind of macroeconomic instability, as developing countries' ability to service their new debt on market terms became very sensitive not only to how they managed their own economies, but also to changes in the international economic environment. The latter were driven not just by exogenous events, but also by the policies of industrial countries. And because when debt-servicing difficulties arose the affected parties were not just the indebted developing countries, but also the financial institutions in the industrial countries that had played the role of intermediaries, these difficulties had worldwide (systemic) implications. Thus the resolution of these problems involved all the players in the international system – industrial as well as developing countries – with the IMF playing a central coordinating role in allocating resources to countries in difficulties as well as overseeing their policy adjustments. While this was a natural evolution of the IMF's role under changed international circumstances, it was a far cry from the one-on-one lending in response to "temporary" balance of payments difficulties envisaged by its founders.

## 16.3    Changes in the International Macroeconomic Environment in the 1990s

The New Surge in Capital Inflows

Several factors combined to make the early 1990s a period of renewed capital flows to developing countries. The first of these was, of course, the resolution of the international debt crisis for middle-income developing countries through the Brady Plan. The elimination of the large overhang of unserviceable debt helped restore the creditworthiness of many of the heavily indebted countries. That creditworthiness was also enhanced by a second factor: the improved domestic macroeconomic policies that the urgency of the debt crisis and the Brady Plan itself had induced among the indebted countries. A third contributing factor was that these improved policies took the form not just of fiscal, monetary, and exchange rate policies that were more conducive to macroeconomic stability in those countries, but also of an enhanced role for the private sector in these economies as productive activities previously conducted by the government were turned over to the private sector, restrictions on the domestic financial system were removed, and private capital markets were developed. In addition, restrictions on private capital flows were weakened or eliminated in many developing countries, following a process of capital-flow liberalization that had begun in the industrial countries in the 1970s.

There were also structural changes in the industrial countries, where institutional investors became more prominent, and restrictions on access to capital markets by developing-country borrowers were eased. All of these factors contributed to increased capital mobility between industrial and developing countries. A major push was also given to capital flows toward developing countries by low domestic interest rates in the industrial countries, driven by a desire to combat a recession that had emerged in the early 1990s.

The combination of all of these factors resulted in a new surge of capital flows to developing countries in the early 1990s, concentrated in a small number (15–20) of middle-income developing countries whose enhanced links to international capital markets caused them to be dubbed **"emerging" economies**.[2] But this time, in contrast to the 1970s, capital flows tended to go directly to the revived private sectors in the developing countries (rather than to their governments), and they took the form not of syndicated bank loans, but of a combination of foreign direct investment and portfolio capital inflows (recall from Chapter 3 that these involve the purchase by foreign residents of bonds and equities issued by the domestic private sector) as well as short-term claims on developing country banks. Figure 16.2 shows the surge in debt (bonds and bank loans) and portfolio equity flows to all developing countries over the period from 1972 to 1997. The surge in flows during the 1970s, their sharp reduction in the 1980s, and strong revival in the early 1990s are all readily apparent.[3]

---

[2]    The main recipients of capital inflows during the early 1990s were Argentina, Brazil, Chile, Colombia, Costa Rica, Hungary, India, Indonesia, Korea, Malaysia, Mexico, Morocco, Pakistan, Peru, Philippines, Poland, Sri Lanka, Thailand, Tunisia, Turkey, and Venezuela. See World Bank (1997).

[3]    As we saw in Example 8.3 ("The Capital-Inflow Problem") these new capital inflows presented a strong macroeconomic challenge to the countries receiving them. Since the vast majority of these countries maintained fixed exchange rates, the arrival of capital inflows (which were modeled in Chapter 6 as a reduction in the international interest rate facing these economies) would have tended to expand the domestic money supply and exert a sharply expansionary pressure on aggregate demand unless the inflows were sterilized.

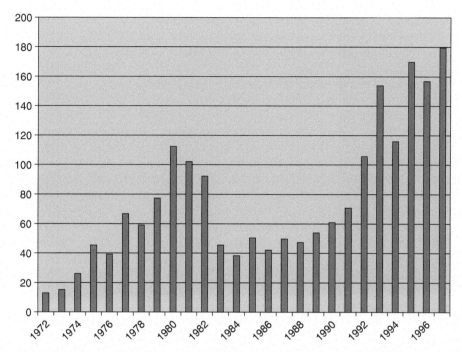

**Figure 16.2**    Net debt and portfolio equity flows to developing countries, 1972–97

Notice from Figure 16.2 that capital inflows to developing countries increased consistently during the early 1990s, but fell off in 1995. The reason for this is that the new order of things, in which emerging market economies became increasingly integrated with international capital markets, hit its first stumbling block at the end of 1994, in the form of a major currency crisis in Mexico.

## Emerging-market Crises in the 1990s

The Mexican crisis turned out to be the first of a succession of crises in emerging-market economies that had benefited from surges in capital inflows during the early years of the decade of the 1990s. As described in Box 9.4, the Mexican crisis was followed by crises in several important East and Southeast Asian countries in 1997, by an important crisis in Russia in 1998, a crisis in Brazil in early 1999, one in Turkey in 2001, and one in Argentina in 2002. Many of these crises had severe implications for living standards in the countries affected, and several characteristics of these crises led knowledgeable observers to the view that the international financial framework needed to be redesigned so as to prevent a recurrence of these problems in the future. Before moving on to consider proposals for revamping the international financial architecture, therefore, it is useful to provide a brief overview of characteristics of the crises of the 1990s to consider what it was about them that called the prevailing international financial framework into question.

In every case, these crises took place in the context of officially determined (fixed) exchange rate regimes, and in countries that had open capital accounts. Each crisis was preceded by large capital inflows. The crises consisted of sharp reversals of those capital flows (referred to as **"sudden stops"**) that created pressure on the central banks' stocks of foreign exchange reserves, eventually compelling central banks to abandon fixed exchange rates. When they did so, the currencies of the crisis countries typically depreciated very sharply, and in most cases the depreciation was accompanied by a severe contraction of economic activity.

All of these features had also been present in the debt crises of the 1980s. But the crises of the 1990s were different in some important respects. As indicated in Box 9.4, in the first emerging-economy crises of the 1990s – the Mexican and Asian crises – the situation in the affected countries was very different from that which prevailed at the onset of the previous decade's debt crisis. Specifically, the affected countries did not appear to be grossly mismanaged from a macroeconomic perspective. Fiscal deficits and public sector debt were not large, inflation rates were relatively low, and in some of the countries, at least, current account deficits were not large either by international standards or by the standards of the countries' own past history.[4] Partly for this reason, these crises came as a surprise to most observers, especially in the case of the Asian economies (Thailand, Korea, Malaysia, Indonesia, and the Philippines), whose previous economic performance had been described as a development "miracle."

One clue to the origin of these crises, however, is that they tended to be **"twin" crises**, in which a currency crisis coincided with a crisis in the domestic financial system in which many domestic financial institutions became insolvent. Why should this have been so? Prior to the 1980s, most developing countries not only maintained closed capital accounts, but they also imposed very strict controls over the actions of *domestic* financial institutions, especially banks. Banks were restricted in the interest rates that they could pay their depositors and charge on their loans, and they were subject to tight government regulations regarding to whom they could lend money. These types of policies, known as **financial repression**, have long been criticized by economists for their adverse effects on the allocation of financial resources and thus harmful effects on economic growth.

In a process referred to as **financial liberalization**, these restrictions began to be removed during the late 1980s as part of the growth-oriented macroeconomic reforms implemented by many emerging-market economies in an attempt to resolve their debt-servicing difficulties. However, the process of financial liberalization was not well managed in many countries. The problem is that, while excessive (and wrong-headed) regulation of the financial sector can harm economic growth, financial transactions have special characteristics that create a role for (appropriate) government regulation of the financial sector. In particular, financial intermediation involves **moral hazard**, the notion that when people are protected from the harmful consequences of their actions, they will be less likely to behave so as to avoid those consequences. Essentially because they are investing other people's money, financial intermediaries are subject to moral hazard. Since most of the funds they lend come from depositors, bank owners do not suffer the bulk of the losses when loans go bad. On the other hand, because deposits pay fixed interest rates, bank owners reap the bulk of the gains when loans yield very high returns. Moral hazard thus creates strong incentives for banks, left to their own devices, to engage in excessively risky lending. When this situation is allowed to proceed unchecked – that is, without government regulations that require bank owners to invest a substantial amount of their own money and that prohibit excessively risky lending – the banking system can become highly vulnerable to changes in the economic environment, and potential losses are even greater when a country's capital account is open, since banks can then expand their deposits by drawing on overseas funds.

---

[4]    There were exceptions. Current account deficits were large in Mexico in 1994, in Thailand in 1997, and, to a lesser extent, in Malaysia in 1997.

This is essentially the situation that prevailed in most of the major crises of the 1990s, especially those of Mexico and the countries affected by the 1997 Asian crisis. Inappropriate liberalization of the domestic financial system – that is, liberalization without the appropriate safeguards in place to minimize the risks associated with moral-hazard lending – made these economies vulnerable to even relatively minor adverse changes in their economic environments.

Finally, another important characteristic of these crises is that they tended to spread, in some cases regionally, and in at least one case – that of Russia in 1998 – internationally. This phenomenon, known as crisis **contagion**, was limited in scope during the Mexican crisis (though as we saw in Box 9.2, events in Mexico in 1994 had significant impacts on Argentina in early 1995), but was quite important after the Asian and Russian crises.[5]

The mechanisms through which contagion happened have proven to be controversial. One possibility is that what appears to be contagion is actually many countries responding to a shock that is common to all of them. This is likely to have been important, for example, in explaining the widespread nature of the debt crisis of the 1980s, since as we have seen, adverse changes in international financial conditions affected many heavily indebted countries at the same time. A second possibility is that crises spread through normal trading channels, as an economic downturn in one country reduced its demand for the products of another, thus spreading the downturn to the second country. Alternatively, a sharp depreciation in a crisis country's real exchange rate may have made its products more competitive in international markets, adversely affecting the demand for goods sold by countries exporting similar products and thus transmitting an economic downturn to such countries.

A third mechanism, however, is that contagion may simply reflect **panic** in international capital markets, when one country's difficulty in servicing its debts may create the suspicion that similarly placed countries would encounter similar difficulties, as is the case with bank panics in the domestic economy. Panics can create crises because the loss of resources associated with a sudden withdrawal of funds from a country as a result of a panic can make it difficult for creditors in that country to meet their debt service obligations, even if they would normally have been able to do so in the normal course of business. Essentially the panic creates a situation of illiquidity.[6] The solution to a panic is for some entity not affected by the panic to make loans to countries suffering from illiquidity as a result of the panic, allowing them to meet their payment obligations until the panic subsides, at which time the loans provided by that entity can be repaid. This is precisely the mechanism that protects the banking systems of many countries from panics, known as **bank runs**. The entity that provides loans to banks suffering from panic-driven withdrawals of funds is known as the **lender of last resort**, and in most countries that function is performed by the central bank.

## An International Lender of Last Resort?

The closest thing that the international financial community has to a lender of last resort for countries, however, is the International Monetary Fund. The IMF indeed became involved

---

[5] Empirical Study 16.1 compares the incidence of international contagion during recent years with the gold standard era (1880–1914).

[6] Remember that this was indeed the original (mistaken) diagnosis by the international financial community of the international debt crisis of the 1980s.

in the resolution of many of the crises of the 1990s.[7] The model for IMF involvement was quite similar to that followed during the debt crisis of the 1980s. In particular, the IMF was at the center of international cooperative efforts to resolve these crises, coordinating the actions of the industrial creditor countries and the affected emerging-market economies. It lent money to the crisis countries out of its own resources, and cooperated with the main creditor countries to raise loans from industrial-country governments. As in the 1980s, these loans were extended under strict policy conditionality.

In contrast to the 1980s, however, the IMF's role in these crises was sharply criticized by many observers. Among other things, the Fund was criticized for not having adequately foreseen or prevented the emergence of the crises, for having attached inappropriate policy conditions to its loans, for not having provided lending on an adequate scale, and for not having disbursed its lending quickly enough.

One particularly serious criticism is that the IMF may actually have helped to *cause* the crises. The alleged mechanism relies on moral hazard. In the context of currency crises, the allegation is that the crises were caused by borrowing countries taking out loans from international creditors that they had little realistic prospect of repaying. The question, of course, is why lenders would have made these loans if that were true. The answer given by these critics is that the lenders did so counting on IMF bailouts. In other words, even if the countries themselves lacked the resources to repay, the availability of IMF money for the borrowing countries would provide the resources with which lenders could be repaid, so the lenders would actually be protected from the consequences (at least for them) of their actions in lending money where the prospects for profitable uses of the funds were not very promising. Thus, IMF lending is perceived as creating moral hazard in international capital markets, driving capital flows that must eventually culminate in a crisis that triggers IMF lending.

Proponents of this view cite as evidence the surge in international lending to developing countries after 1995 that we already noted in Figure 16.2. The Mexican crisis at the end of 1994 created substantial uncertainty in international capital markets at the beginning of 1995, but the resources lent by the IMF and industrial country creditors to Mexico in early 1995 proved to be enough for Mexico to repay all the bond debt that it had accumulated. In the view of proponents of the moral hazard argument, this suggested to international creditors that their lending to emerging-market economies was "backstopped" by the resources of the IMF and the industrial countries, and thus resulted in even larger capital flows to emerging market economies in 1996 and 1997.

The moral hazard story may have particular force when applied to Russia, which had received a succession of loans from the IMF and industrial countries during the 1990s despite its less-than-stellar economic performance. The view apparently taken by many participants in international financial markets was that Russia was too big and "too nuclear" (i.e., had too many nuclear weapons) for the international community to countenance the likely chaos that might ensue within the country as the result of a massive Russian default on the country's external debt.[8] In the event, however, the Russian crisis in August 1998 was in fact triggered by a policy decision taken by the IMF and the industrial countries to cease making resources available to the country, in light of its unsatisfactory policy performance.

---

[7]   The 1997 crisis in Malaysia, the 1998 crisis in Russia, and the crisis in Argentina in 2002 were exceptions.
[8]   In fact, lending to Russia at high interest rates before August 1998 was at times described by international financial market participants as a "moral hazard play."

A further piece of support for the moral hazard view is that the Russian default actually sent off shock waves around in the world, in the form of a substantial reduction in lending for risky activities (including to emerging-market economies). In the view of many observers, this was because the withholding of funds from Russia indicated that the international "rules of the game" had changed, and the resources of the IMF and industrial country creditors would no longer be available to backstop lending to emerging market economies.

## 16.4    Proposals for Reforming the International Financial Architecture

Domestic financial liberalization in emerging market economies increased the likelihood of financial crises, and enhanced globalization (in the form of intensified trade and financial linkages) during the 1990s increased the importance of spillover effects. These links increased interest in the oversight of each country's policies by the international community as a whole. But the experience of the 1990s suggested that under the prevailing international financial system, opportunities for meaningful oversight might be limited. Thus, the stage was set for proposals to revamp the international financial system in order to reduce the incidence of crises. These proposals have covered a number of different areas. In this section, we will briefly review some of them.

### Exchange Rate Regimes

As noted in the previous section, the major crises of the 1990s afflicted countries that maintained fixed exchange rate regimes. And as we discussed in detail in Chapter 9, that observation, together with the "second generation" currency crisis theory that we reviewed there, has driven many observers to the conclusion that soft pegs are not sustainable under conditions of high capital mobility. Thus, one proposal for reform of the international financial system, directed at the emerging-market economies themselves as well as to the IMF as crisis-resolution coordinator, is that countries that become financially more integrated with world capital markets should abandon soft pegs before they are forced to do so in the context of a currency crisis. During the late 1990s and early 2000s, this proposal was framed in the form of the "bipolar view" (see Chapter 9), suggesting that countries should opt either for floating exchange rates or for hard pegs. The role of the IMF in this proposal is that its policy advice should seek to guide countries away from the use of exchange rate regimes that high capital mobility would render untenable.

Recall from Chapter 9 that Argentina adopted a currency board in 1991. The Argentine currency board collapsed in a crisis in early 2002, in part because the currency board was unable to impose sufficient fiscal discipline on the Argentine government to avert a government debt crisis reminiscent of those of the early 1980s. This experience has polarized exchange regime choices even further in the eyes of many observers, and emerging market economies are now often advised to float their currencies or to abandon them altogether by dollarizing (recall from Chapter 9 that this term also encompasses the use of currencies other than the US dollar). Thus, one reform proposal is that the IMF exert moral suasion or condition its loans to guide countries to the extreme polar ends of the spectrum of exchange rate regimes.

## Rules for Transparency and Disclosure

Recall from the previous section that one interpretation of the international contagion that characterized several of the major crises of the 1990s is that it was induced by panic. One way to define panic is as an overreaction to new information. Individuals are likely to overreact to new information of a negative character, say, if they interpret it as a signal that there is more negative information that has not yet come to light. One proposal to reduce the likelihood of panic in international capital markets, then, is to induce countries to compile and disclose more information about their macroeconomic and financial conditions. This move to enhance **transparency** has already begun to be implemented through the IMF. The Fund has begun to publish some (for the countries that have granted it permission to do so) of its periodic reports on economic conditions prevailing in individual countries on its website (you can read some of these at imf.org), and it has also promulgated various sets of standards for the compilation and disclosure of economic information on issues such as countries' external debt and reserve positions, as well as on the health of domestic financial sectors.

It is important to emphasize that improved transparency and disclosure are important not just to minimize the risk of panic, but also for international capital markets to do their job in the first place – that is, to allocate resources to where they are likely to be used most productively, and to withhold resources from countries where they are not likely to be well managed. In that way international financial markets can more effectively impose discipline on macroeconomic management in individual countries – by providing resources when they are likely to be used effectively and withholding them when they are not. Because few economists question the benefits of transparency and disclosure, this is a reform proposal that has been widely embraced by the international financial community.

## International Lender of Last Resort

As mentioned in the previous section, the presence of a lender of last resort can also protect financial markets from panics. This is because borrowers who are solvent, but face problems servicing their debts due to a panic that deprives them of liquid funds, can obtain such funds from a lender of last resort, thereby staving off default until the panic subsides. To function effectively as a lender of last resort, an institution should have the means to lend in large amounts and should have the ability to distinguish between borrowers who are insolvent and those who are merely illiquid, reserving its lending only for the latter. It should lend at penalty interest rates, to discourage appeals for its funds except in times of emergency.

As also indicated in the last section, the IMF is the institution that comes closest to functioning as an international lender of last resort. But the IMF as presently structured faces handicaps as an international lender of last resort, because it cannot lend quickly and reliably in large amounts. Thus, an additional proposal for reform of the international monetary system is to restructure the IMF so as to provide it with much larger liquid resources and allow it to develop procedures to disburse funds more quickly such as, for example, by pre-qualifying countries for lender-of-last-resort borrowing.

However, this proposal has proven to be very controversial. At issue is the very fundamental question of whether an international lender of last resort would do more harm than good. Some observers have expressed the view that the absence of an effective international lender of last resort may have increased the frequency and severity of crises, essentially by allowing panic to escalate and spread in international financial markets. Recall that one view of the mechanism underlying contagion was precisely that it was panic-induced.

However, opponents of an international lender of last resort emphasize the moral hazard argument. They argue, as we have seen, that crises have been aggravated by moral hazard associated with bailouts. Increasing the scale and certainty associated with the provision of resources to countries undergoing crises would only aggravate the moral hazard problem, according to this view, and not only increase the frequency and severity of crises, but – even in the absence of crises – would distort the international allocation of resources by inducing an excessive flow of resources to countries that have the opportunity to avail themselves of funds from an international lender of last resort.

In addition, the proposal to pre-qualify countries for last-resort borrowing has its own problems. On the one hand, countries that seek such pre-qualification might fear to reveal themselves as potential candidates for crises.[9] On the other hand, for countries that have pre-qualified, the Fund would be under intense pressure not to remove their qualification if conditions in those countries changed, because doing so might influence perceptions in international financial markets in such a way as precisely to trigger a panic-driven crisis of the sort that the facility is supposed to prevent.

For these reasons, the international community has as yet taken only very limited steps to refashion the IMF into an international lender of last resort.

## Standstill Agreements

The need for funds in the context of a crisis and the potential role of moral hazard have given rise to yet a different kind of reform proposal: the implementation of **standstill agreements**. These are essentially agreements among creditors not to withdraw funds from crisis countries (i.e., to "stand still") under a carefully defined set of pre-specified conditions. One possible set of conditions, for example, could involve a simple declaration by the IMF. If the IMF triggers the provisions of the agreement, creditors would be bound to leave funds in the country for some specified period of time, effectively **"rolling over"** (i.e., adding to the principal due on the loan) any payments due to them. Implementing such an arrangement would involve inserting legal clauses in bond contracts suspending the right of individual bondholders to sue to recover their funds if a standstill is declared.

The benefits of such an arrangement, of course, include the fact that they would effectively provide funds to crisis countries when they most need them, by removing the need for funds to make payments to external creditors. The creditors themselves may benefit from such an arrangement – even though it constrains what they can do with their money – to the extent that the declaration of a standstill avoids the economic disruptions associated with a panic-driven crisis and makes it more likely that they will eventually be fully repaid. But there may be benefits even if losses to creditors *cannot* eventually be avoided. Standstill agreements would in effect "bail in" private creditors rather than allow them to be bailed out by official international lending. By forcing creditors to share some of the losses (rather

---

[9]   Indeed, a limited move in the direction of increasing the IMF's lender-of-last-resort function took the form of the creation of a Contingent Credit Facility (CCF) shortly after the Asian crisis. This was a special lending facility for which countries could pre-qualify to be entitled for a limited amount of quickly disbursing funds in the event of a crisis. Precisely because of the fear mentioned above, no countries sought this qualification, and the facility was abandoned in 2003.

than shifting them all to taxpayers in the crisis countries and any industrial countries that provide resources on less than market terms), standstill agreements may help to ameliorate moral hazard problems in international lending.

However, critics of such proposals maintain that uncertainties associated with such agreements may turn this particular "benefit" into a serious cost. They argue that the prospect of a standstill will make the returns from international lending so much more uncertain that they would significantly diminish capital flows to developing countries. Moreover, they argue that standstills may actually trigger the very crises they are designed to prevent or ameliorate, by giving creditors an incentive to pull their funds out of borrowing countries before a standstill is declared. Again, because of these conflicting views, no general procedures have as yet been implemented for "bailing in" private creditors through standstill agreements.

## Capital Controls

Finally, the rash of currency crises during the 1990s has led to some rethinking in the international financial community about the costs and benefits of capital controls. At the time of the Asian crisis in 1997, the IMF's governing body (then known as the Interim Committee) was considering a proposal to amend the IMF's Articles of Agreement to give the Fund a mandate to work for the removal of capital account restrictions. The argument for the benefits of doing so was essentially that restrictions on capital flows impeded the allocation of productive resources to their most efficient uses.

However, the frequency and severity of crises among emerging-market economies that had opened their capital accounts at the end of the 1980s gave the international financial community pause regarding the wisdom of rapid transitions to open capital accounts, and the proposal before the Interim Committee has been shelved. Not only does theory suggest that capital account restrictions can reduce susceptibility to currency crises (see Chapter 9), but the experience of the 1990s, in which several countries with relatively closed capital accounts (notably China and India) avoided currency crises despite having many features in common with countries that succumbed to such crises, has also driven home the point that an open capital account can be dangerous if the quality of domestic macroeconomic management or of the domestic financial system potentially suffers from serious shortcomings. Thus the new conventional wisdom on this issue is that countries should not necessarily rush to open capital accounts, but should do so only when the quality of domestic economic policies is sufficiently strong.

---

## Empirical Study 16.1    Contagion Then and Now

An important factor driving the rethinking of the international financial architecture during recent years has been the cross-country spread of financial crises, especially in the cases of the Asian and Russian crises of 1997 and 1998 respectively. The increased real and financial integration of the world economy in the last decades of the 20th century may have been an important factor facilitating the cross-country spread of such crises. But, as we saw in Chapter 5, the world economy was also highly integrated during the heyday of the gold standard (1880–1914). How does the contagion phenomenon during recent years compare to the experience during that early wave of globalization?

This question was investigated by Bordo and Murshid (2006). Bordo and Murshid used three empirical approaches: they looked at the international co-movements in spreads on long-term bonds as well as in indicators of **exchange market pressure** (EMP, to be described below), they looked at measures of global crises in financial markets, and they used VAR impulse response functions to examine the direction and impact of financial shocks among countries. Their gold standard sample included 15 countries (5 advanced and 10 "emerging" economies), while their post-Bretton Woods sample included up to 23 (5 G-8 economies, and 15 emerging economies, plus Greece, Portugal, and Spain). The index of exchange market pressure was a weighted average of movements in exchange rates, short-term interest rate differentials, and reserves, the idea being that pressure for capital outflows, say, would tend to show up in some combination of exchange rate depreciation, higher domestic interest rates, and reserve losses, depending on the exchange rate and monetary policies pursued by the country that is under such pressure. The weights used were based on the ratio of the reciprocal of the standard deviation of each variable to the sum of the reciprocals of the standard deviations of all three variables. These weights are constructed so that they sum to one and no single variable dominates movements in the index.

To determine the degree of co-movement in the long-term bond spreads in the two periods, Bordo and Murshid estimated the **first principal component** of the spread time series in both periods.[10] In both samples the first principal component captured about 60 percent of the variation in the data, suggesting that the degree of co-movement was similar in the two periods. However, the degree of co-movement was much lower for EMP in both periods, although there was more co-movement during the gold standard (36 percent of the variance explained by the first principal component) than in the post-Bretton Woods period (25 percent).

Bordo and Murshid constructed a global crisis index based on the first principal component of the EMP data. Global crises were defined to have happened when the first principal component exceeded a threshold value that was set to be the same for both periods. They found that the incidence of global crises, measured as the percentage of monthly observations that exceeded this threshold value, was higher in the first period (12 percent of all observations) than the second (only 2 percent).

Finally, to examine the geographic pattern of transmission in the two periods, Bordo and Murshid estimated VARs based on weekly interest rate data for several groups of countries. They found that during the gold standard era, shocks to the United Kingdom and Germany were transmitted to other countries, whereas shocks to emerging economies were not transmitted back to the advanced economies or to each other. In the more recent period, shocks tended to be transmitted among the advanced European countries to each other, and among the emerging European countries to each other, but not between advanced and emerging economies in Europe. In a separate grouping containing the United States, Japan, and several Asian emerging economies, shocks were largely transmitted from the United States to the others.

*(Continued)*

---

[10]    To estimate the principal components for $N$ time series of length $T$, run a regression where the dependent variable is a $NT \times 1$ vector with the $N$ series stacked on top of each other, and there are $N$ independent variables, each consisting of one of the series stacked on itself $N$ times. The $T \times 1$ vector containing the fitted value of this regression for the first $T$ observations is the first principal component, and the $R^2$ of this regression is the percentage of the total variance of the $N$ series explained by the first principal component. To extract the second principal component, run a similar regression, but this time using the residuals from the first regression as the dependent variable.

**Empirical Study 16.1**    *(Continued)*

Overall, "contagion" appears to be an important phenomenon in both "globalized" eras, but the geographic pattern of transmission was more centralized during the gold standard years than it has been during the post-Bretton Woods period.

## 16.5    Summary

The post-Bretton Woods international monetary system has been described as a "nonsystem" because of the relatively large discretion that it left individual countries with respect to their macroeconomic policies. However, the increased integration of international economies that has accompanied the process of globalization has created important spillover effects of events in one country on other members of the international economic system. These spillover effects have increased the perceived benefits of various forms of international cooperation, which essentially involves the voluntary acceptance by individual countries of limits on their policy discretion for the sake of benefits to the international community.

In the immediate post-Bretton Woods period, such cooperation was conducted through the activities of the International Monetary Fund (IMF), which served as the conduit through which the international community provided assistance to individual countries in exchange for commitments to resolve domestic macroeconomic difficulties in ways that were not destructive of international prosperity. During the decade of the 1980s, however, the increased flow of resources from industrial-country banks to developing countries eventually resulted in a generalized debt crisis that was resolved only through the combined efforts of the indebted countries themselves, the IMF, and industrial countries. As financial integration increased during the 1990s, new and different kinds of crises emerged – crises that proved to be difficult to predict, severe in their effects, and that had a disturbing tendency to spread beyond the borders of individual countries. This changed set of circumstances has created strong incentives for enhanced cooperation in the form of redesigning the "rules of the game" governing international financial relations. In this chapter we have reviewed several proposals for reforming the international financial architecture, but most of these proposals are still in their infancy.

These rules pertain largely to macroeconomic and financial relationships between industrial and developing countries. However, international cooperation has been proceeding at the same time among industrial countries themselves, and this type of cooperation has focused not just on "rules of the game" – that is, on the framework within which countries interact with each other macroeconomically – but has actually gone further, addressing specific policy choices made by individual countries. This type of international policy coordination among industrial countries is the subject of the next chapter.

**Questions**

1    Show how the equilibrium level of real GDP in a small open economy that maintains a fixed exchange rate and is imperfectly integrated with world capital markets would be affected by a reduction in world interest rates.

2   How would a relaxation of capital controls that resulted in a higher degree of substitutability between domestic and foreign bonds affect your answer to question 1?

3   How could the phenomenon of "contagion" described in this chapter be represented in the fixed exchange rate-imperfect capital mobility model of Chapter 8?

4   In Chapter 9, you learned that "second generation" currency crises could sometimes be self-fulfilling. How would the existence of an international lender of last resort affect the likelihood of self-fulfilling currency crises?

5   Would you expect the implementation of effective "standstill" agreements to increase or decrease private capital flows to emerging economies? Explain your reasoning.

## Further Reading and References

### On the evolution of the IMF after Bretton Woods

Fieleke, Norman (1994), "The International Monetary Fund 50 Years after Bretton Woods," Federal Reserve Bank of Boston, *New England Economic Review* (September/October), pp. 17–30.

### On capital flows to developing countries in the 1990s

World Bank (1997), *Private Capital Flows to Developing Countries: The Road to Financial Integration* (Oxford: Oxford University Press).

### On contagion

Bordo, Michael D. and Antu Pannini Murshid (2006), "Globalization and Changing Patterns in the International Transmission of Shocks in Financial Markets," *Journal of International Money and Finance*, Vol. 25, pp. 655–74.

### On the IMF and capital controls

Fischer, Stanley (1998), "Should the IMF Pursue Capital-Account Convertibility?" International Finance Section, Department of Economics, Princeton University, *Essays in International Finance* No. 207 (May).

### On proposals to reform the international monetary
### system after the crises of the 1990s

Couere, Benoit and Jean Pisani-Ferry (2000), "Events, Ideas, and Actions: An Intellectual and Institutional Retrospective on the Reform of the International Financial Architecture," paper prepared for the CDC-CEPII-CEFI international conference on reshaping the architecture of the international financial system (Sienna, May 23–24, 2000).

Goldstein, Morris (2001), "An Evaluation of Proposals to Reform the International Financial Architecture," paper prepared for NBER conference on "Management of Currency Crises," Monterrey, California, March 28–31.

Little, Jane Sneddon, and Giovanni P. Olivei (1999), "Why the Interest in Reforming the International Monetary System?" *New England Economic Review* (Federal Reserve Bank of Boston), November/December, pp. 53–84.

Little, Jane Sneddon, and Giovanni P. Olivei (1999), "Rethinking the International Monetary System: An Overview," *New England Economic Review* (Federal Reserve Bank of Boston), November/December, pp. 3–24.

# 17

# G-8 Policy Coordination

In the last chapter we examined two forms of international policy cooperation: agreement on a common set of rules to govern international financial transactions, and special *ad hoc* arrangements among the IMF as well as particular groups of industrial and developing countries to help resolve emerging-market financial crises. These types of international financial cooperation had three features in common: they involved cooperation among industrial and developing countries, they featured an important role for the International Monetary Fund as an intermediary, and they were designed to prevent and/or resolve extreme macroeconomic events. From the perspective of constraining domestic policies, the special *ad hoc* arrangements that emerged to handle crises had the property that they were asymmetric, in the sense that they caused only one of the parties to the arrangement – the developing countries in crises – to modify their domestic policies relative to what they otherwise would have been.

This is, however, not the only form that international cooperation has taken in the post-Bretton Woods period. Institutional arrangements have also arisen to foster macroeconomic cooperation among the industrial countries themselves. As we will see in this chapter, this form of cooperation is quite different from that examined in Chapter 16. It takes place both inside and outside the framework of the IMF and it concerns the formulation of fiscal and monetary policies during normal times, rather than during times of crisis.

In this chapter we examine why industrial countries may find it desirable to coordinate their macroeconomic policies. As we will see, the basic reason is that when the small country assumption fails, the effects of macroeconomic policies in one country can spill over to other countries, thus giving each country an interest in what other large countries do. We will explore these interactions in the next section by extending our analytical framework to the **large-country** case – that is, the case in which the country under analysis has sufficient weight in the world economy that its actions can appreciably affect macroeconomic outcomes in the rest of the world. We also briefly survey the history of cooperative arrangements among industrial countries that potentially fit the ''large country'' definition, in the sense that their macroeconomic actions may have significant spillovers on each other. As we will see, these cooperative arrangements have been very loose indeed, consisting largely of **surveillance** over (sharing information about) each other's policies through various means, as well as the exercise of **moral suasion** (peer pressure) to induce countries to adopt specific policies or to change current policies in certain ways in the context of periodic meetings among representatives of the Group of Eight (G-8) countries, consisting of the largest industrial economies (the United States, Japan, Germany, the United Kingdom, France, Italy, and Canada), plus Russia.[1]

## 17.1 Why Coordinate? Theory

International policy coordination becomes an issue when the policies adopted by one country exert spillover effects on the rest of the world. In the small open economy models that we have been analyzing in the book up to this point, the issue of policy coordination does not typically arise outside of the context of the crisis ''contagion'' that we discussed in Chapter 16, because any single country is too small to have any impact on the rest of the world. Thus, our first task in addressing this issue is to consider the macroeconomics of the large-country case – that is, the open-economy macroeconomics of a country that is large enough for its domestic policies to influence what happens macroeconomically in the rest of the world.

To do so, in this section we will go back to our basic analytical framework and explore how it has to be modified in order to describe the macroeconomics of a country that is large enough for its policies to affect macroeconomic outcomes in its trading partners. As we will see, the complications that arise in this case are that if a country's policies can actually affect macroeconomic outcomes in the rest of the world, then our model will need to be able to explain macroeconomic outcomes in the rest of the world, as well as the feedback effects of those changed outcomes on the first country.

### A Large-country Model

As a point of departure, notice that what we want to model are policy interactions among industrial countries. As we have already noted, such countries (or country blocks, in the case of the **Eurozone**, the set of countries that have adopted the euro as a common currency) tend to maintain floating exchange rates among each other. That is true, for example, between the Eurozone and each of the non-euro members of the G-8 (the United States, Japan, the United Kingdom, Canada, and Russia). Moreover, as we have seen, under contemporary circumstances financial links among these countries are well described by the assumption of perfect capital mobility. Thus, in describing the large-country case, we will adopt the floating exchange rate–perfect capital mobility framework of Part 3 of this book. To concentrate on the macroeconomic stabilization issues that have historically been the focus of policy

---

[1]  This group was known as the G-7 until 1997. Russia was added to the group in that year. Its economy is relatively small compared to the others, and its influence is primarily on political rather than economic issues.

---

### Box 17.1    The Small-country Model under Floating Exchange Rates

**Money market equilibrium**

$$M = PL(R, Y) \tag{17.1}$$

**Uncovered interest parity**

$$R = R^* \tag{17.2}$$

**Goods market equilibrium**

$$Y = \phi(SP^*/P)A(Y - T, R) + G + X(\theta, SP^*/P) \tag{17.3}$$

---

coordination, we'll go back to focusing on the sticky-price short run and, to keep matters simple, we will abstract away from the assumption of slow goods-market adjustment that we considered in Chapter 12. Finally, for concreteness and simplicity in studying policy spillovers we will concentrate on the analysis of the effects of permanent policy changes.

Thus, our analytical point of departure is the permanent-shock model of Chapter 11. Recall that the compact version of the permanent-shock model for a small country with floating exchange rates consisted of three conditions listed in Box 17.1. In this model, the small-country assumption made the world interest rate $R^*$ and the ''shift factor'' in the foreign demand for domestic goods $\theta$ exogenous, precisely because the domestic economy was too small to affect them. Thus, we could solve this three-equation model for three endogenous variables consisting of the domestic interest rate $R$, the level of real output $Y$, and the nominal exchange rate $S$.

What changes are required to adapt this model to the large-country case? First, for a large country, it is no longer legitimate to use an exogenous catch-all variable such as $\theta$ to describe the factors driving foreign demand for domestic exports, since treating the factors affecting foreign export demand as exogenous precludes any effects that changes in the domestic economy may have on foreign economic conditions that may affect the demand for domestic exports. Thus, as a first step we have to be more explicit about the factors affecting foreigners' demand for the domestic economy's exports. The most natural way to do this is to assume that the foreign economy is exactly like the domestic economy. In that case, foreigners' demand for the domestic economy's exports (which are, of course, *imports* from the foreigners' point of view) is determined in exactly the same way as the domestic economy's demand for exports from the foreign economy. Thus, we can write $X$ as:

$$X = (1 - \phi^*(P/SP^*)) A^*(Y^* - T^*, R^*)SP^*/P$$
$$\phantom{X = (1 - \phi^*(P/SP^*)) A^*(Y^* }{+}\phantom{- T^*,}{+}\phantom{, }{-}\phantom{)SP^*/P}$$

This equation requires some discussion. It describes foreigners' demand for domestic exports in exactly the same way as the domestic economy's demand for imports was described in Chapter 4. Real foreign private absorption (measured in units of the foreign good) is given by $A^*$. As we have done for the domestic economy, it is taken to depend positively on foreigners' income $Y^*$, but negatively on foreign levels of taxation $T^*$ and the foreign interest rate $R^*$. Like domestic residents, foreigners are assumed to devote a positive fraction $\phi^*$ of private absorption to the purchase of their own goods, with the remaining $(1 - \phi^*)$ devoted to purchasing imports from the domestic economy. The fraction $\phi^*$ depends positively on the real exchange rate which, from foreigners' perspective, is the price of the home country's goods in terms of foreign goods, or $P/SP^*$. The quantity $(1 - \phi^*)A^*$ therefore represents the rest of the world's demand for the home country's goods, measured in units of the foreign good (since $A^*$ is measured in units of the foreign good and $(1 - \phi^*)$ is unit-free). To convert this quantity into units of the home country good (the units in which $X$ is measured) we have to multiply it by the relative price of foreign goods in terms of domestic goods, which is given by the real exchange rate $SP^*/P$. Notice that, consistent with what we assumed about the effect of the real exchange rate on exports from the domestic economy, in this equation an increase in $SP^*/P$ (a real exchange rate depreciation) increases foreign demand for domestic goods. It does so both because it reduces $\phi^*$ and because it increases the value of foreign private absorption measured in units of domestic goods.

With this modification, equation (17.3) becomes:

$$Y = \phi(SP^*/P)A(Y - T, R) + G + (1 - \phi^*(P/SP^*))A^*(Y^* - T^*, R^*)SP^*/P \qquad (17.3')$$

Thus, our revised model consists of the money-market equilibrium condition (17.1), the UIP condition (17.2), and the new goods-market equilibrium condition (17.3').

The second change to our model concerns the identification of what is exogenous and what is endogenous. If the small country assumption does not hold, then we have to treat the foreign interest rate $R^*$ and foreign output $Y^*$ as endogenous. However, that would give us five unknowns ($S$, $R$, $R^*$, $Y$, and $Y^*$) to solve for with our three equations. How could we solve such a model? The obvious answer, as you know by now, is that we cannot do so without adding more restrictions. In particular, we have to explain what determines $R^*$ and $Y^*$. Once again, the natural way to do so is to assume that they are determined in the same way that their domestic counterparts $R$ and $Y$ are, that is, by financial and goods market equilibrium in the rest of the world. Thus, treating the rest of the world as a foreign economy that looks just like the domestic economy, we would have to add to our model the conditions for financial and goods market equilibrium in the rest of the world.

Adding these two conditions, the complete large-country model takes the form indicated in Box 17.2, where all the symbols with asterisks denote foreign variables. Equations (17.4) and (17.5) are just the foreign versions of (17.1) and (17.3'). That is, they are the foreign country's money and goods market equilibrium conditions, respectively. Notice that this model now contains five equations in the five unknowns, $R$, $Y$, $S$, $R^*$, and $Y^*$.

## Solving the Model

How do we solve this model? We will proceed as we have in previous chapters: by collapsing it into two relationships in two endogenous variables that we can plot and solve graphically. To do so, we begin by using the UIP condition to replace $R^*$ by $R$ in (17.4) and (17.5). This eliminates $R^*$ from the model, leaving us with four equations in the four unknowns $R$, $Y$, $S$, and $Y^*$.

## Box 17.2   A World Model

**Domestic money market equilibrium**

$$M = PL(R, Y) \tag{17.1}$$

**Bond market equilibrium**

$$R = R^* \tag{17.2}$$

**Domestic goods market equilibrium**

$$Y = \phi(SP^*/P)A(Y - T, R) + G + (1 - \phi^*(P/SP^*))A^*(Y^* - T^*, R^*)SP^*/P \tag{17.3'}$$

**Foreign money market equilibrium**

$$M^* = P^*L^*(R^*, Y^*) \tag{17.4}$$

**Foreign goods market equilibrium**

$$Y^* = \phi^*(P/SP^*)A^*(Y^* - T^*, R^*) + G^* + (1 - \phi(SP^*/P))A(Y - T, R)P/SP^* \tag{17.5}$$

*Goods-market interactions*   Our next step will be to rewrite the goods-market equilibrium conditions (17.3') and (17.5) in simpler form. To do so, we begin by plotting the relationship between $Y^*$ and $Y$ in the market for the home country's goods. Notice that if foreign output $Y^*$ increases by one unit, the demand for home country goods will increase by an amount equal to the marginal propensity to absorb in the foreign country (measured in units of the home good), times the share of foreign absorption devoted to imports. That is, the demand for home country goods will increase by $(1 - \phi^*)A_Y^* SP^*/P$, where $A_Y^*$ is the foreign marginal propensity to absorb, measured in units of the foreign good. This increase in demand for home country goods requires an increase in the supply of such goods in order to restore equilibrium in the market for home goods. Thus the relationship between $Y$ and $Y^*$ in the market for the home country's goods must have a positive slope when plotted in $Y$-$Y^*$ space. This curve is labeled DG in Figure 17.1.

But how steep is this curve? That is, by how much does the output of home goods have to increase when the output of foreign goods increases by one unit? To answer this question, remember that each additional unit of output of home goods leads to an increase in domestic absorption that is given by the domestic marginal propensity to absorb $A_Y$, and thus to an induced increase in demand for home goods equal to $\phi A_Y$. Thus, for every unit of increase in domestic output, only the excess of domestic output over the induced demand for home goods, or $1 - \phi A_Y$, is available to satisfy the increased foreign demand for the home country's goods. Under our assumption that the two economies that we are describing are initially identical, we must have $\phi = \phi^*$ and $A_Y = A_Y^* SP^*/P$ – that is, the shares of private absorption devoted to each country's own goods and the marginal propensities to absorb must be the same in the two countries. Now notice that, while each unit of increase in foreign income creates excess demand for the home country's goods equal to $(1 - \phi^*)$

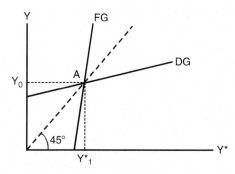

**Figure 17.1**   Equilibrium in the domestic and foreign goods markets

$A_Y{}^* SP^*/P = (1 - \phi)A_Y$, each unit of increase in domestic output creates excess supply equal to $1 - \phi A_Y$, which must be strictly larger than $(1 - \phi)A_Y$ as long as $A_Y$ is less than unity, as we have been assuming. That means that a less than one-unit increase in $Y$ is necessary to satisfy the excess demand for home goods caused by a one-unit increase in $Y^*$, which in turn implies that the slope of the DG curve in Figure 17.1 must be less than one. Thus, this curve is drawn flatter than a 45-degree line from the origin in Figure 17.1.

What determines the position of the DG curve? The answer is that the curve must be shifted vertically by any shock that affects the demand for domestic goods at a given value of foreign output $Y^*$, since such a shock will require an adjustment in the supply of domestic goods. You can see, therefore, that increases in domestic government spending and/or tax cuts (expansionary domestic fiscal policy) will shift the curve vertically upward, as will foreign tax cuts, which increase foreign private absorption and thus increase the demand for exports from the domestic economy. The DG curve will also be shifted vertically upward by a reduction in the world interest rate $R$ or by a depreciation of the domestic economy's real exchange rate $SP^*/P$.

Figure 17.1 also contains a curve labeled FG. This is simply the equilibrium condition in the market for *foreign* goods, given by equation (17.5). Because of the symmetry of our model, if you reversed the axes so $Y^*$ is on the vertical axis and $Y$ on the horizontal one, the properties of the FG curve would be exactly the same as those of the DG curve. Thus, with the axes as they are, it must be the case that FG has a positive slope that is *greater* than unity, and that anything that would cause DG to shift upward instead causes FG to shift to the *right*. There is one exception to this, however. Remember that a depreciation of the domestic economy's real exchange rate $SP^*/P$ is actually an *appreciation* of the real exchange rate of the foreign economy. Thus, while an increase in $SP^*/P$ shifts DG upward, it shifts FG to the *left*, rather than to the right.

We can now use Figure 17.1 to analyze the interactions between the domestic and foreign goods markets. In particular, consider the effects of the following shocks:

1. *Changes in domestic fiscal policy*

An increase in domestic government spending shifts the DG curve upward, as we have seen, leaving the FG curve unchanged. The effects on output in the domestic and foreign economy are shown in Figure 17.2. Notice that both domestic and foreign real GDP increase, with effects being larger on domestic than on foreign real output. You can see that the effects on domestic output must exceed the effects on foreign output, because the

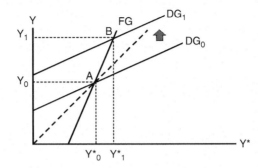

**Figure 17.2** Goods-market effects of an increase in domestic government spending

point B lies to the left of the 45-degree line, along which changes in domestic and foreign output would be identical. You can also see that feedback effects on foreign real GDP actually *magnify* the effects of the fiscal expansion on the domestic economy. To see this, notice that the direct effect of the fiscal expansion on domestic real GDP would correspond to a point directly above A on $DG_1$. But the new equilibrium at B is above and to the right of such a point. The rightward movement along $DG_1$ to the point B is the result of the induced increase in foreign GDP, which creates additional demand for the domestic good.

The effects of a domestic tax cut are a little more complicated. Since a tax cut affects the level of private absorption for a given level of real GDP, and since changes in private absorption affect the demand for foreign as well as domestic goods, changes in taxation directly affect both the DG and FG curves. If each country's private absorption is primarily devoted to that country's goods (that is, if $\phi > 0.5$), then the magnitude of the upward shift in the DG curve will be greater than that of the rightward shift in the FG curve, as shown in Figure 17.3. In that case output in both countries will rise, but effects will be larger on the domestic than on the foreign economy, as was the case for the change in government spending.

### 2. *Changes in the world interest rate*

Next, consider the goods-market effects of changes in the world interest rate. For concreteness, consider a reduction in the world interest rate. It is easy to see that, because a reduction in the world interest rate would increase demand for each country's goods, given

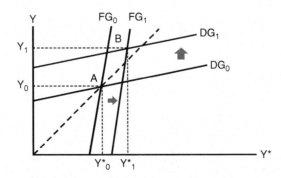

**Figure 17.3** Goods-market effects of a reduction in domestic taxes

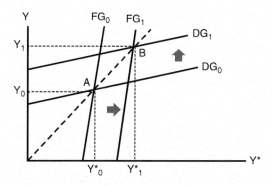

**Figure 17.4** Goods-market effects of a reduction in the world interest rate

the level of real output in the other country, the DG curve would shift upward, while the FG curve would shift to the right. Under our symmetry assumption, the two shifts would be equal in magnitude, as in Figure 17.4. Thus, output in both countries would increase by similar amounts.

### 3. *Changes in the nominal exchange rate*

Finally, consider the effects on the two goods markets of a depreciation of the domestic economy's exchange rate, shown in Figure 17.5. As mentioned above, this would be associated with an *upward* shift of the DG curve, but a *leftward* shift of the FG curve of the same absolute magnitude, since the associated real exchange rate depreciation switches spending from the foreign to the domestic economy. Domestic real output increases and foreign real output falls. It is easy to see, however, that the increase in domestic real output is not as large as it would have been if foreign real GDP had not contracted. As before, the direct effect on domestic real output is at a point on $DG_1$ directly above A, but in this case the point B is to the *left* of that point, indicating that this direct effect is somewhat offset by the effect on demand for domestic goods of the induced contraction in the foreign economy.

Based on these results, we are now ready to rewrite the goods market equilibrium conditions of our model. After taking into account the interactions between the domestic

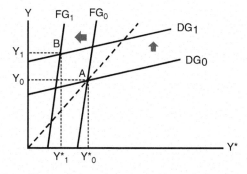

**Figure 17.5** Goods-market effects of an exchange rate depreciation

**Box 17.3    The Modified World Model**

**Domestic money market equilibrium**

$$M = PL(R, Y) \qquad (17.1)$$

**Domestic goods market equilibrium**

$$Y = Y(\underset{+}{G}, \underset{-}{T}, \underset{+}{G^*}, \underset{-}{T^*}, \underset{-}{R}, \underset{+}{SP^*/P}) \qquad (17.6)$$

**Foreign money market equilibrium**

$$M^* = P^*L^*(R, Y^*) \qquad (17.4)$$

**Foreign goods market equilibrium**

$$Y^* = Y^*(\underset{+}{G^*}, \underset{-}{T^*}, \underset{+}{G}, \underset{-}{T}, \underset{-}{R}, \underset{-}{SP^*/P}) \qquad (17.7)$$

and foreign economies through the goods markets, the equilibrium condition in the market for domestic goods becomes:

$$Y = Y(\underset{+}{G}, \underset{-}{T}, \underset{+}{G^*}, \underset{-}{T^*}, \underset{-}{R}, \underset{+}{SP^*/P})^2 \qquad (17.6)$$

And the corresponding equation for the foreign economy is:

$$Y^* = Y^*(\underset{+}{G^*}, \underset{-}{T^*}, \underset{+}{G}, \underset{-}{T}, \underset{-}{R}, \underset{-}{SP^*/P}) \qquad (17.7)$$

*The HH and FF curves*    We can now replace our previous expressions for equilibrium in the markets for the two types of goods with these new ones. The resulting model is listed in Box 17.3.

Recall that this model contains the four endogenous variables $R, S, Y$, and $Y^*$. To eliminate the last two we can substitute the domestic goods market equilibrium condition (17.6) into the domestic money-market equilibrium condition (17.1), and do the same thing for the foreign equations (17.7) and (17.4). The results can be written in the form of "general" (financial and goods markets) equilibrium conditions for the domestic and foreign economies. This produces a compact, two-equation version of our world model, which is contained in Box 17.4.

This is the compact version of our large-country model. Notice that these equations can be interpreted as "generalized" money-market equilibrium conditions that, while expressed as

---

[2]    The effects of foreign fiscal policy on domestic real GDP in this equation are inferred from the analysis above of the effects of domestic fiscal policy on the foreign economy, relying on the symmetry between the two economies.

**Box 17.4   The Compact World Model**

**General equilibrium in the domestic economy**

$$M = PL[R, Y(G, T, G^*, T^*, R, SP^*/P)] \qquad (17.8)$$

**General equilibrium in the foreign economy**

$$M^* = P^*L^*[R, Y^*(G^*, T^*, G, T, R, SP^*/P)] \qquad (17.9)$$

an equality between the supply of money (on the left-hand side) and the demand for money (on the right-hand side) also incorporate equilibrium in the goods market by expressing real output $Y$ as a function of the variables that determine it.

Since equations (17.8) and (17.9) only contain two endogenous variables, consisting of the nominal exchange rate $S$ between the domestic economy and the rest of the world and the world interest rate $R$, we are now ready to complete the solution of our model graphically. We will do so by plotting the set of all combinations of $S$ and $R$ that are consistent with general equilibrium in the domestic economy as well as all combinations that are consistent with general equilibrium in the foreign economy, and then find the unique combination that is consistent with equilibrium in both economies at the same time.

Let's begin with the domestic economy. As a first step, notice that the world interest rate plays two roles in equation (17.8): it affects the domestic demand for money both directly as well as indirectly. It does so directly in the usual fashion – that is, through its role as the opportunity cost of holding money. But in this general equilibrium equation, it also does so indirectly through its effects on the equilibrium level of domestic output, as shown in the function $Y(\ )$. Notice that both effects operate in the same direction: an increase in the world interest rate would reduce the demand for money both by increasing its opportunity cost as well as by reducing the level of domestic output.

With this observation in hand, we can now plot equation (17.8) in $S$-$R$ space. Since an increase in the world interest rate $R$ reduces the demand for domestic money through the two channels just described, the domestic money market can only clear if the exchange rate adjusts in such a way as to restore the demand for money to its original level, since the money supply $M$ is unchanged. Since the interest rate is higher, maintaining equilibrium in the money market requires a higher level of output, and this can only be brought about through a depreciation in the exchange rate. Because a higher interest rate thus requires an exchange rate depreciation in the domestic money and goods markets, the general equilibrium condition for the domestic economy, labeled HH (for ''home'') in Figure 17.6, must have a positive slope.

However, repeating this analysis for the foreign economy, an increase in the world interest rate requires an *appreciation* of the domestic currency (a reduction in $S$) to restore general equilibrium in the foreign economy, because that is what is required to reduce the relative price of the foreign good and thus increase demand for it, increasing output so as to restore money market equilibrium in the foreign economy. It follows that the set of all

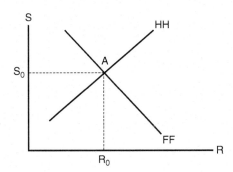

**Figure 17.6**    Short-run world equilibrium

combinations of $S$ and $R$ that is consistent with general equilibrium in the foreign economy, labeled FF in Figure 17.6, must have a *negative* slope.

The world equilibrium is depicted by the intersection of the HH and FF curves at the point A in Figure 17.6. This equilibrium determines the relative values of the currencies of the domestic and foreign economies $S_0$, as well as the world interest rate $R_0$. It is easy to see that, since the domestic and foreign interest rates must be the same, the solution for $R$ determined in this way also determines the value of $R^*$. Moreover, once we have solved for the world interest rate, given that the domestic and foreign real money supplies $M/P$ and $M^*/P^*$ respectively are exogenous, we can go back to equations (17.1) and (17.4) to solve for domestic and foreign equilibrium levels of real output.

## 17.2    Comparative Statics

We have just seen that the world equilibrium can be represented by the intersection of two curves depicting general equilibrium in the domestic and foreign economies. To see how this model works, we can now analyze how the world economy reacts to policy shocks in each of the two countries. We will consider both monetary and fiscal shocks. Remember that our assumption in building the model was that these shocks are anticipated to be permanent. Since the roles of the domestic and foreign countries in our model are completely symmetrical, it is sufficient to analyze changes in monetary and fiscal policies in the domestic economy. The effects of changes in monetary and fiscal policies in the foreign economy, both for the world and for the domestic economy, will then be easy to infer.

As a preliminary matter, we need to investigate how the HH and FF curves are affected by changes in domestic and foreign fiscal and monetary policies. Again, since the model is completely symmetrical, we can focus on changes in domestic policies.

Consider then, the effect on the HH curve of an increase in the domestic money supply. We can examine the effect of this shock on the (horizontal) position of the HH curve by asking what must happen to the domestic interest rate in order to maintain equilibrium in the domestic money and goods markets at an unchanged value of the exchange rate. From the general equilibrium condition for the domestic economy (17.8) you can confirm that an increase in the money supply must be offset by a *reduction* in the interest rate to maintain general equilibrium in the domestic economy since, as we have seen, a reduction in the interest rate would increase the domestic demand for money both directly and indirectly. Thus an increase in the domestic money supply must cause the HH curve to shift to the *left*. Alternatively, to interpret the effect on the vertical position of the HH curve, note that at a given world interest rate, an expansion of the domestic money supply requires an increase in domestic output in order to maintain equilibrium in the domestic money market. To generate an increased demand for domestic output at a given world interest rate requires a depreciation in the home country's currency, requiring the HH curve to shift *upward*.

Since changes in the domestic money supply have no direct effects on the foreign economy, the FF curve is unchanged by changes in domestic monetary policy.

The effects of changes in fiscal policies are a little more complicated. Since an increase in government spending $G$ increases the level of output of domestic goods, thus increasing the demand for money, it must be offset by an *increase* in the interest rate to maintain equilibrium in the domestic money market, implying that the HH curve must shift to the *right*. However, as we have seen, for given values of the world interest rate and the nominal exchange rate $S$, an increase in government spending in the domestic economy will also have a positive impact on output of the *foreign* good as well, so the FF curve must also shift to the right, essentially for the same reasons that the HH curve does: with increased output of the foreign good, clearing the foreign money market requires a higher world interest rate. The important point to note is that the rightward shift in the FF curve must be *smaller* than that in the HH curve in this case. The reason is that, as shown in Figure 17.2, an increase in domestic government spending must have a smaller impact on foreign than on domestic real output, so a *smaller* increase in the world interest rate is required to restore equilibrium in the foreign than in the domestic economy. A similar analysis, relying on Figure 17.3, yields a similar result in the case of a domestic tax cut: the HH curve shifts to the right by more than the FF curve.

With these results in hand, we can now investigate the international transmission of monetary and fiscal policies in our large-country model.

## Effects of a Domestic Monetary Expansion

Consider, then, how the world economy would be affected by a monetary expansion in the domestic economy. As we have just seen, at a given value of the nominal exchange rate $S$, an increase in the domestic money supply requires a decrease in the world interest rate to clear the domestic money and goods markets, so the HH curve must shift to the left, leaving the FF curve unchanged. The new world equilibrium is depicted at the point B in Figure 17.7.

At point B the world interest rate has fallen and $S$ has risen, implying that the domestic currency has depreciated and the foreign currency appreciated. The combination of a lower interest rate and more depreciated currency must be associated with an increase in domestic real output, since both changes tend to increase aggregate demand for domestic goods. Notice, by the way, that even though the monetary shock was assumed to be perceived as permanent, in the large-country case monetary transmission operates through both the interest rate as well as the exchange rate, in contrast to the small-country model of Chapter 11.

What happens to the domestic economy's net exports? The depreciation of the real exchange rate implied by the higher equilibrium value of $S$ would tend to cause net exports to increase, but the higher value of domestic real output and lower interest rate would

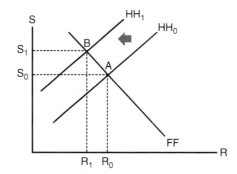

**Figure 17.7**   Effects of an increase in the domestic money supply on the world economy

have the opposite effect. The absorption approach does not help us sign the effect on net exports in this case, because the association of the lower interest rate with a higher value of real output leaves room for the possibility that absorption increases by more than real output. However, as we shall see below, we will indeed be able to pin down effects on the domestic economy's net exports by examining the effects of the monetary expansion on the foreign economy.

What about effects on the foreign economy, then? Because the world interest rate $R$ falls and the foreign money supply $M^*$ does not change, it is easy to see from the foreign money market equilibrium condition (17.4) that foreign income $Y^*$ must actually *fall* in this case. This is the large-country counterpart of the result we previously derived for a small economy under floating exchange rates – that is, that increases in world interest rates were expansionary while decreases were contractionary. But how can foreign output fall, since the lower world interest rate would tend to increase absorption in the foreign economy? The answer is, of course, that the foreign country's real exchange rate has appreciated. We can indeed show that the foreign economy's net exports must deteriorate as the result of the appreciation of the foreign currency. This must be so because $Y^*$ is lower despite the increase in foreign private absorption that would tend to be caused by a lower world interest rate.

We can now go back to the impact of the shock on the domestic economy's net exports. We have just seen that the foreign country's net exports must deteriorate. But of course, if the foreign economy's net exports deteriorate, those of the domestic economy must improve.

## Effects of a Domestic Fiscal Expansion

Since increases in domestic government spending and reductions in domestic taxation have qualitatively similar effects on the HH and FF curves, in considering the effects of a domestic fiscal expansion we can focus on just one of these. Consider, then, the effects of an increase in domestic government spending. An increase in $G$ increases demand for the domestic good, causing domestic real output to rise at given values of the nominal exchange rate $S$ and the world interest rate $R$. As we have seen, the HH curve must shift to the right, because a higher world interest rate is required to maintain equilibrium in the domestic

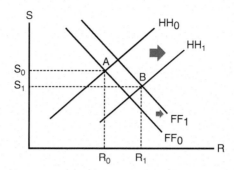

**Figure 17.8** Effects of an increase in domestic government spending on the world economy

money and goods markets at a given value of the exchange rate. Because the higher value of domestic output at given values of $S$ and $R$ increases domestic demand for the foreign good, the FF curve must shift to the right as well, though as we have seen, this rightward shift must be smaller in magnitude than that of the HH curve, as in Figure 17.8.

As is evident from Figure 17.8, the increase in domestic government spending causes the world interest rate to rise and the domestic currency to appreciate. Once again, note that though the shock in this case is expected to be permanent, the outcomes for domestic interest rates and the exchange rate are quite similar to those that we derived in Chapter 10 for transitory shocks in the case of a small economy. The increase in the world interest rate and appreciation of the currency imply that the increase in government spending will give rise to crowding out of other sources of aggregate demand. However, domestic real GDP must nevertheless rise, in contrast with the small-country case, where a permanent domestic fiscal expansion has no effect on domestic output. You can see that domestic output will be higher from the domestic money market equilibrium condition (equation 17.1). Since the money supply is unchanged and the world interest rate is higher, the domestic money market can only continue to clear after the fiscal expansion takes place if domestic real output increases.

The domestic fiscal expansion has spillover effects on the foreign economy. Again, effects on foreign real GDP are easiest to see from the foreign money market equilibrium condition. Since the foreign money supply is unchanged but the foreign (that is, world) interest rate is higher, foreign money market equilibrium requires an increase in foreign real GDP. How is this possible, with a higher interest rate prevailing in the world economy? The answer is that the reduction in $S$ represents a depreciation of the foreign economy's exchange rate. Thus the additional demand for foreign output must come from an increase in the foreign country's net exports. This implies, of course, that the domestic economy's trade balance must deteriorate.

In summary, in the large-country case, a domestic fiscal expansion raises income in both countries, increases world interest rates, causes the domestic currency to appreciate, and causes the domestic economy's net exports to decrease. A domestic monetary expansion, on the other hand, lowers world interest rates, depreciates the domestic currency, and raises income in the home country while lowering it in the foreign country. In this case the domestic economy's net exports increase. The key point in all of this is that both types of policies have spillover effects on the foreign country, giving the latter an interest in what the home country does and creating the incentives for policy coordination among large economies.

## 17.3    Post-Bretton Woods International Policy Coordination among the G-8 Countries

The question of how international macroeconomic interactions such as those described above should be managed among the major industrial countries has been a recurrent one during the post-Bretton Woods era. One answer that the international community has given is that it has been done through a multilateral system of **surveillance**. This refers to formal mechanisms through which industrial countries monitor each other's policies and engage in discussions about changes in macroeconomic policies in individual countries that may be viewed as desirable by the group as a whole in light of the world economic conditions prevailing at the time. The system of multilateral surveillance typically takes the form of group discussions of each country's economy based on annual reports on that country's economy prepared by the staff of an international organization. The two international organizations that host such discussions are the IMF itself, as well as the Organization for Economic Cooperation and Development (OECD), which is an international organization of industrial countries created in 1960 to promote cooperation among such countries and to coordinate and monitor the economic assistance that these countries provide to developing countries. These discussions provide forums through which the group of industrial countries can attempt to exercise diplomatic pressure to influence the policies of individual members of the group. Pressure is also applied to influence the policies of individual countries by publishing the proceedings of these discussions as well as periodic reports on the state of the world economy prepared by the staffs of these organizations.

But the most visible mechanism through which the industrial countries attempt to coordinate macroeconomic policies is through periodic summit meetings of the heads of state of the major industrial countries as well as ministerial meetings involving finance ministers and central bank governors. The Leaders' summits, which are held annually, were initiated not long after the collapse of the Bretton Woods system.[3] The first of this series of summits was held among the United States, the United Kingdom, Germany, Japan, and France – then known as the G-5 – at Ramboulliet (outside Paris) in 1975. This summit formally acknowledged the then-new floating rate system, sanctioning occasional intervention in foreign exchange markets by the participating countries to maintain order in those markets.

Subsequent summits explicitly took up the issue of coordinating macroeconomic policies among the industrial countries. Table 17.1 provides a list of such summit meetings through 2007. Typical issues discussed were the placing of primary responsibility for altering world aggregate demand on countries whose domestic situations seemed to call for aggregate demand policies consistent with those required by the world economy, or coordinated demand expansions in some countries and contractions in others designed to alter current account balances and exchange rates while maintaining desired levels of world demand.

For example, at the 1977 London summit Japan agreed to undertake fiscal expansion to try to help bring the world out of the 1974–5 recession. By contrast, in the 1978 Bonn summit, Germany agreed to expand government spending, while the United States agreed to decontrol domestic oil prices and take anti-inflation measures. The purpose was to stop the

---

[3]    The ministerial meetings are held in advance of the spring and fall meetings of the World Bank and International Monetary Fund.

**Table 17.1**    G-8 summit meetings

| Summit | Date | Host country | Location |
|---|---|---|---|
| 1 | November 15–17, 1975 | France | Ramboulliet |
| 2 | June 27–28, 1976 | United States | San Juan |
| 3 | May 7–8, 1977 | United Kingdom | London |
| 4 | July 16–17, 1978 | West Germany | Bonn |
| 5 | June 28–29, 1979 | Japan | Tokyo |
| 6 | June 22–23, 1980 | Italy | Venice |
| 7 | July 20–21, 1981 | Canada | Montebello |
| 8 | June 4–6, 1982 | France | Versailles |
| 9 | May 28–30, 1983 | United States | Williamsburg |
| 10 | June 7–9, 1984 | United Kingdom | London |
| 11 | May 2–4, 1985 | West Germany | Bonn |
| 12 | May 4–6, 1986 | Japan | Tokyo |
| 13 | June 8–10, 1987 | Italy | Venice |
| 14 | June 19–21, 1988 | Canada | Toronto |
| 15 | July 14–16, 1989 | France | Paris |
| 16 | July 9–11, 1990 | United States | Houston |
| 17 | July 15–17, 1991 | United Kingdom | London |
| 18 | July 6–8, 1992 | West Germany | Munich |
| 19 | July 7–9, 1993 | Japan | Tokyo |
| 20 | July 8–10, 1994 | Italy | Naples |
| 21 | June 15–17, 1995 | Canada | Halifax |
| 22 | June 27–29, 1996 | France | Lyon |
| 23 | June 20–22, 1997 | United States | Denver |
| 24 | May 15–17, 1998 | United Kingdom | Birmingham |
| 25 | June 18–20, 1999 | West Germany | Cologne |
| 26 | June 21–23, 2000 | Japan | Nago |
| 27 | June 20–22, 2001 | Italy | Genoa |
| 28 | June 26–27, 2002 | Canada | Kananaskis |
| 29 | June 2–3, 2003 | France | Evian-les-Bains |
| 30 | June 8–10, 2004 | United States | Sea Island |
| 31 | July 6–8, 2005 | United Kingdom | Gleneagles |
| 32 | July 15–17, 2006 | Russia | St. Petersburg |
| 33 | June 6–8, 2007 | West Germany | Heiligendamm |

rapid dollar depreciation of that time, which had been associated with expansionary monetary and fiscal policies in the United States. Expansionary policies in Germany, which had a strong currency at the time, were agreed in order to compensate for the more restrictive policies to be adopted in the United States.

International policy coordination among the industrial countries, however, has had an uneven history. The decade of the 1980s illustrates this experience. International macro-economic performance during the 1980s was heavily influenced by political events at the end of 1970s. These included the Iranian revolution at the end of 1979, which led to a reduction in Iranian oil exports, causing a sharp upward spike in the world price of oil in early 1981. It also included the election of Margaret Thatcher in the United Kingdom in May of 1979, of Ronald Reagan in the United States in November of 1980, and of Helmut Kohl in Germany in 1982. All of these elections represented changes in political regimes that set the

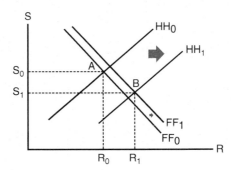

**Figure 17.9**   The early 1980s once again

stage for tight monetary policy in the United Kingdom, tight monetary and loose fiscal policies in the United States, and tight fiscal policies in Germany. The discovery of oil in the North Sea and the adoption of tight monetary policy under Thatcher caused the British pound to appreciate sharply in 1980–1, while the loose fiscal-tight monetary policy mix in the United States with tight fiscal policies in Japan and Germany resulted in large current account deficits for the United States in the early 1980s (recall Figure 3.2 in Chapter 3), with surpluses for the other countries. As we saw in Chapter 3, the sharp increase in the US current account deficit was accompanied by a strong appreciation of the real effective exchange rate of the US dollar in the early 1980s.

These developments are well explained by our world model. Assume, for example, that the United States is the home country, and the rest of the world is the foreign country. As we saw in the last section, a domestic fiscal expansion shifts both the HH and FF curves to the right, with the rightward shift in the former dominating the shift in the latter. The effect is to cause the home country's exchange rate to appreciate and its net exports to fall, as well as to raise the world interest rate. A domestic monetary *contraction* shifts the HH curve further to the right, reinforcing all of these effects. Thus the dramatic loose fiscal-tight monetary policy combination adopted by the United States in the early 1980s can be illustrated by a large rightward movement in the HH curve, coupled with a smaller rightward movement in the FF curve, as illustrated in Figure 17.9. Notice that the sharp appreciation of the US dollar and dramatic increase in world interest rates that occurred at that time both are well explained by our large-country model. Notice also that, according to our model, both fiscal expansion and monetary contraction would tend to be associated with reductions in net exports, so the sharp deterioration in the US current account position during the early 1980s is also well explained by our model.[4]

Despite these rather dramatic developments, a largely uncoordinated floating exchange rate regime prevailed among the industrial countries until 1985, partly because of philosophical commitments to limited roles for activist government policies in the new governments of some of the key countries in the system, and partly because of the primacy these governments

---

[4]   The fiscal contractions in Japan and Germany that took place at this time would have tended to shift FF to the left, accompanied by a much smaller leftward shift in HH. This would have ameliorated the increase in the world interest rate, but magnified the appreciation of the US dollar, as well as the deterioration of the US current account position. However, both because Japan and Germany were significantly smaller economies than the United States, as well as because the shift in their fiscal positions were not as dramatic as that of the US, these effects would have been small compared to those depicted in the figure, and they are omitted from the figure to avoid clutter.

gave to domestic economic goals. During 1980–5, for example, the United States called for other countries to deal with the dollar appreciation created by the US fiscal expansion by adopting measures to strengthen their own currencies. Since the other countries, attendant to their own domestic priorities, refused to do so, there was in effect little active macroeconomic policy coordination among the major industrial countries during this period.

However, the situation had changed by 1985, as new US Treasury Secretary James Baker was more open to active coordination than his predecessors had been. Large coordinated interventions intended to slow the dollar's appreciation were undertaken by United States as well as the central banks of other industrial countries from January to March of 1985. To address the factors that were driving dollar appreciation, the-then G-5 countries (Canada, Italy, and Russia had not yet joined the group) pushed Japan to stimulate aggregate demand while the United States reduced its fiscal deficit. As a result, the value of the dollar peaked in February of 1985. On September 22, 1985 the United States, the United Kingdom, France, Germany, Japan reached an accord known as the Plaza Agreement (after the hotel in New York where the meeting took place). The communiqué issued by the participants after this meeting stated that dollar depreciation was desirable, and that the participants would engage in joint intervention if necessary to bring it about. Central banks of the industrial countries sold a substantial number of dollars over the next few weeks. As we saw in Figure 3.2, the year 1985 indeed marked the beginning of a period of sharp dollar depreciation in nominal effective terms. Box 17.5 describes how joint foreign exchange market intervention can work in our world model.

Closer policy coordination was on the agenda at the May 1986 Tokyo summit.[5] The United States sought to secure macroeconomic stimulus by Germany and Japan in order to offset an intended fiscal contraction in the United States. As a "stick" to induce the cooperation of other countries, Secretary Baker held out the prospect of additional dollar depreciation from the adoption of a tight fiscal-loose monetary policy stance to sustain economic activity in the United States. As our model suggests, this policy stance in the United States would have had a contractionary effect on the other industrial countries if such cooperation was not forthcoming. In the fall of 1986, Japan indeed adopted more expansionary monetary and fiscal policies, causing Baker to agree to a statement that the depreciation of the US dollar had gone far enough. In the Louvre Agreement signed on February 22, 1987 the G-5 plus Canada agreed to seek to stabilize exchange rates, in a context in which stimulus in Japan and Germany would seek to offset the contractionary effects on the world economy of budget deficit reduction in the United States. In the event, however, though the sharp depreciation of the US dollar (in nominal effective terms) that had been taking place since 1985 indeed slowed down, because the dollar remained more appreciated in real terms by some 10 percent than it had been in 1980, and the United States still had a substantial current account deficit, the depreciation of the dollar continued at a more moderate pace until the mid-1990s (Figure 2.4).

Another notable outcome of the Tokyo summit was that the participating countries agreed to meet once a year for economic policy consultation, basing their surveillance of each other's economies on a set of seven indicators (economic growth, the rate of inflation, the trade and current account balances of the balance of payments, the behavior of exchange rates, the stance of monetary policy, and the state of government budgets). As shown in Table 17.1, regular consultations have continued since the Tokyo summit. However, the record of international policy coordination among the industrial countries since that time has

---

[5]    Italy and Canada joined the G-5 at the Tokyo summit, causing it to become the G-7.

## Box 17.5    Joint Foreign Exchange Market Intervention in the World Model

The effects of joint intervention in foreign exchange markets by the central banks of two large countries (e.g., the United States and the rest of the world) can be analyzed with our world model. Recall that the model assumes that perfect capital mobility prevails between the home country and the foreign country. As we saw for the small-country case in Chapter 10, when capital mobility is perfect the macroeconomic effects of foreign exchange market intervention depend on whether the intervention is unsterilized (i.e., is allowed to affect the domestic money supply) or sterilized (has its money supply effects neutralized by an offsetting open-market).

The same is true in the large-country case. As you can see from equations (17.8) and (17.9) in Box 17.4, effects on the exchange rate $S$ and the world interest rate $R$ ultimately depend on the magnitudes of the domestic and foreign money supplies $M$ and $M^*$, not on the composition of the balance sheets of the domestic and foreign central banks. Thus, sterilized intervention that leaves $M$ and $M^*$ unchanged would have no effect on the exchange rate or the world interest rate.

On the other hand, unsterilized intervention can be used to alter the exchange rate between the domestic and foreign economies while leaving the world interest rate unchanged. To see how this would work, consider Figure 17.10. For concreteness, assume that the domestic and foreign central banks' intention is to depreciate the home country's exchange rate while leaving the world interest rate unchanged.

Suppose that the domestic central bank intervenes in the foreign exchange market by buying foreign currency and selling domestic currency, but does not sterilize the effects of this transaction on the domestic money supply. Since the central bank has to print domestic currency to buy the foreign currency, the supply of domestic money in the hands of the public increases, while that of foreign currency decreases. If intervention is uncoordinated, the foreign central bank may prevent the foreign money supply from contracting, say through open-market purchases of its government bonds. In this case, the only effect in our model is that the HH curve shifts vertically upward, say from a position such as $HH_0$ to $HH_1$.

But if intervention is coordinated with the foreign central bank, the foreign central bank would allow its own money supply to contract, shifting the FF curve upward as well. By together engaging in unsterilized purchases of the home country's currency, the domestic and foreign central bank can in principle increase $M$ and reduce $M^*$ in such a way as to ensure that the FF curve shifts upward by an amount exactly equal to the upward shift in the HH curve. In this case, the world economy would move from A to B in Figure 17.10, with the increase in the supply of domestic currency and reduction in that of the foreign currency increasing the relative price of the latter in terms of the former – i.e., depreciating the domestic economy's exchange rate – while leaving the world interest rate unchanged.

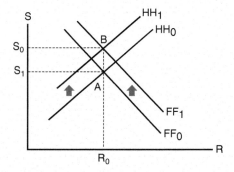

**Figure 17.10** Effects of coordinated unsterilized intervention

at best been mixed. Differences in national economic priorities, and the absence of any real inducements for countries to deviate from those priorities, except for the moral suasion exercised by others, make it difficult to identify many clear instances in subsequent years when industrial countries have substantially deviated because of international pressures from macroeconomic policies that they would otherwise have adopted on their own.

## 17.4 The US Current Account Deficit in the 2000s

The situation of the world economy in the early years of the 21st century illustrates this point. As we saw in Chapter 3, just as was true in the early 1980s, the United States once again has a large current account deficit that has become a source of concern for international macro-economic policymakers. But there has been little progress made to date on a coordinated international approach among the major industrial countries to reduce the current account deficit in the United States without triggering a worldwide recession (this scenario is sometimes referred to as a **soft landing** for the US current account deficit). Part of the reason for this is that there has been no agreement on a diagnosis of the cause of the deficit. Our world model can help us sort out the plausibility of some contending explanations.

First, it is important to note that during the first half of the decade of the 2000s, the large US current account deficit was accompanied by low world interest rates and a depreciated US dollar. Thus, explanations for the emergence of the US current account deficit need to be compatible with those observations as well. In effect, what needs to be explained is the combination of all three phenomena: a large US current account deficit, a depreciated US dollar, and relatively low world interest rates. There are two competing single-cause explanations for the emergence of the large US current account deficit, but as you will see below, a combination of factors is required to account for the facts.

### Expansionary Fiscal Policy in the United States

The United States had achieved a fiscal surplus by the year 2000, and at that time was projected to run large fiscal surpluses over the near future.[6] After 2001, however, partly as the result of tax cuts and increased defense spending following the 9/11 terrorist attacks, and

---

[6] For a perspective on the US fiscal situation from that time, see Viard (1999).

partly as the result of a recession, the US federal budget went into deficit. One interpretation of the increase in the US current account deficit at the same time attributes it to this switch to expansionary fiscal policy in the United States.

Does this explanation square with the facts? Our world model suggests not. As we saw in Figure 17.8, a domestic fiscal expansion in a large country such as the United States would indeed result in a deterioration of the country's current account balance, but it would tend to be accompanied by an *increase* in world interest rates and an *appreciation* of the home country's currency. As we have seen, both of these were counterfactual for the United States in the early 2000s. Thus, while this does not exonerate US fiscal expansion, it suggests that by itself, American fiscal expansion is not enough to explain the facts.

### The "Savings Glut"

An alternative explanation has been proposed by Federal Reserve Chairman Ben Bernanke (2005). Bernanke argues that the increase in the United States current account deficit primarily reflects changes not in the United States itself, but rather in the rest of the world. In particular, after the spate of currency crises that characterized the late 1990s, many countries – especially emerging market economies – sought to protect themselves from future crises by accumulating financial claims on the rest of the world – i.e., by improving their international investment position. To do so, as we saw in Chapter 2, they had to run surpluses on the current account of their balance of payments. Since world current account balances have to add to zero, the increase in the United States current account deficit is simply the counterpart of the larger current account surpluses desired by the rest of the world in the aggregate. Because countries generate current account surpluses by increasing their saving relative to their investment (again, recall our discussion in Chapter 2), this hypothesis is known as the "savings glut."

We can again evaluate the plausibility of this explanation using our world model. An increase in rest-of-the-world saving can be captured in our model in the form of a decrease in the foreign country's absorption. As shown in Figure 17.11, this would have the effect of shifting both the FF and HH curves to the left, with the shift in the FF curve exceeding that in the HH curve. The world interest rate would fall from $R_0$ to $R_1$ in Figure 17.11, and the foreign exchange value of the US dollar would appreciate from $S_0$ to $S_1$. With a lower world interest rate and appreciated dollar, both expenditure increasing and expenditure switching effects would indeed cause the US current account balance to deteriorate, but as

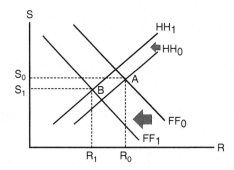

**Figure 17.11**    Effects of the savings glut

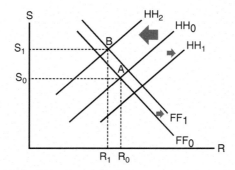

**Figure 17.12**     Effects of the US fiscal-monetary mix

we have already seen, the appreciation of the dollar predicted by this mechanism is counter-factual. Thus, like the fiscal expansion hypothesis, the "saving glut" hypothesis does not fit all the facts.

## The US Fiscal-monetary Mix

A third explanation relies on the fiscal-monetary mix pursued by the United States in the early 2000s. In contrast with the early 1980s, the expansionary fiscal policies adopted by the United States during the early 2000s were accompanied by a similarly expansionary monetary policy. The effects of this policy mix are illustrated in Figure 17.12.

As we saw before, expansionary fiscal policy by itself would have shifted the HH and FF curves to positions such as $HH_1$ and $FF_1$, explaining an increase in the current account deficit, but counterfactually predicting higher world interest rates and US dollar appreci-ation. A contemporaneous monetary expansion in the United States, however, would have shifted the HH curve to the left, leaving it in a position such as $HH_2$. Under these circumstances, the world economy would have moved from A to B, with a lower world interest rate and a depreciated dollar, as were actually observed.

While this scenario seems to fit all the facts we have considered so far, it has two problems:

a   With a depreciating dollar and lower world interest rate, the effect of this policy mix on the US current account deficit is ambiguous. A deficit would have emerged under this policy combination if the expenditure-switching effects in the United States associated with the dollar depreciation had been relatively weak compared to the expenditure-increasing effects of the lower world interest rate.
b   While this is plausible, the combination of a cheap dollar and low interest rates should have meant a high level of aggregate demand in the United States, and a booming economy. However, the United States economy did not boom in the early 2000s.

## Putting it All Together

Both of these problems with the fiscal-monetary mix explanation can be addressed by bringing the savings glut back into the picture. Relative to the point B in Figure 17.12, a reduction in foreign absorption would tend both to increase the US current account deficit as well as to reduce aggregate demand in the United States. Thus, the emergence of a ''savings glut' in the rest of the world at the same time as the United States was pursuing expansionary fiscal and monetary policies would help to explain why expansionary fiscal and monetary policies in the United States were not associated with an economic boom, but *were* associated with a large deficit in the current account.

In the language of previous chapters, this explanation suggests that the US current account deficit in the early 2000s was the result of a combination of an expansionary goods market shock in the United States and a contractionary one in the rest of the world. It therefore also suggests the outlines of a cooperative international strategy to engineer a ''soft landing'' for the US current account deficit: what is required is tighter fiscal policies in the United States and looser ones overseas. Whether the G-8 policy coordination process will be able to produce such a result remains to be seen at the time of writing.

## 17.5   Summary

In the last chapter we reviewed the relatively loose forms of ''north-south'' international macroeconomic policy coordination among industrial and developing countries that has characterized the post-Bretton Woods period. This type of coordination, consisting of specifying the ''rules of the game'' governing international financial flows and the creation of *ad hoc* mechanisms for dealing with developing-country financial crises, has partly been motivated by the fear that such crises could spread, as the debt crises of the 1980s appeared to do. The case for policy coordination among the major industrial countries, on the other hand, is based on the perception that for large countries, domestic macroeconomic policies have spillover effects even during normal times. In this chapter we have developed a large-country model that illustrates how this can happen, and have also seen how our previous results about the effects of policies on small open economies need to be modified in the large-country case.

The upshot is that systemically important (large) countries have good reasons to have a strong interest in each other's macroeconomic policies. As we have seen, this interest has manifested itself in a systematic, but somewhat weak, process of international policy coordination among industrial countries, in the form of continuous surveillance of each other's policies and ''moral suasion'' exercised in a variety of forums to influence each other's macroeconomic policies. While this represents a continuous attempt by the international community to constrain the macroeconomic policies adopted by individual countries for the sake of improved performance in the world economy, these constraints have been weak at best and have fluctuated with the political tides in individual countries. The large US current account deficit in the early years of the 21st century represents a significant challenge to this process, and it remains to be seen whether the system of policy coordination among the major industrial countries will rise to the challenge.

In the next chapter we will examine a much more constraining form of international macroeconomic cooperation than those that we have examined so far, in the form of monetary unification.

# Questions

1 Policy coordination among industrial countries has been an important issue on the international macroeconomic policy agenda since the collapse of the Bretton Woods system. Use any of the floating exchange rate models we have developed in this book to explain separately how the fiscal and monetary policies followed in the rest of the world affect macroeconomic outcomes in an open economy under floating exchange rates.

2 Consider a large open economy operating under floating exchange rates. Contrast the effects that (permanent) expansionary fiscal and monetary policies in such an economy have on the level of economic activity (real GDP) in the rest of the world and explain any differences that you find.

3 Assume that a country maintains a floating exchange rate and is linked to international capital markets under conditions of perfect capital mobility. Compare the power of a permanent fiscal expansion to affect real GDP in this country if its economy is very small relative to the world economy to what you would observe if the economy is very large, explaining the economic reasons for any differences you find.

4 Compare the transmission mechanism under floating exchange rates for permanent changes in the money supply in a small open economy and in one that is large enough for its actions to affect the rest of the world. What accounts for the difference in the two cases?

5 Consider a *large* open economy operating with floating exchange rates and characterized by perfect capital mobility. Explain what effects a permanent increase in private absorption in that country would have on:
   a That country's nominal exchange rate and the world interest rate.
   b Real GDP at home and in the rest of the world.
   c That country's current account balance.

6 The large current account deficit of the United States is arguably the most important issue on the international macroeconomic agenda today. Based on what you have learned so far in this book:
   a Explain how the large US current account deficit came about.
   b Describe a set of policies that could be undertaken in the United States and the rest of the world to reduce the US current account deficit (and the rest of the world's current account surplus) before a crisis is potentially created for the world economy by a loss of creditor confidence in the United States' ability to repay the debts it is accumulating through its deficits.

For both parts of this question, be sure to use diagrams and to explain how the policy actions you analyze are linked to US current account outcomes.

# Further Reading and References

### On US foreign exchange market intervention

Belongia, Michael T. (1992), ''Foreign Exchange Intervention by the United States: A Review and Assessment of 1985–89,'' Federal Reserve Bank of St. Louis *Review* (May/June), pp. 30–51.

**On the effectiveness of intervention**

Batten, Douglas S. and James E. Kamphoefner (1982), "The Strong U.S. Dollar: A Dilemma for Foreign Monetary Authorities," Federal Reserve Bank of St. Louis *Review* (August/September), pp. 3–12.

Batten, Douglas S. and Mack Ott (1984), "What Can Central Banks Do about the Value of the Dollar?" Federal Reserve Bank of St. Louis *Review* (May), pp. 16–26.

Bonser-Neal, Catherine (1996), "Does Central Bank Intervention Stabilize Foreign Exchange Rates?" Federal Reserve Bank of Kansas City *Economic Review* (First Quarter), pp. 43–57.

**On the G-8 process**

Dobson, Wendy (1990), *Economic Policy Coordination: Requiem or First Step?* (Washington, DC: Institute for International Economics).

Espinosa, Marco, and Chong K.Yip (1993). "International Policy Coordination: Can We Have Our Cake and Eat It Too?" Federal Reserve Bank of Atlanta *Economic Review* (May/June), pp. 1–12.

Fieleke, Norman S. (1988), "Economic Interdependence between Nations: Reason for Policy Coordination?" Federal Reserve Bank of Boston, *New England Economic Review* (May/June), pp. 21–38.

Frankel, Jeffrey (1990), "The Making of Exchange Rate Policy in 1980s," National Bureau of Economic Research Working Paper No. 3539 (December).

Meyer, Laurence H., Brian M. Doyle, Joseph E. Gagnon, and Dale W. Henderson (2002), "International Coordination of Macroeconomic Policies: Still Alive in the New Millennium?" Board of Governors of the Federal Reserve System, International Finance Discussion Paper Number 723 (April).

Putnam, Robert and Nicolas Bayne (1987), *Hanging Together: The Seven-Power Summits* (Cambridge, MA: Harvard University Press).

**On interpreting the US current account deficit in the 2000s**

Bernanke, Ben S. (2005), "The Global Savings Glut and the US Current Account Deficit," remarks at the Homer Jones Lecture, St. Louis, Missouri, April 14, 2005.

Viard, Alan D. (1999), "The New Budget Outlook: Policymakers Respond to the Surplus," Federal Reserve Bank of Dallas *Economic and Financial Review* (Second quarter), pp. 2–15.

# 18

# Monetary Unification

The last two chapters have examined mechanisms for post-Bretton Woods international macroeconomic cooperation both among industrial and developing countries, as well as among the larger industrial countries themselves. As we have seen, mechanisms for cooperation among industrial and developing countries, consisting of agreement on the ''rules of the game'' under which international capital flows take place, as well as of *ad hoc* cooperation in times of crisis, tend to impose few constraints on the normal formulation of domestic macroeconomic policies in individual countries. On the other hand, mechanisms for cooperation among the larger industrial countries, in the form of continuous surveillance over macroeconomic policies and the exercise of moral suasion to modify domestic policies in the interests of the world economy, can potentially be somewhat more constraining in their effects on the formulation of domestic macroeconomic policies in the participating economies, even if their actual effectiveness in practice has been problematic.

We now turn to a form of international macroeconomic cooperation that imposes significantly stronger constraints on the domestic macroeconomic policies that the participating economies can pursue: monetary unification. As we shall see, this form of cooperation has been undertaken both among groups of industrial countries as well as of developing countries. Box 18.1 lists the major international monetary unions in the world as of end 2007. As you can see there, these unions have involved groups of both industrial and developing countries. We will see in this chapter that the unification efforts that have been undertaken to date among industrial countries have been more successful than those among developing countries.

As mentioned in Chapter 5, **monetary unification** – the adoption of a common currency by sovereign countries – represents the multilateral adoption of a ''hard'' exchange rate peg, and as such has implications not just for exchange rate policies, but also for the conduct of both monetary as well as fiscal policies in the participating economies. We have already studied the

## Box 18.1   Major International Currency Unions

### I.   North-North Currency Unions

**The Euro Zone**

Austria, Belgium, Finland, France, Germany, Greece, Ireland, Italy, Luxembourg, Netherlands, Portugal, Spain.

### II.   South-South Currency Unions

**The Eastern Caribbean Currency Union (ECCU)**

Antigua & Barbuda, Dominica, Grenada, St. Kitts and Nevis, St. Lucia, St. Vincent and the Grenadines.

**The West African Economic and Monetary Union (WAEMU)**

Benin, Burkina Faso, Cote d'Ivoire, Guinea-Bissau, Mali, Niger, Senegal, Togo.

**Other countries in the French Franc Zone**

Cameroon, Central African Republic, Chad, Republic of Congo, Equatorial Guinea, Gabon.

*Source*: The Annual Report on Exchange Arrangements and Exchange Restrictions, International Monetary Fund, 2002.

macroeconomics of hard pegs in Chapter 6. In this chapter, we will review the implementation of this type of exchange rate arrangement among various groups of countries. As we will see, monetary unification may impose even stronger constraints on the formulation of domestic macroeconomic policies than the unilateral adoption of a hard exchange rate peg.

We begin by reviewing what is perhaps the most well known of the international experiences with monetary unification: the creation of the euro as a new currency for 15 of the member countries of the 27-country European Union (EU). We then review the history of the process that led to the creation of the European Monetary Union (EMU) and to the adoption of the euro as a common currency among member countries. We also survey experiences with monetary unification in West Africa as well as the Eastern Caribbean.

## 18.1   Economic Integration in Western Europe

As we have seen, after the collapse of the Bretton Woods system, most industrial countries abandoned fixed exchange rates. However, a large and important subset of such countries in Western Europe soon committed itself to restricting exchange rate fluctuations among themselves and eventually returning to a fixed exchange rate arrangement, at least among the countries in the group. This commitment eventually took the form of the formation of the European Monetary Union and subsequently led to the creation of a new currency, the **euro**. This section will describe the evolution of the process that culminated in the creation of the euro to replace the national currencies of 11 participating economies in 1999, and of 15 EU countries by 2008.

## Motives for Real Integration in Western Europe

The adoption of a common currency in most of Western Europe represented the culmination of a long process of economic integration among European countries. In the first part of this section, we will review the real (goods market) aspects of this process, before turning to a discussion of monetary integration itself.

As we saw in Chapters 6 and 7, during the decade of the 1930s, industrial countries implemented steep barriers to trade in both goods and services (tariffs and quotas) as well as in financial assets (capital controls). Many of these restrictions were still in place among countries in Western Europe after World War II, severely limiting both real and financial links among these countries. The process of economic integration in Western Europe, which was undertaken not long after World War II, began as an attempt to reverse some of these policies. It was motivated by a number of factors, including the desires to reap gains from trade, to expand the size of the market for domestic firms, to have a larger voice in international economic negotiations, and to reap the political benefits of having a united Europe.

*The Desire to Reap Static Gains from Trade*    Trade barriers reduce national income, essentially because they distort the allocation of both production and consumption. To show the production costs of trade barriers, consider the example described in Table 18.1. Suppose that France, Germany, and the United States can all produce a good that French consumers buy, with the cost of production in each country given (in US dollars) along the first row of the table. In the presence of a French tariff of $1.00 per unit, French consumers would face the prices for the good from each potential source of supply that are given along the second row of the table. With such a tariff in place, they would buy the product from a domestic supplier at a cost of $1.60, instead of from an American firm at a cost of $2.00, even though the American firm would actually be the lowest cost supplier ($1.00) in the absence of the tariff. However, the tariff makes France worse off, because $1.60 worth of

**Table 18.1**  Gains from trade and European integration

|                   | *France* | *Germany* | *United States* |
|-------------------|----------|-----------|-----------------|
| Production cost   | $1.60    | $1.20     | $1.00           |
| With $1.00 tariff | $1.60    | $2.20     | $2.00           |
|   Customs Union   | $1.60    | $1.20     | $2.00           |
| With $0.30 tariff | $1.60    | $1.50     | $1.30           |
|   Customs Union   | $1.60    | $1.20     | $1.30           |

French resources has to be devoted to the production of the good, instead of the $1.00 that would be required to buy it from the United States (notice that French consumers would pay $2.00 to buy it from an American supplier, but since $1.00 of this amount goes to the French government in the form of the tariff, France actually pays the rest of the world only $1.00).

If tariffs between France and Germany are eliminated, however, then as shown in the third row of the table, French consumers would be induced to buy the good from German firms instead, since the cost to French consumers of importing the good from Germany would be $1.20, less than the cost of buying it from domestic forms. In this case, France would be better off than in the previous case, because only $1.20 of French resources would now be required to produce the product. Implementing free trade with Germany is thus like an increase in French productivity – the same amount of goods can be produced with fewer resources.

The desire to achieve this kind of social gain was one of the driving forces behind the move to eliminate tariffs and other restrictions to free commerce in goods and services within Western Europe. However, it is important to emphasize that this favorable outcome of removing barriers to trade among a subset of countries is not necessary. Notice that in this case, the removal of taxes is **trade creating** – that is, trade emerges between France and Germany, where previously it did not exist. Suppose, however, that the tariff was originally $0.30 instead of $1.00, so that French consumers found American firms to be their lowest cost supplier ($1.30). Then eliminating tariffs between France and Germany would cause German firms to replace American firms as the most attractive sellers from the standpoint of French consumers, and trade in this good would be diverted from the United States to Germany. What would happen to economic welfare in France? It would actually fall, because the country would now be acquiring the good from a higher-cost supplier, and thus devoting more resources to its production than it did before the tariff was reduced. This example shows that gains from trade will only be forthcoming if the customs union is trade creating, rather than **trade diverting**. This is exactly what would have happened in this example – regardless of the original tariff rate – if Germany rather than the United States had been the lowest cost supplier.

*The Desire to Expand the Size of the Market for Domestic Firms*   A separate motivation for removing barriers to trade was to expand the size of the market facing domestic firms. This can increase national income in two ways. First, if there are **economies of scale** in production (that is, if the unit costs of production falls as the scale of production expands) such that a single firm comes to dominate the domestic market, the firm will maximize its profits by exercising monopoly power, reducing national income by artificially restricting production of its good. Opening up the domestic economy exposes the firm to competition from foreign firms, and reduces the scope for monopoly power. Second, if there are economies of scale that cannot be exploited because of the limited size of the domestic market, then the reduction of tariffs by other countries in the union would expand the size of the market that can be serviced by the domestic firm, permitting it to expand its scale and produce at lower cost. Indeed, one reason why the United States suppliers may have been the lowest cost sources in Table 17.2 may have been precisely because the large size of the American market permitted them to take advantage of economies of scale.

*The Desire to have a Larger Voice in International Economic Negotiations*   We saw in Chapter 17 that large countries could influence economic outcomes in other countries through their fiscal and monetary policies. Because such countries could thus offer large benefits to others by adopting the polices that other countries would desire, large countries would have substantial bargaining power in international macroeconomic policy negotiations. Moreover, a country whose tariff reductions would open up a large market would also wield more influence than smaller countries. Thus, a third motivation for economic integration in Western Europe has been to increase the influence of the countries from the region in such negotiations by allowing them to act both macroeconomically and in trade matters as a single large country in international negotiations, thereby allowing European countries to pursue common interests in these areas more successfully than they would be able to do independently.

*Political Benefits*    Finally, the last (but probably not least) motivation for European economic integration has been political. Both world wars of the 20th century began in Europe and devastated the continent. One aspiration of the proponents of European economic integration has been that closer economic ties among the countries in the region, as well as the need to work together in common European institutions, would reduce future conflicts in Europe.

## Chronology of Integration Measures

The earliest postwar institution designed to promote European economic integration was the **European Coal and Steel Community**. The Coal and Steel Community was established in 1952, with six member countries (Belgium, France, Italy, Luxembourg, the Netherlands, and West Germany). Its purpose was to promote free trade among the member countries in coal and steel products in order to take advantage of the economies of scale believed to exist in these activities. By allowing the reduction in unit costs that would be associated with a larger scale of operations, the expansion in the size of the coal and steel markets was expected to lower the price of coal and steel within the Community, and thus facilitate the postwar reconstruction of the European industrial base.

The next step in real integration was the establishment of the **European Economic Community (EEC)** among the six members of the Coal and Steel Community by the Treaty of Rome in 1957. The EEC was intended to become a **customs union**, a group of countries with no trade barriers among themselves but with a common external tariff applied to imports from the rest of the world. Its purpose was to encourage more extensive economic integration among the six member countries than had been achieved through the Coal and Steel Community by gradually reducing tariff barriers among the member countries. As mentioned previously, it was also intended to increase the negotiating power of European countries in international tariff negotiations by allowing them to speak with one voice, and offer access to a far larger market than any single EEC country could do. An important development within the EEC was the introduction of the **Common Agricultural Policy (CAP)** on December 31, 1961. The CAP eliminated trade barriers in agricultural products within the EEC and imposed common barriers against outside agricultural goods, in addition to implementing an extensive series of subsidies and price support programs for agricultural commodities within the EEC. The United Kingdom, Denmark, and Ireland joined the EEC in 1973, Greece in 1981, and Portugal and Spain in 1986.

An important date for the EEC's integration objective was March 1985. On that date the EEC Council of Ministers agreed to dismantle barriers to trade in goods, services, and financial assets within the Community and to allow the free movement of people as well. This agreement was formalized in the **Single European Market Act of 1987**, intended to take effect by the end of 1992. The single market formally went into effect on January 1, 1993, though its objectives were still incomplete at that time. Importantly, one component that was implemented early was the removal of restrictions of capital flows, which was accomplished in mid-1990. The static gain from the implementation of the single market has been estimated to amount to about 4 to 6 percent of regional GDP. Some economists have also estimated that growth in the region would accelerate by 1/4 to 1 percent per year as a result of the reductions in barriers to commerce.

## 18.2    European Monetary Integration

The European Monetary System

The movement toward monetary integration in Western Europe also has a long history. The objective of restricting exchange-rate movements among Western European currencies was officially articulated even before the collapse of the Bretton Woods system. Indeed, the Werner committee (headed by finance minister Pierre Werner of Luxembourg), which began work in 1970, proposed fixing intra-European exchange rates in a report adopted by the European Council (the heads of government of the EEC and its successor, the European Union) in March 1971. The objectives driving monetary integration consisted of the following:

1  To facilitate intra-European trade by eliminating exchange-rate uncertainty.
2  To enhance Europe's role in the world monetary system.
3  To reduce the costs of managing the price support system incorporated into the CAP.

Exchange rate uncertainty had prevailed in Western Europe even within the narrow (+/− 1 percent) bands that were enforced in the Bretton Woods system. Within such bands European currencies could move by 2 percent relative to the US dollar without changes in their official parities. This meant that if one European currency was at the top of its band while the other was at the bottom, the cumulative exchange rate change between the two currencies could amount to as much as 4 percent without a parity change. Uncertainty about exchange rates was perceived as the equivalent of a tax on international trade within Western Europe, discouraging the process of real integration that was being sought by other means.[1]

Consequently, international arrangements among West European countries to restrict exchange rate fluctuations among themselves began early. European countries maintained an arrangement referred to as the "snake in the tunnel," after the collapse of the Bretton Woods system resulted in the Smithsonian agreement in December 1971. Under this arrangement European currencies were maintained within margins of +/− 1.125 percent against each other, though they were free to fluctuate by +/− 2.25 percent against the U.S.

---

[1]    See Chapter 15.

dollar.[2] The objective was to prevent large fluctuations of these currencies relative to each other. The "tunnel" was the relatively broad band around the dollar parity for any particular participating currency, and the "snake" was the range around each country's dollar exchange rate within which the dollar exchange rates of the other participating currencies could be found. However, this arrangement soon fell apart, as European currencies abandoned their pegs against the US dollar (the United Kingdom and Ireland did so in mid-1972, and Italy followed in early 1973).

The **European Monetary System (EMS)** was the successor to the "snake in the tunnel." It was introduced in March 1979. Eight of the nine countries then members of the EEC (the original six plus Denmark and Ireland, but not the United Kingdom) initially participated. The core of the EMS was the **Exchange Rate Mechanism (ERM)**. This was essentially a multilateral system of fixed exchange rates. A central rate was established for each of the participating currencies relative to a basket of member country currencies called the **European Currency Unit (ECU)**. The ECU consisted of fixed amounts of each of the participating currencies, intended to reflect the relative size of the economy in the EEC. Its composition was decided by finance ministers. A set of bilateral "central" rates against all other participating currencies was implied by the set of individual currency pegs against the ECU, called a **parity grid**. Each currency was allowed to fluctuate within a band of 2.25 percent on either side of its central parity against each other currency. Within the bilateral band, intervention to maintain the bilateral parity was typically carried out by the central bank of the weak-currency country, but at the margins of the bilateral bands, the ERM obliged both central banks to intervene.

The United Kingdom ultimately joined the ERM in October 1990, availing itself of an option to allow the pound to fluctuate within margins of 6 percent. Spain joined in June 1989, and Portugal in April 1992. The currencies of both countries were also allowed to use the 6 percent margin on each side of their central parities.

Under the ERM arrangement, member countries were not permitted to alter their parities unilaterally. Instead, realignments of the central parities were negotiated within the EEC's ruling body, the Council of Ministers, and were decided by consensus. Rules limited the frequency with which devaluations could take place, as well as the extent of any permitted devaluation. Specifically, devaluation was not allowed to be sufficient in magnitude so as to offset any cumulative real appreciation of the currency that had taken place since its last realignment.

This fairly rigid fixed exchange rate mechanism embodied in the ERM was intended to capture some of the benefits of hard pegs by enforcing monetary discipline and enhancing the credibility of the anti-inflation efforts of the participating central banks. However, inflation rates were initially quite different among many of the member countries, and despite extensive capital controls that were kept in place until 1987, there were 15 ERM realignments between 1979 and November 1992. Overall, the Dutch guilder stayed close to the German deutschmark from the inception of the system, but France, Italy, Ireland, Belgium, and Denmark all saw their currencies depreciate over time. After 1986 or so until 1992, however, all of the ERM currencies tended to move fairly closely together as – except for Greece and Portugal – inflation rates tended to converge among member

---

[2]    Under this arrangement, the maximum bilateral fluctuation of each participating currency against any of the others amounted to 2.25 percent, as opposed to the maximum bilateral fluctuation of 9 percent that would have been possible if each currency was only restricted by its dollar band.

countries (see Figure 18.1). The range between the highest and lowest inflation rates indeed narrowed dramatically over the course of the ERM's existence, just as our analysis of fixed exchange rates would suggest (see the appendix of Chapter 13). Convergence of inflation rates took place in the context of gradual disinflation for the region as a whole after 1982. The extent to which the monetary discipline imposed by the ERM was responsible for this result remains controversial, however, since such convergence also occurred outside the EMS.[3] Empirical Study 18.1 at the end of the chapter describes the ambiguous results of one prominent study.

## The European Monetary Union

Despite this inflation convergence, increased financial integration in the context of the single European market for financial assets made the emergence of currency misalignments the cause for substantial speculation on realignments, and this speculation was increasingly associated with large capital flows. The solution to this problem was perceived to be **monetary unification**, a movement to an extreme form of fixed exchange rates that would render realignment impossible and take the "hardness" of the exchange rates among European currencies to the extreme.

On April 12, 1989 the *Delors Report*, the report of a committee composed of Jacques Delors, then President of the European Commission, the governors of the central banks of all member states at that time, and three experts, recommended that the 12 countries then in the EEC move through a succession of three stages to the adoption of a single currency with a single central bank. The three stages were to be as follows:

1   In the first stage, all EEC currencies would join the ERM under an identical set of rules (implying the end of disparate fluctuation margins).
2   The second stage involved setting rules determining the acceptable size and financing of government budget deficits for countries that aspired to join the EMU. A European System of Central Banks (ESCB) would be established at the same time that would represent the precursor of a European Central Bank (ECB).
3   In the third stage, irrevocably locked exchange rates would be adopted by all members.

At a summit meeting in Madrid in June 1989, the EEC countries agreed that the first stage of monetary unification would begin on July 1, 1990. In December 1990, the Intergovernmental Conference (IGC) agreed on the establishment of a European Monetary Institute, to be located in Frankfurt and to serve as the forerunner to the ESCB. The IGC also established criteria that would determine when stage III could begin. In a summit meeting at the Dutch city of Maastricht in December 1991, EEC members reached final agreement on a blueprint for monetary union. This blueprint was spelled out in the Treaty on European Union, also known as the **Maastricht Treaty**. After this date the EEC became known as the **European Union (EU)**.

The Maastricht Treaty specified four stages to monetary unification:

1   In the first stage, the EMS would be strengthened by adding all remaining EU currencies into the system, and the new treaty would be ratified by the EU member countries.

---

[3]   See Belongia (1988).

2    In the second stage, the European Monetary Institute was to begin operations. This was to happen on January 1, 1994. It would pool the reserves of member countries and intervene in the foreign exchange market to maintain the fixed exchange rates prevailing under the ERM.

3    To advance to the next stage of irrevocably fixed exchange rates, countries had to satisfy a set of **convergence criteria** (known as the Maastricht criteria), which consisted of:

- The achievement of price stability (defined in terms of a CPI inflation rate not more than 1.5 percent above the average of the three lowest-inflation EU countries).
- Long-term interest rates had to be less than or equal to 2 points above the average of those of the three countries with the lowest inflation rates.
- The achievement of exchange rate stability (this meant remaining within the ERM band for a period of two years).
- The achievement of a sustainable fiscal position (defined as a fiscal deficit of less than 3 percent of GDP, and a stock of public debt amounting to less than 60 percent of GDP).

4    The goal was set that by January 1, 1999 the European Monetary Institute would become the European Central Bank, with legal independence. Exchange rates were to be fixed permanently by that time.

Unfortunately, the path to monetary unification did not prove to be a smooth one. As we saw in Chapter 9, the ERM was struck by a severe exchange rate crisis in the fall of 1992. The crisis was triggered by Denmark's failure to ratify the Treaty of Maastricht in a referendum held in June of that year and by the fear that French passage of the treaty in September of 1992 was by no means assured. As a result of the crisis, the United Kingdom, Spain, and Italy dropped out of the ERM, and both Sweden and Finland, which, though not participants, had "shadowed" the ERM by pegging their currencies to the ECU in the hope of eventually joining the ERM, were forced to devalue. A new crisis erupted in July 1993, triggered by very high French unemployment figures, suggesting that France would be tempted to drop out for the same reasons that the United Kingdom and Italy had done so in 1992. Germany's reluctance to support the franc in the summer of 1993 led to a widening of ERM margins to +/− 15 percent.

After mid-1993, however, tensions within the ERM abated. Austria, Finland, and Sweden joined the EU in 1995, and Austria joined the ERM in January 1995, while Finland did so in October 1996. Italy rejoined in November 1996. As shown in Figures 18.1 to 18.4, convergence among the EU countries along the macroeconomic dimensions specified in the Maastricht Treaty indeed advanced very rapidly over the course of the 1990s. By May 1998, 14 of the then 15 EU countries were deemed to have satisfied the Maastricht criteria for joining the European Monetary Union. These included Austria, Belgium, Denmark, Finland, France, Germany, Ireland, Italy, Luxembourg, Netherlands, Portugal, Spain, Sweden, and the United Kingdom. Only Greece was deemed not to qualify. The new head of the European Central Bank, Dutchman Wim Duisenberg, was appointed to an eight-year term in 1998 and the Bank's Board of Directors named.

Despite qualifying for monetary union, the United Kingdom, Denmark, and Sweden chose not to participate immediately when the EMU was launched on January 4, 1999. Thus 11 countries of the 15 EU members participated initially. On January 1, 1999, the

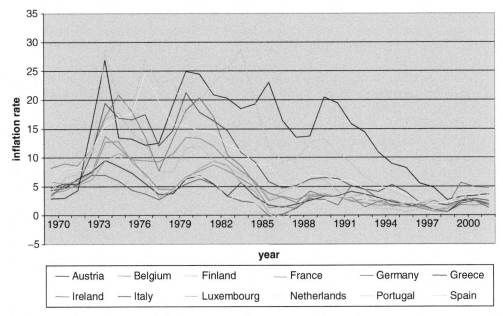

**Figure 18.1**    Eurozone: CPI inflation

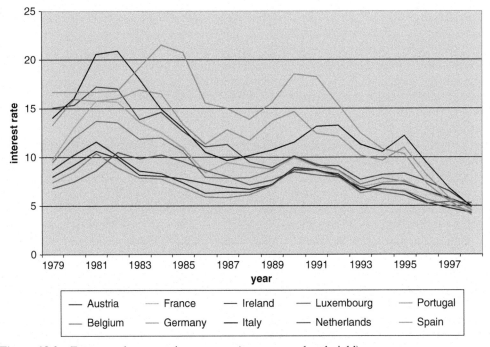

**Figure 18.2**    Eurozone: long-term interest rate (government bond yield)

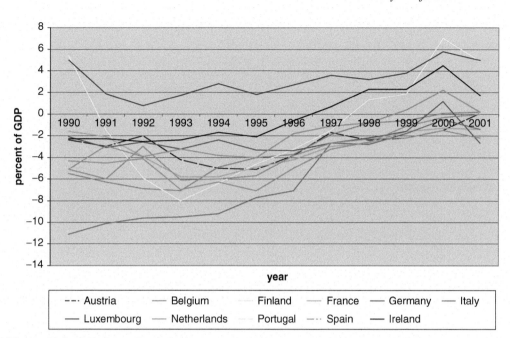

**Figure 18.3** Eurozone: fiscal surplus

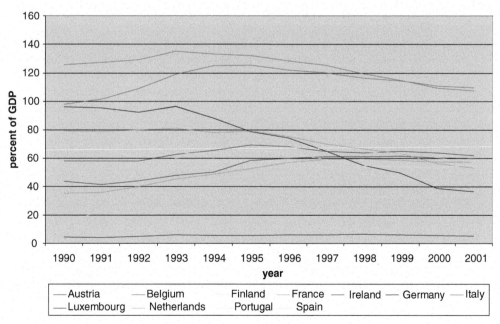

**Figure 18.4** Eurozone: public debt

currencies of the participating countries were irrevocably linked with fixed exchange rates, and monetary policy began to be framed and implemented by the ECB. From that date on, new public debt of member countries was denominated in euros, and financial markets in participating economies began to use euros as their unit of account. Thus, after January 1, 1999, the euro effectively became the unit of account for EMU member countries, though the individual national currencies continued to circulate.

However, euro notes and coins began to circulate alongside national currencies on January 1, 2002, and on July 1, 2002, the changeover to the euro was completed and national currencies were dropped from circulation. The Eurozone grew to 15 countries with the adoption of the euro by EU members Cyprus (2008), Greece (2001), Malta (2008), and Slovenia (2007).

## Monetary Unification as International Policy Coordination

What have the macroeconomic implications of the EMU been for member countries? It is easy to see that, in comparison to other forms of international policy coordination that we have studied, monetary unification imposes the tightest constraints on domestic macroeconomic policy formulation in the participating economies. First, since monetary unification is a form of hard exchange rate peg, individual member countries not only lose the option of responding to macroeconomic shocks by altering their exchange rates, but they also lose all national discretion over monetary policy formulation. Monetary policy is set for the entire monetary union by the governing board of the European Central Bank, and individual countries can influence Eurozone monetary policy only through their representation on that board.

Second, although fiscal policy was not similarly coordinated at the Eurozone level by a single fiscal authority – so fiscal policy continued to be formulated at the national level – the Maastricht criteria had important implications for the flexibility of fiscal policy as a macroeconomic policy instrument for EMU countries. The tight limits on public sector debt and deficits imposed under the terms of the Maastricht treaty impose strict constraints on the national formulation of fiscal policies over and above those that are imposed under other forms of hard peg. Under dollarization or currency boards, the government is deprived of financing by the central bank, but it can implement any fiscal deficits that it can finance by borrowing from other potential lenders. However, the Maastricht criteria imposed limits not only on the outstanding stock of government debt, but also on annual fiscal deficits.

This is an important point, one that illustrates a key policy tradeoff that countries make when they opt to join a monetary union rather than one of the other forms of hard exchange rate pegs: under a monetary union, they retain some voice over the region-wide conduct of monetary policy, but at the expense of giving up additional policy discretion in the fiscal area. Why is this so? The motivation for fiscal constraints in monetary unions is that overly expansionary fiscal policies on the part of some subset of the union can impose costs on other members of the union. If some part of the currency union maintains overly expansionary fiscal policies, then the central bank can try to stabilize aggregate demand by adopting a tighter monetary policy, or it can maintain interest rates unchanged by adopting a more expansionary monetary policy. In the first case, all members of the union will suffer from higher interest rates, while in the second case they will all suffer from higher inflation. Thus the economic costs of fiscal irresponsibility in one country would be partly borne by other participating economies. These spillover effects – and the resulting moral hazard incentives that they might create for countries to avoid difficult fiscal decisions under a monetary union – provide a rationale for fiscal coordination in monetary unions.[4]

Thus, it is clear that monetary unification, at least as practiced in the context of the EMU, indeed represents an extreme form of international policy coordination. By completely foregoing independent exchange rate and monetary policies, and by tightly circumscribing the scope for independent fiscal policies, monetary unification under the EMU has all but eliminated macroeconomic policy discretion on the part of participating economies. In comparison with other forms of hard pegs, monetary unification provides participating economies with a voice in zone-wide monetary policy formulation, but at the cost of an additional loss of fiscal discretion.

Given these constraints on traditional macroeconomic policies, and in the absence of a supranational fiscal authority than can redistribute income among the EU countries (as does the federal government among the states of the United States), the only mechanisms left for national adjustment to shocks among the EMU countries will be price level flexibility (to adjust relative prices without nominal exchange rate changes, as analyzed in Chapter 9) and labor mobility among countries. Ultimately, the test of the EMU will be whether these mechanisms function sufficiently smoothly to promote adjustment of external imbalances without tempting member countries to abandon the monetary union.

## 18.3   Monetary Union in West Africa

As shown in Box 18.1, monetary unification has not just been a form of international policy coordination among industrial countries. Several monetary unions have been formed or are under discussion among developing countries. In this section and the next we will look at the experience of monetary unification among developing countries in West Africa and the Caribbean.

### The West African Monetary Union

Six former French colonies in West Africa (Benin, Burkina Faso, Ivory Coast, Niger, Senegal, and Togo) formed the **West African Monetary Union (WAMU)** in 1962. These countries had shared a freely circulating common currency, the CFA franc, since pre-independence times.[5] After 1962, under the WAMU, the CFA franc was issued by the Central Bank of West African States (known by its French acronym of BCEAO). As is easy

---

[4]   Indeed, the explicit motivation for the fiscal criteria in the Maastricht Treaty was to limit pressure on the European Central Bank to buy the debt of a participating government that ran into fiscal difficulties (when the treaty was signed both Belgium and Italy had very large stocks of public debt relative to the sizes of their economies, as shown in Figure 18.4). Under the floating exchange rate regime that prevailed for the euro, such "monetization" of a member country's debt would create inflation in the Eurozone as a whole. Such an outcome would have been strongly resisted by Germany, which insisted on the inclusion of the fiscal criteria.

[5]   CFA is the French acronym for the African Financial Community in West Africa and for Central Africa Financial Cooperation in Central Africa.

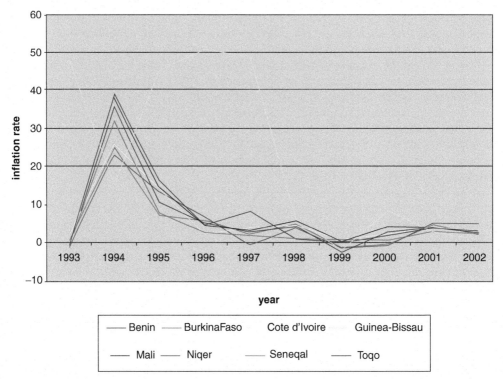

**Figure 18.5**    WAEMU: CPI inflation

to see from Figure 18.5, inflation rates among the six original WAMU countries have moved together for some time.[6]

Unlike the euro, the CFA franc has not floated against currencies outside the union. Instead, from 1948 –before the creation of the WAMU – to 1993, the CFA franc was pegged to the French franc at the value of 50 to 1. A major devaluation was implemented in January 1994, when the official parity of the CFA franc was changed to 100 to 1. The fixed exchange rate against the French franc – and after its creation, the euro – has effectively been guaranteed by France: the BCEAO maintains its foreign exchange reserves at the French Treasury and the latter ensures unlimited convertibility of the CFA franc into euros through an "operations account" that essentially lends the BCEAO the euros required to ensure convertibility. In return, France is represented on the BCEAO's Board of Directors. The fixity of the exchange rate against the euro reflects, at least in part, the desire to minimize transactions costs emphasized as a motivation for "hard" exchange rate pegs in Chapter 15 since, as the former colonial power, France has historically dominated the external trade of the member economies of the WAMU.

The WAMU, unlike the Eurozone, did not impose explicit fiscal conditions for membership in the union. However, some coordination of fiscal policies to prevent the spillover problems described in the last section has been attempted through the lending policies of the

[6]    The inflation rate for Guinea-Bissau, which joined the union in 1994, also appears in Figure 18.5. As you can see, its inflation rate was originally very different from that of the other WAMU countries, but over time has tended to converge with that of the other members of the union.

BCEAO. This has taken two forms. First, outstanding central-bank credit to the governments of each of the member countries is restricted to be no more than 20 percent of that government's tax receipts in the previous year. Second, each year the BCEAO's Board of Directors formulates plans for credit expansion to each member country that includes a ceiling on the flow of credit to each government. Notice that, if effective, these restrictions would indeed help to safeguard the BCEAO from pressures for excessive monetary expansion driven by the fiscal needs of individual member countries, but unlike the Maastricht treaty, which circumscribes overall fiscal deficits and total public debt, they still leave individual countries with substantial discretion over their overall fiscal policies, because member country governments retain the latitude to finance fiscal deficits through means other than borrowing from the BCEAO.

## The West African Economic and Monetary Union

The **West African Economic and Monetary Union (WAEMU)** was created in 1994 as a successor to the WAMU. It currently consists of eight countries (the six countries that belonged to the WAMU in 1962 plus Guinea-Bissau and Mali). The goal of the establishment of WAEMU was to build on the accomplishments of the WAMU by developing other aspects of regional integration beyond monetary unification. Thus, the evolution of the WAEMU, where monetary unification has preceded explicit policies to promote "real" economic integration, has been the reverse of that of the EU, where measures fostering "real" integration – beginning with the Coal and Steel Community – were well advanced before monetary unification was attempted. The WAEMU aims to extend integration from the monetary area to the entire scope of economic interactions among member countries, and in particular envisions the creation of s single domestic market. Initiatives under the WAEMU have addressed trade policy, the banking system, legal harmonization, and regional policies to promote investment.

A key objective of the WAEMU has been to promote intra-regional trade while deepening the integration of member countries with the world economy. An important component has been the goal of eliminating trade barriers among member countries and harmonizing trade practices with third countries. To further these goals, a common external tariff was implemented during 1998–2000. The WAEMU has also attempted to address structural problems in the banking systems of member countries. Several of these banking systems lack competition, as evidenced by high spreads between deposit and loan rates. Moreover, the legal systems of some member countries undermine lending by making loan contracts hard to enforce in cases of default. Therefore, the WAEMU aims to develop inter-bank markets, to introduce a single, zone-wide banking license, and to improve the judiciary environment. A regional Banking Commission supervises the banking system. The WAEMU has also adopted regional strategies to promote investment. Member countries have implemented common accounting frameworks, policies have been adopted to harmonize laws relating to business, and a regional court system has been established. In addition, the WAEMU has decided to create a regional securities exchange. Finally, common initiatives have been developed on sectoral policies in the areas of human resource development, transport, telecommunications, the environment, agriculture, energy, industry, and mining. Thus, just as has been true in Western Europe, monetary unification in West Africa has been only one component of a process seeking much deeper economic integration.

Of importance for the purposes of this chapter, the implementation of the WAEMU has involved a move toward greater regional harmonization of fiscal policies. The WAEMU has adopted a set of five indicators for the union to use to monitor the convergence of fiscal policy among individual member countries, in order to facilitate the working of the common currency. Those indicators include the civil service wage bill, the level of public investment financed by domestic resources, the size of the primary (non-interest) fiscal surplus, and the level of the government's domestic as well as external arrears. The WAEMU has also sought to harmonize the statistical methodology for keeping track of the government's accounts and to develop a disciplinary system to punish countries that fail to achieve the fiscal objectives specified by the Union. Thus, like the EMU, the WAEMU seems to be moving to closer oversight of each country's fiscal policies.

## The Economic Community of West African States

From a monetary perspective, West Africa consists of two groups of countries: the CFA franc zone as well as non-CFA franc zone countries. The CFA franc zone countries consist of the WAEMU and the other countries listed in Box 18.1 that use the CFA franc but are not members of the WAEMU. In April 2002, six West African countries outside the CFA franc zone (Nigeria, Ghana, Guinea, Liberia, Sierra Leone, and The Gambia) undertook to form a monetary union (referred as the "second" monetary union) by 2003, as a first step toward a wider monetary union for all countries in the **Economic Community of West African States (ECOWAS)** in 2004.

The April 2002 Accra Declaration by the six non-WAEMU countries represented the West African counterpart to the Maastricht Treaty. Participating countries agreed to set up three phases of transition to monetary union:

1    In Phase 1, countries would harmonize exchange controls, liberalize capital and labor markets, form an exchange rate mechanism similar to the ERM, establish a regional central bank, and meet a set of macroeconomic convergence criteria.[7]
2    In Phase 2, countries would reduce fluctuations of exchange rates and harmonize taxation.
3    Finally, in Phase 3 irrevocably fixed parities would be adopted with exchange rates managed by the regional central bank.

In the recent past, the non-WAEMU countries have experienced high inflation due to money creation to finance government deficits. Some of them have only recently moved toward market-determined exchange rates and trade liberalization, and none of them has a credible currency governed by a strong central bank. Moreover, although these countries are mainly agricultural, their production structures are quite different. Each country in the group specializes in different export commodities. Nigeria, for example, is a major oil exporter, while the remaining countries are net oil importers. As a result, changes in the prices of their

[7]    The Declaration established convergence criteria for the six countries that were similar in some respects to those of the EMU, but different in others: maximum budget deficits of 4 percent of GDP, rates of inflation below 5 percent per year, central bank financing of governments limited to 10 percent of the government's tax revenues, and stocks of gross foreign exchange reserves equal to at least six months of imports.

primary export goods are not well correlated among these countries. Finally, intra-regional trade is relatively minor.[8]

Perhaps not too surprisingly in light of these characteristics as well as of the experience of Western Europe, these countries have found it difficult to meet the convergence criteria in the short period of time stipulated by the Accra Declaration, and they are still far from achieving them. Moreover, the WAEMU countries have set more comprehensive and more demanding convergence criteria to be satisfied before a regional monetary union including the WAEMU as well as the six non-WAEMU countries can be formed. Therefore, the future of the ECOWOS monetary union remains unclear.

## 18.4    The Eastern Caribbean Currency Union

The **Eastern Caribbean Currency Union** consists of eight member countries and territories: Antigua and Barbuda, Dominica, Grenada, St. Kitts and Nevis, St. Lucia, St. Vincent and the Grenadines, Anguilla, and Montserrat. These countries share a common currency known as the Eastern Caribbean dollar, which has been pegged against the US dollar since 1976 at a rate of 2.70 to 1. The **Eastern Caribbean Central Bank (ECCB)** implements regional monetary policy. Unlike the WAEMU, the members of the ECCU pool their foreign reserves, the exchange parity of the EC dollar has never changed, and the currency is completely self-supported.

The countries in the ECCU have a long history of monetary cooperation, dating to the pre-independence establishment of the British Caribbean Currency Board (BCCB) in 1950. The BCCB was replaced by the Eastern Caribbean Currency Authority in 1965, at which time the EC dollar was pegged against the pound sterling. The peg was changed to the US dollar in 1976. The countries in the union are very small, with agricultural economies specialized in exporting bananas and sugar, though tourism has become increasingly important. These economies are very open, trading mainly with the United States and the European Union. They are exposed to a variety of shocks, both economic as well as in the form of natural disasters. Though there have been periodic deviations in response to shocks, inflation has historically been low in the region (see Figure 18.6).

The ECCU incorporates a different relationship between the currency of the currency union and that of the rest of the world than either the EMU or the WAEMU. Recall that the euro is a freely floating currency, while the CFA franc is fixed against the French franc and supported by France. By contrast, the fixed exchange rate of the EC dollar is maintained under a quasi-currency board arrangement, since the ECCB is obliged to maintain "the level of pooled reserves at not less than 60 percent of its demand liabilities." In practice, the ECCB actually holds much higher levels of foreign exchange reserves, as the result of fiscal discipline among member governments and conservative lending practices implemented by the ECCB itself. Its excess of foreign exchange reserves over the statutory requirement leaves the EECB room to act as a domestic lender of last resort for banks and to lend to governments during natural disasters.

Unlike the EMU, the ECCU has no formal fiscal harmonization scheme. Nevertheless, there are several mechanisms that serve to impose fiscal discipline within the ECCU.

---

[8]    However, informal trade, which is not included in the official data, may be large.

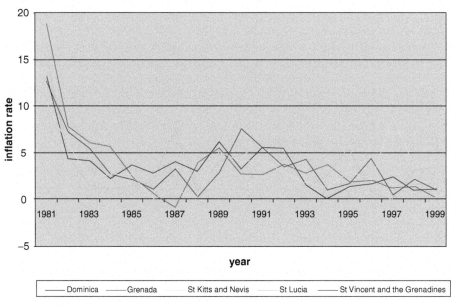

**Figure 18.6**    ECCU: CPI inflation

Foremost among these, of course, is the quasi-currency board structure of the ECCB. Fiscal discipline among member countries has in part resulted from a long tradition under quasi-currency board arrangements. But in addition, though the Articles of Agreement of the ECCB do allow it to hold some domestic assets (thus making it a *quasi* currency board), like the WAEMU, lending to member governments in various forms is restricted to specified ratios of tax revenues. As a result of these constraints, government deficits have primarily been financed from external sources.

More recently, as part of its efforts to promote efficient region-wide financial markets (see below), the ECCU has created a Regional Government Securities Market (RGSM) to facilitate government issuance of Treasury securities and the emergence of **secondary markets** (i.e., markets where existing securities are traded, rather than newly issued ones). The ECCB recognizes that the creation of the RGSM could aggravate the moral hazard problem that member governments face in a currency union, inducing them to issue more debt. In response, the ECCB has adopted the practice of only purchasing treasury bills to replace bills that are maturing at the same time, thus maintaining its stock of government securities at existing levels and safeguarding the currency board arrangement in the form in which it has been managed to date.

As in the case of the EMU and the WAEMU, monetary integration under the ECCU is just one component of a broader effort directed at regional economic integration. In particular, the ECCU aims to create a "single financial space" to attain greater economies of scale in financial markets and to enhance the efficiency of capital mobilization. Member countries are working on harmonizing taxation as well as business laws, eliminating restrictions on the capital account of the balance of payments, and introducing uniform accounting standards. The ECCU aims to improve the flexibility of goods and factor markets, accelerate trade and capital account liberalization, strengthen financial systems, and maintain fiscal discipline.

---

## Empirical Study 18.1   Disinflation Under the EMS

As described in the text, the interpretation of inflation convergence under the European Monetary System remains controversial. Inflation convergence is an observed fact. What is controversial is the extent to which the creation of the EMS contributed to this outcome. How can we bring empirical evidence to bear on this issue? Giavazzi and Giovannini (1988) proposed one approach. Their results indicate why the issue has been difficult to settle.

Giavazzi and Giovannini argued that EMS membership could have facilitated inflation convergence by lowering inflationary expectations in the member countries. They noted that a credible change in a country's monetary policy regime – such as participation in the EMS could potentially produce – would tend to create a change in private sector expectations about future inflation. The empirical question is whether joining the EMS indeed caused a reduction in inflation expectations in the participating countries. Unfortunately, such expectations are not directly observable. However, precisely because inflation expectations affect actual inflation outcomes in most macroeconomic models, there is a way to test for a change in expectations indirectly. Specifically, such a change in expectations should show up in the data as a shift in the relationship between inflation and its observable past determinants. If inflation turns out to be lower in the member countries after the implementation of EMS than it would have been predicted to be based on the past relationship of inflation to its observable determinants, this would provide indirect evidence that these countries underwent a reduction in inflationary expectations.

Giavazzi and Giovannini implemented this approach as follows. Using quarterly data for Denmark, France, Germany and Italy, they estimated a reduced-form system of equations for changes in prices, wages and output for each country in the pre-EMS period of the form:

$$\mathbf{Y_t} = A(L)\mathbf{Y_{t-1}} + B(L)\mathbf{Z_{t-1}} + u_t$$

where $\mathbf{Y_t} = [\mathbf{p_t}, \mathbf{w_t}, \mathbf{y_t}]'$ is a vector of the endogenous variables (price inflation $p_t$, wage inflation $w_t$, and growth $y_t$), $\mathbf{Z_t}$ is a vector of exogenous variables (money growth, changes in the relative price of imported raw materials and of imported finished goods, a trend, and several dummy variables), $u_t$ is an error term, and $A(L)$ and $B(L)$ are polynomials in the lag operator L, making the equation a vector autoregression with several exogenous variables. This VAR was estimated with available quarterly data over the period up to the implementation of the EMS, and was then used to forecast post-EMS inflation. Giavazzi and Giovannini argued that if the pre-EMS equation overpredicts post-EMS inflation, this provides evidence consistent with the proposition that the adoption of the EMS lowered inflationary expectations in the member countries, and thus facilitated inflation convergence.

*(Continued)*

**Empirical Study 18.1**    *(Continued)*

Their findings were not unambiguous, however. Their estimated equations actually *underpredicted* wage and price inflation for Germany. Though they overpredicted inflation for Denmark, consistent with the hypothesis of reduced inflation expectations, the results were more complicated for the other two countries. For France, overprediction starts only after 1982 (the sample extends to the end of 1986), while for Italy underprediction prevails until much later in the sample period. To add to the ambiguity, when the exercise was conducted for the United Kingdom, which did not participate in the EMS during this period, both wage and price inflation were overpredicted for most of the sample period. This raises the question of whether even in those cases where overprediction was found for EMS countries, this can be interpreted as due to the role of the EMS.

## 18.5   Summary

Monetary unions represent a very strict form of international macroeconomic cooperation. In a spectrum of degrees of cooperation at one end of which is simple agreement on "rules of the game" to govern private capital flows and ad hoc arrangements in times of crises (as in Chapter 16), monetary unification occupies the other end. Under monetary unification, all three of the key macroeconomic policies that governments have at their disposal – fiscal, monetary, and exchange rate policies – are restrained by international agreements. Countries that participate in monetary unions do not have an independent currency, so they have no exchange rate policy. They have no independent monetary policy, but may have some voice in the policies pursued by the union as a whole. This is more meaningful if the union as a whole maintains a floating exchange rate, as in the case of the EMU, but is much less so if the exchange rate regime pursued by the union is one in which an independent monetary policy is either precluded by the exchange rate regime – as in the case of a currency board such as that adopted by the ECCU – or is rendered ineffective by the Impossible Trinity, as would be the case for a fixed exchange rate arrangement such as that of the WAEMU with a high degree of capital mobility.

The novelty in this case, unlike in those of single-country currency boards or dollarization, is that the moral hazard created for domestic fiscal policy by membership in a currency union typically induces such unions to place restrictions on the fiscal discretion that member countries can exercise as well. These restrictions are very explicit in one of the currency unions that we examined in this chapter – the EMU – but mechanisms for restricting domestic fiscal autonomy have also been implemented in other currency unions.

This means that currency unions must rely for macroeconomic adjustment on domestic wage and price flexibility as well as on international mobility of factors of production such as labor and capital. It is thus not too surprising that some of these regional experiments in "globalization" have heavily emphasized measures to integrate regional labor and capital markets, as well as to make these markets more flexible. But the harmonization of national macroeconomic policies and the reform of regional labor and capital markets that currency unions require to work effectively are by no means easy tasks. Thus, whether the world will see new and broader currency unions in the future remains an open question.

## Questions

1  The inflation rates of the member countries of the Exchange Rate Mechanism (ERM) of the European Monetary System tended to converge since the system was set up in 1979. Based on what you know about how fixed exchange rates work, what role – if any – do you think the ERM played in bringing about this convergence?

2  In what ways did the macroeconomic policy options that were available to a representative member of Euroland (the Western European countries that have adopted the euro as a common currency) after it adopted the euro differ from those that would have been available to the same country under the Bretton Woods monetary system adopted at the end of World War II?

3  In what ways does participation in a monetary union impose constraints on domestic policies that differ from those of unilateral dollarization?

4  The adoption of specific numerical targets for member country fiscal deficits proved to be a very controversial component of the Maastricht framework. Make the best cases you can for and against the imposition of such constraints on fiscal policy in a monetary union.

5  Explain how the flexibility of domestic wages and prices in the individual member countries of a monetary union may influence the ability of the union to sustain itself over time.

## Further Reading and References

### On the benefits and costs of monetary unification

Eudey, Gwen (1998), "Why Is Europe Forming a Monetary Union? Federal Reserve Bank of Philadelphia *Business Review* (November/December), pp. 13–21.
Tootell, Geoffrey M.B. (1990), "Central Bank Flexibility and the Drawbacks of Currency Unification," Federal Reserve Bank of Boston *New England Economic Review* (May/June), pp. 3–18.

### On the history of monetary unions

Graboyes, Robert F. (1990), "The EMU: Forerunners and Durability," Federal Reserve Bank of Richmond *Economic Review* (July/August), pp. 8–17.

### On the evolution of the EMS

Bean, Charles (1992), "Economic and Monetary Union in Europe," *Journal of Economic Perspectives,*" Vol. 6, No. 4 (Fall), pp. 31–52.
Chriszt, Michael J. (1991), "European Monetary Union: How Close Is It?," Federal Reserve Bank of Atlanta *Economic Review* (September/October), pp. 21–8.
Eichengreen, Barry (1993), "European Monetary Unification," *Journal of Economic Literature* (September), Vol. XXXI, No. 3, pp. 1321–57.
IMF (1986), *The European Monetary System: Recent Developments*, Occasional Paper 48, International Monetary Fund.
IMF (1990), *The European Monetary System: Developments and Perspectives*, Occasional Paper 73, International Monetary Fund.

Klein, Michael W. (1998), ''European Monetary Union,'' *New England Economic Review*, Federal Reserve Bank of Boston, (March/April), pp. 3–12.
Pollard, Patricia (1995), ''EMU: Will It Fly?'' Federal Reserve Bank of St. Louis *Review* (July/August), pp. 3–16.
Schelsinger, Helmut (1994), ''On the Way to a New Monetary Union: The European Monetary Union,'' Federal Reserve Bank of St. Louis *Review* (May/June), pp. 3–10.
Whitt, Joseph A., Jr. (1997), ''Decision Time for the European Monetary Union,'' Federal Reserve Bank of Atlanta *Economic Review* (Third Quarter), pp. 20–3.
Wynne, Mark (2000), ''The EMU at 1,'' Federal Reserve Bank of Dallas *Economic and Financial Review* (First Quarter), pp. 14–28.
Wyplosz, Charles (1997), ''EMU: Why and How It Might Happen,'' *Journal of Economic Perspectives*, Vol. 11, No. 4 (Fall), pp. 3–22.
Zaretsky, Adam M. (1998), ''Yes, This EMU Will Fly, But Will It Stay Aloft?'' The Federal Reserve Bank of St. Louis, *The Regional Economist* (July), pp. 5–9.

### On economic performance under the EMS

Belongia, Michael T. (1988), ''Prospects for International Policy Coordination: Some Lessons from the EMS,'' Federal Reserve Bank of St. Louis *Review* (July/August), pp. 19–29.
Collins, Susan (1988), ''Inflation and the European Monetary System,'' in F. Giavazzi, S. Nicosi, and M. Miller, eds., *The European Monetary System* (Cambridge: Cambridge University Press), pp. 112–36.
Giavazzi, Francesco, and Alberto Giovannini (1988), ''The Role of the Exchange-Rate Regime in a Disinflation: Empirical Evidence from the European Monetary System,'' in F. Giavazzi, S. Nicosi, and M. Miller, eds., *The European Monetary System* (Cambridge: Cambridge University Press), pp. 85–107.

### On the single european market

Fieleke, Norman S. (1989), ''Europe in 1992,'' Federal Reserve Bank of Boston *New England Economic Review* (May/June), pp. 13–26.

### On the ERM crisis

Whitt, Joseph A. Jr. (1994), ''Monetary Union in Europe,'' Federal Reserve Bank of Atlanta *Economic Review* (January/February), pp. 11–28.
Zurlinden, Mathias (1993), ''The Vulnerability of Pegged Exchange Rates: The British Pound in the ERM,'' Federal Reserve Bank of St. Louis *Review* (September/October).

### On the future of the Eurozone

Eichengreen, Barry (2007), ''The Breakup of the Euro Area,'' NBER Working Paper 13393 (September).

### On Monetary Union in West Africa

Bhatia, Rattan (1985), ''The West African Economic and Monetary Union: An Analytical Review, IMF'' Occasional Paper 35.
Clement, Jean A.P. Johannes Mueller, Stephane Cosse, and Jean Le Dem (1996), ''Aftermath of the CFA Franc Devaluation,'' IMF Occasional Paper 138 (May).

IMF (1998), ''The West African Economic and Monetary Union: Recent Developments and Policy Issues,'' IMF Occasional Paper 170.

Masson, Paul and Catherine Pattillo (2001), ''Monetary Union in West Africa (ECOWAS): Is It Desirable and How Can It Be Achieved?'' IMF Occasional Paper 204.

## On the Eastern Caribbean Currency Union

IMF (2000), ''The Eastern Caribbean Currency Union: Institutions, Performance, and Policy Issues,'' Occasional Paper 195, International Monetary Fund.

# Part 5

# The New International Macroeconomics

# 19

# Intertemporal Issues in International Macroeconomics

......................................................................................................................

In this book we have considered a variety of ways in which specific characteristics of open economies affect the way that such economies behave. We have examined, for example, the effects of differences in exchange rate regimes, the degree of capital mobility, and the degree of domestic wage-price flexibility, as well as the role of the expected duration of shocks. Throughout the book, however, we have retained the basic macroeconomic framework introduced in Chapter 4. This framework has long been the workhorse of international macroeconomics. It has yielded many powerful and robust insights about the way that open economies ''work'' from a macroeconomic perspective, and it remains widely used in policy analysis, especially for short-run stabilization issues.

All simple macroeconomic models need to be extended if the range of issues to which they are to be applied is expanded, however, and our framework is no exception. In our framework, the behavior of economic agents, especially with respect to private spending decisions, was not explicitly grounded in a careful microeconomic analysis of how households and firms try to achieve their economic goals subject to the constraints that they face. Rather than conduct such an analysis, we simply stipulated a private absorption function in which the current period's level of private spending was described as depending on current period income, current period taxes paid to the government, and the real interest rate. In recent years, however, international macroeconomists have increasingly become concerned with the **intertemporal** dimension of the decisions made by economic agents in an international macroeconomic setting, and with the consequences of those decisions for economic welfare. To address these issues, they have worked with an extension to our analytical framework that goes back to microeconomic first principles by deriving descriptions of the economic behavior of private agents from their explicit maximizing behavior. An important aspect of this **new international macroeconomics** is that since such behavior typically emerges from plans that economic agents make across different periods of time, a multi-period planning horizon, the resulting macroeconomic framework is explicitly intertemporal.

To introduce you to recent analytical developments in international macroeconomics, in this chapter we will explore some of the results derived from this new framework. In order to make the analysis as transparent as possible, we will begin by analyzing consumer behavior and macroeconomic equilibrium in the simplest possible framework: a one-good "real" model. We will subsequently add more features that move the model closer to the level of realism captured by the analytical framework of Chapter 4. In particular, we will extend the initial framework to take into account two goods that are imperfect substitutes for each other. Finally, we will go beyond a purely private economy to explore the role of the government in our intertemporal framework.

## 19.1    A Simple One-Good Model

To derive the new intertemporal framework, let us return to our small open economy. We will assume that this economy is highly integrated with the rest of the world in both goods and assets markets. To capture a high degree of goods market integration, we will proceed as we did when we explored the Monetary Approach to the Balance of Payments in the appendix to Chapter 9, that is, we will assume that the domestic economy produces a single good that is a perfect substitute for what the rest of the world produces. To capture high financial market integration, we will simply assume that the economy operates under conditions of perfect capital mobility, as we have done for most of this book.

To keep the focus on how goods market equilibrium is affected by the intertemporal framework that we will be exploring in this chapter, we will also assume that we are in a nonmonetary environment. That is, we will assume that all trade is carried out through barter, and all borrowing and lending is conducted by selling and buying bonds that are denominated in units of the single good that exists in the world economy (we can call these **real bonds**). We will split up time into two periods: the present (period 0) and the future (period 1). In each of these periods, the economy will be assumed to produce an exogenous level of real GDP, so we will be working under the assumption of full employment. We will set real GDP equal to $Y_0$ in period 0 and $Y_1$ in period 1. The interest rate (domestic and foreign, real and nominal) is $R$.

### The Intertemporal Budget Constraint

The next step – and the step that differentiates what we are about to do from what we have done up to this point in the book – is to ask how the private sector determines its demand for goods in each period. The representative household in our economy will be assumed to face the following problem: it has to decide how much to consume in the present (we will call this amount $C_0$) out of its current income. Whatever it does not consume is saved, and the household uses these savings to buy real bonds. The return on these bonds next period (principal plus interest), plus the stream of future income $Y_1$ represents the resources the household has available to use for period 1 consumption. Thus consumption in period 1 must be given by:

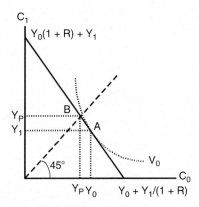

**Figure 19.1**    The household intertemporal budget constraint

$$C_1 = (Y_0 - C_0)(1 + R) + Y_1 \tag{19.1}$$

This expression captures the household's **intertemporal budget constraint**, that is, it describes all the feasible combinations of consumption in each of the two periods, given the income that the economy produces in each period and the world interest rate.

The household's budget constraint is depicted as the downward-sloping straight line in Figure 19.1. As just indicated, it depicts all the combinations of present and future consumption that the household can afford given its two-period income stream $(Y_0, Y_1)$ and the market interest rate, $R$. Notice that since more consumption in the present means that less is saved to finance consumption in the future, the budget constraint must have a negative slope. And since for every dollar not consumed (and therefore, saved) in the present the household receives $(1 + R)$ dollars of income in the future, its slope is given by $-(1 + R)$. It is also evident, as shown in the figure, that the intertemporal budget constraint must pass through the point $(Y_0, Y_1)$, identified as the point A in the figure.

The reason is the following: since the household does not save when its present consumption $C_0$ is equal to its current income $Y_0$, its future consumption $C_1$ can only be equal to its future income $Y_1$. From the fact that the budget constraint passes through the point $(Y_0, Y_1)$, it follows that if $Y_0$ were to change, the budget constraint must shift *horizontally* by the amount of the change in $Y_0$, while if $Y_1$ were to change, it would shift *vertically* by the amount of the change in $Y_1$.

Figure 19.1 also shows the maximum values of consumption in each of the two periods, given by the point of intersection of the budget constraint with the horizontal and vertical axes. If the household wants to maximize its present consumption, it can set $C_0 = Y_0 + Y_1 / (1 + R)$. That is, it can consume its current income plus the *present value* of its future income, discounted at the market interest rate $R$. This provides the horizontal intercept of the budget constraint line. Alternatively, the household can maximize its future consumption by saving all of its current income. In that case, its future consumption will be given by $C_1 = Y_0 (1 + R) + Y_1$, the intercept of the budget constraint with the vertical axis.

Dividing both sides of equation (19.1) by $(1 + R)$ and collecting the consumption terms on the left-hand side and the income terms on the right-hand side we have:

$$C_0 + C_1/(1 + R) = Y_0 + Y_1/(1 + R) \tag{19.2}$$

This is an alternative way to write the household's intertemporal budget constraint. It states that the present value of the household's consumption stream, with future consumption discounted at the market interest rate $R$, must be equal to the present value of its income stream, discounted at the same interest rate. It basically states that the amount that the household can consume is determined by its resources, with the equality between the two expressed in present value terms, because both consumption and income have components that occur at different points in time.

A concept that we will find useful later is that of **permanent income**, defined as a stream of income that is the *same* in every period, but has a present value equal to the present value of the household's income stream. Thus, permanent income $Y_P$ is defined by:

$$Y_P + Y_P/(1 + R) = Y_0 + Y_1/(1 + R)$$

Factoring $Y_P$ out of the left-hand side of this equation and dividing both sides by $1 + 1/(1 + R)$, we have:

$$Y_P = \beta(R)Y_0 + (1 - \beta(R))Y_1 \tag{19.3}$$

where $0 < \beta(R) = 1/[1 + 1/(1 + R)] < 1$, which is an increasing function of $R$. Thus permanent income is a weighted average of current and future income. Notice that this weighted average gives more weight to current income the higher the interest rate.

We can also show permanent income in Figure 19.1. To do so, draw a 45-degree line from the origin, and extend it to cross the budget line. Then permanent income can be identified as corresponding to the (equal) present and future income levels where this line crosses the budget constraint line (that is, at the point B in Figure 19.1), since this identifies a combination of equal incomes in the two periods that has the same present value as the actual income combination $(Y_0, Y_1)$. As drawn in the figure, current income exceeds permanent income, while future income falls short of permanent income, that is, the economy's income stream is skewed toward the present. This does not have to be so, and we will explore later in this section what difference the time profile of income makes for macroeconomic outcomes.

Notice that, given its intertemporal budget constraint, the only independent choice that the household can make is how much to consume in the present $(C_0)$. Once it has decided this, since both its income stream and the market interest rate are exogenous, its choice of consumption in the next period $(C_1)$ will be determined by the budget constraint.

## The Household Utility Function

How does the household decide how much to consume in the present? Notice from equation (19.1) that the more the household decides to consume in the present, the less it will be able to consume in the future. Indeed, as we have seen, for every additional unit of current consumption, the household must give up exactly $(1 + R)$ units of future consumption. The question, then, is how much the household values current as opposed to future consumption.

To answer this question, we need to describe the household's preferences between the two different kinds of consumption. As you know, economists (even international macroeconomists!) describe household preferences by means of utility functions. In particular, we will assume that the household's "tastes" for present and future consumption can be summarized by the utility function:

$$V(C_0, C_1) = U(C_0) + U(C_1)/(1 + \rho), \; \rho > 0 \qquad (19.4)$$

We will assume that the utility of consumption in each period i, given by $U(C_i)$, increases with $C_i$. However, the *marginal utility* of consumption – that is, the extra utility derived from an extra unit of consumption, which we will denote $U'(C_i)$ – decreases as the level of consumption rises. You will recognize this as the assumption of diminishing marginal utility. The parameter $\rho$ is called the **rate of time preference**. It is simply a measure of the relative value that an individual places on future utility compared to present utility. The positive value of $\rho$ means that the household discounts (in terms of its preferences) the value of future consumption relative to current consumption. That is, other things equal, people prefer to consume more in the present than in the future, and they have a stronger preference to consume now (they discount future consumption more heavily) the larger is $\rho$.

In addition to showing the intertemporal budget constraint of the representative household, Figure 19.1 also shows an indifference curve between current and future consumption, describing all the combinations of present and future consumption that can provide the household with a specific level of utility. The indifference curve in Figure 19.1 is drawn for the arbitrary level of utility $V_0$. However, we could draw an infinite number of such curves, each corresponding to different levels of utility. The properties of this family of indifference curves are the following:

1   Indifference curves corresponding to specific levels of utility must have negative slopes, since to achieve the same level of utility it would take an increase in future consumption to make up for a reduction current consumption. More specifically, to derive the slope of an indifference curve at any given point $(C_0, C_1)$ notice that a reduction in current consumption by a small amount, say, $dC_0$, would mean a loss of utility equal to the marginal utility of consumption $U'(C_0)$ (the loss of utility per unit of consumption) times the change in current consumption, or $U'(C_0) \, dC_0$. Similarly, the gain in utility from some extra future consumption equal to $dC_1$ is given by $[U'(C_1)/(1 + \rho)]dC_1$. (Remember that the utility of future consumption is discounted.) To keep utility constant the sum of these changes in utility must be zero, or:

$$U'(C_0)dC_0 + [U'(C_1)/(1 + \rho)]dC_1 = 0$$

Thus, the ratio of the change in future consumption to the change in current consumption required to keep utility constant (the slope of the indifference curve) must be given by:

$$dC_1/dC_0 = -(1 + \rho)U'(C_0)/U'(C_1) \qquad (19.5)$$

Since marginal utilities are positive, you can see that the slope of the indifference curve must be negative.

2   The slopes of individual indifference curves must become flatter as future consumption falls and current consumption rises – that is, the curves must be convex with respect to the origin. To see why this must be so, look at equation (19.5). You can see that as

current consumption increases, the marginal utility of current consumption $U'(C_0)$ must fall, while as future consumption falls, its marginal utility $U'(C_1)$ must increase. Thus, the slope $dC_1/dC_0$ must become smaller in absolute value as $C_0$ increases and $C_1$ decreases.

3   Indifference curves that correspond to higher levels of utility must be further away from the origin. This must be so, because higher levels of utility can be attained only by consuming more, either in the present or in the future.

4   Individual curves corresponding to different levels of utility cannot cross each other. If they did, it would mean that the household would have to be indifferent between two sets of combinations of current and future consumption, of which one set involved higher levels of consumption both in the present as well as in the future. That would contradict our assumption that marginal utility is positive – that is, that the representative household prefers to consume more rather than less.

## Optimal Consumption Plans

With these tools in place, we can now analyze how the household determines its optimal consumption plans. Its objective is to choose the combination of present and future consumption that provides it with the maximum amount of utility over its planning horizon, that is, it seeks to choose the combination $(C_0, C_1)$ that maximizes $V(C_0, C_1)$, subject to its intertemporal budget constraint. Since the budget constraint determines all the feasible consumption combinations, the optimal combination must be the point on the budget constraint that touches the highest possible indifference curve. You will recall from introductory microeconomics that this is determined by the point at which an indifference curve is just tangent to the budget line, as at the point A in Figure 19.1. No higher indifference curve could be reached while remaining on the budget line, and any lower curve, while feasible, would provide a lower level of utility. Thus the optimal consumption plan must satisfy the tangency condition:

$$-(1 + R) = -(1 + \rho)U'(C_0)/U'(C_1)$$

which can also be written as:

$$U'(C_1)/U'(C_0) = (1 + \rho)/(1 + R) \tag{19.6}$$

This expression is known as the **Euler equation**. Its interpretation is very simple. Suppose, first, that $\rho = R$, that is, the rate at which the household discounts the utility from future consumption is exactly equal to the market interest rate. Now consider what happens when current and future consumption levels are equal, so that they yield the same marginal utility in each period. In this situation, the extra future consumption that could be obtained by sacrificing one unit of current consumption (by investing in bonds that pay interest) is only just enough to compensate for the fact that the utility of future consumption is discounted, so the household cannot achieve higher levels of utility by deferring more of its present consumption. The household also cannot gain by consuming *more* in the present, because even though it values an extra unit of current consumption more than an extra unit of future

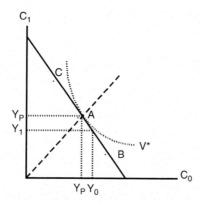

**Figure 19.2** Optimal intertemporal consumption plans

consumption, the amount of extra future consumption that it has to give up (because of the foregone interest earnings) exactly compensates for the lower value of each unit of future consumption. Thus, when $\rho = R$, it is optimal for the household to plan to consume the *same* amount in the present and in the future. Put another way, when $\rho = R$, it is optimal for the household to plan to consume an amount exactly equal to its permanent income in the present as well as in the future. This is the case shown in Figure 19.2.

By contrast, when $\rho$ is not equal to $R$, the household will prefer to tilt its consumption path over time, choosing to consume more either in the present or in the future. If $\rho > R$, for example, the Euler equation tells us that it is optimal for the marginal utility of future consumption to exceed that of current consumption. Because of diminishing marginal utility, this means that it is optimal to consume more in the present than in the future. Thus, the household consumes *more* than its permanent income in the present, which it can do simply by borrowing, and then *less* than its permanent income in the future, when it has to save to repay the debt it incurred in the first period. In this case, the optimal consumption point would lie along the budget line somewhere to the southeast of the point A in Figure 19.2, at a point like B. This should make intuitive sense to you, since a relatively high value of $\rho$ means that the household discounts the utility of future consumption relatively heavily, so that it would tend to prefer to consume in the present.

Correspondingly, if $\rho < R$, according to the Euler equation this means that the marginal utility of future consumption should be small relative to that of current consumption, that is, the household should prefer to consume more in the future, rather than in the present. The optimal consumption combination would be at a point like C in Figure 19.2. You can see intuitively why this should be so, since $\rho < R$ means that the market interest rate is relatively high, so deferring consumption in the present is rewarded with enough additional consumption in the future to more than compensate for the fact that future consumption is discounted.

We have seen, therefore, that the household must plan a stream of current and future consumption that satisfies its intertemporal budget constraint, and that subject to that constraint it will be optimal for it to plan to increase consumption over time if $\rho < R$, to consume equally in every period if $\rho = R$, and to consume more in the present than in the future if $\rho > R$. Next, we will look at the macroeconomic implications of this analysis of household choice.

## Macroeconomic Implications

Recall that we are working with a one-good model in which the single good is traded internationally. Since our small open economy is a very small part of the world market for the good, what happens at home has no perceptible impact on the world market. Thus, in modeling the domestic economy we do not have to describe the full goods market equilibrium for this international commodity. Given the domestic output of the good in each period, and consumer demand for the good, the domestic economy will simply generate an excess supply of or demand for the good that will manifest itself in the form of positive or negative values of net exports. The counterpart of positive or negative values of net exports will be negative or positive values of financial flows (i.e., outflows or inflows). Thus in the present setup, the macroeconomic implications of our analysis boil down to its implications for the balance of payments accounts.

In order to explore the implications of this new perspective on private spending behavior for the economy's balance of payments accounts, let us focus for concreteness on the case in which $\rho = R$. It is straightforward to extend the analysis to the other two cases.

Recall that the absorption approach to the balance of payments (Chapter 2) links the balance on goods and services (which we have called net exports) to the excess of GDP over domestic absorption. Since in our current framework domestic absorption consists only of consumption spending by households, net exports in the first period must be given by:

$$N_0 = Y_0 - C_0$$

Since with $\rho = R$ we know that $C_0 = C_1 = Y_P$, it follows that net exports will be positive in the present period if current real GDP exceeds its permanent value, and negative if the opposite is true. That is, net exports are positive when domestic income is temporarily high and negative when it is temporarily low.

Why should this be? The answer is that optimizing consumers facing the condition $\rho = R$ will wish to smooth their stream of consumption over time in order to maximize their lifetime utility, as implied by the Euler equation. Thus, when their income is temporarily high, they save some of it in order to consume it when their income is temporarily low. In an open economy, they can do this by running a current account surplus and thus acquiring claims on the rest of the world, which they then repatriate when their incomes are low in order to sustain their level of consumption. If they didn't do this – if they simply consumed out of their current income – they would violate the Euler equation. Specifically, if they consumed all of their high income in the present, they would find themselves driving the marginal utility of current consumption far below that of future consumption, foregoing the opportunity to increase their lifetime utility by reducing consumption at times when its marginal utility is low and increasing it when its marginal utility is high.

Notice two immediate important implications of this analysis:

1 The domestic economy benefits from openness in the nonreserve financial account of its balance of payments, because borrowing from and lending to the rest of the world creates opportunities for optimally allocating consumption over time that would not be present if the economy's financial account was closed and it simply had to consume its current income each period.

2 Current account deficits are not necessarily harmful, even though they imply increasing indebtedness to the rest of the world.

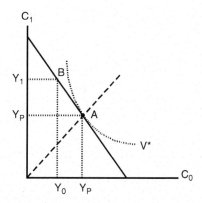

**Figure 19.3** Optimal current account deficits

To see why the second of these implications is true, notice that in the analysis that we have just conducted, current consumption depends only on (is exactly equal to, when $\rho = R$) permanent income. Thus, the optimal value of current consumption would not change no matter where the point A lies in Figure 19.1, that is, no matter what combination of current and future incomes are used to pin down the position of the intertemporal budget constraint, as long as that position itself does not change, which is the same thing as saying that the optimal value of current consumption will not change as long as permanent income does not change. Thus, if the domestic household's income configuration were like that at point B in Figure 19.3 – with a low value of current income and a high value of future income – its optimal consumption path would be the same. In this case, however, net exports would be negative in the current period (they would be given by the distance $Y_0 - Y_P$). The economy would be borrowing to sustain consumption in the present, repaying in the future when its income is much higher. As we have seen, this would actually be optimal from the perspective of domestic consumers, since doing otherwise would violate the Euler equation for optimal intertemporal allocation of consumption. Thus, this analysis confirms the assertion made in Chapter 2 that a current account deficit is not necessarily harmful if it simply serves to transfer consumption from periods when it would otherwise have a low marginal utility to periods when its marginal utility is much higher.

Next, consider how net exports would be affected by shocks to current or future income. The analysis appears in Figure 19.4. Specifically, suppose that from an initial position such as A, where both current and future income are equal to permanent income, current income increases by $dY_0$ holding future income constant, so the budget constraint shifts to the right by $dY_0$, passing through a point such as B. Since the Euler equation still requires current and future consumption to be equal to each other, the optimal consumption point moves from A to C. The change in consumption will be equal to the change in permanent income, which will be only a fraction $\beta(R)$ of the change in current income (recall equation 19.3). Thus the increase in current income will give rise to an increase in current expenditure by households that is only a fraction $\beta(R)$ of the change in current income. The economy consumes some of its extra income, but saves the rest. As a result, even though domestic absorption increases, because the increase in absorption is less than the increase in current income net exports will increase.

Suppose that instead the shock takes the form of an expected increase in future income of sufficient size as to move the budget constraint to the same position that it occupied under

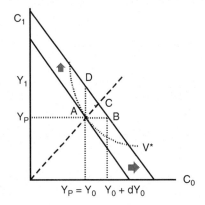

**Figure 19.4**    Effects of income shocks

the previous shock, passing through point D. In this case, once again current and future consumption would be at point C. Now, however, the increase in current consumption is not matched by an increase in current income: consumers have increased spending in anticipation of a higher future income. Since current income has not changed but current consumption has increased, it follows that net exports will fall. The economy is running an (optimal) current account deficit in order to smooth consumption intertemporally, because it expects to be richer in the future than it is in the present. An application to the US current account deficit of the late 1990s is described in Box 19.1.

Finally, suppose that current and future incomes both increase by the same amounts, say, from point A to point C in Figure 19.4. Then it is easy to see that permanent income increases by exactly the same amount, as does consumption in each period. The increase in current period consumption is exactly matched by an increase in current income, and the absorption approach indicates that net exports will remain unchanged.

## 19.2    A Two-Good Model

Now let us return to the production structure that we have been using throughout most of this book: one in which the domestic economy is completely specialized in the production of a single good that is an imperfect substitute for what is produced by the rest of the world. In this case, we can write total consumption expenditure in each period, measured in units of the domestic good, as:

$$C_0 = C_0^D + Q_0 C_0^* \text{ and } C_1 = C_1^D + Q_1 C_1^* \tag{19.7}$$

where $C_0^D$ and $C_1^D$ are domestic demand for the domestic good in the first and second periods, respectively; $C_0^*$ and $C_1^*$ are domestic demand for the foreign good in the first and second periods; and $Q$ is the real exchange rate. It is measured, as in the rest of the book, as the price of foreign goods in terms of domestic goods. $Q_0$ and $Q_1$ are the values of the real exchange rate in the first and second periods. Thus, $C_0$ and $C_1$ should now be understood as

## Box 19.1    The US Current Account Deficit in the Late 1990s Once Again

In Box 2.5 we discussed the reemergence of a US current account deficit in the second half of the 1990s, and attributed it to the expectations of rising future incomes in the United States associated with productivity improvements that accompanied the high-tech boom. We now have the analytical tools to see how this would work: the anticipation of higher future productivity levels result in an increase in $Y_1$, increasing household permanent income and shifting households' budget lines to the right. Household consumption rises, as we have seen, but since current income is not yet affected by the anticipated productivity increases, the result is an increase in domestic absorption relative to income – i.e., a reduction in net exports. The increasing US current account deficit in the second half of the 1990s was indeed associated with a strong increase in the share of household consumption in GDP (a **consumption boom**) and a reduction in the US household saving rate.

Notice two other things:

1   As shown in Figure 2.4, the emergence of a current account deficit in the United States in the late 1990s was associated with *increases* in US fiscal surpluses. This is very different from the role we attributed to expansionary fiscal policy in explaining the increase in the US current account deficit in the early 2000s in Chapter 17. Why the difference? One interpretation is that the consumption boom and the fiscal surplus of the second half of the 1990s were both driven by a common third factor: the favorable productivity shock. Anticipated improvements in productivity created a stock market boom in the United States, and stock market-driven capital gains contributed to a strong increase in federal government tax revenues that drove the US fiscal surplus. By contrast, the fiscal deficit that emerged in the 2000s was largely policy-driven, arising from legislated tax cuts and increases in defense spending.

2   We can interpret the consumption boom as a positive shock to private absorption in our "world model" of Chapter 17. Analogously to a tax cut in the home country, this shock causes both the HH and FF curves to shift to the right, with the HH curve shifting more than the FF curve. Our model would predict that the anticipated favorable productivity performance in the United States would be associated with an appreciated US dollar and higher world interest rates. As shown in Figures 19.5 and 19.6, this is exactly what happened. The dollar appreciated in real effective terms from 1995 to 2001, and this period was associated with relatively high interest rates, compared both to those that prevailed before as well as after.

composites of domestic consumption of both types of goods in the first and second periods, measured in units of the domestic good.

With this change in notation, the intertemporal budget constraint remains exactly as it was in equations (19.1) and (19.2). However, the utility function of the representative household

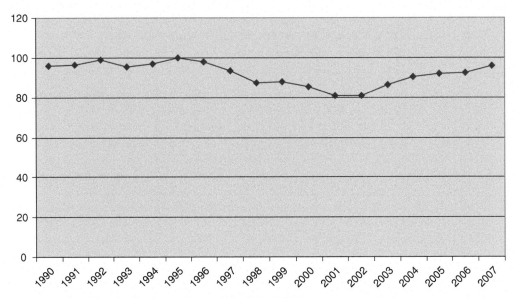

**Figure 19.5**  US real effective exchange rate, 1990–2007

must change to reflect the fact that the household must choose not just *when* to consume, but also *what* to consume. Thus equation (19.4) becomes:

$$V\left(C_0^D, C_0^*, C_1^D, C_1^*\right) = U\left(C_0^D, C_0^*\right) + U\left(C_1^D, C_1^*\right)/(1 + \rho) \qquad (19.8)$$

The household's problem is similar to what it was before: it has to maximize utility over its planning horizon, given by (19.8), subject to the intertemporal budget constraint (19.2). The difference is that now it has to make the *intratemporal* choice of what to consume in addition to the *intertemporal* choice of when to consume.

We can simplify analysis of the household's choices substantially by assuming that the utility function $U\left(C_i^D, C_i^*\right)$ takes a particularly simple form. Specifically, when the utility function is characterized by constant elasticity of substitution, the household will allocate its total consumption each period between domestic and foreign goods in a simple way: each period it will devote a share of its total consumption expenditure to domestic goods that depend only on the relative price of the two goods (and not on its total consumption in that period). Under this assumption, then, we can write:

$$C_0^D = \varphi(Q_0)C_0 \qquad (19.9a)$$

$$C_0^* = (1 - \varphi(Q_0))C_0/Q_0 \qquad (19.9b)$$

$$C_1^D = \varphi(Q_1)C_1 \qquad (19.9c)$$

and

$$C_1^* = (1 - \varphi(Q_1))C_1/Q_1 \qquad (19.9d)$$

where the fraction $\varphi$ is an increasing function of the real exchange rate $Q$. In essence, this assumption separates the intertemporal and intratemporal choices of the representative

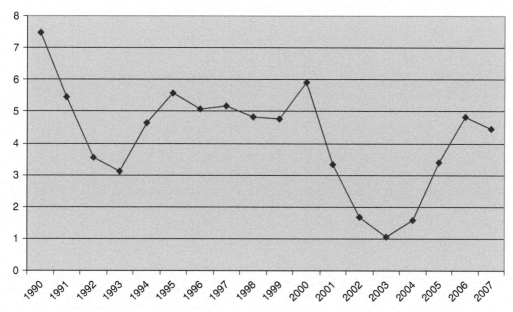

**Figure 19.6** US six-month treasury bill rate, 1990–2007

household. In other words, we can envision it solving its intertemporal problem as in the last section and then allocating its total consumption between domestic and foreign goods each period according to equations (19.9a)–(19.9d).

To see how the two-good model works, notice that we could have summarized the results of the last section, describing the determinants of current consumption expenditure, in the form of a consumption function given by:

$$C_0 = C_0(\underset{+\ -}{Y_P, R})$$

Substituting this expression into equation (19.9a), we can write the demand for domestic goods by domestic residents as:

$$C_0 = \varphi(\underset{+}{Q_0})C_0(\underset{+\ -}{Y_P, R})$$

The rest of the world presumably solves its own intertemporal problem, but from the standpoint of the domestic economy, other than the real exchange rate the factors driving foreign demand for domestic goods in the current period are exogenous. Thus we can write the current period's equilibrium condition in the market for domestic goods as:

$$Y_0 = \varphi(\underset{+}{Q_0})C_0(\underset{+\ -}{Y_P, R}) + X(\underset{+\ +}{Q, \theta}) \tag{19.10}$$

Alternatively, by adding and subtracting $(1 - \varphi) C_0$ from the right-hand side of this equation, we can write the goods market equilibrium condition as:

$$Y_0 = C_0(Y_P, R) + [X - (1 - \varphi(Q_0))C_0]$$
$$= C_0(Y_P, R) + (X - Q_0 C_0^*)$$

or

$$X - Q_0 C_0^* = Y_0 - C_0(Y_P, R) \tag{19.11}$$

The latter allows us to implement the absorption approach to investigate the effects of shocks on net exports $(X - Q_0 C_0^*)$.

We can now repeat the analysis of the shocks that we studied in the last section, assuming as before that $\rho = R$. The difference is that in our two-good framework, in which the domestic economy is not a small player in the world market for the good in which it specializes, we have to describe not just the balance of payments, but also the determination of equilibrium in the market for domestic goods. We can use equation (19.10) to determine what happens to the equilibrium value of the real exchange rate in response to shocks, and equation (19.11) to determine what happens to net exports.

Using these two relationships, we can establish the following results:

1    A current-period (temporary) increase in output of domestic goods increases the permanent income of domestic residents, and thus their total current-period consumption, by less than the increase in output of domestic goods, specifically, by a fraction $\beta(R)$ of that increase, as we have seen before. Moreover, only a fraction $\varphi$ of the increase in domestic consumption will be devoted to demand for domestic goods. From equation (19.10), the result is an excess supply of domestic goods that requires a real exchange rate depreciation to maintain equilibrium in the domestic goods market. With respect to net exports, the shortfall in domestic absorption relative to domestic output in equation (19.11) means that the domestic economy must experience an increase in net exports in the current period.

2    An expected future increase in domestic output, on the other hand, increases permanent income (again, by a fraction of the expected increase in output) and thus stimulates an increase in domestic consumption. Since current domestic output remains unchanged, the resulting excess demand for domestic goods implies that the real exchange rate must appreciate in the current period to clear the market for domestic goods. In turn, the increase in private absorption with an unchanged value of real GDP means that net exports must fall.

3    Finally, an equal increase in domestic output in *both* periods increases permanent income, and thus domestic consumption, by the same amount. Net exports are therefore unchanged. But since some of the increase in domestic consumption is devoted to purchasing foreign goods, at the original value of the real exchange rate there would be an excess supply of domestic goods. Thus, the real exchange rate must depreciate in both periods. The depreciation of the real exchange rate tempers the increased demand for foreign goods by domestic residents and offsets it with an increase in exports.

## 19.3    Introducing the Government

The next step in generalizing our framework is to introduce a role for the government. As we have done throughout the book, we will assume that the government essentially buys domestic goods, levies taxes, and borrows to finance the difference between its revenues and expenditures. However, our new framework introduces two important new issues relating to the role of the government in the economy.

First, since the economy's households are explicitly assumed to behave so as to maximize their utility, we have to take a position as to how the goods and services provided by the government affect their utility. We will assume that government spending has no direct effect on household utility. In effect, the implicit assumption is that the goods the government buys essentially disappear, with no positive or negative effects on households. This is obviously an extreme assumption, and we make it primarily for simplicity, with no pretense at realism.

Second, we have to incorporate into our model the fact that the government, like the private sector, also faces an intertemporal budget constraint. We can describe the constraint as follows: given its expenditures in periods 0 and 1, which we will denote $G_0$ and $G_1$, respectively, as well as its revenues $T_0$ in period 0 (and thus the amount of borrowing that the government has to do in that period), the government must plan to raise enough revenues in period 1 so as to repay the debt it incurred in period 0 as well as to finance its spending in period 1. Thus the government's intertemporal budget constraint is:

$$T_1 = (G_0 - T_0)(1 + R) + G_1 \qquad (19.12)$$

Proceeding as with equation (17.2) we can write this in present value terms as:

$$G_0 + G_1/(1 + R) = T_0 + T_1/(1 + R) \qquad (19.13)$$

We will assume that the government sets $G_0$, $G_1$, and $T_0$ exogenously, and then chooses $T_1$ so as to satisfy its intertemporal budget constraint.

How does the introduction of the government affect our model? The answer is that it does so in two ways: taxation affects the private sector's budget constraint, and thus the household's planned consumption path, and government spending represents an additional source of demand for the domestic good.

To see how taxation affects the private sector's budget constraint, note that when the government levies taxes, in each period the household's disposable income becomes $Y_i - T_i$. Thus we can write its intertemporal budget constraint as:

$$C_0 + C_1/(1 + R) = (Y_0 - T_0) + (Y_1 - T_1)/(1 + R)$$

It is easy to see that the effect of introducing taxation is simply to shift the household's intertemporal budget constraint in Figure 19.1 so that it passes through the point $(Y_0 - T_0, Y_1 - T_1)$, rather than through $(Y_0, Y_1)$. Thus, as a result of taxation, the budget constraint must shift inward, with its slope remaining unchanged. Thus permanent disposable income, which we can call $Y_P^D$, now becomes:

$$\begin{aligned} Y_P^D &= \beta(R)(Y_0 - T_0) + (1 - \beta(R))(Y_1 - T_1) \\ &= [\beta(R)Y_0 + (1 - \beta(R))Y_1] - [\beta(R)T_0 + (1 - \beta(R))T_1] \\ &= Y_P - T_P \end{aligned}$$

where $T_P$ is the permanent level of taxation that the household expects to have to pay, given by $T_P = \beta(R)T_0 + (1 - \beta(R))T_1$.

Since taxation only affects the position of the private sector's budget constraint, it is now easy to see how the previous analysis of household intertemporal consumption choice would be affected. Specifically, the previous analysis goes through with permanent disposable income replacing permanent income. This being so, we can summarize the determination of current period private consumption in the same way that we did before, that is, as:

$$C_0 = \underset{+}{\varphi(Q_0)}C_0(\underset{+}{Y_P - T_P}, \underset{-}{R}) \qquad (19.14)$$

This has some interesting implications. First, notice that a change in current taxes with no change in the path of government spending would have no effect on private spending. The reason is that if, say, taxes were cut in the current period with government spending unchanged in either period, taxes would have to be raised in the future by an amount exactly equal in present value terms to the current tax cut in order to satisfy the government's intertemporal budget constraint. But since the present value of tax revenues would not be affected by this switch in the timing of taxation, the switch would have no effect on permanent taxes, thereby leaving spending unchanged, according to equation (19.14).

Second, a change in government spending that is transitory (it is only implemented during the current period) would change the level of permanent taxes by the amount $\beta(R)$ times the change in government spending. Thus private consumption would be affected directly even if there were no change in current taxes. For example, with $\rho = R$, private consumption would be equal to permanent disposable income. Thus, a current period increase in government spending by the amount $dG_0$ would reduce private consumption by $\beta(R)\,dG_0$.

Third, an anticipated future change in government spending would also affect private consumption in the present, again because of the implications of the government's intertemporal budget constraint for permanent taxes. In this case, the level of permanent taxes would rise by $(1 - \beta(R))\,dG_1$.

Finally, a change in government spending has a larger impact on private consumption (changing it in the opposite direction as the change in government spending) if the change is expected to be permanent rather than transitory. The reason is, of course, that permanent changes in government spending have larger effects on the permanent level of taxes than do transitory ones.

With these observations in hand, we can now look at the macroeconomic effects of fiscal policies in our intertemporal model. As in the last section, we can do so by examining the goods market equilibrium condition written in two different ways. Incorporating the government into equations (19.10) and (19.11), these become:

$$Y_0 = \underset{+}{\varphi(Q_0)}C_0(\underset{+}{Y_P - T_P}, \underset{-}{R}) + G + \underset{+ \ +}{X(Q, \theta)} \qquad (19.15)$$

and

$$X - Q_0C_0^*) = Y_0 - C_0(Y_P - T_P, R) - G \qquad (19.16)$$

These alternative expressions for goods market equilibrium allow us to consider how the real exchange rate and the level of net exports are affected by the fiscal shocks whose effects on private consumption we examined above:

*A tax cut with an unchanged path of government spending*

As we have seen, a tax cut with no change in government spending has no effect on private consumption, because the level of permanent taxes is not affected. The reduction in public saving caused by the tax cut is exactly offset by an increase in private saving, a result often referred to as **Ricardian equivalence**, and neither the real exchange rate nor the trade balance is affected by the tax cut. Ricardian equivalence is a controversial proposition in macroeconomics, and Empirical Study 19.1 describes one of several ways that economists have tried to test its empirical relevance.[1]

1 *A temporary (one-period) increase in government spending.*

We showed previously that, because it implies an increase in the permanent level of taxation, a temporary increase in government spending would trigger a reduction in private consumption that is smaller than the increase in government spending. As a result, equation (19.15) implies that an excess demand for domestic goods would be created, which would require a real exchange rate appreciation to clear the domestic goods market. In addition, equation (19.16) tells us that the net increase in domestic absorption created by this policy would be associated with a reduction in net exports.

2 *An anticipated future increase in government spending.*

We also showed that if the private sector anticipates a future increase in government spending, then it would perceive an increase in its permanent taxes. This would induce households to reduce consumption in the present, and the resulting decrease in demand for domestic goods would result in a depreciation of the real exchange rate. At the same time, the reduction in private absorption with no actual increase in government spending in the current period would lead to an increase in net exports.

3 *A permanent increase in government spending.*

A permanent increase in government spending would be associated with an increase in permanent taxes of equal magnitude. With $\rho = R$, private consumption would fall by an equal amount. As a result, there would be no change in total domestic absorption, and net exports would remain unchanged. However, since the government consumes only domestic goods, while the private sector consumes both foreign and domestic goods, the net effect of the increase in government spending and reduction in private consumption in the current period would be to increase demand for domestic goods, causing the real exchange rate to appreciate.

The upshot is that the effects of fiscal policies in this framework, like those of the real output shocks that we examined in the previous section, depend critically on how the private sector interprets them – specifically, on what households believe a current change in policies indicates about the likely future stance of fiscal policy. For example, while we have seen that a tax cut unaccompanied by a change in the path of government spending would be expected to leave private spending unchanged, our analysis suggests that one that is interpreted as signifying a future *decrease* in government spending should be expected to be expansionary.

---

[1]  Why might Ricardian equivalence fail to hold? Some macroeconomists have argued that the fact that households have finite lifetimes while government debt can be serviced over the indefinite future, and that households use different rates to discount future taxes than the rates at which the government can borrow, would tend to substantially weaken its effects.

## Empirical Study 19.1    Testing Ricardian Equivalence

As described in the chapter, Ricardian equivalence is the proposition that consumers take the government's intertemporal budget constraint into account when they assess their own lifetime resources. This implies that they reduce their estimates of their own resources by the present value of the future tax revenues that the government has to raise to meet its financial obligations. These obligations include not only planned future government spending, as analyzed in the text, but also any pre-existing value of government debt, which the government will have to service in the future. The implication is that government debt held by households does not add to the resources that the households can devote to consumption, because the value of such debt that households hold as an asset is offset by their liabilities in the form of the present value of the taxes that the government will require to service that debt – that is, government bonds held by domestic households are not net wealth, as proposed by Barro (1974).

One way to test the validity of Ricardian equivalence has therefore been to determine whether the government debt that households own actually does affect private consumption. If it does, such bonds must be regarded by households as net wealth, in violation of Ricardian equivalence.

Berben and Brosens (2007) recently conducted a test of this proposition for 17 OECD member countries. They postulated a long-run relationship among the (logs of per capita) consumption $c_{it}$, household disposable income $y_{it}$, equity wealth $w_{it}^{e}$, housing wealth $w_{it}^{h}$, and government bonds $b_{it}$ of the form:

$$c_{it} = \beta_0 + \beta_1 y_{it} + \beta_2 w_{it}^{e}, + \beta_3 w_{it}^{h}, + \beta_4 b_{it} + u_{it}$$

where the subscripts $i$ and $t$ denote the country and time period, and $u_{it}$ is a random term. They further assumed that per capita consumption can deviate from this long-run relationship in the short run, and that short-run changes in consumption can be described by an **error-correction** mechanism. This is an adjustment mechanism in which changes in consumption each period depend (negatively) on the gap between the actual level of consumption and its long-run value, as well as on lagged changes in the variables that determine the long-run level of consumption (i.e., disposable income and the three wealth variables in this case). This error-correction equation is estimated using a **panel** approach, in which the parameters are assumed to be the same for all countries and all time periods, so they can be estimated using all the observations for all countries.

They found that household consumption was positively related to disposable income, stock market wealth and housing wealth in the long run, but negatively related to government debt. This last result might seem surprising, since Ricardian equivalence suggests that government debt held by households should not affect consumption, rather than actually reduce it. But note that the debt variable used by Berben and Brosens refers to the total amount of government debt outstanding, rather than the amount of such debt held by households. In an open economy in which part of the government debt outstanding is held by foreigners, the future tax liability implied by such debt is not offset by a corresponding asset in household balance sheets, so Ricardian equivalence would imply that the effect on household consumption should indeed be negative. Berben and Brosens' results are thus consistent with Ricardian equivalence.

However, Berben and Brosens speculated that the extent to which households discount future tax obligations associated with government debt may depend on the amount of such debt outstanding, with households being more likely to factor such liabilities into their consumption plans if government debt is high than if it is low. To test this conjecture, they divided the countries in their sample into low-debt, middle-debt and high-debt groups and tested whether the coefficient $\beta_4$ was the same for all groups. They found that the effect of debt on consumption was actually *positive* for low-debt countries, but negative for middle and high-debt countries. The implication is that Ricardian equivalence effects on household consumption spending may become important only when government debt is sufficiently high. In Berben and Brosens' sample, the cutoff point between the low-debt countries and the others was at a debt-to-GDP ratio of 55 percent.

## 19.4   Summary

This chapter has provided a brief introduction to the new international macroeconomics, which emphasizes intertemporal planning by optimizing economic agents. We have adopted a particularly simple framework, with a two-period horizon, with only households as private decision makers (that is, we have not explored the role of firms) and in a strictly non-monetary setting.

What does the new international macroeconomics add to the analytical framework that we have used throughout this book? Its key contribution is to add an intertemporal perspective to private absorption. The intertemporal perspective adopted in the new international macroeconomics does not replace, but rather extends, the basic analytical toolkit used by international macroeconomists. It does so by identifying the conditions under which the assumptions about spending behavior built into that model would actually be observed under an explicitly optimizing framework. You can see this most readily by comparing equation (19.15) with the goods market equilibrium condition used in other parts of this book, all of which are based on equation (4.4) of Chapter 4. As you can see, the key difference is the role of expectations in determining private sector perceptions of permanent income and permanent taxation.

Thus, the critical new insight of this recent approach to international macroeconomics is an enhanced appreciation of the critical role that private sector expectations play in determining the macroeconomic effects of exogenous and policy shocks. International macroeconomists are now at work trying to understand how this new set of insights can help design better policies in increasingly open economies.

### Questions

1   In a world in which Ricardian equivalence holds, would you expect an increase in the fiscal deficit to result in an equal decrease in a country's net exports (i.e., in "twin deficits")? Explain why or why not.

2   Suppose that the government in our model consumes only foreign goods, rather than the domestic goods assumed in this chapter. Under these conditions, what effects would you expect a permanent increase in government spending to have on an economy's equilibrium real exchange rate? Why?

3   Consider our one-good model. Show graphically how an increase in the world interest rate would affect the household budget constraint in this model. Would you explain the country's net exports to increase or decrease under these circumstances? Explain why.

4   Consider the two-good version of our model. Suppose that the representative household receives a constant flow of workers' remittances from the rest of the world each period. How would a permanent increase in this flow affect the home country's real exchange rate? Its net exports? Its current account balance?

5   Using diagrams, show how moving from a situation of financial autarky (no international borrowing or lending) to one with a completely open nonreserve financial account can improve economic welfare in a country.

## Further Reading and References

### On productivity and the US current account deficit

Tille, Cedric, Nicolas Stoffels and Olga F. Gorbachev (2001), "To What Extent Does Productivity Drive the Dollar?" Federal Reserve Bank of New York, *Current Issues in Economics and Finance* (August), pp. 1–6.

### On the intertemporal approach

Obstfeld, Maurice and Kenneth Rogoff (1994), "The Intertemporal Approach to the Current Account," NBER Working Paper No. 4893 (October).

### On applying the intertemporal approach

Olivei, Giovanni P. (2000a), "Consumption Risk-Sharing across G-7 Countries," Federal Reserve Bank of Boston, *New England Economic Review* (March/April), pp. 3–14.
Olivei, Giovanni P. (2000b), "The Role of Saving and Investment in Balancing the Current Account: Some Empirical Evidence for the United States," Federal Reserve Bank of Boston, *New England Economic Review* (July/August), pp. 3–14.

### On Ricardian equivalence

Barro, Robert (1974), "Are Government Bonds Net Worth?" *Journal of Political Economy* (November–December), pp. 117–27.
Berben, Robert-Paul and Teunis Brosens (2007), "The Impact of Government Debt on Private Consumption in OECD Countries," *Economics Letters*, Vol. 94, pp. 220–25.

# Index

.....................................................................................

# LIST OF BOXES

# EMPIRICAL STUDIES